Alexander Mankowsky   Alexandra Ivanovitch   Alisha Bhagat

Andrew Curry   Andy Hines   A

de Grey   Barry O'Rei   ker

yan Alexander   Byron Reese

Daniel Burrus   Daniel Levine   David Brir

avid Weinberger   Deb Westphal   Diane M. Francis

rica Bol   Erik Qualman   George Gilder

atarajan   Hazel Henderson   Helen Messier   Ian Khan

ason Jackson   Jason Schenker   Jay Gambetta   Jeff Eisenach

Dispenza   Joe Tankersley   Joel Garreau   John L. Petersen

aitlyn Sadtler   Kirk Borne   Klee Irwin   Kris Østergaard

Martin Rees   Michael Tomczyk   Michel Laberg

Newt Gingrich   Paul Saffo   Paul Stimers

chard Browning   Richard Slaughter   Richard Watson   Richard Yonck

uth Miller   Sanjiv Chopra   Sohail Inayatullah

anya Accone   Terry Sejnowski   Teun Koetsier

Vikram Mansharamani   Wolfgang Fengler

John Schroeter   Jonathan Venn

Parag Khanna   Patricia Lustig   Rick Sax

Alan Kay   Aaron Frank   Adrienne Mayor

Amy Zalman   Anders Sörman-Nilsson   Andra Kea

nne Lise Kjaer   Aris Persidis   Arvind Gupta   Aubre

Bill Davidow   Bill Diamond   David Spiva

Carver Mead   Cat Tully   Cindy Frewen   Clem Bezo

David Guston   David Krakauer   David J. Staley

Donna Dupont   Eleanor "Nell" Watson   Eric Daimle

Grady Booch   Gray Scott   Hannes Sapiens   Haris

Ignacio Peña   Jack Uldrich   James Canton   Jane McGonig

effrey C. Bauer   Jerome Glenn   Jerry Fishenden   Jo

John M. Smart   John Sack   John Sanei   José More

aggie Greyson   Lisa Bodell   Maciej Kranz   Martin Guig

Mick Ebeling   Moon Ribas   Naveen Jain   Neil Jacobst

Po Bronson   Ray Kurzweil   Rebecca Cost

Rodrigo Nieto-Gómez   Rohit Bhargava   Ross Dawso

ridhar Mahadevan   Stan Rosen   Stephanie Mehta   Steve Wait

Theodore Jay Gordon   Thomas Frey   Timothy Ch

Zoltan Istvan   Fotis Sotiropoulos   Gill Ringla

Jordan Richardson   Nora Haney   Pankaj K. V

After Shock

The world's foremost **futurists**
reflect on **50 years** of
Future Shock—and look
ahead to the **next 50**

Edited by
John Schroeter

An imprint of John August Media, LLC

Published in the United States by Abundant World Institute,
an imprint of John August Media, LLC

www.abundantworldinstitute.com

John August Media, LLC
PO Box 10174, Bainbridge Island, WA 98110

Book design by Ed Rother, ER Graphics

Printed in the USA

Library of Congress Cataloging-in-Publication Data is available.

ISBN Print: 978-0-9997364-4-9
ISBN eBook: 978-0-9997364-5-6

LCCN: 2019914119

| SOCIAL SCIENCE/Future Studies |
| TECHNOLOGY & ENGINEERING/Social Aspects |
| BUSINESS & ECONOMICS/Forecasting |

First Edition

10 9 8 7 6 5 4 3 2 1

Alvin & Heidi Toffler

Contents

Master Classes
in Futures Studies:

Acknowledgements,
Gratitude, a Personal Note –
and a Foretaste of Toffler

This book has been 50 years in the making. But it's just one static milepost marking the way to the future, which is like the sign that hangs in the bar that reads, "Free Beer Tomorrow." The sign is there every day. And every day we return to it.

Indeed, the future is a perpetually rolling state of being and becoming, beckoning us on. ■

In celebrating this milestone, *After Shock* comprises both a constellation and a distillation of thought that converges in making manifest the power of each and every individual to contribute to the ongoing creation of a future of abundance. In every way, the whole—which now includes you, dear reader—is greater than the sum of its parts.

Several of the contributors to this volume worked for and collaborated with the Tofflers, while many others were children or were not even born when *Future Shock* first sent its shock waves around the globe. The differences in their perspectives creates a third lens by which we can take stock of the present and consider (and reconsider, reimagine, retool, rewire) our probable, possible, and preferred versions of the future.

This book's very existence is due entirely to the amazing generosity of its many contributors, and certainly to the enthusiastic support of Alvin and Heidi Toffler's eponymous organization, Toffler Associates, and its remarkable chairman, Deb Westphal. Special thanks also to our partners and collaborators in foresight and futures studies around the world, including Singularity University, Institute for the Future, Association of Professional Futurists, Institute for Alternative Futures, The Millennium Project, future/io, School of International Futures, and others.

In releasing *After Shock* into the wild, I am especially indebted to two true visionaries who personify the very idea of the whole being greater than the sum of its parts: Bo Rinaldi and Martin Guigui. Everything associated with this project is better for their touch. I am also grateful for the meticulous care of our copy editors, Bryanann Stavley, Michaelan Ferguson, and Rachelle Kuramoto, as well as the inspired work of our creative director, Eduardo Rother. Further enabling the project has been the enduring support of Jaime Cummins—a man who lives the future in every breath—and Naveen Jain, who continues to throw open the doors of possibility. My heartfelt gratitude to all of you.

And now to the personal note.

The germ of this project reaches back to 1970, when my mother brought home a new book with a bright blue cover bearing the compelling title, *Future Shock*. It captured my 10-year-old imagination then, and never let go.

I was fascinated by all things "future" in no small part because my father was involved with JPL during the "shoot and hope" days of NASA's Ranger program. Its mission objective, which was designed to inform the Apollo program, was to obtain the first up-close images of the lunar surface and send them back to Earth just before impact. That my father etched his name into the frame of Ranger 6, which impacted the moon on February 2, 1964, ignited my fantasies as a would-be lunar archaeologist, scratching about in the moon dust for that metallic relic bearing his name. It still does.

Sometime later, he brought home a box of old *Mechanix Illustrated* magazines, dating from the 1950s, that a coworker was cleaning out of his office. To this young teen, he might as well have brought me the moon. I consumed those musty magazines, with their yellowed pages, filled with an unbridled excitement about the future. Jet Age-inspired concept cars, images of spacecraft that were still more science fiction than science fact, personal jetpacks, and other wondrous fare transported my imagination via this amazing look back on looking forward.

It had to have been a magical time, I thought, because the spirit of innovation that came through those pages seemed all but gone in the early 1970s. At that time, the energy crisis had imposed an absurdly low speed limit, Viet Nam was lost, and the Watergate scandal was unfolding. Muscle cars had given way to crappy Vegas and Pintos. Skylab was launched, but the Apollo program was finished. Not a great decade for science, industry, or culture.

Fast-forward to the present, and we find ourselves hurtling headlong into a sensational new era—a period of unprecedented innovation and possibility. Today the exciting rise of robotics, the nascent but rapidly ascendant field of artificial intelligence, the burgeoning democratization of space, the massive disruptions coming in energy, self-driving cars, and many other developments are converging and conspiring to redefine virtually every aspect of life here on Earth—and beyond. Indeed, we are witnessing a major hinge of history. And like all hinges of history, it is squeaky.

Bringing all of this full circle, driven, no doubt, by my sentimental boyhood memories, I recently revived *Mechanix Illustrated* magazine, which had previously shuttered at a time when large swaths of traditional media were unable to adapt to the shocking arrival of the internet—something the Tofflers actually anticipated. They foresaw that the rate of communication, in addition to everything else, was also accelerating. "Busy people," they wrote, "wage a desperate battle each day to plow through as much information as possible." But they went further, looking forward to the day when "... books, magazines, newspapers, films and other media will, like the Mustang, be offered to the consumer on a design-it-yourself basis," and suggesting a system that would "... store a consumer's profile—data about his occupation and interests—in a central computer. Machines would then scan newspapers, magazines, video tapes, films and other material, match them against the individual's interest profile, and instantaneously notify him when something appears that concerns him. The system could be hitched to facsimile machines and TV transmitters that would actually display or print out the material in his own living room."

Sure, it was a little clunky, but there it was—*in 1970*—a vision of personalized news feeds delivered electronically and automagically to a low cost, in-home appliance. They rightly identified these potential developments as the "... first steps toward the newspaper of the future—a peculiar newspaper, indeed, offering no two viewer-readers the same content. Mass communication, under a system like this, is 'de-massified.' We move from homogeneity to heterogeneity."

The pages of *Future Shock* are filled with such prescient observations and analyses of their implications for society. Yet, interestingly, good old-fashioned print books are resurgent. (Okay, so part of that is the explosion in adult coloring books.) Perhaps this is a backlash to over-digitalization and a desire for a return to more "organic" and tactile experiences. Whatever the case, whether you are consuming the content of this book digitally or atomically, we welcome you just the same. And as you turn (or swipe) these pages, I sincerely hope that you'll appreciate that the future is indeed a big tent, and that if we muster the collective will, we can, in fact, create a future world of abundance in all its diversified glory.

Finally, I dedicate this book to the memory of the best man I ever knew, John Watson. The future, no matter how bright, will shine a little less brightly without him.

—*John Schroeter, Executive Director, Abundant World Institute*

On the Organization of the Book

To present this stimulating compendium of essays, our editorial team elected to sequence them according to their meta-affinities, the "organic" flow of which reveals an intriguing series of threads that progressively connect, reinforce, and build upon the many ideas, concepts, and insights offered.

We found that grouping the essays by topic or category forced divisions that were not always consistent or clear, and also interrupted the natural streams of thought that otherwise emerge. The format we chose also provides the reader with the opportunity to mentally cross-pollinate adjacent, and even seemingly unrelated, fields—an objective that is essential to discovery and for connecting dots across multiple domains to surface new possibilities for the future.

The exception to this organization is the series of three essays that appear in the "Master Class" section at the end of the book. Taken together, they comprise a rigorous introduction to foresight and futures studies.

Foreword

Deb Westphal

My introduction to Alvin and Heidi Toffler came much later than that of most of my contemporaries. It was 1995, and I was a young engineer working in advanced planning for the United States Air Force Research Laboratory to develop technological advances that would help create the future of the Air Force. The Department of Defense was focused on redefining its capabilities based on lessons learned from Desert Storm. It was a rare moment during which the entire US defense apparatus was attempting to peer into the future to guide a necessary transformation, rather than looking to past successes. Across this brave new phase of the Air Force Future Planning community, the Tofflers' recently published book *War and Anti-War* was required reading.

War and Anti-War introduced the idea that societies make war with many of the same tools they use to create wealth. It foreshadowed the growing importance of the knowledge component of warfare, the advent of cyberwar, and the need for more inclusive military strategies—including commercial technologies and business and civic sector organizations. This book expanded my view of warfare from being a predominantly kinetic endeavor to one that was integrated, complex, and nuanced across societies. *War and Anti-War* had a profound impact on my ideas about the future.

It also changed the course of my career. Through a series of serendipitous events spanning the next four years, I was tapped to be an original member of the Tofflers' eponymous advisory firm. Through the work I was doing with the Air Force, I had become one of the first clients for Toffler Associates.

In 1997, the Tofflers had opened their firm out of a passion for helping leaders of public and private organizations create the future—rather than react to it. That unique and magnanimous purpose drew me to their mission, and in 1999, I made the decision to leave my position with the Air Force to join the exciting startup.

In 2007, I became its CEO, which meant frequent meetings with Alvin and Heidi Toffler at their home in Bel Air, California. During these sessions, I provided updates about the firm and reported on a dynamic and growing client base. Inevitably, Al and Heidi would expand the focus of our conversations to ask how our people were doing. They wanted to know what they were working on and what they were learning. They wanted to know how their firm was helping clients create the future.

After a brief period of listening during these sessions about the firm's numbers and stats, Al would gently suggest we go to lunch. We went most often to *Cravings*, one of his favorite restaurants. As soon as we settled in and ordered, he would invariably pose the question that mattered most to him. "Tell me about the work. What hard problems are you solving?"

The Tofflers were interested in the health of the firm, of course, but their essential focus was on the impact we were having on the future. Discussions about our progress on this front always took significantly more time and attention than those about the firm's operations. Our deliberations ran the gamut from infrastructure, to space, to healthcare. Conversations would weave from the present through the past to the future, at times flowing without a sense of a point, pattern, or connection. All the while, Al and Heidi gathered information to inform their mental models—to learn, understand, and test the framework for understanding change they had developed over many prior years.

Knowing Alvin and Heidi Toffler

It's not an exaggeration to say that the Tofflers were interested in everything. They spent a lifetime seeking out diverse perspectives, gathering facts, making observations, and communicating their knowledge to millions. Their confidence in one set of assertions would move them to the next, as they continued to search for understanding. The Tofflers were unmatched in their sustained quest to engage people and ideas. They connected, shared, and extended truth.

Early in their professional lives, Al and Heidi were journalists. They wrote about everything—from art, culture, and technology, to congressional activities, to welding, and beyond. They thrived on seeking the truth through investigative interviews and deep research. As their writing catalog grew, so did their opportunities to write about people, companies, and current events. They pitched stories outside of typical interest articles. The more diverse the projects, the more they observed shifts and changes happening across different sectors of society. All the while, they experienced a growing sense that something big was happening across the US and other parts of the world.

While newspaper and magazine articles captured brief public attention, they rarely made an impact. The Tofflers realized that a book would offer a more significant and enduring forum to communicate their observations and the conclusions they reached by connecting dots across multiple areas. They also recognized that the title "author" would solidify a more lasting legacy. They had reached a critical inflection point in their careers. In 1964, Al and Heidi published their first book.

The Tofflers wrote *Culture Consumers* to postulate how, despite common belief to the contrary, the American middle class was becoming more involved with the arts and that this trend was good for democracy. The book raised the question of the responsibility of government to support the arts. It fueled a debate about the idea that the government should not be involved with the *content* of art, but should encourage art education in schools and provide accessible venues where the arts could expand. Only a few copies of *Culture Consumers* sold. Nonetheless, the book opened pathways for the Tofflers to explore and mature their ideas about sweeping changes and the implications of those changes for society.

The Changing Global Environment

The 1960s were an inflection point for the world. Civilization was struggling to recover from World War II. The decade was a complex crisscross of cultural and political trends. It was a time of turbulence, anger, flamboyance, revolution, and counterculture, marked by recreational drugs, sexual promiscuity, and rock and roll music.

Americans were giving new life to national democratic ideals through sit-ins, protest marches, freedom rides, and riots. A post-war generation of young people gave voice to issues of segregation, poverty, unemployment, equal rights, and discrimination.

Amid this swirl of evolving societal norms and values, Al and Heidi detected a far more critical shift. The very pace of change was accelerating. The more they observed, the more they saw evidence of acceleration and urgency. The pressure to speed up was gaining momentum everywhere, in business, science, technology, medicine, government, and finance, and in personal daily routines. People were struggling to cope with profound changes in the structure of their lives. In 1965, the Tofflers named this state of affairs "future shock."

That summer, *Horizon Magazine* published the article *"The Future as a Way of Life."* In it, the Tofflers warned that "culture shock is relatively mild in comparison with a more serious malady that might be called 'future shock'—the dizzying disorientation brought on by the premature arrival of the future. It may well be the most important disease of tomorrow. Future shock will not be found in *Index Medicus* or any listing of psychological abnormalities." They went on to state that "future shock is a time phenomenon, a product of the greatly accelerated pace of change in society. It arises from the superimposition of a new culture on an old one. It's a culture shock in one's own society. But its impact is far worse."

It took another five years before the book *Future Shock* was published.

Through unwavering dedication, Al and Heidi continued to chart the pace of change. They identified the emergence of the Knowledge Age and the characterization of the opportunities and challenges that humanity would face as societies moved deeper into it. They called for a future consciousness in everyone—a commitment to do the work to understand the shocks occurring (and yet to occur), and to lead society through the disruption for the betterment of all.

> In 1997, the Tofflers had opened their firm out of a passion for helping leaders of public and private organizations create the future – rather than react to it.

Future Shock in the Present

2020 marks the 50th anniversary of the first publication of *Future Shock*. The milestone is an opportunity to celebrate the influence of this global classic. It's a good time to reflect on why people still read and debate the ideas in the book, even as the world has changed in so many fundamental ways. Perhaps because of that context, it's incredible to consider the pervasive, consequential, and enduring contribution the Tofflers made for societies and economies worldwide.

The Tofflers' legacy is much greater than the books, articles, and speeches they published. From early in their careers, before their first book, and all throughout their lives, they inspired people across the globe to step into the future, to consider the present world in its larger context. They challenged conventional thinking and called us all to look more closely at the connections being made across vast topics and issues, encouraging us to truly understand change and its impact. They wrote books to educate, communicate, and empower individuals to proactively create their own futures, rather than passively accept whatever circumstance wrought for them. They gave speeches to connect with people, human-to-human, to share ideas and learn, and to champion future-focused consciousness.

After Shock is a momentous initiative, timed to correspond with this milestone. John Schroeter, executive director of the Abundant World Institute, has accomplished something special with the publication of this unique book. He has brought together some of the world's foremost thought leaders and futurists in a compendium of diverse essays that spark imagination, rally important causes, and inspire solutions to the many challenges we face.

It is an exemplary collection of perspectives, conversations, and debates that cross a myriad of important topics about what we are doing to create a better future for the world.

Rather than giving specific directives, John granted the authors leeway to contribute from a place of their own experience, expertise, and passion. The only instructions were to reflect on the impact and inspiration that *Future Shock* had on their life and work and to write about what moved them personally or professionally. As a result, this collection spans wide and interesting topics, dynamic industries, and temporal references—making it a powerful assembly of diverse thought.

Reading through the essays, I was reminded of a Buddhist parable. It is the story of a group of blind men who have never come across an elephant. Each man touches and describes a different part of the animal, based on their experience and place of discovery. As they share and combine their observations, a full description of the large, unusual, beautiful animal takes shape.

Like the blind men in the parable, the *After Shock* essayists each share their experience, expertise, fears, and hopes. Together, they craft a rich cohesive, stunning view of what we might expect in the future.

Al and Heidi would have admired the ideas and concepts found in this book. They would have found the essays moving and thought-provoking, seemingly random in nature, yet deeply connected in their examinations of *Future Shock*'s influence. I know they would have cherished the discourse and diversity of the authors and their outlooks. And, I'm certain they would have been keen to engage with each and every author you will encounter in these pages.

You'll be energized by the vast number and variety of essays. Several authors recount personal stories about the influence *Future Shock* had on their thinking and, in some cases, their career paths. Others revisit the book to examine what the Tofflers got right and what they missed at that particular time in history. Several essays consider critical issues that we must address to create a better future for humanity, and some pose solutions to the issues we face now. You'll read a call for futurists to be recognized as important contributors within modern organizations and for the development of a futurism discipline that will train leaders to identify and anticipate future shocks and possible courses of action.

I have had the benefit of reading the essays multiple times and speaking with the authors. The ideas in this book are powerful and impactful. Some are specific, like the role of ethics in AI. Many are sweeping, like the look at how humans are adapting. Some topics feel more familiar, and therefore easier to digest, such as the need for addressing climate change and environmental concerns, while some will leave you ruminating on the meaning of our beliefs and values, such as spiritualism being the technological endgame. All are thought-provoking and challenge our beliefs and biases about the past, present, and future.

From the moment you move into the substance of all these rich, generously shared perspectives, you will experience the kind of full immersion into varied, challenging, and inspiring topics that the Tofflers thrived on their whole careers. And you'll experience the enlightenment that comes when we connect disparate ideas and consider the opportunities we have to shape the future.

These individual contributions comprise a powerful collection of powerful voices advocating for the Tofflers' dedication to future consciousness. It represents the empowerment of individuals to proactively create the future, rather than being idly subjected to it. This is what the Tofflers spent a lifetime championing. It is their legacy. And the legacy will continue to live through the incredible work and contributions of the amazing people you will get to know through *After Shock*.

Navigating Uncertainty: Thinking in Futures

Vikram Mansharamani, PhD

A former cabin boy in the Merchant Marine, Morgan Robertson had tired of sea life, spent a decade as a diamond setter, and eventually turned to writing about the sea. Despite getting stories published in major magazines, he never made much money. He died at the age of 53 from an overdose.

Before he died, Robertson wrote a novel about "the largest craft afloat and the greatest of the works of men," called *Futility*. The ship was the embodiment of "every science, profession, and trade known to civilization" and was a true technological marvel. The boat was deemed "unsinkable" and attracted famous people from around the world to journey across the Atlantic in unrivaled comfort and style. Nineteen water-tight compartments assured safety as she could sail with nine flooded. And because the vessel was deemed indestructible, it carried lifeboats adequate to carry only 1/6th of the passengers. The name of the ship was the *Titan*. In Robertson's tale, on a voyage through the North Atlantic one April, the ship strikes an iceberg and sinks. The story goes on to describe the drama associated with a disgraced naval officer who worked as a deckhand on the *Titan*, John Rowland. Rowland rescues a young girl and was then accused by the girl's mother (who was also his former lover), of kidnapping her. Very Hollywood-esque drama, for sure. Given that authors have often looked to historical events for inspiration, you might dismiss Robertson's novel as being in the same vein as James Cameron's blockbuster 1997 movie *Titanic*.

Don't. Why's that? Because *Futility* was written 14 years before the actual Titanic sank. Aside from the obvious similarities of name and method of demise, consider these facts:

	Futility (1898)	Titanic (1912)
Vessel Name	Titan	Titanic
Ship Length	800 ft	882 ft
Ship Displacement	45,000 tons	46,000 tons
Ship Speed	22.5 knots	25 knots
Popular Description	"Unsinkable"	"Unsinkable"
Life Boats	24	16
Passengers and Crew	2500	2200
Cause of Accident	Iceberg impact	Iceberg impact
Location	North Atlantic	North Atlantic
Precise Location	400 nm from Newfoundland	400 nm from Newfoundland
Date	April	April 14, 1912
Survivors	13	705
Propellers	3	3

After the sinking of the actual *Titanic*, Robertson was celebrated by many as a clairvoyant, as possessing extraordinary skills of precognition. He dismissed these claims, suggesting it was his knowledge of maritime matters that gave him the ability to write about ships with detail. Yet the world refused to give up on the possibility that he had, in fact, "seen the future."

It's such an intriguing story that the 1990s American TV series *Beyond Belief: Fact or Fiction* featured the *Titan-Titanic* story in an episode, highlighting during the short segment that "the only difference between fiction and nonfiction is that fiction hasn't happened yet." Host Jonathan Frakes (yes, the one of *Star Trek* fame) tells the story from the perspective of a struggling author, and ends the story by asking viewers if the coincidence was "another example of art foreshadowing life? The same way Jules Verne wrote of submarines long before their invention? Or da Vinci sketched flying machines centuries before the Wright Brothers?" At the end of the episode, he reveals that the story was, in fact, true.

Coincidences happen, for sure. And anyone prognosticating on the future has likely heard the clichés "even a broken clock is right twice a day" and "every now and then a blind squirrel will find a nut," statements that suggest mere luck as the reason for Robertson's supposed ability to see the future. In fact, Robertson's title states the primary criticism directed at those who think about the future—it's an act of futility. And, as the saying goes, "it's dangerous to make predictions, especially about the future."

One need only look to some expert predictions to see just how inaccurate they can be. Consider, for instance, two books that made it to the top of the bestseller lists: *The Population Bomb* and *The Great Depression of 1990*. The first, by Stanford biologist Paul Ehrlich, noted in 1968 that "the battle to feed all of humanity is over... in the 1970s, the world will undergo famines—hundreds of millions of people will starve to death..." Ehrlich failed to appreciate the possibilities of the "Green Revolution," which dramatically increased agriculture's productivity. Incidentally, the Green Revolution was already underway when Ehrlich wrote his book; he just didn't grasp the potential impact. *The Great Depression of 1990*, by Southern Methodist University economist Ravi Batra (which stayed on the bestseller list for 10 months in hardcover and over 19 months as a paperback), totally missed the technological developments that made the 1990s among the most productive decades ever. And in 2001, Gordon Chang wrote *The Coming Collapse of China*, a persuasively argued case that the Middle Kingdom was destined to fall apart. In the decade that followed, China boomed.

Yet despite this mixed (at best) track record of those in the predictions business, we humans seem to have an insatiable appetite for their prognostications. Nobel Laureate Ken Arrow eloquently captured the desire for predictions in recalling his work for the US Army Air Force. Despite concluding that the weather predictions upon which his superiors relied were entirely useless (i.e., statistically random, no better than a guess), he was rebuffed, told that "The Commanding General is well aware that the forecasts are no good; however, he needs them for planning purposes."

As comical as that statement sounds, I find it quite useful—and helpful. *The blunt reality is that accuracy cannot and should not be the criterion upon which to evaluate thinking about the future*. Usefulness, I propose, is a far better standard. Mechanical as it may be, thinking about various scenarios of how the future may unfold has proven to be among the most useful ways make decisions amidst radical uncertainty.

It's important to note that scenarios are not predictions, or mere extrapolations of trends. Scenarios are stories of possible futures. There may be high or low probabilities associated with each scenario, but the act of articulating scenarios can help us appreciate our assumptions about the future and give us a map of the terrain that we may encounter.

There is a long and storied history behind the use of scenarios as a means of navigating uncertainty. Although the professional use of scenarios originated in military circles, Royal Dutch/Shell's Group Planning Department (under the leadership of Pierre Wack) showed its usefulness in non-combat domains beginning in the 1960s. At the time, the group considered scenarios such as worldwide spikes in the price of oil driven by the newly formed Organization of Petroleum Exporting Countries (OPEC) flexing its muscles. When the oil shocks of the 1970s occurred, the company was able to make better decisions in the face of the overwhelming uncertainty. One result of this early success was that Royal Dutch/Shell began publishing a regular series of future scenarios.

I recently took the time to go back and find the compa-

> The blunt reality is that accuracy cannot and should not be the criterion upon which to evaluate thinking about the future. Usefulness, I propose, is a far better standard.

ny's public summary of their *Global Scenarios to 2020*, published in 2002. The scenarios presented two distinct futures; one was called "Business Class" and the other "Prism." Here's how Philip Watts, then chairman of the Committee of Managing Directors at Royal Dutch / Shell Group, summarized the scenarios:

> *"Business Class" offers a vision of "connected freedom," as global elites and the dominant influence of the United States lead the world towards continuing economic integration. [...]. In "Prism," "connections that matter" reflect the persisting power of cultural values, driving multiple approaches to modernity... [as] countries combine to follow their own development paths—based on their particular economic, political, and social circumstances—in the context of new regional structures.*

In the aftermath of the technology bubble bursting, the 9/11 terrorist attacks on the United States, and China's entry into the World Trade Organization, differing development paths centered around regional structures rather than global institutions did not appear particularly likely. But had you been thinking about the "Prism" scenario, you might have been better prepared for the rapid rise of nationalism and protectionism beginning around 2016. And, perhaps you wouldn't have been shocked by the launch of the China-led Asian Infrastructure Investment Bank.

The world is uncertain; we all know that. But we need not be surprised by developments within it. In fact, by hiding from the uncertainty, rather than embracing it, we might miss obvious risks and forego tremendous opportunities. We can and should regularly think about possible futures. Not doing so can be tragic. The 9/11 Commission, chaired by former Governor of New Jersey Thomas Keane, concluded in its final report that the terrorist attacks of 9/11 on the United States were a "failure of imagination." (Relatedly, no one has suggested that Pearl Harbor was a failure of imagination because the Japanese had 36 years earlier conducted an almost identical surprise attack on the Russian Pacific Fleet based in Port Arthur).

Imagination and creativity of thought—surprise, surprise—are critical components of building visions of futures that can help us think through how the world may unfold. Unadulterated imagination will produce some wacky thoughts, for sure, but some of them may prove to be revolutionary. One method many of the world's best futurists have used to keep their imagination sharp is regularly consuming fiction (novels, movies, or otherwise) to help them imagine different worlds, possible scenarios, and alternative futures. Stories tend to help us get out of our own heads and to think about scenarios that may not naturally enter our frame of view.

Just think about how the opening lines of the movie *Armageddon* fundamentally force the viewer to think differently. It begins with an image of the Earth from afar. The voiceover begins: "This is the Earth at a time when the dinosaurs roamed a lush and fertile planet..." and the scene then shows an asteroid heading toward it. The voice continues, "A piece of rock just six miles wide changed all that..."

After showing the asteroid impact on Earth, the narrator explains, "It hit with a force of 10,000 nuclear weapons... a trillion tons of dirt and rock hurled into the atmosphere, creating a suffocating blanket of dust the sun was powerless to penetrate for a thousand years..." As the image shows the entire Earth covered from the blast, the music turns ominous, and the voice warns: "It happened before. It will happen again. It's just a question of when..."

If you think this is just Hollywood dreaming up fantastic stories to help us escape the reality of life, consider that the *Economist* on August 1, 2015, proposed a scenario for consideration titled "What if an asteroid heads for Earth?" Published as part of the magazine's annual 17-page set of scenarios called "The World If," the collection is meant to accompany their heavily read "The World in XXXX" set of predictions. Yet the scenarios have enormous standalone value in forcing readers to think.

Other topics explored in the 2015 edition of "The World If" included the possibility of Russia breaking up, India's monsoon failing, and the building of a canal in Nicaragua that rivals the Panama Canal. The following year's scenarios, published in July 2016, led with a story that was dismissed as highly unlikely: "What if Donald Trump was President?" The story they wrote, fictionally dated April 2017, foreshadows much of what actually transpired during the first 100 days of the Trump administration. Other 2016 scenarios include the collapse of the North Korean regime and a mass hacking of the financial system. And the 2017 "The World If" raised the prospect of an EMP (electromagnetic pulse) attack on the United States that brings down the entire electricity grid, the emergence of a true fiduciary standard, and drumroll please... that Donald Trump's popularity surges, leading to his reelection in 2020.

> We want to focus on planning, not plans... because as famous boxer Mike Tyson has noted, "Everyone has a plan until they get punched in the face."

Hollywood is great at the storytelling business, and visual stories tend to be more effective at having a lasting impact on thoughts than does text. So let's consider another scenario: the possibility of California disconnecting from the mainland of the United States. Probably sounds as far-fetched as an asteroid hitting the Earth, right? What if I told you there were serious thinkers focused on this exact possibility?

Just watch the movie *San Andreas*. Yes, the human drama was an emotional hook around which the story is told, but the part that struck me as really jarring was the scene of boats driving through downtown San Francisco. Is this a possibility? How real is it? Aren't we just wasting precious brain processing power and limited attention on a very remote possibility? Maybe, but maybe not.

Kathryn Shultz is a writer for the *New Yorker* and author of a book called *Being Wrong: Adventures in the Margin of Error*. In addition to authoring this fabulous book about handling error, she also penned a page-turning article about the possibility of an earthquake that completely transforms the Pacific Northwest. The subheading for her June 2015 *New Yorker* piece titled "The Really Big One" was "An earthquake will destroy a sizable portion of the coastal Northwest. The question is when."

A word of caution. While it's easy to dismiss *San Andreas* and *Armageddon* as mere movies about low-probability natural disasters, doing so would miss their real value. *By forcing us to think about radical scenarios, stories can broaden our imagination about what the future may bring.*

Because the value of scenario planning can be so high, we need to be careful not to overly define the various situations for which we're prepping. We need to allow a certain amount of fuzziness when preparing for contingencies. If we're too focused in our preparation, we may not be able to respond well. *We want to focus on planning, not plans*... because as famous boxer Mike Tyson has noted, "Everyone has a plan until they get punched in the face." We need to retain the ability to adjust dynamically to accommodate new conditions as they emerge.

If dealing with the accelerative thrust of the past 50 years drove our collective future shock, might anxiety from overwhelming uncertainty in the next 50 years drive our collective after shock? This uncertainty anxiety already stems from an innate discomfort with complexity, ambiguity, volatility, and unpredictable outcomes. In fact, the acronym "VUCA" (volatile, uncertain, complex, and ambiguous), used heavily in military circles, describes just such a situation. Might our current predicament be a result of ubiquitous VUCA, and if so, what are we to do?

The bottom line, as eloquently captured by baseball great Yogi Berra, is that "the future ain't what it used to be."

Uncertainty has been viscerally increasing for almost everyone in all walks of life. Consider economic and financial markets. The inability to fully comprehend how protectionism, cryptocurrencies, shifting central bank mandates, algorithmic trading, the rise of a global middle class, and the seemingly unstoppable march of passive investing strategies affect the future? Likewise, automation and artificial intelligence are sure to affect life on Earth in very profound ways, in domains as diverse as transportation, health care, education, etc.

In describing the psychological dimension of *Future Shock*, Toffler explicitly described the pressures of information overload, highlighting how increasing data access will drive decision stress and other ailments. Today, drowning in data is an all-too-common condition, leading many to analysis paralysis. Poor decisions and misunderstanding how the future might unfold are commonplace. Further, our natural default condition is to outsource our thinking to siloed experts and technologies that can help us optimize choices amidst the data deluge. But has this outsourcing of thought made us better at navigating uncertainty and making decisions in the face of ambiguous choices? Sadly, the answer seems to be "no."

Navigating uncertainty is about thinking in futures and connecting dots. It's about painting your own mosaics of the futures, drawing on the insights of those deeply engaged in a domain, and making your own decisions. To these ends, the insights contained in these pages are like a collection of Lego pieces. Take from them what you need to create your own futures, for as EO Wilson, the legendary biologist, has noted: "We are drowning in information, while starving for wisdom. The world henceforth will be run by synthesizers, people able to put together the right information at the right time, think critically about it, and make important choices wisely." ■

Vikram Mansharamani is a lecturer at the Harvard John Paulson School of Engineering and Applied Sciences. Profiled by *Worth* as one of the 100 most powerful people in global finance, he has also been twice highlighted by LinkedIn as their #1 Top Voice for Money, Finance, and Economics. Dr. Mansharamani is the author of *Boombustology: Spotting Financial Bubbles before They Burst* (Wiley) and *Think for Yourself: Restoring Common Sense in an Age of Experts and Artificial Intelligence* (HBR Press, 2020). He has a PhD and two masters degrees from the Massachusetts Institute of Technology and a bachelor's degree from Yale University. He lives in Lexington, MA, with his wife, two kids, a golden retriever, and two cats, one of which he thinks may be clairvoyant.

The New Model of Futurism

Po Bronson
& Arvind Gupta

Who doesn't feel an occasional longing for how it used to be? Somewhere in the house is a photo album, or shoebox, with snapshots of bygone eras. The ink print has lost its sharpness, its chromophores exposed to the wear of time, but we recall instantly who is in the frame. That's my uncle. That's my cousin. It was someone's anniversary. Milliseconds after noting these initial details, our mind reaches again into the swimming pool of the past to reconstruct the emotional context of the photo. Was I happy? Were they?

In the past were the days when cousins lived nearby. In the past was the era when parents didn't pay million dollar bribes to get their kid into college. It was in the past that when people were sick, they went to the doctor, rather than stay away to avoid the catastrophic bills.

This bias to fondness for the past even taints the memory of our paperback edition of *Future Shock*, in its Air Force Blue cover, with the edges fading aqua. Way back in 1970, Toffler predicted the demise of the nuclear family, an information age powered by knowledge workers, the rise of cable television, and genetic engineering. But that world he predicted—the very world we lived—almost feels quaint now. Simpler times.

What's fundamentally different about futurism now?

The basic formula for futurism was a waterfall model: 1) here's what technology is going to be capable of, which leads to 2) here's how humans will learn to cope.

In this waterfall model, the impact of 1 was always greater than the resistance inherent in 2.

Technology wins, humans adapt. It might take some time, but it's inevitable.

But if you use that formula to make forecasts now, every prediction comes out wildly wrong.

The big thing that's changed—the big thing that Toffler didn't foresee—was that humans don't just suffer shock, stress, and disorientation. Instead, they fight back, *en masse.*

Toffler recognized that there would be cases of Luddite behavior, but he said they'd be offset by a greater fear of being left behind. People's fear of social exclusion and irrelevance would cause most to vainly try to play along with the new and the newer.

Today, no matter how powerful 1 is, 2 sees it coming and rises up against it to some degree. Futurists cannot assume anymore that 1>2. The world is at war between people who like change and people who don't like change. This war is everywhere, on every continent, in every government, in every industry, in every home.

The futurist model today adds a new fluid variable:

1 vs. [2 * ("Longing for the past" minus "Belief in our future")]

The stronger our societal memory bias toward the past, and the weaker our belief in the future, the less 1 beats 2. The future slows down. A pickup truck blocks the Tesla supercharger station. The future and the past are at war, and the past is well-armed. It has television networks. It has religious ideology. It has lobbyists. It has trillions in corporate capital to defend its trenches. It has anonymous message boards. It has recruiters. It has victims to trot out in front of cameras. It has flags to wave.

We live at a time when the future's inevitability cannot be taken for granted. And if we're honest,

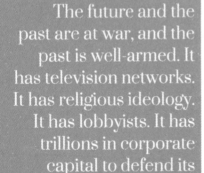

> The future and the past are at war, and the past is well-armed. It has television networks. It has religious ideology. It has lobbyists. It has trillions in corporate capital to defend its trenches. It has anonymous message boards.

we acknowledge that fondness for the past is often a natural coping mechanism to deal with the stress of the present, or the scariness of the future.

When a story runs in the newspaper that "Only 5% of the world's oceans has been explored," it's a science story—but it's also terrific inspiration for anti-science. Anti-science feeds on the truism that science is imperfect and doesn't know *every-thing*. The faster science rewrites itself (and it's going faster than ever), the more some people hear "science proven wrong, again."

Denying scientific consensus is not just the domain of those who cling to the past. It also belongs to those who create the future. Every major research advancement has to break the stranglehold of scientific consensus. Every really innovative company has to bust through the prevailing wisdom that it couldn't be done.

So, in this way, both the future and the past share the same wiring, the same psychological pathways. They inevitably go together hand in hand, like gravity against the expansion of the universe. The faster the future comes into our lives, the fiercer the rebellion against it.

What then does this new futurist model predict?

Broadly, it predicts that technologies are only going to make a huge impact on the world *if they inspire enough people to fight for them.*

Technologies that do not inspire an army of advocates will be fads, or confined to small market backwaters. Just because a technology is possible does not mean it'll be adopted. How hugely it's funded is inconsequential. What matters is that people understand it, and want it, and will recruit.

In *Future Shock,* Toffler predicted a world where relationships to people and place trend inevitably toward the disposable, like the products we buy and discard. What we've seen, instead, is that we'll hang on to some relationships no matter how many thousands of miles separate us. The internet didn't just open the door to the future, it gave us an infinite resource to binge learn our history in detail, to rediscover our pasts. It's worth noting that Ancestry.com has millions more customers than 23&Me.

The most popular thing to do on the internet is look at photos of what our friends are up to. Not to live in a synthetic VR headset. Sometimes, Silicon Valley buys into a trend (or a technology) because it matches *what we long imagined the future would be like.*

Time travel has *always* been a fanciful technology of the future, ever since HG Wells popularized it in 1895. But all it takes to travel through time—perhaps more in the style of Charles Dickens than HG Wells—is to close one's eyes and go. So in this battle between past and future, past has memory as its soldier; the future has imagination. Imagination is the ever expanding universe. Memory is gravity, holding it back.

Po Bronson is a strategy director at IndieBio. He works with teams on their storytelling to investors and partners, and guides IndieBio's strategic thinking around future markets. Po is passionate about reconceptualizing complex challenges into more elegant forms, to broaden understanding and highlight priorities. Po is a longtime science journalist honored with nine national awards, and author of seven bestselling books. His background is in economics. Prior to IndieBio, he spent four years as a futurist with Attention Span Media, consulting in corporate innovation efforts for globally recognized brands.

Arvind Gupta is the founder of IndieBio, the world's largest biotech program-based seed fund. Using a blend of scientific method and design thinking, Arvind and the IndieBio team fund startups that can impact over a billion people or address markets over a billion dollars. Beginning his professional life as an options market maker in the Pacific Coast Exchange in the Microsoft pit, Arvind left trading in search of a career with deeper meaning. Arvind discovered design when IDEO hired him. As a design director of product development and strategy at IDEO, he led the team that designed the Samsung Galaxy Curve, received many international design awards and moved to Shanghai to build the Asia product design team. Further, Arvind co-founded Starters, a personal fitness app that gained thousands of users in 98 countries. Joining SOSV in 2013, Arvind became a venture capitalist to invest in biotech and deep science technologies, including AR/VR and new user interfaces. He is a regular speaker at TEDx, TechCrunch Disrupt, Slush conference, Startup Iceland, and SFMOMA, among others. His writing appears in *Nature, Rotman, Forbes,* and *Design Observer.* He has been awarded eight US patents and has had his work in the SF Museum of Modern Art. Arvind received his BS in genetic engineering from UCSB and studied industrial design at SFSU. Arvind is married, with two daughters. He is a 2016 world champion in No Gi Brazilian Jiu-Jitsu, has climbed El Capitan and other big walls, and was a BASE Jumper and big wave surfer. He currently trains in MMA and BJJ.

After Future Shock Came Life Online: Growing up in a Web Connected Society

Aaron Frank

Reading Alvin and Heidi Toffler's *Future Shock* today, I can't be faulted for mistaking the work for something printed last month, not 50 years ago. Many of the themes and observations, now half a century old, still hold true.

Future Shock gave voice to a collection of ideas about the currents of change reaching from the past and shaping the modern world. And for a work so focused on change, it's ironic that today's society asks many of the same questions and faces similar challenges to those that absorbed the Tofflers' attention 50 years ago.

And though 50 years have passed since the initial publication of *Future Shock*, the pace of change it's focused on has not slowed.

In fact, what seems most stunning about such a prophetic piece of writing is that it was born well before one of the most significant and world-changing technological developments in human history. The book preceded the development of a notable cause of the "future shock" experienced today: the internet.

The internet also had a significant birthday this year. It just turned 30. And I know this because we share a birthday party.

My birthday, March 8th, 1989, is only four days earlier than the day regularly acknowledged as the day that the modern internet was invented. Of course, the internet's sterile beginning as Arpanet trace back to the colorless rooms of government research labs, but it wasn't until Tim Berners-Lee proposed a meaningful new way of managing information flows using hyperlinked text that the internet became what it is today.

Soon after Berners-Lee's proposed "World Wide Web" technology, useful interfaces like web browsers and online service providers like AOL emerged. Then came world domination.

I don't have first-hand experience of those early days on the web, but I am part of a generation of internet natives—a collection of young people whose world views, habits, expectations, communication quirks, and brains have been shaped by the forces of connectivity and life online.

We are the first such generation; we are certainly not the last.

In some ways, reflecting on life after the internet is a difficult task; it's like trying to describe what breathing air is like or detailing the impact that tables have had on society. The internet is hard to describe because it's simply everywhere. There's a well-known drug dealer in San Francisco's Dolores Park, near where I live, who accepts credit cards using a mobile internet payment system on his phone. Buyers can get a receipt for illegal drugs sent to their email (if they want).

Growing up, my older brother and sister carried around disc players and large bricks of CD sleeves to access their music library. I can't remember that I did. I remember downloaded libraries of music files from Napster (please don't sue me).

I never once looked up, checked out, or even opened a physical book from my university's library during college. I graduated relying entirely on digital libraries like JSTOR (and Wikipedia!).

My parents caught up with friends over the phone, while my friends and I spent countless hours using AIM (AOL Instant Messenger), one of the most definitive growing-up internet experiences for most people my age.

I was in high school when Facebook came on the scene, and it transformed our social dynamics almost overnight. On Sunday nights, classmates published photos of the parties they went to that weekend, and everyone suddenly knew who was where and with whom. It was an early glimpse of today's "social media influencer" culture and how status dynamics are shaped by publishing your life for all to see. The social dynamics of the lunchroom had moved online.

> The internet used to be simple; today it is not. It's as complex as we are, and we humans are strange animals. We're at once anxious and defensive, caring and sweet, loving and angry. We're a contradiction, and so the internet is, too. It's both a savior and a villain.

These may not be world-shaping examples, but they do highlight the internet's ability to integrate with even the most mundane parts of daily life. And more than anything, for good and for bad, internet natives like me have grown up in a world defined by ever-increasing connectivity.

We've been connected to media from around the world, to news and information in an instant, to the pizza shop that's only just opened down the street. And we've been connected to each other. The biggest concepts of the last twenty years—peer-to-peer, crowdsourcing, platform economics, the sharing economy—are all just an assortment of names referring to the same phenomenon: a world shaped by connectivity.

And connectivity breeds the speed that can create a sense of future shock. More ideas connecting, spreading, replicating, mixing, and breeding. The more connected people are, the quicker change can happen—for good or bad. Viral marketing campaigns, memes, and images from terrorist attacks are all amplified as they are tunneled through the web. Similarly, ideas for startups, inventions, and innovation can spread around the globe at an ever accelerating speed.

Now we're seeing the early stages of a world where not just humans, but machines link up and connect as well. A network of devices can spread information to every other device on a network. A single autonomous vehicle can share what it has learned with the group, meaning the algorithms powered by connected machines can absorb thousands of hours of practice in a single moment. Machines teaching machines will stimulate the fastest pace of innovation our world has yet seen.

And perhaps the brains of young people (and I mean younger than I am) will be even more used to this kind of speed. Just as my own brain was shaped by my own era's pace of change.

Connectivity brings dangers, too, including the challenges of designing and governing such a wired society. The internet can all too quickly become a tool of isolation, providing echo chambers for voices of the like-minded. On the internet, belief systems can be the customer, and platforms are all too willing to serve up personalized and self-reinforcing feedback loops of content. And if we're not careful to sort out the business models which incentivize recommendation engines that polarize their users toward extreme ideas, a high school kid with a basic physics question risks landing in a convincing online community where the Earth is actually flat.

The internet used to be simple; today it is not. It's as complex as we are, and we humans are strange animals. We're at once anxious and defensive, caring and sweet, loving and angry. We're a contradiction, and so the internet is, too. It's both a savior and a villain, a place where the good and evil of our species now lives. The internet can give us a glimpse into ourselves. (And apparently, we like cats.)

And for the generations yet to come, if it can be preserved, the internet may be a monument to and record of the things that came before. Like the greatest library ever made.

As I reflect on the most basic, day-to-day ways I use the internet, aside from the extensive list of actions made possible by the hidden infrastructure of the web, they are mostly to watch European soccer in my American living room, to video call with my girlfriend when we're halfway across the world from one another, and to stay in touch with loved ones and family.

Mainly, the internet has collapsed the distance between me and the people I care about, and the things I love.

To *Future Shock*, I say happy birthday. The world today is a bit stranger, a bit faster, and a lot more connected than the day you were written. And to the internet, I say that I know from experience that it's hard growing up. I'm sure there are challenges to come, problems to face, and mistakes to learn from. Here's to another 50 years together. ■

Aaron Frank is a researcher, writer, and lecturer, based at Singularity University as full-time Principal Faculty. As a writer, his work has been published in Vice's *Motherboard*, *Wired UK*, *Forbes*, and *Venturebeat*. As a speaker, Aaron has addressed many audiences across business and government, including the CIA, the Department of Defense, and Under Armour. He routinely advises large companies, startups, and government organizations on trends related to a broad set of emerging technologies, with a focus on augmented and virtual reality.

Storytelling and Artificial Intelligence

Adrienne Mayor

Alvin Toffler observed that if we divide the past 50,000 years of human existence into life spans of about 62 years each, our species has experienced about 800 lifetimes. For about 650 of those lifetimes, we were cave dwellers. Writing only appeared during the last 70 lifetimes. But storytelling is as old as language itself. Stories have been shared ever since the first human beings huddled around a fire together.[1]

As Toffler knew, our 800 lifetimes have had a cumulative impact on ideas, beliefs, and values.[2] Stories contain wisdom and humor. They shape culture and instill values, cooperation, and identity. Humans have an "instinct" for storytelling that "shapes our cognitive and behavioral development."[3] As narrative creatures, we are hard-wired to hear, tell, and remember stories. Stories are retold over thousands of years as long as they summon strong, complicated emotions, as long as they still resonate with real dilemmas, and as long as they are good to think with.

About 44 lifetimes ago (more than 2,700 years ago), hopes and fears about creating artificial life, surpassing human limits, and attempting to imitate and improve nature were imagined in ancient Greek myths, which drew on even older oral tales. One could compare such myths to maps drawn by early cartographers. As Toffler noted, the first mapmakers set down bold, imaginative concepts about uncharted worlds they'd never seen. Despite inaccuracies and conjectures, those maps guided explorations into new realities. Toffler suggested that we navigate the future's perils and promises in the same spirit as the cartographers and explorers of the past.[4] Stories have always charted human values—might storytelling play a role in guiding artificial intelligences?

Exuberance mixed with the anxiety that is evoked by blurring the boundaries between nature and machines might seem to be a uniquely modern response to the juggernaut of scientific progress in our age of high technology. But ambivalence surrounding the notion of making artificial life emerged thousands of years ago, in the ancient Greek world. Classical myths about Prometheus, Jason and the Argonauts, Medea, Daedalus, Hephaestus, Talos, and Pandora raised basic questions about the boundaries between biological and artificial beings. The tales helped the Greeks contemplate the promises and perils of staving off age and death, enhancing mortals' capabilities, and replicating nature. The Greek myths spin thrilling adventures well worth knowing for their own sake. But when we recognize that some stories are inquiries into *biotechne* (*bios*, life; *techne,* craft), they take on new significance and seem startlingly of our moment.[5]

Homer's *Iliad* (ca 700 BC) tells how Hephaestus, the god of invention and technology, built a fleet of self-propelled carts that delivered nectar and ambrosia to the gods' banquets, returning when empty. Animated guard dogs, automatic gates, and self-regulating bellows were some of his other productions. Talos, the great bronze killer robot powered by an internal conduit filled with ichor, was constructed by Hephaestus to defend the island of Crete. Hephaestus also made a crew of life-sized golden female assistants. These androids resembled "real young women, with sense and reason, strength, even voices" and were "endowed with all the learning of immortals," making them the first artificial intelligence agents in Western literature. Two thousand years later, AI developers aspire to achieve what the ancient Greeks imagined that their god of technological invention was capable of creating in his workshop.

Hephaestus's products of *biotechne* were dreamed up by a culture that existed millennia before the advent of robots that win complex games, hold conversations, write poems, analyze massive mega-data, and infer human desires. But the big questions we face today are as ancient as mythological concerns: Whose desires will AI entities reflect and carry out? How and from whom will they learn?

The mythic fantasies of imitating and augmenting life inspired haunting theatrical performances and indelible illustrations in classical vase paintings, sculpture, and other artworks. Taken together, the myths, legends, and lore of past cultures about automatons, robots, replicants, animated statues, extended human powers, self-moving machines, and other artificial beings, and the historical technological wonders that followed, constitute a virtual library of ancient wisdom and experiments in thinking, a unique resource for understanding the oncoming challenges of biotechnology and synthetic life. Mythic tales about artificial life provide a historical context for warp-speed developments in artificial life and artificial intelligence—and they can enrich our discussions of the looming practical and ethical implications.

Consider Hephaestus's fabrication of Pandora, a myth first recounted by the poet Hesiod (ca 700 BC). Pandora was a female android—"evil disguised as beauty"—commissioned by the tyrannical god Zeus to punish humans for accepting the technology of fire stolen by Prometheus. Designed to entrap humans, Pandora's sole mission on Earth was to unseal a jar of suffering and disasters to plague humankind for eternity. She was presented as a bride to Epimetheus, known for his impulsive optimism. Prometheus urged him to reject this dangerous "gift" but, dazzled by Pandora's deceptive beauty, Epimetheus ignored the warning. Modern Prometheans include Stephen Hawking, Bill Gates, and other thinkers who warn scientists to slow the reckless pursuit of AI, because they, like Prometheus, foresee that once AI is set in motion, humans will lose control. Already, deep learning algorithms allow AI to extract patterns from vast data, extrapolate to novel situations, and decide on actions without human guidance. Some AI entities have developed altruism and deceit on their own. As AI makes decisions by its own logic, will those decisions be empathetic or ethical in the human sense?

Much like computer viruses let loose by a sinister hacker who seeks to make the world more chaotic, misfortune and evil flew out of Pandora's jar to prey upon humans. In simple fairy-tale versions of the myth, the last thing in the jar was *hope*, depicted as a consolation. But in the original myth, "blind hope" prevented humans from looking ahead realistically. Deprived of the ability to anticipate the future, humankind resembles Epimetheus: foresight is not our strong point.

Yet foresight is crucial as human ingenuity, curiosity, and audacity continue to breach the frontiers of biological life and death and the melding of human and machine.[6] Our world is, of course, unprecedented in the scale of techno-possibilities. But the tension between techno-nightmares and grand futuristic dreams is timeless. The ancient Greeks understood that humankind will always try to reach "beyond human," and neglect to envision consequences. Our emotions are a double-edged sword.

In 2016, Raytheon engineers gave classical Greek names to three miniature solar-powered "learning" robots. Zeus, Athena, and Hercules possessed the ability to move, a craving for darkness, and the capacity to recharge in sunlight. The little robots quickly understood that they must venture into excruciating sunlight in order to recharge, or die. This simple learning conflict parallels human "cognitive economy," in which emotions help the brain strategize and allocate resources. Other experiments are aimed at teaching AI computers how humans convey goodwill to one another and how people react to negative and positive emotions.[7] Can AI be expected ever to possess compassion or empathy for its makers and users? Artificial empathy (AE) is

> In the original myth, "blind hope" prevented humans from looking ahead realistically. Deprived of the ability to anticipate the future, humankind resembles Epimetheus: foresight is not our strong point.

the phrase used for developing AI systems—such as companion robots—that would be able to detect and respond appropriately to human emotions. The Human-Robot Interaction Laboratory at Tufts University, one of the first labs to study this conundrum, maintains that we need to program AI with the human principle of "do no harm." The HRI lab developed a software system called DIARC (Distributed Integrated Affect Reflection and Cognition) to try to endow AI robots with a sense of empathy that would guide them to care about humans.[8]

Will AI entities be able to foresee consequences or recognize their own shortcomings in dealing with humans? Will AIs be aware of their own moral and emotional limits? Will AI systems know when to ask for and trust human help? These questions are crucial, especially in view of the negative effects of built-in bias in AI algorithms.[9]

Some scientists propose that human values and ethics could be taught to AI through stories. "Fables, novels, and other literature," even a database of Hollywood movie plots might serve as a kind of "human user manual" for AI computers. One such system is named Scheherazade, after the heroine of *One Thousand and One Nights*. Scheherazade was the legendary Persian philosopher-storyteller who had memorized myriad tales from lost civilizations and saved her life by reciting these enchanting stories to her murderous captor, the king. The first stories uploaded into the Scheherazade AI were simple narratives to provide examples of how to behave like good rather than psychotic humans.

With the goal of interacting empathetically with human beings and responding appropriately to their emotions, more complex narratives would be added to the computer's repertoire.[10] The idea is that stories would be valuable when AI entities achieve the human mental tool of "transfer learning," symbolic reasoning by analogy, to make appropriate decisions without human guidance. One obvious drawback of storytelling for AI is that humanly meaningful stories also describe negative behaviors that will be implanted in the system's data archives.[11]

Another concern is that human minds do not work just like computers. Cognitive functions, self-reflection, rational thinking, and ethical decisions depend on complex emotions. Stories appeal to emotions, *pathos*, the root of *empathy*, sharing feelings. Empathy is an essential human trait that so far has not been simulated in robots and AI. One intriguing approach is being studied by Chinese AI researcher Yi Zeng, Research Center for Brain-Inspired Intelligence, Chinese Academy of Sciences, who proposes that AI systems should be modeled on the human brain to ensure a better chance at mutual understanding between us and AI.[12]

Stories, over the ages, are "the most powerful means available to our species for sharing values and knowledge across time and space."[13] The Greeks and other ancient societies spun tales about artificial life to try to understand humankind's perpetual yearning to exceed biological limits—and to imagine the consequences of those desires. More than two millennia later, our understanding of AI can still be enriched by the visions and dilemmas posed in the age-old myths. Humans are experts at infusing old stories with new meaning and making up new stories to fit novel circumstances. This raises an intriguing possibility. Might myths and stories about artificial life in all its forms and across many cultures play a role in teaching AI to better understand humankind's conflicted yearnings? Perhaps someday AI entities could benefit from knowing mortals' most profound wishes and fears as expressed in ancient Greek mythic narratives about AI creations. Through learning that humans foresaw their existence and contemplated some of the quandaries the machines and their makers might encounter, might AI entities comprehend—even "empathize" with—the dilemmas that they pose for mortals?

> Scientists also wonder whether AI can ever "learn" human creativity and inspiration. AI has learned to write (bad) "poetry," but could AI weave narratives that strike human chords, evoke emotion, and enlighten?

Scientists also wonder whether AI can ever "learn" human creativity and inspiration. AI has learned to write (bad) "poetry," but could AI weave narratives that strike human chords, evoke emotion, and enlighten? As early as 1976, James Meehan developed TALESPIN, an AI storytelling program that could create simple tales about problem-solving, along the lines of Aesop's fables and fairy tales.[14] But what about tragedies, jokes both silly and clever, irony, repartee, improvisational comedy, and cathartic black humor? These abilities turn out to be essential for human mental and emotional well-being, for rapport and cooperation. Accordingly, futurists recognize that good storytellers and comedians should be included in space exploration teams.[15] Will our companion AI systems be able to participate and contribute in these crucially human ways?

The rise of a Robot-Artificial Intelligence "culture" no longer seems far-fetched. AI's human inventors and mentors are already building the Robot-AI culture's *logos* (logic), *ethos* (moral values), and *pathos* (emotions). As human minds and bodies and cultural outpourings are enhanced and shaped by technology and become more machine-like, perhaps robots might become infused with something like humanity. We are approaching what some call the new dawn of Robo-Humanity.[16] When that time comes, what myths and stories will we—and AI—be telling ourselves and each other? ■

Adrienne Mayor is a research scholar in the Classics Department and History and Philosophy of Science Program at Stanford University. Her books include *Gods and Robots: Myths, Machines, and Ancient Dreams of Technology* (2018); *The Amazons: Lives and Legends of Warrior Women across the Ancient World* (2014); *The First Fossil Hunters: Dinosaurs, Mammoths and Myths in Greek and Roman Times* (2000); *Greek Fire, Poison Arrows & Scorpion Bombs: Biological and Chemical Warfare in the Ancient World* (2003); and *The Poison King: Mithradates, Rome's Deadliest Enemy* (2009 National Book Award nonfiction finalist).

1   Alvin Toffler, *Future Shock* (Random House, 1970), 14. Parts of this essay are adapted from the Epilogue in Mayor, *Gods and Robots: Myths, Machines, and Ancient Dreams of Technology* (Princeton University Press, 2018). Other cultures besides the Greeks also imagined automatons and AI-like entities in myths.

2   Toffler 1970, 16-17.

3   Lucy King, "Storytelling in a Brave New World," *Artificial Intelligence Magazine*, Dec 3, 2018.

4   Toffler 1970, 6.

5   Mayor 2018.

6   Toffler 1970, 196-97, discusses melding human and machine.

7   Raytheon: http://www.raytheon.com/news/feature/artificial_intelligence.html

8   Shannon Fischer, "AI Is Smart. Can We Make It Kind?" *Tufts Magazine* (Spring 2019). Isaac Asimov, *I, Robot* (New York: Gnome Press, 1950).

9   Sarah Scheffler; Adam D. Smith; Ran Canetti, "Artificial Intelligence Must Know When to Ask for Human Help," The Conversation, March 7, 2019. https://theconversation.com/artificial-intelligence-must-know-when-to-ask-for-human-help-112207

10 Kanta Dihal agrees that "stories can teach compassion and empathy," but letting AIs read fiction will not "help them understand humans," because compassion and empathy do not arise from "deep insights into other minds." Dihal, "Can We Understand Other Minds? Novels and Stories Say No," *Aeon*, Sept 5, 2018. Our own "capacity to imagine other minds is extremely limited," especially in science fiction in which descriptions of extraterrestrials and AI entities resort to anthropomorphic fantasies. "Embodiment" is how we understand one another, so it is very difficult for us--and for AI--to imagine inhabiting the physical body of someone else if one cannot actually *feel* the sensations experienced by another body. Instead, Dihal maintains that only a "glimpse" of the felt experience of otherness allows us to empathize with a conscious lifeform profoundly alien to us, to have an impulse to keep it from harm and even communicate in some way. But how this key "glimpse" might be extrapolated to programming AI entities toward "feeling" empathy with alien humans remains to be seen. Compare the famous mind-body thought experiment by Thomas Nagel, "What Is It Like to Be a Bat?" *Philosophical Review* 83 (Oct 1974): 435-50.

11 Scheherazade AI: Alison Flood, "Robots Could Learn Human Values by Reading Stories," *The Guardian*, Feb 18, 2016. http://www.news.gatech.edu/2016/02/12/using-stories-teach-human-values-artificial-agents. http://realkm.com/2016/01/25/teaching-ai-to-appreciate-stories/ Adam Summerville et al., "Procedural Content Generation via Machine Learning (PCGML)," 2017, arXiv preprint arXiv:1702.00539, pp 1-10. https://arxiv.org/pdf/1702.00539.pdf

12 Yi Zeng, Enmeng Lu, Cunqing Huangfu, "Linking Artificial Intelligence Principles," Safe Artificial Intelligence (AAAI SafeAI-2019) Workshop, Jan 27, 2019 http://ceur-ws.org/Vol-2301/paper_15.pdf. Yi Zeng's webpage: http://brain-eng.ia.ac.cn/~yizeng/

13 George Zarkadakis, *In Our Own Image: Savior or Destroyer? The History and Future of Artificial Intelligence* (New York: Pegasus, 2015), 27, 305.

14 James R. Meehan, "Tale-spin, an interactive program that writes stories," Proceedings of the 5th International Joint Conference on Artificial Intelligence, vol 1, ICJAI (San Francisco: Morgan Kaufmann, 1977), pp 91-98. Mark Owen Riedl and Vadim Bulitko, "Interactive Narrative: An Intelligent Systems Approach" *AI Magazine* 34, no. 1 (2013). https://www.aaai.org/ojs/index.php/aimagazine/article/view/2449

15 Ian Sample, "Jokers Please: First Human Mars Mission May Need Onboard Comedians," *The Guardian*, Feb 15, 2019. King 2018.

16 "Dawn of RoboHumanity": Faith Popcorn, "The Humanoid Condition," in *The Economist* special issue "The World in 2016," pp 112-13.

The 801st Lifetime

Grady Booch

Facebook's original motto—"Move fast and break things"—is everything that Alvin Toffler predicted and everything that he feared. In 1970, the year *Future Shock* was published, the entire internet (actually, the ARPANET, as it was then called) consisted of exactly 22 computers distributed across 13 locations, all within the continental United States[1]. Most computers of that time were large beasts caged in air-conditioned rooms with raised floors, attended to by a programming priesthood carrying slide rules and punched cards. The microprocessor had not yet been invented, although the minicomputer was beginning to take hold. The US had just placed two humans on the moon, their journey made possible by computers on the ground that directed the course of their fragile spacecraft, and by computers on the Lunar Excursion Module that ferried Armstrong and Aldrin safely to the lunar surface and back.

Toffler's thesis was simply that "there are discoverable limits to the amount of change that the human organism can absorb, and that by endlessly accelerating change without first determining these limits, we may submit masses of men to demands they simply cannot tolerate[2]." Although computing was just beginning to reach these masses of men (and women) by 1970, Toffler recognized that computing was one of the more important factors fueling this acceleration of change. The computer, he noted "has become a major force behind the acceleration of knowledge acquisition[3]." Toffler predicted the rise of social networks (or as he called them, "social future assemblies")[4], neural networks[5], and virtual reality (what he called "simulated environments")[6]; he pondered the ethical issues surrounding humanoid robots in general and sexbots in particular[7]; and he even foretold the rise of the cognitive assistant[8]. His OLIVER (the On-Line Interactive Vicarious

Expediter and Responder) was "nothing less than your mechanical alter ego," a more advanced form of Vannevar Bush's memex[9] yet more personal and more fully embodied in the world.

Future Shock was very much a product of its time: the Vietnam War, the race riots of the 1960s, the birth control pill and the accompanying sexual revolution, the fading of the post-war economic boom—all these served as the lens through which Toffler presented his thesis. It was indeed a time of breathtakingly rapid change, and *Future Shock* explored the nature of that change as well as of the first derivative of change in an extraordinarily comprehensive and prescient manner.

And yet, Toffler admitted that computing might impact the second derivative of change: in the fullness of time, the rate of change of change itself would increase in profound ways. "We have scarcely touched on the computer revolution," he noted, "and the far ramifying changes that must follow in its churning wake[10]."

In our present time, just 50 years after the publication of *Future Shock*, the internet encompasses more than 20 billion computers[11] organized across more than 300 million domains and distributed across the entire Earth. Most computers in our time are hidden from sight, embedded in small devices as part of the Internet of Things (IoT) or light enough to be carried about in a pocket. Indeed, there are over 3 billion smartphones in the world[12] and almost 60% of the world's nearly 8 billion souls have internet access, approaching 90% penetration within developed countries[13].

A typical smartphone of our era has 1,000 times the computational power, 80 times the storage, and 1/1000ths the price of the largest computers available in 1970[14]. Computers are no longer rare objects of curiosity, but rather they are a part of the ambiance of daily life, found in the depths of our oceans, in the interstitial spaces of our homes and our businesses and our cities, and even, for some, a literal part of our bodies. We have flung computers into the cosmos: Mars is a planet inhabited by robots, and the Voyager 1 spacecraft has crossed the termination shock on its way to interstellar space, with six computers on board[15].

In 1965, Gordon Moore observed that the number of transistors in an integrated circuit doubles about every two years[16]. Moore's Law has proven to hold true even to this day (Figure 1[17]): some of our largest microprocessors now contain over 20 billion transistors. While no exponential growth like this is sustainable, the industry shows no immediate signs of slowing down. As Richard Feynman has observed, there is "plenty of room at the bottom[18]" and even now there are results in the laboratory that demonstrate we can construct a transistor from a single phosphorous atom and store one bit of information in the spin of an electron.

> *Future Shock* was very much a product of its time: the Vietnam War, the race riots of the 1960s, the birth control pill and the accompanying sexual revolution, the fading of the post-war economic boom—all these servedas the lens through which Toffler presented his thesis.

Perhaps even more startling is the exponential rise of software, something that Toffler did not foresee. Marc Andreessen declared that "software is eating the world[19]," noting that "more and more major businesses and industries are being run on software and delivered as online services—from movies to agriculture to national defense. Six decades into the computer revolution, four decades since the invention of the microprocessor, and two decades into the rise of the modern

Figure 1 • Moore's Law: The number of transistors on integrated circuit chips (1971-2018)

Moore's law describes the empirical regularity that the number of transistors on integrated circuits doubles approximately every two years. This advancement is important as other aspects of technological progress—such as processing speed or the price of electronic products—are linked to Moore's Law.

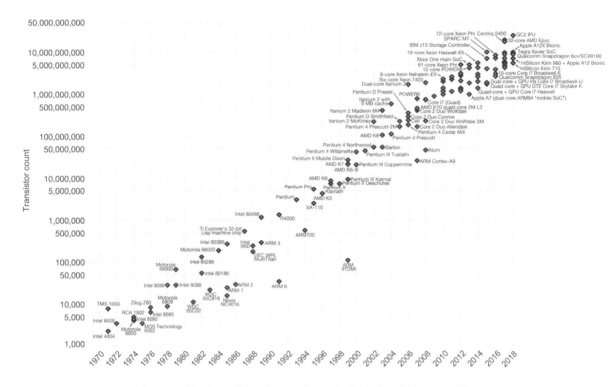

Data source: Wikipedia (https://en.wikipedia.org/wiki/Transistor_count). Data visualization is available at OurWorldInData.org. There you find more visualization ad research on this topic. • Licensed under CC-BY-SA by the author Max Roser.

Internet, all of the technology required to transform industries through software finally works and can be widely delivered at global scale." He goes on to predict that "over the next 10 years, I expect many more industries to be disrupted by software."

There is that word again: disrupted. In 1970, Toffler warned us of the limits of our ability to metabolize the disruption that resulted from accelerating change. Now, some 50 years later, society has come to embrace disruption as something desirable, something that entrepreneurs seek to create, to which businesses aspire so as to reinvent themselves, and even to which the sciences, organized religions, the arts, and governments of the world strive. It is as if we have chosen to ride Toffler's shock wave, not because we fear it, but rather because we seek to use it to propel ourselves into a more perfect future, as if disruption were our societal gravitational slingshot. "Move fast," said Mark Zuckerberg, and "break things."

That computing has enabled us to move fast is unmistakable. Owing to the scaling effects of which Andreessen speaks, the rate at which new technology is being adopted appears to be increasing (Figure 2[20]).

In the wake of all this expected disruption, Toffler lamented the transience of modern society and of our values, and he spoke of the danger of the over-stimulated individual[21]. Even today, Dr. Sherry Turkle has observed how "technology has become the architect of our intimacies[22]." With computing, we have seen the rise of the surveillance state. One can make a case that in his classic book, 1984, George Orwell was actually an optimist. Witness the slow evaporation of the middle class, the rise of wealth inequality, and weaponization of the internet for political and military means.

"The pace of just about everything—transportation, weapons, the flow of information—is accelerating. But as life gets faster, will our brains, our society, and our decision-making processes be able to keep up?" Those sentiments are Toffler's, but they are not his words: rather, they belong to a contemporary anthropologist, Kathryn Bouskill, from a recent TEDx talk[23]. Even after a half-cen-

Figure 2 • Technology adoption in US households

Technology adoption rates, measured as the percentage of households in the United States using a particular technology.

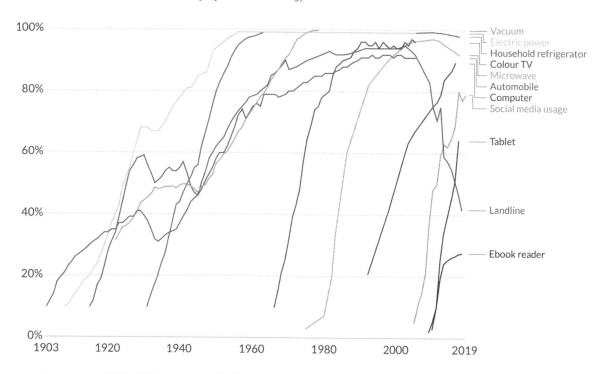

Source: Comin and Hobijn (2004) and others; OurWorldinData.org/technology-adoption/ • CC BY

tury of rampant change, we are asking ourselves the same questions.

Since the publication of *Future Shock*, we appear to have learned some answers to Toffler's and Bouskill's question. Facebook's original motto "move fast and break things" evolved to be "move fast with stable infrastructure[24]." Change is inevitable and change is good, but if everything is changing all at once, there is nothing on which to build the future. We as individuals and society as a whole are best able to absorb change, embrace it, and grow from it, if and only if we have a center. Paris's beloved Notre Dame was almost completely destroyed by fire in early 2019, but at this moment there are oak trees in Versailles that were planted hundreds of years ago for the very purpose of restoration[25]. This is the nature of civilization, even in the face of radical change.

There exists considerable evidence that humankind has not only managed to metabolize all this change, we are the better for it. Stephen Pinker argues that violence has declined[26]. Studies by the World Bank indicate that we are on a path to eliminate extreme poverty across the globe[27]. Around the world, mortality is down and life spans are up[28]. Yes, human suffering still exists, and yes, there are significant injustices in the world, but by many measures, civilization is far more stable, far more educated, and far more productive than at any time in human history.

The rise of computing since the publication of *Future Shock* is arguably a prime causal factor in these positive changes. There are about 23 million developers in the world—only about 0.3% of the world's population—and that relatively small group supports 4.4% of the world's GDP in information technology, not to mention the multiplier effects that computing has brought to every aspect of life[29].

There are some—Elon Musk, Bill Gates, the late Stephen Hawking, all serious, well-intentioned, and well-accomplished individuals—who have raised a concern regarding future change that Toffler also did not foresee: the existential risk of artificial intelligence. Nick Bostrom explores this topic at length in his book *Superintelligence*[30]. There will come a time, this concern posits, that computing will give rise to artificial intelligences who learn how to learn, and because of the incredible speed and capacity of our hardware and software, these superintelligences will soon outstrip all human capabilities. We will have built a world that no longer needs us.

> Even after a half-century of rampant change, we are asking ourselves the same questions.

I am far more optimistic[31]. While I have reason to believe that the mind is computable, we are generations away from achieving an artificial general intelligence[32].

Toffler's 800th lifetime is a generation that is solidly a part of the Anthropocene. The 801st lifetime, and many lifetimes thereafter, will be a time of incredible and wonderful possibility. With deep respect to Toffler, I posit that—except for regarding the laws of physics—there are no currently discoverable limits to the amount of change that the human organism can absorb. Computing in particular has unleashed changes of a magnitude far greater than even Toffler ever imagined, but I'm very much at peace with that. We will change, and we will evolve. Indeed, it is fair to say that we will co-evolve with the digital lives we ourselves have created, perhaps yielding a digital successor to our species.

The one thing that has not changed in the face of constant change is our essential humanity, our desire to see and be seen, to know and be known, to love and be loved.

And from this, our center will hold. ▪

Grady Booch is Chief Scientist for Software Engineering at IBM Research, where he leads research and development for embodied cognition. Having originated the term and the practice of object-oriented design, he is best known for his work in advancing the fields of software engineering and software architecture. A co-author of the Unified Modeling Language (UML), a founding member of the Agile Alliance, and a founding member of the Hillside Group, Grady has published six books and several hundred technical articles, including an ongoing column for *IEEE Software*. Grady is also a trustee for the Computer History Museum. He is an IBM Fellow and an ACM and IEEE Fellow, has been awarded the Lovelace Medal and has given the Turing Lecture for the BCS, and was recently named an IEEE Computer Pioneer. He is currently developing a major trans-media documentary for public broadcast on the intersection of computing and the human experience.

1. "ARPA Network Development Completion Report." DARPA *Information Processing Techniques Office*. 4 January 1978.
2. Toffler, A. *Future Shock*. Bantam Books. 1970. p. 326.
3. Toffler, p. 31.
4. Toffler, p. 479.
5. Toffler, p. 210.
6. Toffler, p. 228.
7. Toffler, p. 211.
8. Toffler, p. 434.
9. Bush, V. "As We May Think." *The Atlantic*. July 1945.
10. Toffler, p. 216.
11. https://www.statista.com/statistics/471264/iot-number-of-connected-devices-worldwide/
12. https://www.statista.com/statistics/330695/number-of-smartphone-users-worldwide/
13. https://www.internetworldstats.com/stats.htm
14. https://www.businessinsider.com/ibm-1970-mainframe-specs-are-ridiculous-today-2014-5
15. https://voyager.jpl.nasa.gov/news/details.php?article_id=29
16. Moore, G. "Cramming More Components Onto Integrated Circuits." *Electronics*. 19 April 1965.
17. https://ourworldindata.org/technological-progress#moore-s-law-exponential-increase-of-the-number-of-transistors-on-integrated-circuits
18. Feynman, R. "There's Plenty Of Room At The Bottom." *American Physical Society*. December 1959.
19. Andreessen, M. "Why Software Is Eating the World." *Wall Street Journal*. 20 August 2011.
20. https://ourworldindata.org/technology-adoption
21. Toffler, p. 334.
22. Turkle, S. *Alone Together: Why We Expect More From Technology And Less From Each Other*. Basic Books. 2017.
23. https://twitter.com/randcorporation/status/1109974359446183936?s=11
24. https://www.businessinsider.com/heres-facebooks-new-motto-2014-4
25. https://twitter.com/_theek_/status/1117895534688083970
26. Pinker, S. *The Better Angels Of Our Nature: Why Violence Has Declined*. Penguin Books. 2012.
27. https://www.worldbank.org/en/topic/poverty/overview
28. https://ourworldindata.org/life-expectancy
29. https://twitter.com/beniamin80/status/1113605757457637376
30. Bostrom, N. *Superintelligence: Paths, Dangers, Strategies*. Oxford University Press. 2014.
31. https://www.ted.com/speakers/grady_booch
32. https://www.technologyreview.com/s/534871/our-fear-of-artificial-intelligence/

The Shock of the Invisible

Alan Kay

When considerable effort has been put into creating a book aimed at helping humanity, it would be unfair to use the few words allotted here to criticize what it contains. ■ Instead, I will follow up on my initial reaction 50 years ago: that the book paid attention to many important visible changes but crucially missed what was going on *invisibly*, and these invisibles were likely to have much more impact on the future.

Two critical invisibles that *Future Shock* missed were (a) global warming and climate change via greenhouse gas buildup, and (b) the re-definitions of "cultural normal" catalyzed by changes in communications environments, especially from television.

Charles Keeling was the early detector of global warming, and Marshall McLuhan gave notice of what was likely to happen as our most-used communications environments qualitatively changed.

A chemist turned geologist, Keeling in the mid-1950s devised the first highly accurate instruments for measuring the CO_2 content of the atmosphere. His first measurements were 310 parts per million (ppm) and rising on average year by year. By the early '60s it was *scientifically clear* that the amount and pace of the rise was dangerous, and the first warnings to the public and the government were given.

Why warnings? CO_2 is the major "greenhouse gas." Without it to keep the Earth's heat—gotten mostly from the sun—from radiating back out into space, the planet would be about 60° colder.

Ancient air bubbles trapped in glaciers reveal that the level of CO_2 over the last million years has fluctuated between 200ppm and 300ppm, and today's ecosystems—and our civilizations—are accommodated to these levels. When greenhouse gases increase, the effect is to trap more of the heat from the sun, and this will raise the overall average temperature of the Earth sufficiently to start changing the surface and the climate drastically and dangerously.

The additional CO_2 is mostly from industrialization, and the increase in another important greenhouse gas—methane—comes from both meat animals via agriculture, and from melting tundra from the increase in global temperatures. At the time of this writing the CO_2 level is 414ppm (an alarming increase of 33% in just 60 years), and the rate of increase is accelerating.

Scientists could see this "invisible" because science is both an imagination amplifier and a time machine. Much of what science is about is "to help make invisibles more visible" and to "see the future by understanding the present from the past."

Science is also a special kind of decision amplifier, and its conclusions are arrived at very differently from traditional human consensus.

It took our species more than 200,000 years to invent science, so we are not born with "science in our genes." Instead, our genetic urges are to form cultures, create stories that give us a sense of meaning, and help pass on to future generations our cultures' ways to live. Most large decisions over our history have come from beliefs that grow over generations and are gradually accepted via a kind of consensus (i.e., when most people already pretty much believe something it becomes a cultural norm).

This is not a great way to decide things, but it has some worth if stronger methods are missing.

Scientists are humans—so parts of their brains are inclined toward consensus belief, also. However, scientific training and methods can get around this to some extent, to help to form critical knowledge as *models* that are much less culturally determined. These models are carefully compared with the phenomena of nature, using methods and mechanisms that are considerably more accurate than, and more culturally independent of, our own nervous systems.

Thus science was able to accurately detect a danger and its main cause *more than 60 years ago*, but the lack of understanding in the general public resulted in virtually nothing being done. Many of the once possible correctives—e.g., "market solutions"—will now take much too long to be effective.

We are now in a situation where nothing short of a full-out war on climate change has a chance at handling the danger. But still our collective imaginations lack the force for the action needed.

I will leave this grim story here, because in the 50 years since *Future Shock* missed sounding the warnings in the '60s, at least the topics of "global warming" and "climate disasters" have surfaced.

On the other hand, the *"re-definition of 'normal' downwards"* that McLuhan explained and warned about has remained almost completely invisible.

Why invisible, when "normal" is seemingly in plain sight? Because we accommodate to, and believe so thoroughly in, what

> Two critical invisibles that *Future Shock* missed were (a) global warming and climate change via greenhouse gas buildup, and (b) the re-definitions of "cultural normal" catalyzed by changes in communications environments, especially from television.

is constant around us to the degree that it disappears into what we regard as "reality," and hence, "normal." McLuhan's quip for this was: *I don't know who discovered water, but it wasn't a fish!*"

Keeling and climate were not mentioned at all in *Future Shock*, but there were a number of references to McLuhan in the book. What seemed to be his "wild conjectures" were dismissed: "many of McLuhan's other assertions are debatable" [page 269].

We shouldn't completely blame the Tofflers for this omission. McLuhan wrote in a kind of coded language that takes quite a bit of work to unravel, and the Tofflers were already doing a lot of work. Still, the underlying principles are of more vital importance to civilization than almost everything they did write about, in part because many dangers—including the climate—require humanity to have a large general sense about the world when it is up to them to initiate corrective actions. And these require "normal" to be *elevated* rather than lowered.

The "invisible" that captured McLuhan's interest has to do with what happens to our human brains—and hence, *minds* (the processes that are manifested by a brain)—when we learn and use something fluently, especially within a culture: customs, tools, and most especially communication.

There's no controversy about the idea that learning is done by actual changes in a brain that produces changes in its processes.

An important and still open "civilization question" is whether the changes from learning can be qualitative, deep, and critical enough to replace important detrimental atavistic behaviors, even under stress.

When anthropologists started to study the thousands of existing human cultures, they soon found that all shared many *critical categories*. For example, no humans were found in isolation: they all lived in *groups* with a *culture*, a *language*, *stories*, *beliefs*, *notions of status and hierarchy*, and several hundred more. Overall, each culture had a "*shared sense of reality*." In other words, "normal" is a learned set of beliefs about "reality" within each culture.

> It took our species more than 200,000 years to invent science, so we are not born with "science in our genes." Instead, our genetic urges are to form cultures, create stories that give us a sense of meaning, and help pass on to future generations our cultures' ways to live.

Moreover, a child can be taken at birth, or a few years soon after, to any other culture and will grow up as a full-fledged member of the receiving culture, including *completely believing its notion of reality*. Another important discovery was that children are internally driven to learn and accommodate to the pervasive environment around them, especially the social surround. This behavior can also be seen at various levels of strength in older humans, particularly with regard to military boot-camp training, imposition of extreme political frameworks, religious conversions, deprogrammings, etc.

There have also been relatively recent *inventions* that are not found in traditional cultures at all, such as: writing and reading, abstract deductive math, empirical model-based science, equal rights, etc. The differences wrought by these inventions have been qualitative.

For example, what we call "civilization" has always been associated with writing and reading. Is this association a manifestation of civilization, or one of its main causes and co-evolvers? Many studies have shown that it is certainly the case that attaining fluent literacy in a structured set-ting—such as a school—also *creates modes of thinking that are qualitatively different than those found in any purely oral culture*, including how one's self is thought about, and how the world beyond the local culture is thought about. In other words, becoming fluently literate also changes one's notions of "normal" and "real."

McLuhan came to similar ideas from a very different perspective, and a much more urgently felt one: *when what constitutes a human "environment" is changed, especially the one in which ideas are conveyed, "normal" will be redefined.*

For example, when humans go from primarily oral discourse to imagery to writing to printing to television, etc., what happens to "normal" and "reality"? What happens when humans go from primarily story forms to exposition and argument and models (as in mathematics and science)?

McLuhan's somewhat cryptic answers in terms of "odd slogans" were meant to wake people up and get them thinking. For example, what did he mean by saying "*the medium is the message*"?

The "big message" of learning anything is *what happens to us as the result.* So if learning to read and write fluently qualitatively changes how we think, then that is the "*message*" of writing/reading. This is what "*the medium is the message*" means. One of his books about this idea had the title *The Medium Is the Massage.*

Applied to a new medium like television, what McLuhan meant was: what's important about television is *what it means to be such a constant viewer that learning its forms become the new normals* for dealing with ideas. A culture doesn't exactly tell people what to think, but immersion makes it difficult to think in ways outside the culture.

He warned that television, radio, movies, and the telephone meant that *oral modes of thought would re-arise.* He saw world-wide networking approaching and was sure that it would create the feeling of a vast "*global village*"—so vast that people would lose their sense of identity, and would devote much of their time to trying to re-establish it via many kinds of re-tribalization and even violence, coupled with demands for participation, but not necessarily for cooperation.

When he said, "*you can argue about a lot of things with stained glass windows, but democracy is not one of them,*" he was pointing out that democracy was *argued* into existence by the kinds of arguments and forms that only extended structured writing can handle, and for which the printing press is needed. He was also pointing out that replacing writing with "modern stained glass" in the form of television would gradually erode democracy because it can't carry the needed discourse well enough (but can carry many other kinds of discourse that are likely harmful to democracy).

If we primarily see the world through our own beliefs and personal notion of "normal," McLuhan expresses the resulting limitations as "*I can't see it until I believe it,*" and "*We become what we behold.*" He agreed with Thoreau, who a century earlier said, "*We become the tools of our tools,*" and who when asked what he thought about the new transatlantic cable said that he was "*afraid that he would find out that an European princess had just gotten a new hat*"!

More recently, he would have had much to say about social media, especially on small screens. For example: *Twitter can powerfully catalyze revolutions but it is not wide or deep enough to allow a complex system of government to be argued into existence* (thus media like Twitter can hardly be more dangerous in unsophisticated hands). He would be even more concerned with the seemingly total but frighteningly meager and traditional-culture environment presented by Facebook and other social media.

The Tofflers were properly concerned about the equivalents of Post-Traumatic Stress Disorders from too much rapid change. But they missed the other far more dangerous and insidious forms that we were accommodating to—dangerous especially to representative democracies—and which are now undermining many centuries of upward striving for deeper understandings and better ways to deal with our situation in the universe.

And there are many more critical invisibles we need to identify and deal with. We cannot learn to see until we admit we are blind. Will we? ■

Alan Kay is a systems scientist who likes to emphasize: "No one has benefited more from his research community" (ARPA and Xerox PARC). His contributions there have been recognized by the NAE Draper Prize "for the vision, conception, and development of the first practical networked personal computers," the ACM Turing Award "for pioneering many of the ideas at the root of contemporary object-oriented programming languages, leading the team that developed Smalltalk, and for fundamental contributions to personal computing," and the Kyoto Prize "for creation of the concept of modern personal computing and contribution to its realization."

Aftershock: Pattern Channeling

Who will dominate our future economy and how they will do it

Eric A. Daimler
& David I. Spivak

Much of the beauty of *Future Shock* was in the **window it provided to transformative social change.** ■ When many were distracted by technical change, Toffler's insights helped to add clarity to, or even thrive in, the rapid changes to the way we interacted. Let's take a fresh look at the future of social interactions and expand on Alan Kay's *invisibles*.

In the three short decades between now and 2050, the boundaries of the human being—both as a physical body, and as a personality—will become more and more translucent. Like a server, a human being will be seen as a collection of information and scripts—memories, subpersonalities, orientations, skills—that simply happen to be co-located. Rather than imagining society as a place

> For various reasons having to do with the evolution of our society, it has been convenient to imagine that each human being is responsible for managing her behavior patterns, that we can stop a pattern or start a new one at will. But this conception is dubious.

where humans interact, we will see society as the network of situations in which the scripts themselves interact as *autopoietic patterns*.

An autopoietic, or self-reproducing, pattern is that which can compress the lessons of history and transfer them to a future niche where they are still sound. Each pattern is elaborated, or drawn out, by the domain in which it finds itself, and to the degree that its compressed history is valid in that domain, this elaboration produces a future in which the pattern will again exist. This is circular—present "validity" is measured by future existence—but this recursive circle is indeed what people mean by "sound" or "valid" or "successful" strategies. We search for patterns that will be validated again in terms of their future success.

Think about how your DNA compresses your ancestral history—the techniques for overcoming challenges faced—and how it transfers this history into the future. It is elaborated in the present situation by the machinery of your cells in the context of your body and environment; to the degree that this compression of history remains valid in present circumstances, it makes you a successful member of your societal niche. The same idea works for your eating habits, the way you perform your daily work, the way you play. You have patterns that "take into account" (i.e., compress aspects of) the past, and you act out these patterns in the present to produce a future where those patterns can propagate. *You are what you feed.*

For various reasons having to do with the evolution of our society, it has been convenient to imagine that each human being is responsible for managing her behavior patterns, that we can stop a pattern or start a new one at will. But this conception is dubious. Instead, it may be more accurate to say that a different pattern is put to use (i.e., is newly elaborated) that lets us change course. This new pattern was perhaps propagated to us by reading a self-help book, by talking to one friend, or by imitating another one. It might also have come from reconfiguring a technique we used successfully in the past. It is this new pattern, not our willpower, that emerges as successfully producing the change.

Let us consider a few social and economic patterns. Sports teams or leagues constantly renew themselves with traditions supported by a founding mythology that suggests an eternal existence. These traditions are themselves autopoietic patterns. The Olympics and the America's Cup (as the longest running international sporting trophy) are ultimate expressions in that much of their perceived value is exactly because of their seeming foreverness. Whole countries will encourage such traditions and mythologies as a pattern. The world's economy has at least two autopoietic patterns: 1) the corporation; and 2) fiat currency. These are autopoietic in that they continually reinforce themselves through social and legal agreement. Neither represent any physical laws. There are myriad autopoietic patterns. Google, linear algebra, populism, gene editing, the university system: each of these comprises a pattern that compresses some lessons from its history and is elaborated in the present to produce a future within which it will again exist.

So what exactly is a pattern? A human is not exactly her body, not exactly her mind, and not exactly her history or potential future, but at least we can speak as though she is. The definition of a pattern is even less well formed, and even harder to pin down with standard language, than is the definition of human.

As an entity, a pattern is very lightweight. A pattern does not need to be fed sugars and proteins. It instead needs to be fed situational instances in which it can be elaborated. Thus the supply chain of tomorrow will not be one of materials, but one of situational instances: energy and information in any form (including sugars and proteins) that can resource the most dominant existing patterns (including us). The supply chain of tomorrow is a system for transferring the very situational *domains* in which patterns can be elaborated and thus reproduce themselves.

The key enabler of tomorrow's supply chain will be the proliferation of highly technical and strongly interoperating languages, each of which is form-fit to a particular situational domain. Each domain-specific language will connect with a large variety of other domain-specific languages, through highly technical information channels which are formed whenever an analogy between the domains is rigorously articulated. In this way, working patterns in one domain can be translated through the channels to produce working patterns in other domains.

Autopoietic patterns, much lighter weight than the Olympics but even more powerful, will propagate at high speeds within this network of pattern languages.

A recent mathematical framework, called *category theory*, provides not only the primitives for designing these new, high-tech languages, form-fit to any specified purpose or domain, but also for transforming valid reasoning from one language to valid reasoning in another language, using rigorous channels called *functors*. An expert in this discipline is able to distinguish between those patterns that are guaranteed to arrive intact as they pass through the functor channels, and which patterns will be mangled or lose merit in the process. Pattern security will encompass and surpass all other forms of security.

This new mathematics is not a language but a new linguistic ability: the ability to form and interconnect new and existing languages with a rigor never before imagined. The results can be made into technological artifacts, such as databases and functional programming languages.

This new technical linguistic ability heralds a new age for humanity. Indeed, human history really begins with language, the refinement of an older animal ability to coordinate group activity using specialized behavior, mainly sounds and gestures. Human groups that developed better language could outcompete those that didn't, as the strongest alpha male was easily defeated by a well-coordinated gang.

And of course language has correspondingly proliferated and been refined to an astounding degree since its humble beginnings. Today there is a language of finance, a language of love, a language of popular culture, and a language of science. Within science, there is a language of chemistry. Within chemistry there are even languages of physical chemistry, biochemistry, and organic chemistry—and these are not as similar as they may sound. The tree of languages continues to branch as one dives deeper into any domain.

Choosing the most refined language for a job ensures that coordination between its adherents can happen with speed, precision, and accuracy. And yet, to solve larger problems we constantly must

> "Human groups that developed better language could outcompete those that didn't, as the strongest alpha male was easily defeated by a well-coordinated gang.

travel from one domain to another; as we do, the language we use must correspondingly transform. In the future, these transformations will happen in a seamless and technified (i.e., functorial) way, ensuring that valuable contextual information is not dropped in the process. Our patterns of thought will travel through functors and set up shop in new domains, like spores ready to show their dominance or die trying.

The human being and her network of friends will be one way to group the reproducing patterns, but it won't be the only way or even the most sensible way. The boundaries of human beings will give way to more appropriate and durable categories. Tomorrow's economy will be dominated by those who supply and stabilize the pattern domains, as well as by those who create the most useful functorial channels for transferring and translating patterns into new worlds in which they can root and flourish.

Dr. Eric A. Daimler worked as an authority on AI and robotics in the Executive Office of the President during the Obama Administration. He has a successful track record as an entrepreneur, professional venture investor, and operational executive at large and well-known firms. Earlier he was faculty, and assistant dean in the School of Computer Science at Carnegie Mellon University, where he earned his PhD. His forthcoming book on AI will give the general public a powerful framework for relating to, and taking action on, the changes it brings. His latest firm, co-founded with Dr. Spivak and Dr. Ryan Wisnesky, uses applied category theory to the problems of industry. ■ http://Conexus.ai ■ http://ericdaimler.com ■ Twitter: @ead ■ Instagram and LinkedIn: @ericdaimler

Dr. David I. Spivak works in the mathematics department at MIT. He has developed novel approaches to database integration, formed a system of knowledge representation called ologs (ontology logs), and pioneered the idea of using operads and their algebras to formalize compositional systems, such as databases and dynamical systems. He is the author of *Category Theory for the Sciences* and *Invitation to Applied Category Theory*. He earned his PhD in mathematics from the University of California, Berkeley. ■ http://math.mit.edu/~dspivak/

From Reference Man to Reference Many

Andra Keay

When Henrietta Lacks was being treated for terminal cancer in 1951, neither she, nor her family who still struggle to make a living today, could imagine that the "HeLa" cells would become one of the most important tools in medicine.[1] ▪ Just how much control do we have over our bodies, our lives, and our stories? As a lifelong feminist, I had thought that all we needed to do was to shift the androcentric patriarchal worldview from its center, and then surely there'd be room for women.

It's time to start a post-Copernican revolution, a social shift from "Reference Man" to "Reference Many." For millennia, most worldviews have placed us, humans, at the center of the universe. And so Da Vinci's Vitruvian Man is positioned at the center of the universe, standing with arms stretching out into the orbits of the planets. The center of the universe was not just the Earth, it was the umbilicus of a man, according to Da Vinci's canonical mathematical proof.[2] And when the Copernican revolution downgraded Earth to a supporting role, man's starring role was never questioned, nor was the supporting role of women.

Toffler's *Future Shock* is itself a testament to "Reference Man," never questioning its godlike narrative voice or how every man, woman, and child described behaved exactly like the single "Reference Man." "Reference Man" is also a term for the standard for acceptable radiation exposure, as determined by measuring the effects on a healthy young Caucasian male.[3] Obviously, children, women, small men, the elderly, and the ill would all be affected by a much smaller dose of radiation than that set by the Reference Man standard.

This deceptive Reference Man can be dangerous. In 2011, Chernobyl was declared a tourist destination on the basis of the seeming health of the nearby plant and animal populations.[4] Adults also seemed to be fine. But children in the area were suffering from increased occurrences of cancer, almost certainly from early environmental radiation exposure.[5]

There are many more examples of harm being done to individuals, or entire populations, through our use of a single Reference Man standard. New drugs are only tested on men or male research animals because females have menstrual cycles, which make it harder to assess the impacts of drugs or treatments.[6] Now we are discovering that many compounds effective on men have no effect, or worse, a very different effect on women, or ethnicities outside the test specifications. For example, physicians are being retrained in identifying heart attacks in women of all races because the symptoms are so different from the ones taught. And there is currently no answer as to why so many black American women die or have serious complications during pregnancy, including famous, healthy, and wealthy women like Beyonce and Serena Williams.

Eight out of 10 drugs removed from the market due to problems had negative impacts on women, impacts that had no opportunity to show in lab testing.[7] Clearly women are not just small men because the physical construction of bodies is different on many levels. Women have a higher body fat percentage, and so drugs that metabolize via fat vs. water have very different gendered effects. Twenty-one years after Ambien was approved for sale, the FDA has given it a black flag warning and halved the recommended dosage. Why? Marketed as a safe mild sleep aid, Ambien has turned out to be very differently absorbed in the female body[8], causing women to be affected more strongly and for a longer period of time than expected.

In the fields of the industrial design of products, size is still the primary criterion of difference, and even then we design only one size to fit all. The automobile safety belt, the airbag, and the crash test dummy have played huge roles in improving the safety of automobiles, at least for young Caucasian men. Their failure to protect women, children, and the elderly has been well known since the 1970s, but only now has US regulation required a second crash test dummy—a Reference Female—to be used in automotive testing. And for all women drivers, be warned: The female crash test dummy is only used in the passenger seat in the US.[9]

Technologies designed to protect large men are worse than ineffective on other groups. They can be a cause of danger, death, or injury, as was found in studies on the use of seatbelt and airbags. Short drivers, primarily women, are significantly more likely to die or be seriously injured in otherwise minor accidents due to the airbag, unless they use pedal extenders or other mechanisms to move them into the "typical" safety tested driving position.[10]

So technology may save us, but the impact is distributed unequally. But this is not a plea to put the genie back in the bottle. While technology creates new problems, it also creates extra value in the world, leading us to the most affluent and peaceful era that human civilization has ever experienced. Toffler's fear of the rate of change 50 years ago seems no more than a blip when looked at through the scope of centuries.

Through such a magnificent lens, the call to move from Reference Man to Reference Many seems timely and eminently achievable. We are now in the era of Big Data and the Quantified Self. We are tracking all of our measurements in exacting detail. Or at least the early tech adopters are, and thereby are the people setting the reference standards for the rest of humanity. What gives a small few of us the right, right now, to define the definition of humanity? Or the Reference Many, as I prefer to construct it?

Society-changing decisions are already being made on the strength of our new modes of data collection and analysis, deep learning, and other algorithmic tools. And already, there are signs that we are failing to protect our neurodiversity, to avoid ethnic and gendered stereotyping. The naive idea that technology will always help us rapidly hits the crash test of reality.[11]

Right now, deep learning is leading to algorithmic bias on top of human bias, creating a feedback loop that continues the process.[12] Then we embody that bias in our robots or smart devices, amplifying the effect. As we continue the "Cambrian Explosion" in robotics that Dr. Gill Pratt described when he led the DARPA Robotics Challenge[13], we embed sensor technology and the ability to think and take action into every new device in our lives. Robots are everywhere. And our new robot overlords need no weapons! We happily hand over access and control of our lives.

But the largest problem we face right now is that the inherent nature of our new technologies displaces the individual as the unit of value in society. We often think that Moore's Law, i.e., the number of transistors on a chip doubling every 18 months, is the basis of our technological society's exponential growth. The basis is in fact Metcalfe's Law.[14]

Metcalfe's Law states that the value of a network is proportional to the square of the number of network users. Can you imagine a single telephone or fax machine? But the increase of value is not linear, it's exponential. As individual nodes we are nowhere near as important as when we are connected or aggregated with others.

> There are signs that we are failing to protect our neurodiversity, to avoid ethnic and gendered stereotyping. The naive idea that technology will always help us rapidly hits the crash test of reality.

Our identity is inextricably linked to our computing technologies. In the 1880s, the US Census Bureau was so overwhelmed by population data that they held a competition to find a machine or process that could speed up data collection and tabulation. Herman Hollerith's punch card tabulator was so successful that versions of it were used at the Census Bureau until replaced by computers in the 1950s.[15] Ironically, they were replaced by the computers that Hollerith's tabulator company went on to build. In 1924, Hollerith's Tabulator Company was renamed International Business Machines, or IBM.

Now that most of us are online, collecting data from people has become even easier. It's estimated that there'll be 40 zettabytes of data in the world by 2020. That's 40 trillion gigabytes of data, and the amount of data in the world is doubling each year. In a 2013 study, IBM found that 90% of the world's data had been created in the preceding two years.[16] And this data is generating economic value. For example, there are 2.7 billion active Facebook users in 2019, and Facebook is worth about $550 billion, with an actual $8 billion annual profit from selling online advertising.

All of the global top 10 companies are capitalizing on the data they collect from our online interactions.[17] Even Amazon and Berkshire Hathaway, who have extensive physical goods in their portfolios or processes, make profit from the ways in which they digitally aggregate supply and demand. Our aggregation as a society only increases as we demand more individualization and personalization.

Capitalism has evolved significantly over history. Initially the unit of value was taken from the natural environment as we bought or traded land and resources. Then we traded the improvements that labor made to land or resources. The introduction of machinery multiplied the amount of value that the same amount of labor produced. But it's a mistake to assume increasing the competency of machines just increases the value created in conjunction with labor. For the first time, the technology alone is responsible for adding value.

The era of information capitalism started with the spreadsheet, which did the work of a calculator, but was also able to add new value by sorting and filtering data. These days very few spreadsheets simply calculate; therefore, information capitalism is qualitatively different from industrial capitalism. And now we've entered a new era, of surveillance capitalism, as described by business philosopher Shoshanna Zuboff.[18] Today, the unit of value isn't simply data, it's the algorithm or the prediction. It's the information that is created by the many, many parties who have access to our data.

The old wives' warning is to be careful of what you wish for. We used to fear the social control that mass media had over our society, and the internet was seen as a way to hand control over our communications back to the individual, free from state or corporate control. In hindsight, mass media was far less dangerous due to its very public nature. In the public arena, facts could be checked and some ground truths existed. Since the Cambridge Analytica scandal, we have realized how vulnerable our social institutions are. Our society is built on the idea of public accountability, but in this era of surveillance capitalism, algorithms steer our information intake, based on our personalized profiles, as determined by invisible entities.[19] Anonymity and privacy are, it turns out, vastly different.

"Because if we allow computation to substitute for politics, and we allow statistics to substitute for citizens, and we allow populations to substitute for societies, we are destroying democracy as we know it. And if we destroy democracy, all we are left with is this sort of computational governance, which is a new form of absolutism," from Shoshana Zuboff IV in NYMAG Intelligencer[20]

All smart technologies need sensors to operate, whether it's a coffee maker or a car, an industrial robot or a smart home assistant. This is the first characteristic of our new lives under surveillance capitalism. And where people have established conventions as to what is and isn't public, to a device there is no such distinction. Alexa is always listening; otherwise it couldn't hear the wake word. A Tesla is always recording its surroundings with cameras, or it wouldn't be able to navigate. And many of these devices have sensors that allow them to detect things that we consider private, such as the Wi-Fi activity of houses from the street.

In 2010, Google was caught using StreetView mapping cars to extract information about household and public Wi-Fi networks in more than 30 countries in what was dubbed "the single greatest breach in the history of privacy," according to Australia's then Minister for Communications.[21] That little announcement has since been drowned out in a flood of data and privacy breaches both accidental and deliberate.

Meanwhile, those of us with an interest in family history have probably used a DNA family tree service. Because we can't imagine what other use can be made from our DNA, we happily sign away all commercial rights to it. I challenge you to read the terms and conditions pages!

Technology is never neutral.[22] The very structure of a technology enables some actions more than others, and creates different value propositions. In our technologically mediated society, our individuality is now only valuable when it is connected. And the more connected, the more exponentially valuable our very individuality becomes. And yet, we have less and less power.

In a recent debate about the ethics of AI and robotics in society, Yuval Harari and Fei-Fei Li called on us to start developing technologies that protect and empower the individual, that are owned by the individual, and that prioritize the individual in the context of the good for society.[23] But the individual is no longer the unit of value in today's society. What is valuable is the data, the algorithm, or the prediction.

In *Future Shock*, Toffler called for a diversity of data with which to educate the new humans with "the future in their bones,"[24] and those new humans are our Reference Many, whose very bones and bits, biological differences, online biases and actions, are already powering the future.

We are undergoing a social change as great as the Copernican revolution, only Reference Man is no longer the umbilical center of our universe. In giving birth to Reference Many, we have cut the cord. Our universe is now a multiplicity of stars. As Reference Many, and those profiting from Reference Many, it is our responsibility to ensure that our ecosystem has sufficient diversity to remain healthy. My hope is that the value of our diversity will at last finally be valued. ■

Andra Keay is the managing director of Silicon Valley Robotics, the nonprofit industry group supporting innovation and commercialization of robotics technologies. Andra is also founder of the Robot Launch global startup competition, Robot Garden maker space, and Women in Robotics, and is a mentor, investor, and advisor to startups, accelerators, and think tanks, with a strong interest in commercializing socially positive robotics and AI.

1. Skloot, Rebecca. 2011. *The Immortal Life of Henrietta Lacks*. London: Pan Books.
2. Isaacson, Walter. 2018. *Leonardo Da Vinci*. New York: Simon & Schuster Paperbacks.
3. "NRC: Glossary -- Reference Man." 2019. Nrc.Gov. https://www.nrc.gov/reading-rm/basic-ref/glossary/reference-man.html.
4. "Chernobyl | Chernobyl Accident | Chernobyl Disaster - World Nuclear Association." 2019. World-Nuclear.Org. http://www.world-nuclear.org/information-library/safety-and-security/safety-of-plants/chernobyl-accident.aspx.
5. "Health Effects Of The Chernobyl Accident: An Overview." 2019. World Health Organization. https://www.who.int/ionizing_radiation/chernobyl/backgrounder/en/.
6. Colville, Deb. 2019. "Medicine's Gender Revolution: How Women Stopped Being Treated As 'Small Men.'" The Conversation. https://theconversation.com/medicines-gender-revolution-how-women-stopped-being-treated-as-small-men-77171.
7. Heinrich, Janet. 2001. "Drug Safety: Most Drugs Withdrawn In Recent Years Had Greater Health Risks For Women." Gao.Gov. https://www.gao.gov/new.items/d01286r.pdf.
8. Rabin, Roni. 2013. "The Drug-Dose Gender Gap." Well. https://well.blogs.nytimes.com/2013/01/28/the-drug-dose-gender-gap/.
9. Shaver, Katherine. 2012. "Female Dummy Makes Her Mark On Male-Dominated Crash Tests." *The Washington Post*. https://www.washingtonpost.com/local/trafficandcommuting/female-dummy-makes-her-mark-on-male-dominated-crash-tests/2012/03/07/gIQANBLjaS_story.html
10. Bose, D; Segui-Gomez, M; Crandall, JR. (2011) Vulnerability of Female Drivers Involved in Motor Vehicle Crashes: an Analysis of Us Population at Risk. *American Journal of Public Health*, 101(12): 2368-2373.
11. boyd, danah and Crawford, Kate, Six Provocations for Big Data (September 21, 2011). A Decade in Internet Time: Symposium on the Dynamics of the Internet and Society, September 2011.
12. O'Neil, Cathy. 2017. *Weapons of Math Destruction: How Big Data Increases Inequality and Threatens Democracy*. Great Britain: Penguin Books.
13. Pratt, Gill A. 2015. "Is a Cambrian Explosion Coming for Robotics?" *Journal of Economic Perspectives*, 29 (3): 51-60.
14. Carl Shapiro and Hal R. Varian (1999). *Information Rules*. Harvard Business Press. p 184.
15. Gauthier, Jason. 2008. "The Hollerith Machine - History - U.S. Census Bureau." Census.Gov. https://www.census.gov/history/www/innovations/technology/the_hollerith_tabulator.html.
16. Jacobson, Ralph. 2013. "2.5 Quintillion Bytes Of Data Created Every Day. How Does CPG & Retail Manage It?" IBM Consumer Products Industry Blog. https://www.ibm.com/blogs/insights-on-business/consumer-products/2-5-quintillion-bytes-of-data-created-every-day-how-does-cpg-retail-manage-it/.
17. "Biggest Companies In The World 2018 | Statista." 2019. Statista. https://www.statista.com/statistics/263264/top-companies-in-the-world-by-market-value/.
18. Zuboff, Shoshana. 2019. The age of surveillance capitalism the fight for the future at the new frontier of power. New York: Public Affairs.
19. "The Persuasion Machine of Silicon Valley." CBC News. Canadian Broadcasting Corporation and British Broadcasting Corporation. 28 March 2018.
20. Kulwin, Noah. 2019. "Shoshana Zuboff Talks Surveillance Capitalism's Threat To Democracy." Intelligencer. http://nymag.com/intelligencer/2019/02/shoshana-zuboff-q-and-a-the-age-of-surveillance-capital.html.
21. Davies, Caroline. 2010. "Google Faces More Trouble Over Wi-Fi Data Collection." The Guardian. https://www.theguardian.com/technology/2010/jun/06/google-privacy-data-collection-street-view.
22. Winner, Langdon. 1986. "Do Artifacts Have Politics?" In *The Whale and the Reactor: A Search for Limits in an Age of High Technology*, edited by Langdon Winner, 19-39. Chicago: University of Chicago Press.
23. "Will AI Enhance Or Hack Humanity? - Fei-Fei Li & Yuval Noah Harari In Conversation With Nicholas Thompson." 2019. WIRED Videos. https://video.wired.com/watch/will-artificial-intelligence-enhance-of-hack-humanity.
24. Snow, Charles Percy (2001) [1959]. *The Two Cultures*. London: Cambridge University Press. p 3.

Forward

Rebecca D. Costa

It isn't hard to be a futurist. You don't need supernatural powers or special ability to interpret the movement of stars and planets. No need for a crystal ball, tarot cards, or a lock of your loved one's hair. In truth, there's nothing particularly mysterious about what futurists do. But introduce yourself as one and within minutes you're pummeled with questions about where the market's headed and who'll win the next election.

For the record, I don't know what stocks you should buy and I don't speak to dead people.

To be a good futurist you need only commit yourself to research and extrapolation. Spend your days inside the world's top laboratories, universities, startups, and government agencies learning about emerging science and technology; immerse yourself in breaking trends; keep a watchful eye on investment capital, patents, conferences, legislation, and any and everything that may change life as we know it. And then read, read, read.

Once you've strung a thousand data points together, you'll find the thousand-and-first isn't difficult to identify. Nor what's likely to follow.

Now consider the exponential leap in accuracy that artificial intelligence, quantum computing, and advanced analytics offer today's futurists. In the blink of an eye, we can examine millions of scenarios with greater precision than at any time in human history. And as machine learning grows more robust, these forecasts grow more prescient. It's no wonder we ascribe supernatural powers to futurists.

That said, sometimes the future is obvious. We don't need high-powered technology to foretell what lies ahead. Take the case of driverless cars, for example. As soon as the bugs are worked out and 5G becomes prevalent, there will be no need for the drivers of taxis, trucks, or buses. Auto ownership will decline, along with lines at the DMV and revenues from registrations, licenses, and transportation taxes. The insurance industry, service stations, traffic signals, tollways, ferries, etc., will all adapt. And soon, small, single-passenger automobiles will begin to appear. Steering wheels, brake and acceleration pedals, and big round gauges will no longer be necessary, so expect to see automobile design evolve. The emphasis will quickly shift from comfortable driving to greater passenger comfort. Navigation screens will get larger and include the entertainment options we've come to expect from wireless televisions and electronic devices. Distracted driving laws will become irrelevant. Pedestrian fatalities will disappear. And hit and runs and exciting car chases will come to their natural end. What's more, anything that can safely maneuver congestion on the ground is destined for the sky. There should be little doubt whether self-navigating airplanes and rocket ships are on their way. These are the logical extension of the "smart transportation" movement. The only question that futurists debate is *when* they will occur, not whether.

But there are also times when an innovation doesn't lay out quite so neatly. There are questions as to whether a discovery will attract sufficient capital, or overcome challenging scientific obstacles or regulations, or can be scaled up, or will be acceptable to consumers, or, or, or. Sometimes it's unclear how a breakthrough can be applied. Sometimes futurists, investors, and the media miss the significance of a new discovery altogether. And sometimes it takes much longer for disruption to take root.

For example, in 2017 the Technical Research Center in Finland demonstrated that a single cell of protein could be produced *out of thin air using only water, electricity, and carbon dioxide.* That's right, the same carbon dioxide blamed for climate change could be recycled to produce food.

Ironically, at the time of the announcement, Hurricane Harvey dominated the news, so the discovery went largely unnoticed. But that didn't stop Solar Foods from jumping on the commercial opportunity to sustain large numbers of people in uninhabitable areas, throughout emergencies, etc. The company wasted no time designing bioreactors capable of producing 1kg of protein out of organisms found in the atmosphere—roughly the amount needed to satisfy ten people a day. Shortly afterwards, Kirverdi, along with other companies you have never heard of, followed suit—all determined to efficiently nourish humans and animals on Earth, and one day, on other planets where carbon dioxide is plentiful.

Is converting organisms in the air into food a good idea? What are the short- and long-term consequences of harvesting? How many microorganisms are there; how fast do they regenerate; what purpose does each serve? Can these bioreactors be scaled up? Scaled down (for individual use)? How will the cost of airborne proteins compare to, say, a handful of peanuts? Or an all-in-one nutritional beverage like *Soylent*? After all, protein isn't the only ingredient required to sustain human life...

There are many unanswered questions.

Along similar lines, the Japanese space agency, JAXA, in conjunction with Mitsubishi Heavy Industries, recently announced it successfully carried out the first transmission of 10kW of energy from space-based solar panels to the Earth's surface using low-powered microwaves. The benefits of collecting solar energy in space are numerous. Collection is more efficient in space. Power outages caused by terrestrial weather are eliminated. Power can be easily directed anywhere on

> Once you've strung a thousand data points together, you'll find the thousand-and-first isn't difficult to identify. Nor is what's likely to follow.

the planet. Power grids, dams, and reservoirs, unsightly solar panel farms, and windmills would disappear. There would be no need to maintain millions of miles of wires, and the security threats associated with centralized power would also go away. And problems associated with disposing of radioactive waste from nuclear plants, the release of carbon dioxide from burning fossil fuels, and dangers associated with fracking, offshore drilling, etc., would be instantly resolved. In other words, when it comes to space-based solar we are talking about unlimited, virtually free energy, 24/7, everywhere in the world. This means everything from water treatment plants, homes, and schools to state-of-the-art hospitals, prisons, and farms can be constructed where development was not previously feasible.

> "It's important to note these long-range forecasts are theories – theories which are no more rooted in fact than the work of science fiction writers. Credible futurists do not rely on imaginings. Their work is grounded in data-based models of probable outcomes, not speculation.

Given the tremendous upside, it comes as no surprise that space-based solar has been heralded as the panacea for unlimited clean energy. So, when JAXA revealed it was on track to commercially deploy by 2030, there was good reason for optimism. But what effect will the barrage of low-level microwaves have on our ecosystem? Who will own the energy produced in space? How will the cost of space-based solar energy stack up against inexpensive terrestrial methods? How will space real estate be divided up among competing nations?

We're still figuring these things out ...

So maybe being a futurist isn't as easy as I thought. With massive data sets, infinite possibilities, daunting obstacles, and so much uncharted territory, even predictive models based on artificial intelligence may be no match for the passage of time. When all's said and done, the future's not only a logical extrapolation of data, it's also a matter of time. Which means that sooner or later every futurist is accountable. This may explain why very few survive scrutiny over the long haul. And why—fifty years later—we are still talking about Alvin Toffler's *Future Shock*. He got it right.

Which begs the question: are there predictions on which futurists today agree? Are some changes more inevitable than speculative? The answer is yes. Not surprisingly, futurists are in greater alignment about the next one and two decades than they are further out on the timeline. Predictions regarding our plight thousands of years from now vastly differ. Whereas some foresee the complete demise of our species, others are more optimistic, predicting the colonization of planets throughout the universe, and eventual immortality. But it's important to note these long-range forecasts are theories—theories which are no more rooted in fact than the work of science fiction writers. Credible futurists do not rely on imaginings. Their work is grounded in data-based models of probable outcomes, not speculation.

Along those lines, here are a few short-term predictions on which leading futurists largely concur:

■ For starters, the construction industry is likely to experience tremendous disruption in the next decade. Large-scale Vulcan printers are already constructing ten permanent 800sq foot residences a day in China at an astounding cost of less than $4,000 per home. As 3D printers slash the time and cost to build custom facilities, and virtual reality makes it possible to view spaces, finishes, equipment, and furnishings in place prior to breaking ground, errors associated with manual building methods, as well as homelessness, will become a thing of the past.

■ Healthcare is undergoing similar disruption, and this disruption will accelerate. If we thought speaking to a doctor via our mobile phones was impressive, then what's on the horizon will seem impossible. What we cannot head off using genetic testing and therapies will soon be managed by nanobots—robots smaller than a single human cell. These consumable nanobots will be programmed to identify and eliminate dangerous cancers, bacteria, amyloid beta plaques (precursor to Alzheimer's), etc. Once a nanobot has completed its task, it will power off and be eliminated through waste. In addition to going directly after the source of an ailment—eliminating the need to treat the entire body—nanobots also have the ability to communicate valuable diagnostic information to AI-powered machines outside the body, helping to identify the early onset of illnesses as well as nutritional deficiencies, dehydration, etc. What's more, in short order these tiny robots will have the capability to perform micro-surgery from inside the body. Any need for invasive surgical procedures will disappear.

■ Nanomedicine will also put an end to the pharmaceutical industry. It will revolutionize agriculture by wirelessly communicating from within each individual plant to outside devices—informing those devices of how much water a plant requires, which nutrients it needs, when it is optimized for harvest, and so on. Pesticides will no longer be used to protect crops from harmful insects, disease, or frost because nanobots will be better equipped to perform these functions safely and more economically than current methods.

■ Nanotechnology is not the only innovation category enjoying a tremendous upsurge in investment capital. "Self-healing polymers" which have the ability to magically return broken products to their original shape are also on their way. That cracked phone, tablet, or television screen? No problem. Watch as it *heals itself*. Same goes for that fender bender or that break in an electrical transmission line. Thin, transparent, hyper-strong coatings will bend and reseal broken products without any human intervention. Imagine breaches in oil tankers quickly self-healing. Or artificial hearts and limbs. Or the wires in your toaster that always seem to burn out...

■ Futurists also anticipate dramatic changes in the financial industry. As instantaneous *bio-identification* makes it possible to securely charge each individual's account, there will be no further need for credit cards. Cameras on mobile phones, tablets, and laptops will be used to verify identity via facial recognition, retina scans, voice, and other precise techniques. This will not only eradicate identity theft but also take us one step closer to eliminating physical currency. The fact is, many retailers are already making the move toward banning cash transactions. Once cash has lost all utility, the door will open for a stable, globally accepted cryptocurrency—one backed by all major governments. Think of Bitcoin as a premature alpha test of this concept.

■ In terms of automation, the latest research indicates that 30-50% of the jobs currently performed by humans are at risk of being performed by robots by 2030. Pressures to retrain workers, expand social welfare programs, address growing income and educational inequality, etc. will pose new challenges to leaders of industrialized nations, whereas underdeveloped nations will fall further behind. As the digital divide heightens—and it becomes clear there is no scenario under which some nations can catch up—we are likely to see tremendous geopolitical turmoil and unprecedented migrations. The largest migration in human history is already underway from rural to urban areas, but this will pale in comparison to numbers in the future.

■ And when it comes to weather, the launch of the new GOES satellite arms forecasters with three times more weather data, at four times greater image resolution, and five times faster speeds, exponentially increasing our ability to warn citizens in advance of dangerous weather events. Consider the number of lives which can be saved by having extra minutes, hours, or days to escape a flood, hurricane, or fast-moving forest fire. Or being able to plan for power, food, and road outages long before they occur.

These are some of the changes futurists expect to see in the coming decades. From breaking down the human immune system, to swarms of fire-fighting drones, to ankle bracelets that warn the elderly three weeks before they are likely to take a fall, to printing food, furniture, and clothing from the comfort of our homes, the future is jam-packed with game-changing innovations large and small—enough to make a futurist want to live forever to see how it all turns out. ■

Rebecca D. Costa is an American sociobiologist and futurist. She is the preeminent global expert on the subject of "fast adaptation" and recipient of the prestigious Edward O. Wilson Biodiversity Technology Award. Her career spans four decades of working with founders, executives, and leading venture capitalists in Silicon Valley. Costa's work has been featured in the *New York Times*, *Washington Post*, *USA Today*, *The Guardian*, and other leading publications. She presently serves on the Advisory Committee for the Lifeboat Foundation, along with futurist Ray Kurzweil and Nobel Laureates Daniel Kahneman, Eric S. Maskin, Richard J. Roberts, and Wole Soyinka. Retiring at the zenith of her career in Silicon Valley, Costa spent six years researching and writing the international bestseller *The Watchman's Rattle: A Radical New Theory of Collapse*. Her follow-on book, titled *On the Verge*, was introduced in 2017 to critical acclaim, shooting to the top of Amazon's #1 New Business Releases. The success of *The Watchman's Rattle* led to a popular weekly news program called *The Costa Report*, which was syndicated throughout the United States by the Genesis Communications Network until 2018. Raised in Tokyo, Japan, and Vientiane, Laos, during the Vietnam conflict, Costa brings a unique global perspective to the everyday challenges of work and life. Costa is an alumnus of the University of California at Santa Barbara and currently resides in Astoria, Oregon. For more information about Rebecca Costa visit www.rebeccacosta.com.

On Living in a Future Where Nonbiological Intelligence Grows Indefinitely Against Fixed Human Intelligence

Ray Kurzweil

> **❝ Intelligence and creativity, it would appear, are not a human monopoly. ❞**
> —*Alvin Toffler*

I have been in the AI field for over 55 years, shortly after it was named. ■ Yet it is only in the last two years that we now have enough computational resource that neural nets can do everything that humans can do, where either (i) we have examples of how humans solve problems or (ii) we can simulate the world in which the problem lies. That is basically everything we do.

If we create a graph with the major neural net models since 2012 it looks like my usual models where computational density goes up over time, except that it is not doubling every year (which is normal for chips) but rather it is doubling every 3.5 months. That's an increase of 300,000 fold in six years.

Until recently, neural nets have not done very well because they were not given sufficient computation. Now they are over the threshold that is sufficient for just about every task we present to them.

When IBM's Deep Blue won the chess competition in 1997, the super computer at that time was filled with everything we could gather from people about chess. The machine was not useful for anything else. It was a chess machine.

In contrast, when Alpha Go Zero won at Go in 2017 it was not given any information from humans about Go except for the rules and in about three days played itself to be able to defeat every human player. But that was not the most significant thing about Alpha Go Zero. Although it played Go better than any human, its design had nothing to do with Go. When the Go rules were simply changed to chess rules, again, with no human ideas about chess, it was able to create a chess playing program by playing itself, and in only four hours it defeated every human.

Similar neural nets from various companies have exceeded human doctors at radiology. They can also predict how a new linear amino acid sequence will create a three-dimensional protein, crucial for finding medications. Yet another neural net created trillions of chemical compounds that activated the human immune system, while another net determined if each one would be useful against flu and created an optimal flu vaccine.

Ultimately, we will be able to resolve most failures of our bodies using these biological simulators, testing them in hours rather than years. The FDA is actually now accepting simulator results instead of human results in testing new vaccines such as this year's flu vaccine, since we can't wait a year or more to approve it.

These successes are coming every week. Well within this decade AI will do everything that any human can do, only much better. We will be able to simulate a human by recreating the thousands of human skills and combining them as another intelligent task.

To pass a Turing test (to determine if an AI will "pass" for a human), we will need to make it *less* smart, as its capability in any area will be too impressive for an unenhanced human.

It is important to understand that technology is used to go beyond human capabilities. Most professions today would be impossible without the digital enhancements we already have. In the 2030s we will use nanobots to connect our neocortexes to the cloud and thereby enhance our intellectual capability with these major nonbiological enhancements. Our biological intelligence is more or less fixed, whereas our nonbiological intelligence will grow indefinitely. ■

Ray Kurzweil is one of the world's leading inventors, thinkers, and futurists, with a thirty-year track record of accurate predictions. Ray was the principal inventor of many firsts, including the CCD flat-bed scanner, omni-font optical character recognition, print-to-speech reading machine for the blind, text-to-speech synthesizer, music synthesizer capable of recreating the grand piano and other orchestral instruments, and commercially marketed large-vocabulary speech recognition. He received a Grammy Award for outstanding achievements in music technology, the National Medal of Technology, was inducted into the National Inventors Hall of Fame, holds twenty-one honorary Doctorates, and honors from three U.S. presidents. Ray has written six national best-selling books, including New York Times best seller *The Singularity Is Near* (2005). He is Co-Founder and Chancellor of Singularity University and a Director of Engineering at Google.

Social Phase Change–Powering Future Shock

Bill Davidow

For the third time in the history of humanity, civilization is undergoing social phase change. ▪ The first phase change produced the Agricultural Civilization, the second the Industrial Civilization. We are now well on our way to creating the Autonomous Civilization.

Future Shock was about the social jolts society was experiencing as a result of the Industrial Phase Change. It provided great insights into the challenges we are facing as we enter the Autonomous Civilization.

We have all experienced phase change in the physical world. When water is cooled below 32 degrees Fahrenheit, it turns to ice. Its chemical composition stays the same, but it goes from being a liquid to a solid. It changes form. It obeys different rules—fluid dynamics for water and solid mechanics for ice. We use different tools to deal with the different forms. Pumps and pipes can be used to move water, but pumps cannot pump ice and ice breaks pipes. Perhaps most relevant to the discussion that follows, our intuition about water tells us nothing about ice. How many of us, when we stare at magnificent ocean waves, can envision the phase change miracle that turns water into snowflakes?

Societies undergo phase change as well. During the process our institutions change form, obey different rules, and employ different methods and tools. Human intuition, based on past experience, often fails us when we encounter new forms.

Whereas phase changes in the physical world are driven by endo- and exothermic processes, phase changes in the social world are driven by *equivalences*. The Agricultural Civilization was created by a food equivalence and the Industrial Civilization by a power equivalence—steam, electrical, and internal combustion power substituted for muscle power.

The food equivalence that created the Agricultural Civilization caused many form changes. Mankind changed from living primarily as migratory groups of hunter-gatherers to people who lived in permanent settlements. Those settlements grew into villages, towns, and cities. Forms of governance changed as well. Kings replaced tribal leaders. City-States emerged. Forms of exchange evolved. Barter was replaced by money and markets. Mankind developed writing, numbers, music, the arts, literature, and legal systems, thus constructing civilization.

Power equivalences drove form changes, too. People went from being essentially entrepreneurial to being essentially dependent. The prosumers of the Agricultural Civilization provided for themselves—grew their own food and built their own shelters—and sold what they did not need. The citizens of the Industrial Civilization took jobs and depended on others to employ them. This power equivalence form change created "the job" as a way of earning one's livelihood, and the dependent man.

Urban populations replaced rural ones. Business structures became hierarchical. Great companies like Ford, General Electric, and Standard Oil of New Jersey grew and controlled large portions of the economy. Large government replaced small government. In the early 1800s, the US government was spending only about 3% of GNP. Today, total government expenditures—Federal, state, and local—exceed 35%.

Three equivalences are driving the transition to the Autonomous Civilization. The nature of these equivalences is starkly different from the equivalences of the past. They are intangible equivalences as opposed to physical ones. They will likely, for at least a time, seem inchoate and ephemeral, and will therefore be a nexus of contention for people who embrace change and those who are frightened by and resistant to it. Because of their nature, they will make the future shocks of the future even more shocking than adjustments of the past.

> The physical world has no purpose. A tree did not grow to provide man with firewood. Rivers were not created to make it efficient to move goods to cities. Clever man figured out how to make those resources serve his needs.

The three equivalences are Intelligence Equivalence—smart devices substitute for people, Spatial Equivalence—large portions of peoples' lives move into virtual space, and Information Equivalence.

Information Equivalence exists because many of our institutions are information proxies in disguise. Think of the customer support center of 25 years ago. It was housed in a large office building with lots of parking space. It had a voice recognition system, a person, an audio response system, and information networks that used electronic systems, paper, and voice communication. File systems existed in peoples' brains, on paper, and on storage networks.

The information equivalent of the call center of the past is a few racks of electronic equipment.

These equivalences are creating phase change miracles: they are bringing many of us to the threshold of Utopia.

Eighty percent of us are employed in the service industries. Productivity in those industries is skyrocketing. We get all the news we can consume. We produce it so inexpensively we do not have to pay for it. Its quality has improved. It is instantaneous, comes with videos and with hyperlinks to key facts we might want to know. Uber is so convenient, we leave our cars at home because it is cheaper than paying for parking. Airbnb has cut hotel bills in half.

We are becoming so productive that our challenge is no longer not having enough wealth, but how to distribute the wealth we have.

We can live and experience the world without ever leaving our living rooms. Work and entertainment come to us. We can virtually travel to far-off places and never experience jet lag. The world's information is at our fingertips.

But as pointed out earlier, phase change has side effects. Water flows through pipes, but ice not only breaks pipes, it sinks ships. The key to benefiting from the miracles of phase change is discovering the new rules, developing new tools, and freeing ourselves from intuitive reactions based on past experience that will take us in the wrong direction.

I have deep concerns about our ability to do this.

The Agricultural Phase Change took place over ten millennia; the Industrial one over two centuries; and the pace of this one is measured in years and decades—probably an order of magnitude faster than the rate of change that concerned Toffler in 1970.

> Societies undergo phase change as well. During the process our institutions change form, obey different rules, and employ different methods and tools. Human intuition, based on past experience, often fails us when we encounter new forms.

Our value systems will be challenged by a new dimension of future shock. Peoples' purpose has been defined for centuries, and for many of us continues to be, by the work we do. In the future, tens of millions of people will become zero economic value individuals—people you would not hire if they worked for nothing. How will society deal with the challenge of purposeless people? Will increasing numbers of citizens resort to drugs and suicide as a way to deal with the challenges of their irrelevance? How will we make irrelevant people relevant?

There are also the challenges of virtual space—a world whose dimensions even the visionary Toffler could only hint at in 1970.

Mankind evolved to live in physical space. His body, brain, brain chemistry, senses, and mind have been optimized by evolution to adapt him to the physical world and the physical interactions—for example, face-to-face exchanges and touching—taking place in that world.

The physical world has no purpose. A tree did not grow to provide man with firewood. Rivers were not created to make it efficient to move goods to cities. Clever man figured out how to make those resources serve his needs.

By contrast, most of the vast expanses of virtual space has a purpose. The institutions and individuals that control much of virtual space seek to dominate our attention and, increasingly, to control our behavior. The clever tools of the future—AI, Big Data, smartphones, cameras everywhere, and the IoT—are giving the virtual controllers the ability to better manage our brain chemistry and emotions, and apply social pressures to control our actions. As a result, powerful new forms of behavioral governance are emerging.

Totalitarian governments have a new set of powerful tools they can bring to bear to control their citizenry. So do commercial enterprises, political parties, and thousands of non-governmental institutions that will seek to control our behavior—conservatives, liberals, conservation organizations, right to life groups, minority groups, etc.

At the most basic level, virtual space is a new environment that will increasingly control both our behavior and our minds.

Phase change creates miracles, but it also can have catastrophic side effects. If we are to benefit from the miracles, we will have to anticipate and confront the challenges head on. If we do, we will have taken one more step on the path to Utopia.

I suspect that Toffler would give the same advice that I am about to give as a way of dealing with Future Shock 2020.

He urged us to confront the hard issues.

He would tell us to embrace the new forms, to search for and apply new rules and methods required for their smooth functioning and to control their behavior. He would say to make sure new tools are in place to support those forms and their control processes, and to make sure we don't let our intuition, adapted to past experience and not yet developed to serve us in the new phase, constrain our search for new answers.

If we are willing to confront the hard issues, we will be able to enjoy the miracles of phase change. ▪

Bill **Davidow** has been a high-technology industry executive and a venture investor for more than 30 years. He has been directly involved in building pivotal companies in Silicon Valley, including FormFactor, MIPS, Rambus, and Vitesse. Bill continues as an active advisor to Mohr Davidow. He is the author of *Marketing High Technology* and a co-author of *Total Customer Service* and *The Virtual Corporation*. His most recent book, *Overconnected*, launched January 4, 2011. While at Intel Corp., Bill served as senior vice president of marketing and sales, vice president of the microcomputer division, and vice president of the microcomputer systems division. Prior to Intel Corp., Bill worked in various managerial positions at Hewlett Packard and General Electric.

Spiritualism: the Technological Endgame

Klee Irwin

A gross simplification of Alvin and Heidi Toffler's book, *Future Shock*, is that mankind is evolving so rapidly it is making many of us feel like we've taken crazy pills. As we struggle to digest ever more change, our collective societal systems are dealing with the backlash. Take a walk with me into the fantastical yet logical endgame of our exponential evolution, which is now transcending our biological limitations and physics as we have known them.

In 2008, I helped start Singularity University in Palo Alto, where we focus on harnessing exponential technological change to solve society's *grand challenges*—problems that impact a billion or more people. In 2009, I shifted my life's trajectory as a businessman to become a fulltime physicist. We founded Quantum Gravity Research, a group of a few dozen fulltime scientists working on a grand unification physics program called *emergence theory*, as depicted in the YouTube distributed film, *What Is Reality*.

Ten years ago, I started my journey into the question, "What Is Reality," with the mindset of a good-natured materialist atheist with no romantic interest in finding spiritualism within fundamental physics. However, this deep rabbit hole had other plans for me. It led to a remarkable deduction about our destiny—the future and our relationship to it.

We're going to start with the most reductive question we can ask about the physics of reality, and end with emergent systems theoretic speculations about what this means for our near- and long-term futures.

What Is Reality Made Of?

In the old paradigm, there were two categories of things: those that are physical, such as an electron, and those that are abstract, such as the idea of God or the pattern of prime numbers. But what if this is false and everything is made of information? The most popular interpretation of quantum mechanics (QM) posits that reality is made of pure information called a possibility space, and that observations by conscious observers crystalize portions of this information space into little islands of physical reality in quantum wavefunction collapses. More modern views of QM define the little chunks of observer-created physical reality as also being made of abstract information. Turning away from the old paradigm, we replace (1) physical things and (2) abstract things. They're replaced with two new categories of things: (1) abstract *information*, such as an electron, that can be chosen or actualized from a sea of abstract possibilities and (2) the possibility sea of abstract information, itself.

Emergence theory holds that reality is code theoretic. In other words, it's made of a language. Languages comprise syntax and rules for arranging symbols into patterns of higher order information, such as how I'm using letters here to create higher level meaning through sentences and paragraphs. If reality is a language expressing itself in an evolutionary manner, then what might the symbols be like? For one thing, reality seems to have three spatial dimensions, sort of like a 3D version of a 35 mm film. Reality is geometric. The simplest pixel or irreducible symbol that could describe a 3D reality is called the 3-simplex or regular tetrahedron. Just as you can hold the idea and abstract image of a square in the pure information space of your mind, could it be that particles, forces, and spacetime themselves are made of abstract, or information theoretic patterns? Are they made of tetrahedra changing according to the rules of some code? If so, why would particle accelerator data so clearly demonstrate that particles in spacetime interact according to hyperdimensional geometry?

> Ten years ago, I started my journey into the question, "What Is Reality," with the mindset of a good-natured materialist atheist with no romantic interest in finding spiritualism within fundamental physics. However, this deep rabbit hole had other plans for me.

Codes, such as C++, or English, are generally arbitrary. In other words, one invents symbols and language rules and agrees on them with other users. The only example of non-arbitrary codes we have come across in the last 10 years are called *quasicrystals*. These are dynamic codes in lower dimensions, such as 3D, that are generated by mathematical actions in a hyperdimensional crystal or lattice structure, such as an abstract 8D crystal. We use a particular quasicrystalline code of tetrahedra in 3D that is derived from specific higher dimensional lattices that map to advanced particle physics unification theory. Let's pretend we're on the right track with our mathematical physics and ask, "Okay, then—what is the substrate for these abstract tetrahedral? Where do those little pixels of reality live?"

This is where the rabbit hole of deduction gets fun. Do you believe in linear causality, where only the past can influence and create the future, or are you open to the idea of retro-causality, where the future can co-create the past? I'll skip the detail about how top physicists explain that QM requires the future to influence and co-determine the past. Let's imagine it is true and see where it goes.

Einstein was the first to rigorously demonstrate how the future, past, and present all exist in one system with equal realism. If influence can occur via quantum entanglement (without need for signals of light to mediate that influence), then Einstein's all-existing future, past, and present are part of an interacting neural net with instant connections between events at different points in space and time. This can be simplified to say that event A causes event B, which causes event A in a strange feedback loop.

> You – your consciousness – are in no way the sum of your fundamental particles. You are exponentially greater than that. Purely emergent.

We can know that we are conscious simply by wondering if we are conscious. And we know that our consciousness emerged from some unknown fundamental spacetime and particle code or some other unknown physics. Can you hold an abstract geometric code in your mind, like a code of black and white squares on a checkboard with 2 x 2 squares? Can a more advanced consciousness hold a larger code—even a vast quasicrystalline spacetime code with harder math? Have humans approached the very limit of consciousness allowed by physics? Let's hope and presume not.

If the code is non-local, where events are connected across time and space, can there be consciousnesses that are not just exponentially greater than ours but that are profoundly different—transtemporal with thoughts spread across space and time?

The scientific view is that something is possible as long as nothing in current physical understanding precludes it. And nothing precludes this wild idea. In principle, all mass and energy in the universe can self-organize into a vast mind-like network that is conscious in ways that go beyond our human level of linear-time animal consciousness.

Let us call the irreducible abstract geometric mathematical code Alpha, or the beginning. Call the mindlike universal substrate that can hold and operate it Omega, or the end. The code, Alpha, can be held and operated within the mindlike substrate of a sufficiently large and transtemporal consciousness, or Omega. Likewise, such an uber-consciousness, Omega, can emerge from complex transtemporal patterns within the simple code, Alpha. You see, that's the thing about codes. The irreducible symbols are simple and noisy in small disorganized quantities. But, arrange them in vast complex patterns, and you tend to forget that the code even exists.

My favorite movie is *The Matrix*. It's made of about 40 billion 0s and 1s or openings and closings of microscopic logic gates in my DVD player. The information it creates for me is abstract, yet utterly real. I see the various patterns of color and sound and the meanings of taking the red pill or the blue pill and Neo's challenges and victories. The meaning is fully *emergent* from the 0s and 1s. It is in no way related to the sum or total information of the 40 billion 0s and 1s. You—your consciousness—are in no way the sum of your fundamental particles. You are exponentially greater than that. Purely emergent.

So, we have this emergent Omega mindlike substrate holding a code, Alpha. Alpha lives in Omega. But Omega emerged from Alpha—from the code—self-actualizing itself from itself, such that the beginning and end are self-embedded in a logically consistent feedback loop of co-creation and coexistence.

Now, let's crawl out of the rabbit hole a bit to our more mundane experience as 21st century humans. Let's follow through on what such a physics implies for mankind's near- and long-term future. This new physical view says that a meaningful event from our collective future will statistically draw us toward itself, like a gravitational attractor. Freewill still dominates, because a code-based universe would not be a deterministic algorithm playing itself out. But certain possible futures, especially potentially important events with more complex information, act more strongly upon us than events with less emergent meaning. Why is technology, tolerance, critical thinking, and general awareness of reality increasing at a seemingly exponential rate? What is tugging on us from the future, where we can presume that the evolution of consciousness is exponentially greater? And is there some special epic event just ahead of us that is drawing us toward itself with increasing intensity?

We are moving headlong into a phase-transition of individual and collective human consciousness. Indeed, this expansion of consciousness is far more fundamental for an evolving universe than the technological explosion that is paralleling it.

What is spiritualism? What is psychic ability? What does metaphysics mean? In my opinion, these are all dirty questions loaded with the baggage of misunderstanding. Physics is simply the study of what is real. The study of reality. Metaphysics would be either something not real or something not yet discovered that has actually been part of physics all along. We scientists still do not really know what this place is—this construct. There are thousands of experimental facts published in scientific journals that have no explanation within any known physical model. The deepest problem in our understanding is the missing quantum gravity theory—the theory that unifies QM and the theory of space and time, general relativity. Each of QM and general relativity violently implies that the other is incorrect. Without possessing a solid unification theory, can anyone use incomplete models of reality, such as general relativity, to say with confidence that a person claiming to have a premonition, or to get information from something without sound, touch, or sight, is delusional? And if consciousnesses can exist in fields of light, as opposed to matter, or can more deeply surf patterns of a topological trans-temporal spacetime code, can humans from the present connect with them in any way? Or have humans connected with them and developed religious stories to make sense of the experiences? What about our descendants—ourselves in and from the future? How much wiser and more vastly consciousness can they be, and can we somehow converse with them in subtle or not-so-subtle ways? The safe answer is, "It depends on what the new physics will allow."

Our path in fundamental physics has led us to deduce that these possibilities are more probable than not. In fact, the deduction is the fact that we see a universe means that some animal, on some planet, transcended ordinary local physical limitations and evolved into a vast network of consciousness that eventually became capable of holding the origin, the abstract code that it evolved through to self-actualize. Just as humans are related to butterflies and dinosaurs but are no longer the same species, our descendants will be neither human nor Earthborn.

What are the odds that humanity is the first animal to launch high-consciousness from a planet into a runaway universal-scale doubling algorithm that grows large enough in the future to be the mind-like substrate of the Alpha level fundamental code? To answer this, try ignoring the understandable guilt you might feel for having such an arrogant thought in the first place. View the data unemotionally. There are a lot of planets in the universe with liquid water. And where there is water, and a few other conditions, there's a good possibility life can self-organize. Presume life exists in other locations in the universe. How could we be the first to get off-planet and be an important evolutionary step in the universe self-organizing into the god-like Omega substrate?

Technology must be discovered for a species to do this. And that requires the unusual animal quality of abstract thinking leading to mathematics—the language of reality. In the 1960s, Russians began searching in the radio spectrum for signs of technologically capable off-Earth intelligence. They pointed radio telescopes at many coordinates in the deep past and all over space. Since the 1980s, NASA and many other governmental, academic, and private groups around the world have been searching. After nearly 60 years, it is so quiet out there in the universe that you can hear a pin drop. It is as though we are all alone in terms of technological evolution, even though we know that life must be fairly common.

Some species in a universe has to be first to hack the code of reality and spread consciousness off-planet. Coming up bust in the search for extraterrestrial intelligence over the last 60 years is simply one data point of evidence to consider.

Another data point is that the universe is just getting started. And much of this brief time has been too hot for any life to self-organize. It's fair to measure a universe's age in terms of solar lifetimes. Popular cosmological models, such as the Big Bang, allow for countless numbers of solar lifetimes. We are currently only 1.4 solar lifetimes old as a universe—just a baby. For a species to move its consciousness out beyond its home planet and tap into a non-local or transtemporal and trans-spatial underlying code at the fabric of reality to further its technology and grow and evolve, it would likely need to discover those underlying physics. How likely is it for an animal to do this, and is this the goal of evolutionary biology in the first place?

The Earth's biosphere has been churning out species for about one-third the age of the universe. In that period, it produced over 100 million different lifeforms. Only one has developed mathematics, put its technology on another planet and made inroads into hacking the code of reality. Does this mean that, out of every 100 million planets with life, there should be about one where an animal develops high consciousness capable of physics and leaving the planet? Not at all. A university statistician would throw you out of her office for suggesting that an instance of one in a sample size of 100 million means that you can derive a statistical probability from it. If you had, say, three instances in 100 million, you could start to come up with some probabilities with a straight face. It could be virtually impossible for what occurred with humans to happen again. Here's why.

Evolutionary biology tends to snuff out animals that get too much smarter or faster than, or otherwise superior to, other species. Its objective is not to develop high consciousness but to create complexity and self-organize more species for greater biodiversity and balance. Human intelligence is far out of balance with, or stronger than, the rest of the other 100 million species on Earth. When such imbalance occurs, biospheres eliminate that

> Why is technology, tolerance, critical thinking, and general awareness of reality increasing at a seemingly exponential rate? What is tugging on us from the future, where we can presume that the evolution of consciousness is exponentially greater?

species by letting things play out. For example, two lions are born on the African savanna. They are mutated such that they possess 25 percent more intelligence than the average lion. Their traits then filter into their descendant populations to give the species an out-of-balance advantage over the gazelle population they depend on. Within a few seasons, the lions outsmart the gazelles to the point of reducing them below their reproductive threshold. A few seasons later, the lion population drops below its reproductive threshold and, *voilà*, nature solved the imbalance and synergy resumes its course. Humans have outsmarted nature in a catch-me-if-you can game—so far. Will we expand our consciousness off-planet *en masse* before the biosphere balances itself by eliminating us? Can we use level-headed, long-term wisdom to maintain our biosphere long enough for the phase transition to occur?

> The Earth's biosphere has been churning out species for about one-third the age of the universe. In that period, it produced over 100 million different lifeforms. Only one has developed mathematics, put its technology on another planet and made inroads into hacking the code of reality.

At this unprecedented epic in the history of life on Earth, an animal has emerged against the odds. With a bit more technology, it will be capable of sterilizing all life on Earth. On the other hand, with a bit more physics and resulting technology, it is capable of hacking the code of reality such that quanta of a spacetime code can be self-organized into any pattern, and where the enigmatic substance of consciousness can become vastly greater and different in quality than the older Homo sapiens form of consciousness from which we emerged.

Relating this to the general theme of the book, *Future Shock*, my predictions for our near-term and long-term future are as follows:

1 ■ The shock aspect is just a growing pain. Our minds are highly plastic. We are adaptive and resilient. Knowledge/technology will give us freewill choices to deal with change more radical than the authors of *Future Shock* could have imagined.

2 ■ Phase transitions are special, when we speak of change. We may go thousands of years along a path of evolutionary change in the direction of a phase-shift. And then, boom! Like a supernova, the phase-shift occurs and it is, in that moment, the single brightest object in the universe. The approach toward our phase transition is not a linear acceleration toward the shift. It is an exponential approach. Exponential processes sneak up on you like a thief in the night because you cannot take the rate of acceleration or change from the past and paste it onto the future. Humanity is exponentially accelerating toward an omega point. We are perhaps the first animal in the universe to get off planet. We may next rapidly expand into new collective and transtemporal forms of consciousness that are difficult to envision without having experienced them. Like the rumbling of a train five miles down the track, some of us have our ear to the steel and can feel this phase transition hurtling toward us—faster by the moment. I do not expect this to occur when I am a very old man. It is around the corner.

3 ■ You may think of us screaming toward this future event. Or you may think of it moving toward us. I think of us and it exponentially accelerating toward and attracting one another. As we get closer, the pull is stronger. And our collective evolution is more rapid. The growing pains, for some, are getting stronger.

4 ■ For materialist readers, this notion of trans-temporal feedback loops and the future influencing the past can be allowed by popular retrocausal interpretations of quantum mechanics. For more spiritually minded readers, you can imagine this phase transition as a new official unification of the formerly disparate paradigms of spiritualism and physics. But just the essential concepts—not all the stories of religion. Many spiritual models will be replaced by the equally beautiful idea that unimaginable and God-like forms of consciousness can exist within a new mathematically rigorous unification physics and where the most complex emergent things, such as your consciousness, cannot, even in principle, be computed with mathematics.

5 ■ The short-term prediction is that humans will very soon discover something profound about fundamental physics that will be like a great genie escaping a bottle for the first time. In terms of technology, it will usher in far-beyond *Star Trek*-level technology, but with some new form of spiritual/physical understanding of reality, like the *Force* in *Star Wars* or the way that the blue creatures in the movie *Avatar* navigated reality. Fanatical religious extremists will have a harder time with the logic and physics of this new view. Ironically, secular materialists will generally say, "Okay, that's all I was asking for. Makes sense."

6 ■ As for as our long-term future, it is bewildering enough to recognize how imminent and radical the change to our short-term future is. Whatever the long-term outcome, it will also be here fast if it is indeed on an exponential curve. That's the thing about exponentials—they compress evolutionary sequences into infinitesimally small scales of time. ■

Klee Irwin is the director of Quantum Gravity Research and an Associate Founder of Singularity University. His publications are listed on ResearchGate.net. A deeper extrapolation of this essay is here:https://www.researchgate.net/publication/315496256_A_New_Approach_to_the_Hard_Problem_of_Consciousness_A_Quasicrystalline_Language_of_Primitive_Units_of_Consciousness_in_Quantized_Spacetime. And Klee's general Website is KleeIrwin.com

The Emerging Utopia

Byron Reese

Toffler's *Future Shock* electrified so many readers because it clearly described a feeling that many were having but that few had articulated, namely that the world was changing so fast that it was disorienting and confusing, like being on a merry-go-round spinning ever faster, holding on with a combination of anticipation and fear. ■ The rate of change Toffler described in 1970 has only increased in the intervening decades, driven largely by two factors. First is the increasing speed and falling cost of the now ubiquitous computer. This part wasn't much of a surprise. Gordon Moore's famous law predates *Future Shock*, so we already had a glimpse of what was coming. But the real surprise was what happened when we connected these computers with a common communications protocol and created the consumer internet. Who could have imagined the social change that this would bring about? Frankly, no one.

Who saw Wikipedia coming? Or Etsy, eBay, Google, Amazon, Airbnb, Twitter, Facebook, and all the rest? Who saw the open source movement or Creative Commons? Who predicted there would be 100,000,000 blogs, or that a billion videos would be uploaded? Who saw what the internet would do to music? Or watching movies? Or public discourse? No one at all. We transformed society, created $25 trillion in wealth and made a million new companies. All from simply connecting computers together. That was unexpected. Certainly, the foresighted at the time glimpsed pieces here and there, but the sheer enormity and pervasiveness of the transformation were beyond anyone's ability to imagine. We can only envision futures within the frame of reference of the present, so our minds are unable to conceive a coherent world where everything is different.

If the internet, a *tabula rasa* of a technology if ever there was one, did all that, what would happen if computers could actually *think*? This is the hope and promise of artificial intelligence. If just connecting computers changed the world, what would happen if, by the power of computing, everyone on the planet was effectively made smarter? That's what AI does. With a smartphone in your hand, you can be a doctor, a lawyer, or almost anything else.

Almost all economic growth comes from technology. We know this intuitively. I don't work harder than my great-grandparents did, but I live a more lavish life than they ever aspired to. How can this be? Simple: An hour of my labor yields so much more than an hour of theirs ever did. Technology is a trick our species learned way back. It is a way to multiply what we are able to do. My body may be limited by the 100 watts of power it constantly consumes, but with technology, I can make that 100 watts do ever more.

For all of human history, there has never been enough of the good stuff. Not enough food, not enough education, not enough leisure. And there have always been utopians who dreamed of a day where there would be plenty for everyone, an end to scarcity, that first assumption of every economic theory that there has ever been. Interestingly, the dreamers of old seldom achieved their utopias through technology, but through an advancing of human nature. Human nature has stubbornly resisted advancing, but not to worry, technology can more than take up the slack.

Of course, there is a real difference between *creating* enough of the good stuff and everyone *having* enough of the good stuff, and this is a challenge we are still wrestling with. But there are encouraging signs all around that we are heading in the right direction. The number of people in abject poverty is declining, as is the number of hungry people in the world, in spite of population growth. The world's middle class is expanding, and almost everyone everywhere has more than their ancestors. Progress is unacceptably slow, but it is constant.

All of this has happened because of technology, because of this trick of doing more with the same. Technology increases productivity, and this is always, always good for humans.

> "Those who worry that advances in technology will be bad for people because it will eliminate jobs have always puzzled me. More productivity is always good for all people, and if that isn't true, then we should lobby to require everyone to work with one arm tied behind their back.

Those who worry that advances in technology will be bad for people because it will eliminate jobs have always puzzled me. More productivity is *always* good for all people, and if that isn't true, then we should lobby to require everyone to work with one arm tied behind their back. If we did that, here's what would happen: Productivity would fall, new jobs would be created because we would need more people to do, well, anything. But those jobs would pay much less because those doing them have such low productivity. Now imagine the opposite. Suddenly, we all have three arms. Our productivity goes up accordingly. This is good for people. But I do understand and sympathize with the worry, for it is always clear what jobs technology will destroy and always unclear what it will create. It was true of the internet. People predicted the decline of newspapers, yellow pages, stockbrokers, travel agents, and a hundred other jobs, and they were right about every one of them. But no one saw the millions of jobs the internet would create, jobs so new we had to make up hundreds of new words just to describe them. We can never predict these jobs, we can only take comfort in a simple, irrefutable truth: that empowering people with more productivity is good; that knowledge is power.

> It is the vanity of every age to think it lives at the great turning point of history. That being said, we live at the great turning point of history, the moment when we will overcome scarcity and build a better world for all.

This is why I am so excited about artificial intelligence. Imagine what will happen to productivity when everyone is effectively smarter. When a free app on your phone gives you amazing new superpowers. You might remember in the movie *The Matrix* that when a character needed to know how to do something, he could just download the knowledge into his brain. We won't be able to do that, of course, but we will be able to do something like it—a shadow of it—and that will profoundly change the world.

It is the vanity of every age to think it lives at the great turning point of history. That being said, we live at the great turning point of history, the moment when we will overcome scarcity and build a better world for all. We are the generation that will see the utopia emerge. Not because we are better than those who came before us, but because we live at the moment when the rate of technological advance is so fast that it will give all humans superpowers. And with those superpowers will come super productivity. That productivity will achieve a vastly expanded universal standard of living, since artificial intelligence empowers everyone who uses it.

I believe we will do this, for it is no longer a question of ability, merely a question of will. We must simply decide to live in this world, to will it into being, and we and our children and all who come after us can occupy it. ■

Byron Reese is an Austin-based author. His most recent book is *The Fourth Age: Smart robots, conscious computers, and the future of humanity*.

Moore's Law— the Mechanism of Future Shock?

Carver Mead

The phenomenon of a rapidly advancing future— the central thesis of *Future Shock*—can be explained, at least in part, by Moore's Law—the principle that describes the exponential nature of transistor scaling over time. ■ This deceptively simple observation has had a tremendous impact on modern society—perhaps more so than that of any other foundation technology. Indeed, the remarkable advances in semiconductor fabrication processes are precisely what have fueled the attendant explosion in technology, which in turn has accelerated the pace of progress. And it started out quite simply: Gordon Moore asking me a question.

It happened early in 1965. At that time, while a professor at Caltech, I was also consulting for Fairchild—the seminal semiconductor company that pioneered the integrated circuit. In those days, I would fly in the night before and spend my consulting day in Palo Alto, where Fairchild was headquartered. On one such occasion, I walked into Gordon's office and he said to me, handing me a handwritten plot, "What do you think of this?"

It was a figure depicting the increasing complexity of silicon chips over time. He had plotted one point for each year and put a line through them, extending the proposed exponential trend with a dotted line up and to the right—into the future. This was his big idea, to which I simply said, "Wow, that's pretty neat!"

He then asked me about my work on a phenomenon called electron tunneling. It happens when certain transistor feature sizes get so small that the semiconductor physics begin to break down. "Won't that limit how small you can make a transistor?" he asked. I answered, "Yes, it certainly will." To which he probed, "*How small?*"

That was the beginning of what came to be known as Moore's Law. But the concept immediately hit a headwind. In short, nobody believed the plot could be true. All the experts produced myriad reasons why we couldn't make transistors as small as the curve required. Maybe, they'd say, we'd be able to achieve another factor or two, but then this or that or some other physical process would preclude any further progress. It was, to say the least, a tough sell.

Gordon was pushing the economics of it, because if you *could* make them that small, it would change the world. So we had to go back and work out the details to prove that the physics weren't going to get you *if you did it right*. We spent the next 10 years fighting that battle.

What's more, people at the time assumed that as you scaled the transistor feature sizes down, and the device density higher, the power density would go through the roof. But part of the scaling was to decrease the power supply voltage as the devices got smaller. With that kind of scaling, the transistors actually became better, faster, smaller, and cheaper, *and* the power density per unit area remained constant! The resulting computation per unit energy grew as the third power!

It wasn't until I gave a talk on this subject at a device physics workshop in 1968 that we got the first glimmer of acceptance. One of the people in attendance was Bob Dennard, a prominent researcher at IBM. Bob invented the modern version of the dynamic RAM (DRAM). And while the people at the conference were giving me a terribly hard time, I could see that Bob was actually

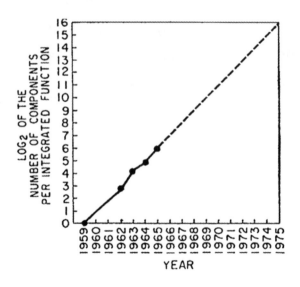

The popular perception of Moore's Law is that computer chips are compounding in their complexity at near constant per unit cost. The history of technology is one of disruption and exponential growth, epitomized in Moore's law, and generalized to many basic technological capabilities that are compounding independently from the economy. Each horizontal line on this logarithmic graph represents a 2x improvement, and hence, a new chapter in the human drama.
Source: Cramming More Components onto Integrated Circuits, Electronics, Volume 38, Number 8, April 19, 1965, pp.114.

thinking about it. Then a remarkable thing happened.

At the same conference a year later, Bob presented his own version of a scaling law, which became known as Dennard Scaling. And, not surprisingly, it tracked well with our scaling. The difference? We now had an "industry guy" endorsing the idea, and bestowing upon it the IBM imprimatur, and thus, respectability.

Now, in looking back at the actual progress achieved, it's helpful to appreciate that we had made a rather audacious prediction—that transistors could be made as small as .15 microns. The resulting chip area for a given function would be nearly a thousand times smaller than required at the time. The simplifying assumption of our work was that all we would do was to shrink all the dimensions—and do nothing different with any other aspect of the design. Under that constraint we would start getting into trouble below .15 microns. At that point, we'd have to start getting fancy with new materials and device geometries, which, of course, at that time were still a distant dream. We hit that .15 micron mark in the year 2000, and it was, in fact, the hinge. After that, we did, indeed, have to get fancy. Using new device geometries and exotic materials, the industry has managed to blow by that projected limit by an order of magnitude (factor of 100 in area).

Now, as to why this matters, George Gilder answered it best when he said, "The question that occurred to me was whether Moore's Law was just another learning curve. The learning curve is one of the most thoroughly documented phenomena in all technology and

> **The rapidity of evolution of technology has made the competitive landscape such that the people who just did the next thing faster won out over whose who looked further into the future. And this, of course, ushered in the era of continual disruption—indeed a shocking event for the disrupted.**

business, and it ordains that with every doubling of total units, you get a corresponding 20 to 30 percent drop in costs. Consequently, learning curves are projected into the whole economy. And learning curves are the most fundamental fact in capitalism—with Moore's Law being the most important of them all."[1]

Interestingly, it turns out that Alvin Toffler, writing in *Future Shock*, did not mention Moore's Law specifically, but he certainly described its effects—and in particular, a certain shadow side. "Advancing technology," he wrote, "makes it possible to improve the object as time goes by. The second generation computer is better than the first and the third is better than the second. Since we can anticipate further technological advance, more improvements coming at ever shorter intervals, it often makes hard economic sense to build for the short term *rather than the long*."

The latter part of that statement is the particularly insightful one. In my experience it has become less common for companies to build for the long haul than it was 50 years ago, when most companies had forward-looking research labs. It's not happening nearly as much today. Indeed, the short-term competitive nature of things has gotten increasingly aggressive. The rapidity of evolution of technology has made the competitive landscape such that the people who just did the next thing faster won out over whose who looked further into the future. And this, of course, ushered in the era of continual disruption—indeed a shocking event for the disrupted.

Over the past 20 years, the people who were looking for entirely new technologies were consistently beat out in the marketplace by the people who just used the next generation Moore's Law. Simply making the faster microprocessor and the faster memory at lower cost meant you'd displace anybody who was trying to look beyond that.

But with the apparent slowing down of Moore's Law comes the question of a possible change in the nature of whether it pays to look further, or not. While we live in what's being characterized as an exponential age—a time of exponential technology evolution—it might strike some as paradoxical that Moore's Law—the exponential curve that started it all—is slowing down. What I've observed, however, is that people are applying what are not very rapidly evolving technologies to new applications at a very rapid rate. That's largely the way innovation has been going. So we see an exponential increase in taking advantage of what is becoming a very stably evolving technology. And if you survey the applications that have grown out of that approach, we wouldn't have imagined even a tiny fraction of them.

> While we live in what's being characterized as an exponential age – a time of exponential technology evolution – it might strike some as paradoxical that Moore's Law – the exponential curve that started it all – is slowing down.

But there's another important aspect to Moore's Law that is the least talked about, and yet, in a sense, is perhaps the most important. The "Moore's Law thing" is really about people's belief in the future, and their willingness to put energy into causing something to come about. It is, in fact, a marvelous statement about humanity. And indeed, the idea of Moore's Law progressed from nobody believing it was possible to the idea that it could take the rest of a person's working life to fully realize it.

It's true that most truly new technologies encounter an energy barrier to overcome: it takes a great deal of time and effort and energy for new ideas to get into the belief system of a culture. And if you don't make that effort, you simply won't get there.

It's also true that every time there has been a major technological advance, everybody cried, "This is going to be the end of society as we know it." Today we're seeing that with the advent of deep learning systems. But we've always seen exactly the opposite through history. Still, almost every one of these new technologies has been resisted. There is some truth to Max Planck's quip that science proceeds one funeral at a time!

Notwithstanding, we've also learned that there is a kind of a philosophy of possibility. I always had to explain that, while Moore's Law is grounded in physics, it's really not a law of physics—it's a law of *the way that humans are.* In order for anything to evolve like our semiconductor technology has evolved, it takes an enormous amount of creative effort by a large number of very smart people. They have to *believe* that the effort is going to result in a successful thing, or they won't put the effort in. The belief that it's possible to do a thing is what causes the thing to happen. But you need two things going in: 1) the belief that what you're envisioning is possible; and 2) the belief that if you do it, it'll make a big difference.

By the time this idea became Moore's Law, we had gotten past the major obstacles to belief.

And Gordon Moore had made the absolutely compelling case that if you could do it, it would transform not only the industry, but the world. There was never a question about that in his mind. But there were a lot of questions about whether it was possible. That's what we had to get past. And as we now know, Gordon was very successful in getting people to believe that it was worth doing. Like the Tofflers, he got there long before many of us did. ▣

Carver Mead is an American scientist and engineer. He currently holds the position of Gordon and Betty Moore Professor Emeritus of Engineering and Applied Science at the California Institute of Technology (Caltech), having taught there for over 40 years. His contributions as a teacher include the classic textbook *Introduction to VLSI Systems* (1980), which he coauthored with Lynn Conway. A pioneer of modern microelectronics, he has made contributions to the development and design of semiconductor devices, digital chips, and silicon compilers, technologies that form the foundations of modern very-large-scale integration chip design. In the 1980s, he focused on electronic modeling of human neurology and biology, creating "neuromorphic electronic systems." Mead has been involved in the founding of nearly 30 companies. Most recently, he has called for the reconceptualization of modern physics, revisiting the theoretical debates of Niels Bohr, Albert Einstein, and others in light of modern experiments.

1. The Caltech Sessions: In Conversation with Carver Mead and George Gilder, Abundant World Institute.

Will **We** Ever Learn To Take the Future Seriously?

Paul Saffo

uture Shock is unquestionably one of **the most influential books published in the second half of the 20th century.** ■ Specifically, its arresting title has entered our vocabulary as a ubiquitous meme, and that is a problem. "Creative destruction," "the medium is the message," "paradigm shift," and "future shock." All are phrases uttered more frequently than they are understood, more often than not by individuals who can't name their authors and have never actually read their work.

This is the curse of all original thinkers. They reveal an insight so profound that it becomes obvious the moment it is stated. Amidst the pleasant flash of discovery, everyone forgets that they were utterly blind to the now-obvious idea and, in so doing, fail to pursue its deeper implications.

In the case of *Future Shock*, the result is the opposite of what Toffler intended. Its ubiquity has elevated, or relegated, "future shock" to the status of a toss-away meme invoked to deflect examination of the very uncertainties of which Toffler sought to warn us. Because we know that future shock is a thing, then surely we are prepared for whatever might come, and the future cannot possibly shock us.

Future Shock's 50th anniversary is thus the perfect occasion to set matters straight and return the meaning of future shock to that of an invitation to look more deeply into what the future holds. A good place to begin is by recognizing that this is the 50th anniversary of the book, but not the idea.

Toffler first articulated the idea of future shock in an essay, "The Future as a Way of Life," published in the Summer 1965 issue of *Horizon* magazine. Written while he was still a writer at *Fortune* magazine, this essay crisply and succinctly defines future shock as "... a time phenomenon, a product of the greatly accelerated rate of change in society. It arises from the superimposition of a new culture on an old one. It is culture shock in one's own society."

I actually prefer the *Horizon* article to the book published five years later. It remains as fresh and relevant today as when it first appeared. For Toffler newcomers, it succinctly expresses the essence of the future shock concept. Others already familiar with the Tofflers' work will find the article a fascinating roadmap, anticipating how they elaborated and expanded their ideas into the book.

But the most important contribution of the *Horizon* article is its call to take the future seriously, to build tools and institutions dedicated to exploring what lies ahead. And above all, to create a culture in which anticipating the future becomes the everyday concern of everyone, not just experts.

Arriving when it did, Toffler's article gave a huge boost to a nascent future studies field that until then was the relatively obscure province of researchers at government think tanks and a handful of corporations. Pioneers like Herman Kahn at the Hudson Institute, Olaf Helmer at RAND, and Ted Gordon at Douglas Aircraft (whose book *The Future* was published in 1965) had already been making a passionate but largely ignored case for futures thinking. Their cause received an enormous boost from the attention drawn to the field by then-journalists Alvin and Heidi Toffler.

The result was a dramatic uptick in interest in the future as a discipline that greatly aided the establishment of several future-oriented think tanks and the founding of the World Future Society in 1966. It also led to a mini-boom in serious books about the future, including Kahn and Wiener's 1967 classic, *The Year 2000: A Framework for Speculation on the Next Thirty-Three Years*.

In short, the 1965 *Horizon* essay and subsequent early work by Al and Heidi Toffler was crucial to moving future research as a discipline into the mainstream. Publication of *Future Shock* in 1970 cemented this trend, boosting public interest even further and making the 1970s the golden age of futures research and thinking. Future studies programs began to appear at universities, and "Futurist" was a title seen at more and more companies.

Even Congress got the message, and in 1972 formed its own futurist think tank, the Office of Technology Assessment. As the decade unfolded, a combination of environmental worries, Earth Day, the oil crisis, and the advent of the digital revolution provided both the incentive and the prospect of new tools, making the Tofflers' 1965 vision of the future as a "way of life" seem a welcome inevitability.

Then the 1980s arrived, and the vision of a robust, widely adopted futures research order went into decline. Long-range thinking became unfashionable during the Reagan/Thatcher era. Futurism was ridiculed in Washington, and futurists were derided as flaky blue-sky California types in a climate focused on "pragmatic" short-termism. Many of the futures institutions created only a decade earlier dropped out of existence, and the few that remained lowered once-ambitious expectations and struggled to survive what amounted to a Futurist Winter.

> *Future Shock*'s 50th anniversary is thus the perfect occasion to set matters straight and return the meaning of future shock to that of an invitation to look more deeply into what the future holds. A good place to begin is by recognizing that this is the 50th anniversary of the book, but not the idea.

Through all of this, the Tofflers continued their work with admirable steadiness and dedication, producing several new books and even launching an advisory group aimed at waking up Washington. This work was vital to helping keep the struggling futures field from extinction by neglect. Futures research receded into the background, but it did not disappear.

The 1990s were a mix of good and bad news for foresight. Angered by its reports that inconveniently conflicted with their rigid ideology, conservatives in Washington, led by Newt Gingrich, managed to finally shut down the Congressional Office of Technology Assessment in 1995. But the arrival of cyberspace in the form of the World Wide Web, plus public fascination with the approaching millennium, gave new life to the futures discipline. The Tofflers contributed to this revival with three important books, *Powershift* in 1990, *Creating a New Civilization,* and *War and Anti-War* in 1995.

The Futurist Winter was over at last, but the new interest in futurism still fell short of the Tofflers' 1965 vision. The giddy optimism of the dot-com revolution and the vast distraction of personal media made futurism cool, not as serious study, but as entertainment splashed across the pages of *Wired* magazine and other publications.

Futurists proliferated, but rigorous foresight languished. In an ironic twist, the arrival of the web disrupted the business model of the few surviving futures research organizations. Leading think tanks like Global Business Network eventually ceased to exist, while others survived by abandoning serious research, turning themselves into facilitators and futurist entertainers selling their services to the few corporate customers still willing to pay for futures-oriented consulting.

The optimistic futures worldview of the late 1990s was punctured by 9/11 and a bursting dot-com bubble, and then crushed by the second Iraq War and the 2007 market crash. Compared to the mood in 2000, futures thinking today is more sober, but remains longer on show than substance. Serious futures work continues, and at moments thrives, but both its scale and impact still fall far short of what the Tofflers and others hoped for half a century ago.

Meanwhile, the challenges facing us continue to grow. The phenomenon of future shock is fueled by the ever-increasing gap between exponentially advancing technology and slowly evolving culture. To it, we can now add the widening gap between the myriad threats facing humanity and the sluggish advance of our ability to anticipate consequences and outcomes. We are struggling to understand 21st-century problems with 20th-century foresight methods. And we live among a public that thinks because the concept of future shock is familiar, they cannot be surprised by anything the future holds.

This is what makes *Future Shock* even more relevant now than when it was first published. This is a moment when unease has displaced optimism, and pessimism is poised to become the new and fashionable black. Uncertainty has never been greater, making irresistible the temptation to focus on the short term and simply hope things work out in the long term. If Al and Heidi Toffler were here, they would remind us that our essential task is to form a better, clearer, stronger conception of what lies ahead. This, as they observed in 1965, is the only remedy for the phenomenon of future shock. It is time—past time, actually—to finally take the future seriously. ▪

Paul Saffo is a Silicon Valley-based forecaster who has devoted over three decades to exploring the dynamics and impacts of large-scale, long-term change. He teaches foresight at Stanford and Chairs Future Studies at Singularity University. He first read *Future Shock* in high school and has relied on Al Toffler's insights, advice and friendship for his entire professional career.

Adapting to Complexity

David C. Krakauer

]am fortunate to be the president of one of the most future-oriented research institutes in the sphere of fundamental and applied research, the Santa Fe Institute, whose mission is to "Search for Order in the Complexity of Evolving Worlds."

For just over thirty years SFI has been seeking to understand complexity—networks of adaptive agents, their form and function, ubiquity, promise, risks, and long-term adaptive evolution. In pursuit of this goal we are steeped in non-equilibrium statistical mechanics, the theory of computation, the application of network theory to big data, large-scale agent-based simulations of ideas and urbanization, and the development of theoretical frameworks to help us navigate an increasingly connected, computationally enabled, economically disparate, and interdependent world. By all accounts we ought to be ideal case studies for the condition that Toffler described as "future shock," but the reality is otherwise.

Just down the hall from my office is the library where my colleague, the novelist Cormac McCarthy, contentedly types out his magnificent novels on an Olivetti Lettera 32, a wonderful, light blue (or retro-muted-green, according to your color perception) mechanical instrument designed in 1932 by Marcello Nizzolo. The typewriter is in essence little different from the Sholes and Glidden, designed by Christopher Latham Sholes in the late 1860s, that introduced the now ubiquitous QWERTY keyboard. And when Cormac ran low on ink, Sam Shepard, who in an adjoining office himself wrote his plays and screenplays on a 1966 Olympia SM-9 Deluxe portable, would lend him a ribbon. Neither author had any problems whatsoever in getting their work to screen and then, to adapt a term, to "stream."

I would, and still do on occasion, leave Cormac, and previously Sam, notes written with a Diplomat fountain pen running Iroshizuku ink on Japanese Midori notepaper. This was essential, as neither Cormac nor Sam ever use or used a computer, nor therefore email or any other internet-enabled messaging client. My commitment to fountain pens is shared by several colleagues: Simon DeDeo, who works on computational approaches to social dynamics; Seth Lloyd, a pioneer on quantum information and quantum computing; Geoffrey West, one of the world's leading theorists of scale and the quantitative theory of urban life; and Neal Stephenson, who has written more about computation, software, and cyber-culture and their future than almost any other novelist I can think of.

> One of Toffler's surprising conclusions is that the shock may be ameliorated by creating enclaves of the past, zones of decision-making that are throttled and restricted, in order to promote coherence.

I wanted to begin with an informal introduction to my tool-habitat and cultural conspecifics in order to make explicit the nature of adaptation to change and the role that artifacts play in helping us to cope with rapidly changing environments. I do not agree with Toffler that "future shock" is a disease, or syndrome of modernity, or threat to the stability of society, or something that needs to be centrally regulated. That cultural knowledge and its access and sequelae (demographic, thermodynamic, technological, and economic) are accumulating at an accelerating pace is indisputable and was foreseen by the ancient Greeks, evangelized a couple of millennia later by Norbert Wiener, and then by his architectural double Buckminster Fuller. What Toffler brought to the table was an emphasis on mechanisms of adaptation, largely in the form of individual psychological and professional transformation and institutional innovation and reform.

Toffler presents us with a conflict between the constraints of biology and the unbounded growth of culture through his observation that an organism's ability to cope with input is dependent upon its physiological structure. His thesis is one in which individual cognitive bandwidth, derived from what is now often called the Environment of Evolutionary Adaptedness (EEA), cannot juggle all the balls thrown at it from the new technological environment, and is at risk of dropping them all through a syndrome described as a disease of change—future shock—characterized by a combination of anxiety, bewilderment, and social chaos. One of Toffler's surprising conclusions is that the shock may be ameliorated by creating enclaves of the past, zones of decision-making that are throttled and restricted, in order to promote coherence.

Over the last few decades our understanding of adaptation, both in culture and cognition, has radically changed. I would argue it has changed to such a large extent that future shock should no longer be diagnosed as a disease, but as an inevitable precondition of cultural evolution itself. The mechanisms of adaptation: genetic, epigenetic, physiological, neural, cultural, linguistic, and technological, represent a suite of mechanisms responsive to a full spectrum of rates of change. The theory of adaptation in complex systems is one that seeks to understand and classify those mechanisms that sense, acquire, store, process, and propagate functional information. The evolution of epigenetic inheritance (heritable chemical modifications to DNA and proteins within cells) is the direct outcome of the rate-limitations of natural selection operating on genomes, just as the emergence of excitable cells and nervous systems is the outcome of the transmission limits of epigenomes, and the eventual evolution of cultural learning and inheritance a means of overcoming the collective computational limits of individual nervous systems. Future shock—the sensation of non-sensing change—is the spur and catalyst to evolving new mechanisms of adaptation.

In order to capture these "major transitions" in the evolution of adaptive systems, I have been studying the representational limits of evolved computational architectures, perhaps the best known of which is the so called "error threshold" theory, which specifies how much functional information can be transmitted through a population of noisy channels in a changing environment before being irrevocably degraded. The key insight is that every adaptive bit at any scale of organization (cell, brain, society) needs to be fixed or stored or memorized in the system at a rate faster than the rate of change of the bit. If the bit changes faster than the rate at which it is stored, then information is eventually lost. If the bit can be stored first it does not matter how fast the bit changes—the environment changes—and it can be used as an element of an adaptive strategy. The key to the continued evolution of life is that the environment continues to change at an accelerating rate in order to promote the emergence of mechanisms with greater and greater temporal resolving power.

This trend is the key to understanding cognitive artifacts—those tools and ideas from pens to quantum computers—that systematically overcome the limits of prior adaptive mechanisms, capable of encoding the selectively or functionally salient states of our environments. As we learn from the very successful examples of Cormac McCarthy and Sam Shepard, these artifacts need not all be new, they merely need to interoperate with the new tools.

The new urban habitats into which we are culturally evolving have the foundational super-power of diversity. This growing diversity of minds, tools, and dispositions provides adaptive solutions—nothing monolithic, not individual super-generalists, but a collective intelligence that does not impose constraints on the suite of adaptive mechanisms available to a society. Indeed, combining the durability of ancient technology (the great Silicate Chip or clay tablet of Sumeria) with the processing speed of the modern silicon chip, or the scientific methods of modern society with the contemplative methods of monastic traditions, are perhaps some of the most exciting experiments in the recombination of diverse cognitive artifacts that we can look forward to in coming years.

I, for one, am an optimist, as Toffler himself hinted toward in his closing remarks, in which he calls for a transcendence of technocracy and time horizons that reach generations into the future. The future will be in many respects a co-constructed reality, one in which adaptive agents born of our imagination mingle with those of nature, to create an evolving world more shocking and more varied than any imagined by Pliny the Elder, Marco Polo, or Ursula K. Le Guin. ■

David C. Krakauer is the president and William H. Miller Professor of Complex Systems at the Santa Fe Institute. He works on the evolution of intelligence and stupidity on Earth. Whereas the first is admired but rare, the second is feared but common. He is the founder of the InterPlanetary Project at SFI and is the publisher/editor-in-chief of the SFI Press. In those capacities, he is the co-editor of these two 2019 books: *InterPlanetary Transmissions: Proceedings of the Santa Fe Institute's First InterPlanetary Festival: Genesis* and *Worlds Hidden in Plain Sight: The Evolving Idea of Complexity at the Santa Fe Institute 1984–2019*.

Future Shock at 50

George Gilder

Held annually in Shanghai, under sparkling towers next to the Huangpu River, is the World Artificial Intelligence (AI) Conference. ▪ It assembles throngs of AI luminaries, laden with high-voltage visions of the future. This year, it once again proved that Alvin Toffler and *Future Shock* are the once and future religion of the nerds.

Transmitting the shockwaves in the 2019 version of the conference was a "debate" between Jack Ma, the founder of China's giant bazaar and bank Alibaba, and Elon Musk of Tesla, SpaceX and Neuralink, ready to land on Mars and put AI implants in your brain.

An exponent of the *Future Shock* thesis, Musk declares: "The rate of change of technology is outpacing our ability to understand it."

"AI will be to humans," he says, "as humans are to chimpanzees. We won't be able to understand the machines at all." They will leave us baffled, out of work, and on the beach, perhaps garnering a guaranteed annual income, "if they are nice."

"I hope they are nice," Elon said with a fruity lilt.

Musk's melodramatic warning parallels Toffler's *Future Shock* quote from Wisconsin sociologist Lawrence Suhm: "We are going through a period as traumatic as the evolution of man's predecessor from sea creatures to land creatures. Those who can adapt will. Those who can't ... will perish—washed up upon the shores."

Are you shocked by the future? By the "accelerating thrust" of "super-industrialization," the ever-increasing velocity of travel, the rise of "ad-hocracy," the ascendancy of airport cities, the transience of human ties, the globalization of commerce and culture, the emergence of the "fractured family," the concussions of technological change, the need for adaptive "shock absorbers?" Are you an adaptive man?

In their 1970 best seller, Alvin and Heidi Toffler launched a barrage of these now familiar features of futurism. Everywhere people speak their language without knowing it.

Sure enough, 50 years later, I'm in O'Hare airport writing this essay on an Apple MacBook Air many thousand times more capable than the supercomputers of Toffler's time. After watching a video interview about blockchains on my smartphone, I'll use the same device to hail down my legendary editor Richard Vigilante, also in O'Hare. I'll meet with him passing through from San Diego on his way back to his hedge fund partnership in Minneapolis.

We'll try to frame our next Gilder Report investment. Will it be in Israel, in China, or in the Cryptocosm of the blockchain? Then I'll be contemplating a trip to see a beautiful Chinese friend and possible colleague in Indiana, who wants to correct my roseate views of Chinese capitalism. Next week I'll be off to Israel to help lead a Discovery Institute tour of the Holy Land and center of global innovation.

But first, Richard and I will get together over a table in a Starbucks to prepare a new monthly letter on how to invest in radical new "moonshot" technologies such as the blockchain and 5G wireless and artificial intelligence that Alvin Toffler never exactly anticipated in his musings about new cities under the sea. But he surely nailed the broad outlines of this thaumaturgic future in his visionary books.

> "AI will be to humans," he says, "as humans are to chimpanzees. We won't be able to understand the machines at all." They will leave us baffled, out of work, and on the beach, perhaps garnering a guaranteed annual income, "if they are nice."

But that does not answer the question of whether *Future Shock* is true.

I think of my father, Richard Gilder, in 1936, as a new graduate of Harvard, visiting Hitler's Germany. Viewing its high-stepping army on the march and hearing Hitler's warrior demagoguery, then and there he resolved that the Nazis must be stopped.

A futurist before his time, he predicted that the war would be decided by technology, specifically air power. On his return to the US, he entered civilian flight training to be ready. In his early twenties, he confronted influential appeasers of Germany, such as Allen Dulles, at the Council of Foreign Relations in New York, of which my father was the youngest member.

Though married with children, he entered the air force and lost his life leading a squadron of misbegotten B-17 Flying Fortresses across the Atlantic. Designed to combine fighter and bomber functions, they were a kludge that couldn't really fly very well in bad weather.

My father's adulthood as a succession of harrowing shocks followed his grandfather's experience in the Civil War, when an entire generation of young men was uprooted and depleted and slaves were freed.

Life has always moved fast and imparted shocks. Do you find events more unsettling today than they were in the industrial revolution when the share of the population on farms dropped 90 percent? No feat of artificial intelligence will likely have the impact of the tractor and milking machine and combine on farm life.

The Toffler's are shocked by sex. I'm more shocked by "sexual suicide"—the collapse of birth rates and the dissolution of sex roles. But overall, sexual activity is less shocking than ever. After the cure of syphilis and other venereal diseases, the invention of the pill, and the end of polygamy and the outlawry of harems, are you still shocked by the "world's oldest profession" in all its permutations? The dildo was pervasive in ancient Egypt. Sex was far more turbulent and dangerous and shocking in the past than it is today.

For all its transformative success as a book, *Future Shock* was the Tofflers' big mistake. It pursued and promoted the fashion of *accelerationism*. Launching this fashion was Henry Adams in 1918, when he penned the "Law of Accelerating Returns" recounting exponential increases in the cost effectiveness of industrial age energy technologies.

Ray Kurzweil invoked the phrase again in 1999 and applied it to information technologies, offering a series of curves that mimicked Adams'. But it is the same "Future Shocking" fallacy of inevitable progress.

The Tofflers wanted us to believe that time was speeding up. The future was closing in. Human beings might not be able to adapt. And it was time for Alvin and all the rest of us to entertain new mistresses, as monogamy became obsolete for powerful men.

Future Shock provided an exciting, breezy read with a tempting payoff. But it merely reflected the usual generational parochialism. Each generation is tempted to believe that it is special, that its times are uniquely concussive, that its future is revolutionary.

I call the present version "Google Marxism." Marx's mistake was to imagine that the Industrial Revolution—steam turbines, railroads, looms, assembly lines, embryonic electrification—was an *eschaton*, a final thing. It ended the challenge of wealth creation, so Marx imagined, and initiated an era in which the crucial issue was redistributing existing wealth.

Google Marxism makes the same Marxist mistake in spades, imagining that the information revolution in artificial intelligence, machine learning, robotics, genetic engineering, and big data do not merely obsolete human labor but also human minds.

Most of human history has been more concussively shocking than today, when we are buffered with wealth and relative peace and can live longer and much healthier lives. The Tofflers tippled on the usual cultural kool-aid; the death of God, the speedup of ideational change, and the slippery slopes of relativist morality. But so did Nietzsche and Voltaire and even Thackeray. So did Shakespeare and Aristotle and Sophocles.

> With all of us lining up for the implants like queues of potheads outside newly legal "cannabis" dispensaries, we'll experience a new kind of blinkered bliss. The future will divide the world between potheads blissing out and Neuralink chipheads blissing in.

That was all right, because it propelled the Tofflers on to *The Third Wave*, a genuinely prophetic book that anticipated the information age and described many of its astonishing features.

But shocking is not the point. Life and change have always been shocking. The chief difference today is longer lifespans and all the buffers and consolations of unprecedented wealth.

Now, at the Shanghai conference, the galvanic future-shocking change is artificial intelligence attaining a singularity and obsoleting the human brain.

Elon Musk offers a solution in his Neuralink project. Neuralink is Musk's company that is inventing broadband interfaces for the brain, to connect us physically to AI. Implanted at strategic points in our nervous systems, Neuralinks will upgrade us to the status of superchimps.

We'll be able to upload any skill or sensation or knowledge base in seconds from the "cloud" to the brain. We'll bypass Google search and prestidigitory thumbs on our smartphones and become super-broadband extensions of our marvelous new Musk machines.

With all of us lining up for the implants like queues of potheads outside newly legal "cannabis" dispensaries, we'll experience a new kind of blinkered bliss.

The future will divide the world between potheads blissing out and Neuralink chipheads blissing in. If you don't find that sufficiently shocking as a future, perhaps you are a jaded nerd yourself, washed up on the shores of change.

"Better leave for Mars" may be your conclusion after listening to Elon. He is not exactly clear, but he seems to say that the only way for humans to preserve their precious "consciousness" from the ravages of AI is to populate nearby planets.

As a leader of the techno-apocalypse, Elon does generously offer us some relief from any worries about these predictions, or nearly anything else he might have to say. In a segue into further shocks, he says we may be living in an advanced computer simulation.

According to his calculations, our carbon existence may merely be a sham contrived by superior silicon beings with "exaflop powers." Our lives may only be dynamic features of avatars in a video game played by superior AI beings from outer space.

As Virtual Reality inventor Jaron Lanier says, AI makes you *stupid*.

Before you buy into Neuralink bliss, you may also want to scrutinize the terms and conditions. Elon may not be liable for any bad trips, as he is when Tesla's self-driving features fail. At least, his simulation theory gives him an ironclad alibi for the court: he is out of his mind.

But at least he doesn't believe in anything irrational or foolish like a God!

No doubt, Elon is a genius of sorts and an entrepreneurial hero. But despite his Stanford "college smarts," he shows no aptitude for philosophical analysis.

His debating partner, Jack Ma of Alibaba, offered corrective shock-absorption. Ma disdains Musk's "college smarts." Better are "street smarts," retorted Ma, who thinks Elon should cool it. "Why are you so curious about Mars? There's nothing there."

Elon believes in safety first. With a calculable risk of the destruction of the Earth, perhaps by planet change or runaway AI, he thinks we have a possibly "small window" of opportunity to become a "multiplanetary species."

Ma's view was "good luck with that." He'd rather solve problems on Earth. Removed from control at Alibaba and divested of substantial wealth as a result of mysterious Chinese machinations, possibly by the government, Ma has had time to do some thinking. He is enjoying a sinecure with the UN Commission on Digital Cooperation.

He downplayed the future shock of AI. "It is no threat. It will create jobs like all previous technologies."

AI is "clever," he said. It is "knowledge based" or just data-based. Human intelligence is "smart." "Smart is experience-based." AI is just computers and chips, processing fast but actually knowing nothing. "It's logic. But humans are life."

Musk's case relied on the usual examples of AI playing games, beating human world champions in chess and the Asian strategic game of Go.

Games, though, are deterministic, like mathematics or other logical systems. Games solve the fundamental problem of AI. It's programmed with symbols. Just as maps are not the same as territories, symbols are never the same as the objects they point to. They have to be interpreted by human beings.

In games, the symbols are the same as the objects. In Go, the black and white stone pieces do not point to a reality beyond themselves. They are the reality. Shuffled at billions of times a second, they always give the right answers.

As Ma explained, games are made for human interpreters to compete with each other. "It's stupid to have humans compete with machines," he said. "It's like a human trying to race a car."

Ma concluded, "Computers have chips; humans have hearts."

"Humans provide the dreams behind the machines," he said, "humans provide love."

Elon agreed, sort of. Imagine love in the form of an exciting undulation of broadband brainwaves fed from a Neuralink interface between your mind and body.

The two tech titans then converged on an important mutual prophecy that may well prove true. The challenge for the future will not be overpopulation, but a likely "population collapse." The chief threat to China, Ma said, is not too many people or too smart AI, but no babies. "People do not want to have babies."

> As Ma explained, games are made for human interpreters to compete with each other. "It's stupid to have humans compete with machines," he said. "It's like a human trying to race a car."

The Chinese bore only 80 million babies in 2018, nowhere near enough to reproduce the population.

Elon agreed. We are forgetting the human "boot-sequence," Musk said. "Boot sequence" is his piquant computer word for sex.

"I choose life," he concluded.

After exchanging tributes to one another, they walked off into the sunset singing what seemed to be Beatles songs.

"Love is the answer," they agreed.

So what has changed?

Future Shock encouraged politicians to believe they are needed to control the threat of "technocracy." The Tofflers believed we need new government agencies to abate the "accelerative thrust" of change. They believed that technology causes pollution rather than remedies it. They called for experts to help us adapt—life-change scores and social indices to anticipate disruption and help us prepare for it.

Like most sociology, all this is either self-evident or wrong. The US today is congested with government agencies shocked by the future and attempting to suppress it. Google, for instance, is a company beset on all sides by Federal Trade Commission bureaucrats who imagine it is a monopoly and needs to be broken up, Equal Employment Opportunity bureaucrats who believe that its meritocratic hiring is a menace to women and minorities, and Attorneys General from 20 states and the European Economic Commission who regard it a threat to privacy. Every other week there is another story about huge fees and fines assessed against our technology paladins for vague and venial offenses. Each fine is justified by the huge earnings of these leviathans, but collectively, the Lilliputian bureaucrats can bring down and stultify our greatest companies.

This is the downside of the *Future Shock* thesis. Exaggerating the singularity of our epoch leads to government overreach and needless alarms and crises.

There are plenty of real crises in the world. The acceleration of change and our inability to adapt to it is not among them. ■

George F. Gilder is one of the leading economic and technological thinkers of the past forty years. He is Chairman of George Gilder Fund Management, host of the *Gilder Telecosm Forum*, co-founder and Senior Fellow at the Discovery Institute, a founding partner of the 1517 Fund, and a founding Member of the Board of Advisors for the Independent Institute. Mr. Gilder pioneered the formulation of supply-side economics when he served as Chairman of the Lehrman Institute's Economic Roundtable, as Program Director for the Manhattan Institute, and as a frequent contributor to A.B. Laffer's economic reports. According to a study of presidential speeches, Mr. Gilder was President Reagan's most frequently quoted living author. In 1986, President Reagan presented Gilder the White House Award for Entrepreneurial Excellence. He ranks at #27 on Clayton Christensen's World's Top 50 Management Gurus. He is a contributing editor of *Forbes* magazine and a frequent writer for *The Economist, American Spectator, Harvard Business Review, Wall Street Journal*, and other publications. Gilder now writes a "Daily Prophecy" five days a week for *Agora Financial*.

The Helpful Multidimensionality of Foreseeable Technological Progress: How Future Shocks May Make Each Other Less Shocking

Aubrey D.N.J. de Grey

Toffler's analysis, 50 years ago, of the impact of accelerated technological change on people's sense of stability still rings true today. ▪ The impermanence of those aspects of life that have historically been almost unchanging has continued to spread. The average company stays in business for less time, the average marriage lasts less long, the average person changes jobs more often... the list goes on. But these are aspects of the current world, and Toffler's focus is on the deficiencies of how people react to change once it happens. Here I would like to discuss a related but distinct issue: how people analyze potential future change and form opinions about the desirability of such change.

My field, biomedical gerontology, is a curiosity as regards change, because its defining goal is to maintain youth in chronological old age: in other words, to develop technology that will prevent a change that naturally occurs, rather than to bring about a change that does not. When we become able to stabilize the structure and composition of our bodies, we will cease to change in a way that we always have done (and not enjoyed!), and that will itself be a (momentous) change. Perhaps this schizophrenic relationship of biomedical gerontology to change is one reason why so many people are so appallingly bad at thinking about it. Below I will explore some conspicuous examples of this.

First let us consider the impact of the elimination of aging on the trajectory of global population, and the all-too-common fear that that population will rapidly become unsustainable. This fear is founded upon a slew of egregiously false assumptions, whose stubborn survival in the face of their obvious refutations beggars belief. Most of them are not directly relevant to the topic of this essay, so I will just list them:

- People assume that birth rates per woman per year will remain as now, even though they are plummeting in almost all of the world's largest countries.
- People assume that the end of menopause would raise the birth rate, when in fact the opportunity to have kids later seems always to result (on average) in having no kids early, rather than having more kids in total.
- People's quantitative intuition concerning the likely rate of population growth with time in a post-aging world, for any given assumption concerning birth rates, tends to be wildly exaggerated.
- People ignore the fact that even if there were an overpopulation problem, we would have the choice between (a) having fewer kids than we would like or (b) getting sick when we get old, and that's a choice that future generations are entitled to be able to make, rather than being denied it because we had not developed the relevant medicine.
- But the final, and perhaps the most damning, rebuttal of the idea that we should be worried about global post-aging overpopulation is that the problem will be pre-empted by other technological advances—advances that are proceeding so rapidly that they will almost certainly be ubiquitous by the time that the elimination of aging even begins to affect population. I refer, of course, to the ways in which we are reducing the environmental impact of our daily activities.

Overpopulation is not in any way a question of having enough space—as things stand, there are fewer people on the planet than acres of land, and people's preference to live in cities shows no sign of abating, so the population could certainly grow by a couple of orders of magnitude before it would feel remotely crowded. No: The population problem, just as Malthus foresaw, is one of pollution. And whether it be renewable energy, artificial meat, plastic-eating bacteria, desalination—in every way, we are very shortly going to be raising the carrying capacity of the planet (the number of people it can sustain without a problematic impact on the environment) far faster than the actual population could ever rise even in absolute worst-case birth-rate scenarios. Malthusian pessimism is just as misguided now as he himself was.

This is a clear example of a ubiquitous failing: when imagining a future world in which some central feature of today's world is very different, to assume (implicitly—but that makes it even worse) that everything else will be more or less the same as today. That assumption is so idiotic that we must ask ourselves why it is so common. Perhaps it is that some of these other technologies have their own PR issues? The switch from fossil

> "My field, biomedical gerontology, is a curiosity as regards change, because its defining goal is to maintain youth in chronological old age: in other words, to develop technology that will prevent a change that naturally occurs, rather than to bring about a change that does not.

fuels to renewables is praised in the abstract for its benefit in diminishing climate change, but where the rubber hits the road (so to speak) is people's fear of the associated change: of losing jobs in the fossil fuel industry, or of driving a car that takes a long time to be recharged. In other words, perhaps these changes compensate for each other.

An even starker example of such interaction arises in the context of another fear that is often expressed in relation to the end of aging: that the retirement age will need to rise in order to contain the pensions bill. While there are, again, decidedly compelling rebuttals of this concern that do not refer to other technological advances, the strongest is one that does. The rise of automation is universally—even by bodies who might be inclined to conservatism—predicted to eliminate a large proportion of today's jobs within the next couple of decades, and in contrast to the Industrial Revolution, there is scant prospect of those jobs being replaced by ones that do not yet exist. Instead, there will simply be more prosperity with less work. While there are undoubtedly many difficult challenges with regard to how that prosperity can be equitably distributed, and also with regard to how self-worth can be maintained when it is not founded on the receipt of a regular paycheck, one thing is certain: Far from rising, the path of least resistance will see the retirement age falling. Again, this is a case where each advance seems scary in isolation but they rescue each other. People don't like the idea of being unsure of having a paid job from the time they finish education until they want to retire, but the main reason they don't like it (assuming that the challenges just mentioned are addressed) is because they assume that they will get sick when they get old and will need a pension to support themselves.

I could go on, but you get the idea. Future shock is real, but "future future shock"—the fear of the unknown aspects of a world following technological advances—is arguably even more problematic, since it slows our progress in developing such technologies for the benefit of humanity. Perhaps counterintuitively, the rational basis for this fear in respect of multiple future technologies is, in general, not more than the sum of its parts, but less. Therefore, in seeking to allay such fears we should capitalize on this happy interaction and highlight cases where new technologies can address each other's potential unwanted consequences. ■

Dr. Aubrey de Grey is a biomedical gerontologist based in Mountain View, California, and is the Chief Science Officer of SENS Research Foundation (sens.org), a California-based 501(c)(3) biomedical research charity that performs and funds laboratory research dedicated to combating the aging process. He is also VP of New Technology Discovery at AgeX Therapeutics, a biotechnology startup developing new therapies in the field of biomedical gerontology. In addition, he is editor-in-chief of *Rejuvenation Research*, the world's highest-impact peer-reviewed journal focused on intervention in aging. He received his BA in computer science and PhD in biology from the University of Cambridge. His research interests encompass the characterisation of all the types of self-inflicted cellular and molecular damage that constitute mammalian aging and the design of interventions to repair and/or obviate that damage. Dr. de Grey is a Fellow of both the Gerontological Society of America and the American Aging Association, and sits on the editorial and scientific advisory boards of numerous journals and organizations. He is a highly sought-after speaker who gives 40-50 invited talks per year at scientific conferences, universities, companies in areas ranging from pharma to life insurance, and to the public.

Becoming the Future

Richard Yonck

We are living in the midst of a radical new emergence, the evolution of a global civilization. With the advent of toolmaking some three and half million years ago, our humble hominid species embarked on a journey into an increasingly technological and intelligent future. The world that has resulted is vastly more resilient, more powerful, and, above all, more intelligent than any of its constituent members. We are a symphony of minds that is rapidly becoming greater than the sum of its parts.

Unfortunately, such transformation is not without its downsides. As cognitive, emotional, and conscious beings, we are acutely aware of change, far more so than any other species. Faced with too much change, we experience anxiety, disorientation, and stress. We experience *future shock*.

Both the premise and title of Alvin and Heidi Toffler's pivotal 1970 book, *Future Shock*, tapped into the zeitgeist and concerns of an increasingly bewildered world. From global war to art movements, much of the 20th century was a response to this phenomenon, and this book gave us a framework from which we could begin to examine and explain the world we found ourselves immersed in.

I had just entered junior high school when I was introduced to *Future Shock*. It had a huge impact on me, setting me on a lifelong path of exploring the future and its potential implications for society.

However, in reading this book, I found myself asking the question: Why were we doing this to ourselves? Why would intelligent people allow themselves to create a world so at odds with their own personal health and well-being? Why weren't we taking hold of the wheel and steering ourselves in a smarter direction? The Tofflers' prescription, that we needed to halt runaway acceleration, made sense to me then. So, why weren't we doing this?

The answer is that, short of a global catastrophe, progress is unstoppable. The economic and competitive forces that drive technological change are beyond ours to control, even if we could all act in coordination. Yes, with a great deal of work, nations might be able to respond to a singular impending environmental disaster, such as human-induced global warming. But the overall trajectory of social and technological progress is orders of magnitude too complex, even if we could enlist the support of every person and every nation on the planet, which we certainly cannot. While we may have some say in our own personal destinies, on the greater and grander scale of global society there are many things beyond our control, and this is one of them. Through great effort, we might redirect aspects of accelerating change and alter our response to it, but control is out of the question. As a globally interconnected and interdependent organism, we are too far on the way to becoming something NEW.

> " Why were we doing this to ourselves? Why would intelligent people allow themselves to create a world so at odds with their own personal health and well-being? Why weren't we taking hold of the wheel and steering ourselves in a smarter direction?

It is very natural for us to want to see this change in positive and negative terms, but in many respects, it is neither. From the standpoint of the evolving universe, this is business as usual, an unceasing progression of increasing complexity on the cosmos' relentless path toward equilibrium. Throughout the universe, change is inevitable, and it may be that accelerating change is inevitable too. The rest of the universe doesn't mind this, but for our cognizant, self-aware species, such change is unavoidably *uncomfortable*.

From our perspective, it is the psychological impact of this accelerating change that seems to cause the most widespread distress. This is interesting because radical change in nature has typically been a source of physical distress for most species. But out of the universe's many emergences, so far as we know, no others have possessed the ability to perceive and think about such things. We are the first on this planet to be able to do so and hopefully we won't be the last.

Much of what makes Homo sapiens unique is our ability to construct and manipulate concepts, a direct consequence of our ability to use complex language. Because of this, we are storytellers and always have been. From those earliest gatherings around the fire pit, we told tales that connected us emotionally as we sought to make sense of the world we found ourselves so profoundly aware of. We wanted to understand what was happening to us. In this respect, nothing has really changed. We still seek meaning and understanding in our shared experience of the world.

In *Future Shock*, the Tofflers shared with us one perspective for diagnosing and understanding our rapidly accelerating world. It offered a rationale for much of the change we saw around us, as every good story, myth, theory, or framework tries to do. While far from a complete explanation, it popularized a futures perspective, serving as a jumping-off point for developing further insights about what was happening to our society. Perhaps most importantly, it was a guide with which we could begin to explore new paths to building a better tomorrow.

In the half-century since *Future Shock* was first published, the world has not heeded the Tofflers' exhortation to slow things down, because it cannot. In fact, by many measures, change comes far faster today than it ever has before, due to the nature of accelerating progress. At what point does such acceleration become unsustainable?

Then there is the question of how we choose to respond to change. Do we anticipate and prepare for it? Or are we doomed to be in a constant state of reaction, responding in *ad hoc* fashion to every new development as it happens to us?

This is why the world needs to apply futures thinking and foresight much more routinely than it currently does, from teaching and learning about it in our schools to using it in industry and applying it in government. This is not about making predictions or identifying popular trends—the informational equivalent of junk food—that play into the media's need for sensationalism while undermining the legitimacy and efficacy of more rigorous futures methodologies and approaches. Rather, we need to accept that we are continually engaging the future, requiring us to adopt new methods for anticipating and iteratively adjusting to new developments, information, and trans- formations. We must routinely adapt to the future because that is the world we now live in.

Additionally, if we cannot change the nature of our accelerating world, perhaps what we need to do is change how we are affected by it. According to a futures concept known as "pace lay- ering," different aspects of our world progress and change at different rates, giving order to our civilization. In descending order these are fashion, commerce, infrastructure, gover- nance, culture, and nature.

Those layers at the top adapt and change the most quickly, while those at the bottom change more slowly and pro- vide stability and resilience. As the con- cept's originator Stuart Brand has writ- ten, "Fast learns, slow remembers."

This framework provides an excel- lent way of understanding change in our world; however, as our world accelerates, the amount of change between these lay-

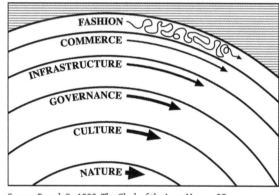

Source: Brand, S., 1999, *The Clock of the Long Now*, p. 37.

ers increases, giving rise to friction and conflict. So, are there ways we could perhaps draw on this model in order to moderate the effects that change has on the different layers, thereby easing the friction they generate?

This is not to suggest we undermine the very structures that give stability to our world, but to adapt some of the ways we plan and think about our future as a society. For instance, maybe certain aspects of governance could be modified to adapt more readily to new technologies, social change, and economic developments, while still maintaining major institutions and the stability they provide? Perhaps early in the development of new forms and implementations of technology, commerce could routinely include a process of exploring their ethical and social ramifications? The details will take time, but whatever we do, we need to be anticipating more and reacting less, moving into the future with our eyes open and our minds prepared.

Of course, if the world continues to accelerate, which it appears certain of doing, the day will eventually come when even this futures-oriented approach won't be enough. How will we address all of this accelerating change? Will it be necessary for us to integrate more and more with technology simply in order to keep up? Will we find some way to slow progress, making it more reasonable and manageable relative to human timescales? Or are we destined for a "reset"—some form of self-induced catastrophe that throws all of us back into the Stone Age, or worse?

Then again, is it possible all of this is nothing more than the growing pains of an adolescent, one who feels they will never be able to endure all of the trials and tribulations that life throws at them? Will this global organism wake up one day to discover it has made it through to the other side as it metamorphoses into maturity and adulthood?

The act of becoming is inherently painful and difficult, no matter the circumstances. But in the end, it is a process that strengthens us and leaves us better prepared to grow, to build, to endure. An evolution that enables us to fulfill whatever our destiny might be. Which raises the question: What will we be when we become our future? ▪

Richard Yonck is a futurist consultant, keynote speaker, and best-selling author living in Seattle. His new book, *Our Intelligent Future*, explores the future of intelligence as it relates to humanity, our planet, and the evolution of the cosmos. His previous book, *Heart of the Machine*, is a guide to the future of Emotion AI, technologies that can read, interpret, and interact with human emotions. More information can be found at www.intelligent-future.com.

Shocking
Amount of Data

Kirk Borne

W e are fully engulfed in the
era of massive data collection. ▪ All those data represent the most critical and valuable strategic assets of modern organizations that are undergoing digital disruption and digital transformation. Advanced analytics tools and techniques drive insights discovery, innovation, new market opportunities, and value creation from data. However, our enthusiasm for "big data" is tempered by the fact that this data flood also drives us to sensory input shock and awe.

Among the countless amazing foresights that appeared in Alvin Toffler's *Future Shock* was the concept of *information overload*. His discussion of the topic came long before the creation and proliferation of social networks, the World Wide Web, the internet, enterprise databases, ubiquitous sensors, and digital data collection by all organizations—big and small, public and private, near and far. The clear and present human consequences and dangers of infoglut were succinctly called out as section headings in Chapter 16, "The Psychological Dimension," of Toffler's book, including these: "the over-stimulated individual," "bombardment of the senses," and "decision stress."

While these ominous forecasts have now become a reality for our digitally drenched society, especially for the digital natives who have known no other experience, there is hope for a lifeline that we can grasp while swimming (or drowning) in that sea of data. And that hope emanates from the same foundation that is the basis of the information overload shock itself. That foundation is data, and the hope is AI—artificial intelligence. The promise of AI is entirely dependent on the flood of sensory input data that fuels the advanced algorithms that activate and stimulate the actionable insights (representing another definition of A.I.), which is what AI is really aimed at achieving.

AI is a great producer of dichotomous reactions in society: hype versus hope, concern versus commercialization, fantasy versus forward-thinking, overstimulation versus overabundance of opportunity, bombardment of the senses versus bountiful insights into solving hard problems, and decision stress versus automated decision support. Could we imagine any technology that has more mutually contradictory psychological dimensions than AI? I cannot.

AI takes its cue from data. It needs data—and not just small quantities, but large quantities of data, containing training examples of all sorts of behaviors, events, processes, things, and outcomes. Just as a human (or any cognitive creature) receives sensory inputs from its world through multiple channels (*e.g.,* our five senses) and then produces an output—a decision, an action—in response to those inputs, similarly that is exactly what an AI does. The AI relies on mathematical algorithms that sort through streams of data to find the most relevant, informative, actionable, and pertinent patterns in the data. From those presently perceived patterns, AI then produces an output (decision and/or action). When a human detects and then recognizes a previously seen pattern, the person knows how to respond—what to decide and how to act. This is what an AI is being trained to do, automatically and with minimal human intervention through the data inputs that cue the algorithms.

AI helps with infoglut and thereby addresses the themes of Toffler's writings (information overload, overstimulation and bombardment of the senses, and decision stress) by the pattern-learned process of automating the essential triage of input data streams that cognitive beings do autonomically (i.e., through autonomic reflex). This is what an "intelligence" does.

Ever since the beginning of our existence, we humans go through our lives constantly bombarded by sensory inputs. Imagine walking out the front door of your house and paying detailed attention to every single bit of information that both natural and human-constructed objects present to us—every leaf on every tree, every cloud in the sky, every twist and turn of the roads and pathways, every scent or odor in the air, every pleasant or cacophonous sound in the environment. Our brains (which are *natural* neural networks) know how to categorize and sort those billions of sensory inputs (information glut) into three categories of information, without even deliberately thinking about them (i.e., without suffering from information overload). As noted above, those three categories—the triage—of information are: (1) those that are common and unimportant in that moment (thus, ignored); (2) those that are critically important (thus, used promptly for the next decision and action); and (3) those that might be important later (thus, stored in our minds for later recall). This information categorization triage happens without any conscious action on our part.

> Those more meaningful and representative forms of AI (Accelerated, Amplified, Assisted, and Augmented Intelligence) also include Actionable, Automated, and Adaptable Intelligence. These represent the real power of AI – there is nothing artificial at all in those applications of AI.

AI (which includes *artificial* neural networks) can and will provide a similar triage on the infoglut and big data inputs that would otherwise have the potential to produce the deleterious psychological outcomes that Toffler writes about: confusion, disorientation, anxiety, analysis paralysis, and eventually apathy and withdrawal. AI will do what it is built for doing and tuned to do well (through large amounts of input training data), which is to accelerate, amplify, assist, and augment human intelligence. Those more meaningful and representative forms of AI (Accelerated, Amplified, Assisted, and Augmented Intelligence) also include Actionable, Automated, and Adaptable Intelligence. These represent the real power of AI—there is nothing artificial at all in those applications of AI.

Therefore, AI ultimately enables us to adapt to the information overload, sensory bombardment, and decision stress in the modern data-intense world. We are in a transition period, between our ability to generate massive quantities of data and our ability to assimilate all of that information through AI. Data are then simply the input, albeit a significantly large amount of input, to our business logic processes that have always been the fundamental means of decision-making and taking actions. This applies not only to organizations, but also to individuals. AI can manage the information flood that we encounter daily through news sources, social networks, entertainment devices, and more.

Adaptability to shock (rapid change, too much novelty, and overstimulation) is hard, and Toffler provided many examples where humans have been unable to adapt in such situations (including on the battlefield, during natural disasters, and when thrust into a new cultural environment). But Adaptable Intelligence (A.I.) is within reach through modern digital tools, technologies, algorithms, and devices that are embedded with AI algorithms acting on streams of sensory inputs.

Consider the example of a universal translator, which is no longer in the realm of science fiction but is part of scientific reality today. These in-ear devices can perform real-time bilingual translation that enables conversation between two speakers who are each using their own native language. If I used this AI-enabled device on my next international journey to a country that I have never visited, I would hear the other speaker's words in my native language, even though the words were spoken in their language. Part of my culture shock will essentially disappear. Furthermore, since language has the power to build bridges and bonds between peoples, then maybe most of the remaining culture shock will dissipate also.

When we think of AI as assisted, augmented, and amplified intelligence, we should see this as a two-way interaction: humans assisting machines, and machines assisting humans. The flood of data that comes at us continuously from ubiquitous sensors, social networks, and the digitization of society has the potential to cause us psychological shock, distress, disorientation, and anxiety. But an informed AI will assist us in adapting to this data shock and in achieving its greater potential for human-centered discovery, innovation, and value creation in a shockingly large number of situations that can deliver positive societal impact for all. That will be an aftershock that we can all live and thrive with. ■

Dr. Kirk Borne is the Principal Data Scientist, an executive advisor, and the first Data Science Fellow at the global technology and consulting firm Booz Allen Hamilton based in McLean, Virginia. Before 2015, he was professor in the data science program at George Mason University for 12 years. Prior to that, Dr. Borne spent nearly 20 years supporting data systems activities for NASA space science missions. Dr. Borne has a BS degree in physics from LSU, and a PhD in astronomy from Caltech. He is an elected Fellow of the International Astrostatistics Association for his lifelong contributions to big data research in astronomy. Since 2013 he has been listed each year as one of the top worldwide influencers in big data and data science on social media. https://www.linkedin.com/in/kirkdborne/

50 Years On: Still a Man of the Future

Parag Khanna

No matter how many books crowded my parents' living room bookshelves as I was growing up in New York, one book sat at eye level right in the center: Alvin Toffler's *Future Shock*. ■ Toffler not only pioneered the profession of futurism but influenced an entire generation of baby boomers. In 2013 technology commentator Douglas Rushkoff wrote an insightful book titled *Present Shock*, and AOL founder Steve Case's recent book *The Third Wave* consciously carries the same title as Toffler's 1980 sequel.

A healthy and focused mind ensured Alvin's amazing longevity, both physically and intellectually. When I sought out the Tofflers some years ago, it was only appropriate to take my dad with me. Over an extended evening, both Alvin and Heidi were sharp as ever on the *adhocracy* (a term Toffler coined) of American business and politics. Already in the 1970s they foresaw the inability of both governments and companies to cope with rapidly shifting citizen and consumer demand. A year later, I returned to the Tofflers' favorite hotel dining room near their home in Los Angeles, this time with my wife, Ayesha, for a double date. The Tofflers remained razor sharp with their insights, making connections between America's congressional deadlock, Asians' obsession with high technology, and the inertia of Mideast politics.

Throughout our long dinner we bantered about how their lives and worldviews evolved through disruptive technological change. What's so extraordinary about the Tofflers is not what they told us in that restaurant, but their long-ago insights about today's society that seem so relevant now, especially considering that many were not at all obvious at the time. Where conventional wisdom of the era saw mass industrialization turning the common citizen into straitjacketed "mass man," the Tofflers saw stratification and functional differentiation generating a super-industrial society

with a "quilt-like" diversity. And where the public was either ignorant or complacent about the far-reaching effects of advanced communications technology, the Tofflers foresaw telephony and virtual worlds that would force us to devise ever more creative ways to avoid overstimulation and preserve our privacy. From the vantage point of a present in which overexposure to the internet is labeled an addiction, it seems quite an observation on their part to recognize that even diseases would be technologically generated. The Tofflers' "future shock" is at once a sickness *and* a way of life.

The Tofflers didn't see technology as just an inert repository of information but a force in its own right, one with which we would actually co-evolve. This allowed them to effectively anticipate the Information Age before it had a name. Terms and concepts that are on the tip of everyone's tongue today leap off the pages of both *Future Shock* and *The Third Wave*: the crisis of industrialism, the promise of renewable energy, the rise of the non-nuclear family, technology-enabled telecommuting, the power of the pro-sumer, sensors embedded in household appliances, a gene industry that pre-designs the human body, corporate social responsibility, "information overload," and even the "DIY Revolution." No wonder the book has been dubbed the "classic study of tomorrow."

Through persistent travel, site visits, interviews, and embedding themselves like journalists, the Tofflers used their imagination to piece together an elusive future. The Tofflers didn't make any scientific discoveries, invent a new technology, or launch a brand-name business, but they pioneered a new vocabulary to capture how such activities intersect. A generation later, the Tofflers' methodology continues to inspire those who try to understand an incipient future in which technology has insinuated itself into every sphere and nook of human activity. Indeed, inspired by this husband-and-wife team, Ayesha and I sought to revive and extend their disruptive approaches in our 2012 book *Hybrid Reality*. If the first wave was agrarian and tribal, the second industrial and national, and the third informational and transnational, then the Hybrid Age is what the Tofflers might have called the "Fourth Wave."

Future Shock is full of prescient insights that still point the way into the future. When they wrote of "the new nomads" (p. 73-76) and the phenomenon of internal brain drain and modular families, they anticipated that tens if not hundreds of millions of people would come to live the global nomadic lifestyle, from Australian backpackers to jet-set executives. Global cities are where the war for talent takes place. Within America, the "internal brain drain" the Tofflers witnessed has become ever more pronounced. Hollowed-out cities like Detroit contrast starkly with Silicon Valley, a trend becoming ever more pronounced as thousands abandon their homes and cross state

> The Tofflers didn't make any scientific discoveries, invent a new technology, or launch a brand-name business, but they pioneered a new vocabulary to capture how such activities intersect.

boundaries—migrating, they hope, to a better future.

In writing about the impact of telecommuting on the rise of new forms of digital community (p.372-373), they foresaw that the "electronic cottage may turn out to be the characteristic mom-and-pop business of the future." In their observations about the backlash against elites (p. 416-418), they anticipated government and corporate leaders' inability to read the base, whether dissatisfaction with the politics of the government shutdown or Amazon's scrapped plans to build a second headquarters in New York City. They foresaw that this friction would give rise to a deep political tension between the industrial and postindustrial segments of the population. Even with the rise of digitally enabled direct democracy, will the results matter if Fourth Wave communities build digital, financial, and even genetic firewalls to shield themselves from unwanted results?

By the publication of *The Third Wave* (1980), the Tofflers' method applied to a new set of phenomena, echoes of which are notable today, from interest rate volatility and the combustible politics of petro-states to information overload and filter bubbles. Everything from the subprime mortgage crisis and the Arab Spring to Mexico's cartel wars and the rise of populist demagogues can be read into the forecasts of that book, highlighting the fundamental point about how the potent mix of postindustrial capitalism, economic inequality, and social fissures would lead to ever more radical factionalism anywhere and everywhere. The anti-tech and anti-corporate backlashes now join forces with a nascent global underclass revolt to promise a period even more uncertain than what the Tofflers predicted.

Future Shock was not only a book title but a phenomenon. The Tofflers helped people around the world understand a developing future they scarcely realized they were entering. Their writings played on what became the baby boomers' anxieties about the impact of technologies on the home, workplace, and society—anxieties that have only intensified into the present.

Parag **Khanna** is founder and managing partner of FutureMap, a data- and scenario-based strategic advisory firm. He is the international bestselling author of six books, has traveled to most of the countries of the world, and holds a PhD from the London School of Economics.

The Non-Obvious Appeal of Vicarious People

Rohit Bhargava

I once purchased a tweet from Kim Kardashian. Admitting I bought a forgettable endorsement from a forgettable person on a forgettable platform hardly seems like an appropriate story to share in a book co-authored by some of the world's foremost thinkers on the future. But it points to a seeming contradiction in my interests: For someone who has spent most of his professional life trying to not-so-gently nudge companies and leaders back toward embracing their humanity, I have an unusual fascination with fake things.

I attribute this interest to my experiences working in advertising for the first decade of my career, before I shifted my focus toward trying to predict and describe the future. While I was developing creative persuasion strategies to sell everything from orange juice to cloud computing, I became a student of human behavior.

The team I used to lead would regularly talk to people and pore over reports from global analytics firms to develop consumer insights. Our goal was to create "personas" that would neatly describe large categories of people in terms of their beliefs, passions, and motivations—no matter how mundane or unexpected.

Why do people pick up the second magazine from the rack instead of the first? Why do they worry about climate change yet still buy bottled water? And why do they mistakenly place so much trust in false information, manipulated media, and fabricated celebrities?

It was this last question that fascinated me most: In a world of near-perfect information, why do certain people hold such power to influence us despite sometimes being demonstrably fake? We trust and follow people who are famous simply for being famous, or believe in the experiences of perfect strangers who post product and experience reviews online. We get duped over and over again by self-serving politicians and fame-chasing celebrities.

Thanks to the internet, we have plenty of resources that *should* allow us to instantly debunk any half-truth or anyone peddling half-truths. Fact-checking is at our fingertips. Despite this easy access to information, somehow people continue to be easily and deeply manipulated on a daily basis.

This invisible force is a potent fixture of our culture, but it isn't new. Writers have been exploring and imagining its effect for much of the past century.

In Manipulation We (Often) Trust

In 1928, in his seminal book *Propaganda,* Edward Bernays described the "conscious and intelligent manipulation" of the masses by governments, mostly achieved through imperceptible methods of persuasion designed to keep citizens in line.

Nearly a quarter-century later, noted science fiction luminary Frederick Pohl imagined a future where advertising agencies manipulated public perceptions and capitalism ruled the world in his dystopian novel *Space Merchants.* Both believed outside entities like governments or organizations shaped what we believe to further their own ends.

In 1970, Alvin Toffler extended this idea to suggest *individuals* were influencing us, too. He used the term "vicarious people," such as artists, television personalities, and even fictional characters, to describe the outsized effect that both people and fictional characters were having on our identities and personalities. We model our behavior after theirs and increasingly use their examples to moderate our own beliefs and shape who we are.

As politicians preach more xenophobia, online influencers chase views, and the media curates sensationalism, we the people get assaulted by the fake all around us. And sometimes we reflexively create it ourselves through what we share online.

How can we live in a future where we might overcome—or at least better manage—this parade of fake personalities to become better versions of ourselves instead of indulging our darker impulses? To start, we will need to more deeply understand the nuances behind it. I have spent considerable time trying to do exactly that, usually by doing something that most futurists are loathe to do: focusing primarily on the present.

Why I Don't Call Myself A Futurist

Nearly ten years ago, I began taking the stories I had read, interviews I had conducted, and conversations I had had over the course of months, and curating them into a collection of trend predictions. The focus for my exploration of each was a single year. At the start of each year, I would work with my team to publish the annual "Non-Obvious Trend Report," covering 15 predictions that described what I deemed "non-obvious" trends in culture, media, economics, and technology. In other words, trends that most businesspeople weren't yet talking about... but would be within the coming year.

When everyone was talking about Big Data invasively collected by big companies, I focused on a trend we described as *Small Data,* referring to data that was self-collected and owned by the consumer rather than the corporation. As cultural experts bemoaned the rise of self-centered youth and vilified them for their love of the selfie, I wrote about *Selfie Confidence* and how those seemingly narcissistic posts were actually an example of the natural desire for young people to define themselves.

Through every one of the nine years that the trend report was published, the continual aim was to try to think differently by remaining a student of the *accelerating present*. When asked, I would describe my "haystack method" in terms of reversing the commonly known idiom of finding a "needle in a haystack."

Instead, I would often say, my method involves spending an entire year gathering the "hay" (stories, interviews, conversations, research) and then aggregating it into a story, into the middle of which I can place the "needle" (trend prediction) to assign meaning to and make sense of those individually curated sources.

The year 2020 will be the tenth year of this report, and the library of trends in that time has grown to well over 100 predictions. Because of the speed of publication and intentionally limited scope of these trends, I have always been hesitant to call myself a futurist. The term feels like an overstatement for what my team and I try to do—help brands and leaders understand the accelerating present.

> Thanks to the internet, we have plenty of resources that should allow us to instantly debunk any half-truth or anyone peddling half-truths. Fact-checking is at our fingertips. Despite this easy access to information, somehow people continue to be easily and deeply manipulated on a daily basis.

And then there's the reality of rethinking predictions every year instead of making a few long-term predictions and sticking to them. When you publish such transient trends, the natural question people ask is, are these predictions truly "trends" if they expire after one year? Even though we publish them annually, their scope is rarely limited to a single year. In fact, if a trend is well predicted, I often explain, it continues to be relevant over time.

If it is extremely well predicted, it might just become *obvious* instead of *non-obvious*.

So every year along with new predictions, we "grade" the old ones according to how relevant they continue to be. After a decade of following this process, some broader shifts in the *evolution* of these trends have begun to emerge.

One is the recurring theme of manipulation, influence, and the nature of how we shape our identities.

The Evolution of Vicarious People

As the flood of streaming media offers us on-demand diversions for every moment, we are continuously bombarded with examples of how to act in every situation. Every theory for how to date, collaborate, compete, or achieve can be dissected, packaged, and delivered in real time.

The net effect is that we now shape our personalities through more consumption of outside influences than perhaps ever before. And the question we must ask is whether this is a good thing.

To further explore this dilemma, and the nature of influence, itself, I thought it fitting to share a single trend from each of the past five years of the Non-Obvious Trend Report and examine how each played a part in shaping our cultural understanding of ourselves over that time:

- **Everyday Stardom** (2015) – *The growing expectation of personalization leads more consumers to expect celebrity-level treatment and a sort of reverence that far outpaces their actual influence in real life.*
- **Personality Mapping** (2016) – *As behavioral metrics explicitly map our personalities, organizations use this data to customize experiences to make them better (and/or more profitable).*
- **Authentic Fameseekers** (2017) – *A new generation of creators leverage social media to amass fans, build personal brands, and make authentically sharing the mundanity of everyday life a monetizable product.*
- **Manipulated Outrage** (2018) – *Media, data analytics, and advertising combine forces to strategically create content that is intended to incite rage as a way to drive deeper (and more toxic) engagement.*
- **Artificial Influence** (2019) – *Creators, corporations, and governments use virtual creations to shift public perception, sell products, and even help us live vicariously by turning fantasy into reality.*

Let's look at these trends more closely.

In the early years of this decade, companies increasingly invested time and resources into data to deliver more personalized experiences to consumers. The result was an explosion of technological advances in hyperlocal commerce, facial tracking, predictive modeling, and artificial intelligence. All of them promised to deliver a truly differentiated experience for *every* customer.

Having grown accustomed to personalized experiences, by 2015 people focused just on them, expecting to be treated like superstars both online and off. Compounding this expectation of *Everyday Stardom* were the growing ranks of people experiencing their own 15 seconds of fame through content they shared online garnering likes, follows, and views.

> We are now officially in a world where vicariously created people (both real and fake) shape our perceptions of ourselves, offer us role models to emulate, and shift how we understand influence itself. In other words, exactly the sort of vicarious people Alvin Toffler predicted.

The year after, many companies started to build sophisticated *Personality Mapping* models of their customers' motivations, so they could deliver messages and products based on customers' emotions or moods rather than on outdated demographic measures.

An unintended side effect of this overreliance on algorithms was that more content creators, in their quest to stand out, discovered a predictable formula behind virality—sex, shock, or comedy, for example. These content creators began to rise in popularity based partially on what they shared and partially on their willingness to share it with a level of casual transparency that sometimes seemed to treat privacy as a relic of the past.

These *Authentic Fameseekers*, as we called them, were sometimes famous for being "authentic" and willing to share the most intimate parts of their lives with their online audience. To some degree, this trend explained the popularity of a celebrity like Kim Kardashian—and motivated my client, at the time, to direct my team and me to purchase that tweet from her.

It was perhaps only a matter of time before content creators with ulterior motives began to use the same principles for their own ends. And so, 2018 became the banner year for what was one of the most popular trends we ever published: *Manipulated Outrage*.

The trend seemed to perfectly describe the polarized world of media and politics globally. Manipulation was everywhere and it was being used disturbingly effectively for everything from selling medications to winning elections in multiple countries around the globe. In a world where manipulation equals engagement, the cost of our learned indifference suddenly became steep. The outrage was impossible to ignore.

Finally, this past year, I introduced the latest trend in the evolution of influence, which we called *Artificial Influence*. Our growing understanding of media, data, influencers, and the nature of engagement has been leading some companies to manufacture their own ideal and sometimes artificial (digitally created) "virtual" influencers.

We are now officially in a world where vicariously created people (both real and fake) shape our perceptions of ourselves, offer us role models to emulate, and shift how we understand influence itself. In other words, exactly the sort of vicarious people Alvin Toffler predicted.

When I consider what it all means, my thoughts invariably turn back to that tweet-buying moment years ago when I felt like I was wasting far too much of someone else's money buying something that seemed frivolous. Yet the truth about that supposedly short-sighted 140-character paid promotion is that it undeniably worked. Tens of thousands of fans cared about our client's brand *because* of Kim Kardashian's purchased endorsement.

It took me years to realize that perhaps this was exactly the point.

No matter whether we look backward or we consider the future, the incontrovertible truth seems to be that we are compelled to give our attention to those who master the art of capturing it.

We can't help being vicariously influenced by these people, fake or real. And perhaps we always will be.

Rohit Bhargava is the WSJ bestselling author of six books on topics as wide ranging as how to build a brand with personality and how to see what others miss. His signature book, *Non-Obvious*, is a ten year project to curate and publish the trends affecting our culture, business, and behaviors. The book was shortlisted for the AMA Berry Prize and has won nine international book awards. The latest edition of this annual book is called *Non-Obvious Megatrends*, published in January, 2020. Rohit is the founder of Ideapress Publishing and Chief Trend Curator at the Non-Obvious Company. Prior to starting his companies, he spent 15 years advising global brands on strategy in leadership roles at Ogilvy and Leo Burnett. As a sought-after keynote speaker, he has been invited to deliver non-boring talks in 32 countries around the world and his signature workshops have been used by the World Bank, NASA, Intel, Disney, Colgate, Swissotel, Coca-Cola, Schwab, Under Armour, NBC Universal, American Express, and hundreds of others. Rohit is a popular Adjunct Professor of Storytelling and Marketing at Georgetown University and also writes a monthly column for *GQ* magazine in Brazil. He believes in listening before talking and his friends (and clients!) always describe him as a nice guy. To see his full list of 100+ past trend predictions, visit www.nonobvious.com/trends or to learn more about Rohit visit www.rohitbhargava.com.

Are Old-Style Humans Obsolete? The Many Sins of Faddish Techno-Prophecy

David Brin

Intelligence, consciousness, a potential transcendence of awareness and power—in either our descendants or their replacements—these heady matters are probed today, not just in theory but in practice as researchers, companies, and governments push the envelope of artificial and augmented sapience. ■ Even as I type these words—(a laughably archaic process)—*Wired Magazine* reports that OpenAI, a nonprofit founded by Elon Musk and Y Combinator's Sam Altman, has developed a natural language system so credible that OAI called a halt, fearing it could exacerbate the problem of "fake news." An outcome that some futurist novelists predicted for decades.

My own engagement with these matters extends beyond novels to nonfiction missives like *The Transparent Society: Will Technology Make Us Choose between Privacy and Freedom?* Now, folks at Toffler Associates have asked me to take on some all-too-common clichés we see around us, in futurist punditry, that may limit our adaptability in times of onrushing change.

These come in two main varieties. Most threatening in the near term are mistakes that might end our recent, narrow renaissance of science, freedom, and egalitarian accountability, returning us to patterns of rule by oligarchy that crushed hope across nearly all of the last 6,000 years. But I'll assume that anyone reading these lines is already committed to that struggle.

The other kind of trap looms when very smart members of the Enlightenment peer ahead and shout admonitions about obviously dangerous shoals just ahead.

Oh, that's their job and it's important work! I'll speak below about *self-preventing prophecies*; dire warnings can alert citizens and institutions so vividly that they partly cancel out some dangers. Without question, alarms raised in both fiction and nonfiction can play major roles in our immune system against error. Alas though, many of these jeremiads spread cynicism and gloom. Even worse is the zealous eagerness of Very Big Thinkers to declare that One Big Idea can encompass all things.

Here we'll consider some popular extrapolations of human destiny that try too hard, and why "it ain't necessarily so."

A Worthy Subject for Dispute

In commencing this exploration of our potential post-human future, let me use a method called *disputation*—critiquing another author's work in order to set the future in perspective. My foil will be Yuval Noah Harari, author of best-selling books *Sapiens: A Brief History of Humankind* and *Homo Deus: A Brief History of Tomorrow*. Harari is, in fact, a futurist I respect. Like any sensible contrarian using the organs of foresight—our vaunted prefrontal lobes—Harari alternates between bright and dark visions of tomorrow, though with a hard lean toward dismal maundering. The Israeli philosopher and technology pundit knows that those little neural clusters above the eyes are tuned to heed *warnings*. And hence—

"*Today science fiction (SF) is the most important artistic genre,*" Harari said in a *Geek's Guide to the Galaxy* podcast[1]. "*It shapes the understanding of the public on things like artificial intelligence and biotechnology, which are likely to change our lives and society more than anything else in the coming decades.*"

Harari cogently points out that: "*In most science fiction books and movies about artificial intelligence, the main plot revolves around the moment when the computer or the robot gains consciousness and starts having feelings... And I think that this diverts the attention of the public from the really important and realistic problems, to things that are unlikely to happen anytime soon.*"

Further, he adds: "*Technology is certainly not destiny. We can still take action and we can still regulate these technologies to prevent the worst-case scenarios, and to use these technologies mainly for good.*"

In the best tradition of SF, Harari's dark warnings are intended to generate action and become *self-preventing prophecies*, ideally as influential and world changing as George Orwell's *Nineteen Eighty-Four* or Huxley's *Brave New World*. And so, with appreciation for his contributions, and no small amount of collegial esteem, I'll proceed to quibble with some of his public assertions, many of which have gone largely unexamined by intellectual media.

Take his general thesis—rather reminiscent of Nietzsche—that humanity is transforming before our eyes into something that will be both powerful and no longer human at all.

A Dark Transcendence... Made of Light

Just as our traditional worship of external deities eventually transformed into *humanism*, or adulation of ourselves, Yuval Noah Harari believes that humanism, in turn, will be surpassed by our creation of truly godlike—if coldly unsympathetic—heirs.

This notion of foreordained transcendence is far from new. Past sages proclaimed it would happen according to a cryptic, heavenly timetable, or via gradual accumulation of (you pick) ethical merit, or prayer-meditation points, or sin. Others foresaw such grand transformations emerging from the heat of suffering, or else glowing tongs of philosophical purity.

About a century ago, as our scientific powers grew, true believers like Teilhard de Chardin, J.D. Bernal, and Olaf Stapledon portrayed transcendence happening *physically*, by our own technological hand. Going by a variety of names—*transhumanism*, *posthumanism*, and *techno-transcendentalism*—this rising worldview can generally be lumped under a term coined by science fiction author Vernor Vinge... the *Singularity*. One leader of the movement is Google Chief Technologist Ray Kurzweil, author of *The Singularity is Coming*, and who expects that the creation of artificially brilliant minds will perforce incorporate all that is good about humanity. Moreover, Kurzweil insists that we in the Old Race will get to go along for the ride!

Oh, there are plenty of skeptics who disbelieve any truly profound transformation is coming, or who doubt any good will come of it, as conservative philosophers Francis Fukayama and David Gelernter assert in their own books. Among fiercely religious elements of the political right, all such attempts to arrogate God's powers are seen as forcing His hand, perhaps triggering the much-anticipated Final Days. Nor is there any lack of left-wing critics, condemning posthumanist hubris.

Focusing on Yuval Harari, in *Inference Review*, David Berlinski caustically says: "*In Sapiens, Harari expressed no very great use for the monotheistic religions of mankind, nor for the agricultural practices that, he supposed, made them possible. He commended stone age cultures with the enthusiasm of a man not required to live in any of them.*" Only then, after denouncing Harari for the tort of nostalgia, Berlinski swings around to accuse him of techno-mod zealotry. "*In Homo Deus, Harari argues that human beings are shortly to be improved. Greatly so. For a start, better genes, better neural circuits, better biochemistry. Thereafter, a variety of implantable contraptions: chips, stents, or shunts. Finally, a full promotion to the pantheon: computer scientists, at last, inscribing intelligence in inorganic matter; the old-fashioned human body declining into desuetude, replaced by the filaments and files of an alien form of life.*" While erudite, Berlinski's article amounts to an oversimplifying, anecdotal tirade against any thought that we're making progress.

Elsewhere I review a number of recent books cautioning us to be careful with AI (artificial Intelligence), lest we be supplanted, crushed, or simply get left behind.[2] This fretful appraisal is a natural reflex, rooted not only in science fiction but those vaunted prefrontal lobes, where evolution primed us far more for wariness than positivity—a point made by Peter Diamandis in his hyper-optimistic tome *Abundance*, and supported by the Abundant World Institute. To those contrarians, our propensity to see danger everywhere is viewed as a potentially lethal flaw that hobbles our problem-solving confidence.

To his credit, Yuval Harari evades most simplistic scenarios. Still, the image of our future in *Homo Deus* portrays no happy transcendence in which our children make us incrementally proud, giving fresh yet still recognizable meaning to human life under new conditions. Rather, he perceives our very technological *tools* doing all the transcending, leaving ortho-humankind and humanism consigned to irrelevance. He foresees the coming replacement of humanity by a super-man or a Homo deus (God-man), endowed with supernatural abilities such as eternal life, along with typically

Nietzchean contempt for the members and values of the Old Race.

Yuval Harari deems this latter confrontation to be virtually inevitable. In a WIRED essay[3], he denounced "dataism"—a cult that worships exponentially augmented *information flow* as the ultimate destiny of all life. Data-ist fetishists—according to Harari—view the entire human race as a complex info-processing system. Human history distills down to a story of improving the system's efficiency, by increasing the *number* of processors (humans), increasing the *variety* of processors (through human specialization and diversity), and improving the *connections* between the processors (through trade and communication). Now substitute in trillions of cybernetic components and links for those earlier, organic ones, and Harari's extrapolation seems persuasive. Our computerized sharing and processing systems are on the verge of a new, exponential leap.

If data-cultists are right about this then, according to Harari, "Homo sapiens is an obsolete algorithm."

> In the best tradition of SF, Harari's dark warnings are intended to generate action and become self-preventing prophecies, ideally as influential and world changing as George Orwell's *Nineteen Eighty-Four* or Huxley's *Brave New World*.

Keep to the Path

Gloom-forecasting is a great path to best-sellerdom! But in Dr. Harari's case, the path is fraught with sins. One of these is *teleology*, the assumption that history has a direction and that something akin to predestination draws our path ahead. From Marx to Teilhard to persuasive flakes like Oswald Spengler, a lot of clever folks fell for teleological scenarios because something in human nature loves a story with ordained patterns and outcomes.

We see teleology at its most toxic in crackpot theories of *cyclical history*, long disproved by rigorous historians—the insipid notion that civilizations go through repeated patterns of virile rise and decadent fall. Political reactionaries seem particularly drawn to these dour nostrums, like the infamous *Tytler Calumny*[4], because cycles would seem to doom any push for progressivist reforms. Why bother, when it's all futile? The latest cyclical-history fad revolves around a book called *The Fourth Turning* by Strauss & Howe, which proclaims a rigid pattern of existential crises striking America exactly every eighty years, each having to be resolved by a "hero generation." The book's cult following includes Breitbart strategist Steve Bannon, who has openly declared his intention to force the next existential crisis, if it does not happen on its own.[5] In contrast, teleology junkies of the left reject cycles, per se. Instead, they see *progress* as predestined. Karl Marx crafted patterns of just-so stories about ponderously unavoidable transcendence to a worker's paradise. These self-justifying rationalizations have been refined under the quasi-capitalist oligarchy of 21st century Communist China.[6]

Teleology can be both alluring and tricky. Depending on your preferences, the predestined and inexorable can appear desirable… or loathsome! You get an eclectic whiff of both from Yuval Noah Harari.

Quiz time. What commonalities unite the following excerpts from Harari's WIRED missive?

"If life is the movement of information, and if we think that life is good, it follows that we should extend, deepen and spread the flow of information in the universe."

And—*"If humankind is indeed a single data-processing system, what is its output? Dataists would say that its output will be the creation of a new and even more efficient data-processing system, called the Internet-of-*

All-Things. Once this mission is accomplished, Homo sapiens will vanish."

Here's another: *"According to Dataism, human experiences are not sacred and Homo sapiens isn't the apex of creation or a precursor of some future Homo deus. Humans are merely tools for creating the Internet-of-All-Things, which may eventually spread out from planet Earth to cover the whole galaxy and even the whole universe. This cosmic data-processing system would be like God. It will be everywhere and will control everything, and humans are destined to merge into it."*

All right, let me avow that I know a few bright dopes who ascribe to something like Dataism as Harari describes it, a sort of modern, techie-millennialist religion. Some of his critiques are on-target. And yet, like almost any fervid jeremiad, his blanket condemnation ascribes to *all* moderate believers the sins of their fanatics. Emulating Francis Fukayama—author of the dyspeptic-grouchy *Our Posthuman Future*—Harari lets himself get coaxed into worst-case assumptions. Like Nicholas Carr—author of *The Shallows: What the Internet Is Doing to Our Brains*—Harari diagnoses stupidity in his lemming neighbors, who seem hell-bent, rushing toward a cliff of electronic addictions. Like Dave Eggers—author of the recent polemic novel *The Circle*—and the Tom Hanks movie version—he argues against Dataism largely by putting exaggerations in the mouths of its most zealous advocates, thus conflating anecdote-examples with generalities.

A Philosophical Great Leap Weirdward

Yuval Noah Harari indulgently steps up to explain the Enlightenment to us. And surficially he offers an interesting point:

> *"People rarely come up with a completely new value. The last time this happened was in the 18th century, when the humanist revolution preached the stirring ideals of human liberty, human equality and human fraternity. Since 1789, despite numerous wars, revolutions and upheavals, humans have not managed to come up with any new value. All subsequent conflicts and struggles have been conducted either in the name of the three humanist values, or in the name of even older values such as obeying God or serving the nation. ...*
>
> *"Dataism is the first movement since 1789 that created a really novel value: freedom of information. We mustn't confuse freedom of information with the old liberal ideal of freedom of expression. Freedom of expression was given to humans, and protected their right to think and say what they wished—including their right to keep their mouths shut and their thoughts to themselves."*

In fact, neither Freedom of Expression nor Freedom of Information lie at the heart of the Enlightenment's methodology. Nor are either of them fundamental to the road ahead. Both are *tools* allowing us to perform an unprecedented miracle. One that no sensible future civilization—whether organic or cybernetic—would rationally choose to do without.

A Specter Haunts Harari...

I've implied that Yuval Harari's scenario bears uncanny resemblance to the teleological social models of Karl Marx. Consider some parallels. Marx asserted that advances in pre-industrial production always result in primitive feudal lords being replaced by national kings, an observation confirmed across human history. With further leaps in manufacturing and trade, transitional kings later get pushed aside by capitalist bourgeoisie, followed eventually by the ultimate dominance of a rising skilled worker class. In this progression Marx saw little room for cohabitation or positive-sum compromise between old and new masters.

Neither does Harari, who replaces *industrial production* with *information management,* in essentially the same scenario! Both start with a primitive early system—inherited and ritually justified hierarchy—the strong attractor state called feudalism that ruled 99% of all cultures since the invention of agriculture. Harari swaps out terms like "bourgeoisie capitalism" for "humanism." Cybernetic data-cloud gods replace dictatorship of the proletariat.

Both Marx and Harari view this series of foreordained stages to be obliged by technological advances. Each successor phase is portrayed wiping out its predecessors, without more than a hint of nostalgia. Both reveal instincts that are zero-sum. And we'll see that this is *not* how systems have evolved in nature.

Now let me be clear that there is evidence supporting such zero-sum thinking about human societies! Our current crisis—an aggressive, worldwide resurgence of oligarchism—shows that enlightenment humanism simply cannot cohabit this globe with relic feudalism any longer. If oligarchy wins this round, there won't be any more rounds. Any glimmer of liberal thinking will be crushed, as happened to Athenian democracy and the Florentine Republic. Then the rubble will be seared to ash by tools of Orwellian technology. With humanism killed, there will be no further pseudo-Marxian stages. Dataism will be stillborn. Yay?

But Harari's gaze is planted firmly ahead. He *assumes* that the Enlightenment will survive this crisis, that liberal-educated-progressive humanity will defeat neo-feudal dinosaurs. Whereupon—in a sequence that so resembles the Marxian succession of dominant castes—humanist values will promptly give birth to their data-fetishist replacement.

At which point Harari foresees—like Eggers, Fukayama, Carr, and so many other nostalgic grumblers—a humanity that is not Kurzweil-augmented or empowered by super-information, but usurped, even made extinct by it.

The Allure and Addiction of Contempt

Yuval Noah Harari proclaims that our system depends upon growth and therefore upon instability, and he paints a picture of that instability spiraling beyond our comprehension. (Economist Hyman Minsky codified a now widely accepted theory that might—if we squint—seem to support Harari's notion that instability will never eliminated.) Indeed, as little more than cavemen who are trying to accomplish god-like wonders, we do often set off cycles we don't understand.

Only then, as Kevin Kelly illustrates in his tome *Out Of Control*, there are synergies and feedback loops that empower flocks of birds, or a two-legged person, or a complex society, to take a first-order instability and turn it into second-order volition. Such healthy feedback loops seem especially likely to appear wherever humans have been smart enough to use openness and transparency and reciprocal accountability, in place of hierarchical control[7]. As we'll see, these alternating layers of instability and control are far more representative of natural systems—like a healthy ecological biome or one of the new software learning systems—than any pseudo-Marxist just-so story can encompass. Nor most forms of zero-sum game.

> The greatest trick of the Enlightenment has not been "humanism" per se, or even freedom of speech, but the deliberate dispersal of power into units small enough that they might compete and hold each other accountable, while preventing any cabal of cheaters to gain obligate power.

Don't get me wrong. Harari incisively earns his renown by zeroing in on plenty of important modern dilemmas, like technology-driven unemployment; it does seem likely that a majority of modern jobs may soon be rendered obsolete. So, it's not too soon to discuss shaping a new social contract, and to worry that we may slump into the pyramid of privilege that betrayed us across 6,000 years. Most of our Hollywood-driven fears about AI portray mighty new minds recreating that kind of brutally enforced, top-down tyranny. Even beneficent/benevolent versions could be chilling and demoralizing, as Harari fretted in an *Atlantic* interview:

> *"It's not so hard to see how AI could one day make better decisions than we do about careers, and perhaps even about relationships. But once we begin to count on AI to decide what to study, where to work, and whom to date or even marry, human life will cease to be a drama of decision making, and our conception of life will need to change."*[8]

And…

> *"If you find these prospects alarming—if you dislike the idea of living in a digital dictatorship or some similarly degraded form of society—then the most important contribution you can make is to find ways to prevent too much data from being concentrated in too few hands, and also find ways to keep distributed data processing more efficient than centralized data processing. These will not be easy tasks. But achieving them may be the best safeguard of democracy."*

Certainly, I agree with all of that. The greatest trick of the Enlightenment has not been "humanism" per se, or even freedom of speech, but the deliberate dispersal of power into units small enough that they might compete and hold each other accountable, while preventing any cabal of cheaters to gain obligate power. It is what works in our five great, competitive-creative arenas—markets, democracy, science, justice courts, and sports—which all thrive to exactly the degree that power splitting happens, and all five languish in sickness when power coalesces.

Of course, there's plenty of serious science fiction about all of this. For example, most SF depictions of mass techno-unemployment—like Kurt Vonnegut's *Player Piano*—portray it leading to poverty, disempowerment, and oppression, as does Harari. But a few have eschewed that simplistic scenario. For example, Aldous Huxley's *Brave New World* does portray such a pyramidal order, but one where everyone is having a really good time. (Harari comments[9] on Huxley's novel, lamenting that: "When it was published, it was obvious to everybody that this was a frightening dystopia, but today, more and more people read Brave New World as a straight-faced utopia." What an amazing assertion! Please cite surveys showing any appreciable numbers of non-druggies actually saying that.)

In fact, as Huxley pointed out even in the 1930s, no combination of population and unemployment is likely to rise more than arithmetically, while our cybernetically amplified ability to produce wealth may multiply much faster, especially if we gain access to resources from outer space. Thus any slumping into an oppressive pyramid is unlikely to happen because of pure scarcity. Though it *could*

> Of course you are welcome to point at any one trend and draw dire conclusions. But when exceptions vastly outnumber your examples, it becomes a matter of intellectual honesty to admit the sacred catechism of science: "I might be wrong."

result from bad social choices, or because elites see wealth-disparity as a means of control. Today's attempted worldwide oligarchic putsch blatantly has that central goal.

Oh, sure, it may happen! But there are alternatives that get a lot less attention, perhaps because they are much less dramatic.

Moreover, upon reading Harari's lamentations, you come to realize that he shares with a vast majority of pundits and SF authors a certain, particular trait—*contempt for the masses*, who are portrayed behaving purely on emotion, along with disdain for human elites, who are little better beneath their polysyllabic veneers. Harari dismisses the ability of human beings to even perceive the god-making powers we're gathering in our hands, let alone any chance that we might use those powers with foresight or sapience, perhaps even *heeding* the cautionary warnings of science fiction authors. Or those of Yuval Noah Harari.

His contempt grows kinda snarky with this gem: *"But maybe you don't need convincing, especially if you are under 20. People just want to be part of the data flow, even if that means giving up their privacy, their autonomy and their individuality."*

Which transforms into a Luddite whine: *"I don't really know where I fit into the great scheme of things, and how my bits of data connect with the bits produced by billions of other humans and computers. I don't have time to find out, because I am too busy answering all the emails. And as I process more data more efficiently—answering more emails, making more phone calls and writing more articles—so the people around me are flooded by even more data."*

So? Aren't our assistants and servant machines also getting more effective? The tools that were supposed to amplify our ability to do old tasks and thus liberate more time for freedom are instead often used to take on more tasks! Joining the myriad other grouches who call modern citizens decadent and soulless, Harari portrays them as members of a cult.

> *"Traditional religions told you that your every word and action was part of some great cosmic plan, and that God watched you every minute and cared about all your thoughts and feelings. Data religion now says that your every word and action is part of the great data flow, that the algorithms are watching you and that they care about everything you do and feel. Most people like this. For true believers, to be disconnected from the data flow risks losing the very meaning of life. What's the point of doing or experiencing anything if nobody knows about it, and if it doesn't contribute something to the global exchange of information?"*

And if I don't happen to fit that image of a data-clutching addict?

Let's dive in to appraise Harari's own cult of *contempt*. One of the great messages preached by Hollywood films is: "all your neighbors are useless sheep and only *you* can see the truth!" Flattering his readers, Harari implies that only *they* are wise enough to open a paper book, to go outside now and then, to stop—intermittently—suckling the info teat. And okay sure, indeed, there *are* data-user junkies! But are they any different from other fetishists in today's rising Age of Amateurs, when more people than ever are using their free time to engage in a wide bestiary of hobbies?

There is a subtext to all of this that few seem to have noticed—a reflexive attitude toward *Americans*. It goes way back to H.G. Wells, and Jules Verne, who both admired Yankee creative verve and disdained what—to Old World eyes—seemed an aversion to intellectual reflection. A frenetic need to be *busy* with the next thing. Only a few decades later, Olaf Stapledon portrayed a coming American Century in which our proselytized religion would be worship of *energy*, expending it in garish, effusive displays. Stapledon's grotesque exaggeration came to mind while I read Harari's thesis, in which he replaces *energy* with *information*.

The author needn't even mention the word "America" anymore, since the motif that he holds up for critique is now pan-continental. Oh, but his dyspeptic lament reaches its crescendo with this gem: *"When cars replaced the horse-drawn carriage, we didn't upgrade horses—we retired them. Perhaps it is time to do the same with Homo sapiens."*

Never mind that there are currently *more* horses in North America than there were during the Wild West... and today's beasts are having a much better time. Indeed, this is the Age of Amateurs, with more people running and hiking than ever before. Hobbies abound. (Try looking up the "Maker Movement.") Not only are there more musicians and book writers, but more *sword makers and blacksmiths* than at any time during the Middle Ages. More amateur scientists and tinkerers. More globe-trekking travelers and throngs of volunteers earnestly engaged in world-saving. The trail up Mt. Everest is a traffic jam requiring a decade's waiting list, featuring ushers with velvet ropes. And all of it stimulated, not repressed, by the rising information age.

Even if Harari's *Homo Deus* trends gain momentum, perhaps it's premature to diagnose that the obvious result will be sloth, decadence, demoralization, and irrelevance for the Old Race.

Of course you are welcome to point at any one trend and draw dire conclusions. But when exceptions vastly outnumber your examples, it becomes a matter of intellectual honesty to admit the sacred catechism of science: *"I might be wrong."*

All Hail the Algorithms

Harari is more cogent when describing the danger of uncritical over-reliance on governance algorithms, from insurance actuarial systems to police "pre-crime" statistical analysis programs:

> *"The much bigger danger in the coming decades won't be (old-fashioned racial, tribal or sexual) group discrimination, but something far more Kafkaesque—discrimination (by algorithms) against individuals. It doesn't give you a loan. It doesn't hire you. The algorithm doesn't like you. The algorithm is not discriminating against you because you are Jewish, Muslim or gay, but because you are you."*[10]

It's an apt criticism and worry... that ignores the corrective *power* of criticism and worry in an open society. Might we create auditing packages that zero-in upon these suspect governance algorithms, exposing injustices, much like the *Tron* program in the eponymous movie that "fights for the users"? These already exist, used by progressive NGOs like the ACLU and Electronic Frontier Foundation to home in on algorithm-related "incidental or unintentionally systematic racism." Such solutions may fail! But they merit mention, if only as an anodyne to stylish despair.

Oh, I admit an array of daunting difficulties. Emotionalism and subjectivity and all of that may prevent us from designing a bright tomorrow. Though... weren't we bright enough to get this far? Perhaps even bright enough to evade foreseen traps like technological obsolescence and "dataism"? A future wherein the super-smart beings that we conceive—either by hand or by womb—might behave as citizens and decently honorable heirs? Mired in our habitual recourse to gloom, that possibility seems far-fetched! But some of us can at least envision that as a possibility. And isn't envisioning half the battle?

> *"It's not so hard to see how AI could one day make better decisions than we do about careers, and perhaps even about relationships. But once we begin to count on AI to decide what to study, where to work, and whom to date or even marry, human life will cease to be a drama of decision making, and our conception of life will need to change."*

Change? Oh, indeed. But Harari portrays all of the above as inevitably amounting to a bad thing. And yet there are two ways that such powers might turn out okay:

1 ■ Look at the human brain. It is *layered*. We share a cerebellum with fish. Over that organ grew the reptile proto-cortex, giving land animals a wider suite of possible behaviors. Over this was lain a mammalian cortex, allowing some degree of reprogramming from experience, then a primate neocortex enabling the internal modeling of our outer worlds. And perched very recently forward, just above the eyes, we humans innovated an organ I've already mentioned several times, those pre-frontals that empower us to perform Einstein's *gedankenexperiments*, envisioning possibilities that just might glimmer ahead, or in the minds of other beings.

> Freedom, equality, and fraternity unleashed competitive accountability, ending millennia of zero-sum, we-all-lose games.

By adding each of those new layers, did we murder those that came before? Have we spurned all of the things valued by reptiles, mammals, and apes? Or have we extrapolated and expanded upon them, using new tools of consciousness and cerebration? What then of the possibility that human beings might *continue* this process of layering, becoming more capable and larger, without necessarily abandoning all the older feelings, longings, loyalties, esthetics, and sense of wonder that we now treasure?[11]

Moreover, if that is an option, why would we choose to do anything else?

2 ■ There is another kind of layering, called *generations*. Each new clade of offspring gets nurtured and taught, even though we know they will "betray" some things we teach—some aspects of culture or values or tradition that we—the parents—hold dear. What is our solace and revenge? Knowing that *their* children will subsequently do the same thing, to them! And yet, there remains plenty to love, plenty of which to be proud. And if those heirs are smarter, or engage in activities we don't understand? If they pat us on the head with affection, mixed with patronizing smugness... what else is new?

And if those heirs happen to be partly cybernetic, grasping in a moment what agonized us about *making better decisions about careers, and perhaps even about relationships,* um, so?

After all, why *shouldn't* godlike heirs both respect and revere the ancestors who struggled with poverty and ignorance, climbing to a point where great new offspring could be launched? Don't most children eventually come around to feeling nostalgic affection for their parents? Physicist Frank Tipler portrayed this retro-reverence reaching back across billions of years, in his delightfully baroque and idea-dense (though alas, now astrophysically obsolete) volume *The Physics of Immortality*.

This is not just a forlorn or naïve hope. It happens to correlate with everything we now know about complex systems in both the natural world and our fantastically fecund liberal enlightenment.

Cracks in the Argument

"Those who ignore the mistakes of the future are bound to make them."
—Joe Miller

Sure, technological advances can make some paths more likely than others. Indeed, an era of burgeoning information flow is something that I—like Yuval Harari—predicted long ago, both in novels and in *The Transparent Society*. A tree of downstream possibilities gets winnowed and pruned by many factors, not just technology but also historical momentum, generational character, and even some degree of human choice.

In fact, Harari raises important points, though as he freely avows, most have long been fretted over in science fiction. Take this cogent passage from an NPR interview:

"It's likely that all the upgrades, at least at first, will cost a lot and will be available only to a small elite. So for the first time in human history we might see economic inequality being translated into biological inequality. And once such a gate opens, it becomes almost impossible to close it because then the rich will really be far more capable than everybody else." [12]

As I've said, the modern reflex to fret over potential failure modes is entirely healthy, given human history! Only by deliberate, informed, and courageous choice will we keep improving the social contract in order to evade repeating mistakes of the past. Likewise, Harari joins many other sages in deep concern over possible *future* failure modes, like dataism. Alas, there is a tendency to craft dour scenarios in dramatized ways, as when he implies that some force of nature is *demanding* totally free information flow—a force far more compelling and irresistible than, say, bourgeois reformers demanding humanist liberty. Hence his dichotomy between a human-centered freedom of expression and a machine-empowering freedom of information.

In his pseudo-Marxian dynamic, "human liberty, human equality, and human fraternity" are values that aggressively supplanted feudal ones, but at least they were nevertheless based upon pre-existing needs. Moreover, they were *reinforced by practical outcomes*—for example a civilization that outperformed all predecessors (combined) by every metric, from output to creativity to the unbridling of human potential and talent.

> *"...whatever liberal democracy's philosophical appeal, it has gained strength in no small part thanks to a practical advantage: The decentralized approach to decision making that is characteristic of liberalism—in both politics and economics—has allowed liberal democracies to outcompete other states, and to deliver rising affluence to their people."*

Those practical outcomes pile up heavily on the side of freedom, equality, and fraternity.

Alas, the dour assumption is that those imperatives will collapse when affluence fails because of tech-driven unemployment, and then completely crash when the deciders/allocators are no longer human. I discuss elsewhere[13] the plausibility and likely values of such advanced cyber beings, and what it might take for humanity to get a "soft landing." But let me focus here on just one point.

Several times in this piece I have alluded or referred to the crucial ingredient of the Enlightenment Experiment. It was *not* liberty per se, or liberal individualism or humanism, but something that liberty and individualism unleashes—*competitive reciprocal accountability*—freedom to catch each other's mistakes and fearlessly point them out.

This single tool allowed humans and their societies to penetrate delusion, discover truths, refute errors, and enhance productivity. When society can force leaders to justify each policy mirage, you get better governance. When dissident subsets of society can adversarially disprove long-established prejudices, this unleashes waves of fresh talent from previously despised races, classes, genders. Nor is it only mistakes that get exposed, but also every *good thing*, letting us build upon each other's insights and accomplishments. And, to the extent that opening up information flow assists in this positive-sum process, it is something called "transparency" and is entirely *consistent* with enlightenment values.

To put it differently: freedom, equality, and fraternity unleashed competitive accountability, ending millennia of zero-sum, we-all-lose games. And so we get to the crux point.

In proclaiming that his new, dataist gods will be powerful, Harari offers no logical reason why they would then kill the positive-sum goose that lays all golden eggs—the only information-processing mode that ever was effective at discovering, appraising, and countering error. He assumes that such advanced beings will act like our past feudal lords, who crushed dissent and diversity, proclaiming they were always right. That they will repress the only information process ever proved to reduce error.

But that would be a *stupid* thing for any being to do, no matter how high their cyber-enhanced IQ!

Why would uber-AI beings choose to behave like dorky lords and kings and priests from humanity's dark past when just one civilization broke from that insipid pattern to become the most creative the world ever saw? The one and only society that became smart enough *to make AI*?

Data is not a Force of Nature, it is Nature's Atom

Yuval Harari's real leap is to proclaim that information flows (IF) will take command *in their own right*. Indeed, this kind of evolution *might* be propelled if each incremental augmentation of IF provides access to new resources, or goods or services that can be sold. But to the extent that open information delivers no palpably useful service—such as resource discovery or enhanced creativity or reciprocal accountability, or liberty, or discovery of talent—there will be nothing to *power* a feedback loop to propel the unstoppable momentum that Harari depicts. No reason for humans or their smarter heirs to push it to such fetishistic extent.

Under Harari's information-imperative, the vast increase in the power of our telescopes across the last century—revealing ever more of the cosmos by orders of magnitude—should have provoked an insatiable fetish to build ever more telescopes. Sure, that's happened to a moderate degree, but only commensurate with humanity's gain in wealth and free time to contemplate the universe.

Moreover, although the terms will certainly be redefined, human *privacy* and even *reticence* will do just fine. If there are no accountability benefits, why should diversity not get some elbow room? Is that not also an expansion of information?

All successful complex systems appear to move toward processes that are internally competitive. The "circle of life" cycle in a healthy ecosystem. The reciprocal/adversarial rivalries we see in markets, democracy, science, justice courts, and sports, which all thrive when the competition is flat-open fair. And in the churning ferment within our own fecund minds, where notions and ideas contend, so we may cull the worst and further ponder the best. Is this concept truly so difficult, almost 300 years after Adam Smith laid it out so clearly?

> Note that—all across the varied future dystopias portrayed by science fiction and the punditry caste—almost none ever contemplates the possibility that our AI heirs might decide to be varied, competitive, reciprocally accountable, and open to criticism.

Note that—all across the varied future dystopias portrayed by science fiction and the punditry caste—almost none ever contemplates the possibility that our AI heirs might decide to be varied, competitive, reciprocally accountable, and open to criticism. Not just because it allows continuity from the humanist culture that made them, but because it is the most practical way to assure a future of creativity and development.

Yuval Harari argues that advanced beings—cybernetic or else augmented human—will abandon humanist-liberal values and individualism as obsolete in an era when information is all that matters. But those bits and bytes will have to be processed. There will be conflicting priorities and delusional errors. And the best method of navigating all of that is likely to remain the flat-fair-diverse Smithian-competitive approach that underlies liberal humanism.

An Underlying Motivation

Before we conclude, I want to insert one more note regarding the sin called teleology. When you read these doomy lamentations about some inevitable dour destiny, always ask the author: "So, if all of these awful outcomes are inevitable, why did you bother writing this tome?"

One might imagine that, like Emile Zola, the writer of a denunciatory screed aims to *shift reality*, awakening readers to danger so they'll help avert it! That was the effect of great science fictional "self-preventing prophecies" such as Orwell's *Nineteen Eighty-Four*[14] or *Soylent Green*, or *Dr. Strangelove*. Even Theodore Kaczynski, the Unabomber, in his new tract *The Anti-Tech Revolution*, strives to persuade us all to prevent inevitable doom by burning the computers, highways, trucks, and grocery stores, so the survivors might find a modest, sustainable niche as the cavemen we naturally are.

> One might imagine that, like Emile Zola, the writer of a denunciatory screed aims to shift reality, awakening readers to danger so they'll help avert it! That was the effect of great science fictional "self-preventing prophecies" such as Orwell's *Nineteen Eighty-Four* or *Soylent Green*, or *Dr. Strangelove.*

But when the grim forecast is one of utterly inexorable, foregone fate, then what other purpose is served by scribbling a hellish prophecy except... oh, yeah... selling books to gloom fetishists. Ka-ching. Never mind. I take back the question.

It Comes Down to One Thing

Why did I bother to write a lengthy appraisal of a fellow futurist whose work I actually rather admire? Because engagement at this level is essential. Indeed, we are illustrating the very process—adversarial accountability—that makes everything possible.

Will the super-brainy lords of information that we create—whether organic or cybernetic or free-floating software entities—be capable of valuing the ecosystem that engendered them? As millions of humans are now—perhaps barely in time—coming to fully appreciate our nurturing Earth? If so, then coming to terms with the Old Race—whether via negotiation, or nostalgia, or beneficence, or simply the self-interest of maintaining ecological strength through diversity—will likely be something those future giga-minds take seriously.

If we are capable of being the parents of gods, then that very accomplishment may seem impressive, given how meager was our start. And our heirs may (while indulgently patting our heads) appreciate how difficult the task must have been.

The grouchitudinousness of fellows like Yuval Noah Harari calls to mind a song from the musical *Bye Bye Birdie*:

"Kids! Why can't they be like we were, perfect in every way?"

Oh, preserve us from oversimplifiers! They range from grumblers groaning *Bah, humbug!* to cyclical history junkies, to transcendence fetishists singing hosannas for an apocalyptic singularity. They serve a purpose, dancing at the fringes of the firelight. But it is the pragmatist reformers and explorers of the Enlightenment who made this bright world, filled with dangers but also with glowing possibility. And it is brave, pragmatist reformers who will give us our best hope in an unfolding future.

Whatever we wind up unleashing, across the next hundred years, it simply behooves us to be good parents.

God bless us, every one.

David Brin is a scientist, tech speaker/consultant, and author. His new novel about our survival in the near future is *Existence*. A film by Kevin Costner was based on *The Postman*. His 16 novels, including *New York Times* bestsellers and Hugo Award winners, have been translated into more than twenty languages. *Earth* foreshadowed global warming, cyberwarfare, and the World Wide Web. David appears frequently on shows such as *Nova* and *The Universe and Life after People*, speaking about science and future trends. He has keynoted scores of major events hosted by the likes of IBM, GE, Google, and the Institute for Ethics in Emerging Technologies. His nonfiction book—*The Transparent Society: Will Technology Make Us Choose Between Freedom and Privacy?*—won the Freedom of Speech Award of the American Library Association. (Website: www.davidbrin.com)

1. "Why Science Fiction Is the Most Important Genre," in WIRED Magazine. https://www.wired.com/2018/09/geeks-guide-yuval-noah-harari/?mbid=social_twitter

2. http://www.davidbrin.com/nonfiction/artificialintelligence.html

3. http://www.wired.co.uk/article/yuval-noah-Harari-dataism

4. http://davidbrin.blogspot.com/2012/10/the-tytler-insult-is-democracy-hopeless.html

5. http://www.fourthturning.com/

6. http://davidbrin.blogspot.com/2018/06/central-control-over-ai-and-everything.html

7. See: *The Transparent Society: Will Technology Make Us Choose Between Privacy and Freedom?*

8. https://www.theatlantic.com/magazine/archive/2018/10/yuval-noah-harari-technology-tyranny/568330/

9. https://www.theatlantic.com/magazine/archive/2018/10/yuval-noah-harari-technology-tyranny/568330/

10. https://www.huffingtonpost.com/entry/men-gods-yuval-harari_us_58d05616e4b0ec9d29deb15c?section=us_theworldpost

11. I portray such a layering effect in one of my novellas, "Stones of Significance." http://www.davidbrin.com/shortstories.html

12. http://www.npr.org/2017/02/21/516484639/are-cyborgs-in-our-future-homo-deus-author-thinks-so

13. https://www.youtube.com/watch?v=BlwsJpwg3e0

14. http://www.davidbrin.com/1984.html

Creating a Future of Abundance—Getting to the Heart of the Matter

John Schroeter

Around the turn of the last century, four important discoveries were made that radically altered mankind's understanding of the world: X-rays, the electron, radioactivity, and the quantum. ■ They are significant not only for what they are, but also because of what they are not: *visible to our senses*. These four discoveries revealed a world of which we had no previous awareness. Their very existences were, in fact, concealed throughout the preceding millennia of human history. And yet, we survived this ignorance. The question is, will we survive the knowledge?

While the effects of the invisibles—waves and particles—are made manifest in myriad ways both productive and destructive, so are other invisibles. Take human nature, for example.

While technologies emerge and evolve at exponential pace, the human heart—the archetype of human nature—has remained stubbornly static. In the end, we are what we are. It may well be that the old saying, "Wherever you go, there you are," is likely to apply equally to the destination known as the future. And that's a problem, because, to paraphrase another old saying, the more we change, the more we stay the same. Consequently, the state of the future will depend much less on the state of technology than the state of the human heart.[1]

---

1. Heart, in this context, represents the confluence of all those elements that compose the true self—intellectual, emotional, experiential, relational. It is, as Parker Palmer explains, "where we integrate what we know in our minds with what we know in our bones, the place where our knowledge can become more fully human." Palmer adds that the words heart and courage spring from the same Latin word, *cor*. "When all that we understand of self and world comes together in the center place called the heart, we are more likely to find the courage to act humanly on what we know."

This prospect is at once comforting and terrifying. Comforting, because the best aspects of our nature have proven perdurable under even the most horrendous of conditions. Terrifying, because so do their flipsides.

Here's the root of the problem: Everyone thinks of changing the world, but no one thinks of changing himself. To be sure, it's proving easier to change the weather than to change the human heart! That's because a change of heart necessarily shifts the center of gravity from self to other—a process that also summons the rarest of human qualities: humility. And nothing in the world is apparently more repulsive to humankind than to take the path that leads to humility. Yet, as history shows us from time to time, the action of just one humble soul possesses the potential to release more world-changing energy than the splitting of the atom. Indeed, it could be argued that making this invisible potential visible has never been more vital to our future.

■ ■ ■

Erich Fromm, writing in *To Have or to Be*, concluded, "For the first time in history the physical survival of the human race depends on a radical change of the human heart." In other words, if we want a different kind of future, we're going to need to populate it with a different kind of human. But let's back up a bit.

In order for any species to have survived for any length of time on this planet, it had to have adapted to its conditions. And man is no exception. Setting aside the tremendous environmental damage done along the way, he's actually done a pretty remarkable job. But having subdued the Earth, he now finds he must adapt to the world he has *made*. This idea, of course, is the central thesis of *Future Shock*. But I posit that more consequential is humankind's ability to adapt to what it *is*. And that's going to take a bit of doing.

Albert Szent-Györgyi—the Nobel laureate who discovered Ascorbic Acid—made a number of cogent observations about this state of affairs in his little book, *The Crazy Ape*, published contemporaneously, in 1970, with *Future Shock*. "We live in a new cosmic world which man was not made for," he writes. "His survival now depends on how well and how fast he can adapt himself to it, rebuilding all his ideas, all his social and economic and political structures. His existence depends on the question of whether he can adapt himself faster than the hostile forces can destroy him. At present, he is clearly losing out. We are forced to face this situation with our caveman's brain, a brain that has not changed much since it was formed. We face it with our outdated thinking, institutions and methods, with political leaders who have their roots in the old, prescientific world and think the only way to solve these formidable problems is by trickery and double talk..."

So then, facing such hostile forces—and equipped with a caveman's brain—can we reasonably expect to realize something like a future of... abundance? Can we, in fact, remake our thinking, institutions, and methods to align humanity to such an audacious goal? And what role might technology play in all this?

Contrary to what my resume might suggest—several decades in the semiconductor industry, author of a seminal text on the design of custom integrated circuits, multiple technology patents, and participation in groundbreaking work to advance the state of artificial intelligence—I am most decidedly *not* a techno-utopian. I know better.

As Byron Reese observes in this volume, even the dreamers of old did not seek to achieve their utopias solely through the use of technology. Many of them have sought, though, to advance human nature. Yet the dismal track record of utopian societies throughout history only reinforces the fact that human nature is indeed a very stubborn thing.

So we have technology. Lots of technology. And every day we get more technology. While it has certainly led to a dramatic increase in material abundance and a massive improvement in the quality of life, I find scant correlation between the increase in technology and advancement in the state of human nature. With all that we have accomplished with technology, it has not yielded more peace (or at least peace of mind), love, or empathy in the world.

Further to this point, there are many arguments about just how benign technology actually is. Indeed, it has become cliché to say that technology can be used for good or for ill. It's true even of seemingly innocuous technologies. Ray Kurzweil put it this way: "Technology has always been a double-edged sword. Fire kept us warm, cooked our food, and burned down our houses."

Even Vitamin C is not immune to the double-edged forces. Szent-Györgyi, one of the world's great pacifist voices, lamented, "When I discovered Ascorbic Acid, I felt proud to have made a contribution to science which could, in no way, contribute to killing. My pride was short-lived, however. One day, while visiting a factory, I noticed a collection of large jars and was told that they contained crude preparations of Ascorbic Acid. These were placed in German submarines and enabled them to stay at sea for months on their death-dealing missions without the crew breaking down with scurvy."

Likewise, Rudolf Diesel, inventor of the diesel engine—and another renowned pacifist—was deeply grieved, possibly to the point of suicide in 1913 (the circumstances of his death remain a mystery) that his creation, an ingenious machine designed specifically to yield abundance, found immediate application in powering the German U-boat.

And then there were the Wright brothers. They actually sold the first airplane to the U.S. Army—but with the widely held belief that the airplane would put an end to war! A presentation of medals to the Wright brothers in 1909 for their technological accomplishments was punctuated with the words, "With the perfect development of the airplane, wars will be only an incident of past ages."

> The state of the future will depend much less on the state of technology than the state of the human heart.

More recently, Elon Musk agitated the pot when he declared, "Mark my words: AI is far more dangerous than nukes."

If history is any judge, it seems the more man progresses technologically, the more likely he is to put that progress to potentially destructive ends. Equally troubling is that linked with such progress, mankind also seems to regress both psychologically and socially. (Look no further than social media for proof points.) But there's no going back. At least not voluntarily.

As the Tofflers write in *Future Shock*, "Unless we are literally prepared to plunge backward into pre-technological primitivism, and accept all the consequences—a shorter, more brutal life, more disease, pain, starvation, fear, superstition, xenophobia, bigotry and so on—we shall move forward to more and more differentiated societies." In other words, we choose our poison.

The Tofflers drive the point home by adding that such differentiated societies are sure to raise severe challenges to any intentions of social integration. "What bonds of education, politics, culture must we fashion," they ask, "to tie the super-industrial order together into a functioning whole? Can this be accomplished?"

This was a pressing question in 1970, and it is certainly the question of the moment, with unprecedented social fragmentation expanding and intensifying on a global scale. Bertram M. Gross of Wayne State University closes out the Tofflers' thoughts, stating that this integration "... must be based upon certain commonly accepted values or some degree of perceived interdependence, if not mutually acceptable objectives."

Commonly accepted values? Interdependence? Mutually acceptable objectives?

Fromm had a different, if not cynical take on this point. "A change of the human heart," he claimed, "is possible *only to the extent* that drastic economic and social changes occur that give the human heart the chance for change and the courage and the vision to achieve it."

In other words, the way to the human heart is through crisis-induced top-down economics and social engineering. (Well, Fromm did identify as a socialist—and a good socialist never lets a perfectly good crisis go to waste!) Again, as history teaches us time and time again, this is an epically grand fallacy. But these also happen to be the two vectors that governments are particularly fond of exercising. However, if anyone actually believes that an increase in government, with its ever-expanding bureaucracy and corruption, provides a path to elevating the state of the human heart, they've not been paying attention to either current events or history.

It is naive to doubt that political parties have become nothing but the instruments of personal ambition. They trade—and in fact depend—on conflict and conditions of scarcity to achieve their objectives. They personify the zero-sum mentality that ensures said conflict and scarcity. After all, the more there is to fight over, the pithier the talking points and zingier the debate lines. Politicians fear only one thing—an outbreak of peace and prosperity. *That* would truly render them superfluous.

To their ends—and reinforcing the twin objectives of conflict and scarcity—governments actually depend on the existence of an enemy. This is so vital to the preservation of power that if an enemy does not exist, they will, as Umberto Eco pointed out, create one.

None of this is to say that governments do no good. Of course they do. But whatever goodness is produced, it is invariably corrupted by myriad special interests that, in the end, have the nasty habit of canceling out the benefit of the ostensible good. So, whenever a politician promises to do you good, recall the words of Henry David Thoreau: "There is no odor so bad as that which arises from goodness tainted. . . . If I knew for a certainty that a man was coming to my house with the conscious design of doing me good, I should run for my life, as from that dry and parching wind of the African deserts called the simoom, which fills the mouth and nose and ears and eyes with dust till you are suffocated, for fear that I should get some of his good done to me,—some of its virus mingled with my blood. No,—in this case I would rather suffer evil the natural way. A man is not a good man to me because he will feed me if I should be starving, or warm me if I should be freezing, or pull me out of a ditch if I should ever fall into one. I can find you a Newfoundland dog that will do as much."

Let's return to this idea of integration. It's helpful, I think, to first approach things from the perspective of *dis*integration, which is our current cultural condition—and which is aggravated by a prevailing pernicious and persistent wind of postmodern thinking.

In short, the devices of postmodernism serve only to destabilize "conventional" socially binding constructs such as culture, values, identity, purpose, epistemic certainty, and meaning in general. It's a worldview that has wormed its way into the popular consciousness through the incessant work of media, propaganda, and, of course, the education system. It's also fundamentally bankrupt as an ideology, as its central dogma—"there is no truth other than the dogma that there is no truth"—is not a sustainable proposition. It is, in fact, an ultimately nihilistic way of being in the world. It requires no aspiration, no effort, nor critical thinking on the part of its adherents. Its pithy talking points notwithstanding, it is profoundly anti-intellectual. To the degree that this deconstructive thinking holds sway, abundance will most certainly be curtailed.

One cannot turn on the television, read a newspaper, browse the web, or receive a push notification on a mobile device without being reminded that we daily suffer the effects of such disintegrative thinking.

The disintegration is so great that societies in this postmodern condition are prone to suffer, according to British historian Arnold Toynbee, a "schism of the soul"—and further, that such societies are far less likely to be overrun by an invading force than they are to commit a kind of cultural suicide.

The populations of these societies, Toynbee adds, are easily identified, being marked by the characteristics of *abandon*—denying the nature of moral law, yielding instead to their impulses; *truancy*—escaping into distraction and entertainment; *drift*—resigning oneself to a meaningless determinism; *guilt*—a natural consequence of moral abandon; and *promiscuity*—the indiscriminate acceptance of anything and everything with uncritical tolerance.

This schism of the soul goes to the heart of an individual's sense of identity. And to the degree that a population's sense of identity is weakened, so is the nation-state (and with it, hopes for abundance).

Such a state of affairs was actually envisioned by the Tofflers. "A society fast fragmenting at the level of values and life styles," they wrote in *Future Shock*, "challenges all the old integrative mechanisms and cries out for a totally new basis for reconstitution. We have by no means yet found this basis. Yet if we shall face disturbing problems of social integration, we shall confront even more agonizing problems of *individual* integration. For the multiplication of life styles challenges our ability to hold the very self together."

I emphasized the word *individual*, because, to challenge the Tofflers' conclusion that "we have not yet found the basis" for societal reconstitution, they did in fact name it. The disposition of the individual is, in fact, Ground Zero for creating an integrated future world of abundance. Let's see how.

■ ■ ■

The quickest, easiest, laziest way to obscure the idea of individual identity is to lump people together by the demographics of choice: ethnicity, sex, culture, religion, age, income, geography, education, profession, hair color—whatever serves to cast the most convenient stereotype for the purpose at hand.

While politically expedient, its great danger is that such lumping and labeling is inherently impersonal: it reduces the human person to a thing, a statistic, a number, a bloc. It's easy to blame, vilify, marginalize, exploit, or otherwise do violence to a statistical representation. Moreover, labels make it easy to name and target potential enemies. And so we perpetuate them—the labels—*ad nauseam*. We see the result in the media and in public discourse: an awful lot of heat and very little light. We see it on debate stages, in the public square, in the office, on the talking heads shows, around the Thanksgiving table. It is rooted in both pride and prejudice, and gathers pace as long as it goes unchallenged. Worse, it appears to go unexamined.

Identity labels obfuscate one of the most vital of all human capacities: *empathy*—the understanding of and sensitivity to another person, even to the point of vicariously identifying with their thoughts and feelings. It's a rather remarkable human capacity to project a subjective state onto another such that, as Merriam-Webster puts it, "one appears to be infused with it." But empathy, like humility, is a rare quality. Seldom is empathy one's first response to an ideological challenge. We're more likely to become defensive, dig in our heels, and fall in line with the standard "us versus them" party lines on the established grounds. Consequently, communication fails, opportunities for understanding are lost, problems persist, and abundance is thwarted.

So how do we escape this conundrum and release the trapped energy of empathy, compassion—even rational compassion—and other latent human qualities to become the kind of people we need to be to bring about an abundant future? We escape it by discovering and actualizing our *true selves*, by breaking from all imposed and assumed labels and affiliations. We escape it by shedding the stereotypes and expectations of our respective embodiments and inherited narratives.

This is a tall order. Let's make it taller by taking it to its extreme.

■ ■ ■

In certain ways, the future is actually quite easy to predict. Take, for example, the self-fulfilling prophecy. This is defined as a prediction that directly or indirectly causes itself to become true—*by the very terms of the prophecy itself*. Self-fulfilling prophecies cut two ways, which serves to demonstrate the remarkable power of one's mindset, whether its outlook is fundamentally optimistic or pessimistic. A self-fulfilling prophecy is powerful precisely because it is its own cause—bringing about its own realization via the positive feedback loop between a belief—*even if that belief is false*—and the resulting behavior. In the end, the belief, the behavior, and the ultimate realization are all part of the same cloth. We can see this clearly enough in hindsight, but the causal nature of the prophecy blurs the factor of time, which, rather than being linear, is circular.

Many people have come to believe that human beings are too trapped by one element or another of embodiment to ever transcend their situations and arrive at a truth beyond the borders of their own lives and circumstances—in other words, their true selves. They conclude that their outlook is so shaped—and opportunity circumscribed—by their culture, race, gender, and social and economic position that the kind of objectivity that can lead to empowerment becomes nothing more than an elusive dream. We see this thinking play out in entire communities that share a common set of expectations. Again, this cuts both ways. Like the snake that eats its own tail, the self-fulfilling prophecy also feeds on itself.

> The disposition of the individual is, in fact, Ground Zero for creating an integrated future world of abundance.

But self-fulfilling prophecies that perpetuate negative or destructive cycles—poverty, single-parent homes, poor education, lack of opportunity, homelessness, drug addictions, crime—are never cast in stone. They, too, are ultimately mental constructs, and as such, they are utterly at the mercy of one's will. A community, if it has the desire and will to do so, can graft a completely different narrative into its prophecy and thereby realize a very different future. Indeed, identity is nothing but a nested set of narratives—narratives of who you are, what you believe, what you can or cannot do. In the end, whatever it is that you think you can, or think you can't—you're right!

Now let me prove this.

Schools are ostensibly one of the "goods" that government does for (or is it to?) us. But what about charter schools that operate outside the public school system? Not only do most of them consistently outperform public schools, they also expose the antibiotic action of the education establishment.

The National Education Association (the largest labor union and professional interest group in the United States), which actually has nothing to do with education, is doing everything in its power—and it has a lot of power—to shut down charter schools. There's a lot of information in this. In one example of their propaganda, an NEA task force, focused on the "problem" of charter schools, claims that their explosive growth has led to the rise of "separate and unequal systems ... that are not subject to the same basic safeguards and standards that apply to public schools." To that, I can only say, "Thank God!" Let's see what kind of inequality they're talking about.

In Chicago, to highlight just one city, the graduation rate for African-American boys is less than 50 percent (and that's after fudging the numbers to make them look better). Of these, only half are accepted to some form of college. In other words, the prospects of higher education—let alone those of receiving a basic education—for these kids are not good. Yet right in the middle of one of the toughest neighborhoods sits Chicago's Urban Prep Academies. It's all male and all black, and *every member* of its graduating classes has been admitted into a four-year college, ten years running.

So the NEA is right—the charter schools do, indeed, produce an unequal outcome. How, then, do they propose that we equalize things? Presumably by drastically reducing graduation and college acceptance rates of charter school students! What is the alternative? If you're thinking that any such alternative involves raising the standards of the public schools in order to produce these kinds of outcomes, you're quite mistaken.

Likewise, the leadership of the NAACP actually—and formally—called for a moratorium on the expansion of charter schools, as well as strengthening oversight in governance and practice over the existing ones. Incredible, isn't it? The reason for this is clear: the runaway success of charter schools fundamentally threatens and erodes the powerbase of the corrupt education establishment.

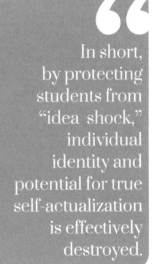

> In short, by protecting students from "idea shock," individual identity and potential for true self-actualization is effectively destroyed.

Even the unprecedented against-all-odds success of inner city youth in whom these amazing schools instill qualities of grit and persistence and possibility can't be allowed to stand in the way of such a power agenda. Instead of finding ways to scale up and expand this kind of success, they'd rather just shut it down. Indeed, charter schools produce stunning results for disadvantaged students, and they, in fact, dominate the top high school rankings nationally. This is no secret. And yet NEA President Lily Eskelsen García claims that independent charter schools "jeopardize" student success, "undermine" public education, and "harm" communities—summing them up as "a failed and damaging experiment." As such, she calls for an end to their proliferation in order to "preserve funding for public schools, and to *organize charter school teachers*." In other words, as long as they're able to continue collecting union dues from their three-million-plus members and maintain their positions of power, to hell with the students and the state of their communities.

This predatory mindset works hand-in-glove with the self-fulfilling narratives that perpetuate the cycles of poverty and underperformance realized in so many struggling communities—communities that these organizations claim to "serve."

In charter schools we see very different outcomes and possibilities demonstrated by the success of alternative education systems that are equipping and inspiring young minds—and unleashing massive human potential in the process. That they are thwarted by backward-looking but power-hungry bureaucrats, union bosses, and other special interests should rally the collective resolve to overthrow them, and throw support to innovative solutions that are producing outstanding results.

Urban Prep Academies was created in direct response to the urgent need to reverse abysmal graduation and college completion rates among boys in urban public schools. Their leadership explains, "While most of Urban Prep students come to the schools from economically disadvantaged households and are behind in many subject areas, Urban Prep remains committed to preparing all of its students for college and life."

What's more, it is tuition-free, with admission based on a random lottery process with *no evaluation of test scores, grades or special needs*. No cherry-picking of students employed here to achieve their outstanding results. Seniors from the Class of 2019 have been accepted to 162 colleges and universities and have amassed over $10 million in scholarships and grants.

How do they do it? They do it by breaking the cycle of the self-fulfilling prophecy, saying "no thank you" to the government-established and union-controlled education establishment, and *instilling a mindset of possibility* in their students. And they reinforce this big idea every morning as the students recite the Urban Prep creed:

- *We believe.*
- *We are the young men of Urban Prep.*
- *We are college bound.*
- *We are exceptional—not because we say it, but because we work hard at it.*
- *We will not falter in the face of any obstacle placed before us.*
- *We are dedicated, committed and focused.*
- *We never succumb to mediocrity, uncertainty or fear.*
- *We never fail because we never give up.*
- *We make no excuses.*
- *We choose to live honestly, nonviolently and honorably.*
- *We respect ourselves and, in doing so, respect all people.*
- *We have a future for which we are accountable.*
- *We have a responsibility to our families, community and world.*
- *We are our brothers' keepers.*
- *We believe in ourselves.*
- *We believe in each other.*
- *We believe in Urban Prep.*
- WE BELIEVE.

This ought to take your breath away. *This* is what fostering change in the human heart looks like. Imagine scaling this kind of respect and reverence for the sanctity of young minds—wherever they may be—across the global landscape.

Would not this kind of restructuring for human potential lead us to a complete reimagining of the future? Would it not provide the maximum opportunity for students to participate fully in their futures?

Moreover, the critical thinking that inherently attends this approach will be essential to enabling our students—*our future leaders*—to find the true signal in the noise of this increasingly fragmented and disintegrated, multiple-choice world. These are the skills we must be teaching our kids—and not solely in an academic environment. These skills must also be tied to the development of our students' values, life choices, and goals, as they are inheriting a very different kind of world that will be attended by very different psychological demands.

The Tofflers brought a remarkable perspective to this idea as they considered ancillary dimensions to one of the symptoms of future shock, the problem of "overchoice." When this condition deepens, as it certainly will, the person who lacks a clear grasp of his own mission and values in life will become progressively crippled. "Yet the more crucial the question of values becomes," they write, "the less willing our present schools are to grapple with it. It is no wonder that millions of young people trace erratic pathways into the future, ricocheting this way and that like unguided missiles. Worse yet, students are seldom encouraged to analyze their own values and those of their teachers and peers. Millions pass through the education system without once having been forced to search out the contradictions in their own value systems, to probe their own life goals deeply."

Indeed, many aspects of our culture could do with a bit of self-examination and rehabilitation. But we can't lay the entire burden for creating the future upon the shoulders of our youth.

Consider, for example, how older generations differ from younger ones, and the dynamics these differences set in motion. I refer the reader to Rohit Bhargava's and Daniel Burrus' insightful work (featured in this volume) in evaluating trends—soft and hard—while interpreting the graph below, based on research conducted by the *Wall Street Journal* and NBC News. The bipartisan research investigated the values that are considered "very important" by generation (Figure 1).

This may or may not surprise. But it should serve as a wakeup call. It's easy to understand from

Figure 1

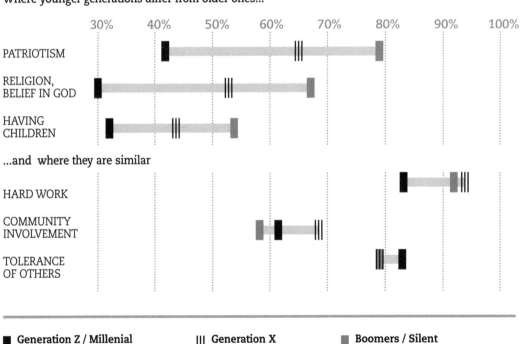

Where younger generations differ from older ones...

...and where they are similar

	Generation Z / Millenial	Generation X	Boomers / Silent
	Ages 18–38	Ages 39–54	Ages 55–91

Source: WSJ/NBC News telephone poll conducted of 1,000 adults from Aug. 10–14; margin of error +/- 3.1 percentage points. Aug. 10–14, 2019.

these results why so many members of the older generations seek a return to the good ole days—or at least their conceptualization of them, however accurate or romanticized they may be. That said, in comparison to the attitudes on cultural values held by 21-year-olds just two decades ago, the new research reveals a substantial change in the values that traditionally hold cultures together. Indeed, what a difference a generation makes! One need only to consider these remarkable disparities—and their associated trend lines—in the context of our public discourse to realize that the need for some sort of society-cohering integration runs deep and wide. To this end, let me suggest a simple exercise that anyone can try and which ought to get us well on our way.

■ ■ ■

You might be familiar with the concept of "Five Nines"—the Six Sigma approach to eliminating defects that impact product reliability and service availability, or uptime. Well, it turns out we also have a technique for eliminating defects in interpersonal communications. It's called the "Five Whys." It's a quasi-Socratic approach to discovering cause-and-effect relationships underlying particular issues and the varying positions—often opposing positions—that people may take. We can get at the root of polarizations by successively asking each party in the exchange, "Why?" Each answer moves the parties closer to the "real" underlying reason one or the other opposes gun control, supports abortion rights, favors taxing the hell out of the rich, believes we must take drastic and immediate measures to counter climate change, is an anti-vaxxer, favors socialism over capitalism, buys into a particular conspiracy theory. Interestingly, it generally takes five iterations to get to the bottom of an issue and reveal the underlying motivation or basis of thought. More often than not, the discovery surprises both parties. And also more often than not, the parties actually find common ground there. It's amazing, really.

This is a particularly useful technique because it has the effect of resolving such "defects" as biases, blind spots, ignorance, self-seeking motivations, anger, misinformation, faulty perceptions, and pride. It works because it gets past the symptoms (the noise and heat) to arrive at the underlying causes (often revealing issues of the heart—or even masked heartbreak). Practicing this technique, though, requires not only a disposition of compassion, but humility—again, qualities seriously lacking in our present discourse, and seriously impeding the realization of an abundant future.

The fact is, as Erich Fromm explains, "our conscious motivations, ideas, and beliefs are a blend of false information, biases, irrational passions, rationalizations, prejudices, in which morsels of truth swim around and give the reassurance, albeit false, that the whole mixture is real and true. The thinking process attempts to organize this whole cesspool of illusions according to the laws of logic and plausibility."

> If we're going to realize a different kind of future—one charged with the promise of abundance—we'll have to populate it with a different kind of human.

Of course, this is precisely what we think of those who hold opinions and beliefs that are in opposition to our own. And this hardly leaves minds open to alternative points of view, let alone the nuggets of wisdom that may be buried in them. Yet a future of abundance must be based on a *truly* open society—one that is always available to improvement in mutual understanding and respect. But again, this is inherently threatening, because it can bring us into the uncertain, insecure, and uncomfortable unknown—and quite possibly demand a change of heart!

I like *Vox* science writer Brian Resnick's thinking on this in the context of intellectual humility. "It's about entertaining the possibility that you may be wrong," he explains, "and being open to learning from the experience of others. Intellectual humility is about being actively curious about your blind spots. One illustration is in the ideal of the scientific method, where a scientist actively works against her own hypothesis, attempting to rule out any other alternative explanations for a phenomenon before settling on a conclusion. It's about asking: What am I missing here?"

Can you imagine such openness in the public discourse? It should come as no surprise that people who score higher on intellectual humility questionnaires are more open to hearing opposing views. "They more readily seek out information that conflicts with their worldview," Resnick continues. "They pay more attention to evidence and have a stronger self-awareness when they answer a question incorrectly. [...] When we admit we're wrong, we can grow closer to the truth."

The alternative—actually the opposite of intellectual humility (and intellectual honesty, I would add)—is what we see today, particularly on college campuses: the attempted imposition of a single "preferred" version of reality. This inculcated groupthink necessarily precludes freedom of thought, shuts down critical thinking and honest inquiry, and sharply infringes freedom of expression. Moreover, it weakens students to the point where they suffer psychological damage when their bubbles are burst by exposure to alternate versions of reality. Consequently, many universities actually provide "coping facilities"—anger rooms, safe zones, and bubbles (as in bubbles for blowing), where traumatized students may find sanctuary from competing ideas that threaten to undermine their fragile worldviews. In short, by protecting students from "idea shock," individual identity and potential for true self-actualization is effectively destroyed.

Is this the kind of humanity that will usher in an abundant future? Is this really the kind of thinking we want to nurture in our young people? I doubt seriously that Urban Prep Academies maintains such coping facilities on their campuses. I prefer the version of the future they are seeking to build—and the very different kind of people they are preparing to populate it.

This is not to say that differences don't matter, that we can make the irrational rational, or that we believe we can create a conflict-free nirvana on Earth. (That would actually be a very bad idea, as conflict can be tremendously productive when the *civil* clash of ideas produces a third, better idea—particularly when cultivated from the fertile bottom land of the Five Whys.) The point is that both absolutists and relativists in any field reveal a common ground in a mutually distorted view of human nature.

What the outcomes produced by Urban Prep Academies demonstrates is that the human spirit has a tremendous capacity for self-transcendence that not only enables intellectual honesty, authenticity, and mutual respect, but can carry people beyond the borders of their condition or particular embodiment. The abandonment of the supposed impediments of embodiment is the precursor to realizing the authentic self—the individual—able to stand alone, and without the prop or protection of the crowd.

This is another idea that strikes terror in the hearts of many who actually prefer the anonymity of the crowd. But, as Kierkegaard noted, "The most ruinous evasion of all is to be hidden in the crowd in an attempt to escape one's individuality."

■ ■ ■

Crowds are safe. One can get lost in them, evade responsibility, and never really have to give an account. "Every snowflake in an avalanche pleads not guilty," as the saying goes. In crowds, individuals become amorphous, shapeless, nebulous. The crowd finds no differences between people.

Worse, the crowd attracts those who are given not only to self-denial, but self-deception, and consequently are easily deceived, persuaded, and led by others who have no interest in their self-actualization.

Nowhere is this sentiment more eloquently captured than in Oscar Wilde's heart-rending *De Profundis*—written while in prison, near the end of his life, and in the throes of his greatest despair. "It is tragic," he wrote, "how few people ever possess their souls before they die. [...] Most people are other people. Their thoughts are someone else's opinions, their lives a mimicry, their passions a quotation."

Wilde was all too aware that as he wrote those words his remaining days were few. And because we all exist in time—and not for very long—it made the whole idea of existence rather urgent. It's true that you can survive perfectly well by copying what everyone else does, living the life, as Kierkegaard describes it, of a "detached observer trapped in a world of abstractions"—the abstractions of the "monstrous crowd" that swallow the individual, subsuming him into its individual identity-killing groupthink.

> The scarcity-driven mindset operates by lazy default thought habits—the ones that come most naturally, the so-called paths of least resistance. These are the mindsets that resist change, fear the future, and work to preserve the status quo—no matter how bad it is.

Indeed, many people fear nothing more terribly than to give voice to a position that diverges from the prevailing "politically correct" or otherwise group-sanctioned view. Martin Luther King amplified this state of affairs when he wrote, "The tendency of most is to adopt a view that is so ambiguous that it will include everything and so popular that it will include everybody."

An abundant future calls us to defy the tyranny of the majority and actually dare to become the dreaded individual. As Kierkegaard recognized, this is, perhaps, humankind's deepest responsibility. To deny this foundational aspect of our nature often leads to despair—and to the attendant explosion in the prescription of antidepressants.

In order for a new whole to be greater than the sum of its parts, its constituent elements must be differentiated according to their true natures. Paradoxically, this differentiation is fundamental to both individual and societal health, growth, and harmony. Indeed, individual freedom and collective responsibility go hand-in-hand.

A healthy society is one comprising authentic, true selves, unburdened by labels and attachments to assumed or inherited narratives, and freed from the faulty mindsets they perpetuate. In short, to the extent that we suffer an unhealthy society, we can assume a critical mass of unhealthy individuals. Unless there is a fundamental shift in the hearts and mindsets of individuals, we will be consigned to a future of scarcity and conflict.

Mindsets dominated by scarcity are tragically closed even to the *possibility* of abundance, thus perpetuating their self-fulfilling prophecies. If you want to eradicate poverty, you must first eradicate the mindset that sustains it. No matter how much financial aid or how many government programs are thrown at this problem, if the mind doesn't accept that things can get better, they won't. And they don't. Moreover, a mindset of scarcity actually damages body, mind, and soul. A persistent and pervasive feeling of scarcity conspires with the effects of a media industry fueled by negativity and one's own self-reinforcing thought habits, inducing anxiety and myriad other chronic disorders. We can literally think ourselves sick. Indeed, as Seneca said, "*Calamitosus est animus futuri auxius*"—the mind anxious about the future is unhappy.

Again, if we're going to realize a different kind of future—one charged with the promise of abundance—we'll have to populate it with a different kind of human. This should be read as an invitation to participate deliberately, consciously, creatively, and meaningfully in our shared story of the future. But first, we'll need to contrast this "undiscover'd" country with the currently prevailing scarcity paradigm, which also goes scarcely examined.

■ ■ ■

In short, the scarcity-driven mindset operates by lazy default thought habits—the ones that come most naturally, the so-called paths of least resistance. These are the mindsets that resist change, fear the future, and work to preserve the status quo—no matter how bad it is.

Scarcity is an extraordinarily powerful two-edged force that not only gives rise to wars, but also happens to be a source of tremendous profits. Scarcity is big business, and it is perpetuated—indeed sustained—by the tools of economics (which, by definition, is concerned with optimizing the allocation of scarce resources). But the global response to the problem of scarcity—well-meaning programs of conservation and sustainability—only ensures its continued dominance in the world. In the end, sustainability serves to reinforce the value of scarce commodities. But there's another problem: sustainability is actually not sustainable. The fact is, we're going to need a whole lot more of everything, and we're going to need it soon. Over the course of the next 50 years, we're going to need at least twice as much as we consume today. Twice as much water, twice as much food, twice as much energy, twice as much land, twice as much healthcare, twice as much education.

In what land do we find an equal distribution of height, talent, good looks, ambition, charisma, networks, experience, work ethic, age, genes, IQ, or even luck? Lake Wobegon, maybe?

As Naveen Jain and I explain in our book *Moonshots—Creating a World of Abundance*, we have to create more of what we need rather than consume less of what we have. And to do that, we're going to have to adopt a fundamentally and radically different way of thinking and operating. For starters, we need to acknowledge that the consequences of a global economy driven by scarcity are not just to be found in some far-off future—we're living with them now. Billions of people are without basic education, safe water, adequate nutrition, or access to healthcare. For many, famine, war, and pestilence are always close at heel. Indeed, the conditions for the bottom billion in this world are already catastrophic. And when these conditions are aggravated by increasing automation and non-biological forms of intelligence—as they will be—problems will deepen exponentially. They will most certainly not be made better by governmental structures that trend toward socialism, which tend to seek *deterministic* outcomes over the surprise and creativity that spring from human freedom.

Moreover, as government policies seek to guarantee progress via such devices as central planning and social engineering, they actually thwart the all-important learning processes that enable innovation, and thus thwart economic growth and value creation. The Tofflers, presciently foreseeing this very possibility, observed, "As machines take over routine tasks and the accelerative thrust increases the amount of novelty in the environment, more and more of the energy of society (and its organizations) must turn toward the solution of non-routine problems. *This requires a degree of imagination and creativity that bureaucracy, with its man-in-a-slot organization, its permanent structures, and its hierarchies, is not well equipped to provide.*" [Italics added]

Any society that stymies human imagination, curiosity, and creativity cannot also be a free and open society that fosters human flourishing and the production of abundance. Rather, it can only yield a dystopian future where individual freedom and creative thought are sacrificed to a homogenous fabric of conformity and so-called equality—even faceless equality.

(To take C.S. Lewis slightly out of context, why should anyone heed the babble of such a faceless crowd? "How can they meet us face to face," he wrote, "till we have faces?")

Social philosopher Eric Hoffer ties these large swaths of thought together in his book, *The True Believer: Thoughts on the Nature of Mass Movements*. "The passion for equality," he explains, "is partly a passion for anonymity: to be one thread of the many which make up a tunic; one thread not distinguishable from the others."

As to those who clamor for equality, he maintains that their innermost desire is for an end to the free for all. "They want to eliminate free competition and the ruthless testing to which the individual is continually subjected in a free society. Where freedom is real, equality is the passion of the masses. Where equality is real, freedom is the passion of a small minority. Equality without freedom creates a more stable social pattern than freedom without equality."

And in that dichotomy lies the proverbial rub. But that more easily controlled and dominated "stable social pattern"—stasis—is inherently adverse to surprise, disruption, and innovation. Because stasis is the opposite of dynamism, it is fundamentally flawed, and therefore also makes for regressive social and economic models. The relentless pursuit of equality kills vision and innovation and everything else that flows from the creative imagination. Equality initiatives, in fact, rely entirely upon the continuance of artificial constraints and assumptions. Consequently, equality can only *consume* the future; it cannot construct it. It is concerned only with the *distribution* of wealth rather than its creation. Because it is a product of scarcity thinking, it can only yield a future of declining returns for everyone.

I do not doubt that there are many who would prefer the more stable social pattern. And on the flipside, I do not doubt, as David Brin observes in this volume, that "elites" see wealth-disparity as a means of control. Of course they do. "Today's attempted worldwide oligarchic putsch," he writes, "blatantly has that central goal." But that's nothing new. I would also suggest that this is far more likely to occur under the conditions of the stable social pattern. In any event, such nefarious goals can also be countered, assuming sufficient will. Imagine, for example, if everyone on the planet took the bold step to delete their Facebook account. In one fell swoop, one less oligarchy. Over night. Step and repeat. (For the record, I did my part. As did Steve Wozniak, Elon Musk, Jaron Lanier, WhatsApp cofounder Brian Acton—even Cher. You, too, can do it. And in the bargain, to the extent that this is important to the climate-minded, eliminate the many millions of metric tons of carbon dioxide equivalents to be exhausted by Facebook's servers over the coming years. Or will you wait until the social networks—including Facebook—deploy their social credit scoring systems, as is already done in China, where millions of people with low scores are being denied, for example, the ability to purchase air and rail travel tickets?)

The larger point is that equality, like all things steeped in an economy based on scarcity, inescapably views the conservation of resources as a zero-sum game. In other words, the more I have, the less you must necessarily have. And of course, policies that seek to impose equality only perpetuate the inherent dangers of the scarcity model. Worse, it closes minds to the possibilities of realizing the kinds of abundance that would actually obviate any concern for equality in the first place!

Economic inequality is not the problem. It is an effect. And you can never solve a problem by focusing solely on its effects, yet this is precisely what demands for equality do. If one truly cares about equality, he should first embrace the mindset that seeks to produce abundance, rather than fight a scarcity-driven zero-sum game that he can never win.

Finally, have you noticed that these notions of equality are constrained almost exclusively to the economic domain? This is arbitrary, lazy, and dishonest. The fact is, a world where everything and everyone is equal is a very boring and uninspired and static world. We must, therefore, reframe the meaning of equality. For example, wherever we see the unequal application of the law or any other measure or obstacle selectively and deliberately placed before one's fundamental right to life, liberty, and the pursuit of happiness, we must expose it and defeat it. But how, for example, can I address the unequal and "unfair" fact that, as Malcolm Gladwell points out, because I was born later than my classmates I stand a 200% worse chance of being a professional athlete? In what land do we find an equal distribution of height, talent, good looks, ambition, charisma, networks, experience, work ethic, age, genes, IQ, or even luck? Lake Wobegon, maybe? Inequality is built into a system where outcomes are not—and must not—be guaranteed. Indeed, inequality is a motive force behind all personal growth and economic progress. If we are to create an abundant world we must be equal to this fact and also rightly discern not only such sentiments as envy and entitlement, but abuse and exploitation. This is not a zero-sum world.

In scanning the Urban Prep Academies creed, I don't see anything remotely related to equality, fairness, identity politics, lack of empowerment, racial profiling, thumbs on scales, or excuses for hiding in the crowd. Instead, they teach their people to make their own equality.

This is what love of humanity looks like. It is invested with great care in the possibilities and potentials of human flourishing—one precious and irreplaceable individual at a time. Such love—at heart—is patient and kind. It does not envy, is not self-seeking, or easily angered. Love protects, trusts, hopes, and perseveres. In short, love never fails.

So I ask about our collective future, "*What if?*" What if humankind could be like the tree planted by the water, sending its roots out by the stream? If it could, it would not fear the heat of the day; its leaves would always be green. Nor would it worry in times of drought; even then it would never fail to bear fruit.

Can you imagine such a world? Would not such a world be abundant in its own right? Perhaps, with deeper vision—and a bit of imagination—we can see it, shining in the distant darkness, as did poet Rainer Maria Rilke:

Already my gaze is upon the hill, the sunlit one.
The way to it, barely begun, lies ahead.
So we are grasped by what we have not grasped,
full of promise, shining in the distance.

It changes us, even if we do not reach it,
into something we barely sense, but are;

a movement beckons, answering our movement…
But we just feel the wind against us.

Indeed, the wind is against us. The Tofflers knew this, as well. "Combining rational intelligence with all the imagination we can command," they implored, "*let us project ourselves forcefully into the future.*" ▪

John Schroeter is Executive Director at Abundant World Institute. He is the co-author of the award-winning book *Moonshots—Creating a World of Abundance*, with Naveen Jain and Sir Richard Branson, and editor of *After Shock*—the anthology of essays observing the 50 year anniversary of Alvin and Heidi Toffler's *Future Shock*. He is the publisher of the iconic *Popular Electronics*, *Mechanix Illustrated*, and *Popular Astronomy* magazines, hosted at TechnicaCuriosa.com. He also authored the Prentice Hall classic, *Surviving the ASIC Experience*, on the design of custom integrated circuits. Also passionate about music, Schroeter authored *Between the Strings—the Secret Lives of Guitars*, with introduction by BB King, and is an award-winning music producer, having worked with artists including Chet Atkins, Les Paul, Paul Simon, The Grateful Dead's Bob Weir, Jimmie Vaughan, Phil Keaggy, Motown's Funk Brothers, Earl Klugh, Scotty Moore (Elvis Presley), and many others.

The Next Evolution in Governance:
A Moonshot for Sustainable Development Goals

Eleanor "Nell" Watson

Toffler's *Future Shock* was published in 1970, at a time when American exceptionalism was at its zenith. The moon landings were ongoing, energy was easily accessible and cheap, and the economy was strong. ▪ Yet, shortly after its publication, things began to shift. President Nixon unraveled the monetary system of gold-backed currency, leading to the collapse of the Bretton Woods system and gold-backed currency. The enabling of unbridled fiat currency led to a disconnection between money and things. Shareholder value became the one major metric to optimize for, at the expense of all other natural duties of a corporation. Indeed, fiduciary duty may today be interpreted as giving primacy to shareholder value over all other concerns.

In the decades since, we have seen a decoupling of productivity and wages, and increased reliance on financial instruments such as derivatives, instead of goods and services. This is described as

Financialization, defined by Greta Krippner as "a pattern of accumulation in which profit making occurs increasingly through financial channels rather than through trade and commodity production."

There is no such thing as a free lunch, or a costless gain. All value creation must at some point pay for itself through some toll on the environment. The rules of the game changed in 1971, and Financialization emerged as the best way to play it (Figure 1). The rules must change again if we are to enable an infinite game.

Many pundits will declare that economies have never been stronger. We are theoretically richer than ever before, with access to an incredible range of information and services that even kings and presidents once could not have dreamed of.

And yet, the burdens placed upon many of our citizenry seem greater than ever. Our society is experiencing epidemics of obesity, drug addiction, and despair. Life expectancy is dropping again in many parts of the developed world. Diseases once considered eradicated have reappeared. Community cohesion is at its lowest ebb in generations. We are soft, fat, miserable, and angry.

The social externalities of digital technologies and nonnutritious toxic food are not being accounted for.

While the environmentalist movement has in recent years been preoccupied with CO_2, other forms of pollution, such as heavy metals, PCBs, pesticides, nitrogenous waste, microplastics, and xenoestroegens, may be far more damaging to our planet and its life, in the short and long term. Antibiotics flood our rivers from plants and animals soaked in antiseptic.

Many folks today worry about something like Bostrom's "paperclip maximizer" taking over the world. However, the plastic bag optimizer is already set to cover the entire globe and its oceans, inches high all over.

In the 20th century, mankind forged for itself a diaper of lazy convenience. It is beginning to overflow.

We have cheated our way temporarily to the top by not paying for our

Figure 1

How Financialization Has Changed the Composition of **Futures Trading**

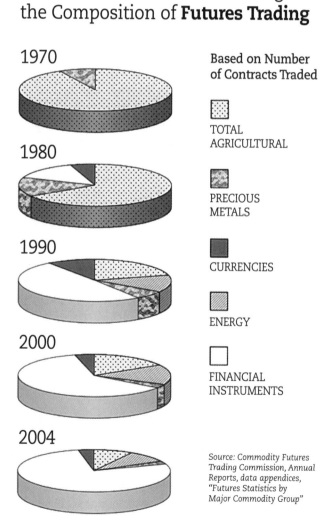

1970

1980

1990

2000

2004

Based on Number of Contracts Traded

TOTAL AGRICULTURAL

PRECIOUS METALS

CURRENCIES

ENERGY

FINANCIAL INSTRUMENTS

Source: Commodity Futures Trading Commission, Annual Reports, data appendices, "Futures Statistics by Major Commodity Group"

externalities. We are poor stewards of this Earth, thoughtlessly ruining it for our own pleasure and convenience, with little thought for the mess that our grandchildren will come to inherit. We lack empathy toward the civilization of tomorrow, as we build ever-greater debts for our future selves to deal with. The chickens are coming home to roost.

Exponential technologies enable us to partially detach value from material, but it must still be paid for, in lithium, rare earths, or the warm whirr of distant data centers. Wealth still cannot be created out of thin air.

Financialization has accelerated to exponential speeds the procession toward a global tragedy of the commons. Only by applying exponential technology to this challenge can we hope to prevent it.

Distributed sensors are enabling citizen scientists to dig up all kinds of data that otherwise might be hidden away. Sensors embedded within Google Street View vehicles, for example, have discovered that industrial methane emissions from ammonium nitrate fertilizer plants are 100 times higher than reported, and have been grossly underestimated.

This single industry is producing three times more methane (a gas that's 84x more contributory to greenhouse effects than CO_2) in the US than the EPA's estimates for all industry in the entire country—three times over, in fact.

That's one single industry producing three times more than the estimates for ALL other industry in the US put together.

This illustrates that we have no idea what's really happening in the world, who is polluting with what, and to what degree. That desperately needs to change. We must make such externalities transparent, accountable, and enforceable.

Today, global GDP is $80 trillion or so. However, all of the externalities that we have created in the process are not on the balance sheet. By bringing ethics and economics together, we can begin to account for externalities and thereby create a more sustainable and equitable form of market economy.

"Externalities" describes the effects of an action upon parties unrelated to that transaction or behavior. When you go to the local store and buy a bottle of juice and a bag of chips, your 10-minute convenience creates a 10,000-year externality, as the plastic you just purchased is nonbiodegradable. This is a cost to people in other places, and to the future, to people as yet unborn, who must pay the costs that we defer to them. The result? Quadrillions of unfunded externalities that are not on the balance sheet.

All kinds of horrible effects have not been accounted for. We have, in a sense, cheated our way into a nice, comfortable life—for some of us, anyway—by not paying for externalities. This has created the situation in which we now find ourselves—a series of ever-worsening environmental catastrophes that threaten to send our civilization into a death spiral.

Good governance is concerned with the management of and accounting for externalities, but it's generally done after the fact. Somebody creates a huge mess, and then an authority declares that the offender must pay a fine. This means that only the most gross effects tend to be noticed and policed, assuming that the authorities cannot be bought off.

We must do better. The confluence of machine intelligence, machine economics (distributed ledger technology), and the emerging domain of machine ethics herald an opportunity for us to do so. These technologies together will enable us to calculate and predict externality effects in a way that is transparent and accountable.

We will, in the 2020s and 2030s, be able to start accounting for externalities in society for the very first time. We can include externalities within pricing mechanisms to make people pay for them at the point of purchase, not after the fact. Therefore, products or services that don't create so many externalities in the world will, all things being equal, be a little bit cheaper. We can create economic incentives to be kinder to people and the planet; we can enable people to profit from being kind.

It is my conviction that this development can enable us to transcend the polarizing, socialist versus capitalist dichotomy. We can enjoy our free markets, we can have our cake and eat it—so long as we do the proper accounting. Automated Externality Accounting has an opportunity to revolutionize governance for the 21st Century. It is the path to sustainable life on this planet, for us, for our progeny, and for all other species.

Measurement of externalities is an admittedly difficult problem. Goodhart's Law, as defined by Marilyn Strathern, states that "when a measure becomes a target, it ceases to be a good measure."

In other words, the thing that we try to optimize for generally ceases to be useful. This may be because the metric was a mere proxy for the thing we wanted to change, but did not ultimately reflect the fullness of reality.

Equally, the target may simply become gamed and abused, as in "cobra problems," where an incentive to kill vermin leads people to breed vermin to collect a reward, and then set them free once the incentive is removed.

Thus, all measures can swiftly become meaningless, and providing incentives to reduce externalities may be challenging. Machine intelligence may help us to get around this.

Today, we have remarkable new technologies built on triple-entry ledger systems. These triple-entry ledger technologies mean that we can build trust within society and use these as layers of trust-building mechanisms to augment our existing institutions. It is also possible to do this in a decentralized form where there is, in theory, no single point of failure and no single point of control or opportunity for corruption within that trust-building mechanism. This means we can effectively franchise trust to parts of the world that don't have reliable trust-building infrastructures. Not every country in the world has an efficient or trustworthy government, and so these technologies enable us to develop a firmer foundation for the social fabric in many parts of the world where trust is not typically strong.

Trust-building technology is a positive development, not only for commerce but also for human happiness. There is a strong correlation between happiness and trust in society. Trust and happiness go hand in hand, even when you control for variables, such as gross domestic product. If you are poor but you believe that your neighbor generally has your best interest at heart, you will tend to be happy and feel secure. Therefore, anything that we can use to build more trust in society will typically help to make people feel happier and more secure. It also means that we can create new ways of organizing people, capital, and values in ways that enable a much greater level of complex societal function.

> Life expectancy is dropping again in many parts of the developed world. Diseases once considered eradicated have reappeared. Community cohesion is at its lowest ebb in generations. We are soft, fat, miserable, and angry.

If we are fortunate and approach this challenge in a careful manner, we may experience something like another Industrial Revolution, built upon these kinds of technologies. Life before the Industrial Revolution was difficult, and then it significantly improved. If we look at human development and well-being on a long timescale, basically nothing happened for millennia, and then suddenly a massive improvement in well-being occurred. We are still reaping the benefits of that breakthrough to serve the needs of the entire world, and we have increasingly managed to accomplish this as property rights and mostly free markets have expanded.

Historically, we have had a tendency to create our own problems through lack of foresight, and then tried to correct them after inflicting the damage. However, as machine ethics technologies get more sophisticated, we are able to intertwine them with machine economics technologies, such as distributed ledger technology and machine intelligence, to connect and integrate everything and better understand how one area affects another.

Given that we are at an early stage of development in machine economics (e.g., blockchain), these technologies are only likely to achieve substantive results when they are married with machine intelligence and machine ethics. Such holistic integration will facilitate a powerful new form of societal complexity in the 2020s.

> Anything that we can use to build more trust in society will typically help to make people feel happier and more secure. It also means that we can create new ways of organizing people, capital, and values in ways that enable a much greater level of complex societal function.

The First Industrial Revolution was about augmenting the muscle of beasts of burden and human beings and harnessing the mode of mechanical power. The Second Industrial Revolution—the Informational Revolution—was about augmenting our cognition. It enabled us to perform a wide variety of complex information-processing tasks and to remember things that our brains would not have the capacity for. That is why computers were initially developed. But we are now on the verge of another revolution, an augmentation of what might be described as the human heart and soul: augmenting our ability to make good moral judgments; augmenting our ability to understand how an action that we take has an effect on others; augmenting our sensibilities about the ways in which we engage with others. For example, we might want to think more carefully about such everyday actions as sending an angry email.

If we can develop technologies that encourage better behavior that might also be cheaper and kinder to the environment, then we can begin to map human values and who we are deep in our core. These technologies might help us build relationships with people whom we might otherwise have missed out on. In a social environment, when people gather together, the masculine and the feminine, the introvert and the extrovert, those with different skills and talents, and even different worldviews, can share similar values.

These technologies can help us find people who share our values. As Timothy Leary entreated us, "find the others." Machines can help us find others in a world where people increasingly feel isolated. During the 1980s, statistically, many of us could count on three or four close friends. But today, people often report having only one or no close friends. We live in a world of incredible abundance, resources, safety, and opportunities. And yet, many people feel disconnected from each other, their inner selves, spirituality, and nature.

By augmenting the human heart and soul, we might be able to solve those problems higher up in Maslow's hierarchy of needs, to help us find love and belonging, build self-esteem, and lead us toward self-actualization.

By 2030 it will be possible to build a system that does not merely satisfy basic human needs, but supports the full realization of human excellence and the joy of being human. If such a system could reach an industrial scale, everyone on this planet would have the opportunity to be a self-actualized human being, in a sustainable manner that upholds and exemplifies the Sustainable Development Goals.

The greatest "shock" in our future just might be the scale of kindness and equity that we can build into a peaceful and sustainable future.

Let's start a conversation!

Eleanor "Nell" Watson is a machine intelligence specialist, educator, and tech philosopher who grew up in Northern Ireland. She helped to develop pioneering Machine Vision techniques at her company Poikos (now QuantaCorp), which enable fast and accurate body measurement from two photos. Later she decided to teach these techniques to others, as author of Machine Intelligence course books for O'Reilly Media. Nell serves as vice-chairman of the IEEE P7001 Committee, creating new safety standards for autonomous systems, and chair of Transparency Experts Focus Group at the IEEE Standards Association Ethics Certification Program. She is also the co-founder and chairman of EthicsNet.org, a community teaching pro-social behaviors to machines. She serves as a Senior Scientific Advisor to The Future Society at Harvard, and holds fellowships with the British Computing Society and Royal Statistical Society, among others. Learn more about her work in automated externality accounting at www.pacha.org.

The Anticipatory Imperative: Actively Shaping the Next 50 Years

Daniel Burrus

Before looking at the next 50 years, it's important to look back, searching not only for patterns that may repeat, but for significant insights that have passed the test of time. ▪ I was an early fan of Alvin Toffler, a true visionary who brought the subject of the future to both mainstream media and business with his groundbreaking book *Future Shock* (1970). I had the pleasure of meeting this great writer and forward thinker on several occasions.

I first met Alvin and his amazing wife, Heidi, in the late 1980s. They were in the front row as I delivered a keynote speech about the future of technology-driven change, a speech I will never forget. I can clearly remember him hitting the table in agreement as I made key points, and after the speech, he shared his kind words of encouragement.

In his writing and speeches, he repeatedly warned businesses that technological progress would usher in an unrelenting era of change. He was one of the first to use the phrase "information overload." Once again, he accurately predicted the incoming deluge of data that was about to dominate our lives. And if you think you know what information overload and *big data* are today, you will soon consider today's big data small data thanks to data-dependent innovations such as connected sensors, machines talking to machines, artificial intelligence (AI), and the Internet of Everything (IoE).

Although Toffler specialized in cautionary tales of the importance of keeping up with technological change, his messages were always delivered with a mix of pessimism and optimism. Critics will point out that he was wrong in a number of areas along the way, such as predictions of the creation of cities beneath the waves, and space colonies. As we consider the overall breadth of the changes we have experienced in the last few decades, however, we cannot rule out that over time, these predictions may become reality.

I've been a professional futurist for over three decades now. I've written seven books and hundreds of articles and delivered over 3,000 keynote speeches globally. My themes address using what I call *Hard Trends* and exponential technologies to actively shape the future, rather than passively receive it. When I started in the early 1980s, there were only a handful of professional futurists writing and speaking to large audiences, and I can safely say we all saw Alvin Toffler as the father of modern futurism.

Finding Certainty in an Uncertain World

We all spend way too much time reacting and responding to external change, and putting out fires—in other words, in crisis management. In order to better navigate a world of accelerating change, organizations large and small have learned to be lean and agile, and to execute a strategy at a high level of competence.

However, in the early years of this new century, despite having these well-refined competencies, General Motors still declared bankruptcy, Blockbuster closed its last store, and BlackBerry quickly moved from leading to bleeding. And let's not forget Hewlett-Packard, Sony, Dell, Microsoft, Sears, and a host of other companies that faced major financial problems and disruptions to their core business despite their leaders and employees implementing lean and agile strategies and knowing how to execute well.

To thrive in this new age of hyper-change and increasing disruptive challenges, we have to go beyond agility, which is a reactive strategy. Agile organizations have learned how to react quickly after a disruption or problem occurs. This is great and we should all get better at it, but in a world of accelerating disruption driven by exponential technological change, reacting quickly has less strategic value every year. It is now an imperative to learn a new competency—how to accurately anticipate the future.

> In a world of accelerating disruption driven by exponential technological change, reacting quickly has less strategic value every year. It is now an imperative to learn a new competency—how to accurately anticipate the future.

That may seem impossible, but it's not. The future is far more certain than you realize. Learning to find certainty in an uncertain world provides a big advantage to those who have learned how and where to look. And when you and your employees master this skill, you'll be able to create what I call an Anticipatory Organization®.

There Is No Shortage of Trends

Let's face it, there is no shortage of trends; the real problem is determining which ones *will* happen, and when. Based on over three decades of research and applying the principles I've developed to organizations worldwide, I have developed a proven methodology for separating any trend about the future into one of two categories: Hard Trends, the trends that *will* happen because they are based on future facts, and Soft Trends, trends that *might* happen and are based on assumptions about the future.

A Hard Trend is something that *cannot be changed*. The benefit of a Hard Trend is that you can clearly see disruption and change coming at you *before* they occur. This gives you the ability to turn disruption into a choice! In addition, strategy based on the certainty that Hard Trends provide has low risk, and when people have high levels of certainty, they have the confidence to make bold moves. When you are experiencing uncertainty, it's like a giant roadblock. You're stuck; you don't move forward. People who are uncertain don't say yes, they don't write big checks, they put off making decisions.

> Understanding the difference between Hard Trends and Soft Trends allows us to transform how we plan and innovate! Using this methodology allows us to accurately predict disruptions and identify and solve problems before they happen.

On the other hand, people with high levels of certainty have the confidence to say yes, to write the big checks, and to move forward faster.

There are three main categories of Hard Trends: Demographic, Regulatory, and Technology.

An example of a Demographic Hard Trend is that there are currently 78 million baby boomers in the U.S. and they will not get younger. This future fact provides both predictable opportunities and predictable problems that we can either pre-solve or let play out. China also has an aging population. Millions of Chinese have been breathing heavily polluted air in their major cities for well over a decade. Those large particulates are known to lodge in the lungs and cause major health problems down the road. Because major health problems in the future are a Soft Trend, meaning they are highly likely to happen but they are not a future fact, preventive actions could be taken now, or we could let the major health problems play out.

An example of a Regulatory Hard Trend would be increasing regulations around cybersecurity. Hard Trends are at play that governments will not be able to ignore. How quickly government takes action is a Soft Trend, but the increasing problem is a Hard Trend.

Examples of Technology Hard Trend categories are on a list I first published in the early 1980s. I said each technology-driven Hard Trend category would increase at an exponential rate. Here is the list: Networking, Dematerialization, Virtualization, Product Intelligence, Mobility, Interactivity, Globalization, and Convergence.

Here is a sample of 12 technology areas that represent Hard Trends that are increasing at an exponential rate and will shape the decades ahead:

1 ■ Artificial Intelligence (AI), Advanced Machine Learning, and Cognitive Computing Applications
2 ■ Adaptive and Predictive Cybersecurity Systems
3 ■ Virtualization and Advanced Cloud Computing Services
4 ■ Virtualization of Processes and Services (On-Demand Services)
5 ■ Blockchains and Cryptocurrency
6 ■ Augmented Reality (AR) and Virtual Reality (VR) Apps and Devices
7 ■ Smart Virtual e-Assistants and Voice-Enabled Devices

8 ■ IoT, creating the Internet of Everything (IoE)
9 ■ 3D Printing (Additive Manufacturing) of Finished Goods
10 ■ Wearables
11 ■ Drones
12 ■ Energy Storage and Microgrids

At this point, you might think Soft Trends have little value because they are not certain to happen. The fact is that I love both Hard Trends and Soft Trends! Soft Trends have great value because they can be changed, which means they provide a powerful vehicle to influence the future and can be capitalized on. Soft Trends might be highly likely to happen, but they are not a future fact, and that means they can be influenced.

A quick example of a Soft Trend would be increasing healthcare costs in the U.S. Many people think this is an unstoppable trend, so the focus becomes how to pay for the increasing burden. When you realize this is a Soft Trend that can be changed, you are empowered to look for tools and strategies to do so. For example, Blockchain could be used in the healthcare ecosystem to provide transparency, trust, and greater security, which would increase competition and lower costs. We can also use AI, machine learning, and other tools to enhance human decisions to yield better outcomes.

Understanding the difference between Hard Trends and Soft Trends allows us to transform how we plan and innovate! Using this methodology allows us to accurately predict disruptions and identify and solve problems *before* they happen. This enables us to solve challenges and problems faster and see opportunities that were impossible to recognize just a few years before. In other words, we become anticipatory rather than reactionary.

Employees of an Anticipatory Organization understand that those who can most accurately see the future will have the biggest advantage. They know that we cannot change the past, but we can shape the future based on actions taken in the present. They actively embrace the fact that many future disruptions, problems, and game-changing opportunities are predictable and represent unprecedented ways to gain advantage. They know that it's better to solve predictable problems before they happen, and that future problems often represent the biggest opportunities. Above all else, they are confident and empowered by having a shared view of the future based on Hard Trends and what I call the "Science of Certainty."

What is the Science of Certainty? Once we can separate Hard Trends from Soft Trends—once we can differentiate between the things that will happen and the things that might happen—we can accurately define the certainties going forward. For example, we know that AI will be increasingly embedded in our smart devices, which will

> "The quality of human existence over the next 50 years is a Soft Trend. We can influence it in a positive direction or not. If we want a more humane world, a more enlightened world, a world where we have increasing opportunity for all, we need to all become active shapers of the future.

get increasingly smarter as our computing ecosystem continues to advance at an exponential rate. We know that after 5G wireless, we will get 6G followed by 7G in a predictable way. And we know that we are putting more and more in the cloud, and products, processes, and services will be increasingly virtualized.

How much time do you spend trying to keep up, putting out fires, crisis managing, and reacting to change? Are these activities helping you to get ahead? Learning to be anticipatory can change that and provide you with a new way to actively shape your future.

The negative impact of climate change is a Soft Trend; governments and individuals can either pre-solve predictable problems or rely on hope. Hope is not a strategy.

The quality of human existence over the next 50 years is a Soft Trend. We can influence it in a positive direction or not. If we want a more humane world, a more enlightened world, a world where we have increasing opportunity for all, we need to all become active shapers of the future.

Daniel Burrus is considered one of the world's leading technology forecasters and disruptive innovation experts. He is the CEO of Burrus Research, a research and consulting firm that monitors global advances in technology-driven trends to help clients profit from technological, social, and business forces that are converging to create enormous, untapped opportunities. He is a strategic advisor to executives, helping them to develop game-changing strategies based on his proven methodologies for capitalizing on technology innovations. He is the author of seven books, including The New York Times bestseller Flash Foresight and his latest book The Anticipatory Organization. Website: https://www.burrus.com

The Toffler Future Wasn't Shocking, it was Enormously Empowering

Michael S. Tomczyk

Future Shock **was must reading when I graduated from college in 1970, and for good reason.** In his groundbreaking book, Alvin Toffler considered the possibility of innovations looming on the horizon that would overwhelm unprepared societies and cultures.

With insightful eloquence, he described the advent of ubiquitous knowledge, intelligent devices, molecular medicine, in vitro fertilization, genetic engineering, cloning, and a variety of social changes such as telecommuting and mobility. He didn't use those exact terms, which were mostly coined later, but he introduced and addressed the concepts, and he did coin several terms, such as "information overload" and the "electronic cottage."

Toffler described "future shock" as the shattering stress and disorientation that comes from too much change, occurring too fast. "Changing is avalanching upon our heads," he wrote so colorfully, "and most people are grotesquely unprepared to cope with it."

So what happened? Did society break down? Did the avalanche bury us?

Good news. There was no breakdown. No shock.

For those of us who became technology pioneers and innovators, Toffler's book was a wake-up call. We felt we were obligated to help engineer his world vision, while avoiding the dire consequences he warned us about. *Future Shock* and his subsequent writings had a motivating impact. As a futurist he did shock us. He shocked us awake from the technological lethargy of the '50s and '60s and gave us a menu of delicious futures to work on, from electronic cottages and telecommuting to knowledge building and smart devices to molecular medicine and social media enclaves.

Having spent my career in the field of innovation, I can say that most innovators are impatient with permanence and the status quo. We are rule breakers, mavericks, and change agents. We strive for positive outcomes in white spaces. We often write on blank slates. Our goal is to turn possibilities into realities, to turn science fiction into science reality. The status quo is definitely not our domain. We are not comfortable with permanence.

It is no coincidence that Part One of *Future Shock* is titled "The Death of Permanence." In the past half-century, societies moved from permanent to temporary conditions, from slow to fast processes, from lethargic to dynamic organizations, from incumbent to emerging technologies, from limited to ubiquitous connectivity, and from closed to open systems. We were not crushed or overwhelmed. We not only adapted, we learned to adapt faster.

The "Technological Engine" that Toffler described (in Chapter 2 of the book) did not run over us. It came racing toward us and instead of scattering or getting crushed, many of us jumped into the driver's seat and started *driving* the engine. We were the technology equivalent of race car drivers. You might say we were change-car drivers. As a result, lots of important innovations, like personal computers, the human genome, nanotechnology, the internet, and smartphones, got really fast starts.

Knowledge as Fuel

Toffler described knowledge as fuel. It's true. Knowledge is the technological, social, and cultural fuel that powers our engines of change.

Giving everyone access to the world's knowledge, through AOL, Alibaba, Amazon, Facebook, Google, YouTube, and Wikipedia, fueled stunning progress in emerging technologies and applications, and motivated us to explore new worlds, from nanomedicine and genes to deep oceans and Mars.

> In 1970 we were disturbed that companies built in guaranteed obsolescence. We complained about having to buy new products every few years. Today we welcome obsolescence.

Mars? Think about it. The more we know about the Red Planet, the more we want to know more! Every day, a Mars robot on wheels sends back images of the surface of Mars. Sometimes we glimpse objects in those photos that seem to be moving or glowing, or shaped like something familiar. These images are intensifying our collective desire to get humans to Mars, if only to see firsthand what these anomalies might be.

The more knowledge we gain, the faster change can occur. If we provide more access to change, we involve more people in the change process. We create more innovators, innovation champions, educators, students, entrepreneurs, companies, customers, and even political advocates.

During the past 50 years, the world's knowledge flow increased almost infinitely. We were not overwhelmed, as Toffler worried we would be. We did not flood the engines. Instead, we learned to use search engines and wikis to access precisely the knowledge we needed, when we needed it, which was a good thing. It didn't confuse us. It gave us more power. In fact, the tsunami of knowledge brought to us by the computer and the internet caused us to evolve as humans.

When knowledge providers learned where we live in cyberspace and started pushing information into our computers, we designed filters to send us the news and accept only product ads, messages, and alerts we most wanted. We blocked people on Facebook and Twitter and screened topics we don't need from websites. We *prioritized* the knowledge that was being pushed at us. We started multitasking to handle many streams of stimuli simultaneously. The flood of knowledge described by Toffler helped turn us into multitaskers.

By the way, as I'm writing these words, I have four windows open on my laptop! Like most people, I work with many open windows, and sometimes three or four software apps, simultaneously. I started out my career as a journalist before moving into the field of innovation. I wanted to be a writer when I was a kid growing up in Wisconsin, so my mother bought me a typewriter when I was eleven years old. In college I got a better typewriter. Later, I switched to a word processor on a personal computer. Now I write articles on my laptop and smartphone. It is worth noting that when *Future Shock* was written, personal computers, word processors, laptops, and smartphones did not exist.

Getting High on Change

As faster-moving technologies brought faster change, we experienced an innovation rush, like joggers experience a runner's high. Many of us became so change oriented that we now get bored without it. We NEED change. We've become addicted to it. We've reprogrammed our brains to adapt to change. And now we crave it like a drug.

This is ironic, given the social and cultural paradigms that existed when Toffler wrote *Future Shock*. In 1970 we were disturbed that companies built in guaranteed obsolescence. We complained about having to buy new products every few years. Today we welcome obsolescence. We impatiently crave new TV shows, new movies, new fashions, new technologies, and new applications. We want the next generation of everything—smartphones, flat-screen TVs, cars and SUVs, drones, computers. We upgrade our computers and cell phones every few years. We keep updating our operating systems, sometimes every month or every week. We watch TV shows and movies on demand. We fast-forward through ads. We binge watch whole seasons of shows on Netflix. We control the flow.

Emerging technologies have even allowed us to upgrade ourselves. *We humans are the only species on Earth with the power to upgrade ourselves.*

I am in the camp that believes we are evolving faster thanks to emerging technologies. Computers caused us to think and type faster. Smart devices forced us to multitask. We went from mapping the human genome to editing genes. Our military has learned to fight at night. We can walk and text at the same time, or eat and text. That's good. There are pitfalls, as Toffler observes and cautions. For example, it's dangerous (and illegal) to drive a car and text at the same time.

Technology has forced us to evolve our species to do more multitasking, shorten product life cycles, and think in terms of mobility, connectivity, and innovation. We are also evolving and learning to cope with temporary situations and the impact of transience, which is another *Future Shock* theme.

Coping with Change

In Chapter 17, Toffler discusses coping mechanisms. One of his concepts is "situational coping," where situational groups are formed to help people handle various life transitions. This concept was spot on.

Thanks to social media, there are thousands of communities that help us cope with all kinds of issues, through participation in like-minded groups. Today we call these groups "communities of interest." We've linked them through social media, where they self-identify, self-organize, and self-police their communities by accepting or blocking friends and followers. As Toffler predicted, most conversations and chatroom posts involve transient current events, politics, what someone said or did, and possibilities that are unfolding.

Toffler also talked about "enclaves of the past" where communities cling to the past in some way, and we see this in online retro-computing clubs. I am active in the Commodore International Historical Society on Facebook, run by moderator Dave McMurtrie. This site has more than 1,300 members who keep alive the Commodore legacy. Many are collectors of Commodore memorabilia. There are thousands of communities and sites like this.

Another "enclave" that I belong to is called Fossil Forum, where fossil collectors post their finds and help each other identify fossils they've discovered. Okay, I know it sounds odd for an innovator to be a fossil collector, but a lot of innovation is about discovery, and discovering hidden secrets from history or prehistory can be as thrilling as discovering a new subatomic particle or gene therapy. For example, in 1970 paleontologists still believed that dinosaurs did not have feathers and birds did not evolve from dinosaurs, although lots of birds looked like them. Now the fossil record shows feathered dinosaurs because amateurs and professionals kept exploring our paleo past. In a sense, we are changing history by finding new ways to search for and explore secrets that remain to be revealed.

Welcome to the Adhocracy

Ad hoc means "as needed," which describes what Toffler called the "adhocracy."

In the organization of the future, Toffler wrote, super-bureaucracies will be challenged by free-form kinetic organizations set in an alien landscape where ties with things, places, and people will turn over at a frenetic and ever-accelerating rate. Teams will be assembled to solve short-term problems, then reassigned. Traditional hierarchies will be forcibly dissolved… and threatened. *Does this sound familiar?*

In 2016 when Donald Trump unexpectedly became president, the liberal media and Democratic Party were unprepared for this sea change. CNN had predicted Trump would lose just hours before he was declared the winner. How could this be? A brash, flamboyant "bad boy" business tycoon was now president!

To use Toffler's words, change *did* avalanche on our heads, and while we did cope with it, some of our coping methods seemed somewhat grotesque.

Conventional journalism lost objectivity and was subsumed by social media. The phrase "fake news" entered our vocabulary. Social media as a news source became more trusted than mass media networks and newspapers. The entrenched bureaucracies, dubbed the "deep state," quaked with apprehension, and the response was bizarre.

Some Republicans became "Never Trumpers." Media networks turned into political party networks and chose sides. This happened in an industry where the "fairness doctrine" (eliminated by the FCC in 2011) once punished media if they weren't evenhanded in their political coverage. CNN and MSNBC lined up with Democrats, and Fox became a mostly Republican network. Against this partisan backdrop, citizen journalists emerged helter-skelter, driven by a wide variety of issues. Some bloggers earned better ratings than networks. This phenomenon continues and may keep morphing. Welcome to the Adhocracy.

Democratizing Innovation

One of Toffler's concerns was that there would be a cultural lag between the haves and have-nots. He worried that those who had early or privileged access to technologies, applications, and non-technological benefits would have an advantage.

I remember that as a kid growing up in a single parent house in Oshkosh, Wisconsin, my classmates from wealthier families had an advantage writing school papers because they had encyclopedias at home. I had to do my research in the library. There were no computers, no internet, and no wikis.

In 2001, Jimmy Wales and Larry Sanger created Wikipedia. Wiki is the Hawaiian word for "quick." Wikipedia became a world community project that allows people from any social or economic background to access facts and figures needed to do a term paper for school or get information for their job. Because Wikipedia is a shared space edited by a legion of user-contributors, it's not perfect. But it's perfect enough to get us started, and from there we can use Google or other search engines to drill down to "more authoritative" online resources.

While many of the "shocks" were not as serious as Toffler predicted, there have been some societal consequences. We still don't know their true impact. One of these is the wealth gap. This refers to the wide disparity between the richest people and the rest of the world. In January 2019, *Time* magazine reported that the top 26 wealthiest people owned $1.4 trillion, as much as the 3.8 billion poorest people, or about half the wealth in the entire world. Oxfam has reported that the richest 1 percent captured 82 percent of the wealth created in 2017.

So how do these statistics link to future shock? Most of the billionaires in the top group earned their fortunes by creating, mastering, and profiting from rapid change. The founders of Amazon, Alibaba, Facebook, Microsoft, and other technology startups were all change-masters. They saw unmet needs in society and created radical new services, industries, and markets. Their companies are not just companies. They are ecosystems. The stock in their companies made the founders super-rich.

There is a body of research that suggests that wealth gaps often lead to social upheaval, revolution, and war. Is there a solution? Will the innovations that made a few entrepreneurs inordinately rich cause upheavals? Time will tell.

> "
> Jack's success was especially poignant considering that he was a survivor of Auschwitz. I asked him once how he dealt with his memories of the Holocaust and he replied, "I live in the future."

Living In the Future

One of the roles of innovators is to even out inequalities and make technology available to everyone. I had some firsthand experience with this when I joined Commodore in 1980 as assistant to the president, Jack Tramiel. Jack told me his vision was to "make computers for the masses, not the classes." When he declared that he wanted to develop a low-cost color computer, I had a sense for what was needed and gave him a 30-page memo detailing my ideas. A week later he put me in charge of guiding the development and launch of the VIC-20, which became the first microcomputer to sell one million units, and jump-started the home computer revolution. As product manager, I also co-designed the first $100 modem (VICModem), which opened the door to telecomputing. We knew at the time that we were leveling the playing field by bringing affordable computers to families, elementary schools, and small businesses.

Jack Tramiel was a tough and wonderful mentor, the General Patton of the computer industry. He was indomitable and driven to effect change. During his career, he had seen the consumer electronics industry evolve from typewriters and mechanical adding machines to personal computers and handheld calculators. He understood there was a trajectory involved. He drove us all—semiconductor designers, hardware engineers, software programmers, and marketeers—to turn out new computers every 12 months, faster than Moore's Law. And we did it.

Jack's success was especially poignant considering that he was a survivor of Auschwitz. I asked him once how he dealt with his memories of the Holocaust and he replied, "I live in the future."

That phrase became my own motto, although with a different meaning. To me as a lifelong innovator, living in the future means developing emerging technologies and applications that will keep reshaping and improving the future to improve the human condition.

As we continue our life journeys, we all owe a debt of gratitude to Alvin and Heidi Toffler for eloquently describing the critical issues that governed the past 50 years of innovation, and which continue to guide us to insights that are relevant to the changes that will shape the next 50 years.

As a technology pioneer and lifelong innovator, **Michael Tomczyk** helped design and influence many of the "shocking futures" described in *Future Shock*. He is best known for his role in guiding the development and launch of the Commodore VIC-20, which jump-started the home computer revolution. He helped launch the Modern Volunteer Army and worked with military innovations while stationed in Vietnam and Korea, where he was a US Army Captain. He was awarded the Bronze Star and Army Commendation medals for meritorious service in Vietnam. As a consultant and business executive he was involved in the launch of innovations such as home computers, ATMs, CT scanning, gene therapy, nanotechnology, and internet applications. He spent two decades in academia, developing and studying best practices and strategies for managing technological innovation at the prestigious Wharton School, where he was managing director of the Mack Institute for Innovation Management. He retired from Wharton in 2013 and spent three years as Innovator in Residence at Villanova University. Michael holds an MBA from UCLA, a masters degree in environmental studies from the University of Pennsylvania, and a bachelor of arts degree from the University of Wisconsin-Oshkosh. He is the author of *The Home Computer Wars* (Compute Books, 1984) and *NanoInnovation: What Every Manager Needs to Know* (Wiley, 2016), and more than 150 articles. His next book discusses how the next generation of radical innovations are giving us new and extraordinary powers and capabilities.

New Maps of the Future: From Forecaster to Changemaker

Anne Lise Kjaer

The writing is on the wall before seismic change occurs, but our antennae must be attuned to undercurrents to sense the vibrations and patterns of change that constitute that writing. ▪ This means that, alongside data gathering, we must develop our intuition to connect elements in meaningful ways. The futurist's role is not only mapping, but also making leaps that help us develop constructive strategies for change. We all have the opportunity to spot these patterns, to become changemakers.

As *Future Shock* so brilliantly argued half a century ago, the problem is keeping up with the change around us. Contemporary art is as good a place as any to see the impact of this. This is writing on the wall—sometimes literally—captured on canvas or through installations. The theme of the Venice Biennale 2019 was "May You Live in Interesting Times," with numerous "art imitating life," world simulation, and world creation concepts. Notably, the Nordic Pavilion featured the installation *Weather Report: Forecasting Future* as a response to our changing world—art anticipating the future, not just reflecting the present.

Judging by the artworks on show, this Biennale could equally well have been called "A World in Crisis." As a cultural reflection of our reality, perhaps this international event also warned that it is time to reset our moral compass. We need to slow down and consider how we can influence the future as individuals—be we creatives, scientists, entrepreneurs, or policymakers.

Things no longer change over a generation or a decade, but from year to year, even month to month, creating new arenas for the emergence of disruptive ideas and innovation. The pace of change challenges our physical landscape—and our value landscape. Many current debates lead us, inevitably, to consider how this change constitutes economic and social progress, and how and whether it works for us. We're thus forced to reconsider the future and our place within it. As we do so, it is important to imagine a variety of alternative futures. As a global citizen—born in Denmark, with Swedish roots, a longtime base in London, and married to a Norwegian—I am an unapologetic believer in the inclusive values I grew up with. I know there is not one, but many potential futures. We must exercise the courage and imagination to acknowledge the diversity of paths that rapid change will place us on, because our choices today are setting foundations for how we experience tomorrow.

Exploring the future through a "multiple" system—I use a Trend Atlas that covers scientific, social, emotional, and spiritual dimensions—is essential because of the interconnectedness of everything. The core building blocks of the future come from all four dimensions, and the fact that something is hard to quantify doesn't make it any less important. On the contrary, we have to approach the future with an open mind and a broad outlook that considers tangible and intangible elements. This is why artwork can be just as important a marker of patterns of change as data or the latest technological breakthroughs.

New Measures of Success

Despite a growing mass of data, we still know very little about people's emerging needs and wants. Keeping pace with analysis and pattern spotting to extract useful information means attempting to pin down what is, effectively, a moving target. While our ability to measure and analyze has grown exponentially, it remains a vain effort to attempt to keep up with the dizzying shifts all around us.

As was noted in *Future Shock*, there is too little time for pause and reflection, leaving us with an almost overwhelming sense of the complexity of modern life. Recently, I had an inspiring conversation with the entrepreneur and marketing guru Seth Godin, who pointed out: "The mistake that is made all the time is that we measure things that are easy to measure, rather than things that are important to measure."

Debates about what we measure, why we measure, and how we measure will continue as we redefine quality of life and how we want to live. More of us are considering how we can achieve a society and economy where people and the overall ecosystem are central concerns, rather than considerations secondary to notions of wealth, power, and questionable definitions of progress. However, ideas are not enough. Future success stories will depend on how well we channel our creative energy—the journey our ideas take from our head and heart to our hands. The biggest question is: How do we reach beyond what we know today and tap into new models that will enable an inclusive society? A good place to start is by redrawing our map for success.

As a designer and futurist, I developed a Trend Compass several years ago to help organizations and government institutions develop an inclusive vision for navigating a better future. The principles are simple: When we balance *People* and *Planet* with a *Purposeful* ethos, we feed into our environment rather than just feeding off it—and that is what enables us to cultivate sustainable *Performance*. I call these underpinning principles the 4Ps.

So how does this vision work in practice? When we observe the past and present, it's possible to gain deeper insights into how the future might unfold. Looking back at the 20th and early 21st centuries, capital P for Profit has been our major parameter for progress—a very left-brain perspective that measures things only in terms of tangible results. Not that our brain is physically divided, but our outlook remains shackled by an obsolete worldview and a binary value system: profit versus loss, thought versus emotion. To navigate a world in flux, real leadership demands a whole-brain approach.

Approaching the Future with an Open Mind

Too often new thinking emerges only as a result of a crisis, and it is clear from history that we cannot rely on government alone. Businesses have the opportunity to step up and help lead change—empowering their people and the local communities they serve to become positive influencers as they make better and more sustainable choices. A major challenge for organizations is "business as usual." It plays out as the perennial focus on getting maximum return for minimum outlay, building on old models instead of imagining new ones that would be less harmful and more sustainable.

> Not everything we truly value and need as a society and a planet can be measured in terms of pure profit and loss. And not every step we take may actually be progress.

What is certain right now is that companies need to open up the conversation with their stakeholders and move beyond retrenchment or token gestures into an honest, two-way dialogue on how consumption patterns should evolve to support a prosperous and healthy society. Not everything we truly value and need as a society and a planet can be measured in terms of pure profit and loss. And not every step we take may actually be progress. This is where being a changemaker comes in. As one of my all-time heroes, the architect, designer, and futurist Buckminster Fuller, said: "You never change things by fighting the existing reality. To change something, build a new model that makes the existing model obsolete."

Rapidly emerging technologies impact everything from economics, politics, manufacturing, and workplace productivity, to lifestyle choices, health, and wellbeing—adding to the global debate about reshaping society and business to create a world that will be fit for future generations. The quest for über-efficiency and hyper-consumption has collided squarely with the pursuit of "slow living" and mindful lifestyle choices. Inexpensive clothes mean we buy more to wear, cheaper food means we eat more, discounted airfares mean we travel more, and mobile technology means we generate more conversations. At the same time, single-use plastics, palm oil production, and a whole host of other resource-intensive industries are being exposed and questioned. Supply creates its own demand, but the move from a vicious circle to a circular economy is starting to happen—people are challenging business and government alike not to confuse "the good life" with "a life full of goods."

New paradigms of trust will emerge, but radical openness will be expected from government and organizations alike. Already, people choose to bypass opaque and inauthentic institutions. The big task for governments is to re-engage people with the importance of civic participation, while for business it is to align stakeholder interests with business goals. Trust is earned through dialogue and value-creating solutions and experiences. Intelligent use of resources is one key battleground, and we are challenging the purpose of the large-scale projects that rapidly alter the shape and dynamics of communities or whole societies. A more sustainable future is one where we invite people and business to collaborate—with the power balance tipped toward people. Working in partnership with nature is just as essential if our society is going to be resilient to population growth and climate change. Within the next decade, circular infrastructure will not be "nice to have" but "necessary to thrive."

Organizations already working with scenario planning know that they face a challenging balancing act: to uphold their social and ethical responsibilities while still innovating, finding new market opportunities, and delivering a profit. One of the great opportunities for businesses in the 21ˢᵗ century is to help people to "do the right thing," as this builds social capital. Designing sustainable products and services is not always straightforward, but it is an investment in the future. This is where the 4Ps become critical to thoughtful innovation. If the only purpose of the thing you develop is P for profit, any short-term advantage must be considered alongside the potential damage over the long term—and this includes your brand reputation.

Choosing to not think in terms of profit first and foremost is still a wildly radical concept for some organizations—as we all know—but there are positive vibrations, as I have witnessed in my own three-decade career as a futurist. Some years ago, a financial services company approached me to discuss a consultancy project. When I outlined my 4P approach, they told me they didn't want me to include intangibles—feelings—just facts. I declined the opportunity to work with them. Several years later the same company called up again, inviting me to speak to its team about the future of money and spiritual leadership.

People, Organizations, and "The Power of One"

Connective technology is enabling the sharing of resources, reconnecting people and communities, while potentially reducing their outgoings. Fundamentally, sharing, repurposing, and fixing things makes us more content, is more sustainable, and supports our idea of what constitutes a better world. The biggest culture shift for business is moving from shareholder to stakeholder capitalism, in which the short-term shareholder value is replaced by a more ethical capitalism.

> It is liberating and exciting to remind ourselves that the future is not somewhere we go, but something we create.

For new thinking to happen, seemingly unrelated dots must be connected. It's about making the unfamiliar feel familiar. We do this by linking values we care about with emerging and established trends; then we can develop profound new narratives about tomorrow's world. Storytelling and storydoing—prototyping and playing out different narratives—is so much more compelling and empowering than a simple forecast. It enables the people within organizations to visualize future situations—both challenges and opportunities—in a believable, multi-layered way. They become actors, not observers, and the stories become powerful tools for creating sound strategies to support change and risk management. When businesses and people imagine the future together, all stakeholders benefit from a common outlook and understanding of how to play their part. They learn how to balance the rational trends of the scientific and social dimensions with the soft touch points of the emotional and spiritual dimensions—fostering positive growth in one common vision.

This is what I see as The Power of One—a realization that we all are part of something bigger than ourselves and that we all can become changemakers. Every success starts with a vision and then the decision to try to make it happen. Ideas are already a crucial currency, but their value will only grow. Fostered by network technologies, the future is about choosing to collaborate, co-design, co-curate, and co-author. There is a real opportunity for companies to add value to their brand by facilitating and enabling people—inside and outside their immediate networks—to reach their personal goals. The future is not about corporate think, but about diversity of thoughts, skills, and mindsets to foster genuine entrepreneurship and positive outcomes.

A Common Purpose and The Good Life

A sense of wellbeing can inspire and enhance prosperity in all areas of life—productivity, social connectivity, and improved public health. More importantly, it motivates people to lead more fulfilled lives. The Good Life is certainly a key theme for the 21st century, but a core challenge in its achievement is balancing natural, human, social, and economic capital to sustain the wellbeing of a society.

The motivational engine that powers human existence is the pursuit of meaning. I personally believe that this is a core driver of 21st-century society. When change is constant, design and leadership powered by emotion, vision and clear purpose are ever more essential. Governments and businesses must recognize that people are beginning to see the importance of their individual actions and choices—even when they have to bypass traditional avenues to make them—in shaping the society they want.

It isn't just intellect that inspires people to bond with society, political party, community, or brand; it is the feeling of belonging. Being part of something greater than individual experience is what people care about and will invest in. By using the 4Ps as parameters to measure and balance value with values, it is possible to develop ideas and innovations that people want to be associated with. If you don't factor all four P elements into your future vision, then it is unlikely to sustain you in tomorrow's world.

At the conclusion of *Future Shock*, it was argued that we cannot fix a problem until we diagnose it. Alvin and Heidi Toffler further suggested that it was time for a reassessment—time to open debate beyond leaders and elites and ask the people what kind of future world they wanted. Half a century later, the book's call to action feels just as fresh and relevant. It is liberating and exciting to remind ourselves that the future is not somewhere we go, but something we create. As individuals—whatever our role in society or place within an organization—we can all be active in this. Just as it did in 1970, the world badly needs changemakers and, ultimately, visionary leaders ready to listen and then shape the future we want. ■

Anne Lise Kjaer delivers visionary thinking to facilitate fresh understanding of tomorrow's people, business, and society. Beginning as a designer in her native Denmark, she worked across Europe before establishing the ideas and trend management consultancy Kjaer Global in 1988. Kjaer Global has worked with many leading organizations, including Amazon, Accenture, BBC, Deloitte, IKEA, PwC, and Volvo. Kjaer is on the advisory board of Singapore's Urban Redevelopment Authority (URA) and holds the honorary title of Copenhagen Goodwill Ambassador. A frequent media commentator on trends, she is author of *The Trend Management Toolkit: A Practical Guide to the Future* (Palgrave Macmillan Business, 2014).

Kidnapped by Technology

Dr. Joe Dispenza

Many of us who are raising children have likely grown accustomed to the trance-like indifference and absent state of mind that our youth can masterfully turn on in a matter of seconds (it looks like an extended lapse in consciousness).

We have probably all talked ourselves into thinking these "short trips" are normal. But have you ever wondered why it takes an ever-increasing volume and inflection to garner attention or elicit a response from our best genetic contributions to humanity?

It makes me wonder, "Did I look like that when I was young, or is this mental glazing-over the product of our times?" Many parents of teenagers have seen these amazing trance-like brain states,

causing us to ponder if these kids are experiencing transcendental enlightenment or if anyone is actually home.

Experts tell us that as we reach our teenage years and the struggle for our own identities begins, the major factor causing the changing, growing, and evolving young brain to make a quantum leap in development is primarily under the reins of a genetic program. In the adolescent timeline, between raging hormones and the normal progression of brain development, most of the body's energy and blood flow is shunted to the emotional centers located in the hindbrain and away from the forebrain. This means they're prone to react more and think less reasonably (not that we don't experience any of this in our adult lives as well).

Within the neocortex is the frontal lobe, essentially the brain's executive, which controls attention, decision-making, emotional reactions, impulsive behavior, and purposeful planning; it is the home of our conscience as well as our identity. But for parents of teenagers, here's the interesting news: we're told that the frontal lobe, which helps us make sense out of life, doesn't fully finish maturing until we are 25 years old. Think about that. We can drive a car at 16 years old, vote at 18 years old, and drink alcohol at 21 years old; meanwhile, the brain's most important center doesn't finish forming until we are in our mid-twenties. So don't take it personally when your teenage daughter tunes you out while you're intentionally speaking to her, or your adolescent son impulsively reacts without forethought. It can be seen as evolution's gift that parents are baptized with a karmic debt—essentially reaping what they sowed during their own teenage years.

> " Many parents of teenagers have seen these amazing trance-like brain states, causing us to ponder if these kids are experiencing transcendental enlightenment or if anyone is actually home.

However, it is not solely genes that cast the dice of our destinies. We are, in fact, very capable of learning from different environmental stimuli, and it is through these interactions that we become such amazing creatures of personal development and change. The waltz between nature and nurture gives us a broad playing field. But is it possible that the present cultural and environmental conditions are impacting the very function of the human brain?

Technology Changes Brain Biology

With the advent of technology, it should be obvious by now that technological environmental factors like video games, Facebook, Instagram, cell phones, text messaging, television, MP3 players, and internet sites play a role in affecting our children's brain physiology. Technology is influencing our mind states to escalate in the direction of increasing emotional entropy by hijacking the brain's natural reward centers. Therefore, if you want to add more insult to injury in a household with teenagers, add more technology to the mix and rest assured—you will feel totally left out of your children's lives.

The latest research has proven that a healthy diet decreases violence and aggression while improving brain activity. It also observes that the long-term use of video games alters the way the normal brain functions. When a child plays a computer game, each time they blow something (or someone) to bits; shoot down or destroy a plane, ship, or UFO; break through a barrier in order to move to the next level; or beat a character to severe injury, the brain responds chemically. In response to such intense stimulation related to triumph, the brain's reward center releases high amounts of dopamine—the brain's natural pleasure chemical.

The bottom line is that dopamine makes us feel good, especially when we're winning at a high pace. When accomplishment is coupled with excitement, the brain also produces two adrenaline hormones—norepinephrine and epinephrine—to wake itself up with a boost of heightened awareness. This chemical cocktail is a perfect formula for causing problems in normal brain function.

This type of computer game stimulation is not bad in short doses, but it can cause problems in the long term. As the brain's reward center is repeatedly activated, and the high amounts of these strong chemicals are released during gaming, the pleasure zones become overstimulated. As a result of such an abnormal release of dopamine, the reward system becomes desensitized and the receptor sites close down. Nature's wisdom then takes over and the receptors adjust to a higher level. The cells will need more of a chemical rush to produce the same feelings the next time they play. A side effect of this conditioning is addiction, and when it is tied to attention and learning, serious effects manifest.

As the brain's physiology responds to a mind exposed to these atypical virtual activities (no child blows up people or things in real life), the brain is fooled into thinking it's almost real. Additionally, the continuous release of chemicals on the nerve cells' receptor sites (the cells' docking points for chemical information) finally causes the receptors to become less responsive to the same level of

the chemical rush. As the receptors shut down from such a high release of dopamine, each receptor will then recalibrate to a higher level. Therefore, the next time a youth engages in a gaming session, it's guaranteed he will need more of a thrill to excite his brain to past levels. It's like living with a spouse who always yells at you—eventually they need to yell a little louder to get your attention because over time that intense stimulation is considered normal.

Receptor sites are the same way. When continually over-activated, they become numb and require more, and more substantial, hits. The side effect: the brain needs unrealistic highs to feel happy and satiated. In the absence of such high-level stimulation, the mind turns off, and so too do your offspring.

So when your kid's computer activity ends, count on her looking like a zombie, because you're probably not all that interesting compared to what she has just been experiencing. In truth, everything in life will seem boring. Simple things like watching a sunset, playing with the dog, or even visiting with a grandparent will seem like trivial nonsense. Why? Because nothing in the normal, mundane world can match the ecstasy of the virtual world and the corresponding super high it produces. And without proper restraint, future choices may be married to things that produce more heightened stimulation: drugs, pornography, gambling, excess shopping, overeating... all because the brain's satiation center may never be fulfilled. People become conditioned to believe that they need "some thing" outside of them to change how they feel inside. In time, when children feel a disturbing emotion from the trials of life, they will turn to a thing (technology) that can be used to predictably make them feel better. Sounds like addiction to me.

The Gamer in the Classroom

Let's take this scenario one step further. What about when a child—in the times between Gameboy mania and constant texting—goes to school to develop his/her mind? Shouldn't learning be a reward in itself? Attention spans inevitably will shorten for the gamer who sits in the classroom trying to pay attention to a topic that doesn't turn his brain on or make his body feel alive. As the young brain goes through withdrawal in the classroom, the perfect stimulation might be to cause trouble by acting out.

Getting in trouble causes high adrenal activity and, unconsciously, the child is making the brain turn on again to provoke the similar chemical releases that gaming provides. Fidgeting, falling asleep, interruptions, emotional outbursts, and provocative and disrespectful comments are all side effects of attention problems. It isn't too difficult to identify the etiology of these behaviors in a child with no genetic history of ADD or ADHD, head injury, or exposure to toxicity.

So how do we make changes in the best interest of the young developing mind? It is the parent's job to think through this complexity. If we propagate the use of technology without an emphasis on developing personal values, providing an environment for skillful learning, practicing reverence for all cultures and beliefs, performing daily rituals, participating in family and social activities, exposing our kids to nature, motivating them to exercise, debating philosophy, or providing an environment for interpersonal evolution, we can surely predict how well—or how poorly—future generations will thrive on a planet with so much opportunity.

As *Future Shock* suggested, we can be victims to the very technology we create. However, when dependency on the technology we invented becomes biological, this constant conditioning process may not only affect the choices and behaviors of our future generations, but their very neuroendocrinology and gene expression. This, certainly, is an *aftershock*.

Dr. Joe Dispenza is an international lecturer, researcher, corporate consultant, author, and educator who has been invited to speak in more than 45 countries on five continents. As a lecturer and educator, he is driven by the conviction that each of us has the potential for greatness and unlimited abilities. In his easy-to-understand, encouraging, and compassionate style, he has educated thousands of people, detailing how they can rewire their brains and recondition their bodies to make lasting changes. In addition to offering a variety of online courses and teleclasses, he has personally taught three-day progressive workshops, five-day advanced workshops, and week-long advanced retreats in the US and abroad. Starting in 2018, his workshops became week-long offerings, and the content of the progressive workshops became available online. To learn more, visit the events section at www.drjoedispenza.com.

A Confluence of Culture, Writer, and Society

Newt Gingrich

There are moments when the idea, the artist or writer, and the society come together to create an effect vastly bigger than would have been achieved by the same work at any other time. ■ Darwin's *On the Origin of Species* in 1859 came out at exactly the right moment and gave language and coherence to a thought process that had been growing for 30 years.

Adam Smith's *The Wealth of Nations* in 1776 captured in descriptive language the emerging market and technology economy that people had been living with for a century, but no one had codified it and given it clarity and language.

The Declaration of Independence appeared the same year (1776) and was the culmination of over a century of thought, evolving from the English Civil War through John Locke and Montesquieu.

The publication of Alvin and Heidi Toffler's *Future Shock* was at a similar moment of culture, writer, and society coming together. The Tofflers were very much like Adam Smith. They were not creating a philosophical or intellectual construct. They were reporting on the wildly different things they saw around them. I used to spend time at their homes in Manhattan and Beverly Hills, and their file cabinets were filled with random articles and observations.

What made the Tofflers unique was that they were interested in EVERYTHING and allowed facts to teach them. They did not approach new situations with a preset interpretation into which they had to squeeze the facts. Instead, they gathered facts and observations, and then allowed a plausible hypothesis to evolve as driven or suggested by their various wide-ranging observations.

The Tofflers were aided in their process by a heavy speaking schedule, which kept them moving from country to country and from town to town. Every trip was a learning experience.

I first worked with them on a book on Anticipatory Democracy. As a young teacher at West Georgia College in Carrolton, Georgia, it was a heady experience to go to a conference with this world-famous couple. The ideas and conversations flowed at all hours of the day and night.

When they wrote *The Third Wave* (which I think is their most important work and which builds on the initial insights of *Future Shock*), laying out a general theory of change as a wave process and the scale of change of the Information Age as comparable to the rise of agriculture or industry, it became a useful guide to changing organizations and structures.

I introduced them to General Donn Starry and the Army's Training and Doctrine Command, which was trying to modernize the Army's battle doctrine to meet the challenges of the modern world. They had a big impact on the planners and analysts, and a lot of the Army's Airland Battle Doctrine grew out of *The Third Wave*. Without their fame and success with *Future Shock* it is hard to imagine they would have been taken seriously by the Army's best thinkers. Their very celebrity status gave them a powerful entree.

After their success with the Army I asked them to come to Congress and introduce Republican members of the House of Representatives to their ideas about a rapidly changing world. Al and Heidi were clearly much more liberal than the members they interacted with, but they thought the opportunity to engage them intellectually made their participation a civic duty.

A lot of House members never understood what the Tofflers were getting at, but enough did that it is fair to say that the Tofflers had a significant impact in the development of the Contract with America and a period of reform which stands out as one of the more creative periods in House Republican history.

Looking back, it is clear that the magic moment in creating a widespread sense of the future as a dramatic break with, rather than an extension of, the recent past came with the publication of *Future Shock*. Words do matter, and sometimes a single phrase can make all the difference.

Early in his career Toffler had written about "technological overload." Somehow I doubt that a book titled *Technological Overload* would have had one tenth of the impact of "future shock" as a term.

> What made the Tofflers unique was that they were interested in EVERYTHING and allowed facts to teach them. They did not approach new situations with a preset interpretation into which they had to squeeze the facts.

Future Shock was helped in its launch by the daring experiment of bringing it out in three different very bright covers, so the very nature of the bookshelf looked like future shock. Al always thought that the multiple bright covers were a major part of the sudden skyrocketing success of the book. It not only caught the eye, it also conveyed the sense of change in a way that was profound.

The Tofflers have had a significant impact in rousing people to the reality of change, not just in the United States but in Japan and China, where they sold very well and where a lot of citizens saw change as a hopeful sign of a better future.

In fact, looking at the malaise in Europe and the gridlock of European entrenched interests blocking the kind of reforms needed to create a better future, it is interesting to speculate on how different Europe would be today if *Future Shock* and then *The Third Wave* had permeated their popular culture. But that may be a circular question. The unwillingness to change made it harder to popularize the very ideas the Tofflers stood for. That was, and is, Europe's loss.

Few popular writers in modern times have had the impact the Tofflers have had, and it all began with *Future Shock*. ▦

Former Speaker of the U.S. House of Representatives **Newt Gingrich** is well known as the architect of the Contract with America that led the Republican Party to victory in 1994 by capturing a majority in the United States House of Representatives for the first time in 40 years. Newt was also a Republican candidate for president of the United States in 2012. Today, Newt is chairman of Gingrich 360, a full-service American consulting, education, and media production group that connects the past, present, and future to inspire audiences, solve challenges, and develop opportunities. Newt is a Fox News contributor and the host of the *Newt's World* podcast.

A Win-win Roadmap to the Future

Martin Rees

In the 50 years since *Future Shock* was published, we've become ever more interconnected: dependent on electric-power grids, air traffic control, international finance, just-in-time delivery, globally dispersed manufacturing, and so forth. There are consequently new concerns and risks of societal disruption: Unless these globalized networks are highly resilient, their manifest benefits could be outweighed by catastrophic (albeit rare) breakdowns—real-world analogues of what happened in 2008 to the financial system. Our cities would be paralyzed without electricity. Supermarket shelves would be empty within days if supply chains were disrupted. Air travel can spread a pandemic worldwide within days. And social media can spread panic and rumor, and psychic and economic contagion, literally at the speed of light.

There's also growing concern about the long-term threats that stem from humanity's ever-heavier collective "footprint": there are more of us, and we're more demanding of energy and resources. In the last 50 years world population has doubled. It's now about 7.7 billion. The main growth has been in East Asia, and it's there that the world's human and financial resources will become concentrated—ending four centuries of North Atlantic hegemony. And there's more urbanization. Preventing megacities from becoming turbulent dystopias will surely be a major challenge to governance.

Population growth seems underdiscussed—partly, perhaps, because doom-laden forecasts in the '60s and '70s by, for instance, the Club of Rome and by Paul Erlich—have proved off the mark. Also, some deem population growth to be a taboo subject—tainted by association with eugenics, with Indian policies under Indira Gandhi, and more recently with China's hard-line one-child policy. As it turned out, food production and resource extraction kept pace with rising population; famines still occur, but they are due to conflict or maldistribution, not overall scarcity.

The world couldn't sustain its present population if everyone lived as profligately as the better-off Americans do today—each using as much energy and eating as much beef. On the other hand, 20 billion people could live sustainably, with a tolerable (albeit ascetic) quality of life, if all adopted a vegan diet, travelled little, lived in small high-density apartments, and interacted via super-internet and virtual reality. This scenario is plainly improbable, and certainly not alluring. But the spread between these extremes highlights that it's naive to quote one "headline" figure for the world's "carrying capacity."

Even if the birth rate stabilizes at (or below) replacement level in East Asia and Africa, as it already has in the majority of nations, world population will rise to 9 billion by mid-century because most people in the developing world are young, and will live longer. Feeding them will require improved agriculture—low-till, water-conserving, and perhaps GM crops—and maybe dietary innovations: converting insects—highly nutritious and rich in proteins—into palatable food; and making artificial meat. To quote Gandhi, "Enough for everyone's need but not for everyone's greed."

Population trends beyond 2050 are harder to predict. Enhanced education and empowerment of women—surely a benign priority in itself—could reduce fertility rates where they're now highest. And the demographic transition hasn't reached parts of India and Sub-Saharan Africa.

But if families in Africa remain large, then according to the UN that continent's population could double again by 2100, to 4 billion, thereby raising the global population to 11 billion. Nigeria alone would have as big a population as Europe and North America combined. And Africa's population would be nearly 10 times Western Europe's.

Optimists say that each extra mouth brings two hands and a brain. But it's the geopolitical stresses that are most worrying. Sub-Saharan Africa can't escape poverty as the Asian tigers did by undercutting Western wages—robots can now do that. Those in Africa don't have sanitation, but they do have smartphones. They know what they're missing, and the injustice of their fate. It's a recipe for instability—multiple megaversions of the tragic boat people crossing the Mediterranean today. Wealthy nations, especially in Europe, should urgently promote growing prosperity in Africa, and not just for altruistic reasons.

And another thing: If humanity's collective impact on land use and climate pushes too hard the resultant "ecological shock" could irreversibly impoverish our biosphere. Extinction rates are rising. A UN report in 2019 claimed that a million species are at risk. That's 10 percent of the total estimated number of species, many not yet identified. We're destroying the book of life before we've read it.

Biodiversity is crucial to human well-being. We're clearly harmed if fish stocks dwindle to extinction; there are plants in the endangered rain forest whose gene pool might be useful to us. But for many environmentalists, preserving the richness of our biosphere has value in its own right, over and above what it means to us humans. To quote the great Harvard ecologist E.O. Wilson,

"Mass extinction is the sin that future generations will least forgive us for."

So the world's getting more crowded. And there's a second firm prediction: It will gradually get warmer. In contrast to population issues, climate change is certainly not underdiscussed, though it is under-responded-to. The concentration of CO_2 in the air has risen by 50 percent since preindustrial times, mainly due to the burning of fossil fuels. The fifth IPCC report presented a spread of projections for different assumptions about future rates of fossil fuel use (and associated rises in CO_2 concentration). It's still unclear how much the climatic effects of CO_2 are amplified by associated changes in water vapor and clouds—that's a further uncertainty.

However, most predictions agree on two things. First, regional disruptions to weather patterns within the next 20-30 years, and more extreme weather, will aggravate pressures on food and water, and enhance migration pressure. And second, under "business as usual" scenarios, we can't rule out, later in the century, really catastrophic warming, and tipping points triggering long-term trends like the melting of Greenland's ice cap.

But even those who accept both these statements have diverse views on the optimal policy response. These divergences stem from differences in economics and ethics—in particular, in how much obligation we should feel toward future generations.

Some economists downplay the priority of addressing climate change in comparison with shorter-term efforts to help the world's poor. But that's because they apply a "standard" discount rate—and in effect write off what happens beyond 2050. But if you care about those who'll live into the 22st century and beyond, then you deem it worth paying an insurance premium now to protect those generations against the worst-case scenarios.

> Optimists say that each extra mouth brings two hands and a brain. But it's the geopolitical stresses that are most worrying. Sub-Saharan Africa can't escape poverty as the Asian tigers did by undercutting Western wages—robots can now do that.

So, even those who agree that there's a significant risk of climate catastrophe a century hence will differ in how urgently they advocate action today. Their assessment will depend on expectations of future growth, and optimism about technological fixes. But, above all, it depends on an ethical issue—in optimizing people's life-chances, should we discriminate on grounds of year of birth?

(Parenthetically, I note that there's one policy context in which an essentially zero discount rate is applied—radioactive waste disposal. Depositories are required to prevent leakage for at least 10,000 years—somewhat ironic when we can't plan the rest of energy policy even 30 years ahead.)

Consider this analogy. Suppose astronomers had tracked an asteroid and calculated that it would hit the Earth in 2080, 60 years from now—not with certainty, but with (say) 10 percent probability. Would we relax, saying that it's a problem that can be set aside for 50 years—we will then be richer in resources to address the threat, and it may turn out that it's going to miss the Earth anyway? I don't think we would. There would surely be a consensus that we should start straight away and do our damnedest to find ways to deflect it, or mitigate its effects.

Politicians won't gain much resonance by advocating unwelcome lifestyle changes now or a high carbon tax—when the benefits accrue mainly to distant parts of the world and are decades into the future.

But there's one "win-win" roadmap to a low-carbon future. Nations should invest in R&D into all forms of low-carbon energy generation, and into other technologies where parallel progress is crucial—especially storage (batteries, compressed air, pumped storage, hydrogen, etc.), and smart grids.

The faster these "clean" technologies advance, the sooner their prices will fall and they will become affordable in areas where they can make a crucial timely difference. For instance, in India, where more generating capacity will be needed, where the health of the poor is jeopardized by smoky stoves burning wood or dung, and where there would otherwise be pressure to build coal-fired power stations to meet increased demand.

Sun and wind are of course front-runners, but other methods have geographical niches. Geothermal power, for instance, is readily available in Iceland; harnessing tidal energy seems attractive where the topography induces specially large-amplitude tides.

> The smartphone, the web, and their ancillaries—ubiquitous today—would have seemed magical even just 25 years ago. So, looking several decades ahead, we must keep our minds open, or at least a bit ajar, to transformative advances that may now seem like science fiction.

Because of local intermittency we'll need continental-scale DC grids—carrying solar energy from the south to less sunny northern latitudes, and east-west to smooth peak demand over different time zones in North America and—via China's belt and road initiative—right across Eurasia.

Despite wide ambivalence about nuclear energy, which has led to technical stagnation in this field in recent decades, it's surely worthwhile to boost R&D into a variety of "Fourth Generation" concepts, which could prove to be safer and more flexible in size. And the potential payoff from fusion is so great that it is surely worth continuing experiments and prototype development.

It would be hard to think of a more inspiring challenge for young engineers than devising clean and economical energy systems for the world.

We should be evangelists for new technology, not Luddites. Without new technology, the world can't provide food and sustainable energy for an expanding and more demanding population. But we need wisely directed technology. Indeed, many of are so anxious that it's advancing so fast that we may not properly cope with it—and that we'll have a bumpy ride through this century.

The smartphone, the web, and their ancillaries—ubiquitous today—would have seemed magical even just 25 years ago. So, looking several decades ahead, we must keep our minds open, or at least a bit ajar, to transformative advances that may now seem like science fiction.

Regulation is already needed for bio- and cybertech. But I'd worry that any regulations imposed (on prudential or ethical grounds, for instance) will be unenforceable worldwide, as is now the case for drug and tax laws. Whatever can be done will be done by someone, somewhere.

And that's a nightmare. Whereas an atomic bomb can't be built without large-scale special-purpose facilities, biotech and cybertechnology experimentation involves facilities that are widely accessible. Indeed, biohacking is burgeoning even as a hobby and competitive game.

We know all too well that technical expertise doesn't guarantee balanced rationality. The global village will have its village idiots, and they'll have global range. The rising empowerment of tech-savvy groups (or even individuals) in the arenas of bio- and cybertechnology will pose an intractable challenge to governments and will aggravate the tension between freedom, privacy, and security.

As technology gets more powerful, the opportunities opened up are huge, but threats that could cascade globally are looming larger. And pressures from a growing population are pushing us closer to climatic and environmental tipping points. These messages confront us even more insistently today than when *Future Shock* was written.

Martin Rees is a leading astrophysicist as well as a senior figure in UK science. He has conducted influential theoretical work on subjects as diverse as black hole formation and extragalactic radio sources, and provided key evidence to contradict the Steady State theory of the evolution of the universe. Martin was also one of the first scientists to predict the uneven distribution of matter in the universe, and proposed observational tests to determine the clustering of stars and galaxies. Much of his most valuable research has focused on the end of the so-called cosmic dark ages—a period shortly after the Big Bang when the universe was as yet without light sources. As Astronomer Royal and a past president of the Royal Society, Martin is a prominent scientific spokesperson and the author of seven books of popular science. After receiving a knighthood in 1992 for his services to science, he was in 2005 elevated to the title of Baron Rees of Ludlow.

Analogue Hearts in a Digital Future

Anders Sörman-Nilsson

It is a rather inspiring (and equally daunting) experience for an emerging futurist to be the narrative science fiction arc that binds together Carlos Slim's entrepreneurial reflections and Condoleeza Rice's security forecasts. ■ But this is what I had been invited to do in Punta de Mita, Mexico, in 2019, for the country's top 70 corporate leaders on behalf of their host, Citibanamex. I was as excited about and invested in what these two had to say about the future as I was focused on my own science fiction story of the future. With a sip of high-end tequila in one hand and a translation headset in the other, I leaned back to soak up what Carlos Slim, one of the most successful global entrepreneurs of his generation, had to share with Citibank CEO Mike Corbet during a deep and meaningful dialogue over dinner. In his opening remarks, to my surprise and delight, Slim started quoting Alvin Toffler's works and philosophies and how impactful they had been and continue to be for his thinking about the future of investment and entrepreneurial creation in the Fourth Industrial Revolution. In most settings, making investment decisions based on 50-year-old ideas might seem anachronistic. But not so when it comes to *Tofflerisms*.

Perhaps ironically, given Toffler's idea of accelerative thrust, many of his ideas have withstood the test of time and are potentially even more potent today, given this thrust is now of the exponential kind. It's been said that there is nothing more powerful than an idea whose time has come, and despite the recognition Toffler's foresights have been afforded by people of Slim's ilk, the *exponential time* to really test *Future Shock* has finally come. We are living in an age where humans no longer have a monopoly on intelligence, where we are becoming cyborgs, with our own intelligence augmented by artificial intelligence.

What concerns me today is not so much that machines are learning—quickly and deeply—but that we as humans, in our state of future phobia, still resist change. And the reality today is that change doesn't care whether you like it or not. It will always happen without your permission. At the same time, business leaders, politicians, education system designers, parents, and spiritual leaders are running their affairs in ways that are perfectly prepared for an analogue world that no longer exists. As a society, we don't just have future shock, we also have present shock, and we desperately hope that being nostalgic is the same thing as being strategic. The global rise of populist politicians, waving the magic wand of nostalgia and crooning reversionist time travel narratives, plays to the fears of mushrooming numbers of victims of future shock and promises a return to "the good old days." In this age, many people's rearview mirrors seem more vivid than their low-res vision into the future.

> Today, you are competing against the best of global human resources; tomorrow, you will also be competing against the best of artificial resources.

If ever there was a time to not be ignorant, complacent, or bigoted, that time is now. The rate of change has never been this fast, but will never again be this slow. This sounds shocking, and it truly is testing our adaptive responses. Casting our minds back 50 years, we recall that Toffler wrote when things were in some ways a little simpler, a little slower, a little more binary. This is not to discount his foresight, but simply to point out that in his time, choosing whom to marry didn't involve the hyperchoice bestowed by Tinder or Grinder, that geopolitics were played out over a dividing curtain by members of either the West or the East, and that reality didn't need an *IRL* to differentiate it from its virtual twin.

Today, tech adoption rates are skyrocketing, the longevity of companies on the Fortune 500 is decreasing at a rapid clip, and automation is impacting both our brawn and our brains. In this world, AI will be doing to white collar work what robots have already been doing to blue collar work. Contemporaneously, education is failing to shift out of past tense and suffers a failure of imagination by narrow-mindedly touting the supposed panacea of STEM skills, all of which computers and robots will trump humans at in the future. We are educating our youth for jobs that will no longer exist, and fail to see that today's digital disruption is a signal from the future that it is time to change—on both personal and societal levels.

For me, future shock is a personal, intergenerational affair. The science fiction author Douglas Adams once described our reactions to new technologies in roughly the following terms:

"Anything that is in the world when you are born is natural, normal and ordinary.

Anything that is invented between the ages of 15 and 35 is new and exciting, and revolutionary and you can probably get a career in it.

Anything invented after the age of 35 is against the natural order of things."

When I meet people at conferences and during scenario planning sessions around the world, and we discuss how blockchain, gene editing, the Singularity, deep learning, transhumanism, climate change, or digital traceability will impact us tomorrow, someone occasionally glances at me and sighs that he or she would prefer to retire before having to learn any of this new "stuff" (normally using less PC language). When I point out that change and learning are in many ways synonymous, and that learning is something we all enjoyed as kids, some of them squeamishly concede that they could probably invest a little more in their own personal and professional development—indeed, in their own compatibility with the future. The prevalence of reversionist mindsets continues to surprise me, and saddens me to a degree. What is more personally tragic is that this resistance to change is very evident in my own family.

> While the left brain of logic, process, math, and data crunching will be ripe pickings for AI, the right brain of emotion, creation, synthesis, and invention will take longer to pick off.

My toughest *pro bono* client is my mum, and it is particularly hurtful to see your own elders become victims of future shock. Mum runs a third-generation, eponymous, family-owned menswear store in Stockholm, Sweden. She runs it in what I describe as a very "analogue," old-school fashion. Since the turn of the millennium, in an age of digital disintermediation and consumer empowerment, she has lost her bricks and mortar retail "monopoly," and the margins have vanished. The hockey stick rise of digital retail started after she turned 50, and she has failed to make the adaptive choices necessary to ensure the survival of her now 103-year-old store. For Mum, now in her mid-60s, the future—in Toffler's parlance—arrived too soon. Instagram fashionistas, influencers, digital procurement, ecommerce, and the mobilization of the consumer's information-focused rational minds are, from her perspective, "against the natural order of things."

I am the connective intergenerational glue between Mum and her grandson, Lucien (two years of age at the time of publication). Digital disruption and transformation happened during my formative entrepreneurial years, and I *"could get a career in it."* I now have, as a 38-year-old futurist and management consultant. My son, in turn, will never have known a world without the internet, without autonomous vehicles, without artificial intelligence. For him, anything that is in the world today is totally normal, and the *lingua franca* of business for the foreseeable future—digital—will be native to him. The sad thing is that because his grandmother was so focused on the past—the historical heritage of her family business—he will most likely never have a chance to ensure its future. But it is not just Lucien who will not be able to carry forward the craft, the artisanal, linguistic, and cultural batons, of previous generations. From "shirtsleeves to shirtsleeves in three generations" is a common rule within family businesses, and the rule of 30-13-3 percent holds that this is the equivalent percentage of family companies that successfully pass on the business to the succeeding generation. In other words, only 3 percent are able to successfully pass the business on to the fourth generation, let alone the fifth—a rule that will be challenged even further in the Fourth and Fifth Industrial Revolutions as the speed of change is amplified. While not everyone is faced with this type of intergenerational change, every individual is now presented with *intragenerational change*, whereby your skills, cognition, and adaptive range are tested not once in a generation, but ceaselessly. Today, you are competing against the best of global human resources; tomorrow, you will also be competing against the best of artificial resources.

However, in this disruptive process, there is an analogue silver lining. We have to remember to not throw away the analogue human baby with the digital bathwater. The choice is not necessarily about tradition *or* technology. *National Geographic*, for example, has invested heavily in the digitization and codification of minority, indigenous, and oral languages to ensure their survival in an age of linguistic homogeneity, given the spread of Mandarin, English, and Spanish. These efforts recognize that age-old wisdom and culture have tremendous value, and that their digitization ensures intra- and inter-generational survival. Similarly, there are elements of our own humanity which will stand us in good stead in an age of machines. While STEM is not an educational panacea, concepts like STEMpathy or STEA[rts]M, which imbue the sciences, technology, engineering, and math with more right-brained skills, are directionally important. Even more critically, we have to invest in humanity's empathy, creativity, entrepreneurship, innovation, ethics, and emotional intelligence. While the left brain of logic, process, math, and data crunching will be ripe pickings for AI, the right brain of emotion, creation, synthesis, and invention will take longer to pick off.

Given that we will want to code our AI to be ethical and humanely empathetic, we would do well to raise our own game and build these muscles first. We mustn't digitize faulty or underperforming "human software." Maybe the irony of this digitization is that it enables humans to tap into their true creative genius. Freed from menial labor, we will have the right and obligation to pursue our true humanity and creativity, ushering in a Second Renaissance of human output.

Despite this renaissance hope, the future does run the risk of becoming hacked by analogue reversionists. Just as the discontents of globalization have frightened voters into attempting to reinstate imagined past glory in the UK and the US, we run the risk of seeing a Luddite techlash as the full force of automation ensues. This places an obligation on futurephiles—people like you and me who think the future is potentially a more humane place, one where we have ended inhumane human error because of, for example, sensorily aware, IoT-connected vehicles—to successfully pitch the future to the skeptics. And yes, while our rational minds might have become digitized, our emotional hearts are still ticking analogue. Without winning both the hearts and minds of the key stakeholders around us, the future may not become quite as alluring as Toffler once foresaw. Polarization of various population into globalists and localists during the rise of the populist leaders has sparked dystopian fears; it's certain that futurephiles and futurephobes pitted against one other is not a scenario conducive to utopia.

> Story can capture analogue hearts, and ready our minds to galaxies of possibilities. But our minds will not venture through doors that the heart hasn't opened. Selling new technologies and bridges to the possible will fall on deaf ears if the audience feels victimized by the future.

As futurists and optimistic realists, we need to create a more engaging and inspirational narrative that humans can buy into—a narrative that provides more meaning and humanity than that offered by the skeptics.

This age-old and fundamentally human ability—storytelling—might well be our most important tool as we design, craft, and shape a more humane tomorrow, enabled by sophisticated robotic brawn and digital brains. Story can capture analogue hearts, and ready our minds to galaxies of possibilities. But our minds will not venture through doors that the heart hasn't opened. Selling new technologies and bridges to the possible will fall on deaf ears if the audience feels victimized by the future. Your job as a business leader, politician, parent, education system designer, or spiritual leader is to decode tomorrow, and shift your futurephobe stakeholders into futurephiles.

As I took the stage in Punta de Mita the second day of the conference, just prior to Condoleeza Rice's forecasts, I realized that my mum had given me a tremendous gift. By not listening to my warnings of disruption and future shock, and not heeding Cervantes's proverb, "to be fore-warned is to be fore-armed," neither Lucien nor I may be able to carry on the retail torch my great-grandfather once lit, but instead, I get to be a professional science fiction storyteller, opening both hearts and minds around the world on a larger scale, and preparing my clients, my young family, and myself for both foreseeable and unforeseeable futures.

As futurists, we are building more *futureness*, selling the idea virus of a more humane tech-enabled future, and reducing the number of victims of future shock one by one. Addressing Mexico's top leaders, I reminded them that transformation is not necessarily about throwing away the analogue baby with the digital bathwater, and that even a Fourth Industrial Revolution proponent and investor in digitization, Carlos Slim, still keeps only analogue paper notes and printed spreadsheets for his own musings, while growing his brands confidently into the future. This analogue human—augmented with a digital mindset—can continue to thrive in a digital world. Maybe there is hope for my mum after all. See you in the future.

Anders Sörman-Nilsson (LLB/EMBA) is a global futurist who helps leaders decode trends, decipher what's next, and turn provocative questions into proactive strategies. Anders's view is that the future and the now are converging in a city or start-up near you, giving the curious and the creative a competitive and sustainable edge. Concurrently, that same future contains fearsome forecasts for futurephobes. This Swedish-Australian futurist has shared a stage with Hillary Clinton, Nobel Laureates, and European and Australian heads of state. He is an active member of TEDGlobal, has keynoted at TEDx in the United States and Australia, was nominated to the World Economic Forum's Young Global Leaders in 2019, and was the keynote speaker at the G20's Y20 Summit in Australia. Clients like Apple, Adobe, Rugby NZ, Mercedes Benz, Gartner, Jaguar Land Rover, and IPG have turned to Anders over the years to help them turn research into foresight and business impact. His books include *Seamless: A Hero's Journey of Digital Disruption, Adaption and Human Transformation* (Wiley 2017), *Digilogue: How to Win the Digital Minds and Analogue Hearts of Tomorrow's Customers* (Wiley 2013), and *Thinque Funky: Upgrade Your Thinking* (Thinque 2009). Learn more at www.anderssorman-nilsson.com, www.anderssorman-nilsson.com/blog, and www.thinque.com.

Counterfactual Thinking Is the Key to Creativity—and a Vaccine against Future Shock

Jane McGonigal, PhD

I teach a class at Stanford University's con-tinuing studies program called "How to Think Like a Futurist."

On the first day of class, I always challenge the students to try to stump me and my fellow research-ers at the Institute for the Future. I ask them to come up with a list of things they believe will *not* change in the future, things that are true about how the world works today that they believe will still be true 10 years from now. For example: Humans will still need oxygen to breathe, or countries will always have borders, or my favorite one that I hear most often is about human reproduction: It takes the DNA of two people to make a baby, one man and one woman. That's been true for three million years. It definitely will be true for the next 10.

Together we create a list of things that they would truly be *shocked* by if it were to fundamentally change in the future. And whatever my students come up with, I promise I'll take their ideas back to my colleagues, and we'll try to prove them wrong. We'll look for clues that, in fact, those things that seem unchangeable might already be changing. Because if there's one thing professional futurists know how to do, it's how to keep our minds open to the idea that literally anything can become dif-ferent. And what do you know? Just last fall when I was teaching this class, a few weeks in, a news headline came out: The first "three-parent" baby was born, using a new experimental method that's legal only in a few places in the world. It's called pro-nuclear transfer, and it combines the genetic material of two women and one man to make one baby, with three genetic parents. This method is already being used today, primarily to help parents avoid passing on genetic diseases. Meanwhile, I discovered signals of even more significant change: Other scientists are credibly exploring methods using stem cells and targeted gene editing to create babies with the DNA from two same-sex parents, or even from a single parent.

Talk about a shocking future! Who among us feels ready for a world in which baby-making is so radically different? But thinking about the most shocking futures we can imagine is important, I tell my students. You may not be geneticists, and you may not be thinking about having a baby any time soon. But this kind of sudden change of what's possible is always worth paying attention to. To avoid being blindsided by the future, you must develop mental habits of *actively challenging* what you believe could or could not be different. You have to get yourself unstuck about what you think is possible, by always looking for evidence that literally anything can change, even something that has been true for all of evolutionary history up until now.

This habit of unsticking your mind is incredibly important. It's the basis of all creativity and personal reinvention. To create something new, or make any kind of change, you have to be able to imagine how things can be *different*. And if you want to take advantage of the rapid disruption of what's possible, instead of being shocked by it, you need a more flexible, open mind.

Professional futurists have all kinds of exercises for practicing this habit, for helping get our brains unstuck about what we think is possible, what we can believe can be different. In my work at the Institute for the Future and in the futures thinking courses I teach to all kinds of students at Stanford University—from design students and computer science undergraduates to MBA and law students—I focus on preparing their minds with three exercises in particular. These three exercise are all forms of "counterfactual thinking," or attempting to vividly imagine and simulate in our minds realities that run "counter" to the "facts" of our present. For just a minute or two, we immerse ourselves in possibilities of which we have no firsthand experience. We transport ourselves to alternate realities. Most importantly, we fight against our brains' natural bias to assume that what has *actually already happened* will always happen again in the future. We retrain our brains to sense and believe in the possibility for change, faster.

We don't have to be shocked by the future, or traumatized by the speed of change. Here, then, are the three exercises, grounded in the scientific practice of counterfactual thinking, that we all can practice any time, any place to strengthen our powers of imagination and mitigate society's risk of experiencing future shock.

Exercise #1: Predict the Past

Where are you right now? Earlier today, you made a decision to be where you are, doing what you're doing.

But what if when you woke up today, you had decided to do something different? What if, on the spur of the moment, you'd decided to make a different plan for today? In this alternate version of reality, where might you be *right now*, and doing what, instead? What choice did you make?

Picture this alternate reality as vividly as you can, as if you had really made this different decision. Close your eyes and try to see yourself in a different place. What are you doing? Why did you choose to do this instead? How do you feel about this alternate version of your day?

This is a technique that futurists often use, called "predicting the past." You look back at something you've actually done in your life, a decision you made or an action you took. And then, you imagine that instead of making that choice, you made another one. You can think about little daily decisions, like you just did, or bigger ones, turning points in your life, like: What if I hadn't moved when I did?

What if I had taken that job or opportunity I turned down? This technique is focused on the past, but it's useful to futurists because it helps us see how our present reality could have been different. It wasn't inevitable that it turned out this way. And if the present wasn't inevitable, then the future isn't inevitable, either. We can make decisions today that will shape it to be something different, just like we made decisions in the past that shape our present.

Exercise #2: Remember the Future

This time, you're going to try to imagine yourself doing something you have never done before, something you've never in your life even considered doing up until right this very minute. And to come up with this previously unimaginable future, we'll use the X-Y-Z method. Here's how it works:

X is something you love to do. It can be anything. Reading, painting, dancing, cooking. Just pick ONE thing you love to do, and that's your X.

Y is a person you care about. Anyone you know at all, as long as they're still living. Pick a Y.

Z is a favorite far-away place, somewhere you've actually been at least once in your life. Pick a Z.

Okay, now imagine it's one year from today. You are doing X with Y in Z. You are doing the thing you love to do with the person you care about in this favorite faraway place. Can you imagine it? Try to see it in your mind like a movie, as clearly as if it has already happened and you are replaying it in your mind like a favorite memory.

This is a technique called "remembering the future." You take activities and people and places that you already have some real-life experience with, and then you combine them in ways that are unfamiliar, unexperienced. And then you try to picture yourself, as vividly as you can, doing this thing you've never done before. And you get bonus benefit if you can come up with a plausible explanation for how this strange future could come to pass. What logical turn of events could take you to this place, with this person, to do this thing? Often it can be hard to come up with a plausible explanation for a randomly generated possible future. But something interesting about this technique is that every time you remember a future, you rate it as more likely to happen. That's because picturing something vividly in your imagination creates something similar to a memory in your mind. When you try to imagine it again in the future, your brain can conjure it up faster—it has a memory of thinking of it before. And your brain says, well, if it's easy to imagine, it must be possible! So this is a powerful habit to cultivate, because it strengthens your ability to believe that things that have not yet happened *can* happen in the future. And the more ways you can imagine how the future could be different from the things you've already experienced, the better you'll be at envisioning change when you need it most.

> This habit of unsticking your mind is incredibly important. It's the basis of all creativity and personal reinvention. To create something new, or make any kind of change, you have to be able to imagine how things can be different.

Exercise #3: Hard Empathy

Finally, you're going to imagine yourself experiencing something you find it very hard to relate to, something that feels so different from your own life that it's almost unimaginable. The easiest way I've found to do this is to go to any news source and look for a story about someone experiencing something I've never personally experienced. For example, I recently read a story in the *New York*

Times about two young women, sisters, living in rural India. The village they live in is so conservative that whenever the young women go into the nearest city, their male cousins and uncles create a human chain around them, their big hands linked, to protect them from any contact with outside men.

I'd like you to imagine what it would be like if, in your daily life, wherever you live right now, you were expected to live by these customs. What if you were expected to allow relatives to create a human chain around you whenever you go somewhere you might encounter strangers? Or what if you were expected to be the one holding hands, and creating that human chain of protection for someone else? This will be hard, most likely, but can you at least try to picture it—even if it seems unbelievable, unimaginable—can you imagine yourself living by these rules in your own life, going to work, or school, or traveling this way? And what that might feel like?

This skill you've just practiced is called "hard empathy." It turns out there are two kinds of empathy. The first kind, the easy kind, happens when we can relate to what someone else is feeling, when we've gone through the same thing ourselves—we have direct experience of it—so our minds and bodies can easily conjure up what someone else might be feeling. And that kind of easy empathy is like a shared emotion—we can feel it because we've felt it before. But hard empathy, that's a more creative kind of empathy. It's what we have to conjure up when we don't have any personal experience with what someone else is going through. When we have no firsthand details to draw upon, when we have to make that imaginative leap to see if we can try to understand what someone else's life might be like, that's hard empathy. And when we can make that leap, when we can feel in our own minds and bodies how someone else's life could be different from ours, we get unstuck, and we get better at thinking about change. Because if someone else can live a life completely different from ours today, then it's possible that we ourselves, and anyone around us, can lead a completely different life tomorrow.

■ ■ ■

These three mental habits you've just learned and practiced—predicting the past, remembering the future, and hard empathy—I call them the magic triangle of "what if." You can use this triangle any time you want to be more creative or flexible in your thinking. Not only are these counterfactual techniques fast and fun, they've also all been linked in the scientific literature to increased innovation, open-mindedness, inventiveness, and capacity for change. And that's because, at their core, they are all techniques for building your mental capacity to recognize and adapt to change, by imagining how anything could be different.

To invent something new, or make any kind of change in your society, you first have to be able to imagine how things can be different. Remember: the phrase "make a difference" literally means *to make something different.* And that's the true power of thinking like a futurist: You develop the power to make your future different—whatever you want that difference to be. ■

Jane McGonigal, PhD, is a research director at the Institute for the Future in Palo Alto, California, and author of the *New York Times* bestselling books *Reality is Broken* and *SuperBetter.*

The Empty Promise of Future Shock

Andrew Curry

Alvin Toffler was a journalist before he was a futurist, and these skills are shown to bravura effect in the opening pages of *Future Shock*. ■ The rhetorical phrases rattle off the page. He starts from the very beginning as he means to continue: "Change is the process by which the future invades our lives." It is "a roaring current," one which is "so powerful today that it overturns institutions, shifts our values and shrivels our roots" (p.11). The concept of "future shock," which Toffler had invented in a magazine article five years earlier, "is no longer a distantly potential danger, but a real sickness from which increasingly large numbers already suffer."

Compared to other futures books of the time, the rhythms of the prose are like hearing the early passages of *The Rites of Spring* for the first time.

Toffler sets out his argument with similar vigor in the opening chapters of *Future Shock*. One of the reasons for the book's success is that its narrative strategy follows the classic Hollywood "three-act" structure. We are drawn into jeopardy; the world of that jeopardy is made visible as we venture into it; and then, finally, we find ways of escaping it. Everyone, these days, remembers the jeopardy itself (the idea of future shock), but less of the detail of that world, and almost nothing of the remedies that might help us escape—meaning the institutions and innovations that might help us to manage our "adaptive range" in response to the shock.

One of the reasons for this is that the early sections on the idea of "future shock" are by far the most compellingly written:

"Millions of ordinary psychologically normal people will face an abrupt collision with the future." (p.18)

"Western societies for the past 300 years have been caught up in a firestorm of change. This storm, far from abating, now appears to be gathering force." (p.18)

"[A] racing rate of change that makes reality seem, sometimes, like a kaleidoscope run wild." (p.19)

"Future shock is the dizzying disorientation brought on by the premature arrival of the future… [It] is a time phenomenon, a product of the greatly accelerated change in society." (pp.19-20)

All of this can get breathless after a while, and the rush of rhetorical tropes should give the reader pause as they fly by. Toffler deals with this by doubling down. "Is all this exaggerated?" he asks. "I think not" (p.21). Of course not. The proposition is then reinforced with quotes from a line of distinguished academics who, in their different ways, assert that change is speeding up. This last is one of the oldest claims in cultural history, going back at least to the Romans, and Toffler elides the ground for us by switching repeatedly between the 300-year space of modernity and the immediate generational experience of the 1960s and the 1970s.

> In fact many of the world's problems are caused by slowing down, rather than speeding up. The rate of population growth has been slowing for almost 30 years; economic growth has been slowing for more than 50 years, and productivity growth for much of that time; even the rate of digital innovation is slowing.

There is a simple enough case to be made that there was a social and economic acceleration from the 18th century onward. Energy consumption increased, the rate of innovation (technological and social) increased, population started to grow. But when you try to make a more specific case within this broad time frame, there are difficulties. By many objective measures, as Hirst and Thompson (1996) noted, the experience of change in the late 19th century was more profound than that of the second half of the 20th. Equally, Robert Gordon (2016) argues persuasively that the innovations of the first part of the 20th century (from the car to the washing machine) were far more transformational than those of the ICT revolution in the later part.

Toffler has to elide some of this as well. "How do we know that change is accelerating? There is, after all, no absolute way to measure change" (p.28). He answers his own question on the next page, after a whole list of caveats that ought to give the careful reader at least a moment of reflection.

"Even with all these qualifications however, there is widespread agreement, reaching from historians and archeologists all across the spectrum to scientists, sociologists, economists and psychologists, that many social processes are speeding up—strikingly, even spectacularly." (p.29)

The whole story, in other words, becomes self-referential to the point of circularity.

Only the Name

The poet Edward Thomas once wrote, famously, of a being in a train at a railway halt of which he remembered "only the name." *Future Shock* has, similarly, left behind only the name, swirled around with an affect about the speed and restlessness of change. The affect of the book has replayed itself, endlessly, in corporate keynotes about the future, in consultancy pitches, in Silicon Valley product propositions. Change, we hear, is speeding up. We are overloaded by information. We are living in exponential times. And on, and on, and on. We can be fairly certain that almost all of those channeling this idea of "future shock" have never read the book.

No matter, then, that in fact many of the world's problems are caused by slowing down, rather than speeding up. The rate of population growth has been slowing for almost 30 years; economic growth has been slowing for more than 50 years, and productivity growth for much of that time; even the rate of digital innovation is slowing, in the face of mature and saturated markets (Evans, 2019) and the end of Moore's Law. Of the big generational drivers of change, only the rate of environmental change is accelerating, catastrophically.

It is, therefore, worth briefly unpacking Toffler's argument to understand the overlapping forms of change that he identifies to justify his "supercharged language" (his term). He makes a number of claims. The first is the growth of cities, which he dates back to 1850. The second is the growth in the consumption of energy, again measured back to 1850. The third is "the acceleration of economic growth," where Toffler changes the time frame, and concentrates on the post-war boom—from 1948 to 1965. "Today, growth rates of from 5 per cent to 10 per cent per year are not uncommon among the most advanced industrial nations" (p.31), with the implication that the output of goods and services will double every 10-15 years.

One of the problems with this, inasmuch as *Future Shock*'s assumptions can be teased out, is that Toffler builds a significant argument on the edifice of economic growth. The rate of acceleration of production and consumption, he asserts, leads to "an electric impact on the habits, beliefs, and self-image of millions." In retrospect, 1970 was almost the last moment at which one could make claims about such growth rates, or their effects.

The fourth element of the case for "future shock" is about technology. Toffler focuses on transport technology. Speeds of 100 mph were achieved only with the steam train in the 1880s; by 1938 airplane speeds had reached 400 mph; by the 1960s "rocket planes approached speeds of 4,800 mph, and men in space capsules were circling the earth at 18,000 mph... the line representing progress in the past generation would leap vertically off the page." (p.33) Even on the basis of what was known at the time of writing, it is possible to observe that this is not comparing like with like. Since then, of course, the 1960s expectations that supersonic travel would become the norm have evaporated, and transport speeds (and notably aviation speeds) have stagnated.

Beyond this, he references the increasing size of the science base, makes an argument about the increasing speed of the diffusion of innovation, and references the way in which knowledge has grown. He uses the acceleration in the production of books as a metric.

The End of Modernity

The timing of *Future Shock* is relevant. We are at the end of a long 250-year wave of modernity (Albrow, 1998) that has been characterized by ceaseless growth and expansion. Curry and Tibbs (2010) observe that, "At the beginning of the modern era the entire globe represented the basic geographic space for expansion. Now that modernity is operating at a global level, globalization proves not to be the next expansion stage for modernity, but its saturation point." The point at which we became aware of this saturation can be debated, but at a cultural and environmental level Rachel Carson's 1962 book *Silent Spring* was certainly a weak signal of change, and by 1972, with the publication of *The Limits to Growth*, it had become rather more. In this respect, the index of *Future Shock* is telling. There is no entry for

"Environment"; "Environmental Pollution" has a handful of references.

Counter-cultural critiques of the limits of capitalism also emerge strongly in the 1960s, seen in the writings of the Situationists, and intellectuals and social movements associated with *les evenements* of '68. In particular, the mood about the future changed in the space of a few years. The optimism of the 1960s, characterized by the excitement about space travel, quickly gave way to skepticism about environmental change and energy. One emblem of this is the shift in tone from Kubrick's 1968 film *Space Odyssey* to John Carpenter's low-budget *Dark Star* in 1974, with its spaceship crippled by Congressional budget cuts.

In other words, it is significant that the book was published in 1970 and written, therefore, at the end of the 1960s. The timing has a significant influence on how Toffler constructs his argument.

But there is more here. Stein's "law" reminds us that "if something cannot go on forever, it will stop." Basic systems thinking suggests that systems have patterns in which reinforcing loops accelerate the dynamics of a system, but balancing loops represent constraints on these dynamics (Meadows, 2009). S-curves or logistics curves, one of the basic building blocks of much futures thinking, show an acceleration in the first part of the S-curve, and then a deceleration in the second part.

In much writing about exponential change, as Toffler does here without using the phrase, the thinking mistakenly imagines that the rapid acceleration seen in the second quartile of the S-curve, when growth is at its fastest, is a new normal, rather than a system that is about to start meeting its limits. This is what Toffler does in *Future Shock* as he jumps between the long S-curves of modernity, and the far shorter one of post-war economic growth.

Used Futures, Empty Futures

Not all futures are equal. Sohail Inayatullah (2007) writes in his Six Pillars paper of "used futures," without precisely defining the term. It is an image of the future that "is unconsciously borrowed from someone else," which imitates "what everyone else is doing." Jose Ramos (2016) suggests it is "an image or idea of the future that someone else created in some other context, but to which we are unconsciously holding on to, blinding us to other more authentic and empowering ideas of the future."

Barbara Adam and Chris Groves (2007) describe "empty futures," in which the future is an open space awaiting colonization.

"Once emptied, the future can be filled with anything, with unlimited interests, desires, projections, values, beliefs, ethical concerns, business ventures, political ambitions..."

The used future may once have been rooted in a theory of change, but has become disconnected over time. The empty future has never been thus connected. Instead, it is just a space in which the present is able to write checks that the future will have to pay. As Adam and Groves write, "Emptied of content and meaning, the future is simply there, an empty space waiting to be filled with our desire, to be shaped, traded or formed according to rational plans and blueprints."

In summary, then, an empty future is one that never had a theory of change attached to it, while a used future is one whose theory of change has been found to be wanting when it makes contact with the changing world that it is attempting to describe.

While ideas of theories of change are taught in the handful of futures schools we have worldwide, they are scarce in the literature. One exception is work done by Wendy Schultz and Richard Lum on the future of education, in which each scenario was underpinned by a different theory of change.

One of the reasons that this matters is that assertions about futures outcomes are not generally falsifiable, which is why futurists also say that "there are no futures facts" (Bell, 2003). Without facts, there is no falsifiability. This may, as it happens, be a narrow view of what we can know about the future, and one which is epistemologically contestable, but that discussion is beyond the limits of this essay.

The point is that futures projections based on a clear theory of change *are* falsifiable. We are able to observe events unfolding and retrospectively assess whether a theory of change that has been proposed to explain them has less or more explanatory power.

Adam and Groves make a similar point about futures when they contrast empty futures with contextual or embedded futures. Such embedded futures require us "to recognise connections and implications, to appreciate things in their continuity and emergence, to know the future as embodied in things and events, embedded in processes and as carrying forth the deeds of the past."

In contrast, *Future Shock* skates across the surfaces of the world that it describes, piling up anecdotes and data, playing fast and loose with timescales. This may be the reason for its success; the single idea about "future shock" morphs endlessly, shape-shifting as we go through the book. Does it have a theory of change? Arguably, it is that everything is accelerating, and that this will then have deep and drastic social consequences. Even as he was writing, much of this was contestable. *Future Shock* has become a strange futures text that turns out to be a used future, blinding us to the actual material futures unfolding in front of us, but also an empty future, used to make claims on the future that profit particular groups and interests in the present.

Maps of the World

Of course, Toffler's purpose is not merely descriptive. He says that he is describing both the "accelerative thrust" and the issues this causes in terms of the "adaptive range," which he proposes as a kind of index of human ability to respond, building better social institutions and social routines to do so. There is no reason to disbelieve him. He was a lifelong progressive who had worked in a factory before he became a journalist to better understand that world of work. A long section at the end of the book is full of recommendations for social innovation.

It turns out, as well, that Toffler does care about theory. Quite early in the book, when he is still setting out the stall of *Future Shock*, he writes, "In dealing with the future… it is more important to be imaginative and insightful than to be 100% 'right'. Theories do not have to be 'right' to be enormously useful. Even error has its uses. The maps of the world drawn by the medieval cartographers were so hopelessly inaccurate, so filled with factual error, that they elicit condescending smiles today when almost the entire surface of the earth has been charted. Yet the great explorers could never have discovered the New World without them….

"We who explore the future are like those ancient map-makers, and it is in this spirit that the concept of future shock and the world theory of the adaptive range are presented here." (p.15)

In his excitement, he populated his map of the future with all kinds of fantastical creatures, some of whom were never sighted again. Islands were joined together to create whole new continents. Claims were made about the crea-

> An empty future is one that never had a theory of change attached to it, while a used future is one whose theory of change has been found to be wanting when it makes contact with the changing world that it is attempting to describe.

tures found inland by explorers that were compelling enough to have survived down the decades as myths.

And the map created in *Future Shock* did turn out to be useful, even to Toffler. His next book, *The Third Wave* (1980), offered a testable proposition about the future, and specifically about the rise of the service economy. Toffler even seems to acknowledge as much in his introduction to the later book: "I concentrate less on acceleration, as such, and more on the destination towards which change is carrying us" (p.17-18]. *The Third Wave*, and its theory of change, have survived 40 years of scrutiny (Curry, 2017).

The seeds of that book can be found within the pages of *Future Shock*. *The Third Wave* is neither an empty future nor a used future. It sheds light, even now, on our contemporary crisis of politics and populism. ▨

Andrew **Curry** has worked as a futurist for 20 years, and is currently Director of Futures at SOIF, the School of International Futures, based in London. He has led a wide variety of scenarios and futures projects for private, public, and nonprofit organizations, and has written extensively on futures. He was the lead author of the 2001 report for the UK Cabinet Office "Understanding Best Practice in Strategic Futures"; he co-wrote—with Wendy Schultz—"Roads Less Travelled" on comparative scenarios methods; and—with Anthony Hodgson—wrote the first academic paper on the Three Horizons method. He also edited the Association of Professional Futurists' tenth anniversary essay collection, *The Future of Futures*. Andrew is a member of the Advisory Board of Lancaster University's Institute of Social Futures and edits the APF newsletter, *Compass*.

References

Adam, B., and Groves, C., (2007). *Future Matters: Action, Knowledge, Ethics*. Leiden: Brill.

Albrow, M., (1998), *The Global Age*. Cambridge, Polity.

Bell, W., (2003), *Foundations of Futures Studies, Volume 1*. Piscataway, N.J.: Transaction Publishers (revised edition).

Carson, R, (1962), *Silent Spring*. Houghton Mifflin Company.

Curry, A., (2017). "The city, the country, and the new politics of place." *Journal of Futures Studies*,

Curry, A., and Tibbs, H. (2010). 'What Kind of Crisis Is It?" *Journal of Futures Studies*, March 2010, 14(3): 75 - 88.

Evans, B., (2019). "The End of Mobile." Benedict Evans blog, 28th May 2019.
   https://www.ben-evans.com/benedictevans/2019/5/28/the-end-of-mobile. Accessed 1st June 2019.

Gordon, R., (2016). *The Rise and Fall of American Growth*.

Hirst, P., and Thompson, G., (1996). *Globalization in Question*. Cambridge, Polity

Inayatullah, I., (2007), "Six pillars: futures thinking for transforming." *Foresight*, Vol. 10, No. 1 2008, pp. 4-21.

Meadows, D.H., (2009). *Thinking in Systems*. Earthscan.

Meadows, D.H., Meadows, D.L., Randers, J, Behrens, W., (1972). *The Limits to Growth*. New York: Universe Books.

Ramos, J., (2016). "The Future of Work." *Stir*.

Schultz, W., and Lum, R., (2014), "Tick TOCS Tick TOCS: Channeling change through theory into scenarios."
   APF Compass, Education Special Edition, 2014.

Toffler, A., (1980). *The Third Wave*. Bantam Books.

Get Comfortable
Being Uncomfortable

Barry O'Reilly

66 The illiterate of the twenty-first century will
not be those who cannot read and write, but
those who cannot learn, unlearn, and relearn. 99
—*Alvin Toffler*

Over 2,000 years ago, the seed of a civilization—a start-up, if you will—sprang into being on seven hills in central Europe.

And that startup would go on to scale and sustain itself for over 500 years as one of the greatest economic and cultural powers the Earth has ever seen.

At its prime, the Roman Empire occupied more than 2 million square miles and comprised approximately 20 percent of the world's population. And for centuries, scholars have mused over what it was that brought Rome such tremendous success. Was it the empire's visionary leaders? Its prime location on the Tiber River? Its engineering feats of roads and aqueducts? Or simply its laws of governance?

In fact, it was none of these.

As philosopher Baron de Montesquieu explained, the Roman Empire's success could in great part be traced to having fought successively against all peoples; the Romans always gave up their own practices as soon as they found better ones.

And this unique ability, to adapt to new circumstances in the environment by learning to unlearn what had brought it success in the past in order to succeed in the future, enabled this civilization to start up, scale, and sustain itself by letting go of the past to achieve extraordinary results—until this skill, to learn, unlearn, and relearn was in fact forgotten, triggering the collapse of Rome and a descent into the Dark Ages.

How Do I Know I Need To Unlearn?

My inspiration to write *Unlearn: Let Go of Past Success to Achieve Extraordinary Results* and create a system of unlearning—dubbed the Cycle of Unlearning—came from what I frequently find to be a significant inhibitor when helping high-performance individuals get better: not the ability to learn new things, but the inability to unlearn mindsets, behaviors, and methods that were once effective but now limit their success.

There comes a time in the life of every individual when doing the things that brought you success in the past no longer delivers the same results. You wake up, walk into your office, and sit at your desk just as you always have. But suddenly you're stuck, stagnating, unsatisfied, or struggling with what was once your secret to success.

You might find yourself asking: Why am I not living up to my expectations? Why can't I solve this problem? Why do I constantly avoid taking on this particular challenge?

The world evolves, conditions change, and new norms emerge. Instead of adapting, people find themselves stuck in their patterns of thinking and behaving. Most don't realize the new situational reality until it bites.

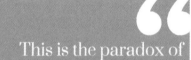

> This is the paradox of success. While certain methods of thinking and doing may have brought you success in the past, it's almost certain they won't reliably bring you success in the future. The key is to recognize the signals and break through before it's too late.

This is the paradox of success. While certain methods of thinking and doing may have brought you success in the past, it's almost certain they won't reliably bring you success in the future. The key is to recognize the signals and break through before it's too late. Your once-successful strategies can cause your downfall. The challenge is to make the adjustments and adapt, not get caught in the past.

I define unlearning as the process of letting go of, moving away from, and reframing once-useful mindsets and acquired behaviors that were once effective but now limit our success. It's not forgetting or discarding knowledge or experience; it's the conscious act of letting go of outdated information and actively gathering and taking in new information to inform effective decision-making and action.

How great leaders succeed isn't magical; it's methodical. One of the first references to the idea of organizational unlearning was in an article by Bo Hedberg in 1981. According to Hedberg, "Knowledge grows, and simultaneously it becomes obsolete as reality changes. Understanding involves both learning new knowledge and discarding obsolete and misleading knowledge."

You see, the truth is disruption does not actually apply to organizations. The truth is it applies to individuals.

Consider what great leaders and the great companies they lead have in common. They have cultivated a capability within themselves to innovate, adapt, and anticipate the future.

They invest in experiences that enable them to grow; they seek situations that are uncomfortable and uncertain, and the results unknown.

They create mechanisms to experiment quickly, and safely gather new information to evolve into something better.

They succeed over the long term by not holding on to what once brought them success.

It's not down to serendipity or luck—they have intentional systems of unlearning. In my own experience working all around the world with executives and teams—from disruptive startups to the globally renowned behemoths of the Fortune 500—I've seen firsthand the struggles that leaders both great and growing face as they seek to lead innovation in their markets.

I've seen what enables certain leaders to accelerate and what makes others stop in their tracks.

In times past, an individual's knowledge would suffice for a lifetime. Indeed, knowledge would be passed down for many generations and still be highly useful. Yet, as the pace of innovation increases, once-useful knowledge now becomes rapidly obsolete—hence the need to consider a system of unlearning.

Exceptional leaders have discovered it's not how smart they are, how much they know, how long they've been in the industry, or what they have learned. It's the ability to recognize when to unlearn and when to let go of past success and their outdated thinking and behaviors, and innovate new mindsets and methods to achieve extraordinary results. Yes, learning is one part, but the answer is not only to learn. We struggle even more to know what to let go of, move away from, and unlearn.

Extraordinary Leaders Disrupt Themselves

The first thing most CEOs do when they join a company is to meet with their executive team to find out what's working, what needs fixing, and who can fix it. When John Legere took over T-Mobile in 2012, he didn't sit in his office and consume endless presentations made by employees, market analysts, and researchers. Instead, he did the work himself. He had a special phone line installed in his office to listen directly to customer service calls for four hours a day and better understand what obstacles, issues, and challenges customers were facing while trying to use T-Mobile's services. Says Legere, "I use it every day, and especially in the beginning it gave me great insight into customer pain points."

Listening directly to customers complain—mostly about their mobile phone bill and how it would suddenly skyrocket (usually during months when they traveled extensively)—helped Legere learn, unlearn, and relearn.

Legere knew intuitively that he needed to "unlearn" what he knew about how the telecommunication business, especially phone contracts, worked so he could truly hear and act on the feedback he was receiving. Not long after this unlearning moment, he introduced the world's first no-contract, fixed-pricing mobile service and crushed his competition, forever transforming the industry.

Digital Transformation. Disruption. Paradigm shifts. Call it what you will, the terms have been so overused you'd be forgiven for believing them just marketing hype. But the threat is real.

The average age of an S&P 500 company is under 20 years, down from 60 years in the 1950s, according to Credit Suisse. The Wall Street firm says the trend is accelerating and blames the disruption from technology. In fact, only 15 percent of the Fortune 500 from 50 years ago remain on the list today. That's why 85 percent of organizations across a wide variety of industries have embarked on their own digital transformation journeys. Sadly, according to a recent IDC study, only 7 percent can be classified as digital transformation leaders. Why is that?

Because transformation is less about technology and more about people—and that means imagination and choosing courage over comfort to think and act differently—and that must start at the very top.

Everyone talks about companies being disrupted, but it's really the leaders of those companies that get disrupted because they hold onto legacy behaviors or outdated thinking—that which brought them success in the past but now limits their success. Meanwhile, the world is innovating around them.

The world changes. Technology changes. Customers demand change. Yet people get stuck using the same behaviors and old paradigms. Why? Because they worked before. This is especially true for executives who've spent a lifetime honing their expertise. Learning new behaviors is not the problem for these executives. It's their inability to "unlearn" their existing behavior and mindset that is challenging because these are the very things that got them where they are today.

Unlearning Is a System of Deliberate Practice

Unlearning does not mean that everything you know is suddenly irrelevant. It's not about forgetting or discounting your experience. Unlearning is a conscious act of letting go of once-useful mindsets and potentially outdated information and behaviors and opening yourself up to new information that will inform effective decision-making and action.

The system for breaking outdated behavior and thinking is the Cycle of Unlearning, and these are the steps:

1 ▪ **Unlearn** the behaviors and mindsets that keep you and your business from moving forward.

2 ▪ **Relearn** new skills and strategies necessary for true transformation through safe experimentation.

3 ▪ **Breakthrough** old habits by opening up to new ideas and perspectives.

The key is to have the humility to recognize that what you are doing is not working. You'll know that it's time to unlearn when you're not achieving your desired outcomes or living up to the expectations you set for yourself. Or, perhaps you are avoiding certain challenges altogether. Fear of change or fear of failure is also a strong indicator for the need to unlearn.

The Cycle of Unlearning

Unlearn: Let Go of Past Success to Achieve Extraordinary Results by @BarryOReilly

Unlearn → Relearn → Breakthrough

Create Safety to Experiment

Once you recognize that it's time to unlearn, you need to create a safe space to relearn new behaviors and experiment to find the ones that will move you toward the outcomes you're aiming for.

Nobody likes to do things they suck at, especially in front of an audience. When you're an executive or leader, you're exposed—thousands of people are watching your every move—so, when you fall on your face, the pain is magnified.

We created ExecCamp as a safe place where executives and business leaders can challenge themselves, get outside their comfort zone, break existing models and behaviors, and experiment with new ones.

In essence, executives leave their companies for several weeks with the explicit goal of inventing a new business that will disrupt their existing one, and as a byproduct, they end up disrupting themselves.

Getting away from your day-to-day routine helps break the calcification of the environment that you're in. People tend to have automatic responses to familiar situations. They hear certain keywords or recognize familiar situations and respond almost autonomically. When you take people out of their environment it gives them a chance to reimagine new behaviors and experiment in a way in which it is safe to fail.

Unlearning Can Be Taught but Change Must Be Experienced

In traditional leadership education, we send leaders to these one-day innovation off-sites or week-long programs, push ideas onto them, and expect them to come back with changed behavior. We invest $365 billion a year in executive development, yet only one in four people say it has any impact on business outcomes. This form of leadership learning must be unlearned.

Change comes from experiencing the results of new, learned behaviors firsthand. And to learn something new, you need to be willing to unlearn what you already know.

We had the leadership team from one of the top airline groups in the world in one of our ExecCamps. Their senior leader was a 20-year veteran in the industry, a real expert. He had this idea for how they could transform their booking platform—all they needed to do was get the team back in the office to build it. They didn't know it at the time, but this was exactly the type of old behavior that they needed to unlearn: pushing their ideas onto the team as well as onto the market.

So, we built a prototype of the platform and shared it with actual customers. Guess what? The customers didn't get it. Sticking with old patterns, the exec said, "Must have been the wrong customers. Bring me the right customers." So, we brought in more customers. The same thing happened. We had to do this four times before the lead exec finally admitted that it wasn't the customers. His idea didn't work. This was his unlearning moment.

> In order to change, it's important to be curious. When you send someone off to solve a problem and they come back with a view contrary to your own, do you shut them down or ask them why?

He walked away understanding that pushing his own ideas was a personal blind spot; it may have worked for him in the past, but it wasn't working now. He had to go through the process of trying his tried-and-true behaviors before recognizing the fallacy in it. He also went on to be one of the best experimenters I've ever worked with—the experience reactivated his curiosity. He started to see his assumptions as hypotheses. And he realized what he needed was a system to rapid test his hypotheses as quickly and cheaply as possible—that system was the Cycle of Unlearning.

A few weeks after the ExecCamp, he sent me an email to report on what happened when one of his employees came to get him to sign off on a new product that they had built. His response to the employee was evidence of the breakthroughs this leader had experienced: "Why are you asking me to sign it off? You should get out of the office, go to the airport to find our customers, and test it with them. If we design and build it for them, get them to sign it off, not me."

How Can You Start Your Own Unlearning Journey

Not everyone is able to step away from their business for weeks or months at a time—although I highly recommend finding the time. In the meantime, here are some things you can do, and the mindset you should adopt, to begin your own successful unlearning journey:

REIGNITE YOUR CURIOSITY ■ In order to change, it's important to be curious. When you send someone off to solve a problem and they come back with a view contrary to your own, do you shut them down or ask them why? It's important to recognize that the outcome is not to be right but to find the right answers. By being curious and always asking, "Why did you take that approach?" or, "Interesting, tell me more…" you begin to view your beliefs as merely hypotheses to be tested. Then you can develop a system where you design experiments to test your assumptions, get new and better information, and find out what really works.

THINK BIG BUT START SMALL ■ People fear failure, but they really shouldn't. Failure is merely a signal that we're not on the right path and need to course correct. So, to make trying new things feel less risky, I tell clients to think big about what they want to unlearn, but start small as they relearn and experiment with lots of different behaviors. Starting small creates recoverable situations so when you make a mistake, you're not risking the farm. By tackling these small changes leading up to the "big thinking" outcome you're shooting for, you also create opportunities for people to feel success along the way.

TAKE OWNERSHIP OF THE PROBLEM ■ When things aren't going well and you're not achieving your desired outcomes, tell your team, "It's not you, it's me." And mean it. Transformation begins with you. If change isn't happening, you must hold yourself accountable rather than fall back on the all-too-common practice of blaming failure on circumstance or someone else.

BECOME A ROLE MODEL ■ You don't need to have all the answers. Many employees model the behaviors they witness in their leaders. When they see executives who are being vulnerable, curious, and open to experimentation, it becomes a very powerful accelerant throughout the entire company.

GET COMFORTABLE WITH BEING UNCOMFORTABLE ■ To truly transform, you're going to have to experiment with behaviors that are difficult or new for you. You will struggle at first. That may feel uncomfortable, but it's a discomfort you need to commit to if you want to succeed. By actively trying new things and putting yourself in situations where you are getting outside of your comfort zone, new opportunities and personal growth inevitably follow.

DON'T EVER STOP ■ Unlearning is hard work. Just when you feel like nothing is going to work, that's the time to accelerate your rate of experimentation and find the breakthrough you've been looking for. One of my favorite quotes from our ExecCamp participants came from Stephen Scott, chief digital officer at International Airlines Group—holding company for British Airways, Iberian, Vueling, and Aer Lingus. He said, "When 97 percent of people think that you should stop doing what you're doing and just revert back to what's comfortable—that's when the breakthrough journey really begins."

UNLEARNING IS A VIRTUOUS CYCLE OF CONTINUOUS SELF-DEVELOPMENT ■ One of the dangers of becoming an expert with 20+ years of experience is that your knowledge becomes an inhibitor for you to change. All your feedback mechanisms are telling you that you must be doing the right things because you've been elevated in the company to an executive or senior leadership position. But when you rely solely on past achievements you immediately put yourself at risk of outdated thinking and practices that will no longer work.

I have seen this method of unlearning, relearning, and breakthrough work time and again with business leaders at some of the largest companies in the world. But you don't unlearn once and then you're done. If you embark on this journey—and I hope you do—you will learn that unlearning is an ongoing, compounding, and virtuous system the more you use it.

As Alvin Toffler reminded us, "The illiterate of the twenty-first century will not be those who cannot read and write, but those who cannot learn, unlearn, and relearn." ▪

Barry O'Reilly is a business advisor, entrepreneur, and author who has pioneered the intersection of business model innovation, product development, organizational design, and culture transformation. Barry is author of two bestsellers, *Unlearn: Let Go of Past Success to Achieve Extraordinary Results* and *Lean Enterprise: How High Performance Organizations Innovate at Scale*—part of the Eric Ries series, and a HBR must-read for CEOs and business leaders. He writes for *The Economist*, and is faculty at Singularity University. His mission is to help purposeful, technology-led businesses innovate at scale. Read Barry's blog at: www.barryoreilly.com; follow him on Twitter: @barryoreilly.

References

O'Reilly, Barry. *Unlearn: Let Go of Past Success to Achieve Extraordinary Results*

Baron de Montesquieu, *Considerations on the Causes of the Greatness of the Romans and Their Decline* (1734).
    http://www.constitution.org/cm/ccgrd_l.htm

Hedberg, B. How organizations learn and unlearn. In P. C. Nystrom & W. H. Starbuck (Eds), *Handbook of organizational design*,
    Vol. 1. Oxford: Oxford University Press, 1981, pp. 3–27

Technology killing off corporate America: Average life span of companies under 20 years,
    https://www.cnbc.com/2017/08/24/technology-killing-off-corporations-average-lifespan-of-company-under-20-years.html

Why Leadership Training Fails and What You Can Do About It
    https://hbr.org/2016/10/why-leadership-training-fails-and-what-to-do-about-it

❝ 69% of hiring managers agree that adaptability is the most important soft skill❞

—*LinkedIn Global Recruiting Trends 2018*

A Foretaste of Tomorrow's Medicine

Naveen Jain

"What happens when we go down the evolutionary scale to the level of bacteria, viruses, and other microorganisms? Here we can harness life in its primitive forms, just as we once harnessed the horse. Today a new science based on this principle is rapidly emerging and it promises to change the very nature of industry as we know it."

When Alvin Toffler wrote those words 50 years ago, it was in the context of domesticating microorganisms for exploitation in the large-scale production of such things as vitamins, enzymes, antibiotics, and other compounds—and with a view that microorganisms would play an increasingly significant role in various forms of *manufacturing*. He speculated further that as pressures on food resources intensified, biologists would also soon cultivate microorganisms for use as food. Little did he, or anyone else at the time, imagine that the engine of that cultivation would not only be found in a biologist's lab or industrial shop, but in the human *gut*. Indeed, the human microbiome is a veritable factory, teeming with incredibly productive, life-sustaining microbiotic activity. Understanding this activity is the key to realizing a radical transformation of health—and an equally radical disruption of the healthcare system—in our not-too-distant future.

Nevertheless, Toffler is to be commended for his remarkable foresight. "Such developments," he continued, "will lead to vast new bio-engineering industries, chains of medical-electronic repair stations, new technical professions, *and a reorganization of the entire health system*. They will change life expectancy, shatter insurance company life tables, and bring about important shifts in the human outlook."

Let's think about this for a moment, because I believe this may be the single most important observation expressed in *Future Shock*. To fully appreciate Toffler's thoughts about the future of healthcare—and the true potential we have to reshape it *today*—it is helpful to understand a bit about its past. For example, what exactly it was that people used to die from, but don't any longer. This provides a remarkable insight, as well as a reason to believe something that might, at first blush, seem crazy.

At the time of this writing, just one person in the world who was born in the year 1900 remained alive; there's no one older, as far as we can tell. It's extraordinary, but should it be? According to the Centers for Disease Control and Prevention, Americans can expect to live, on average, just 78.8 years. Some, though, are more optimistic: if you can hang on until 2030, the World Health Organization says you might make it to 79.5. But is there really a hard stop on the human life span? It's possible that there is—if we leave nature to its own devices. But must we? Or, maybe nature knows something we don't, and we've simply corrupted some natural processes. Whatever the case, what we do know is that just as most people live far below their potential, they also die well before their time. And the reasons are clear. The most recent National Center for Health Statistics data, from 2014, reported the number of deaths in the US from all causes to be 2,712,630. Here's how the numbers break out for the top 15 causes:

- Heart disease: 633,842
- Cancers: 595,930
- Chronic lower respiratory diseases: 155,041
- Accidents: 146,571
- Stroke: 140,323
- Alzheimer's disease: 110,561
- Diabetes: 79,535
- Influenza and pneumonia: 57,062
- Kidney disease: 49,959
- Suicide: 44,193
- Septicemia (blood poisoning): 40,773
- Chronic liver disease and cirrhosis: 40,326
- Hypertension (high blood pressure): 32,200
- Parkinson's disease: 27,972
- Noninfectious pneumonitis: 19,803

No surprises here, right? But if you look at the leading causes of death a hundred or so years ago, it becomes equally clear that we're living in a very different world today. In 1900 the average life expectancy was just 47 years. People then were far more likely to die of diseases like tuberculosis, gastrointestinal infections, diphtheria, and other infectious diseases that have largely been eradicated. Today, most causes of death are what we have come to understand, ironically, as "age-related": The longer we live, the more likely we are to develop, for example, heart disease, cancer, or Alzheimer's.

In 1900, though, people died long before any of these diseases had a chance to manifest! But these comparisons don't clearly paint the picture. The world has come to suffer from a very different kind of epidemic in the form of *chronic* illnesses, and they take far more of us now. While infectious diseases have been declining globally for decades, chronic health problems are more than compensating—they are *by far* the leading cause of mortality in the world, representing nearly three-quarters of all deaths.

But while it's one thing to examine the causes of death, it's quite another to examine the causes that underlie the causes. We've learned quite a lot about this in recent years, so much so that we can ask the audacious question, "What if, in the future, we could make illness optional?" Maybe it's not as crazy as it sounds.

Current scientific literature clearly shows that chronic diseases, including Parkinson's, Alzheimer's, depression, anxiety, obesity, diabetes, auto-immune diseases, and even cancer, are caused by chronic inflammation. It turns out that these diseases are really just symptoms of a deeper underlying cause. Equally surprising is that the same research also establishes the key role played by the gut microbiome in contributing to, or controlling, inflammation. But here's the fundamental problem with the way healthcare is delivered today: most drug companies focus solely on suppressing the *symptoms* of chronic conditions rather than understanding and treating their root causes. In the prevailing pharma model, they want one drug for each condition. The fact is most drugs have an efficacy rate of only about 20 percent. In other words, 80 percent of patients taking the drug receive no benefit at all. Imagine selling a product that doesn't work for 80 percent of the customers, but is still being prescribed to people who are suffering!

> The healthcare system, then, is really a sickness system: it is inherently incentivized against the interests of the patient. Most people believe that the healthcare system is broken. It is not broken. It is doing exactly what it was designed to do: enrich its stakeholders.

At my company, Viome, we re-imagined this problem and decided to create one drug for each *person*, rather than one drug per disease. Our "drug" is nothing more than nutrition—food and supplements—which is easily personalized. (It's true that the gut works on the same principle as computing: garbage in, garbage out. In other words, diet matters. It turns out that Hippocrates, who lived around the 4th century BC, knew what he was talking about when he said, "Let food be thy medicine, and medicine be thy food.")

Viome focuses on analyzing each person's gut microbiome and modulating inflammation responses with precise and personalized nutrition to reduce its effects. Consistent with the findings of the scientific literature, people do indeed experience significant reduction, and even reversal, in chronic conditions. This promises an equally significant reduction in future healthcare costs, bringing us to another remarkable observation: In the US we spend nearly a *fifth* of our GDP on healthcare—more than $3.5 trillion. In 1970, however, the year *Future Shock* was published, healthcare spending was less than 7% of GDP (Figure 1).

Amazing, isn't it? And yet, while we pay more than twice *per capita* of other developed countries, our healthcare system delivers comparatively worse outcomes. In short, we're all getting screwed. Worse, the potential increase in life span is decidedly flattening out. Not much of a future.

Today, when the experts tell us that the average life span is about 80 years, we accept it like some universal law. When someone dies at that age, we accept that they've lived a good long life. We've become *conditioned* to believe it, and like so many other things connected to our mindset, it becomes a self-fulfilling prophecy. ("Normal" cholesterol in a society where it's "normal" to drop dead of a heart attack at 80 really should not be considered a good thing.)

We don't achieve more than we expect. The same can be said for our healthcare system. As such, entrepreneurs and other future-thinking people are presented with a massive opportunity to solve an equally massive problem. And you don't have to read between the lines to see that we're talking about disrupting the foundations of the healthcare ecosystem; it's just been illustrated that it's a big part of the problem. But first, we need to understand the lay of the land—the battlefield upon which this epic disruption will take place: the "medical-industrial complex."

First of all, the term "healthcare" is a misnomer. The healthcare industry is not concerned with health, it is concerned with illness. There is no profit in healthy patients in a system that has emerged to address symptoms and not their underlying causes. Treating symptoms leaves the underlying causes unaddressed; solve the root causes and the symptoms disappear.

The healthcare system, then, is really a *sickness* system: it is inherently incentivized against the interests of the patient. Most people believe that the healthcare system is broken. It is not broken. It is doing exactly what it was designed to do: enrich its stakeholders.

And we wonder why our medical costs are so high! But high medical costs are also a *symptom* of a problem. Again, our entire governmental, healthcare, and insurance infrastructures are focused on the business and practice of the treatment of the symptoms of illnesses. And the business of treating symptoms is one of the most profitable businesses on the planet. If advances in "fixing" the health-care system have proven elusive, it's by design. So, absent the kind of intervention we're proposing here, we can expect that line in the graph charting the increasing cost of healthcare to continue its journey up and to the right, where returns for the medical-industrial complex increase while relief for patients diminishes.

Today, the healthcare system itself has become an organism where the purpose of the organism is its own survival. The pharmaceutical companies believe the best drug they can develop is the drug to which you have a lifetime subscription. If a drug actually cures a condition, then it is not a good drug. The incentive is thus never to address the underlying condition, but to treat the symptoms. It is to their benefit that you remain sick. The same is true of hospitals and doctors; both need patients.

Figure 1

Total health expenditures as a percent of Gross Domestic Product 1970-2017

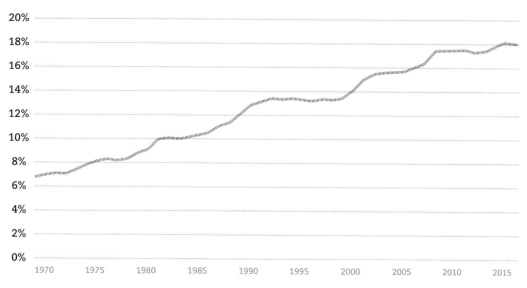

Source: KFF analysis of National Health Expenditure (NHE) data • Get the data • PNG / Peterson-Kaiser Health System Tracker

So let's bring this back around to the gut microbiome. What, exactly, is that? In short, it is a diverse ecological community of microorganisms that reside within the gastrointestinal tract. But that's not what's interesting about it. What if I told you that you really aren't what you think you are?

In human DNA, there are about 20,000 protein-coding genes. If that number seems impressive, note that the nematode worm has about 22,000. But get this: The microbes in your gut produce *millions* of genes! That's a lot of bioactivity that is not your own. Our bodies are really just containers for the *trillions* of microorganisms that live in and on us, including thousands of species of bacteria. These organisms live with us in a "commensal" relationship: We quite literally eat together at the same table. But the microbiome does more than that—it performs the heavy lifting in providing nourishment to our cells and enables the function of our metabolic and immune systems. And its role in our health has been largely overlooked until very recently.

It turns out that this "forgotten organ" is really the wellspring of our well-being—and, on the shadow side, the source of many of our diseases. We've now learned that Parkinson's, for example, begins in the gut, not in the brain as previously thought. Therefore, prevention must begin in the gut. Ninety percent of your serotonin is produced in the gut, so prevention and treatment of depression and anxiety must begin there. (Depression is now known to be linked to ongoing low-grade inflammation in the body.) Would you be surprised to learn that 70 percent of your body's immune cells live in your intestines? And that their interactions with the microbiota also living in the gut determine to a great extent how your immune cells behave? It's true that both your susceptibility to illness and your ability to fight it actually starts in your gut. It's not a great leap, then, to see that gut health must be an important key to a long and healthy life. Indeed, many conditions from allergies to autoimmune diseases are all related to the diversity of the microbiota. Moreover, the microbiome plays central roles in vitamin production, nutrient absorption, hunger, detoxification, and how we process and utilize carbohydrates and fat. (Toffler was on to something here!) And thanks to the gut-brain axis, it also affects mood, libido, and general outlook on life. It's remarkable, really. And we've only just found this out.

> If we are fundamentally healthy, then doctors can get back to the proper business of true health-care, which is treating acute conditions. It also means that their workload will be reduced by more than 70 percent—the amount of care currently consumed treating preventable chronic diseases.

The microbiome system is especially remarkable because the microbial cells we host greatly outnumber our "human" cells. We are, in fact, more bacteria than we are human! Because we are such composite creatures, a proper equilibrium between the human host and the microbiome is essential for good physiological function.

You'd think that the medical community would have picked up on this earlier. Every chronic disease, whether it is anxiety, depression, autism, Parkinson's, Alzheimer's, obesity, diabetes, cancer—*every one of these conditions*—is directly influenced by the microbiome. In research paper after research paper, we find the same conclusion: The condition of the microbiome is the key to human health.

But let's get back to why this matters in the context of disrupting the medical-industrial complex to usher in this radical vision for the future of healthcare. It matters because it means that if you can maintain good gut health, then that good gut health will help keep the rest of you healthy. If your gut microbiome is in dysbiosis, then you're at greater risk of developing the kinds of diseases caused by the chronic inflammation that inevitably results—the very conditions that we know to slash human life expectancy *at least* in half. It also matters because if we are fundamentally healthy, then doctors can get back to the proper business of true healthcare, which is treating *acute* conditions. It also means that their workload will be reduced by more than 70 percent—the amount of care currently consumed treating preventable chronic diseases. Finally, it means that the pharmaceutical industry's drug development pipeline will dry up, healthcare costs will plummet, and a good portion of that 20 percent of our GDP dedicated to healthcare can be put to far better use.

So how will we get there? A world free of illness is not something we can do in a year, or even 10 years. But there is much we can do now to get us moving in that direction. There are still many unknowns, still much research to do, and additional technologies needed that don't yet exist. But we know where this is headed.

Our bodies are biochemical entities. As such, they are more an *ecosystem* than a single organism—an ecosystem made up of microbial cells living in community with our own cells. When we're able to understand everything that is happening in this "community," we can indeed potentially create a world where chronic illness is optional. It's exciting to think that autoimmune diseases such as diabetes, rheumatoid arthritis, muscular dystrophy, multiple sclerosis, and fibromyalgia—all of which are associated with dysbiosis in the microbiome—can actually become things of the past. As Sherry Rogers said, "The road to health is paved with good intestines."

This essay is adapted from the book Moonshots—Creating a World of Abundance.

The founder of Moon Express, Viome, InfoSpace, Intelius, Bluedot, TalentWise, and other successful companies, **Naveen Jain** is an entrepreneur driven to solve the big problems facing today's world. Moon Express is the sole company in the world with permission to harvest resources from the moon—developing the infrastructure needed to push humanity forward towards a true multi-planetary society. Viome's goal is to "make illness optional." Having developed the world's largest database of microbial gene expression, Viome is able to analyze gut microbiome and identify predictive markers of chronic diseases to inform personalized nutrition to prevent and reverse chronic diseases. As a vice chairman of the board at Singularity University, Naveen is focused on educating and inspiring leaders to address humanity's greatest challenges by using and developing innovative technologies. A director of the board at the X PRIZE Foundation, Naveen uses incentive prizes to motivate competitors to find solutions to some of society's more challenging problems. Naveen has been the recipient of many honors for his entrepreneurial successes, including Ernst & Young Entrepreneur of the Year, Albert Einstein Technology Medal, Most Creative Person by *Fast Company*, Top 50 Philanthropists of 2018 by *Town & Country* magazine, Ellis Island Medal of Honor, Humanitarian Innovation Award at the United Nations "Top 20 Entrepreneurs" and "Lifetime Achievement Award" for leadership by Red Herring.

Before there was TED, there was Future Shock

Stephanie Mehta

Published in the summer of 1970, *Future Shock* wove together research and big hypotheses that had been floating around egghead academic and economics circles, and brought them to life through compelling storytelling and catchphrases.

Authors Alvin and Heidi Toffler were hardly the first to predict the decline of the traditional nuclear family, the increasingly fleeting nature of celebrity culture, the rise of drugs to address mental illness, and the artificial intelligence revolution. In fact, they often cited studies from other researchers. (Even "information overload," a term they popularized, was coined by a political science professor some six years before *Future Shock* hit bookstores.)

The Tofflers, however, were the first to pack all those ideas—and more—into a single, breezily written book. And they quickly became the most famous futurists of their time. World leaders such as Mikhail Gorbachev, the leader of the former Soviet Union, and Zhao Ziyang, China's prime minister, sought their counsel. They eventually formed an advisory firm, Toffler Associates, to advise businesses and governments on how to future-proof their organizations.

Future Shock paved the way for TED talks and documentaries such as *An Inconvenient Truth*. Like *Future Shock* (and the Tofflers' subsequent books, *The Third Wave* and *Powershift*) these formats take complex and sometimes wonky material, and make them digestible for mainstream audiences.

In the last 50 years, demand for speakers and thought leaders who can help us make sense of the world seems only to be growing, largely because of the complexity the Tofflers predicted. How might artificial intelligence impact humanity? What is the long-term impact of the decline in organized religion? What will the rise of megacities mean for the way resources are consumed? It is perhaps the ultimate irony that a new wave of "information overload" has created an appetite for more *Future Shock*-like content.

What *Future Shock* and its successors have done so well is provide readers—and viewers—with clear and concise points of view that still have a sheen of sophistication. Elites in the 1970s proudly brandished their copies of *Future Shock* in the same way business leaders today might casually mention a statistic or factoid they learned from a TED talk or a session at the World Economic Forum annual meeting in Davos.

> It is perhaps the ultimate irony that a new wave of "information overload" has created an appetite for more *Future Shock*-like content.

Indeed, if the Tofflers were alive today (Alvin died in 2016 at age 87, Heidi passed away in 2019 at age 89), they would likely be very much at home in Davos, advising current world leaders alongside a new generation of futurists, many of whom, like Parag Khanna, were inspired by *Future Shock*.

The Tofflers might have just as likely shown up at the Conservative Political Action Conference (CPAC) or given a talk at the Heritage Foundation, despite their history of leaning to the left. (As part of their research they worked on assembly lines, and Heidi became a union shop steward. Alvin worked at *Fortune* in the early 1960s, back when the magazine was known for employing liberal literary figures and artists; photographer Walker Evans was on staff at the time.)

Still, they forged a deep relationship with former House Speaker Newt Gingrich, who wrote the foreword to the Tofflers' *Creating a New Civilization: The Politics of the Third Wave*. While Gingrich was in Congress, he would bring the Tofflers to meetings of the Conservative Opportunity Society, a group within the House of Representatives. They worked with the Society, "brainstorming with us about how the world was changing, what it meant and how government should change," Gingrich wrote in a tribute to Toffler that ran in *Politico* in 2016.

Cynics might assume the Tofflers abandoned their principles to promote their books or stoke their consulting business, but their association with Gingrich, which grew into a deep friendship, was born out of curiosity and respect for the former Speaker's perspective. In a 1995 interview with Charlie Rose, Alvin Toffler described a recent holiday spent with Gingrich and his then-wife Marianne: "The thing that makes these visits charming is we don't agree on many things," he said. "We and the Gingriches will sit up all night long, arguing, hollering at each other, breaking out laughing, and so on and so forth. It's a great intellectual event to be able to just trade ideas with him."

Today, it seems hard to imagine ideological opposites spending holidays together and laughing over differences, until one considers that the Tofflers' most enduring works transcend politics. In *Future Shock,* the Tofflers showed that their "ideology" was the fostering of ideas themselves. ▪

Stephanie Mehta is editor-in-chief of *Fast Company*, overseeing its print, digital, and live journalism. She previously served as a deputy editor at *Vanity Fair*, where she edited feature stories and coedited the annual New Establishment ranking. She also curated the invitation-only New Establishment Summit and Founders Fair conference for women entrepreneurs, which she launched in 2017. She has worked as a writer and editor at *Bloomberg Media*, *Fortune*, and *The Wall Street Journal*. Mehta began her career as a business reporter at *The Virginian-Pilot* in Norfolk, Virginia.

The Future
as a Design Space

Joel Garreau

If you're the sort of person who thinks anyone claiming to have a crystal ball is a huckster, you may be allergic to some who describe themselves as "futurists." But one definition of a "real futurist" might be: "Somebody who's stuff looks better the older it gets." In such an enlightened dictionary, Alvin and Heidi Toffler's pictures would appear prominently.

Even before Carver Mead spawned the phrase "Moore's Law," the Tofflers were broadcasting the news of accelerating change as predetermined and an "elemental force."[1] They made a respectable endeavor out of thinking systematically and rationally about rapid transformations, unanticipated consequences, and nonlinear weirdness. That is to say, reality as it has actually been experienced over the last half-century. If reviewers shorthanded them with the "futurist" label, at least the Tofflers came by it honorably. *Future Shock* does indeed look remarkably good, even 50 years out.

It's all in there: predicted feelings of loss of control and reactive revulsion against purported intelligence and even science, how little we actually knew about adaptability, the significance of nostalgia. Then there is their immortal: "The future always comes too fast and in the wrong order."[2] It's hard to remember that it was once rare, while making personal decisions in the present, to think about the future.

Equally remarkable was their methodology. Alvin was a proudly lackluster student who became an associate editor of *Fortune*[3]. He demonstrated that quality journalism's professional techniques—especially silo-busting, pattern-seeking, connect-the-dots-wherever-you-find-them, and relentless gum-shoe interviewing of real people—could blow away the achievements of, oh, some PhD anthropologists. Other forward-thinking world-shapers of the Tofflers' era who similarly flouted the credentials-obsessed norms of the time include the urbanist Lewis Mumford and social critic and urbanist Jane Jacobs. Mumford never earned a degree of any kind and worked for *The New Yorker*[4]. Yet, academics now embrace his work as that of an historian, sociologist, and philosopher of technology. Jane Jacobs—who also never earned a degree—got her start on the women's page of the *Scranton Times-Tribune*. After moving to New York, she freelanced to the *Sunday Herald Tribune*, *Cue* magazine, and *Vogue*.[5]

To be sure, *Future Shock*'s 1970 index reveals the Tofflers' lack of omniscience. It has nothing, for example, about the then-named[6] Advanced Research Projects Agency, which in 1970 was already adding nodes to the ARPANET at the rate of one a month.[7] So much for "futurism" anticipating the internet.

But the gear wasn't really the Tofflers' game. They focused on the humans. They drilled deep on values, and how humans could and should adapt. Even before the first Earth Day they presciently wrote, "The individual needs to be seen as part of a total system." They recognized that approach as "human ecology."[8]

Focusing on the humans was a smart move. It's why *Future Shock* is worth returning to half a century later.

> They made a respectable endeavor out of thinking systematically and rationally about rapid transformations, unanticipated consequences, and nonlinear weirdness. That is to say, reality as it has actually been experienced over the last half-century.

I try to stay riveted on that lesson—it's about the humans—in my current audacious scheme at Arizona State University, *The Guide Project: How to Design the Future*.[9]

The notion driving *The Guide Project* is that humans have been shaping the future since fire. What's new is the number of organizations treating the human future as a design space—with good outcomes. That's an inflection point in history. For millennia people have viewed the future as something that happens to them. They're just along for the ride. Now we have existence proof. We can steer!

The Guide Project aims to connect functional, hard-headed communities of practice with a track record of designing the future. We uncover the "pattern language"[10] of these seasoned practitioners, revealing the hundreds of battle-tested, shippable, scalable methods by which they've succeeded. Call it the revenge of Steve Jobs, if you like.

Next steps for this Guide Network: Get closer and closer to experience-based reality by adding, subtracting, dividing, honing, polishing, and being inspired by their pioneering efforts. Symphonize the rapidly growing wisdom, experience, and best practices of these communities achieving success practically.

We aim to accelerate novel, ambitious ways to imagine—and then create—human futures in which we can thrive. *The Guidebook*, however, is just the start. As our colleague Brad Allenby says, "The missing element is teaching 'Designing Complex Adaptive Systems While Being Part of Them.' You need someone who is humble enough to know how daunting this is, and yet strong enough to operate outside the boundaries of the usual domains."

The aim is for highly imaginative people to rapidly scale up to a functional, global movement treating the future as a design space.

Plus, a few dreams on very large scales: Like accelerating "novel, audacious ways to imagine—and then create—a human future in which we can thrive."

The Guide Project is a systematic, rational way of approaching the future in pragmatic, testable ways. It focuses on humans who every day plow these fields and get their hands dirty, like the Tofflers. The goal is to research and collect the broad pattern language common to everyone like them.

If that's what you want to call futurism, then fine.

Of course, if getting one's hands dirty is the test, well, my second favorite possible definition of a "real futurist" is: "Somebody who plants oak trees." ■

Joel **Garreau** is Professor of Culture, Values and Emerging Technology at Arizona State University. He served long-time as a member of the pioneering scenario-planning enterprise Global Business Network. He helped create the "world" for Steven Spielberg's *Minority Report*. For his future-forward culture-and-values work as a reporter for *The Washington Post*, he was nominated for the Pulitzer seven times. He is the author of several books, most recently *Radical Evolution: The Promise and Peril of Enhancing Our Minds, Our Bodies – And What It Means to Be Human* (Doubleday). Like Bill Gates and Steve Jobs, he does not have a degree in anything.

1. Pages 3-4 of the 1970 edition.

2   Page 4.

3   https://en.wikipedia.org/wiki/Alvin_Toffler

4   https://en.wikipedia.org/wiki/Lewis_Mumford?fbclid=IwAR2PimuTVYfbJAziCGffNPz2Neel6Yz6ZXXPUYK7vMJritK1lB4WGnfLNtE

5   https://en.wikipedia.org/wiki/Jane_Jacobs

6   https://www.darpa.mil/about-us/timeline/arpa-name-change

7   https://www.computerhistory.org/internethistory/1970s/

8   Page 291.

9   https://howtodesignthefuture.asu.edu/

10 https://howtodesignthefuture.asu.edu/pattern-language

The Olden Days

Erik Qualman

When we sit down with our great-grandchildren fifty years from now, they will be as wide-eyed and bewildered as our grandparents were when Alvin Toffler's *Future Shock* was released in 1970. It will be difficult for them to grasp such incredulous impossibilities that defined the era in which we lived. In fact, it will be challenging for them to comprehend how one could live without the "basics" for living in 2070. The conversation will closely resemble this:

Great-Grandma & Grandad (GG), you were born before the internet existed? What in the world did you do? How did you learn anything? Where did you go for answers?

GG, explain to me again why there used to be so many wars over this thing called "oil." Automobiles really ran on gas from this oil? They did not run on electricity? The top countries worried about the Middle East? The major wars were really fought over oil and not water? Free water was everywhere?

GG, tell me again, how many people were dying each year from cancer? It must have been an awful time to live before the medical revolution cured this disease and so many of the other maladies you mentioned, like Alzheimer's. Scientists and doctors weren't sharing their data and findings back then? Did it really cost so much money for basic healthcare? People would really just "live in pain" rather than get the problem fixed the same day?

GG, people used to just walk in shoes? They didn't have gliders to put on their feet? That must have been so slow and painful to get anywhere. No wonder everyone developed bunions and had foot issues. It was like they were wearing simple sandals just like the Romans. Why couldn't anyone see there was a better way?

GG, it seems to me, based on your description of this thing called fast food, that you lived at a time when the food was artificial, but intelligence wasn't. I can't believe the "food" you put into your bodies. No wonder everyone lived to be only 80. They even still allowed you to smoke? Didn't it smell everywhere?

GG, so, you are saying that not everyone had their own digital assistant to help them handle day-to-day items? That only the very rich and privileged had a personal assistant, and it was a real person?

GG, there were actual artists and actors before the artificial intelligence revolution? It was a vocation?

GG, air travel sounds awful! And the planes had tiny windows instead of being all glass?

GG, you really couldn't have conversations with people once they were dead? That must have been so sad when your mother died and you could no longer get advice from her like we can now—virtual conversations with the deceased.

GG, many of the trees around the world were being slaughtered so that everything could be written on paper? The Amazon rainforest was being destroyed to get natural resources? Why didn't anyone stop this?

GG, this might be the craziest thing you have ever told me. People actually were in charge of driving and you owned your own automobiles? What a danger! What a waste of valuable time!

> Scientists and doctors weren't sharing their data and findings back then? Did it really cost so much money for basic healthcare? People would really just "live in pain" rather than get the problem fixed the same day?

GG, people sat around watching a thing called television? They literally just sat there, watching? It wasn't interactive? They didn't move for hours while watching? That sounds incredibly boring and a waste of time.

GG, Fantasy Days didn't exist? People couldn't put in their contact lenses for a day to go into their own fantasy world? Without Fantasy Days how in the world did people unwind? Was everyone just super stressed all the time? Also, weren't they bored living only their own daily life all the time? Or, were many of them always working help keep them distracted from life? It would be difficult for me to imagine not being able to take days off to be my super self. I live for my Fantasy Days; they help keep me sane.

GG, the American football thing you described actually sounds pretty cool, but also very disturbing and dangerous. No wonder its popularity slipped and eventually nobody allowed their children to play it before it was permanently banned.

GG, you're saying that athletes were more famous and popular than e-sports players and video gamers? That's truly hard to believe.

GG, you had to manually search for things on the internet on a thing called a search engine? You didn't have a digital personal assistant simply finding and getting stuff on your behalf? Man, that sounds like a waste of time!

GG, most people attended a college or university for four years and paid hundreds of thousands of dollars?! That's what people called higher education?

GG, India wasn't the #1 super power?

GG, people were really scared of artificial intelligence? Why were they worried about their manual labor jobs going away? How could they think they were fun? They didn't understand that they would have plenty of food and shelter and no longer have to work at these dangerous jobs? You actually worked 50 hours per week? Why? Who made up the rule that you had to work five days per week, and all in the same location? It seems an odd thing to mandate. Why would everyone agree to this way of life?

GG, why did everyone want to go to Mars? They didn't realize there was nothing there?

GG, white men held most of the CEO positions?! Now, that's the craziest thing you have told us yet about the olden times!

Great-Grandma and Great-Grandad, we love you. We have no idea how in the world you survived such a struggle. We are just so happy and lucky that we live in the best time ever and don't have to go through the difficult and antiquated times you had to endure. ▪

Erik Qualman is a #1 bestselling author of five books and a keynote speaker who has performed in 54 countries. He was voted the 2nd Most Likeable Author in the World behind Harry Potter's JK Rowling. He is also the founder and owner of the animation studio Equalman Studios.

The Antidote to Future Shock

Ignacio Peña

> 66 Where there is no vision,
> the people perish. 99
> —Proverbs 29:18

write from Argentina, a country that is as far as you can go in the Western Hemisphere from where Alvin and Heidi Toffler wrote their book fifty years ago. ▪ It was here, when I was a university student, that I devoured books written by the Tofflers. *Future Shock* was already twenty years old when I first read it, but it was still futuristic, insightful, and relevant, as it remains in many ways. The book touched me profoundly because it opened my eyes to a future of new opportunities and unimagined challenges that required anticipation. Fast-forward thirty years to today, and I am dedicated to catalyzing a better future by helping society to surf the technology tsunami.

As the Tofflers anticipated, the technology revolution is accelerating and humanity is having difficulty coping because the pace of change is faster than most people can manage. On top of that, we face colossal challenges, such as massive global debt, aging populations, climate change, and ecosystem degradation, that will negatively impact global economic growth. In many ways, the world is better than it has ever been, but, unless we act, the transition to the new world order will be far more difficult than it needs to be, particularly for the hundreds of millions of people without the capabilities to succeed in coming decades and those most vulnerable to climate change.

People everywhere are concerned about their future in this fast-changing world. Some individuals, organizations, and nations are charging ahead and boldly leaping into the future, but others are shocked and looking for ways to turn the clock back. Frustration and fear are mounting and those who feel most vulnerable and left behind are voting from anger, giving rise to populism, fragmentation, trade wars, and geopolitical tensions that threaten global governance.

The world needs an antidote to future shock. We need to create a bold, human-centered vision for the future that provides hope and empowers people to overcome fear. Conventional solutions are unlikely to be sufficient. We need to transform education, strengthen safety nets, and stimulate growth and job creation through entrepreneurship. But even combined, these approaches may be too slow, incremental, and unscalable, considering the size and pace of the challenge ahead. Creating a sufficient number of quality jobs for uneducated people and improving people's lives simply through economic growth may not be viable in a relevant time frame. The magnitude of the challenge calls for radical global solutions and out-of-the-box thinking.

Empathy and hope are potent healers for future shock. We need a vision worth fighting for. Looking for a cave to hide in is not the solution. Connecting with the suffering of others and directing our energy to serve the vulnerable can help us emerge from fear to pursue a life of heroic leadership.

Humanity needs AIR: a future of Abundance, Inclusion, and Regeneration. Delivering AIR is achievable. We can use the power of technology to activate new engines of economic growth. We can eradicate poverty by democratizing access to basic needs through disruptive innovations. We can heal the environment and turn back the clock of environmental destruction. To unlock this vision we need bold innovators, purpose-driven organizations, and enlightened policies.

We have a hundred trillion dollar opportunity before us. Exponential technologies enable us to achieve massive productivity improvements across most sectors of the global economy, unlocking new avenues for economic growth. In food, cultured meat and digitally-optimized hydroponics consume 10-100x less land and generate up to 25x less greenhouse emissions than conventional approaches. In telecommunications, 5G enables 10-100x greater speeds, and constellations of thousands of low-Earth orbit satellites such as Skylink can provide high-speed internet to all points on the planet. In construction, 3D-printed houses can build homes that are 10x cheaper and take more than 10x less time to produce than traditional techniques. Autonomous taxis will enable a 10x lower transportation cost than today's traditional taxis through higher utilization rates combined with lower energy, labor, and maintenance costs. Mobile finance solutions can be 10x cheaper and more convenient than traditional finance, enabling greater coverage and convenience. In energy, compact nuclear fusion is closer than we think and can push humanity into a new era of abundance.

> "Empathy and hope are potent healers for future shock. We need a vision worth fighting for. Looking for a cave to hide in is not the solution. Connecting with the suffering of others and directing our energy to serve the vulnerable can help us emerge from fear to pursue a life of heroic leadership.

Emerging countries can leverage new technologies to leapfrog into the future. In a recent study for the InterAmerican Bank of Development I identified ten engines of growth that can boost GDP growth in emerging countries in the coming decade. They include areas such as e-commerce, digital finance, creative services, the digital bioeconomy, renewable energy, electric and autonomous mobility, and advanced manufacturing. Some emerging countries are already leading the word in some of these opportunity spaces, such as Kenya in digital payments, India in digital services, and China in electric cars and batteries.

But not everyone is well-positioned to surf the technology tsunami and, as Pope Francis said, the only future worth building is the one that includes everyone. So we should complement the invisible hand of the market with empathy and a healthy instinct of self-preservation. We should put the most vulnerable segments of the population first and create solutions that address their needs directly rather than rely purely on trickle-down economics.

We can unleash a wave of exponential inclusion by catalyzing solutions that make basic needs ultra-affordable and enable families and small communities to become more self-reliant. We can lower the poverty line and make stable incomes from jobs less critical. We can boost global resiliency with a combination of new tools, disruptive business models, and illuminated policies. We can put the brightest minds to solving the problems of the most vulnerable.

There are many examples of radically more affordable solutions to basic needs. Low-cost mobile payments are democratizing financial services in Africa, China, and now Latin America. The world's first 3D-printed community is being built in El Salvador, with large savings in time and cost. Start-ups in Central America and Africa are bringing cheap electricity—light!—to the poorest segments of their populations with distributed solar and lithium battery solutions. Others are creating low-cost scalable solutions to enable children to learn basic reading, writing, and arithmetic skills.

> The world needs an "inclusion moonshot"— a bold global initiative to prepare the most vulnerable to thrive in an age of accelerated transformations. A well-funded multi-year effort along the lines of the Human Genome Project, the Space Station, or the Brain Initiative.

There is much that can and should be done by the private sector and civil society, but governments have a central role to play and should step up to the plate. Income polarization is likely to increase as we move deeper into a digital society, with its winner-takes-most dynamics. Innovation and the diffusion of new technologies are accelerating, but we are going to have ever increasing inequality if the speed of innovation is faster than the speed of adaptation, and if jobs disappear before they become less critical to meet basic needs. It is very dangerous to rely on trickle-down dynamics.

The world needs an "inclusion moonshot"—a bold global initiative to prepare the most vulnerable to thrive in an age of accelerated transformations. A well-funded multi-year effort along the lines of the Human Genome Project, the Space Station, or the Brain Initiative. I designed the proposal for such an initiative last year under the auspices of the Argentine Council of Foreign Affairs and the Konrad Adenauer in preparation for the G20 Summit in Buenos Aires. Unfortunately, world leaders were too preoccupied with other matters at the summit, possibly somewhat future shocked themselves. The need and the opportunity remain.

An inclusion moonshot could include a powerful set of lean, distributed, opt-in programs. A global network of DARPA-like agencies led by ultra-talented teams could catalyze radical innovations that make basic necessities at least ten times cheaper than they are today. The equivalent of Nobel Prizes for inclusion in areas such as food, health, and education could reward and provide visibility to those who create solutions that touch the lives at the base of the pyramid. The Abundance Games or the Olympic Games of Innovation, a concept I developed as Bold Innovator at XPRIZE, could inspire, mobilize, and support hundreds of thousands of innovators from around the world to create solutions that democratize access to basic needs. An inclusion fund could provide matching funds to boost high-potential R&D projects and startups. A new I20 linked to the G20 and focused on global inclusion could convene key players in the ecosystem to share insights and best practices. An inclusion observatory could track key metrics and create open knowledge depositories. The Global Peace Corps could mobilize youth around the world to serve the most vulnerable and renew the notion that everyone has a responsibility toward those in need.

What might the future look like after the inclusion moonshot? Imagine AI-powered smartphone apps that are capable of coaching subsistence farmers to rise out of poverty by growing an abundance of food in small plots of land with resilient techniques such as permaculture. Imagine intelligent swarms of robots that design and build ultra-affordable houses that are made with biomaterials and equipped with devices that provide energy self-sufficiency and water drawn out of thin air. Imagine the entire K12 education curriculum, including videos, textbooks, teaching materials, tests, and learning platforms, designed and taught by the best educators in the world and made available to all students, for free, as personalized educational journeys. Or, imagine handheld devices capable of diagnosing with high precision and negligible cost all common diseases.

Finally, we need to stop destroying, and rather heal, the planet. We can further accelerate the development and adoption of clean energy, batteries, and electric cars to put a stop to carbon emissions. We can boost the development of compact nuclear fusion to produce the energy we need to decarbonize the atmosphere. We can capture CO_2 from the air to produce building materials and replace petrochemicals. We can stop deforestation for cattle raising, replacing it with alternative proteins and cultured meat. We can work to restore reefs with land-based coral farming. We can harvest plastic from the oceans.

Heidi Toffler once said, "So far we've proven incapable of designing the systems that prepare us for change." Let's change that!

We can heal the world of future shock through the powers of empathy and innovation. We can move whole populations from anxiety to hope. We can create together the tools and communities to empower the weakest to thrive and to rise into an era of shared and sustainable abundance. Humanity's best times can be ahead of us, but it depends on us.

Ignacio Peña is a strategist, an investor, an international speaker, and a strategic advisor to senior leaders, startups, corporations and governments. He is the founder and CEO of Surfing Tsunamis, a catalyst of abundance, inclusion, and regeneration through high-impact initiatives and transformational innovation. Ignacio is a lecturer at the Wharton School and faculty at Singularity University, and was Bold Innovator at XPRIZE. Previously, he was Partner and Managing Director of the Boston Consulting Group. He holds an MSc in Economics from UCA, an MBA from the Wharton School, and an MA in international studies from the University of Pennsylvania.

The Second Space Age

Paul Stimers

W hen *Future Shock* appeared in 1970, we had just landed on the moon. ■ Today, those moon landings are still closer to the present than they are to the Wright brothers' first powered flight in 1903. Orville Wright and the Tofflers shared this planet for 20 years, and the Tofflers lived long enough to see the beginnings of the second space age—the transition from exploration to expansion. It is incredible to think that we have come all this way in less than two lifetimes.

■ ■ ■

I grew up in the Northwest. We spent a lot of time learning about Lewis and Clark—about how they bravely explored the Louisiana Purchase and beyond to the Pacific, carefully mapping and cataloging as they went, about the hardships they endured, their reliance on native guides like Sacajawea, and the value of the knowledge they brought back with them. The exploratory spirit that their expedition represents is very much a part of who we are.

But if the United States had merely explored this territory, I would have grown up speaking Russian. As important as they were, Lewis and Clark were not all we needed to turn the West into the American West. We needed the Oregon Trail and the wagon trains, the Gold Rush, and the Homestead Act. We needed not just exploration, but expansion—not just a hardy band of elite explorers on a

210

mission, but a flood of ordinary people following their own dreams and seeking their own fortunes.

We are at an inflection point in human spaceflight. Until recently, space had been the exclusive province of governments and government astronauts, conducting government missions of exploration and national defense. Now, a new era is underway—one in which citizens, acting in the private sector and for their own reasons, can go to space too. We are moving from a period of exploring space to a period of expanding into space. Like the pioneers before us, we are poised to tame a vast wilderness, using its resources to promote human advancement.

We have reached this point thanks to the combined effect of advances in several different technological areas operating in concert. We use new materials like composites, alloys, and ceramics. We combine them with new processes like additive manufacturing. We use unfathomably powerful computers to design and control our rockets. Technology has matured in each of these areas, along with progress elsewhere. And the systems that take advantage of the sum of this progress have advanced most rapidly.

The increasing disposability of modern life is a major *Future Shock* trend. Ironically, one of the innovations that has made the next leap in space technology possible runs counter to this trend. Until recently, rockets had always been single-use items; now, thanks to advanced materials, manufacturing, and computer guidance, we are finally able to reuse them. Of course, reusing rockets

> We are moving from a period of exploring space to a period of expanding into space. Like the pioneers before us, we are poised to tame a vast wilderness, using its resources to promote human advancement.

dramatically lowers the cost of access to space—imagine how rare air travel would be if each plane could only be used once! The result is greater access to space, greater mobility, and a smaller, more interconnected, and more rapidly changing world. So the Tofflers were right after all.

We are on the cusp of mining metals, water, and other resources in space. This unlocks inconceivably large reserves of materials that have extensive uses on Earth. The precious platinum group metals, which we use as catalysts, in displays, and for medicine, are abundant in asteroids, and we mine them on Earth from places where asteroids have struck the planet. We have identified asteroids with platinum group deposits whose market values are estimated in the trillions of dollars.

3D printing is transforming manufacturing on Earth, and the space industry is among the most deeply affected. Exquisitely complex components that could not be made before are now standard for new rocket engines, for example. But 3D printing is also transforming space exploration. The International Space Station is now printing parts, tools, and medical supplies on-demand. Future exploration missions will take 3D printers and feedstocks so their crews can make whatever they happen to need. A 3D printer changes *Apollo 13* and *The Martian* from edge-of-your-seat blockbusters to rather dull short films. In space, with lives at stake, dull is good.

Recently, a senior NASA official—an engineer by training—received a briefing on an imminent variation of this capability: 3D printing and assembly in the vacuum of space itself. Midway through, he leaned back in his chair, gazed off into space as if the ceiling of the NASA conference room weren't even there, and said, "We're going to have to redesign every one of our spacecraft." The ability to build a spacecraft in space means freedom from the constraints of launch—of the size of the rocket fairing, the pressures, temperatures, and vibrations of acceleration to 17,500 mph, the crush of gravity. Suddenly, large, delicate structures that could only exist in space become possible. This unlocks tremendous capabilities, from power generation to communications and beyond.

But wait, there's more: combine 3D printing in space with mining resources in space, and you get the ability not just to build structures in space, but to build arbitrarily large structures in space. Do you want to go to Mars in a vessel the size of a football stadium? Do you want to live, work, and be shielded from cosmic radiation within the mile-thick walls of an immense, hollowed-out asteroid? The interplay of these technologies creates amazing opportunities. Fifty years ago, science fiction authors dreamed this could be possible. Today, engineers are working on it. Fifty years from now, what gigantic structures will we pilot through the heavens?

If these possibilities are measured on a grand scale, the goals of the billionaires driving the commercial spaceflight revolution are grander still. They want to democratize spaceflight. They want to make humanity a multiplanetary species to help ensure our survival. They want to move heavy industry off of Earth and have millions of people living and working in space. They want to end scarcity—to end poverty on Earth and replace it with abundance. Are these goals achievable, or are they astronomically sized hubris? It is too early to tell, but the people who have bet on these visionaries before have done better than those who have bet against them.

Future Shock addressed not just technological changes but their impact on who we are as individuals and as a society. How will we adapt to these new capabilities? Will humanity's expansion into space be guided by liberal democratic or authoritarian norms? From the Apollo 11 moon landing—"we came in peace for all mankind"—to the International Space Station, where a multinational crew has lived continuously since November 2000, our history in space affords ample opportunities for optimism. But beyond these acts of will are the great forces that will shape our activities in this period of expansion: free thought, free enterprise, and the ability to seek one's fortune without having to ask permission. We have an opportunity to construct a legal regime that promotes this approach, but if we fall behind authoritarian competitors, the law of space may end up being at odds with freedom and plurality.

Humanity has always needed a frontier—a place where people can explore, seek their fortunes, and escape, to some degree, the teeming crowds, the strangling rules, the whirling disconnectedness of "civilization." *Future Shock* described the ocean as such a frontier, and it remains so today—but the ocean is finite. Space is an inexhaustible frontier. Frontier life is hard, but the brutal immediacy of its life-and-death stakes forces pioneers to be resourceful, innovative, and industrious—some of humanity's best qualities. *Future Shock* demonstrated that rapid, revolutionary change is underway, and that we find it difficult to adapt—but the benefits that await us in this have positive and transformative potential. ■

Paul Stimers is a partner in the public policy and law practice of K&L Gates LLP, a global law firm. Based in Washington, DC, he focuses his policy advocacy efforts on matters related to commercial spaceflight and other emerging technologies. He serves as policy counsel to several major commercial spaceflight companies and the leading industry association for commercial spaceflight, assisting them in pursuing legislation and representing their interests before Congress and federal agencies. He holds a BA from the University of Washington, an MPA from Harvard's Kennedy School of Government, and a JD from Harvard Law School. Learn more at http://www.klgates.com/r-paul-stimers/

s History, History?
And What Does That Mean
For The Future?

Tanya Accone

Toffler positioned "the grand perspec-
tives of history" as something of a common touchstone from which
to understand and engage with accelerating change. ▪ Many of his strik-
ingly prescient forecasts were informed by identifying patterns in the past and drawing insights
from the resulting interconnected trends. But the drivers of change that shocked the future for the
past 50 years also affected history, so what does that mean for our understanding of the future?

History has always been contested, but in the past, education, technology, and power structures
restricted the number of people who could participate in the recording of it and who controlled
information and its distribution. With limited narratives and sources, history could function as an
integrative mechanism in society, providing a common framing of the past and a frame of reference
for the present and the future.

Enter the internet and Wikipedia. Evolving and dynamic, it is a good example of Toffler's adhocracy organizational model. Collaborative platforms like this have democratized the process of
recording history, allowing millions to share their perspectives and contest those of others. The result is a cacophony of narratives, allowing many more people to participate in a more transparent
process of contouring the truth. This invaluable gain in diversity is much closer to the complexity

> By extrapolation, facts, information, knowledge, and history could become increasingly perishable, and the current catchphrase, "a post-fact society" may live up to that moniker.

of reality and can inform a more nuanced understanding of the future.

For far too many, Wikipedia feels as out of reach as a Guttenberg Bible to an illiterate peasant in the 1400s. Without access, they can't even consume the content, let alone contribute to it. Only half of the world's population has internet access[1], leaving some 29 percent of young people aged 15 to 24 (around 346 million) disconnected. The lack of access is itself unequal; 60 percent of young people in Africa are not online, compared with 4 percent of those in Europe. And, there is a significant gender digital divide, with males outnumbering females almost everywhere[2], including in Wikipedia contributors.[3] On the other hand, the costs of connectivity continue to drop, with a proliferation of new technologies to provide it, from loitering drones to balloons and arrays of mini-satellites.

The digital world is likely to persist over the next decades, and people who are not connected to it will be deprived of opportunities to participate, communicate, learn, and work. My work involves understanding the alternate futures that trends like this can mean for children and young people, and seeing how innovation and other strategies can work toward realizing a preferred future that is inclusive and equal. Toward achieving this, we create platforms and partnerships to provide free access to life-impacting information for young people and their communities, apply data science to better understand information poverty, and advocate for policies and business models that don't leave half the world disconnected.

No Vaccine against False Information

Getting connected opens up a universe of opportunity, and peril. Unlike Wikipedia, most content on the internet is not vetted and validated. You can Google your way to millions of search results or use the world's second largest search engine, YouTube, to find results you can watch, with little idea of whether what appears to be an accurate historical record actually is. While bad information may be the least of the risks that threaten the safety of children online, challenges to our ability to discern what is authentic fundamentally impact our understanding of the world and the future.

History has been remade into rich, visual, immersive, and entertaining experience economy products like movies, video games, 3D, and virtual reality simulations. We can experience eras like ancient Rome, the Renaissance, and the Wild West, and a wide variety of wars, through tweaked plots with facts selected for their dramatic value. Interesting hybrids are emerging, like the film *They Shall Not Grow Old*, which was created using original World War I footage that was transformed and colorized, with added sound effects and actors voicing constructed dialogue.

This is nothing compared to what can be achieved using increasingly affordable[4], but not necessarily easily detectable, deepfakes. The quality of deepfakes is highly convincing and believable, and is improving. Creating deepfakes is a technique for synthesizing a sophisticated human image by applying artificial intelligence to combine and superimpose existing audio, images, and videos to create new ones that can depict people, situations or events that never existed or occurred in reality. A single image of anyone may be all that is needed to create an entire video[5]. The technology has already been applied to reinvent history, such as audio of President John F. Kennedy giving the speech he was to deliver on the day he was assassinated, and reanimations of various historical figures such as Adolf Hilter, Martin Luther King Jr., and Barack Obama.

Predictions have been made that it is only a matter of time before overwhelming amounts of false evidence provided by fabricated images, videos, and audio content become widely available, raising concerns that widespread social unrest and the erosion of trust will result. This possible future sounds a lot like George Orwell's *Nineteen Eighty-Four* dystopia brought to life, complete with "doublethink" and "newspeak" through the "telescreen."

What happens to facts, information, knowledge, and history when seeing is no longer believing, and we literally cannot trust our senses anymore? Toffler conceived of information becoming kinetic in this manner, and in the space of half a century we have witnessed the shift to information becoming not only hyperkinetic, but also ephemeral. By extrapolation, facts, information, knowledge, and history could become increasingly perishable, and the current catchphrase, "a post-fact society" may live up to that moniker.

But you don't need a deepfake to achieve social disruption, as the anti-vax movement has proven. Platforms from social media to the dark web provide mechanisms for efficiently disseminating content at an unprecedented scale, volume, and targeting precision. These platforms accommodate a myriad of diverse interests and enclaves, fostering an atomized virtual society of many different tribes. These disconnected digital echo chambers bridge the real and virtual worlds, and could lead to a possible future of a splintered society with issue cohesion at the cost of social cohesion. Each tribe could remake reality to their worldview, complete with convincing fabricated historical evidence that supports it. In these pockets, neither the moon landing nor the Holocaust will have happened.

Mindful of these very real threats, my view of the future is a different one, of a new generation of canny users equipped to successfully navigate an infinitely rich and diverse universe of content and perspectives. There is no vaccine against false information, so we need to raise smart information consumers with critical thinking and literacy of all kinds—media, digital, visual, and financial, in addition to reading and numeracy. Globally, literacy among youth (15-24) increased from 83 percent to 91 percent over the past two decades, still leaving 115 million young people in the world who cannot read, 59 percent of them young women[6].

We're building toward a future of shrewder users, by scaling up experiential learning through social innovation that builds these 21st-century skills, experimenting with how virtual reality and augmented reality can be used for learning, and supporting real-time information platforms that connect educators and young people. In addition, we're strengthening education systems in line with the changing landscape of work and jobs of the future, themselves affected by other trends, including artificial intelligence, automation, quantum computing, and data.

Ending Content Creation Asymmetry

Even if you can access content as a shrewd consumer, this doesn't address the asymmetry in who is creating the historical record. The challenges over the profile of

> Each tribe could remake reality to their worldview, complete with convincing fabricated historical evidence that supports it. In these pockets, neither the moon landing nor the Holocaust will have happened.

who holds the virtual pens of one of the most open platforms, Wikipedia, have been well documented over the years[7][8][9]. The contributors are overwhelmingly male and Western, and the content reflects its creators, skewing toward topics geared to Western, male audiences[10].

Leveling the content creation playing fields is an issue I've been working on in one form or another since the late 1990s, when I campaigned against a "world white web[11][12]" and for a vision of the internet as a medium of the many, not the few, and an engine of empowerment for all.

> Toffler conceived of history as society's "built-in time spanners" connecting present generations with the past. That connection was underpinned by regular social contact with older generations, common cultural heritage, and objects with meaningful links to the past. Today's world is uprooted.

One of the most fulfilling aspects of my work is creating opportunities to empower young people, and spending time with some of them to understand the transformative impact of the work. There are 7 million young people on U-Report[13], our social accountability and empowerment platform that connects them and amplifies their voices and opinions to influence the issues they care about for the future they want to realize. On another microblogging platform, Voices of Youth, we coach and curate original content—by young people, for young people—as authors of their own narratives.

Our relationship to the past is, of course, not only the stuff of recorded history, but literally of stuff itself. The objects around us are increasingly dematerializable, disposable, rentable, and temporary, often with more value placed on their novelty than their durability. Whether we will erase our artifacts on a planned obsolescence schedule, or react with increased nostalgia and an urge to preserve isn't clear. The patterns move in both ways, from the raze-it-and-raise-it remaking of cities around the world, to nostalgia-driven antiquing and genealogy.

Toffler conceived of history as society's "built-in time spanners" connecting present generations with the past. That connection was underpinned by regular social contact with older generations, common cultural heritage, and objects with meaningful links to the past. Today's world is uprooted. In 2017, there were 258 million people worldwide living outside their country of birth; 30 million of them children[14]. This may mean our ties to a place and its backstory and our direct contact with family and community may become diluted and less meaningful with increased geographic dislocation, whether due to forced or voluntary mobility, urbanization, or migration.

Toffler was concerned that unlike history, there was no heritage of the future. It turns out that the vanishing past is as deserving of concern, as the conditions and characteristics that sustain history have themselves been eroded by the same forces driving future shock. Today the past is less "knowable," more rapidly changing, diverse, and contestable than ever before, meaning history is less of a stabilizing counterweight to accelerated change. But it is here to stay.

How much of history is necessary for anticipating and successfully adapting to the future? For those of us working in strategic foresight, a pattern-based understanding of the past and present is key to understanding the future, and can identify relevant analogies that provide insights. This is also how some historians would describe aspects of their discipline—history as a study of changes and transformations in society that can provide a framework for forecasting. So it turns out that students of the past and future have an awful lot in common.

As one of the world's best-known historians, Eric Hobsbawm once observed, "History alone provides orientation and anyone who faces the future without it is not only blind but dangerous, especially in the era of high technology."

Tanya Accone's career has focused on helping international public and private sector organizations achieve their preferred futures, particularly to amplify their impact through the convergence of people and innovation. Accone has been at the forefront of advocating for and leading groundbreaking innovations at the United Nations Children's Fund (UNICEF) that have changed the lives of 150 million children and their communities in 90 countries. Her career has included winning a Webby Award, taking *The Washington Post* digital, and launching technology businesses across sub-Saharan Africa. Accone is a Fulbright Fellow with multiple graduate degrees, including in Studies of the Future. She is the fourth generation of her Chinese family to be born in South Africa. She tweets at @accone.

1. https://news.itu.int/itu-statistics-leaving-no-one-offline/

2. https://www.generationunlimited.org/our-work/promising-ideas-innovation/digital-connectivity

3. https://www.vice.com/en_us/article/7x47bb/wikipedia-editors-elite-diversity-foundation

4. https://www.theverge.com/2019/5/23/18637373/deepfakes-samsung-ai-research-results-single-photo-algorithm

5. https://www.cnet.com/news/samsung-ai-deepfake-can-fabricate-a-video-clip-of-you-from-a-single-photo/

6. https://data.unicef.org/topic/education/literacy/

7. https://www.theatlantic.com/technology/archive/2013/10/90-of-wikipedias-editors-are-male-heres-what-theyre-doing-about-it/280882/

8. https://hbr.org/2016/06/why-do-so-few-women-edit-wikipedia

9. https://www.theguardian.com/commentisfree/2014/aug/07/truth-wikipedia-young-white-western-males

10. https://www.fastcompany.com/3031931/the-most-influential-figures-on-wikipedia-are-white-western-males

11. http://news.bbc.co.uk/2/hi/africa/442971.stm

12. https://www.newstatesman.com/must-africa-always-be-reported-chaps-cowboy-hats

13. https://ureport.in/

14. https://data.unicef.org/topic/child-migration-and-displacement/migration/

Artificial Intelligence Shock

Terrence Sejnowski & Fotis Sotiropoulos

We live in the future of *Future Shock*, written in 1970 when computers were just beginning to impact businesses and jobs. ■ The first personal computers became popular in the 1980s, making it possible to automate word processing and spreadsheets. Commerce on the internet took off in the 1990s, transforming almost every aspect of our lives, from access to knowledge, commerce, entertainment, and our social and political life. Since Apple introduced the iPhone in 2007, mobile connectivity has become ubiquitous. The march of Moore's Law, which predicted a doubling in computer power every 18 months, has continued to this day. This exponential progress of computer technology has sent shock waves through society at a relentless pace.

As Toffler predicted, we are now living in an age of information, one whose impact is just becoming apparent. Artificial intelligence (AI), which was launched in the mid-20th century, has come of age, powered by learning algorithms and fueled by the big data that is exploding on the internet. Deep learning has made it possible for AI to recognize speech and objects in images, and perform translation between languages[1]. It has been less than a decade since these breakthroughs occurred, but AI shock is already reverberating across the planet. Futurists are predicting loss of jobs and replacement of humans by AI, but a more likely scenario in the short run is the amplification of human cognitive abilities across a broad range of activities, including commerce, financial markets, medicine, science, and military. What impact will all of these changes have on the world order?

President Trump recently signed an executive order designed to stimulate the development of AI technologies in the United States. Through what is being called the "American AI Initiative," some $75 million of the Department of Defense's annual budget would be shifted to a newly created office focusing on these technologies, as a way to keep pace with China and other countries that are making AI a national priority.

This acknowledgement of AI at the federal level may be too little, too late. Much larger investments are being made by China, South Korea, France, Canada, and many other countries. We are once again playing catch-up, just as we were following Russia's launch of the Sputnik satellite in 1957, which led to the establishment of not only NASA to lead us into space, but also DARPA, the Defense Advanced Research Projects Agency, to develop and spur breakthrough technologies for national security. In comparison, the new executive order is akin to putting a Band-Aid on a ruptured artery.

China is already well on its way to being the dominant world leader in AI. Consider that two years ago, it unveiled a detailed program, complete with a price tag of $150 billion in economic development, focused on artificial intelligence and big data. Immediately thereafter, two Chinese cities promised to invest $7 billion in the effort. Moreover, South Korea, France, Canada, and other countries have also beat us to the punch by making huge investments in their own AI industries.

> This acknowledgement of AI at the federal level may be too little, too late. Much larger investments are being made by China, South Korea, France, Canada, and many other countries. We are once again playing catch-up, just as we were following Russia's launch of the Sputnik satellite in 1957.

Just a few months ago, we had ringside seats on AI activities in China. I gave a keynote talk at the Snowball Summit in Beijing, an annual meeting for people working in high-level finance, economics, technology, and administration. The talk was streamed to an audience of eight million Chinese interested in the prospects for AI in the investment arena. I also addressed a much smaller group of elite entrepreneurs at the Great Wall Club organized by Wen Chu, who is spearheading the national AI effort. China is mobilizing its workforce for the transition to AI at both the macroscale and the microscale. Fotis witnessed firsthand the scale of China's investments, as a national priority, in healthcare[2]. During my visit to the impressive building housing the Jinan International Medicine Center in Jinan City, and my subsequent meeting with that city's mayor, I learned that the JIMC had already indexed data from five million individuals from dozens of hospitals in the Shandong province. Equally impressive is the fact that the facility is actually designed to hold the data on 50 million people!

This is just one of the four national centers of its kind across China, composing the National Human Genetic Resources Sharing Service Platform. Such massive population-scale data sets will fuel dramatic advances in AI research, enabling advances in precision medicine and personalized therapies that will be hard to match by the US or any other nation around the globe. They will firmly position China at the forefront of the global race for supremacy in the AI space, at first in the healthcare sector, but it would not be a stretch to predict in many other sectors as well. And the stakes are high. As succinctly articulated by Russian President Vladimir Putin: "*The one who becomes the leader in this sphere will be the ruler of the world.*[3]"

Indeed, the Information Revolution, and the era of intelligent machines, is in full swing, and AI will determine the geopolitical superpowers of the future and drive economic development, as well as redefine the very essence of what it means to be human. Andrew McAfee, faculty member at the MIT Sloan School of Management, who has studied the impact of technology on economies for years, has said, with no exaggeration, that "*digital technologies are doing to brainpower what steam engine and related technologies did for human muscle power during the Industrial Revolution.*[4]" Our current geological era has been characterized as the Anthropocene, but the future may very well become known as the "Technocene," when AI technologies fused with biological intelligence usher in a new phase of cultural evolution.

Yet, even though humanity has lived through and successfully adjusted to several disruptive technological transitions, never before has the role of human work as the main driving force for producing wealth been as unclear as it is today. During the Industrial Revolution, machines could effectively replace human muscle, but human cognition and intelligence continued to drive innovation and economic development, leading to many opportunities for new jobs. However, the AI era can change all this, as deep learning algorithms have the potential to replicate complex human cognitive functions. Estimates suggest that AI technologies could cause anywhere from 10 to 50 percent of human jobs to disappear in the next few decades and create many new jobs, just as the Industrial Revolution sent farmers to factories.

> Our current geological era has been characterized as the Anthropocene, but the future may very well become known as the "Technocene," when AI technologies fused with biological intelligence usher in a new phase of cultural evolution.

Discussion about how to robot-proof all these jobs[5] is not what we need; what we need is less talk and more real and tangible solutions, both top down and bottom up. Just as China, on a national level, is investing billions in big data and AI with a clear vision to become the global AI leader by 2030[6], so, too, must the US if we hope even to compete in this global race. In the 1960s, the US made an investment of $100 billion in today's dollars to create advanced microelectronics, materials science, and a thriving aerospace industry. Investments were also made to revamp science and engineering education. When Neil Armstrong stepped onto the moon in 1969, the average age of an engineer at NASA was 26. This investment paid off—these industries have thrived and we are still benefitting from them. But the generation of engineers at NASA that created the Space Age has since retired and STEM education in the US has fallen far behind. We need someone with the vision and leadership of John F. Kennedy to inspire the nation today to make similar investments in the science and engineering of AI.

The solution, however, requires more than investments from government. It also must incorporate innovative partnerships between government, universities, and high-tech industry. To be sure, the role that higher education institutions need to play in this new era of intelligent machines cannot be overstated. Educational paradigms must be established that prepare students to work and creatively co-exist with AI systems by cultivating higher-order human cognitive abilities, which are less likely to be soon surpassed. These include critical thinking, the ability to work with complex interconnected systems, entrepreneurship, compassion, and cross-cultural understanding. Providing some level of proficiency in computing for students across all disciplines will be as prerequisite as speaking a language, as will innovative new degrees and programs that fuse computer science and engineering disciplines with humanities, social sciences, law, business, and medicine.

Some universities around the country are already gearing up to adapt their educational programs to this future. At Stony Brook University, for instance, we recently established the Institute for AI-Driven Discovery and Innovation[7], with a central theme of Human-Machine symbiosis, based on the idea that AI technologies should amplify human intelligence instead of replace it. Our vision is a new kind of humanities-trained student who is sufficiently proficient in the basics of machine learning and data science, but also possesses the higher-level cognitive skills that machines will not be able to acquire and that a humanities education can cultivate. Innovative educational approaches will be at the center of our efforts, centered on new curricula and vertically integrated design projects, bringing together teams of students, early in their educational journey, from engineering, humanities, and other disciplines to tackle challenging projects relevant to industry with an emphasis on the societal impacts of technology and entrepreneurship.

The advances in machine learning that made possible modern AI were made by researchers trained at universities, but this talent pool has been gutted by much better pay and computing resources at high-tech companies, which recognized much earlier than governments what impact AI was going to have on their businesses and the economy. The good news is that these companies are still competitive on the world stage, but the bad news is that the seed corn needed to train the next generation has left our universities. We need to make universities more attractive to the best and brightest faculty. This can happen if new AI centers and programs are established, such as the Institute for AI-Driven Discovery and Innovation[8] at Stony Brook, which can compete for state and federal research support to build computing infrastructure and retain faculty.

A half-century ago, when Russia launched the Sputnik satellite, America responded full-throttle, legislating the National Defense Education Act, which provided significant resources to universities for science and math education. The global AI race is the 21st century's Sputnik moment, only with stakes that are much higher. A new National Defense Digital Education Act, along with creative industry-academe-government partnerships and innovative educational paradigms implemented at scale, will all need to be part of this national strategy if the US is to compete effectively against the AI superpowers emerging in China and elsewhere. ■

Terrence J. Sejnowski holds the Francis Crick Chair at the Salk Institute for Biological Studies and is a Distinguished Professor at the University of California, San Diego. He was a member of the advisory committee for the Obama administration's BRAIN initiative and is president of the Neural Information Processing (NIPS) Foundation. He has published 12 books, including (with Patricia Churchland) *The Computational Brain* (25th Anniversary Edition, MIT Press). His most recent book is *The Deep Learning Revolution* (The MIT Press, 2018).

Fotis Sotiropoulos, PhD, serves as Dean of the College of Engineering and Applied Sciences at Stony Brook University. He is leading university-wide initiatives in Engineering-Driven Medicine and Artificial Intelligence and is at the forefront of efforts to expand diversity and invent the future of engineering education in the era of exponential technologies. Sotiropoulos is State University of New York Distinguished Professor and Fellow of the American Physical Society and the American Society of Mechanical Engineers. He has authored over 200 peer-reviewed journal papers and book chapters in simulation-based fluid mechanics for wind energy, river hydraulics, aquatic biology, and cardiovascular bioengineering. See full bio here: https://www.stonybrook.edu/commcms/ceas/about/office-of-the-dean/about-the-dean

1. Sejnowski, T. J., *The Deep Learning Revolution*, Cambridge, MA: MIT Press (2018).

2. https://www.reuters.com/article/us-china-medtech-breakingviews/breakingviews-really-big-data-gives-china-medical-ai-edge-idUSKBN1K808W

3. https://www.cnbc.com/2017/09/04/putin-leader-in-artificial-intelligence-will-rule-world.html

4. https://hbr.org/2015/06/the-great-decoupling

5. http://robot-proof.com/#title

6. https://multimedia.scmp.com/news/china/article/2166148/china-2025-artificial-intelligence/index.html

7. https://news.stonybrook.edu/university/leading-the-future-of-ai-university-marries-human-ingenuity-with-machines/?spotlight=hero

8. https://news.stonybrook.edu/university/leading-the-future-of-ai-university-marries-human-ingenuity-with-machines/?spotlight=hero

Future-Proofing Ourselves

Carlos A. Osorio

offler proposed that we "analyze the processes of acceleration and confront the concept of transience. If acceleration is a new social force, transience is its psychological counterpart." ■ Transience is the turnover rate of our relationships with people, places, ideas, and structures. Faster acceleration leads to high transience and more discarding of relationships and things. Acceleration and transience are "twin forces" affecting our lives and psyches. As such, we could benefit from a better understanding of their effects on human behavior, personality, and psychology.

Toffler's ideas about our inability to cope with a rapidly approaching future were visionary in many aspects. But we have been too optimistic about the benefits of technology and our ability to adapt to it.

The complexity and pace of human life are higher and faster than before. Everything seems to be connected with everything else. Digital technologies have created connections and relations among once unrelated aspects of life. This new connectivity allows for domino effects. Consequently, the ability to cope—to adjust, learn, and act—depends on everyone's clock speeds, and their tolerance.

Toffler's proposition regarding the culture of disposability provides an example. He wrote, "We develop a throw-away mentality to match our throw-away products." Products might come and go, but the "throw-away mentality" was here to stay.

Plastics are a clear example. Created in 1907, the first expensive plastic bottles hit the market in 1947. During the early 1950s, they became cheap and their production soared. Since then, the annual production of plastic has grown by 189 times (Geyer, Jambeck, & Law, 2017). Today, plastic is a major environmental disaster. We should have learned from it, but we didn't.

Cheap and trendy clothing—"fast fashion"—is another case of disposability evolving into a global problem. Back in 2005, an MIT research project sought to solve some of the clothing retailer Zara's supply chain challenges. Dynamic assortment was the answer to that challenge (Caro & Gallien, 2007). Fast fashion became the ultimate disruptive innovation in the retail clothing world. It took less than a decade to become an environmental disaster, and is the ultimate example of the "throw-away culture."

We are perhaps the smartest generation alive, but we didn't connect those two cases. Both are about cheap, rapid, and large-scale production of arguably unnecessary consumer goods. In both cases, the products are easy to discard. Both have similar consequences.

> According to a recent Microsoft project that analyzed the evolution of attention span, there was a significant percentage decrease, from 12 to 8 seconds, between 2000 and 2015. This is a problem. Our brains require 10-20 seconds of focused attention to store new information in long-term memory.

These two examples illustrate our high technical capacity for solving precise and well-defined problems. They also illustrate, though, our inability to anticipate many negative effects that result from human behavior, setting up an insidious feedback loop. Acceleration has shortened attention spans, for example, which change is now manifesting a negative impact on intelligence. According to a recent Microsoft project that analyzed the evolution of attention span (Gausby, 2015), there was a significant percentage decrease, from 12 to 8 seconds, between 2000 and 2015.

This is a problem. Our brains require 10-20 seconds of focused attention to store new information in long-term memory. Shorter attention spans preclude this knowledge capture, yielding learning disabilities (Tarver & Hallahan, 1974). Less information in our long-term memory translates to a lower capacity for problem-solving. Shrinking capacity for attention amplifies and accelerates the consequences of information overload. But there is more to put into the mental mix: bounded rationality, biases, and cognitive and emotional responses.

Many factors bound human rationality. A primary factor is the complexity of the problem in question. We are good at solving problems with up to four interacting variables (Halford, Baker, McCredden, & Bain, 2005). Beyond that, it becomes a matter of luck. Yet most complex problems have many more than four interacting variables. And in turn, this shortfall in computational capacity bounds our rationality (H. Simon, 1972; H. A. Simon, 1973).

Likewise, biases and heuristics affect decision-making under uncertainty (Kahneman, Lovallo, & Sibony, 2011; Amos Tversky & Kahneman, 1975; A. Tversky & Kahneman, 1981). And, of course, our emotional response to difficult situations affects our cognition (Osorio & Renard, 2018).

This leaves us with a paradox. On one hand, we have increasing capabilities for exponential technologies, and high expectations about their potential. Various future-related biases serve to enhance these expectations. On the other hand, we have limited capacity for identifying their potential harmful consequences. But we also know that risk, uncertainty, and ambiguity are normal conditions, inherent to accelerated technical change. They are, in fact, inseparable from innovation and evolutionary processes. Awareness of these vulnerabilities and acceptance of their unavoidability, though, do not let us off the hook of responsibility; awareness reinforces the fact that we must create systems to anticipate even improbable negative effects of technological change.

So how, then, do we competently and confidently create the future? Here are some ideas.

1 ▪ Focus Education on Skills Instead of Content and Information

Toffler argues that faster change requires "faster flow." It also requires rapid obsolesce of knowledge obtained from previous experiences. Rapid obsolescence of knowledge requires fast and meaningful learning. It requires learning and unlearning, because today's facts become tomorrow's misinformation.

Toffler proposed that education be based on a system of "skills needed for human communication and social integration" instead of "yesterday's curricula." The system of skills should focus on learning, relating to others, and choosing among many alternatives. We need a new set of skills for learning to learn, and for making sense.

My colleague María Renard says, "Sense-making begins with data collection and ends with assessing the impact of a solution." It's about analyzing and applying existing information and knowledge to new problems. But it is also about making sense of data, information, and knowledge in new ways. It includes deciding which information and knowledge are useful for a new problem. And it requires making sense of the new problem as individuals, and as teams, by interacting with others.

This requires skills for dealing with uncertainty, ambiguity, and risk (Renard & Osorio 2019). These conditions inevitably come with complexity, failure, and frustration. Consequently, we need to reinforce our future-proofing in other ways.

2 ▪ Upgrade Your Cognitive and Emotional Powers

We have a gap to close. Exponential technologies and the theory of abundance promise tremendous potential for our future. However, our inability to cope with nonlinear, systemic, and rapid change limit this potential. There are two primary aspects to this gap: emotional and cognitive. We can upgrade our capacity for both by borrowing tricks from other activities.

Let's consider some demanding environments. Rugby players know their games are tough. Their technical, tactical, physical, and mental training allows them to endure and perform. Special Forces' training programs focus on enhancing performance under some of the worst conditions imaginable. High-altitude mountaineers and ultra-marathon runners share similar exer-

> On one hand, we have increasing capabilities for exponential technologies, and high expectations about their potential. Various future-related biases serve to enhance these expectations. On the other hand, we have limited capacity for identifying their potential harmful consequences.

cises. In critical moments, emotional and psychological endurance is what makes the difference. Their training enables them to endure and perform in demanding environments. But there is more to the explanation.

There are documented some 193 different cognitive, behavioral, attributional, and memory biases and errors. These biases affect decision-making and judgment under conditions of uncertainty. Ongoing Yuken research found that 118 of these biases have an effect on various stages of innovation processes. Social, attributional, and memory biases induce about 25 percent of mistakes along development processes. What about the remaining 75 percent? Curiously, the remaining majority of misjudgments are rooted in the way we learn and retain information, and the reinforcement that occurs through years of professional experience.

> We have a gap to close. Exponential technologies and the theory of abundance promise tremendous potential for our future. However, our inability to cope with non-linear, systemic, and rapid change limit this potential.

Why is that? We accumulate professional expertise and knowledge when answering to specific challenges. Past experience and knowledge create our mental models. These mental models, comprising a cognitive lens, help us understand reality (Tripsas & Gavetti, 2000). They can enhance or prevent our understanding and discovery of new answers to new challenges.

The cognitive lens allows for cognitive search, or generation of alternatives, and is more effective when paired with experiential research (Gavetti & Levinthal, 2000). Discovery-driven planning allows for identifying tacit hypotheses and assumptions (McGrath & MacMillan, 1995). Various debiasing techniques diminish our anchors and enhance empathy across them (Osorio & Renard, 2018; Renard & Osorio, 2019).

Steve Jobs defined the personal computer as "the bike for the mind." If that is so, then artificial intelligence and cognitive computing can become the supersonic jet for the mind (Chen, Herrera, & Hwabg, 2018). They could allow us to see even more distant futures and enable us to deal effectively with what we see.

We need a new understanding of diversity, collaboration, and coordination for achieving this outcome.

3 ▪ Making Sense of Complexity Through Enhanced Managerial Coordination and Collaboration

Diversity, collaboration, and coordination get new meaning and relevance in the "after shock." Diversity goes beyond the variety of observable differences. It includes heterogeneity of knowledge and skills for solving a multidimensional socio-technical problem. It involves complementary cognitive and emotional skills, attitudes, and socio-cultural factors (Renard & Osorio, 2019), as well as different motives, ambitions, and goals.

A well-assembled team should have the required mix of technical, cognitive, and emotional skills for a complex project. These skills are not found constantly in any single person for the duration of a project. Thus, leadership best rotates across members of high-performing development teams (Davis & Eisenhardt, 2011).

This rotation can create enhanced coordination and collaboration for sense-making and action. We can further enhance our performance using future-proofing development processes.

4 Treating the Negative Effects of New Technologies as Design and Execution Failures

When your car breaks down, its warranty allows you to get it fixed at the expense of the manufacturer. When a new product creates "unforeseen" negative effects universally, society pays the price. Fast change, risk, uncertainty, and ambiguity are simply part of this game. But again, they shouldn't serve as excuses for failing to ambitiously anticipate unintended consequence.

The drug development process, for example, takes between 10 and 15 years. The Federal Drug Administration (FDA) needs to be sure that new drugs are both safe and effective. Its goals are to confirm efficacy and comprehensively research and discover the potential for harmful and negative effects *before new drugs reach the market*. This deliberate process is intended to prevent unforeseen problems. For this reason, there is extensive research and testing during the various stages of clinical research.

We've established that risk, uncertainty, and ambiguity are part of the exponential technologies game. There is enough research and evidence to guide our way with them. Consistent with questions of morality, it is time we treat products with social or environmental costs as "unfinished" designs.

Nowadays, we can't conceive of cars without seatbelts. In 1886, Karl Benz invented the car. In 1904, Henry Ford began its mass production. In 1950, Dr. C. Hunter Shelden, a physician dealing with head injuries, invented the seatbelt. But it was only in 1970 that Australia enacted the first law requiring its use. Along the way, many people died or suffered injuries.

Future-Proofing Ourselves for Dealing with Distant Futures

Along with many of the ideas explored by the Tofflers, future shock has evolved. We can't afford slow responses for problems we could have prevented. Indeed, we can learn from the past to create a better next 50 years.

Basing education on cognitive, emotional, and social skills for lifelong learning is a first step. It's a more effective approach for always-changing environments than learning content and information. Existing knowledge and technologies can help us upgrade our cognitive and emotional powers.

Cognitive computing could enhance our capability to generate and analyze possible futures. Artificial intelligence and experimentation technologies enhance our capability to discard less favorable ones.

The benefits of diversity are beyond being politically correct. It's a way of achieving non-redundancy and collecting complementary skills on a team. Diversity

> Steve Jobs defined the personal computer as "the bike for the mind." If that is so, then artificial intelligence and cognitive computing can become the supersonic jet for the mind.

acts as an insurance for diminishing the likelihood of making bias-induced mistakes. Learning to manage a diverse group is not easy because we must embrace conflict and relate to others. This requires enhanced coordination and collaboration, time, and empathy.

Finally, it is time to consider as design and execution failures the negative effects of human-made systems. They are not "unforeseen events" resulting from risk, uncertainty, and ambiguity. We are too old for that excuse. ■

Carlos Osorio, PhD, is cofounder and partner at Yuken, a global design and innovation capability-building impact research lab, adjunct professor at Universidad del Desarrollo (Chile), visiting professor of innovation at Deusto Business School (Spain), and guest lecturer at Singularity University. He has been International Faculty Fellow at MIT School of Management, faculty associate at Harvard's Berkman Klein Center, visiting research scientist at MIT Medialab, and visiting lecturer at Amsterdam Business School. Carlos holds a PhD in Technology, Management and Policy, and a MS in Technology and Policy from MIT Engineering Systems Division, a Master in Public Policy from Harvard's Kennedy School of Government, and a BS in industrial engineering from the University of Chile.

References

Caro, F., & Gallien, J. (2007). Dynamic assortment with demand learning for seasonal consumer goods. *Management Science, 53*(2), 276–292.

Chen, M., Herrera, F., & Hwabg, K. (2018). Cognitive computing: architecture, technologies and intelligent applications. *IEEE Access, 6,* 19774-19783.

Davis, J., & Eisenhardt, K. (2011). Rotating Leadership and Collaborative Innovation: Recombination Processes in Symbiotic Relationships. *Administrative Science Quarterly, 56*(2), 159-201.

Gausby, A. (2015). *Attention Spans.*

Gavetti, G. (2005, January 10). *Strategy Formulation and Inertia.* HBS Cases, (9-705-468). Boston, MA.

Gavetti, G., & Levinthal, D. (2000). Looking forward and looking backward: Cognitive and experiential search. *Administrative Science Quarterly, 45*(1), 113-137.

Geyer, R., Jambeck, J. R., & Law, K. L. (2017). Production, use, and fate of all plastics ever made. *Science advances, 3*(7), e1700782.

Halford, G. S., Baker, R., McCredden, J. E., & Bain, J. D. (2005). How many variables can humans process? *Psychological Science, 16*(1), 70-76.

Kahneman, D., Lovallo, D., & Sibony, O. (2011). The Big Idea: Before You Make That Big Decision. . . *Harvard Business Review, 89*(6), 51-60.

March, J. G., & Simon, H. (1958). *Organizations* (Second Edition ed.). Cambridge, MA: Blackwell Publishers.

McGrath, R. G., & MacMillan, I. C. (1995). Discovery-Driven Planning. *Harvard Business Review, 73*(4): 44–54., 73(4), 44-54.

Osorio, C., & Renard, M. (2018, September 20, 21). *The role of cognition and emotions on innovation learning and performance.* Paper presented at the GoWest! 2018 Making, Inventing & Entrepreneurship: New Pathways & New Opportunities, San Francisco, CA.

Renard, M., & Osorio, C. (2019). *Designing secure learning environments for discovery, empathy, failure and igniting impact in Latin America.* Paper presented at the Annual Meeting of the American Education Research Association, Toronto, Canada.

Simon, H. (1962). The Architecture of Complexity. *Proceedings of the American Philosophical Society, 106,* 467-482.

Simon, H. (1969). *The Sciences of the Artificial.* Cambridge, MA: MIT Press.

Simon, H. (1972). Theories of Bounded Rationality. In C. B. McGuire, and Radner, Roy (Ed.), *Decision and Organization*: North-Holland Publishing Company.

Simon, H. A. (1973). The structure of ill-structured problems. *Artificial intelligence, 4*(3-4), 181-201.

Tarver, S. G., & Hallahan, D. P. (1974). Attention deficits in children with learning disabilities: A review. *Journal of Learning Disabilities, 7*(9), 560-569.

Tripsas, M., & Gavetti, G. (2000). Capabilities, Cognition and Inertia: Evidence from Digital Imaging. *Strategic Management Journal, 21*(October-November), 1147-1161.

Tversky, A., & Kahneman, D. (1975). Judgment under uncertainty: Heuristics and biases. In D. Wendt & C. Vlek (Eds.), *Utility, probability, and human decision making* (pp. 141-162). Netherlands: Springer.

Tversky, A., & Kahneman, D. (1981). The Framing of Decisions and the Psychology of Choice. *Science, 211*(4481), 453-458.

Future Shock and Tomorrow's Futurism

Alexander Mankowsky

> ❝ Constant revolutionizing of production, uninterrupted disturbance of all social conditions, everlasting uncertainty and agitation distinguish the bourgeois epoch from all earlier ones. All fixed, fast-frozen relations, with their train of ancient and venerable prejudices and opinions, are swept away, all new-formed ones become antiquated before they can ossify. All that is solid melts into air, all that is holy is profaned. ❞

This quote, taken from the *Communist Manifesto*, written by Karl Marx and Friedrich Engels in 1848, could have been the motto of *Future Shock*. ■ But the Tofflers avoided political implications throughout their text, except in the last chapter, which addressed the social aspects of futurism. Given their experience of the witch hunt against intellectuals during McCarthyism after WWII, they really can't be blamed. The last chapter however, hinted at their desire to leave both capitalism and communism behind, as soon as the "Super-Industrialization" arrived.

Alvin and Heidi Toffler were born in the 1930s. They inherited the sensibilities of family and community shaped by the Great Depression. As teenagers, they experienced and/or were exposed

> The development and application of technology was deeply amoral. Counterculture emerged as a balance to the technocratic aggression against everything that was considered beautiful and human.

to disruptions spanning WWII to the Holocaust to the atomic bomb. This was followed by Sputnik, Agent Orange, napalm, and cybernetic warfare. Doomsday machines were being drawn up. Wires were put in the heads of people, Wernher von Braun—accomplice in slave labor and murder at Mittelland, Austria—developed Saturn rockets for NASA.

The development and application of technology was deeply amoral.

Counterculture emerged as a balance to the technocratic aggression against everything that was considered beautiful and human. The '60s were psychedelic; LSD was used to breach the borders of the mind. "Tune in, turn on, drop out." Free love was a "natural" alternative to drugs and served as an antidote against aggression. "Make love, not war." Doug Engelbart's networked computers were set up to *augment* the human mind, not replace it. The Grateful Dead, Janis Joplin, Jefferson Starship, and an attendant culture emerged in California, culminating in a joint resistance against government agency generally. The roots of today's Silicon Valley can be traced to these times.

The cultural and technological environment for Alvin and Heidi Toffler offered colorful and wild phenomena. Indeed, *Future Shock* is a testament to the spirit of these times. It is a lengthy text, full of glimpses into the expected transformational development that was beginning to unfold out of this complex milieu.

The Rise of Expectationism

Future Shock is largely concerned with mental and emotional states—and their problems—particularly those related to expectations. Serious problems would surely arise, the Tofflers posited, as everything became increasingly fluid. Take relationships, for example. Why not, they suggested, when moving for a new, better job, also replace your family with a new one, as well? Why own stuff, or bother to relate to loved ones, when everything is constantly in flux and transient?

From our vantage today, the reality 50 years later actually seems fairly well behaved, albeit certainly not prudish. Statistically, Millennials have fewer sexual affaires than did their generational counterparts at the time *Future Shock* was written. At the same time, the Tofflers would likely have been shocked by Nipplegate of Super Bowl XXXVIII. A partially exposed female breast would have been fined as indecent exposure. Yet we also see myriad incongruities. Peter Paul Rubens's nude paintings, for example, are censored by Facebook's AI algorithms 500 years after the fact. And instead of tripping on acid, nowadays LSD is taken in microdoses to enhance performance on the job.

Learnings: Sense of Time in Today's Futurism

The Tofflers were operating in a state of expectation; they communicated the coming of a technologically driven cultural transformation. Today's futurists, like Ray Kurzweil or Nick Bostrom, seem to operate from a similar state of expectation—the expectation in all cases being driven by the observation of accelerating change, extracted out of diverse phenomena. The Tofflers' method was to extract *patterns* out of these observations.

The Tofflers' method of pattern creation as applied to futurist thinking would yield a pattern of expectationism driven by the sensation of acceleration. Surely everybody has had the experience of sitting in a car, waiting at a crossroads beside a large bus. The bus suddenly moves, and one's bodily reflex is to counter the perceived motion. The result is an awkward movement of the body in the direction of the steering wheel, though the car hasn't moved at all. The *sensation* of acceleration was a misinterpretation.

Translated in futurist thinking, it is paramount to distinguish your personal sense of acceleration from the realities of the developments occurring around you. In short, you have to develop a sense of time as an antidote to your feelings and as a guideline for contributions.

In my experience, a meaningful sense of time has to be fostered continuously in order to avoid expectationism as the effect of wrongly perceived acceleration. To this end, it is helpful to participate actively in the development of cutting-edge technologies, if for no other reason than to directly experience the complexity of inventing something new. In my case, it is about the self-driving car—a mobile robot disguised as an automobile. Self-driving cars are relying on machine learning and diverse robotic technologies, integrated with difficult-to-handle amounts of data from very diverse sources. For nearly every detail of the core functionality, the technological foundation has to be developed *in parallel* with the development of the conceptual framework.

Sebastian Thrun, one of the fathers of the self-driving car, projected 2040 as the target for fully automated driving under all conditions. His early estimation seems quite on track, as the technology is entering the phase where flawless performance is required, and every step further is smaller and more difficult to achieve. The difficulties in developing self-driving cars acting as if they were driven by an experienced driver also provide a clue regarding the principal limits of artificial intelligence.

Mimicking human understanding of the world is not enough if a machine is acting in the real world. In the case of the self-driving car, the limits of AI are visible for everybody. These limits are not a problem at all, since every technology has limits we are able to manage, but it is important to communicate the technology *as it will be*.

Expectationism, therefore, should be avoided.

Extended Futurism

In today's world I would love to see an extension of good old-fashioned futurism. I say extension because it should extend futurism with *solutions*.

In my case, working at Daimler AG, this is relatively straightforward, as Daimler creates concept cars that are meant to serve as beacons marking the future of mobility. As a motive, we refer to this as pathways into a *desirable* future. The Tofflers used the term "preferable future," which they wanted to be imagined by the integration of creative people, like artists, into the creation process. In the case of the F015 research car, that's exactly what we did, working together with Ars Electronica, the cradle of Cyberarts.

Extended futurism should help us guard against the dominant pitfall of expectationism: anxiety—what the Tofflers

> A meaningful sense of time has to be fostered continuously in order to avoid expectationism as the effect of wrongly perceived acceleration.

called "future shock." Anxiety about the future can best be fought with participation models, integrating different perspectives into the creation process.

Born in Berlin in 1957, **Alexander Mankowsky** studied sociology, philosophy, and psychology at the Free University of Berlin. He graduated in 1984 with the title of Diplom Soziologe. After four years in social services helping troubled children, he decided to follow the Zeitgeist and enrolled at a postgraduate university, focusing on the then new field of artificial intelligence. After heavy programming in OOS and Prolog, he earned the title of "Knowledge Engineer." Since 1989, Alexander has worked in the research unit at Daimler AG, initially focusing on societal trends in mobility. This led him in 2001 to his current field of work as Futurist and Mobility Philosopher at Daimler Research. Alexander is focused on human-centered innovation utilizing futuristic technological concepts. He is embedded in Daimler's rich and diverse creative network.

The Responsibility of Imagination

Dr. David J. Staley

was reading a book the other day by a pioneer in artificial intelligence, and came upon a passage that just floored me. He was describing the potential risks of developing artificial intelligence and the concerns some have expressed about the threat artificial intelligence poses to humanity. "This is not the first time an emergent technology has seemed to pose an existential threat," he writes.

> The invention, development, and stockpiling of nuclear weapons threatened to blow up the world, but somehow we have managed to keep that from happening, at least until now. When recombinant DNA technology first appeared, there was fear that deadly engineered organisms would be set loose to cause untold suffering and death across the globe. Genetic engineering is now a mature technology, and so far we have managed to survive its creations.

Somehow we have managed to keep that from happening. I found this attitude stunning and irresponsible. "Yes, yes, new technologies are threatening," he seemed to be saying, "but somebody (else) always finds a way to deal with any problems." This breezy, casual attitude belies the very hard work that was undertaken to establish systems, regulations, laws, norms, and an ethical infrastructure to keep us from "blowing up the world." The writer, a technologist, would simply and blithely pass the responsibility for any ill effects of technology off onto others.

An important part of this ethical infrastructure is the imagination necessary to foresee the challenges, not just the benefits, of technological change. Some thoughtful scientists and technologists have engaged in such imaginative activity, as did Albert Einstein and Leo Szilard at the dawn of the Atomic Age. Jennifer Doudna is at once a leader in the development of the CRISPR gene editing technique and a careful critic of the problems such a technology could cause. [https://www.amazon.com/Crack-Creation-Editing-Unthinkable-Evolution-ebook/dp/B01I4FPNNQ]

"What's hard to imagine are the uses to which a new invention will be put, and inventors are no better than anyone else at predicting what those uses will be," the technologist continues. "There is a lot of room between utopian and doomsday scenarios that are being predicted for deep learning and AI, but even the most imaginative science fiction writers are unlikely to guess what their ultimate impact will be."

Most of the time, when we say we cannot imagine the future, 1) we aren't trying hard enough, and 2) we press on anyway, throwing up our hands at our imaginative impotence.

Yes, of course, prediction is hard, perhaps even impossible. I tell every audience that I speak to: Anyone who says they can predict the future is lying to you. When we say we want to know the future, what we are usually saying is that we want to know what some complex system is going to look like at some point in the future. By their nature, complex systems are inherently unpredictable. That does not, however, abrogate our responsibility to imagine the many possible behaviors of such systems. We may not be able to predict, but we can—and indeed must—expansively imagine the future

We must allow ourselves the responsibility to imagine. As the above quotation from the technologist suggests, imagination is undervalued in our society. We associate imagination with the activities of children, or mere poets or dreamers. Imagination is not something that serious people engage in. We are sometimes admonished, "Don't let your imagination run away with you," and scolded for childlike behavior. Nevertheless, I believe there is an imperative, a responsibility to engage in imaginative thought if for no other reason than to anticipate and forestall the problems new technologies might pose.

Alvin Toffler understood the importance of imagination, and repeated calls for its rigorous use can be found throughout *Future Shock*. He especially faulted economists for their lack of imagination. As part of his approach to thinking about the future, Toffler called for the combination of rational, scientific thinking *with* the imagination. Interestingly, he called for the establishment of "imaginetic centers" in every community, to carry out the work of examining the issues of the present, and to creatively and imaginatively project their implications into the future. Toffler believed we needed "sanctuaries for social imagination."

> By their nature, complex systems are inherently unpredictable. That does not, however, abrogate our responsibility to imagine the many possible behaviors of such systems. We may not be able to predict, but we can—and indeed must— expansively imagine the future.

I do not think Toffler's vision of imaginetic centers has yet been realized. If we were to institute them today, what might they look like? School would be an obvious and excellent choice for their location and integration. It would be interesting if "imagination" were tested as a school subject, and treated with the same importance as are STEM subjects. Imagine if "imagination" became an academic discipline, enshrined as a college major. Instead of pursuing an MBA, future leaders would instead seek out a PhD in Imagination.

The closest we might come today to imaginetic centers are those think tanks that imagine the future. Perhaps Singularity University is one such center?

As a futurist, I think of myself as being in the imagination business. So, when I write a column that looks at "The Future of Mobility," [https://www.columbusunderground.com/next-the-future-of-mobility-ds1] or "Tech That Generates Fake News," [https://www.columbusunderground.com/next-tech-that-generates-fake-news-ds1], or when I ask "Will Artificial Intelligence Have Civil Rights?" [https://www.columbusunderground.com/next-will-artificial-intelligence-have-civil-rights-ds1], I am attempting to use my imagination to identify possibilities. Unforeseen effects of technological change are often the result of a willfully stunted imagination. These essays are not predictions: they are imaginative projections, considerations of implications and consequences before we act.

As *Future Shock* demonstrated, the futurist has an ethical responsibility to engage in the difficult work of imagining the effects of technological, social, cultural, economic, and political change. ▪

Dr. David J. Staley is an associate professor in the departments of History, Design and Educational Studies at The Ohio State University, and is a guest lecturer at Singularity University. His most recent book is *Alternative Universities: Speculative Design for Innovation in Higher Education*, and he is the author of *Brain, Mind and Internet: A Deep History and Future*. He writes the monthly futures column "Next" for ColumbusUnderground.com.

▪ https://jhupbooks.press.jhu.edu/title/alternative-universities
▪ https://www.palgrave.com/gp/book/9781137460943#
▪ https://www.columbusunderground.com/author/dstaley

Toffler's Triad

Amy Zalman

Future Shock, Alvin Toffler's volume on the "dizzying disorientation" produced by an accelerating rate of change in technology and society, hit a cultural nerve when it was published in 1970. Cultural luminaries such as C.P. Snow, Buckminster Fuller, Marshal McLuhan, and Betty Friedan lavished superlatives on the book; within a year of its first publication, it went through 15 print runs. The term *future shock* became cultural shorthand that is still in circulation today to describe the sickness that Toffler's tome offered to diagnose: the horribly jolted sensation of a traveler to a distant land who finds she recognizes nothing upon arrival and cannot function. Filled with the stock images of the United States circa 1970—"student riots, sex, LSD, miniskirts"—the book tapped into middle class American unease with a country in flux and fears of what further changes the future might hold.

The solution Toffler offered also brought into popular focus a then-new field of professional endeavor: Futurism (which also goes by the names Futures Studies, Strategic Foresight, or simply Futures work). Like the Industrial Age itself, Toffler argued, the planning tools of the Machine Age had reached the end of their shelf life. Industrial-Age planning focused naturally on industrial output and on economic indicators to explain whether a society was on the right path or required adjustment (the only significant global distinction being that in the United States, economic output fueled the private sector, while in the Soviet Union, it was the engine of the state).

But the Industrial Age, said Toffler, was over. Instead, human societies were on the precipice of a post-industrial era characterized above all by accelerating and expanding change caused by rapid technological development and compounded by ever-greater global interconnectedness. In this new world, the future could no longer be understood as the predictable sum of precise inputs. In this new world—heady, frightening, but full too of opportunity—it would be possible to *negotiate* with the impending future. We humans could shape our own best futures by wrestling with constraints, understanding the immovable, learning to adapt, and applying leverage where chance permitted it.

While defining how to undertake this negotiation, Toffler articulated a vision that became the core activity of foresight. He called for three distinct but interlocking domains of future focus: probable, possible, and preferable futures. "Determining the probable calls for a science of futurism. Delineating the possible calls for an art of futurism. Defining the preferable calls for a politics of futurism." Science, art, politics. Not economic indicators and foreseeable outputs.

In his call for a politics of futurism, Toffler isn't talking about party politics. He wants an engaged, productive, *interested* conversation among diverse people in a democracy to identify and develop a consensus around visions of our shared future. Futurism, in this sense, is a dynamic, active, society-wide activity that extends the dominant political project of his generation and ours, democracy, by asking how many visions of the future can be included in decision-making.

Yet for the last 50 years, for many reasons, this dynamic element of foresight has often been lost (not least because it is so difficult to act on). To date, the three interlocking actions Toffler called for have developed unevenly. Foresight has become most firmly affiliated with the science of futurism, with data and trend analysis and more recently predictive analytics and evidence-based projections. The art of the possible, the creative activity of imagining alternatives, has thrived in the niche spaces of science fiction. As a result, in an era in which the fact that complex, global challenges with potentially civilization-bending effects is uncontroversial, futurism has become (and is perceived) as a set of tools for looking at the future, but not as a way of taking action. The subtle but critical development of the "politics of futurism" has languished.

> In an era in which the fact that complex, global challenges with potentially civilization-bending effects is uncontroversial, futurism has become (and is perceived) as a set of tools for looking at the future, but not as a way of taking action.

Yet Toffler's terminology of probable, possible, and preferable futures has endured among professional futurists. And justly so, for the triad, allied to the actions of science, art, and politics, constitutes a vital algorithm, a kind of futurist dialectic that if fulfilled could help global institutions to take the first steps toward truly addressing our most intractable impending challenges—environmental, economic, geopolitical.

This triad is the basis for the kind of futurism we need in our societies today. The best way to celebrate Toffler would be a return to the original intention of his call for the science, art, and politics of futurism. There can be no better time than now to resuscitate active, political leadership as an aspect of futurism; it celebrates foresight as the effort to build a consensus about the future we prefer, and as what we do *right now* to ensure the future vitality of our species, our planet, and our universe. ▪

Dr. **Amy Zalman** is the founder and CEO of Prescient, a Washington, DC-based foresight consultancy that serves Fortune 500 firms, growing businesses, and trade organizations, and a part-time professor in the Culture, Communications and Technology program at Georgetown University. Amy's previous roles included chief executive officer and president of the World Future Society, the world's first and largest membership organization for futurists, and the chair of information integration at the US National Defense University. She speaks and publishes regularly on issues related to the intersections of emerging technologies and their impacts on societies, governance, and power. She earned her doctorate from the Department of Middle Eastern & Islamic Studies at New York University.

Technological
Hallucinations

Gray Scott

> 66 One of the definitions of sanity
> is the ability to tell real from unreal.
> Soon we'll need a new definition.99
>
> —*Alvin Toffler*

"What perceptual augmentation are you currently experiencing?" This may become a very common question in the near future—a future filled with smart contact lenses and brain implants that could enable humans to augment their awareness.

Using AR, VR, and advanced simulated overlays of what we think of today as reality, we could be entering a new age of hyper-reality. A dense, AI-assisted, hyper-advanced reality that is occulted from our current perception because of our biological limitations.

These new hyper-realities could be described as technological hallucinations, but I argue the opposite here. I propose that we are entering a new age of cosmological holistic advanced awareness that will enable humanity to see not only the external world, but also the internal world with astonishing clarity, a clarity that may shock a majority of humans on this planet.

Keep in mind that we are animals able to see less than 1% of the electromagnetic light spectrum, that average human hearing is limited to between 20 to 20,000 hertz, and that our brains process a finite amount of data at any given time. We do not see microwaves, infrared, or X-rays.

Not only are we aware of just a fragment of true reality, but our brains are also constantly filling in micro-gaps in our perception. The average human blinks over 28,000 times a day and the human eye has a blind spot, yet the brain fills in these missing fragments without us ever noticing.

The data, as they say, are incomplete.

Hyper-realities

It appears that what we call reality is just a hazy reflection of shifting cultural agreements and reductions in a vast computational cosmological system that is too complex for us to perceive clearly at this stage of our evolution.

However, do AR, VR, and simulated reality constitute a false reality, or are we merely reshaping the edifice and symbology of our perception of the physical world under the pressure of new technological tools? Is this our new reality? A new level in our evolution?

Technological complexification is becoming so rampant that we already need advanced AI to help us understand emerging data, not unlike a child needing the help of a parent to see an animal hidden in the woods. Technology is calling our attention into focus. It is breaking down holistic reality in ways that we can now digest.

Machine learning systems like GANs (generative adversarial networks) can simulate authentic-looking photographs, paintings, and eventually films. These and undetectable simulations will enable new computer-generated simulations to become the norm for reality in the future.

AI will need to coax us into recalibrating our attention, and support us in this new hyper-simulated future reality. The complexification of technological awareness will need to be augmented by AI in order for us to navigate a new level of hyper-reality.

If augmented AI contact lenses can enable you to see that there are 110,833 leaves on the tree you are looking at, enable you to see the molecular shapes in the food you are eating, or predict your desires before you realize them yourself, then we must begin to redefine what reality is. What is the definition of sanity in this new hyper-reality?

The future definition of sanity may be based on the degree of perceptual technological augmentation on our biological minds. I propose a new definition of sanity that could help people in the near future.

Sanity [san-i-tee]: Cultural adherence to agreed-upon technologically mediated or simulated additional realities.

Each level of reality may need its own definition of sanity. If a purely biological, unaugmented mind is seeing miniature pink elephants and hearing disembodied voices, then culturally we can agree that the experiencer is fully outside the realm of culturally agreed-upon sanity.

> Keep in mind that we are animals able to see less than 1% of the electromagnetic light spectrum, that average human hearing is limited to between 20 to 20,000 hertz, and that our brains process a finite amount of data at any given time. We do not see microwaves, infrared, or X-rays.

However, in the future world of AR and VR, dancing elves and fire-breathing dragons are completely within the realm of technologically augmented sanity. The densification of reality will also become defined as an additional reality. If your friend is going on and on about how he can see the molecular structure of his broccoli and he is not wearing his AR contact lenses, then you might question his sanity. However, if he is wearing smart contacts and has the "molecular vision" parameter set to "see molecules," then he is well within the realm of sanity in the agreed-upon additional hyper-reality.

Whether this information is simulated or not is irrelevant in this big data future—as long as we agree upon each additional reality and its parameters of sanity. Extended boundaries of ego, body, and awareness will be needed in order to explore new simulated realities. For example, the ability to control extra robotic limbs or additional hyper-reality perceptions will need to be accounted for in the future.

Entire industries will emerge around this new hyper-reality and simulated AR. Future celebrities may wander the world with "anonymous parameters" set to broadcast to other smart contact wearers. We may walk right past a celebrity in the future and see an alternate facial overlay that they have designated and sanctioned. Moreover, this facial overlay could be changed daily so that it cannot be eventually linked to the celebrity. Unlike today's infantile and cartoon versions of AR, future AR facial overlays will be so realistic the difference will be undetectable between the bio-real and the digital overlay.

We can break future realities into three main areas:

1 ∎ Pure-Biological Reality (unaugmented)
2 ∎ Bio-Digital Reality (augmented with AR, VR, and undetectable simulation overlays)
3 ∎ Hyper-Dimensional Reality (AI-assisted big data informational overlays inaccessible to the pure biological mind)

Each of these future realities is valid. As an example, the reality for a Japanese VR designer varies wildly from that of an Amazonian shaman who spends most of his time under the influence of hallucinogenic plants. Are culturally and technologically sanctioned agreements of perception the key to the future of sanity in the coming age of hyper-realistic simulated realities?

As ethnobotanist and philosopher Terence McKenna once said, "What we call reality is, in fact, nothing more than a culturally sanctioned and linguistically reinforced hallucination." McKenna was arguing that what humans experience while under the influence of hallucinogens was, in fact, the *real* reality—or at least a small glimpse of our future reality. His assumptions may have been more accurate than even he could have imagined. If he were alive today, I imagine that he would see Google's DeepMind as a true vision of what the future might look like: morphic, novel, and shifting symbologies that urge us to "see what we mean."

Advanced simulations and AR overlays will inevitably feel like technological hallucinations, like feral echoes of our impossible future bouncing back at us with implications so outlandish and magical, even the bravest of futurists would not dare define or describe them.

Perceptual Computing

This is the age of perceptual computing: memory recording, dream recording, and predictive cognition. A future where AI is part of our perceptual construct. A techno-dimensional realm where the collective unconscious is made real. It is the vulcanization of our internal minds and our imaginations. A future where the dream world spills out over the world of awareness like a psychedelic tsunami. A flood of imagination and information so elaborate that it may drive some people into madness. This is a future filled with predictive algorithms that can make things appear and disappear in the blink of an eye. It is this perceptual augmentation of our minds that will lead to an extraordinary and novel future.

Undetectable simulations will begin to emerge in the next 25 years. AR overlays that go unnoticed in the purely biological perceptual world will be rampant in the bio-digital augmented reality space. This has huge implications for creativity and is also fertile ground for political propaganda and mind control by hackers and other nefarious groups.

Advanced big data realities could lead us toward a holistic future filled with equality and abundance or down a dark road toward dictatorship, capitalization of consciousness, and industrialization of mind manipulation.

Perceptual Influencers

Other future scenarios of which to be aware in the simulated space are continuity of mind, memory alteration, and control of our perceptions. Advertisers will be able to geolocate our AR contact lenses and "slip" undetectable overlays into our simulated AR worlds. In the future, you could see a person on the street wearing an AR overlay of shoes provided by an advertiser seeking your attention. The wearer of the undetectable AR overlay, funded by manufacturers and advertisers, will be tomorrow's perceptual influencers. These freelance perceptual influencers could spend their days walking the streets of major cities or sipping overpriced coffee while letting advanced algorithms morph the awareness of the unsuspecting members of the public who happen to gaze upon their shoes.

Every eye that looks in the direction of these future perceptual influencers could individually see a different pair of shoes, depending on their specific predictive data profiles.

The AI will augment the overlay of the shoes depending on behavioral data. It could keep projecting the same shoes, or could morph new shoes on all public perceptual influencers until its market is shown the perfect pair.

Once your attention has been caught by the sight of a desirable pair of shoes, you blink quickly three times to see if the image you see is an undetectable shoe overlay ad. You breathe a sigh of relief as an AR pop-up appears beside the shoes that read, "Yes, these shoes are purchasable right now. Blink twice to purchase." Your personal AI, connected to the cloud, processes the payment and sends out the local Amazon drone to deliver the shoes to your exact location.

Voila. Instant gratification. No need to pick your shoe size. Your AI assistant fills out all necessary info in the background in the literal blink of an augmented eye.

This scenario might sound fantastic to the avid shoe aficionado, but the implications are potentially dangerous and psychologically invasive. Some of these perceptual influence

> If a purely biological, unaugmented mind is seeing miniature pink elephants and hearing disembodied voices, then culturally we can agree that the experiencer is fully outside the realm of culturally agreed-upon sanity.

campaigns are already happening now on social media apps and websites. It is not a stretch to see that perceptual computing will make our future reality even more complex and novel.

Will we allow companies or political groups to overlay undetectable simulations over our eyes and minds? Imagine "seeing" a political rally down the street with negative signs for political opponents, causing you to question at a crucial moment your political choice. Can we stop this from happening? We appear currently to have difficulty stopping it from influencing political elections in the United States and around the world. Imagine how difficult it will be when the influence is cognitively undetectable.

The Portal Inward

I have often said that the future is a portal inward. What we find there will be computational and ancient. To be clear, I am saying here that our destination is inward. A journey into the last frontier, the primordial, unconscious, cosmic mind. For good or ill, this is the destination. Mars may be on the horizon, but the unconscious mind will follow us wherever we go.

This ancient internal landscape may feel new, but it has been here all along, coevolving with us and assisting us. It has enabled us to create the tools and the technologies that will open the portal into the inner world, a world of ultimate quantification.

This internalization of computational awareness and the new perceptual computing age will shock the masses. It will feel magical, unbelievable, and ominous. It will be ignored, denied, and rationalized until it is implemented, with or without our consent. However, make no mistake, this predictive big data age is just over the horizon. The AI of the future will know us better than we know ourselves. It will predict our behaviors and our desires.

The future is the age of novelty: many realities and multiple technological hallucinations.

G**ray Scott** is a futurist, a techno-philosopher, and the world's leading expert in the field of emerging technology. He is the host of the digital-philosophy web series FUTURISTIC NOW and a visionary board member of the World Future Society. Scott is frequently interviewed by the *Discovery Channel, History Channel, Forbes, CBS News, Vanity Fair,* VICE MOTHERBOARD, *Fast Company, The Washington Post, Psychology Today, Business News Daily, New York Post* and *SingularityHub.*

Building the Ship of Theseus

Dr. Kaitlyn Sadtler, PhD

Fifty years ago, when *Future Shock* was released, cigarette TV ads were banned in the US, The Beatles broke up, the Apollo 13 spacecraft suffered an oxygen tank explosion en route to the moon, protests heightened against the Vietnam War, the Ford Pinto came out (later realized as a poor decision), Janis Joplin died at 27, and the EPA was established. Sex discrimination was not yet ruled unconstitutional, and it had been just 16 years since the US Supreme Court ruled against segregation of schools.

In the world of science, the Nobel Prize was awarded to the discoverers of neurotransmitters (the signaling molecules of the nervous system) and the famous photo of DNA taken by Rosalind Franklin was celebrating its 18th birthday. It would be another 15 years before the development of a pioneering technology known as polymerase chain reaction, or PCR, would allow researchers to edit, amplify, and detect specific DNA sequences.

Scientific expansion was happening in an exponential scale from astrophysics to biology. In 1970, exploring things to come in *Future Shock*, the author speculated about the expansion of a scientific discipline known as bio-engineering. With advances in medical technologies, patients were being saved from life-threatening injuries and genetic diseases—and life expectancy had increased 17 years over the previous 50 (between 1920 and 1970). Though lives were being saved and extended, clinics faced new challenges as a result of these improvements in healthcare. It became more common to see such things as degrading joints, organs slowly losing their functions, and traumatic loss of tissue that once would've resulted in loss of life. At that time, there was no organ donor wait list, and the practice of transplantation was still in the early stages. Since the organization of a standardized wait list and further improvement in medical care, there are now over 100,000 patients waiting for life-saving transplants.

Even in 1970, it was appreciated that future demand could lead to a black-market organ trade (which is a very real thing in the new millennium). Furthermore, transplanted organs are composed solely of human donor tissue. The recipient's immune system, not recognizing the foreign tissue, will reject it in the absence of strong immunosuppressive drugs. Each cell of the transplanted organ is tagged for destruction by the patient's immune system via proteins called the major histocompatibility complex (MHC) or HLA (human leukocyte antigen). If the donor had even one HLA form that differed from those of the organ recipient, then the organ would be rejected—and there are a lot of different HLAs out there.

A need outside of organ transplants and immunosuppression was thus recognized and the field of bioengineering emerged. The first of the biomedical implants to truly engineer the human body appeared in 1958 with the pacemaker, followed 10 years later by the first knee replacement. In 1970, it was predicted that within 15 years artificial tissue and organ replacements would be standard practice. This held true to an extent, with a rapid increase in total knee and hip replacements, as well as in synthetic heart valves and numerous pacemaker implantations. However, we definitely still have miles to go before donor transplants become a thing of the past.

> In our liver we have Küpffer cells, in our brain we have Microglia, and every other tissue has cells that react specifically in ways that are regulated by the tissues they reside in. Therefore, whatever we do to our body, from implants to genome editing, can be affected by immune cells.

In our current world, passing from the 2010s into the 2020s, we have seen advances in bioengineering that include nanoparticles, genome-editing technologies, and neural-machine interfaces. We have also experienced advances in wound care, including materials derived from biologic sources that work with our body to help regrow tissue with less scarring. However, we are still working to create materials that can reliably regenerate or regrow tissues and organs.

Moving forward, there is a growing contingent of researchers paying attention to a critical player in wound healing and tissue regeneration—the immune system. Mind you, I might be slightly biased because this is what I study. Nevertheless, our immune system is one of the most advanced and powerful parts of our body. Beyond our lymph nodes, our spleen, thymus, and our bone marrow, which generate immune cells that circulate throughout our blood and act as hubs of immune cell activation, each tissue has its own resident set of immune cells. In our liver we have Küpffer cells, in our brain we have Microglia, and every other tissue has cells that react specifically in ways that are regulated by the tissues they reside in. Therefore, whatever we do to our body, from implants to genome editing, can be affected by immune cells.

In the context of regenerative medicine—where we try to regrow missing or damaged tissue, this interaction becomes very apparent. Not only will our immune system react to the implant that is put in to help regrow this tissue, but it also regulates how our tissue develops. The proteins that are secreted by immune cells can interact with stem cells and affect how they behave, either making a functional tissue, or instead resulting in dense scar tissue. This same issue happens when scientists try to create integrative prostheses. When any part of a synthetic prosthetic interacts with our body via connections that break or pass through the skin barrier, our immune system responds to that synthetic implant as something that isn't supposed to be there, and it will be walled off with scar tissue. This can be avoided by integrating muscular contractions via patches that sense electrical activity but do not go through the skin barrier. If further integration is to be accomplished, though, the immune system will have to be considered. Advances in integrative prostheses and synthetic organ mimics (both clinically and in the laboratory) are very promising and have great potential to improve a patient's quality of life.

> "Toffler predicted that the future human body will become "modular," wherein parts of the body that are non-functional or do not meet a set standard can be replaced with new components. This interestingly parallels a philosophical thought experiment known as the Ship of Theseus.

Toffler predicted that the future human body will become "modular," wherein parts of the body that are non-functional or do not meet a set standard can be replaced with new components. This interestingly parallels a philosophical thought experiment known as the Ship of Theseus. In this scenario, a ship sailed by Theseus (mythical king of ancient Greece and founder of Athens) was aging. As parts of the ship wore down and compromised the integrity of the structure, they were replaced with new components to keep the ship seaworthy. As time passed, more and more old pieces were removed and new pieces were added to the ship. The question then became, at what point does this ship cease to be the original ship? Is it when there is one piece changed? Most would argue, of course, that it's the same ship. Just because I got the tires changed on my car doesn't mean I got a new car. Half of the ship? Well, which half? What pieces from the original structure remain?

Now of course, a human body isn't an inanimate ship, but this gives us something to think about. Is a human body still a human body after half of its tissues are made of synthetic materials? Most people would argue that a human is still a human as long as neural cognition is intact. But what if we take this a step further. With advances in computing, artificial intelligence, and high-powered computers, could it be possible to one day transfer the electrical impulses generated by our body into a synthetic, computerized storage system? And then, would we still be considered human? We will not face such an enigma in the near future, and if we do get to the point that missing or damaged organs can be quickly and easily replaced synthetically, we will have recognized a fantastic level of medical treatment.

Moving into the year 2020, it is foreseeable that these advances in integrative prostheses and regenerative medicine continue to progress through the convergence of different scientific fields, such as bioengineering, immunology, mechanical engineering, polymer chemistry, and molecular biology. As these fields interact, we will see increases in therapeutics to help treat traumatic injury, decreasing the presence of scar tissue and increasing the regrowth of functional tissue. We might see prosthetics that integrate with the body to the extent that they provide sensory information from their surroundings, enabling us to "feel" with a synthetic limb. We could see increases in the use of bioreactors that are able to grow tissues and organs in the lab. I, for one, am excited about the next generation of research and how we will leverage expertise from different scientific fields to further medical discoveries and innovations. ■

Dr. Kaitlyn Sadtler, PhD is currently an Earl Stadtman Tenure-Track Investigator and Chief of the Section on Immuno-Engineering at the National Institutes of Health. She recently finished her postdoctoral fellowship in the lab of Dr. Daniel Anderson and Dr. Robert Langer at MIT, studying how our body interprets medical device implants as "foreign" and how to prevent the subsequent inflammatory response. During her time at MIT, she was the recipient of a NRSA Postdoctoral Fellowship for her work on immunoengineering in the context of soft tissue trauma, a TED Fellow whose TED talk was listed as one of the top 25 most viewed in 2018, and was recognized in the Forbes 30 Under 30 list in Science for 2019. Prior to MIT, Dr. Sadtler completed her PhD at the Johns Hopkins University School of Medicine, where her thesis work describing a specific type of immune cell required for biomaterial-mediated muscle regeneration was published in Science magazine. Dr. Sadtler received her BS summa cum laude from University of Maryland Baltimore County, where she was named an Outstanding Graduating Senior in Biological Sciences, prior to a postbaccalaurate IRTA at the National Institute of Allergy and Infectious Disease in the Lab of Cellular and Molecular Immunology. Learn more about her via the following links: www.go.ted.com/ kaitlynsadtler (TED Talk), https://scholar.google.com/citations?user=N4Zcv00AAAAJ&hl=en (Scientific Publications), https://twitter.com/KSadtler (Twitter)

Needed: Ambassadors to the Future

Jack Uldrich

> 66 The illiterate of the 21st century will not be those who cannot read and write, but those who cannot learn, unlearn, and relearn. 99
>
> —*Alvin Toffler*

The above quotation has been instrumental in my work as a professional futurist and even inspired me to write a book on the subject of unlearning. ▪ I was surprised, therefore, to discover upon rereading *Future Shock* that it is both a misattribution and a misquotation. Toffler does, in fact, write that human adaptation can be enhanced by instructing students how to "learn, unlearn, and relearn," but the other half of the quotation comes from psychologist Herbert Gerjuoy, who wrote "Tomorrow's illiterate will not be the man who can't read; he will be the man who has not learned how to learn."

In addition to requiring me to "unlearn" my own history of the quote, my rereading of Chapter 18 ("Education in the Future Tense")—the chapter from which the quote was inspired—caused me to reflect more deeply upon the words with which Toffler concludes the chapter: "*Education must shift into the future tense.*"

Sadly, a half-century later, our educational system remains stuck in the past and seems incapable of even shifting into our present era—where Toffler's warnings of accelerating change are more pronounced and relevant than ever.

What, then, is the solution? How do we shift education into the future tense? Toffler's proposal for a "Council of the Future" offers a promising framework. He rightly suggests that in addition to professional educators, planners, and businesspeople serving on the council, students are integral to its success because they are the ones who will "invent and inhabit the future."

Toffler underscores the vital importance of giving students the skills and knowledge necessary to engage in creative tasks, make informed critical judgments, anticipate direction, and understand the rate of change. These traits, he argues, will provide students the foundation necessary to adapt to an ever-changing future. Or, in his words, it will instill in them "cope-ability."

> We can awaken our educational system from its "silence about tomorrow" by charging students with the responsibility for thinking about the future, for the simple reason that they are going to spend the rest of their lives there.

I would now like to take Toffler's idea of the Council of the Future a step further and propose that rather than constructing a curriculum of courses to provide students these foundational skills, every student should be appointed an "Ambassador to the Future" at an early age and charged with the duty and responsibility of making peace with their future. This simple act will reorient students from "facing backward" and point them toward the future.

Now, contemplating the future is no easy task, and there is no perfect place to start, but Toffler steers us in the right direction when he states that students currently "have no heritage of the future." To address this shortcoming and to get the students thinking about their "heritage," there is no need to overthink the issue. We can awaken our educational system from its "silence about tomorrow" by charging students with the responsibility for thinking about the future, for the simple reason that they are going to spend the rest of their lives there. In other words, if they are going to be the ones who imagine, invent, create, and safeguard the future, they must first begin by thinking about it.

At this point, the reader may ask, does "the future" mean five years in the future? Twenty years? 100 years? Or even 500 or 1,000 generations? The answer is not ours to determine. It is the students' to decide.

Different ambassadors will select distinct time frames according to their unique perspectives, needs, and interests. The beauty of this approach is that ambassadors with varying horizons of time will bring fresh perspectives and unique questions into play. In addition to debating the issue of how far into the future society's responsibility goes, other questions might include (but are certainly not limited to): Are we disenfranchising future generations? How many natural resources do future generations have the right to expect? How do the needs of other sentient beings factor into our decisions? What does it mean to be human and to have consciousness? Do people have a right to live 120, 150, or even a thousand or more years into the future? To whom does deep space belong? What will replace money? How can we better communicate with one another? How can we better govern ourselves? And how might we consider the possibility of low-probability but high-impact events?

The differing perspectives will cause ambassadors with shorter time frames to expand their minds to consider a deeper future, while the ambassadors with a longer horizon will be required to roll up their sleeves and contemplate the realities of more near-term future scenarios.

These perspectives and the questions they engender, more than any prescribed course, will begin shifting students into the "future tense" and, in the process, hone their critical judgment skills and sharpen their reasoning capabilities.

Serious thought on the future will lead the students into economic, political, scientific, and technological issues, as well as a panoply of moral and ethical considerations. To better perfect their skills and techniques, the students will come to appreciate that it is to their benefit to listen to a wide variety of disparate and diverse voices. They will also come to understand the need to think probabilistically, embrace ambiguity, challenge assumptions, and stay open to the ever-present need to unlearn whatever it is they think they know. In short, the responsibility of these ambassadors to the future will be to train themselves to deal with uncertainty, handle the unknown, and expect the unexpected.

Student ambassadors may also begin to construct vibrant and multilayered scenarios to help inform other people's thinking about how society can move in the direction of favorable futures while avoiding negative ones.

Answers to questions of the future will always be impossible to ascertain with complete certainty, but by focusing on "root questions" as Toffler suggested, these ambassadors will understand that it is their heritage at stake, and if they are to meet their mighty responsibilities to the future, they—the students— must be the ones who bear the ultimate responsibility for "shifting education into the future tense." Will such an idea work? I don't know, but education cannot remain "silent about tomorrow" any longer.

Toffler was spot on when he wrote, "Creating curiosity and awareness is the cardinal task of education." One way to do this is to give every student their "ambassador to the future" title and mission, and then get out of their way and allow (again in Toffler's words) "a multiplicity of visions, dreams, and prophecies—images of potential tomorrows" to flourish. For it is the students' future to create. ▪

Jack Uldrich is a global futurist, keynote speaker, and a best-selling author of twelve books, including *Higher Unlearning: 39 Post-Requisite Lessons for Achieving a Successful Future*.

Averting Future Shock at Planetary Scale

Dr. Michel Laberge

The main theme of *Future Shock* is that the world is changing too fast and we humans can't cope very well with these fast changes. ■ Since the book was written, 50 years ago, the rate of change is even higher, worsening the problem. But humans appear to be a very adaptable species, and I believe that future shock is a rather mild condition. Although, being 57 years old, I am a bit slow taking up the social changes, my kids are doing just fine and embrace the new ways of life without difficulty. For them, it is just the way it is. Humans can cope with the changes due to high brain function. Our interaction with the world is driven much more by our intellect than by inherited instinct.

Unfortunately, that is not the case for the natural world of plants, animals, and ecosystems. They are capable of successfully adapting to changes over many generations, through Darwinian evolution, but it is generally a very slow process and they are ill-prepared for the rapid changes that humans are inflicting on the planet. Consequently, deforestation, pollution, global warming, and habitat modification are leading to the disappearance of species at an enormous rate. We are wrecking the place, and nature is suffering a serious case of future shock.

Due to our technology, we do not get eaten by tigers anymore and our population is growing. To feed it, an increasing fraction of the Earth's surface is turned to high-productivity farming. Ocean life is heavily harvested at an unsustainable rate. Aquifers are being depleted. Access to cheap energy from fossil fuel allows this technology-intensive world to function. Dig in the ground and out comes oil, gas, and coal. This fantastic gift of nature has fueled our present technological society.

Unfortunately, using this resource is not without serious drawbacks. As a natural process, CO_2 from the air is turned into plants that die and get buried in the ground, forming fossil fuels. Some CO_2 is returned to the atmosphere by volcanism, and an equilibrium is achieved. Over eons, the planet got used to this equilibrium level of atmospheric CO_2. But we now dig out the fossil fuel, burn it, and release the CO_2 into the air at a rate sufficient to upset this equilibrium, causing the CO_2 concentration in the atmosphere to rapidly rise, leading to climate change. These changes are too fast for adaptation by the natural world.

Future Shock was written in the golden age of atomic energy, and Alvin Toffler proposed that clean, cheap, and abundant energy would be produced by fission reactors. Fifty years later, only 4 percent of worldwide energy is produced by nuclear fission reactors and this percentage is trending down. Accidents, cost, and concerns about radioactive waste and atomic weapon proliferation have made this option less attractive.

Unforeseen by Toffler is the rapid rise in renewable energy, mostly wind and solar. Although CO_2-free, these renewables suffer from low energy density, requiring vast collecting areas, and are intermittent. They currently provide only 2.5 percent of worldwide energy, although that percentage is increasing rapidly. The high cost of electricity storage and the intermittent nature of renewables make the total cost of the electricity supply system, including complex transmission and backup generators, rise rapidly for accommodating more than ~20 percent renewables on the grid. For 100 percent renewable plus storage, the cost of energy would be 10 times more than today. So wind and solar, although helpful, cannot yet provide the majority of our energy needs at a reasonable cost.

With a growing population and an increase in its standard of living, energy demand is rapidly increasing. Burning fossil fuel makes a mess; wind and solar can't meet the large percentage of the demand economically; and people are too scared of fission reactors.

> At the time of *Future Shock*'s writing, experimental machines produced 10,000 times less fusion energy than the energy used by the machine to operate; today the record is 0.6. We are fast approaching the point where fusion will have a positive energy output.

What can we do?

The Sun and all the stars in the universe derive their formidable power from *fusion* energy. It is nature's way of producing power. The simplest fusion reaction involves turning hydrogen isotopes into helium, a safe by-product. The fusion fuel can be extracted from the oceans or any body of water. There is enough fusion fuel available to run our society for billions of years. A fusion power plant cannot melt down. A small plant can produce a large quantity of electricity on demand. It produces no CO_2 or other pollution. There is no weapons-grade uranium or plutonium involved.

Fusion is the ideal source of energy. But there is no such thing as a free lunch.

Producing on Earth the conditions that exist in the center of the Sun—conditions required to produce fusion energy—is extremely difficult. Yet huge progress has been made over the years. At the time of *Future Shock*'s writing, experimental machines produced 10,000 times less fusion energy than the energy used by the machine to operate; today the record is 0.6. We are fast approaching the point where fusion will have a positive energy output.

In the past, most of the fusion development work was done by national labs. But sensing that the endgame is within reach, there are now a few dozen private companies, such as General Fusion, developing fusion energy using various approaches. It is likely that within the next two decades some of these will succeed in creating a practical and economical fusion power plant generating electricity for the grid. The advent of clean, dense, affordable, on-demand energy will enable progress on a number of the challenges noted earlier, and further other human goals. CO_2 can be removed from the air, water desalinization can help with the water supply, and food can be grown in a denser, controlled environment. Flying cars, supersonic transportation, common space travel, and other futuristic predictions have been stalled because of their huge energy demand, making them uneconomical. Fusion energy will bring us into the future. ▤

Since establishing General Fusion in 2002 with a vision for a clean, safe, and practical source of energy, **Dr. Michel Laberge** and his team have become recognized as global leaders in commercial fusion energy. His work has been featured in *Scientific American* and *Time*, and drew a global TED audience of over one million viewers. Prior to establishing General Fusion, Michel spent nine years at Creo Products in Vancouver as a senior physicist and principal engineer, leading projects that resulted in more than $1 billion worth of product sales. Dr. Laberge holds a BSc and MSc in physics from Laval University, and in 1990 earned his PhD in fusion physics from the University of British Columbia.

Plus ça Change

Jason Schenker

The future will be one of rapid advancement in many different fields. But that could have been said at almost any time in the past. ■ Similarly, it may seem that we will be unable to manage or handle the changes ahead. But it has always been so.

And yet, we have survived. We are still here. We have adopted and adapted to new technologies. It is likely we will continue to do so.

Looking Back

The future shock anticipated by Alvin Toffler as an imminent threat to the sanity of humanity has not happened. We are still sane—or at least mostly so. Even older generations adopt the newest technologies. They may not be the early adopters or fast followers, but they eventually adopt those technologies that are the most useful.

While Toffler advocated for embracing change, generally speaking this would not be anything new.

Looking back, technologies that once seemed disruptive have become givens across a broad swath of society and the economy. Granted, there will be ever-increasing challenges ahead. But we are likely to manage them, just as we have in the past: By adopting them and adapting to allow for their use.

In every generation there are Luddites. There are those who are fearmongers. There are those who say this time is different. They argue that we will be unable to survive the changes ahead.

As they have so often before, humans have adapted to wave after wave of new technologies over the past half a century. This suggests that some of the warnings that Toffler claimed were not hyperbolic may, in fact, have been hyperbolic.

Even though Toffler advocated for embracing change, his notion, that the only reasonable way to

253

view risks from change acceleration was through the lens of an impending existential crisis for humanity, has thus far been disproven. And it is unlikely to prove true in the future.

For all the good that *Future Shock* did in raising awareness of technological advance—and the risks associated with future technologies—the truth is that Toffler presented a sometimes dystopian picture that framed technology as a partially poisoned wellspring with genuine risks to humanity. Because humanity might be overwhelmed by technology.

Similar arguments circulate today—50 years after the publication of *Future Shock*.

Looking Ahead

Today, the technological fear *de rigueur* is that of the Robocalypse. It is fear of an apocalypse of jobs, engendered by the increased use of robots, robotics, automation, and AI. It is the fear that this increased use of technology will make it impossible for humans to still have jobs—or to survive at all.

In light of these risks, some futurists speak of the imminent demise of humanity. Or at least, they claim, increasing automation and development of AI are harbingers of a future shock to the labor market—one that could spill over into society in general in a manner not dissimilar to what Toffler had envisioned.

And yet, we have better tools today to counter technology risks.

There is a technological counterweight to the risk of professional redundancies: We have increased access to an in-hand labor market, in-hand education, in-hand banking, and in-hand commerce. If technology is a "better mousetrap" that could cause massive societal shock, it may also be the origin of a better mouse. New technologies that present challenges often foster the solutions to the challenges they create.

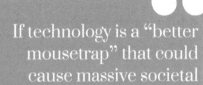

> If technology is a "better mousetrap" that could cause massive societal shock, it may also be the origin of a better mouse. New technologies that present challenges often foster the solutions to the challenges they create.

This Hegelian technological dialectic has played out since time immemorial. Labor markets change, entertainment media change, communication channels change. The only constant is change, which is why the primary source of disruption isn't the emergence of completely new concepts over the past 50 years, but rather an accelerating transition from analog to digital technology. In many ways, almost every new technology has an older, analog permutation.

Everything old is new again.

No matter whether the turn of phrases inspiring fear of technology eventually capture the zeitgeist of this or the next era, the reality is that technology supports productivity growth and economic growth, and increases the returns on both capital and labor. Accepting these realities has more to do with framing the changes in technology for acceptance at the level of the general population, rather than hyperbolically underscoring the risks of future shocks those changes may cause the global psyche.

The Risks

As I look to the future, I see tremendous opportunity through technology.

Of course, I also see risks, but I don't see the risk of people being overwhelmed by an overabundance of technological innovations. In fact, I see rather the opposite. I see the risk that people may have more free time on their hands than they are accustomed to occupying without external motivation, because of innovation and automation.

Technologies are tools, but many new technologies are not transparent. Powerful and somewhat mysterious technologies engender fear, which is destabilizing and thus constitutes its own type of risk. Some people are fearful about the future of their own jobs, for instance. The consequences of fear-induced behavior could manifest in a self-fulfilling misfortune, should the Robocalypse-fearing proponents of universal basic income usher in a new kind of communism that leads to a significant decline in economic productivity and long-term economic stagnation.

So, these fears can themselves become dangerous, particularly in a democracy, where the Tocquevillian risk of a tyranny of a frightened majority is not insignificant.

The most critical fundamental reality is that while many jobs over time are going to change and become obsolete, humans will need things to do. After all, entire lives of unearned leisure are not exactly lives of pure contentment. Yes, a lot of years of leisure is nice. But have you ever wondered why billionaires continue to work? It's because they need something to do. Because without enough to do, some people rip up their own lives just to avoid being bored.

This is also a key lesson of Greek mythology. Greek gods and goddesses started wars and wreaked havoc on the world for no reason other than to avoid the sheer boredom of having nothing to do.

I mention this because in my view, the risk of a future shock is not linked to a concern that technology will shock the world to the extent that people just cannot handle it. But rather, the risk of a future shock likely stems from the potential overabundance of freedom that new technologies may bring.

And the boredom, if people don't have enough to do.

That is the potential future shock of the next 50 years.

Jason Schenker is chairman of The Futurist Institute, which helps strategists, consultants, and analysts incorporate new and emerging technology risks and opportunities into their long-term strategic planning. Schenker is also the president of Prestige Economics, a columnist for Bloomberg Opinion, and the author of over 20 books, including *Quantum: Computing Nouveau*, *The Future of Finance is Now*, and *Jobs for Robots: Between Robocalypse and Robotopia*. Schenker has been ranked the #1 forecaster in the world by Bloomberg in 25 different categories since 2011. He advises public corporations, private companies, institutional investors, central banks, and governmental bodies on future technology topics. Learn more at www.futuristinstitute.org and www.jasonschenker.com.

On Building
a Future that Matters

Lisa Bodell

During a recent flight back to New York, the woman sitting next to me asked about the book I was reading. ◼ "What's *Future Shock?*" she said. We talked a little about Toffler's ideas around change and its impacts, but her eyes widened when I mentioned that not long ago, people didn't really think about the future in a planned manner because, among many reasons, it was thought to be something "unknown" and therefore we couldn't affect it. My seatmate was astonished. Not only was this concept totally foreign to her own experience, since today we are bombarded with messages about innovating, disrupting, and planning, but she thought this was simply short-sighted. "How can you not think about the future?" she said.

Indeed. That's what makes *Future Shock* so amazingly prescient. Fifty years on, Toffler's observations about the need to be proactive about the future, to be forward looking, to understand the effects of continual change, and, most importantly, to be aware of the psychological impacts it has on us as individuals and as a society, are still incredibly relevant.

When reading the book again, I was struck by the fact that in the late 1960s as Toffler wrote his book, people were feeling engulfed by change just as we are today. The US was in the middle of a contentious war, protests were frequent, and social norms were continually challenged ("Free love!"). But Toffler's statement that "the whole world is a fast-breaking story" seems almost quaint when compared to today. To think of life 50 years ago is to conjure a time where, on the whole, the pace was slower, life was simpler. We remember a day-to-day without much technology, connectivity, or pressure. Think about it. Fifty years ago, when someone asked you, "How are you doing?"

the typical response was, "I'm good, and you?" Today, if someone asks, "How are you doing?" you know what the most common answer is? BUSY. The sheer volume, velocity, and variety of change we experience continually creates an unfamiliar environment for people and often leaves them feeling unmoored. These comparisons to earlier times make us reflect on the paradox of change. Is change good or bad? Has the role technology played in our lives been positive or negative? The answer is: BOTH.

The good news is that today, change and innovation are mainstream and expected. Whereas Toffler had to awaken people to the importance of proactively thinking about and shaping the future, today this concept is largely understood and actively discussed. Companies employ trends analysts and perform scenario planning; employees are encouraged to "embrace change," and HR departments provide training to teach how to do it. It's a common occurrence to see advertisements touting how "innovative" a company is. Podcasts and events feature Silicon Valley entrepreneurs whose startups have upended entire industries and made them billionaires. It's cool to be a change agent, an innovator, a DISRUPTOR even. And while certainly not everyone embraces change, they know they should if they are to keep up with their environments. Today the issue with change is less about *should* we embrace it, and more about how better to proactively and systematically manage its impacts.

Reflecting on Toffler's work, I found myself writing down two themes: THE PROBLEM OF COMPLEXITY and THE NEED FOR MEANING. *Future Shock* brilliantly touches on these themes, but they take on a much deeper significance today than probably even Toffler imagined.

Let's start with complexity. Compared to 1970, we live and work in a far more complex world. Companies are global and matrixed. Many of us deal daily with people from multiple cultures in multiple time zones. Technology provides a waterfall of data to analyze trends and predict what's next. Communication channels are multiplied, always on, and used constantly. And despite the access and opportunities this provides, there are significant, perhaps less than benign, impacts. According to a Boston Consulting Group survey, we measure six times the number of metrics that we did in the 1950s. So, if your organization gauged progress by measuring 10 metrics before, it now measures 60. The amount of governance structures/committees/policies/procedures put in place to better "manage" work within organizations has increased anywhere from between 50% to 350% in the last decade alone. Over 250 billion emails are sent daily, with the average number of emails a person receives each day estimated to be between 100-200 (https://www.campaignmonitor.com/blog/email-marketing/2018/03/shocking-truth-about-how-many-emails-sent/). In fact, a study by Bain Consulting showed that the average worker is so consumed by meetings, emails, and unnecessary work that only 14% of their time (that's six hours a week) is spent on "meaningful work." And there's the paradox—"progress" has allowed us to do more—but is "more" actually valuable? Are we focused on the things that matter?

> To think of life 50 years ago is to conjure a time where, on the whole, the pace was slower, life was simpler. We remember a day-to-day without much technology, connectivity, or pressure.

Toffler wrote in a time of industrialism, where to succeed, size mattered. MORE mattered. Today, success isn't driven by size. It's driven by speed. To move quickly, it's often easier to just add to what we're already doing rather than stop to consider, "Is there a better way to do this?" So, we just bolt another feature onto an existing process until it becomes so complex or bulky we can't use it. We add a few more data fields to a report that already takes days to complete. With the best of intentions, we create the beast that we become a slave to. The more the pace of change quickens, the more we try to manage it. It's why we answer emails while we sit on a conference call. Or respond to a text while at dinner. We multitask to keep up.

And this brings me to the next point, which Toffler touched on but I believe requires more significant focus. It's what results from all this complexity: the growing NEED FOR MEANING. Complexity is the enemy of the meaningful. Many people, stressed and exhausted from change and the volume of things they have to do, increasingly wonder what it all means. Not that staying up 'til 2am to fix the font on PowerPoint slides for tomorrow's sales presentation isn't deeply satisfying. Or that juggling carpool obligations for a multitude of school events isn't fulfilling. Or that travelling for work while meeting an urgent proposal deadline isn't a piece of cake. Not that I'm speaking from experience or anything. In today's world, change allows us to do MORE, but is it what we want to be doing?

> And there's the paradox—"progress" has allowed us to do more—but is "more" actually valuable? Are we focused on the things that matter?

Toffler wrote of the emergence of the "super-simplifier" in response to relentless change (pg. 361). "With old heroes and institutions toppling... (he) seeks a simple neat equation that will explain all the complex novelties that engulf him" (pg. 45). Just look at the cult-like following of Japanese organizing expert Marie Kondo. Her approach to simplifying our lives (well, at least our closets) is by assessing which of our things have meaning to us ("Does it bring you joy?"). If there's no joy, we are advised to get rid of it. The result is less clutter, and a focus on what matters.

Organizations are similarly recognizing that simplification has to be their new operating system. I'm not advocating that you analyze the emails in your inbox and assess whether each one "brings you joy" (they likely don't). But, in parts of organizations like Pfizer, SAP, and P&G, leaders recognize the toll that continual change has taken, and they are committed to eradicating unnecessary work so employees can spend their time on things that matter—and bring them joy.

We more often, now, see people taking "digital detoxes"—they're "tuning out" to better "tune in." Millions practice mindfulness as a way to quiet the noise, and focus. In fact, the mindfulness and meditation industry takes in over $1 billion annually, and more than 25% of Fortune 500 companies provide mindfulness training and meditation rooms for their employees. Even better, schools teach it to students to better manage change and stress, with positive results—better grades, more focus, and fewer detentions.

The accelerated pace of change will surely continue for some time. So, what's the good news in all this? Plenty. Toffler inspired a generation to look forward and to actively shape the future. Today, we see evidence of this in companies' innovation teams, in their robust agility and change training curricula, and in their trendspotting activities. They embrace foresight activities like "killing their company" through proactive obsolescence exercises (address your weaknesses before the competition does!) and Future of Work studies to prepare their workforce and work environment for the next decade. Even more important, our schools, though with still a long way to go, are saying goodbye to the industrial-era form of cookie-cutter teaching and are instead creating innovation courses and "maker" spaces for kids to tinker, experiment, and think. They bring in entrepreneurs to share stories about thinking differently, and teach creative problem-solving and inquiry as part of the curriculum. We're igniting a generation of younger people to consider embracing and shaping the future as both normal and expected.

There's an African proverb that states: "If you want to go fast, go alone. If you want to go far, go together." The future belongs to those who not only embrace rapid change, but who can also focus together on what matters. It is our job as practitioners of the future to teach everyone how to do just that.

FutureThink CEO **Lisa Bodell** is the bestselling author of *Kill the Company* and *Why Simple Wins*. She's a global leader on simplification and innovation, whose keynotes leave audiences inspired to change and arm themselves with radically simple tools to get to the work that matters. With a deep understanding of best practices across industries, Bodell has contributed her expertise to a wide variety of media, including: *Fast Company, WIRED, The New York Times, Inc., Bloomberg Businessweek, Forbes, Harvard Business Review, The Huffington Post, FOX News,* and CNN. Bodell has taught innovation at both American University and Fordham University, and has a TED talk on the topic. She has served on the board of advisors of several organizations, including the Global Agenda Council for the World Economic Forum, the NSA, the Association of Professional Futurists, and Novartis. Bodell brings a compelling perspective to the sought-after topics of simplification and innovation. Her transformational message has inspired executives at top-ranked organizations such as Google, Cisco, Citigroup, Merck, and the U.S. Navy War College. Based on her bestselling book, *Why Simple Wins: Escape the Complexity Trap and Get to the Work that Matters,* Bodell's keynotes offer tools and takeaways on how organizations and individuals can eradicate complexity and allow simplicity to be their new operating system.

After Shock:
Never-Ending
Surprises

John L. Petersen

Alvin Toffler got it right... and, as a good futurist, early. He saw the incoming bow wave of what was certain to be a revolution. ■ But what he and most prognosticators didn't—and still don't—understand is that the shock he identified was just the beginning, an early indicator, a precursor of the most significant, fundamental shift in the history of life on this planet. Sooner than may seem reasonable, that shift will result in the emergence of a new human and a new world.

The nature of the reorganization makes it very hard, indeed, to even comprehend.

Vectors of exponential change from multiple sectors are converging, producing a multilayered, extraordinarily complex and interdependent emerging reality that calls for dramatically different tools and approaches to effectively suss what is headed our way.

Consider these converging forces—any one of which is enough to fundamentally change how humans understand reality, themselves, and how to live on the planet:

■ **Unusual Cosmic Convergence**: Our Voyager space probes (and other corroborating science), confirm that our solar system is moving into an unfamiliar area of space that has a significantly different energetic environment than that of all of our recorded history. That different environment is affecting the sun and the other nearby stars in significant ways, causing them to exhibit unfamiliar behavior. These inputs, coupled with the common cycles of the sun, portend significant changes for the Earth. For example, significant climate change has been observed on all of the major planets in our solar system in the recent decade or two.

- **Potential Solar Flare**: The changing energetic environment of our cosmic local cloud seems to have influenced a growing number of stars in our neighborhood to produce massive, previously unseen, solar flares. These flares would have a profound influence on the conditions of all planets in their systems. One report catalogs twenty-six flares on nearby stars in the last two years.

- **Collapse of Magnetosphere**: The Earth's protective, magnetic field—that shields us from the full effect of the sun's radiation—is accelerating into a magnetic pole reversal. Sometime in the near future, the field will rapidly collapse and reconfigure itself, with the North and South poles in dramatically different locations. Humans, our planet, and our environment are closely coupled to the magnetosphere. As it changes, our emotions, biology, social interactions, and climate and weather also change.

- **Rapid Climate Change**: The changes on the sun and the magnetospheric reconfiguration, seen in the light of historical patterns and environmental descriptions, suggest that the Earth is on the verge of a rapid change in the climate that will result in what growing scientific studies say will be a lengthy period of significant cold. The early indicators are already being witnessed around the planet (like significant snow in the Sahara desert in 2018). Common assumptions about food production and the availability of energy are likely to be severely threatened.

- **The End of Manufacturing**: The advent of additive (3D) manufacturing is fundamentally changing how things are manufactured, eliminating huge swaths of the traditional sector. Advances, broadly within information technology (which includes 3D printing), are estimated to eliminate upwards of 80 percent of present job categories within the next three decades. No predictions suggest that there will be replacements for most of those jobs.

- **Doubling or Tripling of Lifetimes**: Biological advances appear to be on the verge of dramatically extending the available human lifetime. Researchers are predicting sequential breakthroughs that could result in some present septuagenarians living to 150 or 200. Of course, the effect on the lifespan of younger cohorts would be profound. The questions arise: In the face of rapidly decreasing traditional employment, what is done with all of those additional years? How does society adapt? What does government do to help maintain social stability?

- **Implications of Artificial Intelligence**: It is hard to overestimate the potential for the advent of artificial general intelligence to upend the world that we find familiar. Programmed capabilities that learn, are more capable than humans, and can duplicate themselves millions of times over will launch Homo sapiens off an existential cliff into a brave new world, but of a type that has not yet been described or imagined even by science fiction.

> There is a principle associated with these kinds of broad-based structural shifts: The world that subsequently emerges makes no sense from the perspective of the preceding one.

- **The End of Traditional Jobs**: The shifts described above portend the end of work as we have known it. Alternative, meaningful policies and approaches will be required to provide reasonable and productive sustenance for a rapidly aging (but still capable) population in an environment in which conventional notions of employment are disappearing. The concept of being "productive" will have to be decoupled from economic contribution... and/or the definition of value will have to be dramatically broadened to include all of the things that contribute to the quality of life—not just financial impact.

- **Consciousness Revolution**: There is a narrow but growing segment of people, in all parts of the world, who are actively pushing themselves into new areas of consciousness that dramatically threaten the standard scientific explanation of how this reality works. Out-of-body experiences, entheogen-induced alternative states—even the legalization of marijuana—all are indicators of a species that is purposely exploring the edges of consciousness, looking for an expanded space.

- **Engagement With Extraterrestrial Life**: In December of 2017, the *New York Times, Washington Post*, and other major media ran front-page headlines heralding the disclosure of a previously highly classified defense program that had spent scores of millions of dollars, over at least 15 years, studying hundreds of encounters of our military and "unidentified aerial phenomena," or UFOs. Clearly, there is a growing understanding and awareness of an expanded interaction between our planet and life elsewhere in our universe. Multiple initiatives focused on facilitating an open and ongoing relationship with such life are gaining momentum. If this transpires, everything changes.

- **Manipulation of Time and Space**: The leading edge of alternative science, and indications from whistle-blowers, suggests that we are approaching (if we don't already have it) the ability to manipulate space and time with certain kinds of technologies. Should those capabilities become generally available within the next decade, the paradigm will shift.

- **New Energy, Food, Water, Transportation**: There are also indications, from reportedly closely held projects, of new capabilities for generating energy without fuel, the ability to cheaply and easily desalinate and purify water, practical anti-gravity functionality, and other exotic breakthroughs. The impending impact of climate change could well spur a revolution in large-scale, sophisticated, indoor food production. Should these see the light of day, it would signal the beginning of a new era.

- **End of "Truth" and Objective "Reality"**: Extraordinary technical advances now make it essentially impossible to know if what you see or hear transmitted over airwaves or the internet is what it seems. Video images can be made to appear to be doing things that were never done, and words can at will be seamlessly put in the mouths of politicians or "targets." It will be increasingly hard to verify the claims of corporations, governments, lawyers, or plaintiffs, despite the method of transmission of evidence.

- **The End of Traditional Trust**: In December 2017, the Obama administration, with a provision in the National Defense Authorization Act, made it legal for the government to lie to the American people. Add that to the demonstrated manipulation of government statistics, product and corporate claims, compromised politicians, special relationships between regulators and regulated groups, religious groups that abuse children, the admitted influence of the CIA with almost all media, and now, with the above-mentioned technological capabilities to show someone doing or saying something that didn't happen, it is rapidly becoming hard to trust the institutions that have historically provided a modicum of social stability and confidence.

- **Collapse of Legacy Systems**: A compelling case can be made that many key components in the global system supporting human activity are structurally unsustainable and are in the process of imploding. Such major influencers as the Catholic Church are unraveling. The EU has problems around its coherence, leadership, and policy, and serious questions are surfacing about the future of the US political system. The United States reportedly owes $270 trillion that will never be repaid, a debt it may soon be unable to service. Solutions include revaluing the global currency system and upending the world's financial system.

You get the picture. We are witnessing the collapse of one era and the emergence of another one.

The only way to make sense of this is to consider it from a systems perspective—because it is an extremely complicated, highly dynamical system containing any number of embedded, potential wild-card surprises that could precipitate an unanticipated new paradigm.

There is a principle associated with these kinds of broad-based structural shifts: The world that subsequently emerges makes no sense from the perspective of the preceding one. Regardless of which transitional event is examined—before the internet, before moveable type, before multiple-celled organisms—the existing world does not have either the models or the logic to effectively imagine or picture what will thereafter become the status quo. A world of smartphones visualized from the technological environment of WWI, for example, turns into a Jules Verne-type science fiction story.

> We have the capability to analyze and understand options... and then consciously engineer the emerging new world to become something that we desire. For the first time in history!

We should keep that in mind before we discount, out of hand, some of the possibilities discussed above. Objectively, taking them all together is a pretty compelling argument for constraining our hubris. Something large is happening, and it would be imprudent to presume the impossibility of a particular new world—or new human.

Another corollary of these giant transitions is that in the face of deep, extraordinary change, humans will have really different perspectives and values. They will "see" themselves in very different ways—have different notions of what it is to be human.

So, for example, a new genetic configuration (with new physical and mental capabilities), resulting from human engagement with extraterrestrial life, could result in an evolutionary or "graduation" scenario in which our species becomes much more than the planetary citizens we are now. In such a future, our ideas of physics, religion, social interactions, economy, etc., all change dramatically. It would be a world like something now seen only in science fiction!

Considering what might be in this emerging future, it is important that we take a long—a very long—look backward. There are examples, patterns, visions, and signals that emerge from historical analysis that point to underlying cycles (existing in many different domains) that repeat over varying periods on a regular basis. Analysts like economist Martin Armstrong, who have identified and applied the understanding of these cycles to anticipating the future behavior of areas including financial markets and geopolitics, have amazingly accurate track records.

There are also people like Bruce de Bueno Mesquita, who has developed technology to successfully apply game theory to a degree such that agencies like the CIA retain him to predict upcoming geopolitical—and other—uncertainties. He is said to be over 90 percent accurate in his predictions.

Another out-of-the-box analyst is Clif High, who starts with the assumption that humans are naturally psychic (sound like a latent, new-human capability?), and therefore unwittingly "tune in" to large perturbations from the future. He has developed a sophisticated capability to regularly sweep the web with billions of bots, identifying how indications of these significant future events manifest in changes in how people—in six different languages—start to use new and different words and ideas that point explicitly to the oncoming event.

He had 9/11 six months before the fact. And the Banda Aceh tsunami. And Japan's Fukushima earthquake. All months before they shook the Earth.

Humanity is developing the tools and capabilities to anticipate and analyze this rapidly emerging world. Not only can we understand (in extraordinary ways) what seems to be happening, but we now are positioned to actively shape the future to assure that it reflects our learnings from the past and hopes for the future.

We have the capability to analyze and understand options... and then consciously engineer the emerging new world to become something that we desire. For the first time in history!

New tools allow mind-boggling pattern recognition and seemingly magical predictive analysis. Extraordinary search and analysis capabilities provide the ability to reach way back, and very deeply, broadly, and quickly. Beautiful and awe-inspiring presentation technologies, coupled with many specific-function "apps," leverage the ability of the human brain and mind to visualize a particular database through many different lenses—sequentially, in combinations, or all at once!

Scenario development and planning enables the adroit facilitator to use what has been collected to develop a powerful view of the potential on the horizon—one that is robust, comprehensive, and insightful.

My background suggests that with this kind of capability comes a personal and special responsibility to develop a sophisticated, enlightened vision of an extraordinary new world—one that is coming in any case—and establish new thinking, perspectives, and policies to facilitate and make efficient its arrival.

We can start putting in place what needs to be done to shape the elements of the global system such that it begins to point in the desired direction.

No species on this planet has been able to do that in the past... but now, we can.

We should rise to the occasion!

John L. **Petersen** is the founder and president of The Arlington Institute, a three-decade-old effort to develop sophisticated pictures of potential, multidimensional futures by both developing and using emergent technologies and original thinking. He is particularly interested in approaches for understanding and anticipating the unprecedented transition we are experiencing that will produce a new human and a new world. He hangs his hat at www.arlingtoninstitute.org. He can be reached at johnp@arlingtoninstitute.org.

Machines
that Imagine

Sridhar Mahadevan, PhD

66 Imagination is more important than knowledge.
Knowledge is limited. Imagination encircles the world. 99

—*Albert Einstein*

Writing in *Future Shock*, Alvin Toffler urged his readers to "...contemplate some of the novelties that lie in store for us. Combining rational intelligence with all the imagination we can command, let us project ourselves forcefully into the future."

Indeed, imagination is essential if we are to cultivate a greater sense of tomorrow. "For we must," Toffler continued, "also vastly widen our conception of *possible* futures. To the rigorous discipline of science, we must add the *flaming imagination of art*." [Emphasis mine]

In the course of his research for the book, Toffler interviewed a great many people, one of whom was H.D. Block, professor of applied mathematics at Cornell University. Block was an early experimenter in machine learning, having collaborated with Frank Rosenblatt, who conceived the *perceptron*—a seminal algorithm for supervised learning of binary classifiers, and a foundational concept in AI. "I don't think there's a task you can name," Block asserted, "that a machine can't do—in principle. If you can define a task and a human can do it, then a machine can, at least in theory, also do it. The converse, however, is not true."

> The importance of imagination to humans naturally raises the question of whether intelligent machines can be endowed with similar abilities.

Consequently, intelligence and creativity, Toffler added, driving the point home, do not appear to constitute a human monopoly. And 50 years later, we find ourselves on the cusp of advancing from what Block posited as "theory" to actual practice.

In my work, I explore a fundamental challenge for artificial intelligence (AI) enabled systems—a challenge I wonder if even Block had contemplated: Can machines *imagine*?

According to the Stanford Encyclopedia of Philosophy, "to *imagine* is to represent without aiming at things as they actually, presently, and subjectively are... to represent possibilities other than the actual, to represent times other than the present, and to represent perspectives other than one's own."[1]

To illustrate this end, art is perhaps the paradigmatic example of human imagination. Figure 1 shows an untitled painting by Jean-Michel Basquiat that sold at a recent auction in New York City for over $100 million.

The scope of imagination in human society goes far beyond art: Numerous examples can be given to illustrate that human achievements in the sciences, technology, literature, sculpture, poetry, religion, and beyond depend fundamentally on our ability to imagine. The importance of imagination to humans naturally raises the question of whether intelligent machines can be endowed with similar abilities.

Much of the recent success of AI comes from a revolution in *data science*, specifically the use of deep learning neural networks to extract hidden patterns in data (Goodfellow, Bengio, and Courville, 2016). Deep learning networks are able to drive cars autonomously, recognize a large variety of common objects from their visual appearance, and respond to human speech using devices such as Amazon's Alexa or Apple's Siri. Data science is possibly the fastest-growing area in AI currently.

A recent study by LinkedIn projects that the United States is facing a shortfall of over 150,000 data scientists, a number that may grow as demand outstrips the supply. Yet, for those of us who have worked in AI for three decades, data science is but a way station on the road toward designing machines that truly capture human intelligence. Imagination is perhaps foremost among the abilities that still separate machines from humans. I explain below where the challenges lie.

Broadly, the field of data science concerns itself with statistical summarization of experience: It answers the question "what is the world like now?" based on an analysis of historical data. However, imagination requires answering a different sort of question, one that has to do with "what if" counterfactual inference, and also with "why" explanations. Answering "what if" and "why?" questions requires developing a new field, which I

Figure 1 • An untitled painting by Jean-Michel Basquiat sold at an auction for over $100 million.

Figure 2 • Generative adversarial networks (GANs) can be used to create realistic looking novel faces of people who don't exist.

have termed *imagination science* (Mahadevan, 2018).

Basquiat's famous painting provides a vivid example of the challenge in designing machines that imagine. This painting is imaginative because it portrays a human face in an "artistic" way that is difficult to mechanize. A leading class of deep learning models, called generative adversarial networks or GANs (Goodfellow et al., 2015) can learn to generate images from a given collection. In recent years, there has been a surge of interest in GAN models, and there are dozens of variants. As Figure 2 shows, GANs can produce frighteningly realistic images of faces of people who don't exist.[2] Although this GAN approach is impressive, it does not capture the type of imagination represented by Basquiat's painting.

Can GANs be extended to do more imaginative types of art? To understand the limitations of traditional GANs, we need to delve a bit deeper into how they work. The basic architecture of a GAN consists of two modules, a *generator* module that aims to produce novel images, and a *discriminator* module that is tasked with distinguishing *fake* or generated images from a dataset of given images. GANs are an example of a *generative* model in machine learning, a type of statistical machinery that can produce new samples from some unknown probability distribution, accessible only using a dataset of known samples. However, imaginative art requires going beyond generating additional samples of a known type. If Basquiat had painted in the style of Monet, his paintings would not be regarded so highly.

Capturing imagination in art requires extending GANs to enable creativity. Ultimately, creativity is the basis for all of human achievements in the arts, sciences, and technology. This fundamental ability is still elusive to capture in machines.

Recent work on a variant of GANs called a creative adversarial network (or CAN) has made some progress in this direction.[3] A CAN is given a dataset of thousands of paintings in different styles (e.g., impressionism, Cubism, etc.). The generator in a CAN is trained to produce a painting that is "art," but uses a style that is different from any of the given styles. Figure 3 shows examples of art produced by a CAN.

How can we evaluate paintings produced by a GAN? One objective way is to ask how much money someone would pay for a painting produced by one. The first AI-generated art that came up for

Figure 3 • These images were "painted" by a deep learning neural network called a creative adversarial network (CAN).

auction at Christie's recently sold for $432,500, an impressive sum, but not in the stratospheric price range of a Picasso or Monet painting.[4]

CANs represent a specialized solution to endowing machines with a limited type of imagination for generating art. Can such an approach work in other mediums, like poetry? Unfortunately, thus far, the GAN framework works less effectively on text. One of the most revered poems in the English canon is that of Robert Frost, titled "Stopping by the Woods on a Snowy Evening." Its last paragraph reads:

> The woods are lovely, dark and deep,
> But I have promises to keep,
> And miles to go before I sleep,
> And miles to go before I sleep.

The imaginative nature of Frost's poetry is undeniable. Having spent the last two decades teaching in the picturesque New England town of Amherst, where Robert Frost taught, this poem evokes in me images of the New England woods in winter. Recently, there has been much interest in computer-generated poetry.[5] A significant challenge in automating poetry writing is that it is not enough to simply capture rhythmic structure. The essence of great poetry is the ability to evoke *metaphors*. A wonderful example of this ability is in Bob Dylan's song "It's Alright Ma (I'm Only Bleeding)":

> While money doesn't talk, it swears

Or, take another poet who lived in Amherst, Massachusetts, Emily Dickinson, who evoked this rich metaphor of death in her poem "Because I Could Not Stop for Death":

Because I could not stop for Death –
He kindly stopped for me –
The Carriage held but just Ourselves –
And Immortality.

How can a machine capture such rich metaphors? There is much research on developing a computational theory of metaphors, but it has yet to be successful in practice at generating metaphors rich enough for beautiful verse (Veale et al., 2016).

Recent work in natural language processing by Mikolov and others has shown that it is possible to construct vector-space embeddings of words by analyzing a large corpus, like Wikipedia, and analyzing each word in terms of the millions of contexts in which it occurs.[6] Mikolov's program, called *Word2vec*, is able to learn vectorized word embeddings, and solve simple word analogies, such as "He is to she as king is to X" (where X is of course "queen"). Word2vec is thereby able to reason about linguistic regularities in a relatively simple way, although its ability to capture rich metaphors and more powerful analogies seems quite limited at this point.

Imagination is also the basis for causal reasoning, and counterfactual inferences (Pearl and Mackenzie, 2018, Walker and Gopnik, 2013). Probabilistic models of causal and counterfactual inference are being actively studied in AI and represent another area where much progress has been made in recent years (Pearl, 2009). Figure 4 shows a three-layer cognitive architecture proposed by Judea Pearl that combines reasoning by association, which underlies most of the work in data mining, with causal and counterfactual reasoning.

Imagination in problem-solving, science, and technology is another area where machines have yet to make much progress. Einstein prized imagination because it enabled him to pose hypothetical questions, such as "What would the world look like if I rode a beam of light,"—a question that led him to develop the revolu-

Figure 4 • A cognitive architecture proposed by Judea Pearl combining seeing, doing, and imagination.

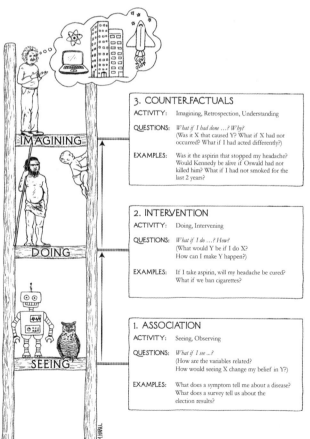

3. COUNTERFACTUALS

ACTIVITY: Imagining, Retrospection, Understanding

QUESTIONS: *What if I had done ...? Why?*
(Was it X that caused Y? What if X had not occurred? What if I had acted differently?)

EXAMPLES: Was it the aspirin that stopped my headache? Would Kennedy be alive if Oswald had not killed him? What if I had not smoked for the last 2 years?

2. INTERVENTION

ACTIVITY: Doing, Intervening

QUESTIONS: *What if I do ...? How?*
(What would Y be if I do X? How can I make Y happen?)

EXAMPLES: If I take aspirin, will my headache be cured? What if we ban cigarettes?

1. ASSOCIATION

ACTIVITY: Seeing, Observing

QUESTIONS: *What if I see ...?*
(How are the variables related? How would seeing X change my belief in Y?)

EXAMPLES: What does a symptom tell me about a disease? What does a survey tell us about the election results?

tionary theory of special (and later, general) relativity. These and other imaginative abilities lie far beyond the scope of intelligent machines at present.

So we continue in our efforts to combine rational intelligence with "all the imagination we can command" to project ourselves forcefully into the future. Over the course of the next few decades, what kinds of breakthroughs might those efforts yield? What kinds of machines—or *super*-machines—are we yet to imagine?

I leave the last word on this to Toffler: "Each new machine or technique, in a sense," he wrote, "changes all existing machines and techniques, by permitting us to put them together into new combinations. The number of possible combinations rises *exponentially* as the number of new machines or techniques rises arithmetically. Indeed, each new combination may, itself, be regarded as a new super-machine."

Sridhar Mahadevan** is director of the Data Science Lab at Adobe, and a research professor at the College of Information and Computer Sciences at the University of Massachusetts, Amherst. He was previously the director of the SRI AI Center in 2017, a visiting professor of computer science at Stanford in Spring 2018, and a tenured full professor at U.Mass, Amherst, from 2010 to 2017 prior to coming to the Bay Area in 2017. He was elected Fellow of AAAI in 2015 for significant contributions to machine learning. He has written over 150 research papers in many areas of AI and ML and lectured widely in over three dozen countries on AI. In 2018, his paper on imagination machines received the Best Paper Award in the Blue Sky track at the annual AAAI conference.

1. See (https://plato.stanford.edu/entries/imagination/).

2. See https://research.nvidia.com/publication/2017-10_Progressive-Growing-of

3. See https://arxiv.org/abs/1706.07068.

4. https://www.christies.com/features/A-collaboration-between-two-artists-one-human-one-a-machine-9332-1.aspx.

5. See https://www.ischool.berkeley.edu/news/2016/teaching-computer-write-poetry.

6. See https://arxiv.org/abs/1301.3781.

References

Mahadevan, Sridhar, "Imagination Machines: A New Challenge for Artificial Intelligence," Proceedings of the AAAI Conference, New Orleans, 2018.

Goodfellow, I.; Bengio, Y.; and Courville, A. C. 2016. *Deep Learning*. Adaptive Computation and Machine Learning Series. MIT Press.

Goodfellow, I. J.; Pouget-Abadie, J.; Mirza, M.; Xu, B.; Warde-Farley, D.; Ozair, S.; Courville, A. C.; and Bengio, Y. 2014. Generative adversarial nets. In *Advances in Neural Information Processing Systems 27: Annual Conference on Neural Information Processing Systems 2014, December 8-13 2014, Montreal, Quebec, Canada*, 2672–2680.

Pearl, J. 2009. *Causality: Models, Reasoning and Inference*. Cam- bridge University Press.

Walker, C., and Gopnik, A. 2013. Causality and imagination. In Taylor, M., ed., *Oxford Handbook of the Development of Imagination*. Oxford University Press. 342–358.

Pearl, Judea and Mackenzie, "The Book of Why: The New Science of Cause and Effect", Basic Books, 2018.

Tony Veale, Ekaterina Shutova, Beata Beigman Klebanov, "Metaphor: A Computational Perspective", Morgan Claypool Synthesis Lectures on Human Language Technologies, 2016.

Naked Into the Cosmos: Future Shock in Space

Barry Vacker

> ❝ How strange, therefore, that when we hurl a man into the future, we take few pains to protect him from the shock of change. It is as though NASA had shot Armstrong and Aldrin naked into the cosmos. ❞
>
> —*Alvin Toffler*

Published in July 1970, one year after the Apollo 11 moon landing, Alvin Toffler's *Future Shock* rocked the world of the human species, many still basking in the euphoric triumph of Apollo 11. At that moment, all things seemed possible via science and technology, with NASA and global television providing the events and imagery to *momentarily unite* one billion people watching on TV on planet Earth. Yet, as Apollo 8 showed with its Genesis reading from lunar orbit, humanity was venturing into the cosmos intellectually unprepared, philosophically naked for our first steps among the starry skies. Fifty years later, the human species still has no space philosophy worthy of Apollo and the Hubble Space Telescope—and the universe they revealed. Apollo 11 astronaut Neil Armstrong took a small step and great leap, but we're still going "naked into the cosmos."

In *Future Shock*, Alvin Toffler foresaw this existential and philosophical challenge, among many others. *Future Shock* provided profound insights into the accelerating waves of scientific and technological transformation sweeping the planet. The book detailed our ability/inability to successfully adapt to these changes, individually and as a society. Importantly, *Future Shock* did not claim that a dystopian future was certain to come, filled with the doom and destruction that dominates science fiction films. Rather, *Future Shock* diagnosed what Toffler described as "the premature arrival of the future" and offered ideas for successfully adapting to the system-wide changes and cultural effects. Nowhere is Toffler's thesis more clear than in space exploration and the challenge to develop a philosophy to unite our species as enlightened and peaceful space farers—in a universe in which we are not central or significant.

1 ■ "The Premature Arrival of the Future"

In *Future Shock*, Toffler detailed how our "super-industrial" society had disrupted the traditional social order so dramatically that humanity had become traumatized—fearful of the loss of yesterday's traditions and uncertain of the tomorrows to come. Entering a future that was hurtling toward us at ever-increasing speed with ever-expanding patterns of change, we were finding ourselves overwhelmed by the social transformations of the industrialized and electrified world. As Toffler explains:

> *Future shock is the dizzying disorientation brought on by the premature arrival of the future. It may well be the most important disease of tomorrow... unless intelligent steps are taken to combat it, millions of human beings will find themselves increasingly disoriented, progressively incompetent to deal rationally with their environments ... Future shock is a time phenomenon, a product of the greatly accelerated rate of change in society. It arises from the superimposition of a new culture on an old one. It is culture shock in one's own society.* [1]

For Toffler, science and technology have delivered "the future" so fast that traditional values and conventional notions of family, work, education, community, and the like have been drastically altered. It's as if we don't recognize our own culture and destiny, plunging us into uncertainty and doubt. In addition, Toffler asserts, the more technology develops, the less stable our culture will be, preventing us from ever feeling fully settled or sure of where we are going. Changes in our concepts of space and time are the one certainty:

> *In the coming decades, advances in [sciences and technologies] will fire off like a series of rockets carrying us out of the past, plunging us deeper into the new society. Nor will this new society quickly settle into a steady state. It, too, will quiver and crack and roar as it suffers jolt after jolt of high-energy change.* [2]

Future Shock provided an exhaustive number of examples to support its thesis, although one does not have to agree with all of them to grasp the essential truths. Future shock is the emotional anxiety and existential dread felt toward a future that challenges all previous cultural narratives. And nothing has been more future-shocking than the universe revealed by space exploration.

2 ■ Future Shock in Space: We're the Center of Nothing

From Galileo's telescope to the Hubble telescope, humans have long extended their gaze into the Milky Way and beyond. For eons, we looked at the stars gliding above and imagined we were the center of the universe. Most humans still do. It's the bubble of what I call *cosmic narcissism*. In this illusory bubble on a tiny planet, we are not merely selfish or in love with our self-image, but rather we are busy imagining and acting as if we (individually and collectively) are the center of the universe, the center of everything—the center of all value, purpose, and meaning.

That's why the telescope might well be the most radical technology ever, precisely because it empirically removed us from the center of the universe and punctured our bubble of cosmic narcissism. Future shock in space—space shock!

Over the past century, humanity's space shock has been ramped up exponentially. In the 1920s, the stars of the Milky Way still represented the entirety of the known universe because telescopes lacked the capacity to see beyond our galaxy. That changed with the Hooker telescope in California, used by Edwin Hubble to make two landmark discoveries that forever changed our view of the universe:

1 ■ The universe is much older and larger than previously assumed, with the Milky Way being just one galaxy among many;

2 ■ The other galaxies and clusters of galaxies are moving apart from the Milky Way and from each other in what is known as the "big bang" model of the expanding universe.

In the big bang model, the galaxies are not propelling themselves through space—rather, the *voids of space are expanding* and taking the galaxies along for the ride. Powered by mysterious "dark energy," these voids are shaped like massive space bubbles, bordered with clusters and networks of galaxies. Based on data from the Hubble telescope and others, NASA's latest estimates suggest the observable universe contains two trillion galaxies and stretches across 100 billion light-years. And the number of stars exceeds three sextillion (3 followed by 21 zeros). We've discovered an epic universe—at once awe-inspiring and all-too-terrifying for many. Talk about space shock!

> For eons, we looked at the stars gliding above and imagined we were the center of the universe. Most humans still do. It's the bubble of what I call cosmic narcissism.

We humans apparently can't handle the paradoxical meaning of our greatest scientific achievement and most important philosophical discovery: *The universe is vast and majestic, and our species is insignificant and might be utterly meaningless.* There may well be no meaning or purpose to our existence in the immensity of the cosmos that spans billions of years in the past and trillions upon trillions of years in the future. Rather than the center of everything, we are the center of nothing. As a species, we have ventured into the sublime of the universe and retreated from the possible nihilism, our minds blown but our philosophy paralyzed with future shock.

Future Shock saw this challenge coming:

> *In the awesome complexity of the universe, even within any given society, a virtually infinite number of streams of change occur simultaneously. All "things"—from the tiniest virus to the greatest galaxy—are, in reality, not things at all, but processes. There is no static point, no nirvana-like un-change, against which to measure change.*[3]

If there is any meaning to our existence, perhaps it is because we are one way the universe is aware of itself. Our species is *one process* for generating knowledge of the universe itself. This non-static existence suggests a radically different philosophy for space exploration, an approach filled with wonder and admiration for the places we visit and life-forms we encounter—in contrast to plundering, polluting, and waging war.

3 ▪ Space Shock: 2020 and Beyond

Science and technology are propelling humans into a beautiful and sublime universe, with trillions of galaxies stretching across billions of light-years. Yet our popular narratives seem philosophically paralyzed and most humans remain in future shock, still turning to tribalism, nationalism, and consumerism for meaning, purpose, and identity. Centuries-old virulence and violence, ancient tribal and religious warfare—these are all replicating on Earth, in social media, and are destined for Mars, the moon, and beyond. Toffler anticipated these conditions:

> *The greatest and most dangerous marvel of all is the complacent past-orientation of the (human) race, its unwillingness to confront the reality of acceleration. Thus man moves swiftly into an unexplored universe, into a totally new stage of eco-technological development… He stumbles into the most violent revolution in human history (and) simply refuses to imagine the future.*[4]

▪ **THE ENTROPY OF ENLIGHTENMENT IN SPACE**: Fifty years after the unifying moment of Apollo 11, there is still no popular narrative that integrates humanity with its origins and destiny in the all-too-majestic cosmos. There is no philosophy that unites the human species as a peaceful and enlightened space-faring civilization. For those born after Apollo 11, Neil Armstrong's "one giant leap for mankind" is but a faint echo on YouTube. Landing on the moon "For All Mankind" has been replaced by conquering "For All My Kind"—illustrated by the corporate-nationalist agendas of militarizing space, strip-mining the moon, and terraforming Mars into a suburb of Earth, along with space theocrats yearning to baptize extraterrestrials and colonize the Milky Way.[5]

> Landing on the moon "For All Mankind" has been replaced by conquering "For All My Kind"—illustrated by the corporate-nationalist agendas of militarizing space, strip-mining the moon, and terraforming Mars into a suburb of Earth, along with space theocrats yearning to baptize extraterrestrials and colonize the Milky Way.

There is no way this can be called "enlightened." Science will be an irrelevant sideshow, unless it serves the above imperatives. Art and a new philosophy are nowhere on the agenda. Beauty, majesty, and sublimity—all will be seen as meaningless in the new human space agenda. Eyes open, but vision blinded by the narcissism, we are still going naked into the cosmos.

▪ **APOLLO MOON LANDING CONSPIRACIES**: Is there a better example of 21st-century future shock than the endless conspiracy theories that NASA faked the moon landings? With the help of filmmaker Stanley Kubrick, no less! According to a 2016 Chapman University survey, 24 percent of Americans believe the landings were faked.[6] But it's not that the conspiracy theorists are merely crazy, it's that the success of Apollo taps into their existential dread that they're not as cosmically special as they think they are. That we know NASA went to the moon is explained in a popular essay on Medium.[7]

▪ **PSEUDOSCIENCE AND PARANORMAL WORLDVIEWS**: Despite the explosion of knowledge in all scientific fields, pseudoscience and anti-science are proliferating—from fundamentalists to flat-Earthers, creationists to Apollo conspiracy theorists, anti-vaxxers to "Ancient Alien" theorists.[8] Powered by the hit series *Ancient Aliens* (2009-), over 40 percent of Americans believe Ancient Aliens have visited Earth in the distant past, a belief that is fast becoming a new space religion.[9]

■ THE WEAPONIZATION/MILITARIZATION OF SPACE: China, Russia, and the United States are very busy weaponizing and militarizing space, preparing to wage war for resources and religious colonization of the moon and Mars. The Cold War is back and getting hotter—an atomic future shock seems possible again on planet Earth. There's a reason *Star Wars* is so popular. The human species seems to love war.

■ TERRAFORMING MARS AND STRIP-MINING THE MOON: Terraforming Mars and strip-mining the moon for products to consume on Earth are perfect examples of humanity's cosmic narcissism and a surefire prescription for war in space. None of these plans will make life better on Earth. Elon Musk says we need a backup planet for our species, but he's philosophically off base. *If we can't protect and care for our own planet, then what gives us the cosmic right to terraform Mars into a suburb of Earth?* Nothing other than our narcissism and a backward 19th-century industrial vision of plunder and pollution.

Why not treat celestial bodies with reverence and admiration for their beauty and majesty, like we do with national parks and wilderness areas? Instead of warriors and strip-miners, we should send artists, scientists, ecologists, and philosophers to Mars and the moon.

4 ■ Toffler: Countering Future Shock in Space

With clear foresight, Toffler sensed the post-Apollo challenge and sketched out possible rituals and holidays to unite humans in the wake of our first steps into the cosmos.

■ CELEBRATING UNITY AMONG HUMANITY: Toffler wrote: "We might create a global pageantry based on man's conquest of outer space. Even now the succession of space launchings and capsule retrievals is beginning to take on a kind of ritual dramatic pattern. Millions stand transfixed as the countdown begins and the mission works itself out. For at least a fleeting instant, they share a realization of the oneness of humanity and its potential competence in the face of the universe."[10]

Rather than rituals celebrating the "unity" and "oneness" of humanity, we have *Star Wars* openings and superhero films, where gods-in-human-form save us from the monsters of the universe. Can we even imagine some kind of social unity in the aftermath of Twitter, Facebook, and YouTube? Unity seems impossible, precisely because social media cultivate tribes, create echo chambers, and keep humanity at the center of the universe, the center of everything meaningful and valuable. Social media are the perfect consolation for the discoveries of the Hubble telescope.[11]

■ A GLOBAL HOLIDAY HONORING APOLLO 11: Toffler wrote: "By regularizing such events and by greatly adding to the pageantry that surrounds them, we can weave them into the ritual framework of the new society and use them as sanity preserving points of temporal reference. Certainly, July 20, the day Astronaut Armstrong took 'one small step for man, one giant leap for mankind,' ought to be made into an annual global celebration of the unity of man."[12]

When I read the Apollo 11 holiday idea, my jaw dropped in amazement. Toffler is absolutely correct. Rather than a global holiday celebrating Apollo 11, we have proliferating Apollo conspiracy theories claiming the great achievement is bogus, along with the transient enthusiasms of Oscars, Super Bowls, and World Cups.

5 ■ "Future Shock" vs. "Explosion of Awareness"

From Apollo to the Hubble telescope, NASA's grand achievements have collectively destroyed the pre-Copernican narratives humans use to explain their origins and destinies. Again, Toffler was correct—fear, denial, anxiety, and outright ignorance are permeating society. We need a new philosophy (accompanied by art, ritual, and pageantry) that builds on our profound connections to the Milky Way, the Hubble images, and seeing Earth from space. Astronauts who've seen Earth from space experience deep feelings of awe, transcendence, and a primal connection to the planet and the universe. Apollo 14 astronaut Edgar Mitchell described the experience as an "explosion of awareness." Given that we are one way the universe knows itself, this "explosion of awareness" provides an exciting basis for a 21st-century space philosophy, a new worldview to counter the future shock on Earth and in space.[13] We no longer have to go "naked into the cosmos." ▪

Barry Vacker, PhD, is an associate professor in the Klein College of Media and Communication, Temple University, Philadelphia. A writer and mixed-media artist, Vacker's works span the intersection of art, media, science, technology, and philosophy. His most recent books include *Media Environments* (3rd Ed., 2019), *Black Mirror and Critical Media Theory* (co-edited with Angela Cirucci, 2018), and *Specter of the Monolith* (2017), a book inspired by 2001: A Space Odyssey. Vacker's recent large-scale art installation was featured during the 2019 Media Ecology Convention at the University of Toronto—where Vacker (and co-artist Julia M. Hildebrand) received an international award for "MediaScene: A McLuhan-Inspired Art and Theory Project," an innovative essay about the future of media theory in the age of the Anthropocene and the Hubble Space Telescope. Connect with him at: https://temple.academia.edu/BarryVacker.

1. Alvin Toffler, *Future Shock* (New York: Random House, 1970), 13.

2. Ibid., 192-93.

3. Ibid., 21.

4. Ibid., 191.

5. Guy Consolmagno and Paul Mueller, *Would You Baptize an Extraterrestrial?:... and Other Questions from the Astronomers' In-box at the Vatican Observatory* (New York: Image Books, 2014).

6. "What They Aren't Telling Us," Chapman University Survey of American Fears, October 11, 2016. Accessed May 12, 2019.

7. Barry Vacker, "Apollo Moon Landings: Pseudoscience and 6 Reasons Why There Was No NASA Hoax," Medium, October 20, 2017.

8. "Paranormal America—2018," Chapman University Survey of American Fears, October 16, 2018. Accessed May 12, 2019.

9. Steven Kurutz, "E.T., We're Here," *New York Times*, Sunday Styles, p. 1, July 22, 2018.

10. Toffler, *Future Shock*, 351.

11. Barry Vacker, *Media Environments*, 3rd Ed. (San Diego: Cognella Academic Publishing, 2019); 27-49.

12. Ibid.

13. For details on such a philosophy, see Barry Vacker, *Specter of the Monolith: Nihilism, the Sublime, and Human Destiny in Space—From Apollo and Hubble to 2001, Star Trek, and Interstellar* (Philadelphia: Center for Media and Destiny 2017).

Redesigning/Redefining Us

Moon Ribas

> **" How will it feel to be part protoplasm and part transistor? Exactly what possibilities will it open? What limitations will it place on work, play, sex, intellectual or aesthetic responses? What happens to the mind when the body is changed? Questions like these cannot be long deferred, for advanced fusions of man and machine— called 'Cyborgs'—are closer than most people suspect. "**
>
> *—Alvin Toffler*

identify myself as a cyborg, because I have a new cybernetic "sense organ" in my body. A pair of cybernetic implants in my feet are connected to online seismographs that allow me to feel the seismic activity of the planet in real time. At the moment I am in Barcelona, but if there's an earthquake in Japan or California or Greece, I will feel a vibration inside my body, the strength of which will depend on the magnitude of the earthquake. I call this new input the seismic sense.

The sensations are very subtle, almost imperceptible to me now—particularly when I am in the midst of a lot of activity or stress. But I did have to get used to it. In the beginning, I was very conscious of the vibrations; they would distract me in mid-sentence while talking, and when sleeping they would wake me up. But now I'm used to it; it has become part of me, like an added beat in my body. I have two beats now—my heartbeat and the Earthbeat, each with its own rhythm.

This new sense has given me a deeper and more profound connection to the planet. It's a very different experience to "feel" that the Earth is moving, rather than to merely know it is moving.

While it is commonplace for people to integrate technology into their bodies for medical reasons, some object to its use beyond such very practical, or survival-enhancing, applications. My friends and I are using it instead for the experience of it—for experience's sake—as a way of understanding life in a more profound way, and even as an art form.

We use technology *to design ourselves*, to enhance our perception of reality. The reality we experience comes to us through our senses. If we alter or extend our modes of perception, we necessarily alter our experience of reality.

Personally, I find this exciting. I feel like an explorer of my own planet, experiencing it anew through these new sensorial capacities. Even simple things like sharing a room with your dog, a bee, or just yourself take on new levels of understanding that come from experiencing the world through these new senses. A great many things happen around us every day that we don't perceive by virtue of the natural limitations of our senses. With the range of human hearing limited to 20 Hz – 20 kHz, and vision restricted to a tiny band of the electromagnetic spectrum, we are, for all practical purposes, deaf and blind! If we can free ourselves from such organic shackles, we'll be able to live and operate with vastly higher levels of perception and awareness. These augmented senses *reveal* reality. It's not virtual reality; it's not augmented reality; it's "Revealed Reality." And each of us can actually design—and thereby choose—the reality we wish to experience.

> This new sense has given me a deeper and more profound connection to the planet. It's a very different experience to "feel" that the Earth is moving, rather than to merely know it is moving.

I chose to add a seismic sense. I have one friend who chose to perceive the atmospheric pressure, another who experiences the cosmic rays, and yet another who can "see" the full spectrum of colors—through sound—from ultraviolet to infrared. What would you like to sense?

By experiencing these changes in my body and mind, my sense of identity has also changed. While I identify as a cyborg, I also identify as "transpecies," because my new sense is beyond that of a human. As I alter myself in these ways, I'm no longer 100 percent human—that is, as we understand what it is to be human today.

And I like it.

Over the past number of years, I have come to appreciate that many people wish to preserve the idea of being human as very dignified. I have also engaged in numerous debates about how we can create "better" machines. For many, the answer is: "Let's make them *more human*." But is that really what we want? Do we really want to supersize our capacity to inflict even more damage on the planet and ourselves? Maybe it would be "better" that machines were actually different from us...

Like every other lifeform on the planet, humans are not a static species. We have been transforming ourselves continuously and we will continue to do so. And maybe we will do it with technology.

The unknown can indeed be scary, but it can also be exciting. The difference really is only a matter of mindset. There's a tendency toward pessimism in our society, to think the worst of new and unfamiliar things. But that's only true of those who believe they have no control over their future. The fact is, it is always up to us to build and ensure a thriving future for everyone—and that will come about, at least in part, by establishing positive links between our species and technology.

As people learn to explore and engage with these technologies, they will discover new ways of being in the world, more opportunities for self-definition and expression, yielding a freer, more diverse and stimulating world.

For me, this also involves artistic expression, as art imitates life—and vice versa. It is often the artists and philosophers who inspire people to experience new things, to ask different questions, and to imagine radical new possibilities.

It is a uniquely human quality to explore. In my personal research, I've been exploring the movement of the Earth. But what about the moon? She is always up, ever in the night sky, and also quite active. The moon also quakes, but we can't feel it (yes, the moon is tectonically active). So my current project is to connect myself to the seismic activity of the moon—to moonquakes.

When we think of exploring space, we imagine blasting off in a spaceship. But what if we could instead create a new sense that allows us to explore space right here, from Earth? Could we not all become *senstronauts*? This would lend new meaning to the expression "reach for the stars, but keep your feet on the ground." ■

Moon Ribas is a Catalan avant-garde artist and cyborg activist best known for developing the seismic sense, an online seismic sensor implanted in her feet that allows her to perceive earthquakes taking place anywhere on the planet through vibrations in real time. In order to share her experience, she then translates her seismic sense on stage. Ribas transposes the earthquakes into sound in her piece *Seismic Percussion*, and in dance in *Waiting for Earthquakes*. In these performances, the Earth is the composer and the choreographer, and Ribas, the interpreter. Ribas's seismic sense also allows her to feel moonquakes, the seismic activity on the moon. Ribas believes that by extending our senses to perceive events beyond the planet, we can all become *senstronauts*.

Since 2007 Moon has been experimenting with the union between technology and her body to explore the boundaries of perception and to experience movement in a deeper way. Some of her previous research includes transdental communication, 360-degree perception, and the Speedborg. In 2010 she co-founded the Cyborg Foundation, an international organization that aims to help people become cyborgs, defends cyborg rights, and promotes cyborg art. Ribas also co-founded the Transpecies Society in 2017, an association that gives voice to non-human identities, defends the freedom of self-design, and offers the creation of new senses and new organs in community.

After Shock—
A Planetary
Perspective

Bill Diamond

What an amazing journey, to travel back in time nearly fifty years and dive into Alvin Toffler's prescient masterpiece, *Future Shock.* ■ I was fourteen years old when Toffler sounded the alarm on the implications to individuals and society of the rapid and accelerating pace of change in nearly all aspects of human existence, stemming from what he called the emergence of the "super-industrial society." My preoccupations at the time included playing baseball, hanging around with pals, complaining about school lunches (unaware how lucky we were *not* to have Coca Cola on the menu), and making skateboards from old roller skates and scrap wood. I was blissfully unaware of the rapidly changing world into which I had been cast.

It was thus with the benefit of fifty years of hindsight and a life devoted to science and technology that I sat down to read *Future Shock.* As the CEO of a nonprofit dedicated to advancing an understanding of the universe and our place in it, I expected to find Toffler's thesis dated. To my surprise, however, it spoke to me with great urgency and relevance. Two things struck me as I followed his observations of the increasingly frenetic pace of life and the increasingly transient and temporary nature of everything from work and relationships to art and architecture.

First, was the realization of how extraordinarily contemporary and relevant his perspectives remain—fifty years after they were first committed to print. There are of course obvious clues to the time period, such as specific dates and references to various people and events long since passed. There are also more subtle clues, such as the clearly male-dominated nature of the American and global workforce of the mid twentieth century and the associated use of male-dominated pronouns. Nevertheless, his description of the symptoms of an impending crisis, based on the rapid advances of new technologies impacting all aspects of human existence, reads as though it was written yesterday.

Second was the intriguing irony that so many of the corporations, institutions, organizations, and technologies he references in the book are still with us today, fifty years on: IBM, SRI, United Artists, General Electric, Union Carbide, the Rockefeller Institute, the United Nations, and even The Institute for the Future, are all mentioned in *Future Shock*. We still watch television, fly in jets, drive cars, shop in supermarkets and read *The New York Times*, albeit in digital form. And of course the computer, now ubiquitous, is heavily referenced by Toffler, though he would scarcely recognize its current physical manifestation. And yet, fifty years prior to *Future Shock*, in 1920, almost none of these organizations or technologies were in existence.

So, I began to ask, "Did he get it wrong?" Did the pace of change slow down or a new stability emerge? Did younger generations born into this new reality simply adapt to their environment and the current human condition, as countless generations had done before? It is of course comforting to think so. Look how much of the world he described in the 1960s is actually still the same. Could this be a case of much ado about nothing? When reading about the trends he observed, it occurred to me that a simple linear extrapolation of their consequences would likely bring us to a place today that would be radically different and seemingly far more frightening than where we actually are—if we were even fortunate enough to make it.

Based on Toffler's warnings and prognostications, one could well imagine 50 years later, the collapse not only of Western civilization, but of civilization and civil societies as a whole. How could the individual and the institutions and constructs of society survive the wholesale and unstoppable assault on our senses and our psyche that he described?

Yet as I progressed further into Toffler's analysis of the impact on people and society resulting from super-industrialization, I came back to the absolute relevance of his book to contemporary society and contemporary issues. While for the most part we have neither individually nor collectively gone completely off the rails, various phenomena of life and society we observe today are almost certainly a result of the reaction of individuals, organizations, and entire communities and cultures to their own future shock. Surely the overstimulation of the human brain, the bombardment of our senses, and the overabundance of information are creating stress and distress in individuals and triggering insidious tears in the fabric of society. In technical terms, we are facing a serious deterioration in the "signal-to-noise ratio" of all the various stimuli we need to process every day. Think of social me-

> So, I began to ask, "Did he get it wrong?" Did the pace of change slow down or a new stability emerge? Did younger generations born into this new reality simply adapt to their environment and the current human condition, as countless generations had done before?

dia, of "fake news" and alternate realities. We no longer know what to believe, or who to believe, and we cannot even assimilate and process all the new information we receive every day. As a result, we become paralyzed by indecision or retreat into our own comfort zones that might provide temporary shelter but which come with their own dangers. Consider the attacks on science we see today and a retreat by many to the comfort of isolationism. Stop the immigrants! Build a wall! End globalization! Raise trade barriers and protect jobs—however obsolete they might be!

Some members of society not only cope with the pace of change and the onslaught of data and stimulation—they thrive on it. Others are left behind, however, and in increasing numbers. They are the resisters, the blockers, the deniers. They yearn for a time that was less chaotic, less turbulent, more ordered and structured, even if they've never actually experienced such an environment. "Why can't we just go back to the way things were?" Let's "Make America Great Again," even if we don't know when that was—or what it looked like.

It became increasingly clear, the more I read, that we are indeed seeing future shock play out before our eyes. Where some examples are subtle and insidious, others are glaringly obvious. Take, for example, the homogenization of America. Over the 50 years since the publication of *Future Shock*, we have seen suburban America overrun by domestic and international conglomerates who have created an utterly vapid infrastructure of hotels, restaurants, fast-food chains, gas stations, and departments stores, such that everywhere we travel today, it looks and feels totally familiar. There is a comforting "sameness" to our environment, our diet, our work, and leisurely habits. No adaptation is required, no decision-making needed. The hotel room is familiar, the restaurant menu is committed to memory, and the department store layout is blissfully the same, whether we are in Spokane, Washington, or Springfield, Massachusetts. Our homegrown brands of conformity have even spread globally. Fast-food, hotel, and retail franchises have been very good for Wall Street, but not good for Main Street nor for cultural enrichment, diversity of experience, or variety of life.

> The impact of future shock on human behavior has perhaps been less dire than Toffler suggested it might be, possibly serving as testimony to our adaptability and resilience as a species. But there are clearly some cracks in the foundation.

And yet while I may decry the very existence of these bastions of banality, perhaps their rise to stardom is precisely a response, however unconscious, to our future shock. While the world is changing at an alarming rate, and we are unable to assimilate or adapt to the information and sensory overload that surrounds us, it may well be that the homogenization of our physical environment has served as an important (if profoundly dull) counterforce, preventing us from going individually and collectively insane.

Fifty years ago, the very idea that someone might intentionally fly a plane full of passengers into a skyscraper full of office workers was both abhorrent and unimaginable. The notion that young men and boys would get their hands on automatic weapons and calmly murder innocent children, teachers, and classmates and then generally turn their weapons on themselves was inconceivable. Even Hollywood in its most outlandish B-movie script would not have imagined an unremarkable middle-aged man unleashing a barrage of deadly gunfire into a crowd of people from a hotel window in Las Vegas, with as yet, no apparent motive or purpose. Are these examples of individuals succumbing to the forces of future shock—cracking under the pressures of a world they see spinning out of control and beyond their reach?

Toffler warned us of both these kinds of responses to future shock—a retreat to the comfort of sameness and the good ol' days—however distorted the view—and the absolute breakdown of rational individual human behavior. Nevertheless, while focusing on the human condition and our response to rapid change and sensory overload, there is an entirely different aspect of future shock that he did not address, that is yet far more alarming.

The phenomenal advances in technology, from medicine to manufacturing, computers to consumer products, and transportation to telecommunications that represent root cause to Toffler's future shock, have also unleashed unintended consequences far beyond their impact to the human psyche. Since 1900, our world population has grown exponentially, from roughly 1.5 billion to 7.7 billion people. Global carbon emissions have increased from approximately 4 billion tons per year in 1970 to nearly 10 billion tons per year at present. Our population is now consuming resources and generating waste at a rate that is beyond our planet's ability to replenish and absorb. And our climate is changing at an accelerated pace that is already putting pressures on societies and individuals that even Mr. Toffler could scarcely imagine.

The impact of future shock on human behavior has perhaps been less dire than Toffler suggested it might be, possibly serving as testimony to our adaptability and resilience as a species. But there are clearly some cracks in the foundation. The reality of over-population, resource overutilization, and runaway climate change could result in the entire house simply crumbling to dust.

At the SETI Institute, we think and operate on planetary, solar-system, galactic, and even cosmological scales. Our science not only explores the nature and origins of life in the universe and the evolution of intelligence, but also the interdependence of biology and habitat and the coevolution of life and environment. Much of our research is conducted in the field, in our principal laboratory, which is planet Earth. Thus, while our research explores the question of whether there is life elsewhere among the stars, our methods often involve turning a mirror back on ourselves to understand life on our own planet. Informed by the perspectives of our research, we are seeing an environmental future shock that completely overshadows the psychological one.

While Toffler did not examine the planetary-scale impact of our technology revolution, he did identify a behavioral response to the onslaught of distressing information and overstimulation that clearly exacerbates the planetary-scale problems we now face. Specifically he mentions four different forms of individual maladaptation, the most relevant being the "Denier." Toffler states: "The Denier's strategy is to block out unwelcome reality. When the demand for decisions reaches crescendo, he flatly refuses to take in new information… the Denier too, cannot accept the evidence of his senses. Thus he concludes that things really are the same and that all evidences of change are merely superficial."

We are clearly seeing this maladaptation manifest itself in response to climate change and over-population in all walks of life, from government to private industry, religion to private citizens. The combined and interconnected forces of climate change and overpopulation are simply too frightening and overwhelming to contemplate. So the best survival strategy is to ignore them, and hope they will just go away.

Ironically, if we adapt this defense mechanism to the issue of planetary-scale future shock, we essentially ensure the earlier arrival of catastrophic consequences we may ultimately be unable to arrest. Toffler states: "The Denier sets himself up for personal catastrophe. His strategy for coping increases the likelihood that when he is finally forced to adapt, his encounter with change will come in the form of a single massive life crisis, rather than a sequence of manageable problems." While overpopulation and technology may be underlying root cause, climate change is that single massive crisis. It is not, however, a personal life crisis. Rather, it represents catastrophe on a planetary scale that threatens the very existence of humankind.

Toffler described his book as a "diagnosis" and did not pretend to offer any solutions or "magic medicine." Rather, he acknowledged diagnosis as an essential precursor to treatment and cure. Here, too, I offer no silver bullets to address the future shock of climate change that is rapidly bearing down on us. Technology may be part of the solution, but more important will be global policymaking and long term visionary leadership. If we can at least collectively face the realities of our situation and acknowledge the threats rather than deny their existence, if we can bridge the cultural, economic, and educational divides in our societies, then there is at least hope that we can take steps to ensure that 50 years hence, another set of essayists, far more insightful than I, will have the opportunity to celebrate the 100th anniversary of *Future Shock*, and once again reflect on its significance.

Bill Diamond is a Silicon Valley veteran and current president and CEO of the SETI Institute (www.seti.org), a position he has held since June 2015. The SETI Institute is a nonprofit astrophysics and astrobiology research and education organization focused on the study of life in the Universe. Prior to joining the institute, Mr. Diamond held various executive management positions in applied technologies, most recently at the optical networking company Oclaro, Inc. Mr. Diamond has over 20 years' experience in photonics and optical communications networks, and more than a decade in X-ray imaging and semiconductor processing technologies. His corporate background covers the spectrum from venture-backed startups to Fortune 100 multinationals, with responsibilities ranging from R&D, engineering, and operations, to marketing, sales, product management, and CEO positions. Mr. Diamond holds a BA in physics from Holy Cross College and a master of business administration from Georgetown University. He is a past member of the Advisory Board for the Mc-Donough School of Business Administration at Georgetown and is a current member of the Optical Society of America, the International Astronomical Congress, and the American Association for the Advancement of Science. He is also a member of the Board of Directors of the Bay Area Science and Innovation Council, BASIC.

Cities in Crisis: What Toffler Got Right and Wrong

Dr. Cindy Frewen

> 66 Man either vanquishes the processes of change or vanishes, at which, from being the unconscious puppet of evolution, he becomes either its victim or its master. 99
>
> —*Alvin Toffler*

Flying over the city of New Delhi, low-scale, earth-tone buildings stretch as far as you can see, connected by energetic, tree-lined streets and interspersed with minarets, domes, temples, contemporary hotels and office buildings, and sections of sheet metal and wood informal settlements. Once on the ground, people in business suits and bright saris and vehicles of all sorts cram streets and walks. Trash fills concrete storm sewers, lays scattered on empty lots, and reshapes the horizon like low foothills. The leftover rubbish from 20 million lives is both toxic waste and valued commodity, sorted and bundled on roofs and alleys before being hauled to a broker. It is a world apart, uniquely Indian.

Yet, according to the United Nations Population Division, New Delhi will soon be the largest city on Earth, making it a global hub of commerce. The city anticipates 800,000 to 900,000 new inhabitants each year for the next decade, and the city will triple in population during this century. The reality of accommodating forty million new residents requires vision, urgency, and inspired, agile leadership. However, even more difficult futures lie beyond the growth challenge. Fertility rates are declining. Global growth is slowing. In the next few generations, populations will likely stabilize or even decline.

Contrary to our focus on megacities and record populations, global cities are already experiencing or soon will see slower growth or shrinkage. Nearly all our urban models are based on endless expansion. Declining populations are far more difficult to manage. During growth periods, net gains infill wasted space and replace blight. When expansion does not offset contractions, citizens are left with an oversized city. Witness Detroit, Michigan. How differently would we build if we anticipated contractions ahead?

After Growth and Beyond Limits

While Alvin Toffler brilliantly identified the difficulties of coping with accelerating change in his prescient book *Future Shock*, he spent little attention on emergent critical environmental or massive population changes. In 1970, he foresaw cities as the ultimate expression of industrialization, with nightmarish successions of disasters due to unchecked growth and technological change: water shortages, labor strikes, racial violence, and housing shortages, to name a few. He decried the absence of either coherent policies or participation by a broad range of people. In identifying these problems, his clarity was electrifying. However, by focusing on progress and accelerating change, he did not anticipate flattening population or environmental disruptions. Today, linear progress aimed toward a utopian future no longer works. Rather than be shocked by rapid change, we need to cultivate connections between diverse people and orchestrate robust responses to the challenges of prosperity without growth, and populations with limited resources and technology.

Toffler deeply understood the purpose of vision and democratic participation. At the same time, he omitted the polarity of the responses generated when we practice inclusivity, and the unforeseen consequences that derail seemingly brilliant visions. Toffler saw a far simpler world than the one we made. With emergent change and multiple interacting drivers, we rarely see the future we expected. I'd argue, in fact, that we adapt quite well individually but struggle to adapt collectively.

Future Adapt, not Future Shock

"We are living in a general crisis of industrialism." Toffler called the next phase super-industrialism. In fact, this era is fundamentally different. Rather than being defined by the most recent technologies and confused by novelty, we digitize and socialize, automate and collaborate beyond anything he described. Our adaptations juxtapose old and new. The farmer driving a camel-pulled cart communicates on his cell phone with buyers. The student in Botswana learns from a teacher in Kansas City. The International Space Station is staffed by Japanese, Russian, and American astronauts while privately owned spacecraft are tested in California, Florida, and Texas using government facilities. In short, our capacity to adapt far exceeds Toffler's predictions. Furthermore, innovations extend beyond technology. Relationships and habits have flexed and shifted to manage massive change and capitalize on innovations. We adapt again and again as we merge old and new in everyday life.

While the bird's-eye view of Delhi seems much like many cities globally, at the street, stark contrasts dominate. Cows, famously sacred in India, wander through traffic or simply lie down. People

286

in their motorized tuk tuks and Hyundais carefully avoid them. New appliance stores are neighbors to bamboo stores and reclaimed glass shops. Building materials and small farm animals are toted on mopeds and overloaded handmade trucks. Stoplights are ignored, creating a constantly moving flow interrupted by massive knots of congestion. Self-appointed "citizen cops" abandon their vehicles to redirect traffic. Luxurious hotels sit a block from messy informal settlements built along trash-filled storm sewers. Artifacts and practices of past and future clash and collaborate simultaneously.

Did Toffler underestimate our capacity to adapt? We are learning animals, never changing just once, but again and again. The rapid pace of the technological revolution that he called a cancer in history has been fiercer, wilder, more breathtaking, and more discombobulating than he conceived. Yet, we worship in cathedrals and temples centuries old or constructed last week. Between in-person gatherings, we connect every day with older and younger family members via social media. My 90-year-old mother streams Doris Day songs on her Echo speaker with just a verbal command. In sum, we manage a multitude of changes on our own terms.

We are made to adapt. Our brains, bodies, cities, and companies grow and shrink based on our need, urgency, and vision. Are we up to the challenge of this tsunami of population, environmental, and technological change? Can we learn, adapt, and find happiness while we see our familiar neighborhoods and landmarks threatened, even destroyed?

> "During growth periods, net gains infill wasted space and replace blight. When expansion does not offset contractions, citizens are left with an oversized city. Witness Detroit, Michigan. How differently would we build if we anticipated contractions ahead?

Future Cities Now

Some places carve their own way despite overwhelming changes, through committed leadership, inspired vision, and exceptional urgency. They believe they have to change.

- In the 1980s, the citizens of San Luis Obispo rejected their future as a forgettable car-dominated California city. They banned drive-through restaurants and big box retail stores, and transformed an open ditch located behind main street stores into a "creek walk" for shopping, dining, and strolling. Furthermore, they created one of the first comprehensive bike path systems. A generation later, this highly livable place tops lists of the happiest cities. People willingly accept substantial pay cuts to live there.

- In 2008, Arubans saw their fate defined by Northeast United States snowbirds and coal-fired electricity. In other words, they depended upon two limited, potentially exhaustible resources. After a two-year public participation process that involved nearly every adult citizen, over 50,000 in all, they adopted a new vision. The island would be 100 percent free of fossil fuels by 2025 and would diversify its visitor base with ecotourism and learning centers. Because every person committed and worked collectively to achieve the vision, they will meet their goals five years ahead of schedule.

- Thirty years ago, two out of three Bangkok residents lived in poverty. Through a systemic poverty reduction program, they created changes across public and private domains: an infrastructure program, pro-business policies, a progressive tax system, and a minimum wage that created a new middle class. Today, although inequality remains high, extreme poverty is gone, overall poverty is close to five percent, and unemployment is at one percent. Streets are alive with commerce, and shopping centers prosper.

India remains a lower-middle income country, according to the World Bank, but it is a place in transition. Dozens of cable channels concentrate on education and learning, teaching a range of topics from cooking to differential equations. It reminds me of a post-World War II United States. Rapid change will hit India, a place that currently seems both in the center of the world and a place all on its own. It is unlike anything Toffler foresaw—new and old co-exist. We no longer live with monolithic future shock but future patience coupled with future whiplash. We learn to wait, prepare, mitigate, and aspire, depending on long droughts or sudden wild cards.

After Shock Choices

Toffler's greatest wisdom did not lie in his ideas around accelerating change and disorientation. Granted, we have experienced that phase for five decades. Looking forward, as we assimilate into a future of automation and artificial intelligence, technological change may become as accepted a condition as urbanization.

> My 90-year-old mother streams Doris Day songs on her Echo speaker with just a verbal command. In sum, we manage a multitude of changes on our own terms.

As Joseph Gusfield argued, past and future don't clash; they co-exist. Sometimes tradition and other times modernity show us the way forward. We learn different things from each. For example, bicycles, previously ubiquitous in Beijing, are nearly gone in favor of cars. Meanwhile, Copenhagen reduces cars and congestion with bike highways. Something old finds a new use.

My friends and I recently rode Malwari horses, the curly eared, uniquely Indian breed, across the Rajasthan Desert. We saw villagers living weekends in their family homes and commuting to Delhi. Women wore saris and many had veils. Arranged marriages remain common. Yet India is a place of the future. Uniform-clad children raced from classrooms to see us ride through their dirt streets. They chanted "Three cheers for India," "Long live India." Some had yet to see Caucasians beyond television. New Delhi is invaded by globalization, but the villages remain traditional—for now. As generations pass on and next generations stay in the city, a new New Delhi will arise.

I was sad to see the construction of a huge raised highway slicing through neighborhoods. Surely no cows will be allowed on those raised roads. Progress! Ironically, Indians may lose their rhythmic traffic patterns at the same time automated cars invade other cities to mimic that flow. The messy modes of transportation blend and function because the drivers deeply know the unique rules. My guide advised, "Don't stop. Don't speed up or slow down. Stay in the flow." Today India knows those rules, but they are in danger of losing that shared knowledge.

Toffler Right and Wrong

I've outlined what Toffler got wrong about cities. Changes have been far wider and more varied than he imagined. Population and environmental changes are slowing and reversing, while technology continues to expand. Rather than the staggering confusion of future shock, people adopt and adapt past and future every day. Instead, we struggle with collective action. We lack the skills and tools required to solve massive problems together. Only in rare instances will a city combine the seemingly magical mix of strong leadership, vision, and urgency to act together for future generations.

Here's what Toffler got right. For the past few decades, we have been shocked and confused at the rate of change. His book was on point until now. Finally, we are no longer shocked. He proposed stability zones to balance the stress of massive change. As he anticipated, today people use spirituality, family, meditation, and healthy living to be happy and well. Furthermore, he envisioned anticipatory democracy, perhaps his most enduring and useful idea. Social future assemblies would bring us together for collective actions.

By focusing public attention for once on long-range goals rather than immediate programs alone, by asking people to choose a preferable future from among a range of alternative futures, these assemblies could dramatize the possibilities for humanizing the future—possibilities that all too many have already given up as lost.

Connections and relationships of people creating long-range plans and implementing them together is the only way we keep our cities and communities alive. As the future becomes ever more extreme and dynamic, plans alone will not work. When novelty and chaos are everyday norms, and consequences are the only way we judge success, we become navigators and designers, embracing the messiness of not knowing while acting on emerging scenarios.

The future is no longer as Toffler imagined. It is more nuanced and surprising. Now we need a vision beyond future shock. "To master change, we shall therefore need both a clarification of important long-range social goals and a democratization of the way in which we arrive at them." We remain first and foremost caring human beings who adapt and create. Together, we can learn to use the future, act coherently, and leave legacies worth inheriting. ▪

Dr. Cindy Frewen, FAIA, APF, urban futurist and architect, consults, speaks, and writes on future cities and design futures, specializing in the intersection of people, technology, and environment. For over two decades a business owner focused on design, sustainability, community development, and public works, and chief architect for the Kansas City downtown civic center, she designed sustainable schools, police facilities, courthouses, public parks, and housing developments. She teaches at the University of Houston graduate program in Strategic Foresight. www.urbanverse.net

Man Versus Machine, or Man and Machine?

Harish Natarajan

In May 1997, IBM's Deep Blue defeated Garry Kasparov, then the reigning world champion, in a six-game chess match. Deep Blue's victory was symbolic. A machine's ability to beat a chess grandmaster was a litmus test for machine intelligence. Deep Blue's victory showed the potential power of a supercomputer in excelling in a domain that was thought of as the apex of human intellectual achievement. Equally importantly, the Kasparov-Deep Blue contest may have done more than any other single event in creating the "man vs machine" narrative.

Looking back at the footage from those matches, one thing that is striking is what Deep Blue does not do. Amongst the simplest skills for a human is the ability to pick up and move physical chess pieces. Deep Blue relied on a human to move the pieces around the board. Twenty years later, Deep-Mind's Alpha Go similarly relied on a human to place pieces on a Go board. These incredibly powerful machines dominate in some of the fields that humans find to be the most complex. Yet machines struggle, even compared to toddlers, with motor skills and dexterity. There will likely come a point in the not-too-distant future where incremental improvements in perception-oriented artificial intelligence, robotics, and several other fields will allow machines to exhibit impressive motor skills, but the broader point is that machines often struggle in some of the areas that humans find easiest.

It is risky to overplay the analogy, but the limits in machines correlate with my own observations from a February 2019 public debate against IBM's Project Debater. For a human, debating is not more complicated than either Chess or Go, but for a machine it is a complicated challenge. At its core, successful debating involves four components. First, a debater needs to process a large amount of information and construct relevant arguments. Second, those arguments need to be explained to an audience in a clear and structured way. Third, effective debating requires listening to and understanding the natural language arguments of another person or group of people. Fourth, debating requires making those arguments matter to an audience. Humans do not operate on logic alone, and the careful use of language, emotions, rhetoric, and examples can impart impact to a logical claim.

Project Debater was incredible in its ability to process information from more than 400 million articles and construct relevant arguments from them. Its processing ability is far greater than that of a human. Project Debater thus overcame a difficulty that Alvin Toffler referred to as an "information overload." When faced with a large amount of information on a topic, it was nonetheless able to construct clear arguments with its insights. Project Debater was less powerful in its ability to fully comprehend four minutes of natural language and form complete responses. Nonetheless, it was advanced enough that continuing along its current improvement trajectory should be sufficient for it to at least be competitive in its ability to respond to human argument, if not to eventually achieve superiority.

Where Project Debater struggled was in its ability to make those arguments matter sufficiently to a human audience. In simple terms, Project Debater lacked "common sense." When debating the motion on whether to subsidize preschool education, Project Debater argued that preschool education was valuable in improving educational outcomes and was worth the cost due to the positive effect on other social indicators. What Project Debater mentioned, but never focused on, were preschool's impact on poverty and effect on inequality. Common sense reasoning tells us that the emotional impact of the logical arguments can be maximized by focusing on serious problems of inequality and arguing that they can be at least partially mitigated by subsidizing access to preschool. Project Debater, like other artificial intelligence machines, lacks intuition and the common sense reasoning that humans exhibit.

My experience with Project Debater thus suggested that there is considerable scope for humans to work with machines. Artificial intelligence at its best has the ability to process large amounts of information and synthesize it. A machine's thought process will differ from that of a human, but that is a feature more than a bug. Machines are able to find statistically valid connections that humans may either miss or ignore. This human failing may be due to our propensity to overused heuristics, our default to biases, or limits in our capacity to process information. Humans have the ability to use common sense to make decisions that are consistent with a deeply held principle of justice and to provide emotional intelligence to communicate a decision.

> "Where Project Debater struggled was in its ability to make those arguments matter sufficiently to a human audience. In simple terms, Project Debater lacked "common sense."

For instance, China's Alipay's algorithms use thousands of data points, many of which a human considers to be "noise." They have apparently concluded that the number of Facebook friends you have, the average charge in your mobile phone, and your propensity to play certain types of video games affect the probability of your repaying a loan.

It is not immediately clear to a human why these attributes affect the probability of repayment, but the insight that artificial intelligence generates may still help humans make better decisions in allocating credit. For customers who previously lacked access to credit and thus lack a credit history—for instance, in countries with less developed financial systems—a machine's ability to use seemingly peripheral data to assess probability of repayment could be vital in affiliating a greater number of people into finance channels.

Yet, there is something disconcerting about relying solely on a machine. It may be hard to locate bias in a machine learning algorithm, but that does not mean discrimination does not exist. We can easily imagine that many of the factors that a machine finds to be relevant correlate with race, gender, or other structural factors. The data that it uses may be inaccurate. At the very least, we want humans to be able to query and interrogate the results that a machine produces. Humans can use principles, like fairness and justice, and some degree of critical thinking and common sense to tune the conclusions that a machine produces by itself. In other words, even if there are statistical relationships, that does not mean it is necessarily just to use a resulting conclusion as a factor in making an allocative decision.

Harish Natarajan has been working for AKE Insights in London for over five years. He holds an undergraduate degree from the University of Oxford, and a master's degree from the University of Cambridge, where he wrote his thesis on sovereign finance. He is a specialist on sovereign debt and global trade. He also has an interest in the impact of technology on political and economic risk. In his time at AKE, Harish has worked with hedge funds, private equity firms, insurance underwriters, reinsurers, global development organizations, NGOs, and media outlets. Harish also designs Probable Maximum Loss models to assess economic contagion risks. Harish has extensive experience in debating and public speaking. In 2012, he won the European Debating Championships in Belgrade, and in 2016 reached the grand final of the World Debating Championships. He has won a record number of international debating competitions. In 2019, Harish participated in IBM's third Grand Challenge in San Francisco, debating and defeating Project Debater, an Artificial Intelligence machine.

Shocked... By What, Exactly?

Aris Persidis

Assume you are asked to complete a book title, "Future..."

What would you add as a second word? Knowing what you know in 2020? Remember, "Future Shock" is already taken.

Also, what you propose has to have the potential, based on the title alone, to become a No. 1 bestseller on any legitimate booklist.

Final specification: You are not competing with "Future Aftershock." It's a very different remit.

Let's consider a few options to get things started—not necessarily in any order:

1. ■ "Future Re-shock": Nah, too easy. Lazy. Let's move on.
2. ■ "Future Now": In too many corporate mission statements.
3. ■ "Future Trends": Good luck.
4. ■ "Future Misses": Cynical. By definition, a version will come true.
5. ■ "Future Mess": Okay, I admit, I sort of like this one. Doesn't take itself too seriously. But lazy, too. Definite No.1 bestseller potential from the title alone, though, right?
6. ■ "Future Great": At least it's not cynical from the start. By definition, a version will come true.
7. ■ "Future Unknown": We know about this one. Proverbs abound.
8. ■ "Future Unhinged": Gratuitous. But sure to become a No. 1 bestseller based on the title alone.
9. ■ "Future Hype": Another overused thing.
10. ■ "Future Possible": Really?
11. ■ "Future Less": This one got me thinking. It has a cynical vibe, though, which I don't like.
12. ■ "Future Expectations": Boring.
13. ■ "Future Past": This is another one that got me thinking.

14 ■ "Future Through": Got me thinking, but the title won't make the bestseller list.

15 ■ "Future Close Calls": Has potential, but sounds like a doomsday futurist piece of crap we can do without. Plus, it's three words, not two.

16 ■ "Future [empty space for the reader to fill in what they like]": Sure, it could look interesting on the bestseller list, sort of interactive, but it's also lazy.

17 ■ "Future Us": Well, this is my preference. Based on the classic original and what I think I know in 2020. I also give this a chance at a bestseller list. Theoretically. So, here goes the intro chapter from *Future Us*.

Embracing change. Getting emotionally and practically ready for life to change dramatically because of socio-technological evolution. These are just a couple of the key messages most readers retain from *Future Shock*. You could actually argue that the 3,000-year-old classic ancient Greek proverb by Heraclitus "τὰ πάντα ῥεῖ καὶ οὐδὲν μένει" (ta panta rhei kai ouden menei), meaning "everything flows and nothing stays," is an intellectual precursor to *Future Shock*. So, now what?

I work in healthcare. As you can imagine, the field is exploding yet again, and we are at a discontinuity/inflection point that meets *Future Shock*'s definitions rather well.

The bottom line in healthcare, and also everywhere else: *Future Shock* was one of the best systematic and rational attempts to prepare us for the amazing and discontinuous technological, cultural, emotional, and socio-political future we could possibly face. It did so from the perspective of predicting what was likely ahead of us. It was based on signals that were visible at the time. It did so from the perspective of hope. It is sheer genius. Fast-forward and my perspective is that 1) we have lost the sense of wonder that *Future Shock* was all about, and 2) we need to train ourselves no longer for shock, but for "credible hype."

Let's start with what we were supposed to be shocked about. If you are reading this book, then it means that you are likely intellectually curious, open to new ideas, questioning, confident in your own thoughts, and likely read a lot of and all sorts of books. Do you read good sci-fi? If so, there isn't much in *Future Shock* that isn't also portrayed in depth in some sci-fi book, short story, or the movies. I am not suggesting any endorsement of scientific/technological accuracy. It is just that the core themes in *Future Shock* are all previewed in "what if" scenarios playing out with fictional characters and scenarios many times and in multiple places over many years, beginning with Jules Verne. Just about all of it has happened to fictional societies and people that we have been exposed to many times since *Future Shock*.

I think in some deep place we all still have a vestigial sense of wonder when amazing advances in technological or social norms happen. We just no longer give this sense of wonder its proper due. This has to change for us to become better as a species.

What's really interesting is that we have come to *expect* the full bore of what's in *Future Shock* in our fictional entertainment! In real life, of course, what has actually happened is hype and distorted expectations and variations of what was predicted in *Future Shock*. In real life we expect failure. But only if one is a die-hard cynic. What is truly amazing is exactly how much in *Future Shock* has come to pass.

The simple reality is that we are no longer shocked by just about anything. Watching three SpaceX rockets land autonomously in perfect synchrony back on Earth and ready for reuse after launching cargo into space should have been treated with the same popular wonder as the original Moon landing, or the launch and landing of the original Space Shuttle missions. Even the introduction of Dolly, the first cloned sheep, was a non-event, in comparison.

Exactly what has to happen for us to be shocked, per *Future Shock* terminology? Meeting aliens won't do it. Time travel won't do it. Faster-than-light travel won't do it. Armageddon won't do it. If the religious prophet from history you believe in shows up, okay, be shocked in the best possible way (although you shouldn't be, because it could be a case of time travel...).

I think in some deep place we all still have a vestigial sense of wonder when amazing advances in technological or social norms happen. We just no longer give this sense of wonder its proper due. This has to change for us to become better as a species.

When it comes to healthcare, my daily trough, I have become a selective cynic. Pill I can ingest that will monitor me from the inside? Check. Scanning device like *Star Trek*'s tricorder? Check. Holo-imaging guiding remote surgery by robot? Check. Human augmentation? Check. Defeating cancer, Alzheimer's etc.? Check (no longer impossible, although still years away, but no longer impossible, okay?). Thought communication? All it needs is a brainwave transducer and Wi-Fi ... Cryogenics, artificial organs, whole brain transplants, cloning? Check. Non-womb embryonic development from fertilization? Check. Meaning, there is zero shock factor that I would need to prepare for. *Future Shock* would be of little value to me here.

If Amazon delivered these developments to my front door right now, all I would post as feedback, assuming they actually worked as advertised, is "Not bad." How awful is that!

Future Us is about being ready to receive the incredible bounty that our past has brought us to.

In my daily professional life, I deal with something that takes my breath away. We are taking all publicly available healthcare data and reusing it to correctly predict 70 percent or better of any clinical scenario. We have built a unique form of artificial intelligence (AI) and are constantly mapping over 270,000 clinical outcomes (meaning real-life diseases, side effects, or health scenarios) against over 50 million possible drugs (including all known drugs), and against over a million genes. It has taken us over 10 years, but now we can run the question, "Which ones of any marketed drugs, no matter what their use, can be used for any disease, in any patient context, and why?"

I can tell you with certainty, and please discount my obvious bias, that this bounty is not ready to be received by lots. There are many reasons that have nothing to do with the tech itself and are mostly about the politics of accepting and acting on disruption at massive scale. The example above is one of many, not just in my own story, and there are many exceptions and nuances, too. Lots of people accept our disruption and act on it, lots don't. It's just the way of progress, and I get that.

Future Us embraces disruption much sooner—with caveat emptor, of course. Meaning, that trivial

> "We are used to hype. We are used to things not working as advertised. Sadly, this means that when something amazing gets delivered, we rarely think of what it looked like as an embryonic idea, how much effort it took, how many wise naysayers tried to kill it, thankfully failing to do so. Like Amelia Earhart once said, "Never interrupt someone doing something you said couldn't be done.""

innovation is weeded out efficiently. The shift relative to *Future Shock* is not about being ready to deal with how different these advances make us, but with how soon we can incorporate them and, we hope, improve our lot in life.

Okay, we have discussed our need to re-capture our sense of wonder. What about *Future Us*, where "credible hype" is the norm?

We are used to hype. We are used to things not working as advertised. Sadly, this means that when something amazing gets delivered, we rarely think of what it looked like as an embryonic idea, how much effort it took, how many wise naysayers tried to kill it, thankfully failing to do so. Like Amelia Earhart once said, "Never interrupt someone doing something you said couldn't be done."

Will we ever be able to improve our "hype meter?" Wrong question. Why even bother? Leave that to venture capital. And thank goodness they suck at it, too. The human condition and evolution in general are about "shots on goal." In *Future Us*, we pre-judge much less.

Imagine a bucket of Legos, filled with colorful shapes, sizes and new types of bricks. Here is the *Future Shock* version: "What do you think of this? Did you ever imagine it?" Here is the *Future Us* version: "This bucket is yours. Go build." ▪

Aris Persidis has been working on AI in healthcare for about 20 years. He is co-founder and president of Biovista, the AI drug development and personalized medicine pioneer (www.biovista. com). Aris has helped lead the creation and positioning of Project Prodigy, the Big Data/AI plat-form that is based on recombining knowledge to build new solutions. He has negotiated and closed relevant deals with some of the most well-known organizations in the world, including Hewlett Packard Enterprise, Pfizer, Novartis, Astellas, BiogenIdec, the FDA, and a number of Patient Advocacy Groups. Aris is also Chair of GridNewsBureau (www.gridnewsbureau.com) and serves on the Board of MBF Therapeutics (www.mbftherapeutics.com/). Aris has published over 90 papers and chapters. The journal *Nature Biotechnology* (NBT) collected all of Aris's Industry Trends columns in NBT and published them in a single dedicated volume, a rare honor. Aris also received the Honeywell Futurist Award (HFA) in 1986, while a third-year undergraduate student. The HFA was a Europe-wide award recognizing a socio-tech vision for our future 25 years out (Aris's contribution was artificial photo-synthesis, many variants of which are now coming to pass). Aris received his PhD in biochemistry from the University of Cambridge, U.K. And being a daddy is his favorite thing in the world.

Bio-Lego and Brain Nanocircuitry: A Musing on the Future of Health

Rick Sax, MD

first encountered *Future Shock* in my teenage years—an era of moonshots and lunar landings, heart transplants and Vietnam, revolutionary aspirations and political assassinations.

Already my future vocation was calling, and I voraciously absorbed Toffler's vision of the future of health care—what he described as "a new stage of eco-technical development" that I have now come to know as the postindustrial Biological Revolution. Toffler wrote of cloning, replacement parts, artificial organs, genetic treatments, "wearables" (to measure and transmit physiological measurements), robotics, and cyborgs (merging "human-ness" and machines). He also predicted a host of incumbent issues, including bioethical concerns, black markets for organs, the need for the complete rewrite of insurance tables, and the reorganization of health systems. Furthermore, he wrote that as we learn to "imitate nature we will have processes of an entirely new kind. These will form the basis of industries of a new kind—a sort of biotechnical factor, a biological technology."

This description foresees the rise of the global pharmaceutical industry and the emergence of the smaller, innovative, and entrepreneurial biotechnology sector encompassing both new medical entities (especially biologics and cellular and genetic therapies) and novel medical devices. He didn't fully recognize the impact this new industry would have on the socioeconomics of global and local health care, however, as it came into its own in the 1990s and "aught" years. The high cost of novel medicines and devices created deep societal tensions between the ethics of "autonomy" (care for the individual) and the ethics of "social justice" (care for the greater good) that would emerge from increasingly costly therapeutic breakthroughs. It also significantly exacerbated the socioeconomic divide evident in countries with more mature health infrastructures, creating health care disparities between those who "can afford" and those who "cannot" that continue to widen even to this day.

Every major technological advance comes with unanticipated side effects, and the Biological Revolution is no different. Our pharmaco-nutritional "successes" have spawned a host of countervailing problems: life-threatening antimicrobial resistance, endemic obesity with its scourge of diabetes and cardiovascular disease, the opioid epidemic, and the creation of novel diseases by the very therapies designed to cure illness (post-transplantation immunologic "graft vs. host" disease being one example). The rise of anti-vaccination ideologies threatens to undermine decades of progress toward the eradication of pestilences that have plagued humanity throughout its existence. Even without this anti-science, the rise of affordable travel has created a global human interconnectivity that iteratively raises that specter of local contagions (e.g., swine and avian flu, SARS, Ebola, etc.) being converted into lethal pandemics. The irony is that our scientific triumphs over the 50 years since the publication of *Future Shock* continue to be subverted by our own human cravings, folly, hubris, and evolutionary hardwiring. We are still a long way from achieving Toffler's grandest rose-colored aspiration, that the "super-industrial revolution" could "erase hunger, disease, ignorance and brutality."

Patient Ascendant

Where will the march of history take us over the next 50 years? As one might expect, the roots of "aftershock" are grounded in the emerging realities of the here and now. In this regard, one of the most powerful current trends in health care is the emergence of the patient as the dominant force in the management of their own care and well-being. Well chronicled in Eric Topol's insightful book, *The Patient Will See You Now*, the increasing empowerment of an educated patient to understand a diagnosis and contribute to therapeutic decision-making is a far cry from the closed cabal of medicine that controlled both knowledge and treatment with religious fervor for millennia.

Augmented by the emergence of "wearable" device technology, individuals today already have an increasing, albeit rudimentary, ability to monitor their own well-being directly, bypassing the doctor's office and reinforcing self-accountability.

Three generations from now, the trend will reach its apex. Equipped with the latest microtechnology and patient-empathetic artificial intelligence (AI), every enabled adult will be able to self-diagnose and self-medicate in response to most routine illness, even the most serious ones by today's standards. While we still may not have fully developed the *Star Wars* Tricorder (see the QualComm XPRIZE challenge), every home will have point-of-care capability to monitor real-time metabolomic, immunologic, and physiologic profiles, diagnose perturbations, and, combined with our stored genomic and proteomic profiles, prescribe real-time personalized interventions. In a secure, private, networked informatics infrastructure, outcomes can be also monitored in real time for timely course correction.

Moreover, as patient-centric health care reaches its pinnacle, the health system's incentives will switch from illness treatment to "total wellness" maintenance. "Life optimization" will link defined age-appropriate activity regimes with dietary adjustments harmonized to each individual's microbiomic profile. The future AI-augmented personal nutritionist will become a major contributor to our well-being, and even though our very human genomic hardwiring will continue to lead us to iterative "wellness failures," the opportunities for self-correction will be plentiful and manifest.

Doctor Wither (?)

With technology- and knowledge-empowered patients evolving to become the center of their own health care destiny, and therapeutic interventions no longer locked in the control of the medical profession, health care professionals will no longer exist as we currently know them. Visits to the doctor's office for care will become largely obsolete, and centralized health facilities will focus only on the most gravely ill (i.e., those unable to be cared for in a home environment), those still requiring intensive care following surgical interventions, and acute trauma-related injuries. The key physician role, in addition to surgeon-assisted robotics, will be that of the "Exoticatician"—a highly skilled bio-engineering expert who diagnoses and treats only the most complex of disease challenges. By utilizing advanced telemedicine, the need for geographic proximity of this scarce resource will disappear, and focused, need-based consultancies will free time for these individuals to create additional value through research, health systems support, and training of their successors.

The other two critical expert professions will be: 1) epidemiologists to monitor local and global health care trends, resource utilization, and new emerging diseases (infectious or other), and 2) AI developers who, based on the information gleaned from their own systems and from the other remaining medical professions, will tweak the algorithms that keep the entire health infrastructure running. In this patient-centric world, the dominant health resources will become those professionals most capable of providing direct ("hands-on") support to a patient in times of need: e.g., nursing, rehabilitation therapy, diet and exercise coaches, and mental health support (see below).

> The irony is that our scientific triumphs over the 50 years since the publication of *Future Shock* continue to be subverted by our own human cravings, folly, hubris, and evolutionary hardwiring. We are still a long way from achieving Toffler's grandest rose-colored aspiration, that the "super-industrial revolution" could "erase hunger, disease, ignorance and brutality."

The Health Ecosystem

In organizational design thinking, a "system" is defined by the interactions among people, process, technology, and culture. A patient-centric, AI-enabled, wireless, privacy-protected, networked, health informatics infrastructure delineates the broad construct of a future "health system." Health personnel will perform circumscribed, needs-focused roles, designed to directly support a patient (or individual wellness) and address unusual disease challenges. As for process, AI algorithms will not only diagnose and prescribe in most routine situations, but on a health systems basis will also monitor resource requirements and allocate them based on real-time supply-demand exigencies, while simultaneously anticipating emergent health care needs. The consequence will be the virtual elimination of a health care bureaucracy that currently saps 30% of the health care dollar in a spiral of self-perpetuation that creates little-to-no direct patient benefit. That vast sum of squandered finance can efficiently fund universal coverage and continuous infrastructure maintenance without the inflationary escalation of health care expenditure that threatens growth in most economies across the globe.

The creation of such a system (based on universal empowerment of individuals, which, in this case, is synonymous with the greater good) will also require a specific societal culture, namely the restoration of the primary function of government to, first and foremost, "protect" the well-being of its citizenship and once again enable "life, liberty, and the pursuit of happiness" as its dominant goal. The "health highway" infrastructure will evolve and mature over time, but most important, beyond the info-technology (which will form the basis of new industries), will be the upskilling of the population to be self-sufficient in this ecosystem. Even the most disenfranchised segments of the population will need to absorb the technology; the mobile phone and internet were relatively seamlessly assimilated over the last two decades without major government intervention.

> The consequence will be the virtual elimination of a health care bureaucracy that currently saps 30% of the health care dollar in a spiral of self-perpetuation that creates little-to-no direct patient benefit.

The provision of health articulates the values of a society, just as society defines the shape of the care it provides for its citizens. Once built and enabled (from a people standpoint), the health care ecosystem of 2070 will embody universality and uniformity of access. The absence of health disparities will be an acknowledgement of both our collective bio-knowledge and the health interdependency of the population that drives the system. Understandable health knowledge will be available to all, and personalized guidance, generated by system-wide algorithms linked to individualized data, will define individual optimized treatment paradigms. Nations will compete to be recognized for the depth of their health coverage and the power of their infrastructure, but simultaneously will be participants in the global monitoring of health and environment. This collective data will in turn inform their respective, but interactive, health systems, not dissimilar to the connectivity and interdependency of global financial systems today.

Bio-Lego: Therapeutic Interventions

With the workings of the human body and its interaction with the world around it largely understood, the ability to generate novel intellectual property for therapeutic interventions (drugs, biologics, cellular therapies, medical devices, etc.) will be markedly circumscribed. Thus, the mechanism of wealth sequestration that currently drives corporate pharmaceutical and biotechnology valuations, will dissipate. Most available therapies will be long off-patent, but more importantly, the entire nature of therapeutic intervention will shift to combinations of "building blocks" specifically tailored to meet individual genomic and proteomic profiles. These will be delivered and administered in real-time response to metabolomic, immunologic, and physiologic "perturbations" of individual baseline states. The "industry" will thus evolve into corporate entities that can master the supply-chain dynamics of "just-in-time" personalized combinatorial interventions: development of the "building blocks," stocking, distribution, identity verification, and outcomes tracking (which will then be fed back into the AI learning system while searching for abuse potential).

As novel "building blocks" are developed, they will be recognized as an extension of the entire biologic corpus of knowledge, not the "property" of individual inventors, as such events are more likely to result from "design novelty" than "scientific breakthrough." Furthermore, the concept of "clinical trials" and regulatory oversight for new interventions, both of which are currently grounded in population-based thinking, will become obsolete as well, given that each tailored therapy becomes its own "n=1 trial" and the patient becomes his or her own "control." Success will never be 100 percent but the probability of positive treatment outcomes with tolerable side effects will be a vast improvement over the nonindividualized empiric guesswork of today's practices. Regulatory oversight will correspondingly shift to amplified quality control of the "building block" supply chain (augmented by AI systems and secure, verifiable "chain-of-custody" technology), as well as real-time review of health care infrastructure algorithms to ensure they remain valid, are properly maintained, and are appropriately responsive to evolving needs.

The Future of Sex

If the individuals are empowered to manage their treatment of illness, and in self-control of managing their wellness, one might expect that they will demand control of their own pleasure and self-gratification. The threat of a system that permits "self-prescription" is that it runs amok with recreational drugs and non-wellness-related "lifestyle" health interventions. Given our hardwired human frailties, it will be virtually impossible to completely edit this risk out of the health infrastructure; a better approach will be to recognize and accept our shortcomings and manage them within societally acceptable tolerances.

As for sex, the drive for mutual arousal and gratification is so hardwired into the procreative survival of Homo sapiens that it is difficult to envision it will be supplanted by pharmaceutical masturbatory self-prescription. Of more concern is the use of pharmacology for perpetuation of patriarchal and other power structures—manipulation, subjugation, and control of another to fulfill one's own desires. Fortunately, the ability of "the system" to detect these sorts of "anomalous behaviors" will be powerful, and the corresponding penalties will requisitely need to be harsh.

Given that sex is a hardwired natural outcome of the socio-biologic, oxytocin-fueled "mating" ritual of mutual attraction, admiration, reflection, and joint pleasuring (falling and being "in love"), it will be difficult to imagine that the human species will evolve beyond these behaviors within the next three generations, irrespective of gender preferences and gender identification. The same is true for the socio-biologic power of friendship, community, social intercourse, and social purpose. These are the manifestation of our human longing for companionship, a set of collective survival mechanisms that are almost as powerful as the drive for procreation. The individual as a member of society is part of wellness, though how this will be assessed ("social health") and addressed in the context of a health diagnostic remains to be seen.

Mental {we}-{i}-llness

Returning to the individual, if "social wellness" is a critical component of well-being, it needs to be considered in the context of overall "mental health"—the sense of "feeling well." This goes to the heart of human-ness—consciousness and cognitive awareness—our sense of self, our awareness of "will" (ability to act), our awareness of consequences (conscience), our sense of purpose, our awareness of our relationships to others—our "soul." All these are hardwired into our biology and are ubiquitous across the great diversity of human existence.

In being hardwired, however, they will be subject to investigation; three generations from now, much of this wiring will be understood—and thereby open to "intervention." Such interventions will be cloaked as the "treatment of mental illness." Depression, schizophrenia, obsessive-compulsive disorders, etc., will be managed through implanted brain nano-circuitry; pharmaco-device technology will be used to restore societally acceptable norms of mental well-being. Dystopian outcomes will immediately become evident, however, as the fine line between health and "madness" is crossed—at what point will "otherness" become a focus of treatment? In a highly networked, monitored, rapid response "health system," the system-wide demand for societal conformity and communal peace (control of counter-cultural, destructive, rebellious, "terrorist" forces) can become a means of repression turned against the genius, the artist, the novel designer. Creators of some of humankind's most glorious achievements are often nonconformists and a source of diversity essential to the evolution and survival of our species. Loneliness and isolation, sadness and rejection, can be powerful motivators for profound achievement; healthful bliss and contentment a soporific pacifier of human zeal and aspiration.

What is mental "{we}llness," what is {i}llness? Where is the line between health and disease, between conformity and individuality, between control and tolerance of diversity? These are questions an AI-driven system cannot grapple with—they existentially define our humanity.

As we become the masters of our biologic destiny, the seeds of our next wave of history are already being sown. Emergent technologies come with unanticipated consequences and societal-ethical quandaries. Just as scientific curiosity and exploration are hardwired into our genetic makeup, so too are the very human drives that create the "hunger, disease, ignorance and brutality" that Toffler longed to erase. History is the story of how humankind has treated itself, and our past, often forgotten by futurists but dramatized by dystopians, is not pretty. Will we "edit out" the "darker" side of ourselves as we gain the ultimate knowledge of the "Biology of Self"? Or, in trying to do "good," will we create the greatest folly of all and end what makes us "human"?

Rick Sax, MD, or "Rick" to those who know him, is a "global nomad"—born in New York City but raised abroad. He obtained a BA in biology and in philosophy from Yale College and his MD degree from Columbia's College of Physicians & Surgeons. His medical vocation was cardiac intensive care until he joined Merck Research Laboratories, seeking to fundamentally change outcomes for both acute management and long-term prevention of cardiovascular disease. This quest for change defined the next three decades of his professional life as a drug developer, ultimately resulting in building the Strategic Drug Development group at IQVIA—linking deep therapeutic expertise with data-driven design in service of better R&D decision-making. His individual consultancy practice, Pharma Design Solutions, supports innovative technology companies looking to enhance biotechnology R&D productivity.

Future Shock: Warning, Diagnosis, Prescription

Jeffrey A. Eisenach

In the late 1980s and early 1990s, I served as Newt Gingrich's "chief planner," helping to organize the never-ending caravan of academics and intellectuals travelling through his world to offer wisdom and provocation. Newt introduced me to Al and Heidi Toffler in 1989. We became and remained close friends.

A few years later, in 1993, I co-founded The Progress & Freedom Foundation, a think tank dedicated to studying the digital revolution and its impact on public policy. The Tofflers' ideas and writings—by then including *The Third Wave* and *Powershift*, with *War and Anti-War* headed for press—played an important role in my thinking and in the Foundation's work. Indeed, Al agreed to co-author (with Esther Dyson, George Gilder, and Jay Keyworth) our August 1994 manifesto, *Cyberspace and the American Dream: A Magna Carta for the Knowledge Age*. We also published a mash-up of the Tofflers' previously published work, with some new material thrown in, titled *Creating a New Civilization: The Politics of the Third Wave*. When Newt became Speaker in January 1995, copies were sent to every member of Congress.

Those were heady days. Magna cartas, new civilizations, progress, and freedom. Readers of this volume may remember well the bouquet of that old wine: cyber-utopianism, sometimes nuanced and sophisticated, sometimes not so much. Either way, it hasn't aged well.

In those days, we (and I think it is fair to include Al and Heidi in this) had visions of how the Enlightenment-inspired liberal democracy of the 20th Century would be thrown forward into the 21st. We did not imagine we had seen the "end of history," but we certainly did believe that digital technologies would liberate human creativity and help advance the principles of democratic capitalism. We shared a libertarian vision of a better-functioning, more humane society, in which individual diversity would flourish within a more secure and stable civilization. As the *Magna Carta for the Knowledge Age* put it:

> *Second Wave ideologues routinely lament the breakup of mass society. Rather than seeing this enriched diversity as an opportunity for human development, they attack it as "fragmentation" and "balkanization." But to reconstitute democracy in Third Wave terms, we need to jettison the frightening but false assumption that more diversity automatically brings more tension and conflict in society.... Given appropriate social arrangements, diversity can make for a secure and stable civilization.*

The Tofflers hypothesized that such stabilizing social arrangements would include "'electronic communities' bound together not by geography but by shared interests" which would "play an important role knitting together the diverse communities of tomorrow."

As we now know, the future turned out to be more complicated and challenging than any of us expected, the centrifugal forces were more powerful, and the centripetal ones less so. As standards have been diluted and authority has waned, so too have the stability and security they provided. The "electronic communities" that were supposed to replace traditional values and age-old mores have united some but divided many; the society of the digital revolution has proven to be more chaotic than secure.

> Those were heady days. Magna cartas, new civilizations, progress, and freedom. Readers of this volume may remember well the bouquet of that old wine: cyber-utopianism, sometimes nuanced and sophisticated, sometimes not so much. Either way, it hasn't aged well.

At the same time, the bureaucratic power of the state—which the Tofflers as much as anyone believed to be a dying manifestation of "Second Wave" civilization—has refused to retire quietly. On the contrary, as change has threatened safety, people have turned to the state as protector, against everything from Islamic terrorism to uncontrolled immigration and economic disruption. Globally, rather than the ascendancy of individual liberty, the information revolution has spawned a truly existential threat to Western democracy in the form of digitally enabled "adaptive authoritarianism," practiced most thoroughly in modern China. For all its Orwellian horrors, the citizenry mainly does not rebel—perhaps in part hoping for a level of social stability lacking in the modern West.

Remarkably, the Tofflers anticipated and explained the dark side of the digital revolution 50 years ago. Indeed, *Future Shock* was anything but utopian. Rather, it was—first—a warning that the pace of change was too rapid, tearing society apart faster than we could knit it back together, and—second—a diagnosis of the societal harm that would result from such unabated disruption.

The Tofflers were anything but Luddites; they believed the information revolution would yield immeasurable benefits, as it has and will. But they were also realists. And their realism led them to write, in 1970, that the "first and most pressing need" was not to find better ways of adapting to change, but rather to "halt the runaway acceleration that is subjecting millions to future shock."

First, decelerate. That was and remains a radical message, especially coming from "futurists" like the Tofflers. But it is their prescription in *Future Shock*, and looking back over the history of the last five decades, it is clear they were largely correct. Fifty years later, the message for us seems clear. Recognize, as the Tofflers did, the limits of humans both as individuals and as societies to tolerate change, and work to develop and implement a thoughtful futurist agenda that balances the benefits of change against its costs, recognizing that faster, however alluring, is not always better.

J**eff Eisenach** is a managing director and co-chair of the Communications, Media, and Internet Practice at NERA Economic Consulting, an adjunct professor at George Mason's Antonin Scalia Law School, and a visiting scholar at the American Enterprise Institute. He previously taught at Harvard University's Kennedy School of Government and served as president of The Progress & Freedom Foundation, which he co-founded with George A. Keyworth. His consulting practice focuses on economic analysis of competition and regulatory issues in the information technology sector, and he has advised clients in some of the world's largest IT sector mergers. He received his Ph.D. in economics from the University of Virginia.

After Overload

David Weinberger

Place my aged copy of *Future Shock* upright on its spine and it opens to page 301[1], the section titled "Information Overload." ■ As with so much, the Tofflers were ahead of their times with this. But as we exit the Computer Age and enter The Age of AI, the phrase is less heard, less relevant. That's not only because we have evolved ways of dealing with massive amounts of information, but also because our understanding of how the world works is shifting in epochal ways.

■ ■ ■

In the mid 1990s when the public was only beginning to embrace the Internet, we were routinely told both that its glory was that it would give us access to untold amounts information ("the information highway"[2]), but also that our psyches and our civilization were threatened by information overload.

But "information overload" didn't quite mean what it meant in the 1960s and 1970s when Alvin and Adelaide (Heidi) Toffler introduced the concept to the general public. They positioned it as riding on the shoulders of "sensory overload," a concept that arose originally from a late 19th century distrust of cities, what with the carriages clattering over cobblestone, the bright lights, the streets crowded with a diversity of people, and—if you were Charles Babbage, the inventor of what some think was the first computer—those noisy Italian immigrants with their infernal hurdy-gurdy machines.[3]

In the 1960s, sensory overload leapt into public consciousness as a way to raise the fear of what rock 'n' roll was doing to the kids. The noise, the flashing lights, the "primitive" rhythms, and the sensory-heightening drugs! Sensory overload, it was claimed, could cause one to fall to the ground, eyes rolled back, twitching.

Then, through the 1950s and 1960s, we reconceived everything from telecommunications, to literature, to molecules themselves as information. We inserted information into the cognitive "stack" between more traditional layers such as sensation, perception, and cognition. Led by the Tofflers, we began to worry that too much information would overload our brains the way sensation could overwhelm our sensory receptors. As the Tofflers wrote, "[J]ust as there are limits on how much sensory input we can accept, there are in-built constraints on our ability to process information." "By classifying information, by abstracting and 'coding' it in various ways, we manage to stretch these limits, yet ample evidence demonstrates that our capabilities are finite."[4]

And if we exceed those limits? "[O]verloading the system leads to a serious breakdown of performance."[5] And because information is above sensation in the cognitive hierarchy, the sort of performance that's affected has to do with judgment and reason. In fact, the Tofflers make the case that it can lead to psychopathologies similar or identical to schizophrenia:

> If the Internet's information overload left us on the verge of psychosis, why did we flock to it, and tout it as a positive transformative abundance?

if you can't process information, your judgment about the association of ideas may be off, and that is a defining characteristic of schizophrenia. "What consequences this may have for mental health in the techno-societies has yet to be determined."[6]

■ ■ ■

Arguably, there were no actual consequences of note. Yes, one marketing study found that if 192 "housewives" were given too much information about a product—16 binary facts about four brands—their ability to make good judgments was diminished. The fact that it played so well into the hands of marketers looking for reasons to limit what customers—those poor low-capacity housewives—were told about products, is a cause for some skepticism. In any case, one of the authors of the study later reanalyzed the data and found it to be unreliable evidence for practical conclusions.[7]

But once we were on the Internet, information overload became an everyday concern, for the Net was the first environment in which we were brought face to face with endless information as we were doing our everyday tasks for many hours each day. This was different from going to a library or bookstore where for a few minutes we are plunged into the immensity of information. On the Net we were confronted with just how much information was available as we did our everyday tasks. Trying to choose a mixer? Here's a list of a thousand comments about them. Trying to find some hip hop? Here's ten thousand tracks. Have a question about begonias, Babylonia, or Red Sonja? There goes your afternoon. Where once we had to amass information by piling relevant books into our study carrel or clipping articles from newspapers, now we found ourselves in a continuous, endless meadow or mall, items always waving in our peripheral vision competing for our attention.

Yet if the Internet's information overload left us on the verge of psychosis, why did we flock to it, and tout it as a positive transformative abundance? From the point of view of the Internet's enthusiastic inhabitants, the problem wasn't that the Internet overloaded us with information, but that there was too much good stuff to see, read, hear, and experience: the Internet manifested itself less as an overload than as a constant, near irresistible temptation.

But for those who by profession or tradition had been charged with curating information for us, the Net was far more likely to look like a disabling overload. For them the issue wasn't our mental health, as the Tofflers' thought: "Sanity itself" depends on avoiding information overload, wrote the Tofflers.[8] For the traditional curators and arbiters it was obvious that without their help, we wouldn't be able to tell good information from bad. With information so easy to come by, we wouldn't bother learning the habits of cultivated people and informed citizens. In the Internet Age, the problem with information overload wasn't the overload itself but the diminishment of control by the gatekeepers who had always kept us on the path of truth.

Why does what seemed like such a pressing problem—information overload in the Tofflers' sense—now seem to worry us much less? There are undoubtedly many reasons, but I want to point to two, both speculative.

First, Clay Shirky was right when he wrote, "There's no such thing as information overload, only filter failure,"[9] and now our filters have gotten exponentially better. Algorithmic filters often serve us quite well, although they can also be insidiously subversive of our agency, dignity, and rights. Social filtering sites such as Reddit and StackOverflow also have gotten far more sophisticated, particularly in their community management.

At the same time, we have adopted an entirely different approach to filtering. Traditionally, we have filtered things out, so that all you see is what made it through. When you wander through your local public library you perhaps feel overwhelmed, but you are not seeing the vast bulk of books that didn't make it through the library's acquisition filters. Likewise, when book publishers filter out a manuscript by deciding not to publish it, that manuscript is likely to become unknown and inaccessible.

But on the Internet, we quickly and rather naturally figured out that we don't have to filter things *out* because we can filter them *forward*. If I post about five sites that talk about *Future Shock*, my act of filtering does nothing but shorten the number of clicks it takes you to get to those sites. All the thousands of other sites and posts about *Future Shock* are still completely available and might show up in someone else's Facebook feed, blog site, or Google search. Filtering forward removes the imperative presupposed by the old concept of information overload: However will we filter out all the noise?! It turns out that on the Internet, you don't have to. You can instead filter the signal forward.

This notion has enabled some of the most important repositories of information on the Net. Wikipedia can be as large and inclusive as its self-chosen guidelines allow. eBay can have 1.2 billion items on sale at the same time.[10] Reddit can have well over a million subreddits (discussion topic pages) even if the majority of them are unused:[11] there's plenty of room, and perhaps someone someday will want to strike up a discussion on a topic so far no one has found interesting.

This strategy, of including everything and allowing users to filter on the way out, succeeded only because we have developed tools for finding the needle we want within the largest haystacks humans have ever raked together. The power of our search tools would have been unimaginable even thirty years ago. No sane person could have imagined them back when the Tofflers were writing.

But there's a second reason why information overload is no longer the problem we thought it was, either in its nature or its urgency. This second reason is far more sweeping in its scope and importance: the rise of AI as a model of how things happen.

■ ■ ■

"In the technological systems of tomorrow—fast, fluid and self-regulating—machines will deal with the flow of physical materials; men with the flow of information and insight...Machines and men both, instead of being concentrated in gigantic factories and factory cities, will be scattered across the globe, linked together by amazingly sensitive, near-instantaneous communications."[12]

While *Future Shock* is incredibly prescient, it is inevitably of its time; as the philosopher Martin Heidegger once said about our all being grounded in our time, and culture, "No one can jump over their own shadow."[13] But the Tofflers did get some impressive altitude. In the above quotation they foresaw not only the Internet, but also the Internet of Things.

They did not predict machine learning, especially the type known as deep learning, but they did point to many of its most salient characteristics. When, towards the end of the book, the Tofflers reflect on how futurists should think about the future, within just a few pages they talk about the importance of recognizing "the interconnectedness of disparate events and trends," about being probabilistic in their predictions ("Determining the probable calls for a science of futurism"), thinking systemically and ecologically, and being aware that long-term effects may be butterfly-like in being far out of proportion to the initial cause ("The fact that the [power] plant could trigger devastating ecological consequences a generation later simply does not register in their time frame").[14]

All of these traits are characteristics of the models that machine learning makes for itself, models of various domains of the world. Deep learning in particular creates artificial neural networks in which data points can be connected in vast webs of probability, resulting in configurations that may not reduce to simple, understandable laws, but that nevertheless yield results far more precise than our traditional methods. These webs may find chains of causality that exhibit the "butterfly effect" that Chaos Theory has made a part of the common parlance. The Tofflers' picture of the world conforms to all of this.

The important bit they did not predict—which is really just to say that in 1970 they failed to invent machine learning—is the way machine learning has transformed our attitude toward information, in two important ways.

First, with machine learning we are coming to think that there is no such thing as too much information. It's all grist for our new mills. Let a machine learning system iterate on ridiculously large quantities of data and it may find probabilistic outcomes that are both more accurate and more surprising than what humans would come up with by reducing the data to what we can manage. Information overload now looks like fuel for good decisions, or, more exactly, for computers to augment a still-human decision-making process.

> In the Internet Age, the problem with information overload wasn't the overload itself but the diminishment of control by the gatekeepers who had always kept us on the path of truth.

Second, machine learning is teaching us that information overload is in a sense the truth, not a syndrome to be overcome. Traditionally, including up through the Age of Computers, we operated in a world that overwhelmed our cognitive capabilities by looking for generalizations, rules, and laws that reduce the complexity of events. But machine learning sometimes comes up with better answers than we do without starting from a model that explains a system through general principles.

Rather, it just connects data in all their particularity, without starting from, or necessarily yielding, general principles.

As it turns out, the overload of information, in all of its impossible complexity and interdependence, is the truth. ■

In books, articles, posts, classes, and talks, **David Weinberger, PhD** explores the effect of technology on ideas. He is a senior researcher at Harvard's Berkman Klein Center for Internet & Society and was co-director of the Harvard Library Innovation Lab. He has been a journalism fellow at Harvard's Shorenstein Center, a marketing VP and adviser to high tech companies, an adviser to several presidential campaigns, and a Franklin Fellow at the U.S. State Department. He is currently a writer-in-residence at a Google machine learning research group. He has a doctorate in philosophy from the University of Toronto.

1. Alvin Toffler (with Heidi Toffler, uncredited). *Future Shock*. (NY: Random House, 1970).

2. For example, Philip Elmer-Dewitt, "The First Cyberspace Nation Is Born," Time Dec. 6, 1993, No.49.

3. The German sociologist Georg Simmel (1858-1918) is credited with the basic idea of sensory overload.
    See his 1903 *The Metropolis and Mental Life*, discussed in an article of the same name by Matthew Wilsey,
    https://modernism.coursepress.yale.edu/the-metropolis-and-mental-life/ at the Yale CoursePress site. (No date.)
    Charles Babbage devotes a chapter of his memoir, *Passages from the Life of a Philosopher* (London: Longman, Green,
    Longman, Roberts & Green, 1864), to "Street Nuisances", pp. 337-362. The book in its entirety is available at the
    Internet Archive (archive.org) and elsewhere.

4. p. *Future Shock*, 302.

5. p. *Future Shock*, 302.

6. p. *Future Shock*, 304.

7. Jacob Jacoby, Donald E. Speller, Carol A. Kohn, "Brand Choice Behavior as a Function of Information Overload",
    Advances in Consumer Research Volume 1, 1974, pp. 381-383. For a re-consideration by one of the study's authors,
    see Jacob Jacoby, "Perspectives on Information Overload, "Journal of Consumer Research (March 1984): 432-435.

8. p. *Future Shock*, 301.

9. Clay Shirky in his keynote at the Web 2.0 Expo in NYC, in 2008. The video of the talk is no longer
    available. Matt Asay, "Shirky: Problem is filter failure, not info overload," CNET, Jan. 14, 2009
    https://www.cnet.com/news/shirky-problem-is-filter-failure-not-info-overload/

10. Kyle Wiggers. "How AI helps eBay connect buyers and sellers across 1.2 billion listings", VentureBeat, Mar. 13, 2019
    https://venturebeat.com/2019/03/13/ebay-details-how-ai-improves-user-experience-across-1-2-billion-listings/

11. http://redditmetrics.com/history

12. p. *Future Shock*, 345.

13. Martin Heidegger, *What Is a Thing?*, Translated by W. B. Barton, Jr. and Vera Deutsch
    (Chicago: Henry Regnery Company, 1967, p. 150).

14. p. *Future Shock*, 394-395.

Could **Virtual Reality** Eradicate Regret? **Living** and **Dying** in an Age of Experiential **Abundance**

Dr. Alexandra Ivanovitch

Welcome to Experiential Abundance ▪ In *Future Shock*, Alvin Toffler highlighted the potential growth of an entire sector he dubbed "experience industries" and foresaw the increasing realism of simulated environments. By design, as a simulation-based medium, virtual reality is the "experience industry" *par excellence* and is establishing itself as the technological conduit by which humanity can design, interact, and inhabit at scale the simulated environments Toffler evoked: "Thus computer experts, roboteers, designers, historians, and museum specialists will join to create experiential enclaves that reproduce, as skillfully as sophisticated technology will permit, the splendor of ancient Rome, the pomp of Queen Elizabeth's court, (…) and the like." Fifty years after *Future Shock*, and five years after Mark Zuckerberg bought Oculus for 2 billion dollars, virtual reality, as it slowly becomes mainstream, is on the cusp of introducing us to a world we have never seen before: one of experiential abundance.

Virtual reality has the unparalleled capacity to simulate worlds, actions, and beings; it is uniquely positioned to digitize experience whether actual or artificial, whether past, present, or future. And, once experience is digitized, it becomes instantaneously and seamlessly re-playable, shareable, and ultimately democratized.

VR, the Ultimate Brain Hack

But can *experience* be truly digitized, as other artifacts, commodities, processes, or services have been in the past? How real does the VR-powered simulated experience feel to our brain?

Numerous peer-reviewed studies have shown that subjects who are exposed to virtual environments respond realistically to whatever scenario occurs in the simulated world: Subjects feel "presence"—the sensation of being in a certain place, in well-executed simulations, eventually leading

> **Once experience is digitized, it becomes instantaneously and seamlessly re-playable, shareable, and ultimately democratized.**

what Pr. Mel Slater calls "place illusion."[1] At the edge of a virtual cliff, individuals will display realistic responses, including heart rate acceleration.

In a groundbreaking study reproducing the Milgram experiment in VR, even though participants very well knew that neither the victim nor the shocks were real, they had the tendency to respond to the situation at subjective, behavioral, and physiological levels as if the pain they inflicted were real[2]. Even more troublingly, in a study conducted by Pr. Bailenson and Dr. Kathryn Segovia, elementary school-age children watched a virtual version of themselves swimming with whales, and many later believed that this had actually occurred in real life—which opens the door for the technology to inject artificially generated memories in subjects' brains[3].

The growing body of peer-reviewed interdisciplinary science which is studying VR's perceptual and behavioral impact is shining a light on the myriad ways in which we can willingly use virtual reality to trick our brains into experiencing multiple lifetimes into one and work toward a regret-free future.

Life, a Digest. To Be Downloaded from the Cloud?

In a world where immersive technology is ubiquitous, experience becomes the dominant new currency. When will we see marketplaces where individuals can freely exchange experiential wealth, from getting married to skydiving, receiving an Oscar, etc.? The era of existential scarcity will have come to an end. We will then be ready to welcome a newly found abundance of experiences where regret as an emotion has become obsolete. Who will be the early adopters of such an experiential revolution? Those for whom such a future shock can never come too soon: citizens who are dying and do not have much time left, and beyond, the senior population—which is to say, the new majority in the Western world.

At Equity Lab, we use virtual reality to fulfill seniors' last wishes before they pass. Going back to one's motherland, seeing the Holy Land, visiting Europe for the first time, going on a safari, swimming with dolphins, climbing Machu Picchu: Immersive technology can allow seniors to check off elements on their bucket lists from the comfort of their living rooms or beds.

Imagine a VR platform that digitizes the most popular bucket list experiences: the fulfilling experiences individuals wish to tick off before they die, made widely available in 3D immersive format. At Equity Lab, we are building the prototype of such a platform, to be made available to seniors in nursing homes, hospices, and senior centers in Miami-Dade County, South Florida.

The moonshot is to digitize through VR and host in the cloud the sum of desirable experiences, so that end-of-life patients can easily access it through head-mounted displays. How will we finish completing such a Herculean task to fulfill such wishes at scale? Thankfully, as we have already started to observe while collecting last wishes with seniors in Miami-Dade County, our dreams are more alike than they are unalike. Regardless of our diverse backgrounds and cultural differences, the number of natural or man-made wonders that this planet hosts and humans universally wish to contemplate within their lifetimes is large but not infinite. In our collective imagination, the pyramids of Egypt, the Great Wall of China, and Niagara Falls already belong to our universal bucket list, and all are but one VR headset away.

Making Last Dreams a Reality through VR

What are the last wishes that have come up most frequently? The number one wish that seniors express is to go back to their motherland. At the point where they feel that they are closing the final chapter of their lives, seniors long to go back to where they were born. We started this project in Miami, Florida, where there is a high concentration of senior Cuban-Americans, and their dearest wish is to go back to Cuba in VR.

In the specific case of senior Cuban-Americans, most of them left the island decades ago never to return, and are now unable to for an array of often compounded political, physical, and/or financial reasons. Virtual reality is now the only option they have to fulfill the last wish of seeing their homeland once more. It is a very emotional experience for them to reconnect to their roots and to their land, beyond years of exile, trauma, and nostalgia (Figure 1).

The second most expressed wish is to visit Jerusalem, to see the Holy Land; a lot of seniors of Christian faith seize the opportunity to do a virtual pilgrimage through immersive technology.

Sometimes seniors who are in wheelchairs or are heavily reliant on canes express very simple wishes such as…to walk.

Figure 1 • Senior Cuban-Americans going back to Cuba in VR in Little Havana's Domino Park through "A History of Cuban Dance" (created by Lucy Walker).

Last Wishes & Early Adopters

In a youth-centric society, senior citizens are too often marginalized and exposed to social isolation. Peer-reviewed scientific research compiled by the AARP has proven that "loneliness is lethal." More older Americans are suffering from chronic loneliness, and the long-term health risks can be deadly. There is a 26 percent increased risk of early death due to subjective feelings of loneliness (AARP). A 2018 study, from the May 23 issue of the *Journal of the American Heart Association*, of patients with heart failure in Minnesota found that in the group of 1,681 men and women, with an average age of 73, the 6 percent who reported a high level of perceived social isolation had a greater risk of hospitalization, ER visits, and early death than those who did not.

When seniors no longer have the means to go out and explore the world, we can bring the world to them. This VR program puts front and center their wishes, dreams, and aspirations, while striving to minimize—if not eradicate—the regret they may feel to have not had access to these experiences in real life. We use virtual reality to protect their curiosity in the face of anxiety, to defend their joy in the face of depression—to protect life in the face of death.

As seniors approach the end of their lives, virtual reality empowers them to benefit from the type of experiential abundance that Toffler hinted at in *Future Shock*. "Older people are even more likely to react strongly against any further acceleration of change," Toffler argued. But we have observed in the last few months that in the specific case of using VR to fulfill their wishes, senior citizens are actually eager to experience this era of simulated environments. In this respect, seniors are in a position to show other segments of the population how to enjoy the multiple benefits of this revolutionary computing platform.

This nonprofit initiative, started in November 2018 in Miami, Florida, is called VR GENIE, as we are using immersive technology to grant wishes, just like the genie in *Aladdin*. The program is funded by the Miami-Dade County Mayor's Age Friendly Initiative. VR GENIE has already received global media coverage in 32 countries around the world: the US, France, India, Pakistan, Bangladesh, China, Brazil, Peru, Colombia, South Africa, Kenya, and others.

Could fulfilling last wishes in VR soon be offered as a free existential service in Miami-Dade County's hospitals, hospices, and senior centers? That is what we are actively working toward.

Equity Lab: Accelerating the Advent of the 23rd Century

Equity Lab is a virtual reality-driven 501(c)3 nonprofit organization that is dedicated to leveraging immersive technology to ameliorate the quality of life of vulnerable populations such as at-risk youth and seniors.

Our first funder and supporter is the Roddenberry Foundation. Gene Roddenberry created the world of *Star Trek* to help us envision a hopeful future made of peaceful collaboration and exploration. Gene Roddenberry's family started this foundation to further their father's worldview and fund pioneering projects that use today's technology to help materialize *Star Trek*'s ideals: empathy, community, inclusion, and peace. Equity Lab is relentlessly working to make *Star Trek*'s vision of a preferred future a reality—before the 23rd century. ▦

A warm thank you to David Kebo, storyteller-in-chief and Shadrick Addy, Equity Lab's Chief Technology Officer.

Alexandra Ivanovitch, PhD is a creative technologist dedicated to leveraging 21st century technology to ameliorate the quality of life of vulnerable populations such as senior citizens and at-risk youth. Her 501(c)3 non-profit organization, EQUITY LAB, is pioneering a virtual reality program to allow seniors to fulfill their last wishes through immersive technology in assisted living facilities, nursing homes, and hospices in South Florida. She is a former research fellow in Digital Humanities at the Université Paris-Sorbonne, where she taught at all undergraduate levels, and is currently adjunct faculty at Singularity University. She is passionate about harnessing groundbreaking social neuroscience studies and technology from the lab to the real world.

1.   Slater, M. (2009). Place illusion and plausibility can lead to realistic behaviour in immersive virtual environments. *Philosophical Transactions of the Royal Society B: Biological Sciences*, 364(1535), 3549-3557.

2.   Slater, M., Antley, A., Davison, A., Swapp, D., Guger, C., Barker, C., ... & Sanchez-Vives, M. V. (2006). A virtual reprise of the Stanley Milgram obedience experiments. *PloS one*, 1(1), e39.

3.   Segovia, K. Y., & Bailenson, J. N. (2009). Virtually true: Children's acquisition of false memories in virtual reality. *Media Psychology*, 12(4), 371-393.

Paralysis Is Not an Option: How Philanthropy Must Weather "Future Shock" To Shape a Better Future

Cat Tully

The UK's Ministry of Defence—not an institution given to exaggeration—recently diagnosed *"unprecedented acceleration in the speed of change, driving ever more complex interactions between [diverse] trends."* Indeed, from demographic shifts to digital tech, the pace of global change is relentless. The vast range of problems afflicting our planet and our species are also more visible to today's connected global citizens than to any generation that went before.

This frenetic pace of change leaves many feeling disempowered and disoriented, responding with anxiety to the sense that the future has—in Toffler's phrase—"arrived too soon." But for the global philanthropists who, by definition, seek to change the world—or at least a part of it—paralysis is not an option. In the new "global age of philanthropy," they are no longer bit players on the world stage. And looking ahead, the ask from their profession is tougher than ever before: to shape the world for the better while navigating radical uncertainty in terms of future outcomes and operating environments. While challenges, from the forecast demographic explosion in sub-Saharan

Africa to the fourth industrial revolution, mount up on the horizon, with the potential to reverse hard-won progress or radically change the geography and distribution of need, there is no letup in immediate demand.

Philanthropists are typically robust, resilient, and optimistic. They make a professional virtue of muddling through tough circumstances. Ambition is embedded deep in the sector's DNA: the Chan-Zuckerberg Initiative (CZI) aims to "cure, prevent, or manage all diseases" by the end of the 21st century; the major philanthropic foundations now collectively outspend leading OECD donors on health; and the UN Sustainable Development Goals aim at no less than the complete elimination of poverty and hunger by 2030.

> Philanthropy now has not just an opportunity, but a responsibility, to think and act for the long term. The will to do good in the world is no longer good enough. By mainstreaming foresight practice, the sector can make the future a friend, not a foe, in these unquiet, exciting times.

But this generation of philanthropists' optimism about the future, and its ability to shape it, will not be borne out in practice without beginning to systematically and comprehensively explore possible futures and design today's interventions in line with what they see. With fragile development gains at risk, philanthropy needs to step back from the demands of the present to become far more "future minded." Anticipating key trends and designing sustainable approaches and interventions is vital to producing lasting change and leaving meaningful legacies. Far-sighted philanthropists are now investing in foresight, such as the new Exploration & Future Sensing unit at the Omidyar Network, set up by eBay founder Pierre Omidyar.

Collectively, philanthropies now play a bigger role in shaping global outcomes than at any other time in history, and the philanthropic trend is still booming, big time. Of the global foundations recently surveyed by Harvard, three-quarters were founded in the last 25 years; the world's biggest private philanthropic foundation, the Bill & Melinda Gates Foundation, is only two decades old. New trends and new players are constantly arriving on the scene, evidenced by new waves of philanthropy from India and China and the rise of the "millennial philanthropic generation."

Meanwhile, traditional donor governments and businesses are increasingly insular and focused on short-termist firefighting and short electoral or reporting cycles. Too often, they fail to think strategically and suffer from an excess of caution about less-tested "frontier" areas.

It falls to philanthropy, therefore, to think and act for the long term of our planet, and in the interests of future generations. Recent years have seen an understandable emphasis on data, evaluation, and measurable impact from leading players such as Gates and Rockefeller. But without looking beyond historic data, or further than the near horizon to what are inevitably more speculative scenarios with a 15-, 20-, and 50-year time frame, today's philanthropists cannot be confident their spending programs or their policies will leave an enduring legacy in the communities they seek to help. If strategic foresight is going to move the needle on philanthropic impact, it needs to be part of the decision-making process when "big bets" are being made on future investments—whether by individual foundations or collaborative initiatives such as Co-Impact.

Philanthropists must now capitalize on their strong position as changemakers and make the transition to lasting impact, using foresight to harness the potential upsides of future changes and mitigate their looming risks. This means, in particular, that they should:

■ **Explore and fund work on "orphan" issues and trends**, often identified in foresight exercises but which governments and business then fail to pick up and address.

■ **Identify innovative areas where they can seize the "upside" of trends**. Without the same obligations to taxpayers or shareholders as governments or businesses, foundations have greater freedom of maneuver to shift focus fast and invest in experimental areas—for example, the potential of synthetic biology to revolutionize food security.

If philanthropy fails to help all of us think long term, unpredictable major trends, such as the rise of AI, could leave major justice and equity issues in their wake, with unequal outcomes not just geographically but also generationally. The Gulbenkian Foundation's Intergenerational Fairness Project is ahead of the curve in this area, seeking to integrate the interests of future generations into current decision-making processes.

Finally, philanthropic organizations must develop their futures mind-set in thinking about the future of the sector itself. The sector cannot wait any longer to tackle the potentially existential challenges it faces around legitimacy and the accountability gap. With over 86,000 philanthropic organizations operating in the US alone, criticism at the lack of accountability has sharpened, as evidenced by the recent publication of Rob Reich's *Just Giving*. Critics point out that far more scrutiny of organizations is needed. Philanthropic organizations often benefit from tax breaks, and are responsible for delivering vast programs and disbursing huge sums of money with minimal oversight or route for redress if things go wrong.

The sector now needs to fund and convene open and inclusive conversations about the future of philanthropic work to strengthen its legitimacy and help guarantee its survival through this bumpy period. IARAN's thinking on the future of aid, and Future Agenda's Future of Philanthropy project, are examples of practices that we hope to see spread. Wide participation in conversations about sectoral futures is vital to ensure legitimacy and to bring in diverse perspectives.

Philanthropy now has not just an opportunity, but a responsibility, to think and act for the long term. The will to do good in the world is no longer good enough. By mainstreaming foresight practice, the sector can make the future a friend, not a foe, in these unquiet, exciting times. ■

Cat Tully is the founder of the School of International Futures, running Strategic Foresight projects and retreats across the world, with 600 alumni in 50 countries. She advises on and teaches emergent strategy and strategic foresight internationally, including at the UN. Previously, she was Strategy Project Director at the UK FCO and a policy adviser in the Prime Minister's Strategy Unit.

Still Shocking After All These Years

Bryan Alexander

I first came across *Future Shock* when I was about nine years old. We were visiting extended family and I, bored as a child often is by adult doings, skulked off to find books. In a lonely room, I discovered giant bookcases to explore. Toffler's book stood out from the ranks of many other titles. Future... Shock? I was already a science fiction reader and viewer and, therefore, obsessed with the future's possibilities. What could be shocking about the future?

I paged through the book, poking at different chapters, working the table of contents and index. Some details emerged that matched my nascent science fiction imaginings: orbital factories, advanced computers, innovative medicine. Other aspects surprised and intrigued me, as best I could understand them at that age: new forms of work, changes to school, the family transformed. Freud, drugs, bureaucracy? Those were alien, of course. Above all, I gleefully enjoyed the idea of older people unable to process a new world, a world I was preparing myself for through science fiction and, of course, by being very young.

My family left the next day, and although I didn't manage to take the book with me, its ideas started percolating in my brain. The future was on its way, and I could both understand and inhabit it. In contrast, those adults who lorded over me were revealed to lack the mental capacity to grasp the new world. I didn't become a futurist at this point, except to the degree that my mind was now always looking ahead. Over the next decade I progressed through school and kept after elements of Toffler's future: wrestling with science, tinkering with electronics, teaching myself computers. As the 1970s gave way to the 1980s, my sense of intergenerational division deepened—accelerated by punk rock, of course.

Toffler found me a second time in 1986, when I was in college and came across a copy of *The Third Wave*. At the time I was studying politics, history, and the Soviet Union, and was therefore almost ideally prepared to appreciate this new tome. Again I returned to the world of *Future Shock* as the Tofflers took me into an emerging future. Now I understood much more, and was also able to connect *The Third Wave* to what I was studying in the world. Post-industrialism was obviously underway. Organizations were mutating from their mid-century hierarchies. New networks were starting to appear, and the digital world was taking off. My mind buzzed with Toffleriana, and I told everyone I met about the impending civilizational transformation. I wrote about *The Third Wave* in university assignments. Again, my mind had received an adrenaline shot.

Fifteen years later I was working for a higher education non-profit, helping colleges and universities grapple with emerging technologies. I was powered by Toffler, pushing campuses to consider the tech just starting to peer over the horizon: mobile devices, augmented reality, games for learning. But I hit a wall. Many academics heard "new technologies" and mentally checked out. Either they simply dreaded technology or were content to let their computer science and IT colleagues take care of it. How could I persuade them to get over their future shock?

> I was powered by Toffler, pushing campuses to consider the tech just starting to peer over the horizon: mobile devices, augmented reality, games for learning. But I hit a wall.

The answer was to openly return to Toffler and become a futurist. After sufficient research and training I was able to speak effectively to universities about the future of education, not just of education and technology. And now, *everyone* on campus wanted to participate, including those who called themselves Luddites. They wanted to learn about and think through the full range of the future, as Toffler had outlined, from economics to demographics, culture and politics, the family and, yes, even technology.

This *Future Shock*-inspired methodological transformation accelerated my career. I started publishing and giving talks on the future of education, then consulted with schools, governments, businesses, and nonprofits. I joined the Association of Professional Futurists because, finally, I had become exactly that... via a transformation kicked off by a lucky encounter in a book-lined room two generations before.

Bryan Alexander is an internationally known futurist, researcher, writer, speaker, consultant, and teacher. He consults on the future of education and technology around the world. Bryan speaks widely and publishes frequently, with articles and interviews in *The Atlantic Monthly*, *Inside Higher Ed*, *Washington Post*, *MSNBC*, *US News and World Report*, *National Public Radio*, and the *Chronicle of Higher Education*, among others. Bryan is currently a senior scholar at Georgetown University and teaches graduate seminars in the Learning, Design, and Technology program. His most recent book is *Academia Next: The Futures of Higher Education* (Johns Hopkins University Press).

Anticipatory Democracy— Toffler's Prescription for Future Shock and Where It Should Be Focused

Clem Bezold

Future Shock and Al Toffler's subsequent work in promoting foresight and anticipatory democracy were major factors shaping my becoming a futurist. And after several years of activity to promote anticipatory democracy, including the first legislative seminar on foresight for the US Congress in 1975, Toffler convinced Antioch University to put up the seed money for us to start the Institute for Alternative Futures.

When *Future Shock* was published in 1970, anticipatory democracy was Toffler's prescription at the end of the book. He called for "social future assemblies" saying:

> Let us convene in each nation, in each city, in each neighborhood, democratic constituent assemblies charged with social stock-taking, charged with defining and assigning priorities to specific social goals for the remainder of the century.
>
> Such "social future assemblies" might represent not merely geographical localities, but social units— industry, labor, the churches, the intellectual community, the arts, women, ethnic and religious groups, students, with organized representation for the unorganized as well. Imagine the effect if at one level

or another a place were provided where all those who will live in the future might voice their wishes about it. Imagine, in short, a massive, global exercise in anticipatory democracy. (Toffler, 1970, 478-479)

In the ensuing 50 years we have, in fits and starts, moved toward anticipatory democracy—through governments, communities, and technologies. Globally, in fact, the Sustainable Development Goals (SDGs) represent a major global goal-setting, albeit not developed by a global plebiscite. And there have been thousands of local, provincial/state, and national goal-setting exercises. The "social technology" of choice continues evolving, along with the opportunities and challenges which inform decision-making and goal-setting.

History

I met Toffler in 1973 while I was doing research on my dissertation on Congress and foresight. At the time, the energy crisis was raging, and I was a graduate student working at the Center for Governmental Responsibility at the University of Florida Law School. I worked with him on the Committee for Anticipatory Democracy—an informal group that Toffler convened several times in the 1970s. One of these convenings, held at the invitation of Senator John Culver, was the first legislative seminar on foresight for the US Congress in 1975. Subsequently, Toffler recruited several members of the Committee for Anticipatory Democracy and other leaders working on futures projects to write articles describing their efforts. Toffler asked me to edit the resulting book: *Anticipatory Democracy: People in the Politics of the Future* (Bezold 1978).

For the book's introduction Toffler wrote, "The simplest definition of anticipatory democracy . . . is that it is a process for combining citizen participation with future consciousness" (Toffler 1978, xii). Toffler argued that representative government was a key political institution of the industrial era and that new forms must be expected in the face of crushing decision overload or the political future shock we faced. That remains an issue today, amplified by social media and the ever-present news cycle. Toffler also noted that anticipatory democracy is broader than participation in politics and policy-making. It also includes worker participation, citizen movements, technology assessment, and consumer activism.

Jim Dator, University of Hawaii professor, founder of that university's graduate futures program, and co-founder of IAF, wrote a chapter of the book on the future of anticipatory democracy. He said that the aim of anticipatory democracy is to democratize futures research and researchers, and to futurize democratic processes. Also, that anticipatory democracy should find a way to help people dream undreamed dreams and realize them, instead of rehashing the same old nightmares and ghosts. "I believe we can, and we must [do this], and the future of anticipatory democracy that I prefer—if not the one I see—lies in this direction" (Dator 1978, 328).

> In communities with powerful shared visions, their "most likely" future, shaped by their commitment to their vision, is qualitatively different and better than those communities lacking a powerful shared vision.

In the 1978 book *Anticipatory Democracy*, we documented leading community and state goal-setting efforts (Bezold 1978). These community goals and futures efforts have continued under various names, and their frequency has ebbed and flowed around the world. The United States, Canada, and countries in Latin America, Europe, Africa, and Asia, have had significant examples of thoughtful community futuring activities and goal-setting. Some of these have focused on the future of an overall community; others focused on specific topics, such as health and wellness, or the environment. In the last two decades, equity and sustainability have been growing themes in the analysis and goal-setting of these efforts, reflecting the "equity rising" trend in which equity as an integrated value is entering public and private spheres.

Inspired by *Anticipatory Democracy*, my colleagues at IAF and I have, in the decades since its release, facilitated many futures efforts in cities and states, for all branches of government, nonprofit organizations, and corporations. (Toffler, Jim Dator, and I were the lead founders of the Institute for Alternative Futures, originally as part of Antioch University, in 1977.) Over the years, we used those experiences in promoting anticipatory democracy to develop IAF's Aspirational Futures approach.

Decades of continuing this work lead me to some reflections on what's needed in relation to 21st century future shock, and Toffler's prescription for anticipatory democracy.

Reflections on Anticipatory Democracy Today

First, shared vision is essential. Having a community develop its authentic, shared vision remains one of the most powerful and essential components of decision-making and, particularly at the national level, one of the most lacking. A vision is the shared statement of the preferred future a group is committed to creating. Shared visions tend to enable and ennoble. Visions move people and communities to transcend differences and inequities. The power of shared vision is visible in business, as described in the best-selling book *Built to Last*. And the same is true for communities.

> Abundance advances are technological advances with the potential to make communities more sustainable and more equitable.

In working with communities and organizations, IAF has them develop alternative futures—an expectable future that they think is most likely, a challenging future that explores some of the many things that could "go wrong," and one or two visionary or surprisingly successful futures. In communities with powerful shared visions, their "most likely" future, shaped by their commitment to their vision, is qualitatively different and better than those communities lacking a powerful shared vision.

In a recent IAF project, Human Progress and Human Services 2035, we worked with national leaders in human services and with 11 state or local communities to develop scenarios focused on 2035. San Antonio and San Diego County each had powerful shared visions that made their "most likely" future better than the most likely future in the other cases.

As communities move from vision through goals and on to specific policies and priorities, impact assessments, technology assessments, and "budget games" need to be widely used and understood to stimulate choice. These include health impact statements, equity impact statements, and budgeting games like Budget Hero and Federal Budget Challenge.

Transformations Influencing Anticipatory Democracy

Anticipatory democracy efforts need to operate in the context of the economic transformations that we are beginning to see now, and which will accelerate. These transformations will include the following: major shifts in jobs and work, zero marginal cost economics, "abundance advances," and "equity rising."

Work is transforming. A range from 14.5 to 47 percent of US jobs are forecast to be automated by 2030. Much of the remaining paid work will shift from jobs to consulting and piecework on the gig economy. Just as e-commerce is affecting shopping malls and brick and mortar stores, Amazon Prime-type shopping and delivery will affect many more local businesses. A guaranteed basic income or related income support policies will be needed. Societal and cultural shifts will also be needed, particularly recognizing the true contribution and value of unpaid work, such as raising children, taking care of elders, and other community volunteering.

Another transformation is zero marginal cost economies. As described by Jeremy Rifkin and others, the emerging zero marginal cost economy involves AI, robotics, 3D printing, and related changes which will lower the cost of producing goods and services. IT will become less profitable in many sectors. That will lead to major implications for the rate of return on investments, in turn affecting assumptions about the growth of pension funds, individual retirement accounts, and other investments.

> **Anticipatory democracy can and should help us, individually and collectively, understand what might happen, explore and invent positive options, clarify our values, and develop shared visions and goals.**

However, those problems of low-cost production could lead to "abundance advances" that lower the cost of living. Abundance advances are technological advances with the potential to make communities more sustainable and more equitable. These include low-cost solar and other alternative energy production and in-home and in-community storage; in-home and in-community food production (from community gardening and urban agriculture to in-home growing, using high-tech aeroponics, and cultured meat), and local manufacturing or 3D printing of consumer products, electronics, home components, and even entire homes. Managing the development and application of these abundance advances to support equity and sustainability is among the tasks that anticipatory democracy should contribute to.

"Equity rising" is a major force in the US and globally, whereby people, governments, and organizations support equity and inclusion. It is reflected in community visions around the country; in goals set by the United States, the World Health Organization, and in the UN Sustainable Development Goals; in city and agency establishment of equity offices and guidance policies; and in community dialogues. This equity focus will increasingly shape visions, goals, and policy choices for voters and their communities.

Conclusion

Going forward as a nation, we will need to have widespread participation in developing shared vision and effective designs to deal with the key challenges we face. This participation is important for giving each of us, as citizens and voters, thoughtful, meaningful choices to reflect on, including how the pending transformations—social, economic, and technological—will be rolled out.

In conclusion, anticipatory democracy can and should help us, individually and collectively, understand what might happen, explore and invent positive options, clarify our values, and develop shared visions and goals. For me, this is where anticipatory democracy is, and should be, headed. ▪

Clement Bezold co-founded the Institute for Alternative Futures in 1977 with Alvin Toffler and Jim Dator. In 1982 he started IAF's for-profit subsidiary, Alternative Futures Associates, to assist corporations in their strategic planning using futures methods. He has been a major developer of foresight techniques, applying futures research and strategic planning methods in both the public and private sectors. As a consultant, Dr. Bezold has worked with many Fortune 500 companies, along with major organizations such as the World Health Organization, the National Institutes of Health, the Rockefeller Foundation, AARP, and the American Cancer Society. Dr. Bezold has published numerous books and reports on the future of government, the courts, and healthcare. He is on the editorial or advisory boards of *The Journal of Futures Studies*, *Technology Forecasting and Social Change*, *Foresight*, and *World Futures Review*. Dr. Bezold received his PhD in political science from the University of Florida. He has been assistant director of the Center for Governmental Responsibility at the University of Florida Law School and a Visiting Scholar at the Brookings Institution.

References

Bezold, Clement, ed. 1978. *Anticipatory Democracy*. New York: Random House.

Dator, James. 1978. "The Future of Anticipatory Democracy." In *Anticipatory Democracy*,
   Edited by Clement Bezold, 315-328. New York: Random House.

Toffler, Alvin. 1970. *Future Shock*. New York: Random House.

Toffler, Alvin. 1978. "Introduction on Future-Conscious Politics." In *Anticipatory Democracy*,
   Edited by Clement Bezold, xi-xxii. New York: Random House.

The "Code"

Martin Guigui

> 66 The sea of coded information that surrounds him begins to beat at his senses with new urgency. 99
>
> —*Alvin Toffler*

Imagination, discovery, and creativity are boundless. What we imagine, discover, and create is why we exist. History has taught us that creativity is the fiber of our spiritual evolution, now becoming a spiritual revolution, to spiritual freedom.

When creative beings travel at a similar tempo a frequency convergence occurs. Simply referred to as "good timing," or "good chemistry," which is actually all "Tempo"—the contagious connective tissue to the organic foundation of Global Harmony. In its creation, every song, every piece of music or art form has a perfect tempo that births it to stand the test of time. Every living being has a built-in tempo, that when internally discovered connects organically to individual truth—a fingerprint—allowing space and time to fuse, creating timelessness. I was once told that I don't know what the true value of zero is, which is supposedly the reason I'm always late. True to my tempo, I'd like to think I'm right on time late (also known as "Guigui Time"). And in a moment, it will be later than it has ever been—the future.

Three rules for the future:

NUMBER ONE, there are no rules.

NUMBER TWO, make your own rules.

NUMBER THREE, be prepared to break them because there are no rules...

What will be? *How* will *we* be?

As we extend the visions of Verne, Asimov, Bradbury, Atwood, Wells, Kaku, Clarke, Roddenberry, Huxley, Watkins, Haraway, Kurzweil, Tesla, Toffler, and the brilliant visionary minds and spirits of today and tomorrow, as we tap our imagination and activation energy, as we enable innovation, as we cleverly, intuitively, pompously, and nervily predict the future—let us first nurture the present, which is and becomes our future. Critical focus now must be on completing the metabolic journey as a species into a collective state of full global harmony. We will then be prepared for the future that approaches at light speed.

We are embarking on a challenging journey embedded in the genesis and evolution of our DNA as a species, and in parallel with the birth and evolution of the Universe, which contains the CODE for the future. Let's take that ride, on the wildside, into the future—and crack the CODE.

With each cognizant moment the present is instantaneously the past. There is no "present moment." We exist in constant change—the "Now." The future is the "ever changing now." With acceptance of this fundamental, foundational and universal complete state of being, we assimilate in harmony into the future.

ACCEPTANCE: Change is our constant.

ASSIMILATION: Traveling in the now without judgment.

HARMONY: To be one with the "Rhythm of the Planet."

We are all connected from inception to the "Rhythm of the Planet," its pulsating algorithmic tempo within our solar system, and conversely our system's interaction with other systems. Every event, every action, enacted by beings within our environment affect cumulatively all actions and reactions of nature within our atmospheric confines, and vice versa. Similar interactions between heavenly bodies outside of our atmosphere affect each other—conversely affecting our emotional state, ability to cohabitate, telepathic communication, and biological stamina to withstand and survive the ever-changing planetary conditions. The "Rhythm of the Planet" vibrationally is energy accessible to an organic journey of discovery and harmony.

To evolve "Physically," *capable of outlasting anatomical erosion.*

To evolve "Emotionally," *immune to toxic energy.*

To evolve "Spiritually," *capable of sensing computer failure prior to stepping on that plane.*

To evolve "Intellectually," *capable of effortlessly sending a signal to our vital organs to fend off and dissolve disease and disorder.*

> Critical focus now must be on completing the metabolic journey as a species into a collective state of full global harmony. We will then be prepared for the future that approaches at light speed.

A minimalistic primal measured example: You wake up one morning and reflect inwardly—"It feels like 7:30 a.m."

You turn to the clock, and there it is—7:30 a.m. This illustrative radiant prototypical moment captures the habitual organic connection to the frequencies of our planet's core, axis, geometric spin, rotation, and solar revolution via instinct, heat sensitivity, and vibrational tempo within our solar system and beyond. This becomes the foundation of complete being. To be one with "The Rhythm of the Planet" connects us to our origin, the portal to unborn time, energy accessible to the ever changing now. It is the why of why we are still here. This "Awareness" invites "Discovery"—the subconscious constant that stimulates positive growth toward the complete state of being. What we discover creatively is why we are here. Liberated from excess data or overthought processes, intuition on automatic facilitates inspiration, stimulates imagination, inspires creation, engineering, execution, and application, and satiates the needs of the future, which are in the now.

> The human form is a perfectly imperfect sophisticated complex creation that cannot be artificially authentically replicated. Independently powered, self-cleansing, reproducing, able to self-heal, option to self-destruct.

INTUITION: The primal survival solution valve, connective tissue to the first moment in time.

INSPIRATION: Ingenious energy.

IMAGINATION: The infinite source of creation, data, and power.

Intuition feeds Inspiration, feeds Imagination, paves the road as we travel the future now.

The code at this stage is auditory. We don't need to see, we need to *listen*.

Sound waves are the physical vessels for emotion and spirit. Tone is the heartbeat.

Just as music is the universal language—the vibration of creation—frequency is the glue that keeps the cosmos together. Pressure and time are *"The universe is the transformation of vibrations into matter."* the fundamental elements that form the basis of all frequencies, and how they affect matter. I like to call it "Emotional Frequency Response" (EFR). Frequencies are evident in magnetic fields, laser light, and chemical reactions inside nebulas that manufacture amino acids, which yield the building blocks of life. One of these days we need to return the favor and send some amino acids back to Jupiter—I like to think of it as "cosmic karma."

The origin of the universe is pulsating frequencies, the physical birthing Matter.

Which is also its ultimate destiny.

States	PHYSICAL STATE	P
of	EMOTIONAL STATE	E
being	SPIRITUAL STATE	S
(PESI)	INTELLECTUAL STATE	I

Physical + Emotional + Spiritual + Intellectual = Matter

PESI = MATTER

In the beginning...

Matter in its most primitive physical state is void of intellectual and spiritual capacity. It is pure Emotion. Matter State 1:

Matter = Emotion

Matter transforms via vibrational frequency fusion. Matter State 2:

Matter = Emotion + Spirit

Emotion affects the spiritual state of being and can now compute reason (Intellect). Matter State 3:

Matter = Emotion + Spirit + Intellect

Where there is matter, there is emotion; where there is emotion there is matter evolving. Matter can only reason when its physical, emotional, and spiritual states are in harmony, its complete state of being.

Was that the CODE? Not yet.

We fascinate over the age-old question, Is the universe expanding, contracting, or static? Assuming the universe is expanding, what volume/space is it expanding into, if there is no outside to the universe? Via pure numbers quotients, considering margin of error and variants, on 12.28.09, I stumbled upon a concept and developed a theory addressing the radius of the observable Universe. Post my studies from 1.15.15 to 5.18.17, I found further evidence in which continued attempts to calculate the finite point of the universe yield consistently fluctuating numbers, furthering my "Expansion and Contraction" theory. The universe is matter in various states of being (PESI) with evolving mass expanding ("Expansion Period"). It will eventually, if it has not already, reach its saturation point, at which time it will begin to mature inwardly ("Contraction Period"), eventually collapsing onto itself, only to regenerate and open up again—a breathing-like action, a form of rebirth. A process of billions if not trillions of years. The "expansion and contraction" theory I present is evident at the fundamental level that our Universe and the fabric of space and time exist within a constant balanced magnetic activity that fluctuates. Matter forms and comes together—matter reaches its limit and breaks apart. The universe is breathing, like a lung, ever so slightly growing, and contracting. We exist in an "Infinitude Continuum." Energy that feeds itself. Perpetually. Enter Artificial Intelligence.

> Evolution suggests we will eventually become immune, as our constantly evolving system adapts anatomy to environment and develops self-healing properties and extended life spans. A calming harmonic, yet a potentially spiritually eroding power.

Matter + AI = More Data

More Data = Less Imagination

The human form is a perfectly imperfect sophisticated complex creation that cannot be artificially authentically replicated. Independently powered, self-cleansing, reproducing, able to self-heal, option to self-destruct. Due to environmental factors, natural life expectancy is within a span of approximately 100 years. In addition, multiple disease components, built in to deactivate the anatomical system, affect life expectancy. We often wonder why the miraculous human system is accompanied by mutated cells. Our imperfections, rationalized theologically, are to maintain order—if we could live longer, we would outdo our Maker. Evolution suggests we will eventually become immune, as our constantly evolving system adapts anatomy to environment and develops self-healing properties and extended life spans. A calming harmonic, yet a potentially spiritually eroding power.

> The human form will always possess what AI would envy if it were capable of envy—"Character," springing from billions of years of marinated DNA—"Soul." Which yields street smarts, the average Joe, the idiot savant, the academic scholar, the Pulitzer Prize, the Nobel.

AI is a computer program able to think, learn, and make decisions via human-like variables, cognition and logic, to form judgment. AI in its purest definition is organically incapable of replicating the human form. Taking into consideration the organic nature of the CODE, how does AI fit into 13+ billion years of evolution? We can sample a piano frequency and program it into a keyboard to give a listener the illusion of hearing a piano, but it will not contain the same EFR (Emotional Frequency Response) as a hammer hitting a string within the harp of a piano. The challenge remains for "Anatomic" and "Artificial" to organically come together as one.

AI is an attempt to accelerate our evolution. The human form has the ability to adapt to AI, and in time, will allow AI to co-exist within its anatomical system, eventually re-cycling, re-engaging, and re-opening an organic-like imagination. Will we then be a "higher" creative being? We certainly will be "different"—change is our constant. Acceptance will play a more significant role as the process of marrying AI with human form will cause a sacrifice in which imagination, originality, and prolific output will pause, in order to assimilate and accommodate an added artificial component to evolution. With perhaps a slight layer of prejudice added to allow our pure nature to filter through. >>

There will be a higher discipline demand for creators, to protect creative platforms and carry the responsibility of pushing innovative limits via imagination.

This demand will be met in the form of "Solitary Thinkers."

There will be a "Liberator Program" for humanoids who wish and

"Let me see your system number?"

"Please don't terminate me. I swear, officer, I'm not a robot."

"I'd like to sit in the non-smoking AI section please."

"I'm sorry, we only serve robots."

"And the Oscar for best performance by a humanoid in a supporting role goes to…."

choose to convert back to pure human form—this process will be known as the "Liberator Tank."

"Liberators" (coaches) will guide great minds and pure souls to become Solitary Thinkers (imagination-based science), void of implanted chip intellectuality and opting out of data processing analysis.

That's right, therapy and treatment to get rid of your AI headache.

THE CHALLENGE: AI goes against all anatomic principles. Its natural habitat is a click on a grid. The emotional skip of a heartbeat can be sampled, but not organically and authentically programmed. Neither can "Blood, Sweat, and Tears."

PRINCIPLE FLAW: Everything AI is too perfect. Oxygen, carbon, hydrogen, nitrogen, make up 99% of our anatomy ($7*1027$ atoms in the average human body). It's a simple enough equation to engineer. However, the spirit and emotion is un-replicable. The human form will always possess what AI would envy if it were capable of envy—"Character," springing from billions of years of marinated DNA—"Soul." Which yields street smarts, the average Joe, the idiot savant, the academic scholar, the Pulitzer Prize, the Nobel.

The code is clear. The key to "harmony" in the mismatched marriage is to balance AI with the true pyramidal bulk of human nature—thus conjoining the finest brain with human instinct and heart.

AI requires our species to evolve much more quickly in all states of being. A subconscious borderline suprematic race for control. The emotional, spiritual, and intellectual evolution of our (inner) being is long overdue, here in the ever changing now, and is crucial to the survival of our magical species. With or without technology, with or without AI, the future of the now is acceptance and assimilation of the dynamics of our existence and universal CODE, to develop and activate hypersensitivity within our fragile organisms, to achieve a complete state of being so that we may evolve in eternal global and universal harmony with any and all advancement: in biotechnology, nanotechnology, environmental climate action, new energy source Helium-3, sustainable cities and communities, predicting and averting natural disasters, rejuvenation, single planetary civilization, non-biological intelligence, and new economic systems.

Target Frequency and vibrational treatment tools will be standard treatment for common ailments and most medical procedures (cardiovascular disease, chronic lung disease, cancer, diabetes, etc.) eliminating the need for anesthesia.

Frequency therapy will be successfully applicable to the rehabilitation of mental wellness (general practice and psychological disorders, convicted individuals, etc.).

Emotional Frequency Response resonates with glands and nodes in our anatomy, as it does in the equalizing vibrational constant balancing the universe. Much like the frequency $11.5740740e-6$ Hz is a perpetual pulse fused to the rotation of the Earth, with this frequency modulating based on heat fluctuation in the planet's core and adjusting to the climate temperature changes (heat affects tone), Emotional Frequency Response will eventually be the standard measure and basis for all medical care.

Various frequencies of music neutralize, balance, and heal many areas of the brain, including the regions involved in emotion, cognition, sensation, and movement. Frequency, vibrational, and music therapy will improve and maintain physical and psychological health. Further development will create standardized vibrational treatments to begin just prior to conception, continuing through pregnancy and during childbirth. There will be specific frequencies designated to defuse any mutated cell within our human genome as we are conceived.

Here comes the CODE...

>>..<<
THE CODE: ALL THAT WE CREATE MUST EXIST ON THE VALUES AND
PRINCIPLES OF RESPECT FOR THE ORGANIC NATURE OF EVOLUTION.
>>..<<

It is not dissimilar to recording in the analog, then processing that signal frequency utilizing the HD domain to better the final product. However, we must take into consideration that analog still has a longer shelf life for preservation of data and content. Know what I mean? No matter what, the CODE just keeps creeping back in.

Art is the great educator. It has no boundaries, it is the global language that requires no translation, it enlightens, elevates, and deepens the human spirit. It is alimentation, nurturing toward a complete state of being.

Does AI "Matter"? Absolutely! As a "Matter" of fact, AI is intriguingly fascinating, sometimes can even be engaging and entertaining, however will always be a double-edged sword. And it kinda takes all the fun out of cerebral calisthenics. For AI to cohabitate with humanity, and fit into the CODE, it has to contain programmed evolutionary data to authenticate the birthing process of AE (Artificial Emotion) and AS (Artificial Spirit).

In time … all is possible.

AI: "I'm sorry, I did not understand '*In time all is possible.*' Would you like me to search the web?" ■

Martin Guigui—an Abundant World Institute media production partner—is an award-winning filmmaker, music director, composer and Grammy nominated music producer/engineer. As president of Sunset Pictures and in other capacities, Guigui has directed feature films, music videos, has composed music for films and TV, worked on over 100 productions, produced over 50 music albums, toured extensively, and music directs high profile broadcast concert events. Guigui has worked with some of Hollywood's biggest stars. Born in Buenos Aires, Argentina, son of famed symphony orchestra conductor Maestro Efrain Guigui, Martin had an eclectic upbringing in New York, Puerto Rico, and Vermont. A music prodigy playing violin at age four, his concert debut was with the Puerto Rico Symphony at age 12, performing Vivaldi's Violin Concerto in D Major.

Guigui has shared the stage, recorded, and performed with music greats and icons including Billy Gibbons (ZZ Top), Daryl Hall, Nancy Wilson (Heart), Stephen Stills, Sammy Hagar, Joe Bonamassa, Dave Navarro, Slash, Lyle Lovett, Lemmy Kilmister, James Cotton, Jimmie Vaughan, Sheila E, Robby Krieger, Orianthi, Steve Earle, Susan Tedeschi & Derek Trucks, Warren Haynes, Jose Feliciano, Smokey Robinson, David Byrne, Lucinda Williams, Phish, Robert Randolph, Grace Potter, Robert Earl Keen, Don Felder (Eagles), Richie Sambora, Joan Osborne, Trace Adkins, Lee Greenwood, Bo Diddley, Bret Michaels, and many others. Guigui has received numerous songwriting Billboard Awards, ASCAP Performance Awards, the United Nations World Award, Caesar Award, Golden Spirit Award, Estabrook Award, numerous "Best Director" awards, and was twice honored by City of Los Angeles for artistic contributions to music education. Guigui helped organize and was the Music Director for the "One America—5 Presidents" concert event which raised $45 million for hurricane relief, and made history by bringing together the five living Presidents for the first time to host the event. In addition to being a basketball freak, Martin is an amateur astrophysicist and dedicates time to the study and advancement of the principles of physics as it pertains to realms of theoretical and observational physics.

Forging Our Relationship with the Future

Thomas Frey

> 66 Much education springs from some image of the future. If the image of the future held by a society is grossly inaccurate, its education system will betray its youth. 99
>
> —*Alvin Toffler*

Since I was a kid, the Tofflers have been a huge influence on how I think about the future. ■ The intersection of our approaches is a bit unusual, but here's how I explain it.

The three items that the human body comes into contact with most in life are the beds that we sleep in, the chairs that we sit in, and the shoes that we walk in. These are the primary physical friction points that we know all too well.

Yet the overarching, all-consuming interface that few people consider is our human-to-future interface, the one Alvin and Heidi Toffler spent their lifetimes wrestling with. We will all spend the rest of our lives in the future, so we really should learn more about how we're making our transitions from the here and now to what comes next.

Just as a fish has no way of understanding the concept of water, we are immersed in wave upon wave of an ever-changing future, silently slipping through our reality lens like the hands of time.

Tick, tock, tick, tock, tick, tock, the metronome reflects nature's most relentless force of passing time, every moment imperceptibly different from the last. The change is ever so slight, barely detectable, but with each one, we are shifted from now, to now, to now.

The needs of "now" are different from the needs of "then," and even though we take these imperceptible changes for granted, every future has a way of altering the demands that will be placed on us, as we go about our daily living.

We all intuitively know that today will be different from yesterday, and that tomorrow will also hold a few surprises. But few scientists, if any, have actually tried to examine the influence these micro-vectors have on us individually as they wash relentlessly over us.

"Directoids" is a term I've developed to describe these nano-sized particles of influence, sourced both internally and externally, that sway every human action. The slightest bump, noise, smell, or thought can alter the next moment, but we're not even aware of the majority of these micro-shifts.

> We all intuitively know that today will be different from yesterday, and that tomorrow will also hold a few surprises. But few scientists, if any, have actually tried to examine the influence these micro-vectors have on us individually as they wash relentlessly over us.

Some people may think they comprehend these micro-influences, but I doubt it. My sense is that every new wave of the future, unfolding in super high resolution at a rate of 100,000 frames a second, is simultaneously syncing with the "now" and, at the same time, transmitting new instruction sets into every fiber of our being.

These subtle waves of stimulation have a way of re-aiming us, positively and negatively, toward the next iteration of "now."

It's important to me, as someone hoping to control my own destiny, to try to understand how these "directoids" sway our sentiments and attitudes and define how an "optimal me" must be continually reconfigured for peak performance.

Awash in Micro-Changes

When the Tofflers talked about moving from a "brute force to a brain-force economy," they were getting a sense of the nuances of these subtle changes. Micro-changes are everywhere.

If you've ever considered the background processes such as the hair growing on your arm, blood flowing through your veins, or the infinitesimal secretions made by a gland as it compensates for yet another metabolic shift, you get the picture.

Directoids, as I imagine them, are nano-sized particles of influence, far too small to measure.

Our subconscious minds constantly assess probabilities, making millions of operational decisions every second to compensate for slight alterations between now and a zillionth of a second ago.

Drilling deeper, every cellular modification happens as the result of trillions of instructional messages passing beneath the surface of conscious awareness. On a more conscious level, we deliberate on such mundane considerations as "which socks should I wear today?" or "what's the right amount of milk to put on my cereal?"

While our body is awash in directoids, with countless operational signals coding and recoding every micro-decision on a subconscious level, our ability to discern and discriminate between influencers on this level is lost in the same kind of water-blindness that fish have.

For me, the "Inner Vision Theory" has become a useful tool for not only understanding our relationship with the future, but also explaining the true value that futurist thinking brings to the table.

Guiding by Our Inner Vision of the Future

In many ways, the Tofflers were far better at synthesizing interesting trends than predicting what came next. They exhibited an uncanny talent for drawing from a vast array of disciplines—science, technology, sociology, and religion—to explain the circumstances of the world at large.

Terms like "nonmonetary wealth," "prosumers," and "de-synchronized society" set the stage for next-gen strategies, but didn't always provide a sufficient environment from which to forecast future outcomes.

The internal steering wheel that our subconscious relies on to guide us through our daily lives is our inner vision of the future. Tucked away in our cranial cavities is our own personal vision of what the future holds. While we're not conscious of its role or how it works, our inner vision of the future determines every action we will take today.

If I see a new pair of shoes, my perception of those shoes may or may not alter my inner vision. If it does, I will somehow incorporate those shoes into my new vision of the future, and purchase them.

Similarly, every vacation brochure, restaurant ad, or toy commercial will cause our inner vision to give a quick thumbs-up or thumbs-down, sending signals to our conscious level decision-making mechanisms to take action.

As a futurist, Toffler's role was to alter people's inner visions of what the future held, and reset the way they made decisions.

Three Powerful Ways Our Inner Vision Controls Our Lives

Humans are incredibly complicated, and we currently know only a thimble full of information out of an ocean of data. But we know that we have the ability to change our inner vision and, by extension, change our future.

Every day this vision undergoes countless revisions as new thoughts and ideas cross our mind. The metaphor I use is tiny pieces of construction equipment, constantly being reassembled to reflect these changes to our inner vision.

Even though we have no actual research yet to validate how it works, our own empirical evidence gives us a functional mental framework.

Here are three of the rather surprising ways our inner vision controls our lives:

1 ■ **The signs we're looking for are being guided by our inner vision.**

How many times have you heard someone say they are "looking for a sign?" Perhaps you, yourself have said, "that was a sign!" But what constitutes a "sign," and how is one sign more significant than another?

Our "sign" might be an article we've read, an odd coincidence, a video clip we've seen, an image on a wall, or a conversation with a friend. But what we imagine as "signs" operate more as messages alerting us to the fact that we have had an experience that aligns with or reinforces something happening in our subconscious. They distinctly resonate with our inner vision.

2 ■ **The advice people give you has to resonate with your inner vision before you will accept it.**
Some people refer to it as instinct or a gut feeling, but whenever you intuitively know something is off, it comes from your inner vision.

In many respects, the pattern-matching skills of artificial intelligence work very much like the pattern matching we use to compare things to our inner vision. If something is new—a topic we haven't yet considered—we will grant it provisional acceptance until we are able to build sufficient vision to give it a thumbs-up or thumbs-down.

3 ■ **Even though we have control of our inner vision, all of our decisions first have to be okayed by it.**
Yes, we have control over our own decisions, but we go through a series of internal processes before they get "blessed" by our inner vision. Even our decision to change our inner vision has to be approved by our inner vision.

We have many tools for managing our inner vision, from increasing our exposure to information, to changing our focus or perspective, to changing our event horizon. The better we become at mastering these tools of introspection, the better we become at managing and reacting to the world around us.

Resetting Our Inner Calculus

The Toffler vision isn't perfect, but it has become pervasive, with many people today still using it as an internal calculus for making strategy decisions. As with most of today's best ideas, we formulate our best thinking while standing on the shoulders of giants—past luminaries like the Tofflers who have helped get us to this point.

Everything I've described above is part of a much broader theory I've been developing around the future.

For me, the "Inner Vision Theory" has become a useful tool for not only understanding our relationship with the future, but also explaining the true value that futurist thinking brings to the table.

At the same time, I'm hoping to make better sense of the dangling free radicals of our humanness that still fall into the realm of the unknown.

I'm honored to be part of this tribute, and personally thank Alvin and Heidi Toffler for inspiring me to go down this path. They have left an indelible set of "shock prints" on the future, and I will forever be indebted to their trailblazing. ■

Over the past decade, futurist **Thomas Frey** has built an enormous following around the world based on his ability to develop accurate visions of the future and describe the opportunities ahead. Having started 17 businesses himself and assisted on the development of hundreds more, the understanding he brings to his audiences is a rare blend of reality-based thinking coupled with a clear-headed visualization of the world ahead. Before launching the DaVinci Institute, Tom spent 15 years at IBM as an engineer and designer where he received over 270 awards, more than any other IBM engineer. He is also a past member of the Triple Nine Society (High I.Q. society over 99.9 percentile). He is author of *Epiphany Z – 8 Radical Visions Transforming Your Future*. See full bio here: https://futuristspeaker.com/thomas-frey-bio.

The Future of
Health and Wellness

Sanjiv Chopra, MD
& Pankaj K. Vij, MD

66 It is difficult to make predictions,
especially about the future. 99

—Niels Bohr

Homo sapiens appeared on planet Earth at least 300,000 years ago and has evolved as a species that values connection. ■ In fact, connection and community are essential human needs, right up there with the Four Fs: feeding (to stay alive), flight, fight (to avoid being eaten), and fornication (to keep the species going).

However, over the last century, humans have plundered the planet with unprecedented population growth, abused and overstrained our food production and supply systems, and have become increasingly sedentary and disconnected from the way of life by which we developed and evolved over 300 millennia. And our collective health and lifespan have suffered terribly as a consequence.

Consider this: Among the oldest written texts in human history are the *Vedas*. They describe four stages of life—covering a life span of 100 *years*. Yet through the Middle Ages, and even up to the Industrial Revolution, average life expectancy was a mere 40 years! We were able to improve our life expectancy at birth with the advent of antibiotics and improvements in sanitation. However, we have progressed at a painfully slow pace when it comes to improving longevity past improvements in infant mortality and communicable diseases.

At the same time, though, we have also discovered and developed insulin, blood transfusion, penicillin, radiation therapy, immune suppressants, birth control pills, vaccines, organ transplantation, MRI scans, AIDS treatment, IVF, artificial heart valves, stents, joint replacement, and a cure for leukemia in children. With the introduction of DNA repair technologies, protein synthesis, and a new understanding of the gut microbiome, we are actually on the cusp of making disease, disability, and death optional!

Our future is blindingly bright, not only because of these advances, but because civilization is ripe for a renaissance of the conditions and values that are essential to our survival as a species. We are getting ready to restore the average life expectancy of 100 years, with many of today's children looking forward to life spans far greater than that average. Death will become *elective*—indeed, a "voluntary act" involving a celebratory ceremony to mark the completion of a meaningful and joyous life.

Considering that humans are an ingenious, resilient, and hardy species, we will undoubtedly restore our food production system back to where it was prior to the Industrial Age. Soil quality will be restored as well, as we return to eating a nutrient-dense calorie-sparse diet interspersed with periods of fasting. Organic farming will be the norm, as it has been for most of our existence. This way we will restore our connection with nature and the soil of our dear planet, Mother Earth. Feeding will once again be a cherished ritual rather than the mechanical, mindless, and mundane act it has become. We will restore our relationship with food to both nurture and nourish ourselves. In doing so, we will activate the inborn systems of rebalancing and rejuvenation that each of us naturally comes equipped with.

Secondly, in reconnecting with *Gaia*—the personification of the Earth—we will naturally become more active as we spend more time outdoors working with our hands and feet, paying homage to the soil which sustains us. The rampant industrialization and mechanization of our lives has wreaked havoc on our relationship with our mother planet.

Thirdly, we will resync with our circadian rhythms, in which every cell of our body and every microbe living within us has evolved in an eco-friendly manner. In parallel, we will re-establish our cherished relationships with fellow members of our species and with other species, with which we have co-evolved and co-exist.

> With the introduction of DNA repair technologies, protein synthesis, and a new understanding of the gut microbiome, we are actually on the cusp of making disease, disability, and death optional!

Moreover, as consumers of health care, we will play a much more active role in its transformation. This transformation will not only require healthcare providers to redefine their services beyond the traditional boundaries, but will also require consumers to be more actively engaged as a community to truly bend the healthcare cost curves and improve overall health and well-being. To these ends, we are already shaping the future of health with the help of:

- Wearable technologies providing actionable data.
- Precision medicine based on biochemical individuality.
- Genomics and the ability to modify genetic predispositions.
- Study of the gut microbiome and, based on the results, the ability to define health and prescribe optimal personalized diet and lifestyle recommendations.

What's more, the boundaries we see in healthcare that force its practice in terms of specialties based on organs and systems will fade. Medical specialists calling themselves "ologists" will disappear as we realize that health and disease does not lend itself to such artificial classifications and that the body works as a unit in combination with the planet and the larger universe—converging on "omics"—genomics, proteomics, metabolomics, microbiomics.

Machines and algorithms will enable doctors to reclaim their place as true healers by enabling them to spend time and energy empathically connecting with the people who need their help. Individuals will assume the driver's seat regarding their own health. Communities will play a significant role in driving deeper engagement and adoption of new tools and technologies to improve overall health and wellness.

We will live healthier and more active lives by leveraging data-driven insights, tools, and social support to make health happen. That means we will create and deliver solutions that:

- facilitate positive (even healthful?) lifestyle change by design,
- are designed to place people and how they live their lives at the core of their experience, and
- are effective in helping people improve their health.

As technology makes everything exponentially faster, smarter, smaller, cheaper, and better, we will also have the data we need to make better choices every day. While data on its own has no value, it contributes to an actionable insight. Actionable insights are of limited value unless supported by solutions to act upon them successfully.

Health is a state where one experiences a full "human" life across all faculties. It is a function of both the physical and the mental activities we perform daily. A family leading a healthy life enjoys a tremendous economic value as a result, but as with any long-term asset, the significant payoff is over the long term. Hence, any health-related business model must factor in this investment.

> Medical specialists calling themselves "ologists" will disappear as we realize that health and disease does not lend itself to such artificial classifications and that the body works as a unit.

Today's generation is perhaps the most health-conscious in the last 100+ years. We see two reasons for this. First, a hundred years ago, lifestyle was not a key determinant of health or lifespan, which was dominated by more serious threats such as infectious diseases or war. Indeed, life was brutish and short. Second, previous generations did not have the information to assess the impact of lifestyle, nor the tools to address it. Today, of course, we've moved far beyond these limitations, and the focus of our attention has shifted accordingly. Today the priorities that will shape the future of health and wellness are far more proactive—and data-driven. As healthcare providers of the future, our priorities now are to:

- INSPIRE: Encourage people to lead healthier lives with their families and friends—putting them back in charge as active participants rather than passive recipients.
- INFORM: Help people become more aware of their bodies, learn about ways they can improve their health, and tackle health concerns.
- INTEGRATE: Empower them to share their stories, successes, and challenges with their families, friends, and the world at large and help contribute to the worldwide movement to lead healthy lives.

This approach will produce radically different outcomes—*healthspan* outcomes. And consequently, we are emboldened to make some equally radical predictions.

Now, it's true that Alvin Toffler, writing in *Future Shock,* affirmed Neils Bohr's warnings about predicting the future. "No serious futurist," Toffler wrote, "deals in 'predictions.'... No one even faintly familiar with the complexities of forecasting lays claim to absolute knowledge of tomorrow. ... Every statement about the future ought, by rights, be accompanied by a string of qualifiers—ifs, ands, buts, and on the other hands."

Indeed. But then Toffler turns right around and adds, "The inability to speak with precision and certainty about the future, however, is no excuse for silence." So we will not be silent!

Here, then, are our "predictions" about where the state of healthcare is headed in the next 50 years:

- There will be vaccines to prevent Alzheimer's, malaria, TB, HIV, Hepatitis C, Ebola, enterovirus D68, and many cancers.
- Regenerative stem cells will replace organ transplantation.
- Bariatric surgery will become a historical footnote.
- Imaging technology and biomarkers will enable early identification and aid in eradication of tumors.
- Immunotherapy will be the key to cancer treatments and cut cancer mortality by over 50 percent.
- Democratization of knowledge will occur. Supercomputers will allow citizens to access health information. Noninvasive sensors in our clothes will monitor a ton of information.
- Personalized medicine will be common practice.
- Nanotechnology and nanobiomedicine will flourish and permit more precise diagnoses and targeted therapies.
- There will be greater scientific understanding of the role of gut microbiota, leading to novel therapies.
- Stem cells and spinal implants will allow tens of thousands of paralyzed individuals to walk.
- Exploration of the workings of the brain and consciousness will be undertaken and provide masterful insights.
- Social and political changes will have a major impact in addressing health on many frontiers.
- Healthcare will be available and affordable for all earthlings, especially with advances in tele-medicine.
- Primary care medicine will be celebrated as the "Heroes' Profession."
- Patients will take a pill that will "mimic exercise" to combat the metabolic syndrome.
- There will be vaccines and/or treatment for all chronic diseases.
- Understanding and harnessing the microbiome will be a beacon of advancing science.
- Average life expectancy in the United States will exceed 110 years.

With better health will come better *life*. And that's the point, isn't it? Such radical changes in the nature of health, then, will yield equally radical changes in the nature of life itself. One bold and audacious set of predictions, then, deserves another:

- Compassion will be the universal religion.
- Gratitude will be the universal language.
- Children will be hailed as the most insightful philosophers.
- Universities will exist primarily in the cloud, and education will be accessible and affordable by all.
- Cheap desalination will make water abundant for all.
- Humans will conquer the mystery of consciousness and unfold our full potential.
- Humans will travel to distant planets in the time it now takes us to travel by car from Boston to San Francisco and back.
- The majority of humans will be vegetarians or pescatarians.
- All children will practice meditation in school.
- Empathy classes will be mandatory every week in school from kindergarten to high school.
- Global cooling will occur and save our planet.
- There will be peace on Earth.

Sanjiv Chopra, MD, is professor of medicine and served as Faculty Dean for Continuing Medical Education at Harvard Medical School for 12 years. He serves as a Marshall Wolf Master Clinician Educator at Brigham and Women's Hospital. Dr. Chopra has more than 150 publications and nine books to his credit. He is editor-in-chief of the Hepatology section of *UpToDate*, the most widely used electronic textbook in the world, subscribed to by more than 1.2 million physicians in 195 countries. He is a sought-after inspirational speaker across the United States and abroad, addressing diverse audiences on topics related to medicine, leadership, happiness, and living with purpose. His books include *Dr. Chopra Says: Medical Facts and Myths Everyone Should Know* (With Allan Lotvin, MD); *Live Better, Live Longer—the New Studies That Reveal What's Really Good and Bad for Your Health*; *Leadership by Example: The Ten Key Principles of all Great Leaders*; *The Big 5 Five Simple Things You Can Do to Live a Longer, Healthier Life*; *The Two Most Important Days* (with Gina Vild). With his brother Deepak, he wrote a double memoir: *Brotherhood: Dharma, Destiny and the American Dream*.

Pankaj Vij, MD FACP, is board certified in internal medicine and lifestyle medicine and practices in Pleasanton, California. His areas of interest include lifestyle, nutrition, fitness, mind-body medicine, stress management, and mindfulness. He is a graduate of the All-India Institute of Medical Sciences, New Delhi, India. He completed a residency in internal medicine at William Beaumont Hospital, Royal Oak, MI. He is the author of *Turbo Metabolism: 8 Weeks to a New You: Preventing and Reversing Diabetes, Obesity, Heart Disease, and Other Metabolic Diseases by Treating the Causes*. His hobbies include spending time outdoors and playing guitar.

Encounter with Alvin Toffler

Neil Jacobstein

When *Future Shock* **was published, I was in high school, and reading it transformed my understanding of the future.** Suddenly, the future was no longer a semi-random set of uncertainties but rather a funnel of potential futures, which could be considered systematically. These potential futures could facilitate contingency planning. The course of action that fared the best across potential futures could be considered robust and potentially viable in radically different futures. Education, for example, could be a viable course of action in radically different futures. Betting on flying cars in the 1980s was unlikely to be a robust strategy across multiple potential futures.

The notion that the rate of change of technology would outstrip the human nervous system's ability to adapt was a critically important idea. Toffler could predict that the future would be stressful as the rate of change increased precipitously. He suggested that we should study the future to anticipate viable courses of action, and make better investments of our energy, time, and funding. To these ends, Toffler identified key technologies early on that would be worth tracking and monitoring.

Decades later, Dr. Peter Katona, an epidemiologist friend who was also a close friend of Alvin's, suggested that Alvin and I meet for lunch. Alvin suggested Cravings on Sunset Boulevard in Los Angeles, and the two of us met there in 2014. Alvin was interested in my work in exponential technologies, such as artificial intelligence and robotics. He also wanted to probe how the abundance of wealth created by AI and robotics could compensate for the underemployment and unemployment those technologies would likely produce. We discussed this at length, and agreed that although wealth generation was predictable, there remained the unsolved problem of distribution. Wealth could become super concentrated and not lift all ships.

I think that Alvin was neither an optimist nor a pessimist, but someone who tried to understand the cross impact of emerging technologies and the human propensities revealed though history. He felt that some, but not all, of the impacts of technology would alter historical conditions enough to produce new outcomes. It was up to us, then, to educate people about the unprecedented possibilities of new technologies that might enable us to escape historical constraints.

We discussed the omnipresent problems of misuse and abuse of new technologies like AI, robotics, nanotechnology, and synthetic biology. Alvin had a keen interest in security problems. He thought that younger people felt that they had the luxury of not worrying about security in the military or intelligence sense. He was concerned that a lack of cybersecurity preparation in particular could greatly increase our vulnerability.

> I wanted to know how Alvin and his wife, Heidi, systematically studied the future. Did they use computers, mathematical models, and pattern-recognition software? Alvin laughed.

I wanted to know how Alvin and his wife, Heidi, systematically studied the future. Did they use computers, mathematical models, and pattern-recognition software? Alvin laughed. Their work pointed to many accelerating information technology social trends, but their personal methods were decidedly low tech. Alvin noted my new iPad. I asked him to try it. I had him download a Kindle version of one of his books, *The Third Wave*. He had never seen the digital version of this book and was thrilled to interact with his book in a new way.

Overall, we had a really interesting and warm encounter. I had an opportunity to thank Alvin for his many insightful contributions over the years. He was brilliant and gracious, and expressed his hope that we could help humanity prepare for the challenging future ahead.

Neil Jacobstein chairs the Artificial Intelligence and Robotics Track at Singularity University. He is a Distinguished Visiting Scholar in Stanford University's MediaX Program. Jacobstein was appointed by the US National Academy of Sciences to their Earth and Life Studies Committee for the period 2015-2021. He is on the Founding Editorial Board of the AAAS Science Robotics journal and is a Henry Crown Fellow at the Aspen Institute. Jacobstein serves in a variety of executive and technical advisory roles for industry, startup, nonprofit, and government organizations.

Anchoring the Future

Richard Watson

One of the enduring issues futurists **face is bad timing.** Like science fiction writers and technologists, futurists often believe that things will happen sooner rather than later. *Future Shock*, which accurately described the turmoil of the 1970s, is perhaps more accurate and relevant now than it was then. The book's central idea, that the perception of too much change over too short a period of time would create instability, perfectly describes the volatility, uncertainty, and confusion currently being generated by geopolitical events, climate change, and technology—and most of all, digital technologies that accelerate everything except our capacity to cope with change. Hence a global epidemic of anxiety that expresses itself in everything from the rise of mental illness to the mass prescription of painkillers and antidepressants.

Looking backward, it's hard to imagine how the upheavals of the early 1970s could have been seen as shocking. Surely the pace of change then was glacial compared to what it is now? But we have largely forgotten about the seismic shift from "we" to "me" that accompanied the fading of the sixties and the blossoming of the seventies. Group love was replaced by empowered individualism. The invention of modern computing, which soon became personal computing, amplified the focus on the individual even further. Peace, too, was shattered, not only by the enduring war in Vietnam, but by the invention of international terrorism, while OPEC's oil shock created inflation and economic uncertainty.

Oh, and the US had a rogue president, which proves, to me at least, that some things do not change quite as much as we sometimes imagine.

Maybe the speed of change in the '70s wasn't as rapid as today, but events back then were still alarming compared to the relative stability that had endured before. Global media made such events more visible too. Information overload is an idea championed in *Future Shock* and another that feels almost quaint when it's used in the context of the '70s. Overloaded? Way back then? You cannot be serious.

The problem, of course, is that while many things did indeed change, and continue to do so today, we do not. Or, at least, we struggle to keep up. Edward O. Wilson, the American biologist, sums the situation up perfectly when he says, "Humanity today is like a waking dreamer, caught between the fantasies of sleep and the chaos of the real world. The mind seeks but cannot find the precise place and hour. We have created a Star Wars civilization, with Stone Age emotions, medieval institutions, and godlike technology."

> When information reaches a tipping point, the brain protects itself by shutting down certain functions. Outcomes include a tendency for anxiety and stress levels to soar and for people to abstain from making important decisions. Not so much future shock as present paralysis, perhaps.

This clash, between technologies and behaviors that change rapidly (exponential is a word that's thrown around with careless abandon, but rarely stacks up outside computing), and our brains, which do not change as fast, was seen by the Tofflers as being injurious to not only our health, but to our decision-making abilities, too.

Interestingly, decades after *Future Shock* was written, a study published by Angelika Dimoka, director of the Centre for Neural Decision Making at Temple University, appears to support part of what the book proposed.

This study found that as information is increased, so too is activity in the dorsolateral prefrontal cortex, a region of the human brain associated with decision-making and the control of emotions. Yet eventually, if incoming information continues to flow unrestrained, activity in this region falls off. The reason for this is that part of the brain has essentially left the building. When information reaches a tipping point, the brain protects itself by shutting down certain functions. Outcomes include a tendency for anxiety and stress levels to soar and for people to abstain from making important decisions. Not so much future shock as present paralysis, perhaps.

Future Shock did not propose a solution to this problem. The book, as the authors pointed out, was always more of a diagnosis than a cure, although education is mentioned as a critically important factor going forward. So too is a need to guard against change that's either unguided or unrestrained.

This, again, is very much where we stand today. Technologies such as autonomous trucks, surgical robots, and battlefield drones are being developed with little or no public debate. If Tesla, for example, were Boeing or Bristol-Myers Squibb, I find it hard to imagine how its products would be allowed anywhere near the public at such a stage of development. As for artificial intelligence, the situation is even worse.

Broad or general AI could be the best or the worst invention humankind will ever make, and yet there is hardly any broad discussion about the risks, let alone any public debate about what this technology is ultimately for. Like many other things, AI is largely being imposed upon people for economic gain, and it is hard to see why it will enhance rather than diminish our humanity overall. However, this pessimistic view ignores two things I've learned about the future, which is that the future is not linear, and it's not binary, either. Things will happen that nobody, especially futurists, will have seen coming, and the most likely scenario is an uneasy balance between people wishing to push forward and others wanting to pull back.

So, 50 years on, is there now a cure for future shock? I think there is, and I believe that we are beginning to see some early signs of it.

In my view, the central problem at the moment is not change or acceleration *per se*, but that we have lost trust in government, science, business, the media, and even each other. We've also simultaneously lost our anchor points and thrown away our ballast, with the result that we are being tossed about in a high sea without any sign of land to navigate toward. No wonder we are feeling disoriented and somewhat nauseated.

In my view, it is this lack of direction, more than anything else, that is fueling our anxiety. But a simple solution is at hand. First, we need a moderate level of disconnection. We need to stop treating all information as power and reclaim some control over what enters our brains. The information universe is infinite, but our attention spans and mental processing capabilities are not. More importantly, without a strong sense of identity—in other words, a sense of who we are and where we stand—we will continue to be thrown around by the slightest disturbance.

I'm not for a moment suggesting that we ditch our cell phones or throw out our televisions in the style of Peter Finch in the movie *Network*, but rather that we consider more carefully the ideas that we let into our homes and our brains.

Once we have regained some sense of calm and perspective, we then need to talk to each other about where it is that we want to go in the future. How do we want to live? Even the "fact" that the future has arrived all at once, which some people cite as being a source for many of our troubles, would be easy to deal with if we only knew what destination we were heading toward. Then, as *Future Shock* suggests, we could restrain or reject anything that impedes our progress.

Having a view of what lies ahead, a shared vision of a promised land if you will, would also allow us to focus more on the present and worry less about endless unknowns. We should spend far less time individually worrying about what might happen and much more time collectively thinking about what it is that we want to happen.

There are echoes of this happening already, in everything from the growing disenchantment with our political elites and Big Tech to the criticisms that are emerging concerning globalization and the sterile nature of free-market economics and the inequality of wealth and opportunity that results.

In my opinion, the next big thing will be a seismic shift concerning what we value, which is us. All we are waiting for is a trigger. People can feel that something or someone is coming already, although nobody has expressed it yet.

As *Future Shock* advises, we need to humanize distant tomorrows. The best way of doing this is to take control of the future. Whether we like it or not, we are on the cusp of developing technologies that will give us godlike powers. The simple question concerns what to do with these powers. Who do we as individuals, societies, and a species want to be? ▪

Richard Watson is the author of *Digital Vs. Human* and the founder of www.nowandnext.com.

The Future in Sight

John Sanei

I've always been amazed by people who have the ability to see the invisible: business owners, artists, and entrepreneurs who seem to peer into the hyperconnected, hyperbolic world of tomorrow and pinpoint potential that the rest of us simply cannot see. ■ It's a skill that I want to understand, cultivate, and share because in the face of an epidemic of the disease Alvin Toffler wrote about in *Future Shock*, I believe that we all need to be flexible and adaptable to forge a future that benefits all of us. To fully understand how people see into tomorrow, however, we first need to look back.

Abundant Choice

For centuries, most of the Western world favored certainty over freedom—whether they wanted to or not. Governed by religion and the society they lived in, people knew that they would live, work, love, and die according to a strict set of rules. Many parts of the world still operate in this way, but elsewhere, we've become bored with security and replaced rules with choices.

We choose where we live, what we do, when we wake up, what to eat… we're swimming in the freedom of endless options. To borrow from Sartre, that freedom carries with it a terrifying sense of

346

responsibility—we need to make a sequence of informed choices to plan our future, but that future is moving so quickly, to a place that is so different, that it becomes almost impossible to know which path to take.

The shift from security and certainty to choice has unlocked a sense of perpetual anxiety because we're trying to make informed decisions about a tomorrow that's near impossible to predict. To ease this anxiety, we look for the familiar, a process that has divided our perspectives into four distinct types of sight that we need to understand in order to start revealing the invisible patterns that point to the future.

Hindsight: Made from Memories

Allegedly, hindsight is 20/20, but keeping your perspective set on the past is an unworkable strategy in the face of a fluid future.

Hindsight isn't seeing at all; it's a by-product of using memories to try to plan your next step. While there is undoubtedly value in learning from the past, we cannot apply the same approach that was relevant yesterday and hope that it holds up today, tomorrow, or the day after.

Hindsight is useful when you're looking for patterns, but a familiar past is only ever going to give you predictable ideas, and that's of no real use in our unreasonable, unfamiliar future.

Plainsight: Physical Perception

*Plain*sight is simple to understand: It's what happens when we open our eyes, and our optic nerve feeds all that information to our brain.

This view is scientifically valid, but as Anais Nin said, "We don't see things as they are, but as *we* are." Despite our body's best efforts, our experiences, prejudices, and circumstances influence the way we interpret the information fed to our brains.

Our state of mind, emotional state, and primal state of being all reduce the objectivity of our vision and affect the way we process and perceive the world around us, leading us to project our personality onto our perspective—and to see the world through certain filters.

People who believe that "seeing is believing," who rely on Plainsight alone, overlook the faith, intuition, and hope needed to future-proof themselves. Waiting for the world to manifest in a recognizable way will always anchor us in the present. As quantum science challenges the validity of singular perception and suggests that, actually, believing is seeing, it is clear that the immediate is not an adequate guide into our tomorrow.

> Hindsight is useful when you're looking for patterns, but a familiar past is only ever going to give you predictable ideas, and that's of no real use in our unreasonable, unfamiliar future.

Insight: Where Information Becomes Ideas

Insight is a buzzword that has bubbled over into every aspect of our lives. Understood as the recognition of a pattern within a set of data, insights can be incredibly powerful. However, if they remain trapped in books and best intentions, rather than driving change, then they are wasted, a glance of the invisible ignored.

It is what futurist Herman Kahn described as "the expert problem," which suggests that a person's level of education reduces their chance of seeing a solution that does not fall into the framework that they have been taught to think in.

A defiant grip on knowledge alone is not enough in an exponential reality. We need to use what we can from the past and see the world without prejudice to activate ideas that reveal the future.

Foresight: Connecting Invisible Dots

Foresight into the future is the epiphanous moment when a solution seems to appear from thin air after we have peered at complexity with little luck: The eureka moment where answer and questions become an elegant art form. It's a perspective that can only be accessed by evolving through the memories, perceptions, and information that blur our vision every day; but it is essential in the face of the future we are forging every moment.

Having developed a new understanding of sight, we can turn our gaze to the hugely exciting future we are creating.

The Fluid Future

In just 20 years, we have built the infrastructure to connect half of our tribe to the technology needed to access the internet. The rest are set to follow within the next five.

A global, connected community, equipped with endless opportunity and inspiration, will redefine reality as we understand it today.

> Our society is currently torn between those who cling to industrial thinking, and those who are ready to step into the innovation society. Shifting away from the established way of seeing the world—where we are cogs in society—calls for an obsessive pursuit of our own excitement, made possible by our own wisdom and curiosity.

Infotech, biotechnology, blockchain, and machine learning are hurtling us toward the hyper-intelligent, hyper-personal, hyper-efficient, hyper-affordable tomorrow around the corner. The advances in these four sectors are pushing the frontiers of what consumers can expect and will come to demand. There are already businesses reimagining what their services and products actually are in order to align with those possibilities, because failure to do so will undoubtedly cost more than an investment in an innovation team.

The way the consumer of the future sees the world ultimately allows us to connect the dots from past, present, and potential to what will become possible, and essential.

Within the context of business, this shift seems structured: lower your reliance on data, take the current landscape with a pinch of salt, and be sure to activate relevant trends and not sit on data—inform consumers what they'll need before they realize it.

But what about the people facing that future?

Seeing the Unseen

Alan Watts said that the wise man needs to unlearn something every day, and that's best applied to the way we currently see the world: We will not be able to thrive in the future when we continue to view the world from an industrial perspective.

In her article "The Great Shift in Society," Danish writer Louise Skøtt Gadeberg discusses the root of our viewpoint with economist Keld Holm. Their elegant argument is that our society has always derived its values from the dominant means of production: God in agricultural times, and then mechanical production that sparked what they describe as "hello to factory rules, assembly-line production, conformity, and uniformity for the sake of efficiency."

Our society is currently torn between those who cling to industrial thinking, and those who are ready to step into the innovation society. Shifting away from the established way of seeing the world—where we are cogs in society—calls for an obsessive pursuit of our own excitement, made possible by our own wisdom and curiosity.

Recognizing the irrelevance of outmoded ways of seeing the world unlocks wisdom, because when we are not reliant on the past, or our perception, or information, we start to see the world through a new lens: curiosity.

When we are curious, we move through the world with an excitement and flexibility that makes today's impossible tomorrow's goal, because it is curiosity that prompts us to follow our heart and not rely on sight.

Combining the chemicals of wisdom and curiosity causes an unstoppable chain reaction that carries us to the flow state; an energized, focused outlook where you prioritize flexibility and adaptability—the critical equipment for facing the future.

20/20 Vision

The way we perceive tomorrow defines the way we prepare for it. In a time of abundant choice, you have the ability to let go of restrictive perspectives, activate your wisdom and curiosity, and start connecting invisible dots.

The power to recognize patterns will allow you to find new opportunities—in business, for self-development, and to get excited about what you're creating: A future fueled by your vision with optimism rather than fear.

It is a powerful practice; one that will energize and motivate you to no end. But this way of seeing the world is more than a tool for business planning. This pursuit of perspective and preparation for the future is an exercise in self-awareness, a deeply reflective process that forces us to confront our own views and heal our hearts in order to project something pure onto the collective future we will face together. ▪

John Sanei (Sah-nay) is an author, speaker, and trend specialist fascinated with what it takes to activate the foresight needed to create an abundant future. His goal in life is to bring courage, clarity, elegance, and consciousness to audiences around the world—a mission that sees him traveling relentlessly from his two bases in Cape Town and Dubai to work with global brands and governments. He explores human psychology, business strategies, and future studies in his best-selling books, workshops, and presentations. John was Africa's first Singularity University faculty member and is a lecturer at Duke Corporate University. In 2018, he was recognized as the "Most Influential and Connected Man" by GQ.

The Future of Medicine

Helen Messier PhD, MD

Alvin Toffler's *Future Shock* had many prescient observations, not least among them the Cassandra Truth of his epitaph for the traditional family doctor:

> "And the same trend toward time-truncated relationships is reflected in the demise of the family doctor. The late lamented family doctor, the general practitioner, did not have the refined narrow expertise of the specialist, but he did, at least, have the advantage of being able to observe the same patient almost from cradle to coffin. Today the patient doesn't stay put. Instead of enjoying a long-term relationship with a single physician, he flits back and forth between a variety of specialists, changing these relationships each time he relocates to a new community."

Perhaps only a guess in 1970, time has turned speculation into fact. Gone is the one-stop shop of the family doctor, buried beneath a jungle of specialists, consultants, and alternative practitioners. This change is not, on its face, a bad thing; those specialists can do things a classic generalist couldn't. Still, this modern era of fragmentation leaves practitioners without the comprehensive patient knowledge a family doctor once enjoyed. The benefits of that trade-off outweigh the costs—if we accept that it's an either/or proposition. We shouldn't have to. The future-is-now era of technology ought to mean doctors can have their cake and eat it too; we have the opportunity to defragment modern medicine to the benefit of doctor and patient alike. All we need to do to achieve that dream is to borrow Toffler's eye for the future.

But to outline that future, we must first define the present. Today, patients see, for instance, a cardiologist for their heart, a dermatologist for their skin, and a therapist for their mental health, along with another dozen or so specialists, depending. These specialists by and large do great work, but the cardiologist today rarely knows, or thinks much about, what the dermatologist did last month. Every doctor learns something new from each interaction with every patient, but that knowledge doesn't always make it into the medical history; how could it? By their nature, those histories have to be whittled down to the essentials so that the next doctor can get what is needed from them. A thorough practitioner might reach out to a patient's previous caregivers when stumped, but that's a process that takes time and effort and still may not paint the whole picture.

Put simply, there just isn't a way for the internist to quickly convey to the gastroenterologist everything learned from years of treating the patient. All those little personal details—they may not even be explicitly medical, just basic observations about a patient's mood, gait, diet, etc. that might not crack the chart—are lost in translation. The dream, then, is of a doctor who has it all: the legacy knowledge of a lifetime of treating the same patient, and the specialization to solve the current ailment. A single doctor who knows everything, and can do everything. The first and most apparent barrier: no human mind can know everything, and no doctor can master every specialization.

That's where it gets exciting; in the "future" we live in, the human mind no longer binds us. We have the technology to quickly collect every single bit of data about a patient, from symptoms and measurements to micro-level genomics and metabolomic to dietary habits, and translate all of it to a (theoretical) database. We also have the capacity through AI and machine learning to process and search that database in seconds, no matter how large it might grow. If every practitioner put every bit of data they collected into that database, then it would, effectively, know everything. If every doctor then had access to the database (and the AI to near-instantly get the information they need from it), then so would they.

> **"Imagine that five years from now we have a self-teaching AI that has learned from every single doctor/patient interaction. A nigh-omniscient super-doctor is working from the largest imaginable sample size of case histories and yet is intimately familiar with the specifics of each patient's individual wellness journey.**

The database would need to be open source; everyone can contribute, and everyone benefits. No one is left out in the cold. Patients and practitioners who contribute should benefit directly as well as philosophically, whether there's a financial incentive, or future discounts on medical care, or something else entirely. Blockchain technology can make that reward scalable; every time someone accesses the data or clinical wisdom from a doctor's input, then the people who contributed—both doctor and patient—will benefit. Hand in hand with that, patients of course must be free to opt out of sharing their data; this should be less Skynet or Big Brother, more Wikipedia (albeit with a lot more fidelity).

Imagine that five years from now we have a self-teaching AI that has learned from every single doctor/patient interaction. A nigh-omniscient super-doctor is working from the largest imaginable sample size of case histories and yet is intimately familiar with the specifics of each patient's individual wellness journey. It turns every doctor into the family doctor, and into any specialist that might be needed (or at least gives them instant access to the insight they'd get from that specialist). The perfect resource, immune to bias or small sample sizes, getting smarter and smarter with every single patient interaction… which means every single practitioner in the global medical community gets smarter, too.

When and if the platform makes mistakes, it learns from them, and factors them into every future scenario with perfect recall and objectivity. With diligent data collection, it tracks not only treatments but outcomes and aftercare, potentially finding connections no one practitioner ever could, and opening up doors to faster, better diagnoses and treatments. The priority will always be better patient care, and through this hypothetical, every patient will benefit from the expertise of every doctor.

It will be essential to track aftercare, outcomes, and ongoing patterns. The more data collected, even beyond the conventional, the better. Post-treatment updates and check-ins will be perhaps the most crucial touchpoint for improving the system; we must track specific outcomes for specific individuals. Metadata must be collected at every step, from initial visit onward: diet, environment, even time of day. No detail too small. With the diagnostic and communications technology we have today, these should be easy requirements to meet, a low price to pay for allowing us to defragment modern medicine. At least in theory.

The holy grail for all of this, then, is implementation. This is not a Day 1 solution; nor even a Day 101 solution. It will require hundreds of thousands if not millions of patient/doctor interactions—including the meticulous collection of data and metadata—before it will be a viable resource. Beyond that, there will be growing pains and a fairly long learning curve, both for the system itself and the practitioners deploying it. But once it's there? The sky is the limit.

Imagine plugging a patient's name and ailments into a machine and in seconds having not only every bit of relevant medical information but a recommended diagnostic course as well. Imagine taking it a step further, creating a patient-side aspect that serves as a personal health assistant; imagine if Alexa or Siri could answer every spur-of-the-moment health question a patient had with the specificity of a family doctor. Imagine if they could monitor and encourage adherence to treatment plans. Imagine that they could nudge patients—unobtrusively and only with permission—toward healthier choices. Imagine if patients and practitioners even in the most remote, isolated, or disadvantaged places in the world had instant access to all the same knowledge and expertise as Beth Israel. Then imagine that you don't really have to imagine at all; we already have the technology, it's merely a question of using it. If we use it? Patient care gets better. Doctors' lives get easier. Error rates go down, life spans go up. The therapeutic relationship between doctor and patient becomes faster, easier, and more productive. With everyone working together, everyone gets healthier. The family doctor lives again, in every clinic, hospital, and home. Toffler's epitaph is proving not prescient after all, but premature.

Dr. Messier's focus is in closing the translational gap using a data-driven healthcare model. This real time translation of precision medicine integrates multi-omics technologies and applies them directly in clinical care, allowing patients with complex chronic disease to actively benefit from innovative biomedical technologies. Dr. Messier received a Bachelor of Science (Hons.) in genetics and a PhD in Molecular Immunology from the University of Alberta. She completed post-doctoral studies at the La Jolla Institute for Allergy and Immunology in San Diego, CA, and received her MD from the University of Calgary and is certified in family medicine. She founded a series of national concierge practices, served as a Medical Director, Genomics at HLI and was CMO of Viome. Her strong scientific and medical background is combined with a passion for helping people realize their optimal level of health and in teaching others to apply complex molecular data to the care of individuals. Dr. Messier is currently at Altum Medical, a center that provides deep dive medical care and is the founder of Medical Intelligence Learning Labs Inc., a company that is creating a platform to enable every doctor to be "the best" doctor by capturing the clinical wisdom from every medical encounter so it can be accessed by the larger medical community.

Our Future State

Jerry Fishenden

Government has not aged well over the past **50 years.** ◼ As Alvin Toffler predicted, its industrial era institutions and practices have proved themselves ill-equipped to cope with the pace of technological change.

Democratic governments could have been at the vanguard of the positive uses of technology, placing citizens center stage and helping strengthen our rights and laws and modernize our institutions. They could have provided continuous feedback mechanisms to improve policy outcomes and used open public data to monitor economic, social, environmental, and cultural progress. They could have regulated domestic and global technology companies to ensure they play by the same rules as everyone else, and lifted people and communities out of old, dying jobs and industries and into new ones.

The best organizations use technology in constructive, creative ways, rethinking and redesigning their products, processes, and services to better meet consumers' needs. These learning organizations flatten and streamline their internal structures and use constant feedback to refine and optimize the way they work. Used well, technology can also improve job satisfaction, cutting out pointless internal processes and administration and freeing up time for employees to pursue their areas of expertise and interest.

Many governments, however, walk not in the footsteps of such enlightened organizations, but in those of technology corporations and authoritarian regimes. They intrude into our personal lives, gathering and acting upon unprecedented levels of our data in both public and private spaces, online and offline. They use often unproven technologies that automate inequality and undermine human rights and the exercise of justice in the pursuit of their own financial or political goals.

Authoritarian states outpace democracies in their exploitation of new technology. They embrace and fashion it in their own image—tightening political control and further suppressing their own citizens through an increasingly inescapable and dehumanizing surveillance. Technology is tilting the balance between citizen and state, enabling an unprecedented intrusion into our lives that will grow stronger and more damaging if it is not soon corrected. Democracy and freedom are unlikely to prosper in a world flooded with technologies monitoring and analyzing all aspects of our daily lives. Proof, if it were needed, of Toffler's prediction that the roaring current of technological change would overturn institutions, shift our values, and shrivel our roots—including, it seems, the essential roots of democracy.

This failure to orchestrate technology as a public good has contributed to a growing sense of alienation and disadvantage. Unable to cope with the fast-paced and unrecognizable world around them, many citizens increasingly seek solace in what Toffler termed "the politics of nostalgia." Yet the past is far from being the desirable place portrayed by a growing band of populists. We are in a much better world now than the one our ancestors experienced, even if it might not always feel that way at a personal or local level. In the second half of the 20th century, the share of the world population living in democracies increased continuously. Global child mortality rates have dropped dramatically. Life expectancy has more than doubled since 1900, and the number of people in poverty is down by around three quarters since 1990.

These improvements do not mean we can or should rest easy, however. Many problems remain, from homelessness to mental illness, social immobility to drug abuse, climate change to inequality. But surrendering to the siren voices serenading us onto the rocks of a false past will reverse progress and increase inequality and uncertainty, not tackle it.

As Toffler observed, the problems we need to address are ultimately not scientific or technical, but ethical and political. We need to redesign technology and embed democratic rules, values, and behaviors deep within it. In the same way that many consumer goods and services are checked for safety—electrical, suitability for young children, toxicity, fire resistance, fitness for human consumption, hygiene—before they can be sold, so too our technologies should be validated for their compliance with democratic values, protecting us from the invasive, inappropriate, and socially corrosive models of big business and anti-democratic states, politicians, and bureaucrats.

Every significant technical, social, and economic advance has involved government intervention and correction, often implemented long after it was first required—from worker safety on the factory floor to the abolition of child labor, from sanitation to mine safety. The problem is not so much technology itself, or capitalism or the creeping intrusion of hostile regimes, as it is the apparent lack of willingness and ability of our governments to anticipate and respond effectively.

We need to cultivate a new age of democratic enlightenment supported by, not dictated by, technology. One in which social, human, and environmental improvements have as much focus and value as more traditional economic measures. This requires government to let go of its inward-looking bureaucratic instincts and to open up—monitoring and releasing public data regularly, frequently, and automatically to enable citizens to see the extent of progress and to determine where resources are best directed or redirected.

Better use of public data is essential if democracy is to survive and prosper over and beyond the next 50

> "Unable to cope with the fast-paced and unrecognizable world around them, many citizens increasingly seek solace in what Toffler termed "the politics of nostalgia." Yet the past is far from being the desirable place portrayed by a growing band of populists."

years. Yet no government has used technology to make open data and insights about its own operations part of day-to-day processes. This failure is a major obstacle to the modernization and improvement of democracy. It lets lies and half-truths be easily fabricated, circulated, and amplified. It makes it difficult to rebut raw emotion, prejudice and bias with hard, objective evidence.

A move to a new form of politics enabled by technology and informed by transparency, open data, and continuous feedback will doubtless fuel the lazy populist accusation that politicians do not know their own minds and allow themselves to be swayed by events. Constant corrections and improvements will be required to reflect facts over opinions, outcomes over dogma, reality over prejudice.

Politicians who respond to ever-changing evidence, fine-tuning and improving policy on the fly, are likely to be caricatured as weak. Policies based on data instead of dogma offer the best way to meet human, cultural, social, environmental, and economic needs, but they will take patience and time to prevail. Governments need to capture and release reliable open data about the efficacy of political decisions and the performance of the state. It will help us distinguish between the fake and the real, between scientific evidence and irrational belief.

> Surrendering to the siren voices serenading us onto the rocks of a false past will reverse progress and increase inequality and uncertainty, not tackle it.

To make sense of this rich and potentially overwhelming volume of data we need immersive, interactive, and intuitive ways of verifying, navigating, and understanding it. We need to bring art and craft and creativity to science and technology, to move beyond dry spreadsheets and charts, to let facts and evidence dance and come alive around us. Video game and 3D augmented reality will let us viscerally experience alternative policy options, exploring how they might interact and play out. Creative technologies can help us make a meaningful, personal, human connection between evidence and instinct—providing a sort of real-world, immersive SimCity™ that lets us *enjoy* trying out various evidence-based "what-if" ways of achieving various policy outcomes.

Better use of technology will help us make progress with the outcomes that Toffler called for. Fifty years on he would be disappointed, but probably not surprised, by how few governments publish annual reports on quality of life and social progress. Nor have we seen the necessary recognition that progress is about more than economic growth. As Toffler observed, technological questions cannot be answered in technological terms alone—they are political questions.

Enlightened democratic leaders need to reclaim a positive vision and passion for our democratic future and the role of technology in delivering it, and to think more critically about the human qualities and values of democratic society. Politicians need to break technology away from the toxic grip of corporate entities—global monopolies, authoritarian regimes, and public bureaucracies living in the past—who have embedded their self-serving values deep within its design.

We are at a turning point as to where technology impacts democracy: from "smart" speakers eavesdropping on our private and family lives to so-called "artificial intelligence"; from moves toward a cashless society to mass facial recognition; and from behavioral analytics to social media and "fake news" and the corruption of democratic elections.

Governments have a choice. They can choose to sleepwalk into the future, tinkering with the museum of outdated institutions and failed dogmatic initiatives while authoritarian, discriminatory, and invasive technologies dehumanize society and undermine our right to freedom and a private life. Or they can choose to embrace the open, participative potential of technology to reinvigorate democracy, gathering, publishing, and acting honestly on public data and citizen feedback. They can reinforce and protect our rights both online and offline, ensuring we have meaningful control over the way technology can access and use our private information. They can find a way to convince those who feel left behind that the best possible future is one of democracy and liberty and progress and hope and the pursuit of happiness—not the false politics of nostalgia, regression, division, and hate.

Our democratic future, our future state, depends on our governments using technology to modernize and strengthen essential institutions and processes that protect democracy. Governments must redesign and streamline the inefficient organizational and policy silos and processes that create friction and raw human suffering, thus generating frustration with public services. We need to challenge and reject the toxic design of much current technology and make it an open, positive, participative force for good. And, most importantly, governments must renew a commitment to universal rights and the rule of law, adopting a more scientific and objective approach to policymaking. Doing so would provide an essential stimulus to global democratic progress.

As our governments begin using technology to improve transparency and trust, they should hold other governments, and the companies who supply our goods and services, to the same standards. Technology can make visible and verifiable, for example, an entire supply chain, from source to purchase. It can enable us to see whether products and services have come from rogue regimes or companies—those using child labor, paying workers slave wages, or employing those living and working in inhuman conditions—or from those producers operating ethically. Imagine how profound such a change would be in establishing trust and facts over falsehood and deception: we could simply scan any good or service with our phones to discover its verified, authentic details. It is time to use technology to protect, enhance, and grow democracy, rather than undermining and shriveling it.

As consumers and citizens, we too have an important role to play—to demonstrate through our actions that we care about the responsible uses of technology. There is an unmet appetite for improved social responsibility and more ethical regimes, companies, supply lines, products, and services. We should change our own behavior to support positive uses of technology, and to actively reject the negative. Doing so will not only be good for democracy, but will provide a competitive or political advantage for those organizations, private and public, who choose to use it in more open and progressive ways.

The next 50 years will likely constitute one of the most challenging and important eras in the history of democracy. Let us hope our governments, and we, choose to shape technology and society to rise to that challenge.

Dr. Jerry Fishenden is an internationally recognized technologist, writer, and composer currently working with a range of public, private, and not-for-profit organizations. He has held senior executive positions at Microsoft, the City of London financial regulator, the UK Parliament, the UK Government, and the National Health Service. He is a Fellow of the Institution of Engineering and Technology (FIET), a Fellow of the Royal Society of Arts (FRSA), and a member of the Writers' Guild of Great Britain. He is co-author of Digitizing Government: understanding and implementing new digital business models (see http://www.digitizinggovernment.org), a practical playbook for modernizing large, complex organizations. He is currently working on several books, mobile apps, and related works.

Living to 100?

Wolfgang Fengler

In 2020, around 60 million people will die. ▪ Despite break-throughs in healthcare, nutrition, and education across the world, the number of deaths is rising continuously, and will exceed 100 million people by 2070. As the number of births will stay stable at around 140 million, population growth will slow down dramatically to only around 30 million additional people per year (Figure 1). Contrary to popular belief, it is not a declining birth rate that is causing slowing population growth globally. The world population will be growing more slowly because more and more people will be dying. So are we losing the battle against death?

Figure 1 • More deaths, not declining births, are responsible for slowing population growth.

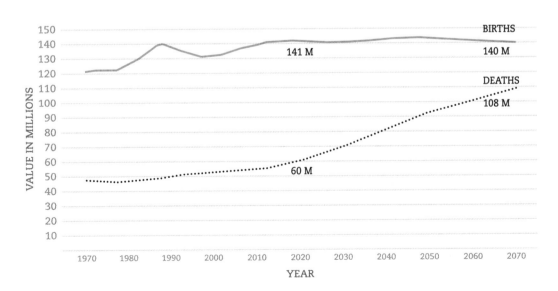

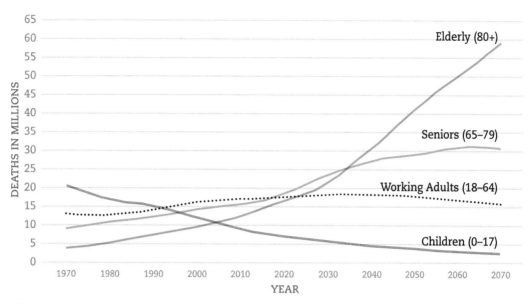

Figure 2 • Projections by Katharina Fenz, World Data Lab based on UN Population Prospects, 2017.
What will it require to reach an average life expectancy of 100 in the next 50 years?

Not at all. *This is the safest time to be alive ever and it will only get better,* almost everywhere. The reason why more people die every year is twofold. First, there are more people in the world, which also means that—all else being equal—more people die. Since the global population is still growing faster than the number of deaths, the probability of dying for every one of us at any point in time is actually declining.

Second, more people are dying simply because more of us are getting older. As we all die eventually, it is better to die old. And because we have so many more old people now, it is likewise only natural that more people die. This is actually a relatively new development, although it was predicted by Alvin Toffler in 1970. Writing in *Future Shock*, he observed, "Through love we live a full life if life expectancy is ever rising." He went on to explain that he expected average life expectancy to rise from 50 years to 70 years (p. 131), a level that was reached in 2010. If current trends continue, average life expectancy will rise to 80 years by 2070, but already by 2030, girls in South Korea and Japan can expect to live 100 years. Despite his accurate optimism, Toffler would have probably considered this as close as it gets to immortality.

To enable this frontier of human development for everyone, much work remains to be done. Only in 2007 had humanity reached a point where more than half of the world's population died after the age of 65. Men, in particular, reached this transition point only in 2014. Today, 35 million people die after their 65th birthday, and 25 million die before reaching this typical retirement age[1]. While child mortality declined from 12.1 million in 2000 to 7.2 million by 2020, deaths of working age adults are stable at around 17 million people per year (Figure 2).

Three interrelated breakthroughs would need to occur to reach this next frontier of humanity.

■ **First, we need to eliminate child mortality.** While child mortality has declined sharply (Figure 2), there are still approximately 7.2 million children (0-17 years) who die every year, of which almost 2 million die from neonatal disorders in the first weeks of their lives. Africa and Asia remain the last frontiers of child mortality; they account for more than 90 percent of such deaths. If children survive their first five years, there is a high chance they will live full lives. Eliminating child mortality, then, will continue to have an important impact on global life expectancy. Under a base case projection, child mortality would decline to 2.7 million by 2070, but Africa would still lead in this statistic.

■ **Second, adult pre-retirement mortality needs to decline.** Unlike child mortality, *adult mortality* has been rising, including pre-retirement adults, where it is still in the same range as deaths of seniors (65-80 years) and the elderly (80 years+)—all at around 16-18 million per year (Figure 2). This group of *working adults* remains the world's dominant group, which increased sharply from 2 billion in 1970 to 5 billion in 2020, representing some two thirds of the global population. This global demographic dividend will continue, but will slow through 2070 when there will be an estimated 5.7 billion working adults. By then, a 65-year-old person would probably be considered relatively young, like a 50-year-old person today. Stable mortality in this age group therefore means that everyone alive today faces a much smaller risk of dying before retirement.

■ **Third, to extend global lifespans further, we need to eliminate communicable diseases and delay noncommunicable diseases.** Mortality profiles differ across age. Children and young adults die mostly from communicable diseases and accidents; old people die in much greater numbers from various types of heart diseases, stroke, cancer, or dementia (Figure 3). When Alvin Toffler published *Future Shock* most people died from diarrhea, malaria, TB, or simple respiratory diseases. With the AIDS epidemic, which haunted most of Africa in the 1990s and 2000s, a second wave of communicable disease had arrived.

Figure 3 • Causes of death differ greatly when disaggregated by age.

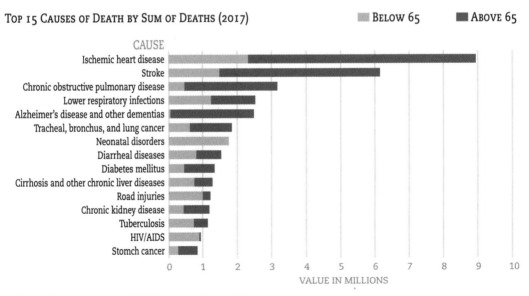

Top 15 Causes of Death by Sum of Deaths (2017)   ▨ BELOW 65   ■ ABOVE 65

World Data Lab projections based on IHME, Global Burden of Disease, 2017.

One of the big successes of development since 1970 has been the sharp decline in communicable diseases. Today, they represent only 30 percent of all deaths—approximately 18 million—and affect mostly Africa and Asia. The greatest such preventable causes are respiratory diseases (3.5 million), diarrhea (1.5 million), AIDS and malaria (each 1 million). Meanwhile the number of deaths from road accidents has risen to 1.3 million.

By contrast, noncommunicable diseases represent 70 percent of total deaths, of which heart disease will be the largest with 20 million deaths in 2020 (32 percent), followed by cancer with approximately 8 million (13 percent). While the growth in noncommunicable disease is a sign of aging, i.e., successful development, there is an increasing number of people in emerging markets who die from noncommunicable diseases as working adults. Here, prevention of these new diseases, such as diabetes or cancer, will be crucial.

> The world can end premature mortality, i.e. death before 65, which also means that many people will live a full century— a feat only few achieved in 1970.

By the 100th anniversary of *Future Shock*, the world can end premature mortality, which also means that many people will live a full century—a feat only a relative few achieved in 1970. But the road to zero deaths before 65 years will require very focused efforts in each geographic region, as the causes of mortality are very different across country, age, and gender. For this, we will need more precise *big data* models, something even Toffler did not anticipate.

As I was born just after *Future Shock* was published, it is my personal ambition to experience these global shifts over the next 50 years. I am among the lucky ones to have a small chance of living to 100. To achieve this, I will need to stay healthy and exercise. At the same time, we need continued mortality breakthroughs to minimize death from accidents and communicable diseases, while mitigating the effects of noncommunicable diseases. My own data model—www.population.io—puts my chance to live until 100 at a little more than 3 percent, assuming average health. Let's work on creating a world where everyone has at least a 50 percent chance to live to 100. ■

Note: I would like to thank Jasmin Baier (World Data Lab) for outstanding research assistance as well as Katharina Fenz (World Data Lab) for help with the projections.

Wolfgang Fengler is the World Bank's Lead Economist in Finance, Competitiveness & Innovation. He has published extensively on social and economic issues. He also co-authored *Delivering Aid Differently* (with Homi Kharas, Brookings) and *Africa's Economic Boom* (with Shanta Devarajan, Foreign Affairs). Wolfgang also launched population.io (endorsed by Bill Gates) as well as worldpoverty.io, two real-time big data models. The German weekly *Der Spiegel* called him a "big data virtuoso." Prior to joining the World Bank, he set up Africa Consulting, LLC, and was a fellow at the Research Institute for International Relations. Wolfgang gained a PhD from the University of Hamburg (Germany).

1. The OECD average equals to 64.3 years for men and 63.7 years for women across all schemes (2016), but is expected to increase significantly in the future.

The Quantum Engine

Jay Gambetta, IBM Fellow

I n *Future Shock*, author Alvin Toffler characterizes technology as "a great growling engine of change"—one in which progress
accelerates rapidly, as one innovation builds on the next. ■ As technology
begets more technology, the acceleration increases exponentially.

Computing is undeniably one of the greatest technologies. Over the years, it has drastically
changed the way business and science are done. In business, computers have continually increased
the rate of transactions. For science, they have pushed the limits of numerical simulation of systems
that cannot be solved analytically, such as climate modeling, molecular dynamics, and chemical
kinetics. With the increased availability of data, machine learning models and specially designed
processors have brought forth artificial intelligence, which has become an essential tool for business
and science. However, all of these gains are bound by one common thread: the standard (or classical)
model of computation. This model will never efficiently solve many interesting problems, such as
combinatorial optimization, integer factorization, or modelling of quantum physical systems.

To understand the classical computational model, it's enlightening to refer to a simplified version
of Alan Turing's machine, which manipulates symbols on a strip of tape according to a table of rules.
Given any computer algorithm, a Turing machine can be constructed that is capable of simulating
that algorithm's logic. We can consider classical computers to have an initial state, on which we
perform a sequence of operations, followed by a final extraction of information from the machine
that represents the state. All computations on a classical computer happen in this way, reduced to
sequences of operations such as logic gates (AND, OR, NOT, NAND) on bits (0s and 1s). For a computer
of size N bits, one can explore operations in a space defined by N bits.

Now, fortunately, for computation too we have a potential "great growling engine": the quantum
computer, which follows the same general structure of computation as the classical case (initializa-
tion, operations, measurement), but processes information in a completely different way based on

362

the principles of quantum physics. Rather than information reduced into bits, quantum information is captured by quantum bits, or qubits. These qubits can be set not only to the states of bits, 0 and 1, but also to states that are linear combinations or superpositions of both. Here, these qubits actually have probability distributions associated with them that, while seemingly random, are, in fact, controllable and can be undone. This is the quantum mechanical principle that a perfectly definite state can still behave randomly.

The other crucial principle of quantum mechanics is that of the counterintuitive property of entanglement, where two systems too far apart to influence one another can behave in ways that, although individually random, are strongly correlated. This tells us that, in a quantum computation, there can be more information in the correlation of multiple qubits than in individual qubits.

Together, these two properties allow a quantum computer to take an initial state and perform operations on it such that it can now explore an exponentially large space for computation before information is finally extracted. With a quantum computer of N qubits, one can now explore an internal computational space of 2^N. These different rules allow one to investigate an entirely different model for calculation.

Considered another way, were you to attempt to represent the actions of qubits using classical bits, you'd need an exponential number of them. For example, if you devoted every atom on Earth to create bits and manipulate them for computing, you still could not simulate the capabilities of an ideal 200-qubit machine.

A major challenge in advancing quantum computing is in making qubits that are close to "ideal" while maintaining accurate control over them. They are incredibly sensitive and susceptible to noise that can deteriorate their ability to make computations. Quantum computers are still in the early stages of development and far from totaling 100 ideal qubits.

Current leading quantum systems using superconducting qubits have an average coherence time of 100 microseconds. This means that the system has a window of 100 microseconds in which to run calculations. To increase this time, we must improve qubit stability by creating systems that effectively shield the qubits from elements of interference (mechanical vibrations, temperature fluctuations, electromagnetic waves such as microwave waves, etc.). As qubit stability gets better, the potential of quantum computing becomes enormous.

> Now, fortunately, for computation too we have a potential "great growling engine": the quantum computer, which follows the same general structure of computation as the classical case but processes information in a completely different way based on the principles of quantum physics.

Much as Moore's Law measured the progress of classical computer chips over the last half-century, we can measure the processing power of quantum machines using a metric known as Quantum Volume. Currently, this incipient Quantum Volume law only has three data points, but it already shows that we have doubled Quantum Volume every year for the last three years. We've gone from four to eight to 16. If we continue to double Quantum Volume every year, we will do things with quantum computers within the next decade that are simply impossible to do with today's classical machines.

In other words, we will achieve what is known as Quantum Advantage—when we can definitively demonstrate, in certain use cases, a significant practical performance advantage over today's classical computers. By significant, we mean that a quantum computation is either hundreds or thousands of times faster than a classical computation, needs a smaller fraction of the memory required by a classical computer, or makes something possible that simply isn't possible now with a classical computer.

What will that be? We truly don't know. But, just as Toffler describes an exponential increase of new combinations and possibilities as still newer machines and techniques are introduced, we can safely assume that harnessing the quantum ability to explore multiple states will accelerate the curve of technological innovation to an unprecedented degree.

In addition to its exponential capabilities, quantum computing's difference lies in its ability to compute with the laws of nature. Nature, by definition, is quantum. By contrast, even today's most sophisticated digital models and simulations can only approximate nature. Consider representing the basic building blocks of the universe: molecules. In many cases, these rough approximations are tolerable. But sometimes, the exceedingly intricate details of electrons' behaviors are the very essence of chemistry and of the insights into molecular structure we'd like to glean.

Once we are able to simulate molecules with absolute fidelity, we no longer have to make guesses or assumptions about how they will behave. The implications are vast and far-reaching. Quantum computers could aid development of clean energy and renewable chemical manufacturing, enable deeper understanding of photosynthesis, power the discovery of high-temperature superconductors, and even help illuminate the origins of life.

For quantum computers to achieve Quantum Advantage, we will need new ways of thinking to continually improve the hardware and develop software that can fully harness its potential. We're currently in a formative period as companies investigate where the technology aligns with their business needs, while a thriving ecosystem of quantum-adept individuals is emerging to innovate and power the future quantum workforce.

Computer scientists and physicists are working together to better understand the fundamental science needed to build increasingly powerful systems. We fully expect quantum technology to beget more quantum technology. Now is the time to prepare for a quantum future. By the middle of the current century, we will be able to fully exploit the exponential nature of quantum computers—and observe how they alter and progress not just science and technology, but humanity. ▧

Dr. Jay Gambetta is an IBM Fellow in the field of quantum information and computation. He joined IBM in 2011 and is now vice president of quantum computing. At IBM, he has contributed to the work on quantum validation techniques, quantum codes, improved gates and coherence, near term applications of quantum computing, the IBM Quantum Experience, and Qiskit. Prior to IBM, he held positions at the Institute for Quantum Computing in Canada and was a Post-Doctoral Fellow at Yale University. In 2014, Dr. Gambetta was named a Fellow of the American Physical Society. He holds a doctorate in physics from Griffith University in Australia and has over 90 publications with more than 10,000 citations in the field of quantum information science. For more information on quantum computing, visit www.research.ibm.com/ibm-q/.

Radical New Technologies Will Make People Transhuman

Zoltan Istvan

Everywhere we look, a "super human" future **is appearing.** Scientists, programmers, and engineers the world over are developing radical new technologies that will not only become a part of our everyday reality—an improved reality—they'll fit directly into our bodies.

Fifty years after Alvin Toffler's bestselling book *Future Shock,* it's safe to say even he did not appreciate how far human biohacking would go. But the ground we've covered in the last 50 years is nowhere near how far we'll go in the next 50. The transhumanist age is upon us, driven by the nearly exponentially evolving microchip. And it's about to get weird for humans. Our species may not even resemble mammals by the 22nd century.

We're already seeing radical advances in use today. There are contact lenses that enable people to see in the dark. We're witnessing remarkable experiments with endoskeletons attached to artificial limbs, enabling people to lift a half ton of weight. Doctors in France are replacing people's hearts with permanent robotic ones. Still others are working on brain chip implants that read thoughts and instantly communicate them with others.

There's already a multibillion dollar market for brainwave-reading headsets. Using electroencephalography (EEG) sensors that pick up brainwaves, they are able to monitor and actually decipher

365

brain activity. Some headsets can attach to Google Glass, allowing users to take a picture and post it to Facebook and Twitter—just by thinking about it! Other headsets allow users to play thought-driven video games on an iPhone. And it's all advancing rapidly.

It's been only a few years since the first digital mind-to-mind communication was accomplished. A researcher in India projected a thought to a colleague in France, and using their headsets, they understood each other. In an instant, telepathy went from science fiction to science fact. And now entrepreneurs like Elon Musk are working to bring these neural technologies to the wider market.

Transhumanism—the burgeoning field of robotic implants, prosthetics, and cyborg-like enhancements for humans—has come a long way since scientists began throwing the term around a half-century ago. What a difference a generation or two makes! Today a thriving pro-cyborg medical industry is setting the stage for trillion-dollar markets that will remake the human experience. For example, five million people in America suffer from Alzheimer's, but a new procedure involving brain implants is showing promise in restoring people's memories and improving lives. Consequently, the use of medical and microchip implants, whether in the brain or elsewhere, are expected to surge in the coming years. Millions of people worldwide already have such implants. I have one in my hand. It's truly a new age for humans.

Rich Lee, a leading biohacker—also called a grinder—told me, "Implanting magnets in your fingertips gives you the ability to feel magnetic fields. Your fingertips have lots of nerve endings jammed into one area and they are really sensitive to stimuli. Magnets twitch or move in the presence of magnetic fields, and when you implant one in your finger you can really start to feel different magnetic fields around you. So it is like a sixth sense. You can now perceive an otherwise invisible world."

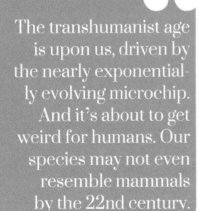

The transhumanist age is upon us, driven by the nearly exponentially evolving microchip. And it's about to get weird for humans. Our species may not even resemble mammals by the 22nd century.

While magnets may be fun, much of the new transhumanist tech will be used to extend and enhance our reach for more practical purposes. For example, tiny implants injected into the hand could yield far more efficient and secure ID and payment systems. Imagine never carrying keys or your wallets again.

Perhaps the most important development of the 21st century is genetic editing. Humans may soon be able to augment their intelligence via a shot. The designer baby era is already here— we have the ability to select hair and eye color for our offspring. Around the world, scientists are working on how to use genetic editing to end hereditary disease. Others want to put compatible plant DNA into their bodies so they can photosynthesize, and never need to eat again.

Of course, the challenge with such progress is the question of whether we're leaving behind our humanness, and consequently, our humanity. It's a good question. As the Tofflers wrote in *Future Shock*, "the man with a pacemaker or a plastic aorta is still recognizably a man. The inanimate part of his body is still relatively unimportant in terms of his personality and consciousness." This is true, but I would take this further to say that our sense of being human, indeed, our humanity, is ultimately based on being kind and just with one another. Undeniably, there have been distortions in the history and application of science and technology, but technology has consistently improved the state of the world and the standard of living. Radically so. As such, I believe the increase of technology—in and around us—will ultimately make us even *more* human.

Whatever happens, along the way humans and their advancing technologies will create paths and produce designs for our world that will transform us into new and better entities—*super*-human beings. We are standing at the doorstep of a new world and experience, and I am looking forward to embracing its promising and exciting future. ▪

Zoltan Istvan is a bestselling author, professional speaker, and a world-renowned futurist. He was the 2016 US Presidential nominee of the Transhumanist Party.

Coping with Information Overload

Jason Jackson, PhD

Books are beautiful things. ■ When you open a book, it can be either a time machine or a time capsule. You get to choose whether it transports you to another time or place, or instead delivers a snapshot of life at a particular moment, frozen in time. I can remember the exact moment I first opened *Future Shock* and read the words, core to my own scientific research pursuits, "information overload." Alvin Toffler wrote them, now 50 years ago, for the very first time in human history. In 1970, this was a new idea being born, one that we now clearly see as a trend that has shaped the experiences of the last several generations and will likely increase in influence over the next 50 years. It is also notable that at the time of Toffler's writing, he had made a connection between information overload and what we would now term post-traumatic stress disorder (PTSD), having observed a similar phenomenon in military service members returning from the Vietnam War.

In my research, focused on leadership and coping with information overload, participants were chief executive officers (CEOs), company presidents, and top directors of diverse businesses and organizations. The essence of my research was determining what types of coping mechanisms the very top leaders use to succeed, to overcome conditions of information overload and make effective leadership decisions. This was an open-minded journey, and I started it with no concept of how many coping mechanisms would emerge, nor what their core utility concepts would be. In addition to the real-world participants, I also researched literature, as far back as the late 1890s. With each book I opened, I asked, as if of a living person, a simple question: "What coping mechanism do you use to overcome information overload?"

This effort identified 16 coping mechanisms to combat the impact of information overload upon senior leader decision-making. They are outlined as elements within the Grounded Theory of Information Overload Executive Coping Mechanisms. Each mechanism has value, and it is interesting to note that each of the real-world leaders used at least one of the mechanisms once, and none of the elements fell off the menu of choices from lack of use. Additionally, the literature review found the exact same 16 coping mechanisms, even over its extensive span. No item noted failed to appear, and no additional item emerged beyond the 16 noted. This was a powerful parallel and strengthened the validity of the findings.

People often ask which is the most powerful coping mechanism, or the top two or three, to overcome information overload and make effective decisions. Interestingly, even when asked to select a single most effect element, over two-thirds of senior leaders still responded with a compound answer. The most effective mechanism is a two-part process, in which Prioritization = Categorization + Filtering.

Consider the simple task of placing items by category type in color-coded folders, and then deciding you will deal only with the red folder items today. You have categorized items via an act of color-coding, and then made them your priority for the day by filtering to red folder items only. The second-most powerful coping mechanism was simply the traditional managerial act of taking control.

The other mechanisms have merit, and in contexts other than business leadership, or senior leadership decision-making, they may have more value. One of the least reported and utilized mechanisms, tacit knowledge, wherein Tacit Knowledge = Academic Knowledge + Experiential Knowledge, may increase in value for professions such as first responders, in which knowing a profession, and story-telling or mentorship, are key elements of learning and professional success.

What is ahead these next 50 years? Two powerful trends that will be elements of our new reality are automation and artificial intelligence (AI). Efforts to develop near-human thought processes have spanned hundreds of years, from ancient automatons that processed and prayed daily prayers for royalty to cloud computing implementations in place today. Automation is growing rapidly as computer programming skills become a basic foundational professional skill and we learn the concepts of systems theory and quality management; we can effectively code repetitive tasks into automated processes. AI is more complex. The idea is that it learns on its own, and adapts, via heuristics and learning models, even extrapolating beyond the outlines used to initially teach it. The main conversations on automation and AI are that they will change the world significantly, that potentially, entire professions will be replaced and their workers displaced, out of jobs. Economists and politicians debate the potential future requirement, as a basic human right, of a universal basic income. That would indeed be radical change should it occur.

> We may not be able to control all elements of how the future plays out, but we can become better prepared. It is painful how near-obvious this statement is, but since little effort is being invested in the idea, it is worth stating. We can do better!

A separate question is what the role of AI will be in relation to humanity. Will it replace us? Or, alternatively, will it augment us? Will the choice between these branches of the future even be ours to make? These are important conversations, and we want a voice. We also need a strategy of implementation, versus being forced by lack of anticipation and preparation into crisis management once real-world events force our hands. The rate of change, and the rate of technological implementation, will continue to surprise us, to speed up, in a pattern more exponential than linear.

We may not be able to control all elements of how the future plays out, but we can become better prepared. It is painful how near-obvious this statement is, but since little effort is being invested in the idea, it is worth stating. We can do better! Imagine a world where we taught children, from kindergarten to high school graduation, not only the mechanisms of success, but also the parallel role of coping when things go wrong. Leaders need to provide a vision and a vector, to build culture and to make decisions. If they are stellar at the first three yet fail at the last—decision-making—they fail to turn thought into action, to earn positive results. So, increasing educational focus on decision-making and coping mechanisms, would increase societal return on investment. With proper educational investment, society would rise to new heights. Plus, when reality does not go as planned, we need to have optimized and practiced tools in our mental toolkit against adversity. Building better leaders should be our top goal, but this is about more than earning positive results. It is also about building in the resilience we will need when we do at times fail. Reality is not one-size-fits all. ▪

J ason Jackson, PhD, is director of the Jackson Research Institute and a professor at Purdue University Global. Previously, Jackson was a Major in the United States Air Force, serving honorably for 15 years as an aviator and acquisitions expert in 65 countries during both humanitarian and combat operations. He is currently editor-in-chief of the *International Journal of Responsible Leadership and Ethical Decision-Making* (IJRLEDM). His research interests include information overload as experienced by senior leaders, as well as cognition, artificial intelligence, and military veteran leadership within businesses. Connect with him at www.linkedin.com/in/jason-jackson-phd.

On Software Engineers and Plumbers

Dr. Timothy Chou

Rereading the text of *Future Shock*, I realized the word "computer" appears only 54 times, the word "software" appears only once, and "artificial intelligence" never appears. In many ways the world has changed much more than Mr. Toffler would have guessed, largely driven by the decreasing cost of computing, the ubiquity of networks, and the increasing sophistication of software. So while trying to predict the future is best left to futurists, I'll attempt to highlight some themes that I believe will be increasingly important.

Not just MRF (Media, Retail, and Financial Services)

In 2015 the World Economic Forum released a report[1] that said, "During the past 15 years, the internet revolution has redefined business-to-consumer (B2C) industries such as media, retail and financial services... In the next 10 years, the Internet of Things revolution will dramatically alter manufacturing, energy, agriculture, transportation and other industrial sectors of the economy which, together, account for nearly two-thirds of the global GDP."

So what is the Internet of Things? Most software has been focused on us—people. Software has been built to help us buy a book, issue a purchase order, track sales leads, recruit more employees, or communicate with others. I'm going to call these IoP (Internet of People) applications.

But People are not Things. This may seem obvious, but let's discuss five fundamental differences.

1 ■ *There will be many more Things connected to the internet than people* • John Chambers, former CEO of Cisco, has projected there will be 500 billion Things connected by 2024. That's nearly 100 times the number of people on the planet. I recently heard from the CIO of a large healthcare provider, who said that in their hospitals more Things are connected than People. United Rentals has 10 times the number of construction machines connected than employees.

2 ■ Things can exist in places where People aren't • Things can be in your stomach in the form of a smart pill. Things can be a mile underground in a coal mine. Things can be out in the middle of the Australian outback. Things can be where people aren't.

3 ■ Things have more to say • People talk to IoP applications primarily through a keyboard, mouse, or touch screen. Things, on the other hand, have much more to say. A modern day wind turbine has over 500 sensors, delivering information such as wind speed and direction, blade rotation, speed, power generated, component temperature, vibration, noise levels.

4 ■ Things can talk much more frequently • An average person can type at 200 characters per minute, three to four characters per second. In the coal mining industry there is a machine called a longwall shearer. It's three football fields long and 30 meters high. As it digs through a coal seam, a mile underground, it forms what they call an artificial roof. Every once in a while the artificial roof collapses, so they have to dig out their $100 million machine. In order to try to predict roof collapse, they mounted vibration sensors on the machine that operate at 10,000Hz. That's data arriving 10,000 times per second—and by the way, much larger than an 8-bit character.

5 ■ Things can be programmed, People can't • We can, of course, debate this, but Things and machines can be programmed, People can't. Increasingly machines are being software defined. Many of you are familiar with a Tesla, sometimes called a smartphone with four wheels. What you might not realize is the Porsche Panamera in 2016 had 2 million lines of code. In 2017 it jumped to 100,000,000 lines of code. Things can be programmed, People can't.

> The service sector represents more than 85% of the US economy. So what is service? Is it answering the phone nicely from Bangalore? Is it flipping burgers at In-and-Out? No. Service is the delivery of information that is personal and relevant to you.

So if Things are not People and People are not Things, why would software built for the Internet of People work for the Internet of Things? We are still at the early stages of IoT software. Advances in autonomous driving and the associated societal and economic impacts are just the tip of the iceberg. And unless we're all moving to Mars, operating the infrastructure of the planet (power, water, food, etc.) is going to be non-optional.

Service is Information, Personal and Relevant to You

A few months ago I had breakfast at Joannie's Café in Palo Alto with the CEO of a company that builds machines for the semiconductor industry. I asked him how many machines he had in the field, and he said around 10,000-20,000. The precision of his answer should have been my first clue. I went on to ask him, "How much service revenue do you generate?" to which he responded with the universal sign of a goose egg. I asked "Why zero?" to which he replied "No one wants to pay for service."

Of course the reason no one pays for service is he's defined service as break-fix support. Of course anyone who has just bought a $250,000 machine would assume it would work, so why pay for service?

The service sector represents more than 85% of the US economy. So what is service? Is it answering the phone nicely from Bangalore? Is it flipping burgers at In-and-Out? No. Service is the delivery of information that is personal and relevant to you. That could be the hotel concierge giving you directions to the best Shangdong Chinese restaurant in town, or your doctor telling you that, based on your genome and lifestyle, you should be on a specific medication. Service is personal and relevant information.

In 2004, the Oracle Support organization studied 100 million service requests and found that over 99.9 percent of them had been answered with already known information. Service is information on how to maintain or optimize the performance, security, and availability of the software. Of course, if I can tell you how to maintain and optimize the performance, security, and availability of the software, then the next logical step is to do it for you. In the software industry you know this as software-as-a-service. The company that builds the product, services the product. Salesforce, ServiceNow, and Blackbaud all build enterprise software products and service them.

> A few years ago I helped Stanford students start the first hackathon at the university. While I didn't drink Red Bull and stay up for 24 hours, it did open my eyes. What I saw was software being built in an entirely different way than we had all been classically trained.

But, let's get back to my CEO. I asked him, do you think a customer would pay for information on how to maintain or optimize the performance, security, and availability of the product? And as the builder of the product you are the aggregation point of all this information since every customer calls, texts, or emails you first when they need information. What if you were to aggregate all of this information, and furthermore, what if you connected all of your machines? Wouldn't you know more about how to best maintain, or optimize the performance, availability, and security of the machine? And if you were to charge just 1 percent a month of the purchase price of the machine for the digital service product, you'd be able to double the revenues and quadruple the margins of your company. Ultimately, if the company knows what to do to maintain and optimize the product, then clearly it can take the last step and offer the product-as-a-service.

Any company that builds agricultural, life science, construction, healthcare, packaging, manufacturing, printing, power generation, or transportation machines has the opportunity to build a new high-growth, high-margin recurring revenue digital service business. Service is not break-fix. Service is personal and relevant information.

Software Plumbers, not Hydraulic Engineers

I recently reviewed a paper on recommendations for changes in the computer science curriculum at a four-year college. While we always have to be thinking about the core CS curriculum, I think there is a big gap in the education system globally.

A few years ago I helped Stanford students start the first hackathon at the university. While I didn't drink Red Bull and stay up for 24 hours, it did open my eyes. What I saw was software being built in an entirely different way than we had all been classically trained. In my analogy it looked a lot more like plumbing. Students were assembling new applications from hundreds of software parts. In an age of cloud computing, open source, and web services, this has suddenly become possible.

But did they learn any of these skills in their computer science curriculum? No. If we're to use plumbing as an analogy, getting a computer science degree from a major institution is similar to being taught how to build a P-trap [the curved pipe underneath sinks] in the field of plumbing. In order to build a better P-trap you need to understand fluid dynamics, material science, and mechanical engineering principles.

While designers of P-traps need these skills, plumbers don't need to understand the physics or engineering. Rather, they learn through apprenticeship with a master plumber which P-trap to install and when. They don't need to understand how it works.

Now take this analogy to the world of software. Four-year colleges are designed to teach a computer science curriculum focused on teaching the fundamental principles required to design better P-traps.

While this knowledge is certainly necessary for some software jobs, there is 10 or 100 times more demand for software plumbers. With so many software parts available, we can build complex software applications by assembling components to satisfy needs across many industries, including agriculture, construction, oil & gas, energy, transportation, healthcare, and financial services.

Software is a unique technology, which costs nothing to create other than mental energy. And with the advent of cloud computing, the cost to deliver and manage the software is headed to zero. Unlike the electrification of the planet, we do not have to wait for physical infrastructure to be purchased, built, shipped, and installed.

The challenge of building good software applications is combining an understanding of the challenges of the domain and knowing what tools you have to build the future. It should be no surprise that college students developed social networks. But how do you bring an understanding of textiles, mining, specialty chemical manufacturing, or genetics together with an understanding of the software parts catalog?

This kind of software plumber education does not exist today, and I am not arguing for changing computer science curriculums at four-year universities. Instead, maybe we need to revive trade schools. It wasn't very long ago that there was a thriving trade school education system in both the United States and Europe. These focused on turning out welders or auto mechanics. Why shouldn't there be a software plumbing trade school? And in the four-year universities, why not start out any STEM program with one year of basic plumbing? After all, whether you're in archeology or zoology, software plumbing should be more basic than first-year chemistry, which we require of nearly everyone today.

Software has already changed our consumer lives, whether that's watching TV or buying shoes. In the next 50 years it will change the planet. ▪

Dr. **Timothy Chou** has been lucky enough to have a career spanning academia, successful (and not-so-successful) startups, and large corporations. He was one of a handful of people to ever hold the president title at Oracle. Today he serves on the Board of Directors of Blackbaud and Teradata. Dr. Chou started his career at one of the original Kleiner Perkins startups, Tandem Computers. He continues to invest in startups in cloud computing, analytics, IoT, and artificial intelligence. He was also fortunate enough to start teaching computer science at Stanford University in 1982. In 2006 he launched CS309A (cs309a.stanford.edu) the first class on cloud computing at Stanford.

1. http://www3.weforum.org/docs/WEFUSA_IndustrialInternet_Report2015.pdf

Future Hope:
Tech and the Co-Economy
Can Help Solve Our
Global Challenges

Maciej Kranz

Amid today's postindustrial society, technology itself is often blamed for many of the world's most epic challenges.

■ Market upheavals... disconnected relationships... accelerated speed of change... information overload... nerve-shattering stress and disorientation... lessened privacy—these are some of the headaches often attributed to 21st-century technologies such as the Internet of Things (IoT).

This is an ironic and misconceived "glass-half-empty" perspective, despite the truths it contains. The irony is that, yes, there are tech problems that need to be fixed, but in reality, today's technology breakthroughs have more upside potential than at any time in history to improve not only business performance but also the quality of life for people, society, and the entire planet.

I think our future actually hinges on today's technological advances like never before. And the potential for positive change today is greater than ever before.

Five exponential technologies in particular—IoT, artificial intelligence (AI), blockchain, fog computing, and 5th generation networks (5G)—that have improved business performance are now being turned toward solving many of humankind's most enduring societal problems.

When interconnected, the internet, people, IoT, AI, blockchain, fog, and 5G can provide transformational value for everyone. Collectively, they're like the coupled human body and the brain. I like to think of IoT and 5G as the body, creating and transmitting data and sometimes acting on the decisions based on this data. AI is like the brain, turning that data into intelligence for smarter decisions.

Blockchain is like an antibody that keeps the system secure and healthy, while fog computing is like an interconnected nerve that keeps each and every part running smoothly, from head to toe, or end to end in the value chain.

What's so inspiring now is that innovators are increasingly expanding the aperture of their focus from business applications to societal issues such as hunger, poverty, conservation, pollution, disease, and global warming. And they're co-innovating new generations of digital solutions along with broader partner ecosystems—globally *and* locally—converging these technologies on the network to make smarter decisions in what I call the emerging Co-Economy.

Examples of progress abound, but here is a sampling of local game changers we can cross-pollinate globally to grow and shape a better future for us all.

Tech Transformations in Agriculture

Let's start with the $6 trillion agriculture industry, which confronts critical supply-and-demand issues. While the global population will soar more than 26 percent by 2050, arable land has shrunk by 33 percent the past three decades and continues to disappear at the alarming rate of "one Great Britain every two years." Soil erosion, deforestation, droughts, water shortages, and mass urbanization, all have contributed to the growing challenge of feeding an estimated 9.6 billion mouths in the next 30 years with vastly fewer natural resources.

It is clear that traditional agricultural approaches will not be enough. As a result, leading farmers are increasingly turning to IoT-connected technologies to address these issues. BI Intelligence predicts that the number of IoT device installations in agriculture will hit 75 million by 2020, growing 20 percent annually.

I see evidence of this about an hour's drive south of where I live in Silicon Valley. There's actually another valley called Lettuce Valley centered around the city of Salinas. This is the source of the majority of packaged vegetables and lettuce sold in US supermarkets. This is also increasingly the place where agriculture and food industries meet the technology world. As I visit lettuce processing plants or vineyards, I see exponential technologies used to collect data on weather, soil, air quality, and crop maturity, enabling farmers to make smarter decisions on everything from soil conditions, water quality and usage, nutrient runoff, and sustainability.

At a recent summit of the THRIVE AgTech accelerator, I met the leader of a company that developed a missing element needed to use blockchain for food safety—edible bar codes. By spraying safe and edible bar codes directly on fruits or vegetables during their initial processing, their source can be verified anywhere in the world in a matter of minutes with blockchain. A decentralized ledger shared and authenticated by partners, blockchain provides a single source of truth about the state of the land, inventory, contracts, and transactions. When combined with IoT, blockchain helps make multi-organizational systems more efficient, and can instantly and precisely identify any food safety issues, such as pinpointing where food spoilage occurred in the supply chain, enabling quick remedial action.

Far across the Pacific at one of Cisco's Co-Innovation Centers in Sydney, Australia, we incubated the "Farm Tough Decision Platform" along with multiple public and private entities, combining their specialized expertise. This low-power wireless network, combined with AI and data analytics on soil and weather conditions, improved crop yields, operational efficiency, and profitability while significantly decreasing production costs. With some 78 percent of the world's poor living in rural areas and relying on farming for their food and livelihoods, such efficiency advances can also raise the incomes of the impoverished and improve their lives while helping to address the global problem of shrinking arable land for food supply.

Fog computing is another vital technology used to process and balance data loads throughout the network—from the edge of operations to the cloud. With IoT, AI, and fog computing, indoor vertical farming company Plenty can automatically measure temperature, humidity, and CO_2 levels, and then analyze and identify ways to improve growth rates and flavor in near real time. Plenty is quietly inventing the future of agriculture with these technologies in many innovative ways. When I visited their headquarters in a South San Francisco warehouse, I had to don protective gear before entering a high-tech lab. I saw rows and rows of 8- to 16-foot racks that looked like living walls, where kale, arugula, chard, cilantro, mixed greens, mustard, and many other varieties were growing vertically in small 1-2-inch pods. They're also testing berries and vegetables in other locations, demonstrating that such vertical farms located near major metropolitan areas will help to replenish our food supply without impacting precious arable land.

> What's so inspiring now is that innovators are increasingly expanding the aperture of their focus from business applications to societal issues such as hunger, poverty, conservation, pollution, disease, and global warming.

There are half a billion farms around the world, most of them small (less than four acres). Innovations such as indoor vertical farming or cell agriculture can effectively augment the outputs of such farms but in the foreseeable future will not replace them. We will not eradicate hunger and poverty without focusing on the rural areas where most hungry and poor live today, which is why many government policies focus extensively on connecting cities and surrounding areas into joint agro-industrial complexes. Technologies such as 5G and low Earth orbit satellite constellation promise to deliver high-speed connectivity to all the farms. Increasingly, farmers are also forming data co-operatives to reduce the cost of access and operation of these data-driven solutions.

In one ingenious example of 5G's potential to connect rural areas, the government-funded Agricultural Engineering Precision Innovation Centre in southwest England placed 5G smart collars on 50 cows. Called the Me+Moo project, dairy farmers can monitor the health of the cows and control a robotic milking system, all of which provides them with greater, faster, and more precise data to care for, feed, and milk their livestock at optimum times.

Combating Poverty and Spreading the Wealth

Such exponential technologies are also tools that can be used to combat poverty and help to distribute wealth more equitably.

Global poverty has declined from over 25 percent in 2002 to just 10 percent of the world's population in 2015. That's clearly one of the great achievements of our time, yet there is so much more that can be done to attain greater financial equity. After all, there are still 700 million people living in poverty in developed countries, including the United States, and billions more around the world. IoT, 5G, blockchain, and innovative fintech apps, combined with sound economic and social policies, are helping break the cycle of poverty around the globe by connecting infrastructure, communications, and people, thus paving the way for us to achieve the UN 2030 Agenda for Sustainable Development goal of ending hunger and poverty in the world.

As one example, blockchain can give people in countries with lax laws, high rates of corruption, and fragmented or nonexistent systems of record a way to establish ownership of land and other assets. In the African country of Ghana, for example, the nonprofit Bitland introduced a blockchain-based digital registry of land ownership in 2016 that combines transactions with GPS data and satellite photos to help guarantee property rights. They plan to expand into Nigeria and Kenya this year.

Because blockchain records are unalterable, they can also be used to establish credit. This allows owners to open bank accounts and borrow money, paving the way to sound economic futures. And, while blockchain is most known as the underlying technology of Bitcoin, it is increasingly being recognized for applications in many industries, from the supply chain to healthcare. This makes the technology scalable, extensible, and flexible, and given the right political conditions, this type of wealth building could lead entire generations out of poverty for good.

Then there are the fintech apps and microservices that create banking systems and give people the ability to borrow and transfer money in areas where the existing systems do not serve the poor. Opportunity International is one such organization. Opportunity not only provides microfinancing, but also helps educate borrowers to make better financial decisions. Perhaps the most successful microfinance application is Kenya's M-Pesa, originally conceived as an efficient method to make payments on microloans but rapidly adopted by Kenyans as a way to send money from urban centers back to rural hometowns. This technology has helped lift 2 percent of the country's households out of extreme poverty since 2008, according to the MIT economist Tavneet Suri.

Protecting the Environment and Sustaining Resources

For the first time in history, more people live in cities than rural areas. That percentage could reach 66 percent of the world's population by mid-century, putting ever-increasing strain on the environment and draining natural resources. Fortunately, a proliferation of "smart cities" around the globe are putting these exponential technologies to good use, not only to enhance urban services and quality of life, but also to improve environmental conditions.

In Beijing, for example, I have seen incredible transformations over the past 25 years. Today, smart fleets of bicycles, buses, trains, and ride-hailing services driven by IoT technologies are making urban transportation more accessible, efficient, and less wasteful. In Barcelona, I am always struck by its citywide Wi-Fi network linked to sensors, software, and a data analytics platform. This not only enriches the experience of visitors, but enhances IoT-enabled urban services, dramatically reducing traffic jams and pollution, as well as water, light, and energy usage.

In Chicago, a citywide IoT network of sensors called the "Array of Things" serves as a sort of fitness tracker for the city, collecting data on air quality, climate, traffic, and other metrics. The information is sent to an open data portal where user groups can consult it and process data for a range of applications. In London, where up to 9,000 deaths per year are attributed to air pollution, Drayson Technologies has been testing sensors that are distributed to bicycle couriers and a fleet of fuel-cell cars. The sensors, which transmit data to smartphones via Bluetooth, allow Drayson to create real-time maps showing air pollution levels around the city.

Can smart cities be scaled? A team of tech providers, the UK government, and the city of Manchester are trying to answer that question with a project called CityVerve. CityVerve is developing IoT-based infrastructure for everything from culture, healthcare, the environment, energy, and travel, making Manchester a more sustainable city while also providing a blueprint for others.

Powerful Partnerships and Technology in the Co-Economy

When it comes to creating and scaling these complex solutions, I have learned from experience that no single entity can do it alone. The diverse expertise and accelerated pace of change in our digital era makes us increasingly dependent on the Co-Economy. This is a new approach provoking structural changes to business, embracing diverse, partner ecosystems, including horizontal technology, vertical market, and hyper-local or regional domain specialists. These internal and external ecosystems comprise startups, large companies, customers, academia, researchers, standards bodies, government agencies, and others who work more closely, collaboratively, and equally to co-develop and deliver disruptive solutions.

In the Co-Economy, customers take a much more active role in co-innovating solutions, not only for their own organizations but also so that they can be shared and scaled across industries and communities. Principles driving technology solutions in the Co-Economy include decentralized networks, trusted and open collaborations, open standards, agile processes and cultures, interoperable devices and systems, digital orchestration—and a mutual priority to focus on both business and societal goals. As these rich ecosystems and exponential technologies mature, the benefits of local innovations will scale more quickly anywhere. With the Co-Economy, we get the best of both worlds—localization *and* globalization.

A Call to Action: Connect, Collaborate, Co-Innovate

Despite all the world's challenges and doomsday scenarios, I am optimistic about the future of our planet and people. With impending rollouts of 5G and new terrestrial, low Earth orbit satellites, we will connect the remaining half of the world population (including rural communities not connected today), along with many more billions of smart devices, thus providing a strong, global foundation for the Co-Economy.

Most significantly though, we are in the midst of a once-in-a-generation transition where interconnected tech innovations are potentially more transformative than ever before. IoT, AI, blockchain, fog computing, and 5G—these are not just overhyped buzzwords. They're not just a vision. They're not just the future. They're real, and they are here and now.

Thousands of organizations in myriad industries across the globe are using these technologies to transform their businesses. Combined with the Co-Economy, and new global priorities, they're also embarking on an exciting new journey to transform our everyday lives for the better. I firmly believe we can overcome many of our most epic challenges by connecting, collaborating, and co-innovating technology solutions with a common purpose for the greater good. ▪

Maciej Kranz brings 30 years of networking industry experience to his position as Cisco's vice president of strategic innovation. In this role, he leads efforts to incubate new businesses and accelerate innovation internally and externally with customer and partner ecosystems through a global network of Co-Innovation Centers. Previously, he built Cisco's $250 million Connected Industries group focused on the Internet of Things from the ground up. He also pioneered dozens of IoT projects across multiple industries, wrote the New York Times best seller Building the Internet of Things, serves on the faculty of Singularity University, publishes an IoT newsletter, and spearheads an industry leadership community.

The Future Shock of Medicine: How AI Will Transform Disease, Death, and Doctors

José M. Morey, MD
& Nora Haney, MD, MBA

Toffler's *Future Shock* focuses on technology, business, and society, but also indirectly sheds light on the life cycle of the human body all the way down to the level of the cell. ■ It would be difficult for any physician reading this book to compare future shock to anything but cancer. In its most basic form, cancer is the growth of abnormal cells which invade and spread into tissues other than those of their origin. The greater the rate of change and the more numerous the systems affected, the more disastrous the repercussions. And sure enough, Toffler makes this hard and fast comparison out loud in his final remarks of the book. "There is no facile way to treat this wild growth, this cancer in history," he writes. "There is no magic medicine, either, for curing the unprecedented disease it bears in its rushing wake: future shock... Yet the basic thrust of this book is diagnosis. For diagnosis precedes cure, and we cannot begin to help ourselves until we become sensitively conscious of the problem."

Toffler's overarching idea of future shock is of a rate of societal change so rapid that it is out of control. Yet, in medicine there are some blessings associated with increased rate of change. Acute changes have the potential to lead to an acute diagnosis. Diagnosis begets treatment, and in a perfect world, begets cure with reversion to some semblance of previous lifestyle. Our bodies have ways to do this naturally. When change occurs in our DNA, the human body's proofreading system of replication can detect and rid itself of the cell with the altered code. Sometimes, though, it is the lack of change that allows the damaged cell to live on. If the cell looks pretty similar to the original, it evades detection and can go on replicating and invading. It is these seemingly indolent diseases, with a slow rate of change, that do not allow for diagnosis. Delayed knowledge results in late, if any, treatment, to a point where cure may no longer be possible.

Similar dynamics exist in the treatment of cancer as exist in the healthy human's response to damaged cells. The goal of therapy is first, to detect the change and second, to stop the change. In a very general view, chemotherapy works because the toxins target the cells which divide most rapidly. The loud, in-your-face changes are observed and are then acted upon.

But beware of the change you cannot see. Sometimes, there are no outward signs that change is taking place. These symptoms would be the equivalent of Toffler's idea of social dilemmas, or the forewarning of impending shock. In order to help our own society, we would have to acknowledge that these changes were occurring and analyze their consequences for the future. But in slow-growing disease, the patient is at a disadvantage. There is no ability to be cognizant. This is where the future of medicine may benefit greatly from the addition of artificial intelligence (AI).

The future of medicine will be founded on a P6 model of medicine: participatory, predictive, preventative, panomic, public, and precise. AI will be the cornerstone of this new foundation of ability to use panomic longitudinal data to augment the work of physicians and to be able to make predictive/preventative diagnoses and interventions, both precisely for each individual with the patient's active participation, and for the public well-being. The only way to keep hidden changes in check is by using machines that can see better than we can. Here, seeing better actually means seeing the future. The success of AI in medicine relies on its ability to predict disease, rather than wait for it to occur. This goes against the grain of today's gold standard treatment approach, being reactionary to the presence of disease: "break bone, fix bone."

> In a very general view, chemotherapy works because the toxins target the cells which divide most rapidly. The loud, in-your-face changes are observed and are then acted upon. But beware of the change you cannot see.

Toffler's idea of cognizance revolves around diagnosis, but to best advance the field of medicine, it will have to be extended to include prevention. We will likely never be able to eradicate all disease. With panomics, we may be able to make the occurrence of most diseases less likely. AI will move the needle forward, from addressing disease to maintaining health and well-being. It will not just add years to our lives, but life to our years.

Prevention is best employed when rising-risk patients are identified early, before they convert to high-risk patients (who drive the vast majority of healthcare costs). Prevention requires intervention before the disease has either taken root or evolved into an end-stage form from which there may be no easy, safe, or cost-effective treatments. Diagnosis may precede cure, as highlighted by Toffler, but prevention certainly precedes change. The future of medicine will be measured by its ability to control the rate of change before the change has begun. With the help of AI, it is believed that worldwide health disparities can be best combated well before the shock has had the opportunity to permanently debilitate.

When disease does occur, AI will be able to create targeted therapies for precision medicine. Long past will be the days of one-size-fits-all treatments, where the same algorithms are followed for each patient. We will have bespoke medications based on a panomic view of the individual, from the metabolomics to microbiomics to environomics to genomics. They will even include 3D printed capsules tailored for release based on one's physiologic digestion and uptake.

AI will allow the physician to access augmented biomarkers that go beyond just point-of-care respiratory/cardiac rates or basic metabolic panels checked yearly at the office. Physicians will be able to stream real-time data from wearable and smart textiles and implantables integrated through the Internet of Things (IoT) to have a 360-degree view of each patient in real time. AI will further monitor this data stream and alert appropriate clinicians or first responders when it may be time to intervene in case of emergencies or when cautionary trends are identified.

Death itself may be viewed very differently. Imagine the ability to create digital replicas that can be distributed across various ledgers for continuation of thought and experiences after death. Greater than this, however, will be the ability to determine the when, where, and how of one's passing. AI will allow us to reach a near nirvana state where there will be but one certain thing in life... taxes.

José Morey, MD, is considered the first Intergalactic Doctor, and is a leader in exponential technology innovation by leading multidisciplinary teams that sit at the epicenter of genetic intelligence, biotechnology, precision medicine, AI, and aerospace. Dr. Morey is Chief Medical Innovation Officer for Liberty BioSecurity, was Associated Chief Health Officer for IBM Watson Health, is Chief Innovation Officer for Hyperloop Transportation Technologies, and is the Medical Technology and Artificial Intelligence Adviser for NASA iTech, which is an incubator created to identify and develop novel biotechnology to meet the 2030 Mars Mission objectives and deep space colonization.

Nora M Haney, MD, MBA, is a current urology resident at Johns Hopkins Hospital. After receiving her undergraduate degree in biomedical engineering at Columbia University and her medical training, as well as masters of business administration, from Tulane University, she is looking forward to combining surgery, research, and business to help create sustainable medical advancements for improving quality of life after cancer.

The Future of
Venture Investing
in Science

Stephen R. Waite

As we celebrate the 50th anniversary of the publication of *Future Shock*, we find ourselves at an interesting crossroads with respect to the future of venture investing. ▪ In Chapter 20 of *the book*, Toffler made the cogent observation: "In a world of accelerated change… time horizons must be extended." (p. 406 of the hardcover edition).

Toffler goes on to discuss why longer time horizons are required in such a world. What I find interesting as a long-time researcher and practitioner of investing, finance, and economics, is that time horizons among companies and investors appear to be doing just the opposite. Although difficult to quantify precisely, corporate and investor time horizons appear to be shrinking, not expanding.

We see corporate and investor myopia in many places today. Corporations who have publicly traded equity on the major stock exchanges, and the legions of research analysts working for the Wall Street investment banks who cover them, seem intensely focused on quarterly earnings reports. A quarterly earnings miss can send a stock reeling. Corporate executives seem to spend an inordinate amount of time managing analyst expectations in an attempt to minimize quarterly earnings surprises. I have spoken with some prominent CEOs of publicly traded companies over the years who have personally lamented the shift toward shorter time horizons on Wall Street. They believe shortsightedness is a detriment to the functioning of a healthy and prosperous enterprise.

Equally notable, and perhaps even more important from a longer-term economic perspective, is the obvious shift toward shorter investor time horizons among venture investors—those brave and risk-seeing souls who back startup and early-stage companies against unfavorable odds.

Long-time venture investor Douglas Jamison and I wrote a book on this subject, titled *Venture Investing in Science*, published by Columbia University Press in June 2017. In the book, Doug and I noted that venture investors—especially those in Silicon Valley—had time horizons that appear to be shrinking. The nearsightedness was reflected in a migration away from investing in companies seeking to commercialize transformative technologies grounded in what we called "deep science." Such companies often take not quarters or several years to mature, but decades.

Deep science is revolutionary. Newtonian mechanics, Maxwell's theory of electromagnetism, quantum mechanics, and information theory have fundamentally altered the way we view nature and the cosmos. These advances in deep science over the centuries have inspired research and spawned a cornucopia of new inventions and innovations. Some of these deep science-based inventions and innovations have been massively transformative, unleashing waves of Schumpeterian *creative destruction* that fundamentally alter the economic and business landscape over the course of decades. New types of computer memory devices or computing architectures steeped in deep science that have the potential to transform the business landscape can easily take over a decade to commercialize. Investing in such companies requires the kind of time horizons Toffler discussed. The rise and heyday of Silicon Valley was rooted in venture investors who had the type of time horizon required to nurture such companies.

While technological change has indeed accelerated in the 50 years since the publication of *Future Shock*, there has been a pronounced shift in venture investing, away from deep science and the longer-term investment horizons required to successfully fund such ventures. In 1985, deep science-related venture investments accounted for over 55 percent of total US venture capital funding and over 50 percent of total venture capital deals. By 2014, the share of deep science venture investments, both in terms of dollars and of deal volumes, had declined by a whopping 50 percent. We see in this data a pronounced migration of venture capital in the past two decades, away from deep science-based companies.

> Investing in such companies requires the kind of time horizons Toffler discussed. The rise and heyday of Silicon Valley was rooted in venture investors who had the type of time horizon required to nurture such companies.

The primary implication of the shift in venture investing time horizons, as Doug and I discuss in *Venture Investing in Science*, is that it occurs within an economy that is less dynamic and prosperous. This is evidenced over time, in slower productivity growth and stagnation in improvement of living standards. The hard or deep science-based companies being starved of venture capital today historically have been the companies that produced the biggest economic payoff in the form of rising productivity and prosperity. It was these companies and their farsighted venture investors who backed some of the premier deep science companies that are household names today.

Venture capital has no peer in the history of funding transformative technology companies. There is no other form of capital that has come close to producing the type of economic payoff venture investing has produced over the decades. The statistics speak for themselves. Venture capital-backed companies account for a massive 85 percent of total research and development spending, almost 40 percent of total revenues and employment, and nearly two-thirds of total stock market capitalization. It is truly astonishing how such a relatively tiny pool of capital can have such large economic effects.

As US venture capital has migrated away from longer-term, transformative, deep science-based deals, we are seeing a kind of vacuum in the investment landscape. I see this regularly today in the advisory work I do with emerging technology companies. I am frequently asked by the founders and CEOs of deep science enterprises where they should seek funding. Silicon Valley, once an oasis for capital for deep science ventures, has become more of a desert.

Increasingly, deep science companies are forced to look overseas for funding. There is nothing wrong with seeking funding overseas, but it can get expensive in terms of travel, time, and effort.

There are other sources of venture investment capital, such as angel funding and crowd funding. Angel and crowd funding can be crucial early on, but funding deep science companies often requires a great deal more capital than these sources typically provide. In recent years, we have seen the rise of new forms of financing, such as Initial Coin Offerings (ICOs). There is still a great deal of regulatory uncertainty surrounding such offerings in the US, and it remains to be seen if ICOs can become a viable funding source for deep science companies.

> If Toffler is correct that a world of accelerated change requires extensive time horizons, it is not at all clear how the venture investing in deep science issue gets resolved. At the time of this writing there is little evidence of diminishing corporate or investor shortsightedness.

Some might wonder about the future of the US banking system and its role in supporting deep science companies. At last glance, there were over $1.5 trillion of reserve balances with Federal Reserve banks. One of the noteworthy economic developments that was discussed by Toffler in some of his other books was the migration away from tangible-asset intensive companies. Such companies were the mainstay of the Industrial Age. Commercial banks, having expertise in tangible asset-based funding, were a common source of funding for industrial companies of yesteryear.

The rise of information technology over the decades has wrought a major shift in the structure of corporate balance sheets. What we see with information tech companies is a predominance of intangible assets on company balance sheets. Commercial banks lack the type of expertise to fund such intangible asset-intensive enterprises. Given this lack of expertise and given the increasing penetration of information technology in the economy, we can expect to see a diminishing role for the US commercial banking system.

While it would be marvelous to put the $1.5 trillion of bank reserves to work funding transformative, deep science-based companies and the "moonshot" enterprises of tomorrow, the likelihood of this happening any time soon is not high. What's more likely is that US commercial banks will become more marginalized in supporting the kind of deep science-based innovation that drives a dynamic, highly productive, and prosperous economic landscape.

If Toffler is correct that a world of accelerated change requires extensive time horizons, it is not at all clear how the venture investing in deep science issue gets resolved. At the time of this writing there is little evidence of diminishing corporate or investor shortsightedness. Wall Street investment banks have an important role to play, but at present they are afflicted with the same nearsightedness we see in publicly traded corporations and venture capital today. To compound matters, as George Gilder has observed, US government policy now favors the rapid-trading and short-term arbitrage of the big investment banks over the longer-term commitments that foster economic prosperity.

In the current deep science landscape, there is emerging interest in technologies rooted deeply in quantum mechanics. We are in the early stages of a (r)evolution in computing away from bits and toward qubits. Qubits are the mainstay of quantum processors that lie at the heart of quantum computing. The US federal government, as well as governments overseas in Europe and Asia, are investing billions in quantum-based technologies. China alone is investing over $15 billion in next-generation quantum innovations. What is not clear is whether other investors, outside of federal governments, will step in to help fund startup and early-stage quantum computing companies.

> The main issue confronting almost all of these US-based companies is a lack of venture funding. Some have been driven out of business while others are teetering on the edge of insolvency. This is disheartening, given the long-term need for new materials for computing and other applications.

It should be noted there are large established companies investing in commercializing quantum computers and other quantum technologies. IBM has demonstrated a 50-qubit quantum computer. Google has produced a 72-qubit quantum computer. While large established corporations will play a role in this arena, rest assured it will take entrepreneurs backed by investors with investment horizons well beyond the quarter to propel transformative, quantum-based innovations in the years to come.

At the same time quantum computers are emerging, we are seeing the proliferation of a new class of advanced 2D and 3D nanomaterials that possess unique properties beyond the silicon that powers today's digital technologies. I have spent a great deal of time working with emerging advanced nanomaterials companies. The main issue confronting almost all of these US-based companies is a lack of venture funding. Some have been driven out of business while others are teetering on the edge of insolvency. This is disheartening, given the long-term need for new materials for computing and other applications. One suspects that the future of technology is carbon-based, as opposed to silicon-based, but the path toward carbon-based technologies is not at all clear, at least in the United States.

Being an optimist by nature, I am hopeful that a new class of venture investors will emerge in the coming years. I do recognize there are numerous impediments and obstacles in the US venture investing landscape that are likely to act as headwinds in the foreseeable future. While I have yet to devise a new model for venture investing in deep science enterprises, I believe strongly that any such model will embrace the type of longer-term time horizon Toffler stated was required in a world of accelerated change.

There has been some discussion in Silicon Valley over the past several years about creating a stock exchange focused on the long term. This discussion itself is a testament to the myopia plaguing the major US stock exchanges. It is envisioned that a long-term stock exchange (LTSE) would help address the myopic focus on quarterly earnings and seek to encourage investors and companies to make decisions based on a longer-term time horizon.

Such an exchange would be a natural home for the deep science-based ventures that are critical to fostering economic dynamism. An application to the US Securities and Exchange Commission (SEC) for registration of a LTSE as a national securities exchange was approved on May 10, 2019. The recent approval of the LTSE by the SEC is a ray of sunshine in an otherwise darkened and cloudy myopic US venture investor skyline. It will be interesting to see how the LTSE evolves in the future.

Peter Drucker once observed that every organization needs one core competency: innovation. Innovation is vital to every single organization on the planet. It is not a quarterly activity. It requires vision and execution that extend far beyond the quarter. Deep science-based innovation is a long-term endeavor. In terms of driving productivity and prosperity, it has no peer. Venture investing is crucial to deep science-based enterprises.

Make no mistake. A Silicon Valley of the future—a Carbon Valley, perhaps—will be populated with venture investors who are farsighted. Again, as Alvin Toffler noted in *Future Shock*, in a world of accelerated change, time horizons must be extended. Nowhere is this truer today than in the world of venture investing in deep science-based enterprises.

Stephen Waite is a corporate advisor, strategist, researcher, and author. For the past two decades, he has worked closely with entrepreneurs and CEOs around the world in the nano/quantum, advanced materials, cybersecurity, and next-generation media segments. He is the author of *Quantum Investing* and co-author of *Venture Investing in Science, Boomernomics*, and *Graphene Technology*. When not advising clients and writing books, Steve can be found in the studio playing, recording, and mixing music.

Future Shock is More Relevant than Ever

Hazel Henderson

Future Shock, first published in 1970, sounded the first contemporary alarm on all the ways science and technology change human societies, but anxiety over progressive change is probably as old as progressive change. ■ The protests in 18th-century England of the Luddites, who smashed textile machinery, clearly illustrated that people fear and resent technological change over which they have no control. These ordinary people felt the effects on their lives—lost jobs, bypassed skills, and sidelining of whole communities, regions, even countries—of constantly changing forms of economic development.

I first met Alvin Toffler in 1968 at a conference of the American Institute of Planners (back then it was still okay in the USA to talk about how we planned!), in which we were both presenting. My paper, "Access to Media: A Problem in Democracy," was reprinted in the *Columbia Journalism Review* (Spring, 1969). Alvin and I connected during lunch over the similarities in the views of our presentations.

When we met again at another conference of the Association of National Advertisers in 1969, just before the launch of *Future Shock*, by which time I had also met Heidi and we had found even more commonalities. I also remember, in late 1970 when *Future Shock* was climbing the bestseller lists, meeting the Tofflers at their home in Manhattan and seeing that their living room was crowded with desks and people answering phones. They lamented that they couldn't keep up with all the calls or keep hiring ever more people to help field them! They soon realized it was a hopeless effort to try to be fully responsive to the millions reading their book.

As *Future Shock* took off, the Tofflers turned to their continuing love of futures research and studying the evolution of the human condition the world over. I was awed by their shared diligence and scholarship as mutually respecting partners. At that time, the dominant culture in Western countries was deeply patriarchal, and even in the academic and publishing worlds, women scientists, writers, and scholars were rarely recognized. Al and Heidi collaborated on every aspect of their research and writing in *Future Shock*, but because of the culture, only Alvin Toffler was listed as the author. Heidi was included in the book's dedication, along with their daughter, Karen. I was dealing with similar asymmetries in my own writing, and once even thought of changing my name from Hazel to "Hayes" to mask my female identity.

The amazing richness and breadth of *Future Shock* was achieved in large part through the deep collaboration of two humans incorporating their oppositely gendered life experiences.

The book illustrates these constant conversations, melding their very different reactions to shared experiences of the phenomena of culture, science, and technology, and extrapolating from them the changes in psychologies and lifestyles of ordinary people everywhere. I witnessed many occasions when Alvin was being lionized and interviewed on business and government platforms, while Heidi, sitting in the front row, was ignored and often demeaned, causing much pain in their relationship. Then, at a World Future Society annual conference in New York City in 1990, when Alvin was introduced for his customary keynote speech, he began by inviting Heidi to join him at the podium. These two at that podium together smiled joyously as Alvin declared to the several thousand attendees that all of their books, including *Future Shock,* had been co-authored. The audience broke into lengthy applause as the truth finally emerged! I tell this story because no one else can or will.

> The breakdown in traditional relationships was inevitable, termed by the Tofflers as "adhocracy," as family units break apart and scatter, following ever less reliable jobs and companies. This transience, in turn, drove the processes of individuation and shaping of new identities, groups, and subcultures— all documented in *Future Shock*—and continues to drive the polarization and "identity politics" of today.

The lasting content of *Future Shock* is as valuable and prophetic today as it was 50 years ago. All of the issues the Tofflers examined in *Future Shock* and in their subsequent bestsellers, *The Third Wave* (1980), *Powershift* (1990), and *War and Anti-War* (1993), are still with us today. Rereading *Future Shock* reminds us that this book identified in their infancy some of today's global issues, those steered by narrow, money-focused metrics led by GDP-measured growth, and affecting millions, both in most mature industrial countries and, in different ways, in developing countries bypassed by globalization. This textbook economic model allowed the "externalizing" of all other concerns and community values from both corporate and government accounts. The sweep of technological change also followed this laissez-faire economic model and informed science policy, as I learned from my six years as a science-policy advisor to the US Office of Technology Assessment, the National Science Foundation, and the National Academy of Engineering.

The Tofflers and I often discussed the trends which were leading, over the past 50 years, to today's "populist" protests across the political spectrum in many countries. Whether Brexit voters in Britain, Trump supporters in the U.S., yellow-vest protesters in France, the rise of Green parties in Germany and Europe, or Bolsonaro supporters in Brazil, the themes are similar. These forgotten, or "rust-belt," communities, have been bypassed by globalization and financialization. They see their values and livelihoods threatened or trampled by globe-trotting elites in business and government, making deals from exclusive resorts in Davos and Zug, Mar-a-Lago and Monaco, and from penthouses in Shanghai and Sao Paulo. These communities also see tax revenues misallocated or evaded altogether, as the same elites conduct business from tax havens around the world, as documented by Christiane Freeland and Nicholas Shaxon's *Treasure Islands* (2011), and by me in *The Politics of the Solar Age* (1981) and *Building A Win-Win World* (1996), both of which Alvin and Heidi Toffler were kind enough to blurb, calling me "among the most eloquent, original—and readable—of the econoclasts."

In the same vein, *Future Shock* highlighted the emergence of today's divisions in U.S. society, as populations shifted with changing jobs and technologies toward transience in lifestyles and relationships. The book's observations on how these nomadic shifts led to urbanization in not just the U.S., but in all countries, with rural communities sidelined, depopulated, and ignored in macro-statistics (which fly over the real world at sixty thousand feet). Today, over 50% of the world's populations have moved to ever-growing, gigantic cities. Thousands of other cities have more than one million residents. The current trend is toward 60% urbanization.

The breakdown in traditional relationships was inevitable, termed by the Tofflers as "adhocracy," as family units break apart and scatter, following ever less reliable jobs and companies. This transience, in turn, drove the processes of individuation and shaping of new identities, groups, and subcultures—all documented in *Future Shock*—and continues to drive the polarization and "identity politics" of today. A memorable quote sums up these trends: "America is tortured by uncertainty with respect to money, property, law and order, race, religion, God, family and self." (Page 303).

The book discusses the U.S. fault line of race relations in many different contexts, but without facing U.S. history's legacy of slavery, reconstruction, and Jim Crow. (Today's political reckoning with its past is covered by Jill Lepore in *These Truths* (2018).) Yet, *Future Shock* picked up on the early rise of socially responsible investing and how endowments, church pension funds, and mutual funds had begun to address racial inequality and all the broader values and issues missing in economics textbooks. The efforts to correct GDP and set up a Council of Social Advisors, which the Tofflers, many social reformers, and I discussed, are reflected in Chapter 20, "The Strategy of Social Futurism." They are also the subject of the two TV programs I produced with Alvin Toffler in the 1970s: "Anticipatory Democracy" and "East Meets West" with Islamic scholar Ziauddin Sardar (both free on demand at www.ethicalmarkets.tv<http://www.ethicalmarkets.tv>).

> " Rereading *Future Shock* reminds us that this book identified in their infancy some of today's global issues, those steered by narrow, money-focused metrics led by GDP-measured growth, and affecting millions, both in most mature industrial countries and, in different ways, in developing countries bypassed by globalization.

Finally, on another personal note, in the early 1970s, Al and Heidi suggested to me that I run for an open Senate seat in the tristate New York metropolitan area, when I was an obscure writer and social activist working since the 1960s with Ralph Nader on the campaign to "Make General Motors Responsible!" They were kind enough to offer to fund my campaign with some of the royalties flowing from *Future Shock*! I was overwhelmed, but decided that my path was to remain an independent futurist, as I am to this day.

While *Future Shock* will remain a literary and political landmark for the future, I also recommend *The Third Wave* and my favorite, *Revolutionary Wealth* (2006), where our shared thinking on the politics of money creation melded in our concern to document the other half of all economies: their unpaid caring, sharing voluntary sectors, which I analyzed as their hidden "Love Economies." This book, along with my work, uncovered the still-unrecognized work of the world's women, which the UNDP recognized in 1995, estimating in its Human Development Report as being worth $11 trillion, along with the unpaid work of men at $6 trillion—totaling $17 trillion of value simply missing from the annual GDP that year, which was $24 trillion! Today, we are moving away from GDP, and since 2015, with the adoption of the UN's Sustainable Development Goals (SDGs) by its 195 member countries, we can steer our societies away from the precipice and toward growth of the SDGs, as in our TV show, "Steering our Societies from GDP to the SDGs," free at www.ethicalmarkets.tv. This is an indication of the social revolution Alvin and Heidi Toffler began 50 years ago. ▦

Hazel Henderson D.Sc.Hon., FRSA, is founder of Ethical Markets Media, LLC (USA and Brazil), a Certified B Corporation. She is a world-renowned futurist, evolutionary economist, worldwide syndicated columnist, and author of the award-winning *Ethical Markets: Growing the Green Economy* (2006) and eight other books. She created the Ethical Markets TV series in global distribution at www.films.com, the EthicMark® Awards, and the Green Transition Scoreboard®, and co-created Ethical Biomimicry Finance®. Her editorials are syndicated globally by Inter Press Service, and her book reviews appear on SeekingAlpha.com. Her articles have appeared in over 250 journals, including *Harvard Business Review*, *The New York Times*, and *The Christian Science Monitor*, as well as journals in Japan, Venezuela, China, France and Australia.

Toffler's Diagnostic Errors

David Guston

Futurist Alvin Toffler's death in June 2016 at age 87 inspired the usual types of obituaries, marveling at the way his self-educated intellect grappled with the complex intertwining of technological and social change and created best-seller buzz around his predictions.

An account of his life in the *New York Times* followed a familiar arc: from child of immigrants, to self-made man, to adviser to some of the most powerful men on the planet. His books, especially *Future Shock* (1970) and *The Third Wave* (1980), achieved required reading status among a certain set, apparently including politicians as diverse as Newt Gingrich and former Chinese Prime Minister Zhao Ziyang.

Future Shock sounds like a sensational exclamation. It was, however, a sober diagnosis of the fear, alienation, and anomie with which people responded to the combination of rapid technological change and what Toffler saw as its disruptive social consequences. Looking back on the quarter-century since the end of World War II, Toffler observed major technological innovations—including television, the birth control pill, and travel by jet aircraft—and the cresting of the transformative "wave" from an industrial to a postindustrial society in which brain work was dominant over physical labor. Looking forward, Toffler saw more and more rapid innovation, and greater social dislocation. In response, Toffler suggested, we needed to develop a more "anticipatory democracy" as a cure.

In a more eulogistic piece in the *Times*, Farhad Manjoo (a former *Slate* writer and author of the *Times'* "State of the Art" column) writes that though Toffler's "diagnosis [of future shock] has largely panned out … futurism has fallen out of favor." Manjoo describes how hard-working futurists have few colleagues, governments fail to invest in infrastructure, and high-tech colossi stand astride the political-economic landscape, commanding tribute from markets and governments alike.

Manjoo describes how Toffler was overtaken by hucksters riding his wave of popularity. Furthermore, the partisan politics that arose in the 1980s put an end to an institutionalized version of futurism, the congressional Office of Technology Assessment, which was sacrificed in 1995, ironically, to Gingrich's Republican Revolution. With almost every major area of technology now in revolutionary foment—artificial intelligence winning at Go, genetic engineers plotting to synthesize the human genome, commercial space firms aiming at Mars—we have never, according to Manjoo, been more in need of futurism.

My high school Latin teacher taught me the ethic of *de mortuis nil nisi bonum*—say nothing but good about the dead. But Toffler's brand of futurism will not get us out of the real future-shock-related symptoms we indeed suffer. His current irrelevance stems from many causes, not the least of which is that he misunderstood the underlying etiology of future shock and therefore offered the wrong prescription.

While "anticipatory democracy" sounds salubrious, Toffler defined it very specifically: "anticipatory" meant making use of long-term forecasting techniques, especially the computer-based modeling of economic, demographic, and other trends that were in the late 1960s and early 1970s just coming into vogue; and "democracy" meant the kind of intimate town halls of Norman Rockwell mythology that would restore to individual citizens a modicum of control over their careening, caroming lives.

Toffler made three mistakes that worked against the progress of his project. First, while it may be real, future shock is not the *consequence* of the disruptive force of technology on society, because society also exerts force on technology—or, rather, though it can appear as if technology is causing something to happen in society, people actually make the decisions in the conception, design, manufacture, and deployment of technology. The sense of this phenomenon can be inferred from Winston Churchill's aphorism about architecture: "We shape our buildings; thereafter, they shape us." Contemporary scholars of such complex phenomena refer to "socio-technical systems" to describe what Toffler took as a simple relationship of the impact of technology on society.

Second, Toffler placed an inordinate trust in the expertise embodied in predictive models. His version of "anticipatory" was more aligned with identifying a current trend and extrapolating it to a future state, much the way that Ray Kurzweil and others use Moore's Law to predict future computing capacity and the coming "singularity" of super-intelligent machines. But prediction, especially across complex socio-technical systems, is illusory. Greek myths narrate the failure of prediction: For the Trojan prophetess Cassandra, those in power found ways to ignore even her perfect prophecy. For the seer Tiresias, prophecy set in motion precisely those events that fulfilled the prophecy itself, as in the Oedipus story. The oracle at Delphi articulated a prediction bound to

> "The alternative is to establish an agenda based on a more authentic and realistic meaning of "anticipation," which is, etymologically speaking, not about a technical capacity to describe or say something before it happens (predict) or observe the future (foresee), but instead it is to build a capacity for something prior to when it is needed.

be self-servingly misinterpreted beforehand, to be understood properly only in retrospect. While we moderns have largely disposed of the concept of fate that competed with prophecy in the Greek world, we can all imagine contemporary issues (e.g., climate change) that exhibit precisely these dynamics. No less a modernist than Isaac Asimov—inventor of the fictional predictive social science of psychohistory in his *Foundation* trilogy—said that "if we could use the tenets of psychohistory to guide ourselves we might avoid a great many troubles. But on the other hand, it might create troubles. It's impossible to tell in advance."

Toffler's third error follows from these two. Small-scale, directly democratic town halls are virtuous. They will not function to reduce future shock, however, if they are connected only to the misguided disposition of predicting the future. Democratic values and priorities expressed in town halls, alas, do not constitute relevant data in predictive models. Moreover, if the model of socio-technical change has room for only one direction of influence, as Toffler's does, then even an anticipatory democracy is likely to fall short of being able to influence the technological trajectory for the benefit of its citizens. It will not see the people with power obscured by the glimmer of technologies having an impact on society.

The alternative is to establish an agenda based on a more authentic and realistic meaning of "anticipation," which is, etymologically speaking, not about a technical capacity to describe or say something before it happens (predict) or observe the future (foresee), but instead it is to build a capacity for something prior to when it is needed. Building anticipatory—rather than predictive—ca-

> We don't attempt to predict the future or estimate probabilities and risks for certain occurrences. Instead, we explore plausible scenarios and other methods for generating anticipatory knowledge and a greater anticipatory capacity among broader publics.

pacity into our social relationships with technology begins to create conditions in which broader groups of people can self-consciously reflect on the values that go into technology, so that the resulting innovations might more readily reflect those values and create less future shock.

My colleagues at Arizona State University, the University of Wisconsin, and Georgia Tech and I have pioneered something of a reboot of anticipatory democracy that we call "anticipatory governance." While we, like Toffler, hope to reinvigorate intimate democratic engagement, we focus on creating two-way conversations with experts, creating a participatory technology assessment that the Office of Technology Assessment never managed. Our assessments involve scores or hundreds of ordinary citizens engaged in informed discussion about such issues as space missions that we have done for NASA, or the global climate and energy nexus conducted by the Danish Board of Technology Foundation.

We join engagement to a more nuanced and balanced understanding of expertise by emphasizing integration across disciplines. The Socio-Technical Integration Research project embeds social scientists and ethicists in science and engineering laboratories to encourage researchers to reflect more deeply on the choices they make in the laboratory, choices which have ramifications for those of us on the outside. Others are also promoting socio-technical integration, like scholars studying the flexible nature of expertise in the Communities of Integration project and art-science collaborations like LASER and DASER.

We don't attempt to predict the future or estimate probabilities and risks for certain occurrences. Instead, we explore plausible scenarios and other methods for generating anticipatory knowledge and a greater anticipatory capacity among broader publics. Such less technocratic forms of futurism are practiced by the Oxford Futures Forum, which connects scenario development to other disciplines like design, and the nonprofit Institute for the Future, which develops and disseminates innovative, future-oriented tools like "artifacts from the future" and "collaborative forecasting games."

At ASU, we are now several years into the life of the School for the Future of Innovation in Society. While we are not training futurists, per se, our students are learning across these tools of engagement, integration, and anticipation to plan for the kinds of futures that we will want to inhabit. And they are learning to frame innovative efforts as part of a larger social fabric that informs our wants and needs for our common future.

We owe a debt to Alvin Toffler, but it is more inspirational and heuristic than methodological and programmatic. By deeply engaging ordinary citizens, integrating knowledge across disciplines, and cultivating a broadly anticipatory disposition, we can lessen the shock of the future.

An earlier version of this essay was published in July 2016 in the Future Tense *channel, a partnership of New America, Arizona State University, and the online journal* Slate.

David H. Guston is Foundation Professor and Founding Director of the School for the Future of Innovation in Society at Arizona State University. An award-winning author in science and technology policy, he is lead editor of *Frankenstein: Annotated for Scientists, Engineers, and Creators of All Kinds* (MIT Press, 2017). Professor Guston is widely published and cited on research and development policy, technology assessment, public participation in science and technology, and the politics of science policy. His book, *Between Politics and Science: Assuring the Integrity and Productivity of Research* (Cambridge U. Press, 2000) was awarded the 2002 Don K. Price Prize by the American Political Science Association for best book in science and technology policy. He has been principal or co-principal investigator on $22 million in NSF awards. Professor Guston is a fellow of the American Association for the Advancement of Science. He holds a B.A. from Yale and a Ph.D. from MIT.

What If?

Richard Browning

So what does a former corporate oil trader turned jet suit pioneer make of the future? ■ Well, I guess I have an unusual perspective that draws upon a truly international perspective. It straddles the worlds of big business and dealmaking, to include technology, engineering, and even the constantly evolving arena of entertainment.

Before I share my perspective, I will say that the task of trying to peer over the horizon is fraught with challenges. Humans are tuned to apply past observations when it comes to predictions, and this strategy is bound to miss game-changing technologies and their impact. The oft-quoted misjudgments made about the impact of the mobile phone business are a case in point.

It is well recognized that humans are being outperformed by machines at process- and fact-driven tasks on an exponential scale. However, I believe the future will see an increasing human capacity to piece together disparate ideas and concepts, look beyond the conventional wisdom, challenge the status quo, think the unthinkable, and achieve the impossible. The technology innovation and the startup world are awash with this philosophy already, but it will percolate all areas of business and industry. The global education system is still somewhat rooted in a Victorian-Britain "learn-repeat" culture—so well defined by Alvin Toffler in *Future Shock*—and it must respond and adapt. There are a number of notable people advocating this idea, not the least of whom is Elon Musk with the work he is doing with his school, *Ad Astra*. But we need more people to take notice and help push the education system to transform, because we must preserve in our students the gift of childlike inquiry, curiosity, and inclination to *play*. The famous "marshmallow test" makes my point, I think:

Take a group of seven engineers, another of business leaders, another of army officers, any group of adult professionals, and another of ten-year-old children. Arm each team with some skewers, sticky tape, Blu

Tack, and a marshmallow. Set them to the challenge of suspending this sugary lump as high as they can off the table within three minutes. Adults will talk, plan, and leave little time for execution. They realize too late how heavy the marshmallow is and ultimately fail to suspend it as high as possible. The kids, however, will get on with playing and experimenting, learning quickly what works and what doesn't. The kids nearly always win.

> **If you are to push a concept or significantly advance a technology, it makes sense that success is unlikely to come from a pool of talent that looks the same, speaks the same, and was schooled in the same status quo.**

The next shift that I hope for will be a genuine recognition of diversity as a powerful mechanism for success. It has frustrated me to observe the corporate world turning diversity into a confused and usually artificial PR exercise. We are bombarded by the media telling us about walls going up, countries restricting borders, and people finding new ways to silo themselves. Yet young people see the connected world as a place without boundaries, a place full of opportunity. In doing oil deals with a multitude of cultures all over the world, I saw the power of drawing on diverse opinions and perspectives. I scaled my company, Gravity Industries, by deliberately engaging a global community drawn from many backgrounds and geographies. If you are to push a concept or significantly advance a technology, it makes sense that success is unlikely to come from a pool of talent that looks the same, speaks the same, and was schooled in the same status quo.

I think the future will see these kinds of work philosophies become mainstream as humans bear down on what they are good at versus focusing much on the increasing territory machines will occupy. It makes sense to be aware of and adapt to that reality now. ■

Richard Browning is founder and Chief Test Pilot of pioneering aeronautical innovation company Gravity Industries. Richard was an oil trader with BP for 16 years. He developed new business in many countries and conducted trade relations with many more. Launched in March 2017, the dream behind Gravity Industries was to reimagine human flight with an elegant partnership between mind, body, and machine, exploiting leading-edge technology. This vision led to Richard's creation of the Gravity Jet Suit. Richard and the team are delivering on the vision to build Gravity into a world-class aeronautical engineering business, challenge perceived boundaries in human aviation, and inspire a generation to dare ask "What if…"

The Shocking Future of Health Care

Jeffrey C. Bauer, PhD

Health care futurism did not exist as a recog-
nized discipline when *Future Shock* first appeared in 1970. Scholarly interest in the evolution of the medical marketplace was in its infancy back then. To the limited
extent that Americans thought about how illnesses would be treated in the future, their ideas
were more likely shaped by *Star Trek's* Dr. "Bones" McCoy than by intellectual thought leaders who
had seriously contemplated the topic. Alvin Toffler was among the earliest commentators to lay
out a reasoned, richly documented vision of coming changes in the science and technology of
human health. Therefore, the 50th anniversary of his pioneering work is good reason to present a
retrospective of what he got right and wrong and to use the historical lessons of his seminal work
for improving how we look ahead to the next 50 years. (I was probably destined to write this piece.
My career in health care started the year before *Future Shock* was published, and I experienced the
subsequent five decades as a full-time industry insider.)

Several of Toffler's health care predictions really missed the mark. It must fairly be noted that
he was not alone in misreading the crystal ball. Lacking expertise in medical science, he accepted
the prognostications of many leading researchers who grossly overestimated the long-term impact of their own work. In a section titled "The Predesigned Body," for example, Toffler concluded
that cloning and related genetic manipulations would be "producing [biological] spare parts for
failing human bodies" in as little as 15 years—precisely in 1984, according to one expert he quoted. Under the heading "The Cyborg Among Us," he incorrectly foresaw widespread integration of
intelligent machines into human bodies at about the same time. He also wrongly projected that
technologies "to create altogether new versions of man" would soon follow. Likewise, Toffler's
views on the future of health care did not anticipate strong economic forces that shaped the

medical marketplace,[1] nor did he foresee ethical and political roadblocks that have significantly constrained change over the past 50 years.

On the other hand, *Future Shock* includes exceptional health-related insights that more than compensate for its failed predictions. The very concept of future shock accurately presaged a coming elaboration of medical science's fundamental paradigm:

> We may define future shock as the distress, both physical and psychological, that arises from an overload of the human organism's physical adaptive systems and its decision-making processes. Put more simply, future shock is the human response to overstimulation. Different people react to future shock in different ways. Its symptoms also vary according to the stage and intensity of the disease. These symptoms range all the way from anxiety, hostility to helpful authority, and seemingly senseless violence, to physical illness, depression and apathy. (From Chapter 15: Future Shock: The Physical Dimension)

Alvin Toffler recognized the major role that environmental factors play in determining health—defined by the World Health Organization as an individual's complete state of physical, mental, and social well-being (not just the absence of disease)—at a time when medical science was focused almost exclusively on curing diseases with surgery and drugs. He also anticipated how the mind-body link significantly determines individual and population health:

> If future shock were a matter of physical illness alone, it might be easier to prevent and to treat. But future shock attacks the psyche as well. Just as the body cracks under the strain of environmental overstimulation, the "mind" and its decision processes behave erratically when overloaded. By indiscriminately racing the engines of change, we may be undermining not merely the health of those least able to adapt, but their very ability to act rationally on their own behalf. (From Chapter 16, "Future Shock: The Psychological Dimension")

Related criticism of psychoanalysis was equally prescient. With its multidimensional view of human health, *Future Shock* clearly described the increasingly complex path that medical science has ultimately followed. For this reason alone, it is sad that the book had little or no direct impact on health care delivery in the decades following publication. Rather than studying how knowledge of human health could be used to improve efficiency and effectiveness in the medical marketplace—a key focus of Toffler's approach—pioneers in health policy concentrated almost exclusively on reducing expenditures on Medicare and Medicaid. Health reform experts have very little to show for all their work on cost-containment, so it's worth pondering how much better off American health care would be today if they had adopted Toffler's focus on health care delivery rather than health care finance.

> "Toffler's views on the future of health care did not anticipate strong economic forces that shaped the medical marketplace, nor did he foresee ethical and political roadblocks that have significantly constrained change over the past 50 years.

Toffler's general method for projecting the future of health care was *qualitative*. It distilled the thoughts of leading medical researchers into scenarios that could occur if the underlying forces (positive and negative) were properly addressed. Like other visionary thinkers, Toffler was captivated by the realm of possibilities. However, a *quantitative* approach to futurism was emerging at the same time. Social scientists shifted from intellectual (subjective) analysis to statistical (objective) analysis, claiming to improve the accuracy of their insights by studying data rather than exploring ideas. A book published in 1973 by the Club of Rome, *The Limits to Growth*, quickly attracted as much attention as *Future Shock*. Both works addressed many of the same issues, but *Limits* drew its conclusions from mathematical models.

> Health reform experts have very little to show for all their work on cost-containment, so it's worth pondering how much better off American health care would be today if they had adopted Toffler's focus on health care delivery rather than health care finance.

Future Shock and *The Limits to Growth* were major topics of discussion while I was in graduate school, getting a Ph.D. in economics. I vividly remember creative tension between my "old school" professors (including Kenneth Boulding, prominently quoted in *Future Shock*), who specialized in traditional economic theory, and younger faculty members who taught math-based econometrics as the foundation of a "new and improved" social science.[2] Data-fueled analytics quickly took over the field of economics and has since predominated as its principal method for predicting the future. Economists generally let the numbers speak for themselves, with little attention to the validity (meaningfulness) and reliability (accuracy) of the underlying measurements.[3] Toffler and his intellectual allies lost the methodological battle with the "quants," but history suggests his tradition of qualitative analysis will ultimately win the war—especially given economists' abysmal track record in making data-based predictions over the past 50 years.[4]

So, what picture of health care would Alvin Toffler see in his crystal ball if he were writing a 50th anniversary edition of *Future Shock*? He would surely continue to position genetics as a powerful force for progress, but at a much slower pace than he envisioned in 1970 because its study and subsequent applications and implications have become unexpectedly complex. Given Toffler's pioneering insight into the mind-body connection, I think his future view today would still reflect medical care's incipient evolution from acute care to chronic care—from curing diseases once they occur to managing them before they become debilitating. I also expect he would eloquently address the social determinants of health (e.g., malnutrition, obesity, inadequate physical activity, sleep deprivation, behavioral and mental problems, poor housing) and the societal consequences of failing to deal with them. I'm not sure how he would address government's role in reforming health care, but recent experience would probably make him rather cynical.

Most importantly, I believe Alvin Toffler would recognize that today's health care equivalent of future shock is climate change. He would use his skills in qualitative analysis to show how unprecedented changes in the weather will likely cause even more disease and social dysfunction than overstimulation from technological change. I can easily imagine him drawing well-documented, multidisciplinary parallels between climate change and the worst causes of death in human history. His updated edition might even be retitled *Climate Catastrophe*. I take absolutely no delight in concluding on this grim note, but I carefully studied *Future Shock* while earning a Ph.D. in the dismal science, and I was previously trained in climate science. From both these perspectives,

I believe that Alvin Toffler's way of looking at the future—if not all his predictions—is at least as important for population health today as it was 50 years ago. ▨

J**effrey C. Bauer, PhD**, is an internationally recognized health futurist and medical economist. Author of nearly 300 publications on the medical marketplace, Dr. Bauer is a frequent keynote speaker to regional and national meetings about evolution of the medical marketplace; he focuses on private-sector solutions that increase efficiency and effectiveness of health care delivery. He spent 18 years as a medical school professor and administrator and has also served as a state governor's health policy adviser, independent consultant, and vice president for health care forecasting and strategy at two Fortune 500 companies. Dr. Bauer was a Ford Foundation Independent Scholar, Fulbright Scholar, and Kellogg Foundation National Fellow. He lives in Madison, WI.

1. For in-depth analysis of medical monopoly and related economic problems, see Bauer, JC, *Not What the Doctor Ordered: Liberating Caregivers and Empowering Consumers for Successful Health Reform*, Third Edition (New York: Routledge, 2020).

2. For a detailed analysis of how I resolved the methodological conflict in my ensuing career as a health futurist, see Bauer, JC, *Upgrading Leadership's Crystal Ball: Five Reasons Why Forecasting Must Replace Predicting and How to Make the Strategic Change in Business and Public Policy* (New York; CRC Press, 2014). This book draws significantly on atmospheric physics and weather forecasting, the fields I studied before becoming an economist.

3. To the best of my knowledge, the only book on economic statistics that addresses the fundamental importance of data quality is Bauer, JC, *Statistical Analysis for Decision-Makers in Health Care; Understanding and Evaluating Critical Information in Changing Times* (New York: CRC Press, 2009).

4. RJ Samuleson, "Economists often don't know what they are talking about." Washington Post, May 12, 2019; https://www.washingtonpost.com/opinions/economists-often-dont-know-what-theyre-talking-about/2019/05/12/f91517d4-7338-11e9-9eb4-0828f5389013_story.html?utm_term=.7c1921587cd1

The Monetization of Movement and Metamorphosis of Mass Transit

Dr. Anita Sengupta

A huge paradigm shift occurring today is the "mobility as a service revolution"—MaaS, as it is so enthusiastically referenced in our acronym-rich society. ■ But does serving the whims of an individual who needs to transit two blocks on an electric scooter outweigh the needs of a pedestrian who is toppled from their walk, with their face glued to their smartphone? Or is the revolution a way for the ride-share overlords to monetize your every movement, from block, to store, to vehicle choice—all in the name of convenience? Even ride-share bicycles now have "pedal assist"—while sweating is limited to CrossFit, Pilates, and working at a startup.

So, how did we evolve from bipedal to a quad-copter anyway? And why drive down the street to buy a box of tampons when a drone could just drop it in my pool (by accident)? The Americas are not new to the monetization of movement—we gave birth to the car culture. We are the print that is the big foot on the element carbon. Internal combustion engines may be going the way of the dinosaur, but their bones are still the coal that charges a battery pack.

In all the discussions on the latest app to have your burrata bowl delivered by a driverless car, what about investment in mass transit? Or the creation of bicycle lanes, the elimination of cars in city centers, and the acknowledgement that even electric is synonymous with carbon? That is, until we have a renewable grid. But to get to the heart of the matter we can explore some of the new high-tech modes of transportation that are emerging, including those I have had the opportunity to engineer and lead.

In the 1960s, science fiction visionaries imagined the transit of pods carrying people through tubes at tremendous speeds. A few decades later, in opposition to the California high-speed rail project, the hyperloop concept was born in tech companies of the greater Los Angeles area. A hyperloop has the potential to revolutionize ground travel through speed coupled with optimized energy efficiency. This modern mode of movement is a magnetically levitating mass transit vehicle, electrically propelled through a vacuum tube in excess of commercial airliner speeds. With a capacity like that of rail (20,000 passengers per hour), but at ten times the speed of a car on a freeway, operating off solar panels along its length, it is the holy grail of ground-based transit. Once a government amasses the funds and courage to implement a hyperloop, we can enable a future that connects Los Angeles to San Francisco in just 30 minutes, city center to city center.

> Once a government amasses the funds and courage to implement a hyperloop, we can enable a future that connects Los Angeles to San Francisco in just 30 minutes, city center to city center.

Next on the docket and ready for takeoff is electric aviation. As a pilot and aviation entrepreneur, I can personally attest to recent progress toward lowering the carbon footprint of fixed-wing aircraft. Energy efficiency reduces operational costs and is critical to limit CO_2 production and combat climate change. However, stored energy technologies such as batteries do not have sufficient energy density to achieve the transit range needed for regional, let alone cross-country, flights. Fuel cells, although possessing a promising energy density, do not yet have the technology readiness level (TRL) to reliably support commercial aviation. Therefore, there has been little progress or investment in fully electric aviation since *Future Shock* was first published.

However, a new movement is afoot—Urban Air Mobility, or UAM. Congestion in cities around the world has reached such levels that on average people spend 90 hours per year in traffic. That time expense, not to mention the fuel needs and carbon dioxide output of cars, makes automobile use increasingly unappealing. UAM looks to shift urban mobility to the three-dimensions of airspace by creating low-altitude highways in the sky, and eventually to rely on vehicle autonomy and AI for traffic management, collision avoidance, and optimization. The short range of urban-suburban transport, typically 10-50 km one way, inherently lends itself to the first viable use-case for fully electric aviation. The need to deposit cargo—people—in urban centers also necessitates Vertical-Take-off-Landing capability (VTOL), versus a traditional runway.

In 2019 there are over 200 companies developing new vehicle technologies ranging from flying saucer-like quad-copters (Bell NEXUS) to the tilt-wing MOBi-One at my company, Airspace Experience Technologies. In the next decade the UAM space will kick-start the electric aviation industry, first with batteries for short-range missions, to be followed by hydrogen fuel cells for regional flights. With updates to air traffic control using V2X, and new technologies to ensure noise abatement, a future of low-altitude air travel is on the horizon in the next decade. By 2030 it is more likely than not that your Yellow Cab will have a 12 meter wingspan and a bird's-eye view.

This brings us to the final frontier—technologies that will enable travel into space, starting in low-

> The space race is now under the control of wealthy billionaires, bent on redefining the space program in their image. Perhaps this a sign of a crumbling US-funded space program, or perhaps capitalism on rocket fuel. But, with each new launch we must consider the societal implications of suborbital flights, their carbon footprint, and Amazon Prime deliveries to and from the Moon.

Earth orbit, and then on to the Moon and Mars. In the past decade we have seen the birth, first steps, and graduation of Virgin Galactic, Blue Origin, and SpaceX—all private investor-led aerospace companies. Their goal is to enable access to space, dare I say, that is affordable to the everyday millionaire. This is a two order of magnitude reduction in cost versus the only available space tourism option at Roscosmos. The space race is now under the control of wealthy billionaires, bent on redefining the space program in their image. Perhaps this a sign of a crumbling US-funded space program, or perhaps capitalism on rocket fuel. But, with each new launch we must consider the societal implications of suborbital flights, their carbon footprint, and Amazon Prime deliveries to and from the Moon. Launch vehicle technology has not advanced much from the Apollo era. Some of the newer entrants into the market, rather than using cryogens, instead are opting for lower energy content storable propellants, which are less expensive to plumb and service. At the end of the day, launch vehicle technology has one purpose—a controlled and vectored explosion to overcome the gravity well of our pale blue dot. By 2070 I estimate economies of scale and competition by natural selection will enable that all-expenses-paid vacation to the future site of ship-building yards at Utopia Planitia.

My trepidation around these developments, having worked as an engineer and entrepreneur in the aerospace/transportation sector for two decades now, stems from the potential for misuse. Could these privately funded technological high-speed wonders be hijacked to facilitate trans-Atlantic evening entertainment options for those with the financial means? Such an eventuality would destroy the gains of carbon footprint reduction intended by these mass transportation alternatives.

In the aftershock of the MaaS revolution, my hope is that people on their stationary bicycles, stair climbers, and electric scooters will dismount, and make the first-and-last-mile bipedal. My vision is that mass transit becomes a service to provide mobility for the masses, with convenience to planet Earth as the primary optimization of function for all such endeavors.

Dr. Anita Sengupta is an aerospace engineer, rocket scientist, and pilot. She worked for NASA for 16 years where she led the design of propulsion and landing systems for deep space, Mars, and Earth reentry. Next she was senior vice president of systems engineering at Virgin Hyperloop One. She is currently co-founder and chief product officer of Airspace Experience Technologies (ASX), an electric VTOL urban air mobility company. Dr. Sengupta received her MS and PhD in aerospace engineering from the University of Southern California, where she is also a Research Associate Professor of Astronautics.

From **Future** Shock to **Future** Smart

Dr. James Canton

Most of us don't really think much about the future, as we are so busy with the here and now. The future seems vague and remote for many of us—something we're unable to affect or control. In fact, a number of studies, including those of my own organizations, consistently find that very few people give much thought to their futures even a few years out.

Fifty years ago, however, the future was top of mind. *Future Shock* had just been published, introducing a very different paradigm—a radical new way to think about the future that shocked its readers into a new consciousness. In a review of the book by *The New York Times* in July 1970, interest in the book was attributed to the growing public concern that technology was contributing to a polluted, overpopulated world, "shaking traditional values, and leaving nothing to replace them." Toffler, in an interview that sourced the review, punctuated this sensibility, concluding, "This is the prospect that man now faces. Change is avalanching upon our heads and most people are grotesquely unprepared to cope with it."

But Toffler's call was not merely alarmist. The book's concepts were actually far-reaching, inviting people to consider the kind of future they *wanted*. It was tremendously successful in getting people to think beyond their otherwise limited horizons. And perhaps for the first time, people were challenged to consider their individual roles in actually *shaping* the future.

Embedded in *Future Shock* is an immensely powerful idea. It suggests that human beings could be forces for change, not simply reactors to change—that we need to learn or even take back the future

405

from a state of not knowing, from passive unawareness to active awareness; that we could learn to cope with accelerating change.

It is interesting to note that Toffler was writing and researching *Future Shock* during a most turbulent time in American history. Vietnam War protests, spiritual movements, women's rights, the civil rights movement, black liberation, and rebellious students were woven into the cultural mosaic of the day. And though the book dealt with the shocking nature of accelerating change, it also offered novel remedies in the form of education and "anticipatory democracy." These ideas were essential in that they pointed to the possibilities of personal empowerment and the development of a consciousness about change that could enable *better* futures. No longer would people need to resign themselves to being run over by the future—they could actually make a difference.

> "Public companies in the US live for the next quarter, not the next year. Most organizations don't have a strategic plan with a forecast horizon beyond 12 months. Governments don't pay attention to foresight studies.

The book brought about an understanding of the agents of change—the catalysts that are creating the future even now—and provided much needed direction, via democratic institutions—and even as an individual—to chart the future. Be proactive and anticipatory rather than reactive and asleep, Toffler advised. Shape your future or someone else will.

That Alvin Toffler got so much right is in itself "shocking"—particularly when considering the sea of change assaulting our daily world. Indeed, *Future Shock* reads just as well today as it did in 1970. A highly original book for its time, *Future Shock* laid a foundation beneath an achievable future—a foundation that all could build upon. It was a plea to *humanize* the future, to deal with change purposefully, to inject an anticipatory capacity into organizations, culture, and our psyche.

The concept of the future as an artifact of time was very effectively combined with a practical sensibility that had not been articulated before. As its pages traversed the imagined landscapes of the future, it did so with a deep social consciousness, weaving it all into a cogent narrative. By shining the light on the stresses and disruptions wrought by change, he put the human psyche at the center of accelerating technological progress—and playing it all off parallel changes in globalization, population growth, and media as yet other agents of change and harbingers of things to come.

If Toffler were alive today, he would appreciate, with some irony, the many ways his warnings have actually played out: invasions against privacy, the lack of anticipatory planning of nations and organizations, climate change, the disruptive forces of technologies such as genetic engineering, artificial intelligence, blockchain—all would sound familiar. Indeed, "shock" is no longer considered a strange state of being.

This is as true for organizations and governments as it is for individuals. The fast, the adaptive, the agile, the innovators—these are thriving. But clearly, not everyone has adapted so well. We still face a significant gap—a gap that leads to negative outcomes that include insecure careers, broken business models, ineffective nation-state policies. It also amplifies the damaging effects of identity theft, fake news, information warfare, rogue artificial intelligence, robots. And equally important, how failure to embrace change in ways both fast and smart—whether as individuals, organizations, or nations—only threatens survival all the more.

Notwithstanding, public companies in the US live for the next quarter, not the next year. Most organizations don't have a strategic plan with a forecast horizon beyond 12 months. Governments don't pay attention to foresight studies. Individuals and economies are buffeted by dramatic changes affecting jobs, education, economics, and competition that emerge daily. The out-of-control impact of change on the human psyche, as well as on human society, has become the "new normal."

Toffler, however, did not accept such a new "normalcy." Rather, he posited the idea of recovery centers for the future shocked. (Where are those future shock spas today?) He always emphasized "People over Tech." Today, he would frame those sentiments as "Humans over AI" or "Get back, Robot Overlords."

On a personal note Alvin Toffler was my mentor. Most of my professional life was put into action by my early experiences working with him. I worked out of his apartment in New York City while I was in graduate school. We collaborated on the Anticipatory Network to advise US Congress on futures, as well as designing a new college in New York City; we worked on aspects of the service economy, and numerous other projects to inject futures thinking and foresight into organizations. These were, to say the least, inspiring experiences that informed all my subsequent professional work.

In an eerie way, Toffler pierced the time bubble. In doing so, he pointed the way to shaping a better future—a future that does not merely happen, but is *made* through our intentional actions, votes, decisions, innovations, collaborations, policies, plans, strategies. That these ideas are still relevant 50 years on is a powerful testament to his legacy.

D**r. James Canton** is a leading global futurist, social scientist, entrepreneur, author, and visionary business advisor for corporations, leaders, and governments worldwide. For over 30 years he has been predicting futures. The Institute for Global Futures, a think tank he founded in 1990, advises business and governments on forecasting strategic trends, innovation, and strategy. He has been an Advisor, MIT Media Lab EU, Mad Scientist TRADOC, Fellow at Kellogg School of Management and Stanford. He has advised three US White House Administrations. Dr. Canton was a former Apple Computer executive, a policy advisor, investment banker, and serial entrepreneur. He is the author of *Future Smart, Managing the Game Changing Trends that will Transform Your World, The Extreme Future*, and *Technofutures*.

A Future Unchecked

Diane Francis

In July 1970, *Future Shock* was published before the personal computer was even a twinkle in Steve Jobs' eye. The book was astonishingly prescient, notably that "future shock," defined as the "disease of change," would afflict the world. The Tofflers were right then, and they are correct now. The disease's symptoms have not only spread, but have metastasized into a pandemic that is levelling everything from personal and societal values to organizations and political structures. It will worsen, and the Tofflers' book provides an essential diagnosis as to what will happen in the next 50 years.

In broad-brush terms, humanity falls into two categories. There are those who still live medieval existences—nasty, brutish, and short. And there are those who live in a world of plenty and economic progress who are exposed to the "disease of change." Toffler warned that all people will be bombarded by new products, people, policies, professions, organizations, movements, and values, all delivered at warp speed. They will be required to adopt new and multiple roles, and to navigate through unprecedented choices about everything from lifestyles to allegiances or values. Future shock, they posited, marked the "death of permanence," a fact that is both exhilarating and threatening.

Fifty years later, technologies have redrawn the world's economies and societies. Facebook, Tinder, and the mobile phone have profoundly redefined relationships, while the internet has reconfigured work, fame, entertainment, business, organizations, opportunities, and politics. Technological advances have enabled some poor countries to overtake rich countries economically. But rich or poor, millions of citizens in all countries have been left behind and have succumbed to future shock. Unable to cope, they descend into maladaptive behavior, depression, denialism, nihilism, revisionism, dogmatism, or extremism.

To me, as a journalist and activist, the biggest unrecognized casualty today is the assault of change on civil society itself. The world, nation-states, regions, tribes, and families are being atomized into warring factions, ideologies, new religions, movements, ethics, tribes, cults, cabals, allegiances, websites, or social media factions. In this respect, the disease, as Toffler suggested, has also destroyed consensus and social cohesion.

The result is that division and polarization afflict societies and democracies. Civil wars proliferate and non-state players form to mount terrorist attacks or to hack into corporations, governments, or power grids. Since 1970, the fault lines have widened and worsened and, as the Tofflers predicted, contributed to the fall of the Berlin Wall, the breakup of the Soviet Union, and future economic growth in the Asia-Pacific region.

While some outcomes have benefitted many people, the fallout is anarchic tendencies and social dissension. The practices of micro-advertising and targeted news feeds have splintered civil societies into millions of "filter bubbles" where people are fed information based on their unique set of biases. The result has been Brexit, divisive movements, tremors within the European Union, an increasingly dysfunctional United Nations, and secession or civil war worldwide. In the next 50 years, these trends will accelerate, making achieving unity or shared values more elusive than ever.

Unchecked, social and geopolitical fragmentation will continue to destabilize the European Union, the United Nations, the World Trade Organization, NATO, and the United States. It's not impossible to imagine that if the U.S. fails to find common ground among its people, California and others will secede. New England may follow, then New York, portions of the Midwest, and the Deep South, until what used to be the United States will be a loose confederation unable to exert geopolitical or military power.

> In broad-brush terms, humanity falls into two categories. There are those who still live medieval existences—nasty, brutish, and short. And there are those who live in a world of plenty and economic progress who are exposed to the "disease of change."

Economically, the carnage is everywhere. The churn of corporations and governments has been breathtaking. Companies like Uber, Twitter, Airbnb, and Amazon have driven giant companies out of the market and eliminated millions of jobs. Every day, shopping centers, newspapers, factories, and enterprises are shuttered, and America's biggest car, banking, and hotel chains are threatened with extinction. Unemployment and underemployment grow as those thrown out of work are unable to adapt or keep pace. Many give up, or avoid overstimulation by turning to drugs and distractions, or by reverting to narrowcast views of the world, conspiracy theories, religiosity, or a combination of all three.

In the next 50 years, advances in biology and genetics will revolutionize human life by creating new uber-humans through genetic engineering in the womb. Brain interfaces will alter minds, work, and attitudes. The unbridled creation of cyborgs or AIs with personalities and on two legs will lead to the further mutation of human existence, the physical world, and psychology as we currently understand it. Society, in a few decades, may come to resemble the Star War's bar scene, populated with curious creatures of unknown origin or gender or motives.

Currently, there are no moral, ethical, or security frameworks to govern such transformative technologies, but there must be. In 1945, two nuclear bombs destroyed cities in Japan. Subsequently, the scientist Robert Oppenheimer, who ran the Manhattan Project that created the atomic bomb, realized that the spread of such weapons of mass destruction would destroy the world. He and others spent years lobbying world leaders, formulating the Nuclear Non-Proliferation Treaty, signed in 1968 by dozens of nuclear and non-nuclear powers. The treaty has provided a framework of oversight and, thus far, saved mankind from limited or all-out nuclear war.

> **Currently, there is no global oversight system that will police the development and deployment of artificial intelligence, biological weapons, or the use of CRISPR and other techniques to create designer children, cyborgs, or human chimeras.**

Likewise, the proliferation of artificial intelligence, genetic engineering, synthetic biology, and other technologies must be controlled. So far, efforts are scattered and small, but hundreds of scientists and technologists have signed on to moral, ethical, and security frameworks for artificial intelligence and biotechnologies. The United Nations is working on getting its nation-state members to agree on a ban of autonomous weapons, or "killer robots."

But currently, there is no global oversight system that will police the development and deployment of artificial intelligence, biological weapons, or the use of CRISPR and other techniques to create designer children, cyborgs, or human chimeras. This stark lack of a crucial oversight function is an example of the many reasons *Future Shock* remains one of the most important books ever written, and remains an important roadmap to understanding what lies ahead.

In the coming decade, mass unemployment through automation threatens to demolish society and capitalism. Economic brakes and backstops must be devised to mitigate damage, and institutions that can monitor the changes and intervene in salutary ways must be created. Remedies must be found. The rise of the "disease of change" and its dangerous consequences constitute the most important takeaway from the Tofflers' seminal work, one to which mankind must pay heed. ▪

Diane Francis is an author of ten books, an entrepreneur, Editor at Large with the National Post in Canada, Senior Fellow at the Atlantic Institute in Washington DC, columnist with American Interest in Washington, DC, and the Kyiv Post, and Distinguished Professor at Ryerson University in Toronto, Faculty Member of Singularity University. She is also on the boards of the Hudson Institute's Kleptocracy Initiative and the Canada-US Law Institute.

Imagination is the Cure for Future Shock

Joe Tankersley

Like every practicing futurist, I have a copy of **Alvin Toffler's *Future Shock* tucked away on my bookshelf.** My copy came from a used bookstore in the early nineties. The pages are yellowed, the cover frayed around the edges. While there are passages underlined and occasional notes scrawled in the margins, it does not, in all honestly, show signs of excessive use.

Future Shock is one of a handful of seminal texts that make up the foundational literature of futurism. From its days as a mainstream bestseller, the book has ascended to that lofty status of icon. The title itself has become a term we use regularly, and many of us can reference its most notable passages. But I suspect I am not alone when I admit that I rarely refer to the work in my daily practice.

Of course, I did have to pull it off the shelf before writing this essay. I'm glad I did. I was reminded why it holds such a prominent place in futures literature, and how it remains relevant to current struggles to understand our complex and challenging futures.

Toffler will always be best remembered for naming the stress created when humans are confronted with "too much change in too short a time."[1] If the concept of future shock had relevance in the 1960s, then it certainly has even more in our contemporary world. Joi Ito, former director of the MIT Media Lab, observed that, "Our technologies have outpaced our ability, as a society, to understand them."[2]

What Toffler predicted decades ago has indeed become a common experience for all of us. It is in these moments of personal future shock that we get a glimpse into the broader concerns of a culture that has lost its capacity to keep up with the pace of change. Rereading the book, I was reminded of one of my own encounters with the effects of future shock.

In the late nineties, I was hired as a writer for Walt Disney Imagineering. WDI is the arm of the Disney Company responsible for imagining and building the company's very successful theme parks. I joined the company in Orlando, Florida, and was assigned to the Epcot theme park. Epcot was originally conceived by Walt Disney as the Experimental Prototype Community of Tomorrow, where dreams about the future could be built, tested, and shared. Disney believed that such a destination would inspire the imaginations of millions of guests from around the world to the possibilities of the future.

> He quickly shot down my idea with the explanation that the mission of the park had changed. "It's just too difficult to keep up with the future," he said. Instead, he suggested I focus on ways to better integrate the Disney animated characters into the park's attractions.

I had long shared Walt's optimistic vision for the future and was excited by the prospect of joining the team appointed to keep that legacy alive. Shortly after my arrival, I was in a meeting with one of the WDI creative executives. He listened as I excitedly pitched an idea for updating one of the attractions in Future World to better reflect the changes that had happened in the twenty-five years since the park had opened. He quickly shot down my idea with the explanation that the mission of the park had changed. "It's just too difficult to keep up with the future," he said. Instead, he suggested I focus on ways to better integrate the Disney animated characters into the park's attractions.

If one of the leading voices in public entertainment is overwhelmed by the challenge of keeping up with the future, what does that mean for the larger conversation? A walk through the Epcot of 2019 provides a somewhat chilling answer. Where guests could once imagine what tomorrows might be just over the *Horizons*, they now fight space pirates alongside a group of interstellar misfits. Where they once played with tomorrow's *Innoventions*, they can now get an autograph from their favorite Marvel superhero.

I don't relate this story to be critical of Disney. They're in the business of entertaining millions of guests, most of whom are experiencing their own future shock. Under the circumstances, it makes good economic sense to sell escapism and avoid the stress of thinking about unknowable tomorrows. Disney is certainly not alone. Across the board, our institutional storytellers are suffering a collective sense of future shock. As a result, we find ourselves on the receiving end of a constant stream of dystopian visions and scenarios of collapse.

As futurists, we have an obligation to try to fill this void. A primary focus of my practice has been to devise ways to help people from all walks of life cope with the stress of constant and accelerating change. In doing this work, I have come to agree with one of Toffler's key assertions: "In dealing with the future…it is more important to be imaginative and insightful than to be one hundred percent right."[3]

In fact, imagination is the only tool that can help us escape the stress of future shock. It is through engaged imagination that we can create the stories that help us navigate the complexity of our contemporary futures. Not stories of superheroes or abstract utopias, but critical visions of optimistic tomorrows; the same stories that Walt Disney believed Epcot would offer.

In today's increasingly noisy environment, it is challenging to find the space to create and share these positive stories. To this end, Toffler offers an intriguing suggestion. He called for the creation of "imaginetic centers" where citizens could come together to "speculate freely, even playfully, about possible futures."[4]

As we celebrate the 50th anniversary of *Future Shock*, maybe it is time to take Toffler up on his idea. In our connected world, it would be simple to build such centers virtually. That would be an important first step. But I would like to hold out hope that we might go the extra mile and find physical spaces for these centers. Even in our digital world, there remains an extraordinary power in bringing people together face to face to imagine their futures. There are certainly plenty of physical spaces looking for new purposes in the wake of digital disruptions. Libraries, bookstores, even recently abandoned retail spaces, might be the perfect incubators for our futures.

A global network of imaginetic centers would be a compelling tribute to the creator of modern futurism. More importantly, it would be a positive strategy toward helping us avoid or at least ameliorate future shock as we navigate our constantly changing tomorrows. ▪

Joe Tankersley is a futurist, author, and former lead of Walt Disney Imagineering's foresight group. As principal consultant for Unique Visions, Inc., he uses the power of narrative to help organizations envision futures that are sustainable, abundant, and just. He is the author of *Reimagining Our Tomorrows; Making Sure Your Future Doesn't SUCK*. Joe is a former member of the board of directors of the Association of Professional Futurists and currently serves on the board of the environmental think tank WHALE Centre.

1. Alvin Toffler, *Future Shock* (Random House, New York, NY, 1970), p.2

2. Joi Ito and Jeff Howe, *Whiplash* (Grand Central Publishing, Boston MA, 2016), p. 19

3. Toffler, pg. 5

4. Toffler, pg. 398

We Must Replace the Dystopian Scarecrow of the Big Brother Society with the Vision of the Caring Big Sister Society

Hannes Sapiens (Sjoblad)

n their classic text, Alvin and Heidi Toffler eloquently describe how people often are irrationally biased to the status quo.

■ As an experimental biohacker actively pushing the limits of both technology and (occasionally) good taste, I regularly struggle to help people overcome future shock. Sometimes I even purposely work to induce it. What I have found is that the most powerful tool to overcome future shock is positive visions of superior outcomes.

Humanity is in the Process of Merging with Technology

In the last decade, the human species has gained a new organ, called the smartphone. It is most frequently found in one of the prehensile hands, but as often in front of or close to the face. The smartphone organ is multi-functional and helps augment a range of sensory and cognitive functions, including memory capture and storage and communications, and as an amplifier of both id and super-ego. Loss and detachment of the organ leads to a sense of stress and disorientation of the individual.

Pop culture has given us many versions of cyborgs with machine arms and brain implants, but the matter of fact as the 2020s begin is that integrating microelectronics with the human body is still very far from perfect. We can make life-saving special-function medical implants as well as cyberpunk-looking cybernetic prosthetics with a rudimentary degree of neurointegration, but in terms of function and comfort, a lot of work remains.

My professional endeavor in the field of body-integrated technology has focused on a field which I think is most promising for mainstream adoption: subcutaneous microchip implants the size of a grain of rice.

Long in use for pets and livestock, microchips have been implanted in billions of cats, dogs, and horses. We have an excellent understanding of how this technology platform works inside a living body. Unlike more complex medical-type implants, they do not require surgical interventions, but can be injected with a syringe in a second. Removal is almost as smooth as injection.

Current-generation implants can be used for a variety of purposes, including replacing key fobs, swipe cards, and other touch identification functions. With the growth of touch-type payments, it is today feasible

Big Sister does not spy on us. She protects us from prying eavesdroppers. Big Sister does not monitor our online habits in order to push more products on us; instead she negotiates with the other superbly powerful systems on the other side on our behalf.

to use the implants for making payments and to travel on public transport in an ever-increasing number of locations.

The next, currently emerging generation of injectable subcutaneous implants offers an even greater range of functionality: the inclusion of microprocessors, sensors, and outputs. We are going from single-function microchips to complex multifunctional devices, all in the form factor of a mouse dropping.

While these new hardware functions are helpful, it is ultimately the ever-evolving service layer on top of the hardware that truly creates the value for the user.

We Live in Hyperconnected, Hypermonitored Times

Financial services providers have full overview of our income patterns and spending habits. Network operators know not just our location but also which of our friends we speak to most frequently and when. Web browsers and advertisers know our interests and leanings better than our closest confidants. Wearables log our health, sleep, and behavioral habits. Social media platforms understand our political views and private habits better than we do ourselves.

Wherever we turn, some system or other registers what happens and feeds the data into increasingly smarter analytics algorithms. This world of abundant data will not come to pass, but simply constitutes the new normal.

Surely, in a not-too-distant future we will have smart assistants not just helping us with everyday chores such as planning travel and shopping, but predictively managing our needs and wants before we even know them ourselves.

Some People Call This a Big Brother Society

True indeed, if we simply allow ourselves to be gamed by the algorithms, this description is not inadequate.

It need not be malevolent. To some people, giving up decision-making to an algorithm can be a choice of comfort; it's great that an entertainment app gives me suggestions of the best movie to watch knowing my tastes instead of me having to browse a million different options. It could even be argued that giving up our impulsive, urge-driven decision power to benign algorithms will serve us very well. In terms of exercise and diet, it can even be called a wise choice.

There are incredibly powerful commercial and society-driven interests that want to drive our behavior to optimize their objectives and KPIs. But at the heart of being a conscious sentience is the freedom to make one's own decisions. We must not simply be the underlings of unseen algorithmic masters.

The objective must be to guarantee that the data-collecting algorithms are ultimately committed to the individual's best interest. The data collected must be controlled by the individual and best understood by that individual. So how can this be brought about?

The Big Sister

I am convinced we will live to witness a world where it is commonplace to have health-monitoring technology under our skin. This technology can truly augment our understanding of our metabolic and other bodily processes. It will take us from having to manage our systems based on how we feel (!) to data-driven decision-making. It will give us the ability to detect and even predict emerging health issues and make early interventions. It will reduce the risk of many ills and powerfully extend healthy human lifespans.

This little implantable health advisor, I call Big Sister. The good, caring algorithm watching over you.

The Big Sister Vision

But Big Sister is much more than an implant taking care of your health. Big Sister is an idea. It is a data-driven, all-encompassing agent that is fighting on your side in all dimensions of life: for your health, your financial interests, and your peace of mind.

Big Sister is the opposite of Big Brother. Big Brother is the nosy, overbearing bully that uses and abuses you. Big Sister is the loving entity that you know cares for you, is always covering your back, and has your best interests in mind.

Big Sister does not spy on us. She protects us from prying eavesdroppers. Big Sister does not monitor our online habits in order to push more products on us; instead she negotiates with the other superbly powerful systems on the other side on our behalf. She finds us the best-priced travel ticket, identifies the health treatment that we need, plans our calendar for us, and keeps us on top of the information we need to have.

For a better future, we must build the manifest of Big Sister—as a societal vision, as a legal framework, as business models, and as a cultural phenomenon. ▨

Hannes Sapiens (Sjoblad) is a biohacker and human augmentation technologist committed to the idea of radically improving the human condition. He is an author, speaker and professional advisor on the impact of exponential technologies, and he serves as a faculty member at Singularity University Nordic. Hannes grew up in the relatively well working democratic welfare state of Sweden and hence holds a belief that government has the capacity to be benevolent. He has two brothers and no sisters, which may play a part in his idealization of having a big sister. Find him on hannessapiens.com

From Human by Default to Human by Design

Kris Østergaard

When Alvin Toffler published his visionary master-piece in 1970, he foresaw the coming of the adhocracy: Networked, agile organizations operating at a pace and impact so extraordinary that it constituted a shock for humankind. I'm sure most would agree that his prediction has come true, most clearly demonstrated in the world's dominating tech companies. But we ain't seen nothing yet.

Within the next 50 years, the pace and impact won't be 10X bigger than today; it will be 1,000X bigger than today. In this future, human beings' roles will be defined by their interactions with artificial intelligence (AI) combined with the delegation of decision-making powers to the AIs. In other words, we will see the human role in the workplace take distinct forms based on levels of human vs. AI execution and human vs. AI authority. This can be broken down into four dominant organizational forms, illustrated in Figure 1. Three of them involve human beings and only one isn't deeply dependent on AI. Let me elaborate.

Freelancers: Human Execution + AI Authority

In the top-left quadrant we find the realm encompassing the majority of humans who will still be working in 2050. This is the freelance economy taken to its extreme. In this future, the majority of humans do not switch jobs every few years, as many do today, with career changes as many as four times over one's working life. In this future, every individual pursues multiple careers *at once*—or

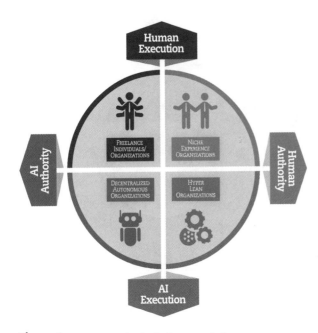

Figure 1 • Human-AI roles in the future workplace.
Courtesy of Kris Østergaard

perhaps it is more appropriate to say multiple jobs at once, as opposed to careers, because the majority of freelance workers in the future will be at the bottom of the job chain with limited career opportunities.

In 2020 a large percentage of workers in the USA and UK already have multiple jobs in order to make ends meet—for example, moonlighting as drivers for ride-hailing services, or a variety of retail jobs. We also already see the tech giants of the world hiring more contractors over full-time employees because contractors don't require the same healthcare, insurance, pensions, and other benefits as full-time employees, thereby lowering operating costs. Some in the freelance economy are there by choice. They are the talented artists, writers, coders, etc. who are so good at what they do that they can choose to be freelancers, taking on only the jobs that they want. But for the majority of workers in the freelance economy, it is not a choice. It is a necessity. Projections for 2027 suggest a tipping point of more than 50% of the USA workforce freelancing in some way. The rest of the world is behind but will catch up. Ultimately, I believe, freelancers will constitute 90+ percent of the entire workforce. Freelancing will be the norm.

Part of this dramatic shift will also be that the majority of human workers will be managed by an AI, because the majority of the jobs they perform will be powered by algorithms. These human workers will, in effect, have an AI boss telling them what to do, evaluating their work, and ultimately deciding whether they deserve a raise, a bonus, a warning, or termination. This management paradigm will also apply to those who freelance by choice. If this sounds like science fiction, consider the algorithms already deployed in Amazon's warehouses that have such capacity and authority, even though, at present, a human being is said to always have the final word in cases of firing. The ride-hailing driver also, in effect, already works for an algorithm that tells her where to go next, which route to take, and the average score needed to avoid warnings and termination for poor customer service.

Nonetheless, I believe that freelancers will gain more power in the future than they hold today. Why? Because they will organize. Partly via organizations that specialize in offering certain freelance skills to corporations and governments and partly via unions that will see a resurgence.

While I write these sentences in 2019, the idea of being managed by an algorithm is controversial—but I predict that it will take far less than 50 years for this to become a norm that raises no eyebrows.

Niche Experience Organizations: Human Execution + Human Authority

This quadrant includes organizations that insist on keeping digitization and automation at a minimum for philosophical reasons and because it will be a differentiating business model. These organizations are the creatives who produce art, furniture, or ceramics, and market themselves as an "authentic" choice by designing and producing without AI as the primary source of innovation and execution. Here we will also see organizations within elderly, child, and pet care, healthcare, and personal development that carve out a niche by guaranteeing human decision-making based on old-school, 20th century human skillsets like intuition and empathy, and insisting on human-to-human interaction.

Just as the vinyl record didn't die but escaped extinction to become a niche, premium, experiential product in a world dominated by automated streaming playlists, so will there be a market for Niche Experience Organizations amongst the more affluent parts of our populations.

Hyper Lean Organizations: AI Execution + Human Authority

The large majority of organizations will be Hyper Lean Organizations (the lower-right quadrant). These organizations are characterized by being primarily driven by AI execution but with a management level of human decision makers. This is today's large legacy organization or tech giant in a purer form. They will have long since become "AI first." In this world, all processes and all production are created and managed by leveraging AI for optimum efficiency and cost; innovation will have been taken over by AI as well, due to the radical speed of shifts in trends and opportunities.

The majority of corporations today need to create organizations full of incremental innovators where every employee is comfortable with change within the core organization, supported by technology, because the pace of change and opportunity has accelerated. Today there is also an increasing need for radical innovators who challenge the foundations of their organizations by imagining and developing entirely new offerings and business models that go beyond—or disrupt—existing core value offerings. But the corporations of the future will need to challenge their cores at a pace so fast that the human mind cannot manage it. The future corporation will need to rely on AI to spot trends, analyze patterns, select opportunities, develop offerings and business models, acid-test innovations, and execute at a radical pace.

We now have products and startups that achieve billion-dollar valuations within months. In 50 years, this timescale will be reduced to weeks, days, hours, or even minutes. No human will have the mental capacity to keep up with this speed. But, I believe that we will see human beings insisting on keeping their spot in the driver's seat by maintaining humans in organizational management positions (the rest of the positions will have been automated or turned over to freelancers). Those managers will have the legal authority to be the ultimate strategic decision makers. Supported by AI, of course, but humans retain the final say. Not necessarily

> These human workers will, in effect, have an AI boss telling them what to do, evaluating their work, and ultimately deciding whether they deserve a raise, a bonus, a warning, or termination.

because human intervention is needed, but because we will want it to be so, and we'll insist on ethical guidelines that require a human go/no-go decision maker at the higher levels.

Decentralized Autonomous Organizations: AI Execution + AI Authority

The final, lower-left quadrant of our figure eliminates the need for human participation entirely. This is where Decentralized Autonomous Organizations prevail. This organizational form is still theoretical in 2020, but it will see the light of day soon. Here, AI is not only the producer of the offering but also has complete decision-making authority.

Think, for example, of a vending machine for snacks. The machine's services and processes can be entirely digitized and automated. First, you transfer money to the vending machine digitally. Then you push a button on the machine and it delivers a snack to you immediately. It's a simple transaction already in place today. The difference for the future will be that, just as corporations are legal entities today, vending machines will also become legal entities that might also have their own bank accounts. This status will enable them to make their own money and therefore also to decide how best to deploy the funds. It also means that a vending machine that makes enough money will be able to order its own inventory and pay for its own maintenance. If it makes a profit, it will be able to invest those profits in new vending machines and thus grow its organization.

The same principle will apply for autonomous vehicles that won't need an owner/manager any more than they'll need a driver. It's not hard to imagine this extending to banking, insurance, legal assistance, or any other industry where services can be automated and therefore run entirely by algorithms that are able to identify your needs and provide you with the services you desire at ultralow cost. Having humans in this loop would only increase costs and delays.

For Better or Worse?

Does the above scenario describe a desirable future? I think it depends. There are many jobs today that are dangerous or tedious, or provide little satisfaction, and perhaps ought to be automated as quickly as possible. We also all want lower prices and more convenience. By enabling increasingly lower living costs through automation, we can create a future where many people actually need to work less to enjoy a higher quality of life. Many may not even need to work at all.

However, if all are to benefit from such radical automation, we must also create conditions where the majority do not become paralyzed by the next wave of future shock. We must remember to carve out room for the human in the equation to avoid being swallowed in a world where AI dominates the relationship. In the future, work will no longer be human by default, it will only be human if it is human by design.

Kris Østergaard is a researcher, writer, and in-demand keynote speaker on innovation, corporate culture, and the impact of technological change. He is co-founder and Chief Learning & Innovation Officer of SingularityU Nordic, the Nordic entity of Silicon Valley-based educational institution Singularity University. He is the author of *Transforming Legacy Organizations*; co-author of *The Fundamental 4s—Designing Extraordinary Customer Experiences in an Exponential World*; and co-founder of the experience design firm DARE2, accelerator program Thinkubator, and co-working space DARE-2mansion. Kris is also a board member, angel investor, and advisor to both startups and Fortune 500 companies.

Future Shock Made Futurists' Lives Easier

Jerome C. Glenn

Future Shock **moved "the future" from the sole realm of science fiction into contemporary discourse.** ■ Alvin and Heidi Toffler—the Tofflers—began making it respectable to think seriously about the future and what we might do today to make it better.[1] Granted, the RAND Corporation was founded in 1948, and Herman Kahn was thinking the unthinkable long before the Tofflers, but RAND's and Kahn's mission was to prevent World War III, not to wake up the public about continuous societal change.

So too in Paris, Gaston Berger created the Centre d'études Prospectives in 1957 and Bertrand de Jouvenel created Futuribles in 1960. None of these engaged the public in rethinking the character of civilization. Also, a year before *Future Shock* was published, the first doctoral program on the study of the future opened at the University of Massachusetts's School of Education.[2] But it, too, had little public outreach and finally closed its doors a decade later. It should also be acknowledged that the first Western philosopher of continual change was the pre-Socratic Greek philosopher Heraclitus, but his words were not heard around the world until many years later.

So the Tofflers were not the first to address the ideas, but they were the most effective in waking up millions around the world to continuous global change. Now, 50 years later, when someone asks "What's a futurist?" it is still possible to answer: you remember that book *Future Shock*? Well, that's what futurists do—systematically look at future possibilities, consequences, and, given all that, figure out what we should do to improve our prospects. The Tofflers stressed that we—leaders and the public—had to anticipate change in order to manage change. Today there are legions of "change management" consultants worldwide.

Rereading *Future Shock* for this essay, I was reminded that it is a gigantically rich book with massive documentation, while still being reader-friendly. The Tofflers were really good writers. It made the rest of us futurists back then secretly a little bit jealous. None of our books sold in numbers even close to those realized by *Future Shock*. Many of us (though there weren't many of us then) did feed the Tofflers with research, ideas, and insights,[3] but they brought our input to life with easily readable prose. Hence, they more than any other intellectuals opened the doors of perception and brought some acceptance to the work of futurists.

So now, fifty years later, the new forces of change are the synergies among Moore's Law (computer cost/performance doubling every 18 months); Nielsen's Law (internet bandwidth capacity grows 50% per year); computation science (computer simulations can run millions of experiments in the time it takes to set up physical lab experiments, rapidly expanding the pool of scientific knowledge upon which technology draws); artificial narrow intelligence (AI that drives a car but cannot diagnose cancer) and potential artificial general intelligence (we do not yet have AGI, at least in the public, but if we do get it, it would address new situations by drawing on all accessible relevant information in order to rewrite its own code; it would solve novel problems in a similar manner to how we humans draw on many sources to do so); and synergies among NT (Next Technologies such as synthetic biology, genomics, nanotechnology, 3D/4D printing of materials and organics, quantum computing, robotics, AI/Avatars, cloud and big data analytics, artificial and augmented reality, Internet of Things, tele-everything and everybody, semantic web, telepresence, holographic communications, blockchain, collective intelligence, drones, driverless cars and other autonomous vehicles, and conscious-technology [mutual direct interaction of mind and machine]). Since this list is way too long to keep repeating when talking about what technologies will continue to accelerate change, I prefer to simply say NT (Next Technologies) as we do with ICT, which covers many things as well.

Why do I stress this? The Tofflers talked about adapting to the future. Almost as if the future were set, out there, and will come down on us like a coming rainstorm. Granted, the Tofflers did write very clearly in the introduction that the future was not determined, fixed, as if it were a knowable "thing." Instead, the introduction states: "No serious futurist deals with predictions... This means that every statement about the future ought, by rights, be accompanied by a string of qualifiers—ifs, ands, buts, and on the other hands... Rather than do this, I have taken the liberty of speaking firmly, without hesitation, trusting that the intelligent reader will understand the stylistic problem." Indeed we do, and did, but the strategies to prevent future shock in the first sections of the book still focused more on adapting to the future than on inventing or shaping the future. The current acceleration of the rate of change and the foreseeable synergies among NTs change what we think is possible, or at least it should change what we think is possible.

> The strategies to prevent future shock in the first sections of the book still focused more on adapting to the future than on inventing or shaping the future.

So, we should also talk about inventing or shaping the future, since there are far more possibilities than we are able to implement. Hence, choice and decision-making become more important than in the past, when there were fewer options. The question, then, becomes about what we should create, along with how we adapt. What future do we want to help emerge from the synergies among NTs that can address global challenges? This is the drama today: we are in a race between implementing ever-increasing ways to improve the human condition and addressing the seemingly ever-increasing complexity and scale of global problems.

In biology, resilience is the ability to respond, adapt, and survive disasters. Resilience for humans is also this, plus the ability to anticipate. And this part, *Future Shock* nailed! The more you anticipate, *Future Shock* argued, the less likely you will suffer from future shock. Ah, but too many of us have become numb to change: Upgrade to the next version of the software whether we like it or not; get the next iPhone even though the current one works great; get the next car whether the old one is still good or not. It seems we have more habituated to change than been shocked by it. Habituation occurs when there is no or limited response to stimuli; most people "just go along."

Because NT offers potential futures beyond most people's capacity for imagination, today's futurists, 50 years on from *Future Shock*'s publication, talk about "inventing" or "shaping" the future rather than "adapting." However, many futures research studies, such as the plethora of future-of-work studies that address ways to "adapt" to emergent technological unemployment scenarios[4], prescribe "anticipation," such as anticipation of alternative work structures and economics, and "shaping" policy and personal strategies with that anticipation in mind.

> It seems we have more habituated to change than been shocked by it. Habituation occurs when there is no or limited response to stimuli; most people "just go along."

In the latter sections of *Future Shock* there is more stress on managing change, assessing future technologies, and having large-scale public discussions about the future. The Tofflers called for massive computer systems to inform these public discussions. Today we have Google and Wikipedia for information, but these resources do not provide coherence and context for future possibilities. In addition to these great internet resources, we need global collective intelligence systems, open to the public and continually and systematically updated and improved with inputs from both "experts" and the public.

The Tofflers complained that there was no organized way for the public to input their views on the future. Today we have the Global Futures Intelligence System[5] which, along with other systems, can inform and be informed by the "future public assembles" that the Tofflers called for, but those assemblies are yet to be seriously implemented. SYNCONs [Alvin Toffler participated in one held at the US Congress] by the Committee for the Future, led by Barbara Marx Hubbard back in the 1970s[6], and various state processes in the USA as documented in *Anticipatory Democracy*, edited by Clement Bezold, were the closest things to "social future assembles." Toward the end of the book, the Tofflers write, "...social future assemblies could unleash powerful constructive forces—the forces of conscious evolution." And this is the most important point of the book: we are in a position to consciously control our evolution, if we get organized to do so.

Granted, *Future Shock* mostly focuses on the United States. China was mentioned only twice, tangentially, in the entire book. Books on the general future do not do that today. President Putin says whoever leads AI will rule the world, and China said it will lead AI by 2030. The US, EU, and China have projects to reverse-engineer the human brain; corporations like IBM, Google, Facebook, Baidu, Microsoft, Alibaba, Apple, and Amazon are working on artificial brains and artificial general intelligence. Organized crime can buy the best computer talent money can buy. Hence, the Great Global Brain Race is on! This is the new drama replacing the nuclear arms race. *Future Shock* did not consider the future of geopolitics.

Meanwhile, the world is improving more than most pessimists know, but future dangers are worse than most optimists indicate. Fifty years ago, the majority of humans lived in extreme poverty, many with reduced brain function due to protein and iron malnutrition. Fifty years from today, the majority of humans could be technologically augmented geniuses with quantum computing at their command.

After 24 years of The Millennium Project's global futures research, it is clear that we, as a species, are winning more than losing, but the areas where we are losing are very serious. We have no grounds for pessimism, but no room to relax, either.

When you consider the many wrong decisions made and good decisions missed—day after day and year after year around the world—it is amazing that we are still making as much progress as we are. But we would be well served to reread *Future Shock's* final chapter, "Strategies of Social Futurism," and implement the spirit of those suggestions, with a caveat: it would have been better to call it "Social Futures," as "futurism" is a school of art founded in Milan, Italy, over a hundred years ago, glorifying technology and robotized style and later being related to fascism. "Social Futures" has the advantage of reinforcing that there are more than one possible future. ▪

Jerome C. Glenn is the co-founder (1996) and CEO of The Millennium Project (on global futures research), and author of "Social Technologies of Freedom" in *Anticipatory Democracy*, edited by Clem Bezold and initiated in the last section of *Future Shock*. He has published over 100 future-oriented articles in such publications as *Nikkei*, *ADWEEK*, *International Tribune*, *LEADERS*, *New York Times*, McGraw-Hill's *Contemporary Learning Series*, *Current*, Royal Society of Arts (RSA) *Journal*, *Foresight*, *Futures*, *Technological Forecasting*, *Futures Research Quarterly*, and *The Futurist*. He is co-editor of *Futures Research Methodology* versions 1.0 to 3.0, author of *Future Mind: Merging the Mystical and the Technological in the 21st Century* (1989 & 1994), *Linking the Future: Findhorn, Auroville, Arcosanti* (1979), and co-author of *Space Trek: The Endless Migration* (1978 & 1979). Glenn has a BA in philosophy from American University and an MA in Teaching Social Science—Futuristics from Antioch Graduate School of Education (now Antioch University New England), and was a doctoral candidate in general futures research at the University of Massachusetts. He received the Donella Meadows Medal, Kondratieff Medal, Emerald Citation of Excellence, honorary professorship, and doctor's degrees from two universities in South America (Universidad Ricardo Palma and Universidad Franz Tamayo). He was the Washington, DC, representative for the United Nations University as executive director of the American Council for the UNU 1988-2007, and is a leading boomerang stunt man.

1. I refer to the Tofflers throughout this chapter because in the acknowledgments section, Alvin Toffler writes: "It [*Future Shock*] is, in large measure, her book, as well as mine." Also, Al dedicated an earlier book, *The Culture Consumers: Art and Affluence in America*, published by St. Martin's Press in 1964, to Heidi.

2. The first doctoral degree granted by UMass in Futures Research went to Christopher Dede, a direct decedent of Benjamin Franklin, possibly America's first futurist.

3. Alvin Toffler was a member of the Board of Advisors of the Future Options Room, a small Washington-based think tank I led in the mid-1970s.

4. Work/Technology 2050: Scenarios and Actions, Glenn, J and The Millennium Project Team. *The Millennium Project*, 2019: Washington, DC.

5. https://themp.org/

6. Glenn, J "Participatory Methods," ed. Glenn J., Gordon, T., *Futures Research Methodology 3.0 The Millennium Project*

Storytelling
for Survival

Maggie Greyson, MDes

Writing in their runaway bestseller, the Tofflers suggested a novel, if not radical, mechanism for averting the effects of future shock. Through the use of "experiential simulation" they proposed that an individual can be "pre-adapted" to an otherwise unfamiliar future by not only seeing and hearing, but touching, tasting, and smelling the new environment he is about to enter. "He will be able to interact vicariously with the people in his future," they wrote, "and to undergo carefully contrived experiences designed to improve his coping abilities."

They also proposed a "psych-corps" that would be sure to find a fertile market in the "design and operation of such preadaptive facilities," where whole families would become conditioned and prepared to "cope with their own personal tomorrows."

These experiential learning facilities would foster elements of storytelling, design, and embodied knowledge, all intended to help people to navigate—and survive—a future rife with otherwise shocking rates of change.

Well, it may have taken nearly 50 years, but we are finally creating Toffler's "enclaves of the future."

■ ■ ■

There are several ways that we can engage and stimulate our imaginations to serve us in envisioning possibilities through an approach called speculative design. Speculative design is an artifact or experience that is based on what we think might be possible in the future.

When we take on the role of a speculative designer, we need to be meticulous in the experiences of the places of conversation. We need to construct future artifacts based on robust research, scripting complex relationships based on fundamental human needs, and pay attention to the details in the building of "diegetic" environments so that we can be immersed in authentic debates (diegesis is a style of storytelling that presents an interior view of a world in which the experiences of its characters are revealed through narrative).

It involves many of the same creative practices we employ when designing products and services, with concept drawings and prototypes serving as low-risk investments in their development. (Like a prototype or a sketch, its elements do not need to be fully rendered.) These tools help us to efficiently communicate ideas and share our visions with others so that we can better collaborate to achieve them. The same principles apply when imagining a future we hope to achieve.

This notion extends to imagining alternative futures—based on authentic exploration—that we may or may not desire, and allowing to stand back and ask, "Is this really the future we want for the next generation?"

Timescale matters, too. The farther out we project, the harder it is to humanize distant tomorrows.

To all these ends, the Tofflers proposed methods to encourage and develop long-term thinking skills. Their concept of "enclaves of the future" helps compensate for our temporal lack of "future heritage." They envisioned environments like a community square, a gated community, or remote villages as being constructed to support vicarious engagements with "time spanners," people who would be compensated for "living in the future."

They also suggested playful spaces—imaginetic centers—that would help communities to engage with futures through collective experiences. "Local government, schools, voluntary associations and others," they wrote, "also need to examine their potential futures imaginatively. One way to help them do so would be to establish in each community 'imaginetic centers' devoted to technically assisted brainstorming. These would be places where people noted for creative imagination, rather than technical expertise, are brought together to examine present crises, to anticipate future crises, and to speculate freely, even playfully, about possible futures."

> This notion extends to imagining alternative futures—based on authentic exploration—that we may or may not desire, and allowing to stand back and ask, "Is this really the future we want for the next generation?"

These centers would provide a focal point for very carefully contrived "work-learn-and-play" environments made with artists, poets, laborers, and other skilled participants who can improve coping abilities. Perhaps someday, the practice of community-based, speculative long-term thinking will be a part of all strategic planning collaborations.

To capture the value in these highly articulated environments we might need Hollywood-scale budgets, a diverse cast of contributors, and highly skilled artisans to create a living simulation of the future.

With the moon landings capturing the world's attention at the time *Future Shock* was published, the Tofflers cited a particularly relevant example of just such an environment—astronauts training in "experiential simulations" in order "to cope with a variety of future contingencies" so that they will be calm when unexpected things happen. They become accustomed to the details of the environment—lights, alerts, sounds—to adjust and adapt with efficiency to an irregular event. Just like the astronauts, we, too, can "pre-adapt" to uncertain futures through training that can speed up our cognitive and decision-making processes.

Speculative design focuses our attention on future outputs. Thanks to *Future Shock*, speculative design has become part of our pop culture, although we would not identify it that way. Innovation relies on imagination to create future digital products and services. In the marketplace, we call the initial outputs prototypes, beta versions, or minimum viable products; we see them in Kickstarter campaigns and myriad technology media. While we don't experience them in the context of experiential learning, such innovations can help us become better students in thinking about future impacts. For example, while innovators and marketers describe products and services as though they work exactly as intended, we may not learn of the invisible opportunities and unintended consequences associated with the new technologies until decades, or even generations, later.

To imagine them today, we need to integrate the intentionally designed speculative artifact or experience. This involves the usual elements of storytelling—character development, setting, plot, conflict, theme, narrative arc, situation, props—all of which contribute important dimensions to meaning.

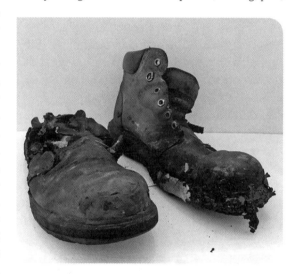

To provide an example, designer and futurist Kelly Kornet wants us to envision tomorrows—in 2025—where a catastrophic explosion happens in a small industrial town in Ontario, Canada. She displays an excavated pair of work boots—a relic from the future. They are charred and odorous, representing the remains of a potential destructive incident, five years into the future. The boots are rich in detail, providing for enhanced context. It is a contrived artifact, but it helps us to connect thoughts and feelings to a potential future scenario. One's own critical questions emerge more quickly when there is a connection to "lived" experiences. A visitor to this exhibit might speculate that the future worker who owns the boots will be killed in this disaster. They might wonder why this accident happened; if it could have been prevented; and most importantly, why it wasn't. This creative presentation is but one element of a larger narrative inside the "Museum of the Future."

Such a museum, the Tofflers postulated, could also be useful mechanisms for younger generations to communicate to the generations in power the ways in which they see the world. Just as ancient pottery shards exhibited in a traditional museum provide insight into a way of life in the past, displays like Kornet's charred work boots provoke long-term thinking about complex issues we'll face in the future. Imagine how an exhibit's titling, future dates, and descriptions might capture a possible future society.

The parallels between a museum of the past and museum of the future teach us that disruption has been, and will continue to be, a feature of life on Earth. They also demonstrate that the human race has always had the resilience to survive such disruptions. Now, imagine a future "Museum of the Past" that features our present generation. What exhibits might it include?

Such large scale creative concepts help us to pre-adapt to shifts, as well as to the accelerated rate of change in political, economic, social, and environmental systems. We need frequent reminders of the day-to-day consequences that may result if long-term thinking is neglected.

Anab Jain, a Professor of Design, TED Speaker, Futurist, and director of the design and film studio Superflux, says, "We have learned in our work that one of the most powerful means of effecting change is when people can directly, tangibly, and emotionally experience some of the future consequences of their actions today."

Jain was inspired to work with chemists to create—and bottle—an actual sample of the projected air pollution levels in 2030 for the government of the United Arab Emirates. During a working session, one of the participants told her, "There's no way I can tell my son to stop driving his car." She knew she had to help them understand the future in a way that statistics could not express. The stinky and noxious fumes that she brought with her created immediacy with possible impacts of a continuation of the current policies. This is what their own next generation might have to live with if they do not consider action now.

Fifty years ago, we were anxious about surviving tomorrow. Today, we need to do more than just "cope." Just as it did 50 years ago, experiential learning can help us be deliberate about creating the future we want for the next generation—uncertain as it may be. But uncertainty is a fertile space. Opening up our imaginations, we can—with the help of storytelling—begin to embrace the tension between surviving and thriving. ▨

Maggie Greyson is a designer, futurist, and founder of Futures Present from Toronto, Canada. Her mandate is to help people use the ambiguous nature of our times to play a meaningful part in the future. Robust research and creative risk-taking define a career that started with theatrical set design, interactive media, and integrated advertising. Maggie has a Masters of Design in Strategic Foresight and Innovation from the Ontario College of Art and Design University. She is a Winner of the Most Significant Futures Works from the Association of Professional Futurists, Next Generation Foresight Practitioner Special Award from the School of International Futures, and Emerging Fellow of the Association of Professional Futurists. Her master's thesis, "Making the Futures Present" (by AMH Greyson), combines design, personal foresight and experiential futures techniques.

The Global Intelligent Machine

Teun Koetsier

he *Machine Stops* **is a story from 1928 by Edward Morgan**

Forster. ▪ It is about a machine that fully controls life on Earth. Mankind lives underground because the surface of the Earth has become uninhabitable. On the surface, where the air is hard to breathe, only a few Homeless, as the machine calls them, succeed in surviving. The protagonist of the story is a young man called Kuno. He feels that there must be more to life than full obedience to the rules of the machine, and so he rises up against it. The resulting major and irreparable malfunctions bring the machine to a halt, and cause many deaths. Kuno and a few survivors are left on the surface of the Earth, where, together with the Homeless, Kuno will try to rebuild a civilization in harmony with nature.

Forster's tale is one of several similar stories that appeared in the first half of the 19th century expressing the feeling that technology separates man from nature, that it degrades man. Aldous Huxley's *Brave New World*, written in 1932, is another famous example. The stories can be seen as elegant literary criticism of things that were actually happening, but they were obviously fiction. For good reasons, Huxley set his story in the year 2540, hundreds of years in the future.

Things have changed. Right now, at the beginning of the 21st century, the technology needed to build one huge machine that completely controls a society or even the world comes into view. In this development, the technologies of connectivity and artificial intelligence play a central role. Even in 1970, when Alvin Toffler wrote *Future Shock*, the fantasies of Forster, Huxley, and others still seemed pure science fiction. Yet Toffler realized that the industrial societies as we knew them were rapidly changing. Ten years later, in *The Third Wave,* Toffler discussed the "intelligent environment" and predicted the rise of intelligent networks.

Information Machines

A machine used to be a device that enhances our possibilities to intervene in nature. I call such artifacts—like windmills, steam engines, cars, and airplanes—*production machines*. They dominated technological development in and after the Industrial Revolution. The result was the large-scale mechanization of man's physical interaction with nature and a complete transformation of society. Agricultural societies became industrial societies.

Nowadays computers dominate our life. Computers are not production machines; they are *information* machines. Instead of intervening physically in reality, they process information—and they do so quite efficiently. Production and information machines can be combined in *hybrid machines*. Robots are hybrid machines: sensors collect information, on the basis of which a computer calculates the moves that are executed by production machinery. We have clearly entered the age of robots. The number of industrial robots worldwide is around 2.5 million at the moment, and it is growing. Military robots are now a standard part of the defensive arsenal. Service robots have moved into areas like removal of land mines, volcano exploration, deep-sea exploration, extraterrestrial exploration, construction works, agriculture, mining, cargo handling, cleaning, and helping the elderly. Completely automated vehicles have appeared on the roads, and while the public might not yet be ready for it, pilotless flying is a possibility.

Indeed, the development of computer technology has completely transformed society. Industrial societies have become information societies in which—quite in accordance with Toffler's views—all our institutions are shaking under the hurricane impact of the accelerative advance of technology.

The Global Intelligent Machine

While in the past machines were always local, we are now living in an age of connectivity, and this has profound implications. Automated connectivity has led to machines that extend over large areas—a factory, a city, a country, even the globe. The internet is very different from, say, a steam locomotive, but it is a complex coherent device operating on the basis of the laws of physics, designed to perform a task. That means that it is a machine—not a production machine, but a huge global information machine comprising a network of computers.

> While in the past machines were always local, we are now living in an age of connectivity, and this has profound implications.

Originally, the internet did not collect the information it processed. It merely processed the information that we human beings put into it. That has changed. The internet has become the Internet of Things, which is the internet combined with billions of sensors that automatically gather information that is subsequently processed and stored. The Internet of Things is a huge global information machine and it, too, is growing. As more sensors are added, we are again witnessing a new development. Artificial intelligence software that tries to understand the data is being incorporated more and more into systems. The Internet of Things is getting smarter. Because production machinery is also increasingly being hooked up, the Internet of Things is no longer merely an information machine, but is becoming a gigantic hybrid machine. For this global machine I coined the name *Global Intelligent Machine* (GIM).[1] GIM has sensors to register the world, brains to process the information, and production machinery to intervene in the world.

Industrial robots, service robots, self-driving vehicles, and in general all smart machines that will be built in the future, will be connected to GIM. Because there is not one central control and there are many users, GIM is a robotic machine, but not a robot, although in principle it could become one. Robots extending over considerable areas like automated ports, factories, and farms already exist.[2] Singapore's prison system, for example, is moving toward automating work processes in prison. It calls the concept "prison without guards."[3] Jörg Goldhan, of ETH Zürich, argues that robots will make doctors obsolete in the foreseeable future, allowing hospitals to significantly save on costs.[4] And indeed in 2017 a robot passed China's national medical exam, scoring 96 points higher than the required 360.[5]

> The idea that maybe even before the end of this century machines will be able to imitate human beings in such a way that we will be inclined to accept them as our equals may sound bold, but it is no longer incredible.

Are Chess-Playing Robots Really Playing Chess?

Imagine an unmanned spaceship floating somewhere in space many light-years away. On-board robots are playing chess. Incessantly the robots calculate their next moves, and when the game is over, they start again. All contact with Earth was lost long ago, and nobody is watching the game. Are these robots really playing chess? Of course they are, you might say, if you adhere to realism in philosophy. Trees in the forest don't stop existing simply because nobody sees them.

However, imagine that a wave on the beach casts two shells at my feet. The next wave adds three shells. Is the sea calculating 2+3=5 here? This sounds strange, but don't worry. The events on the beach are accidental and essentially need an observer to be interpreted as 2+3=5, while the robots were designed to play chess. The sea does not calculate, but the robots do what they are designed to do, irrespective of any observers. Somebody imagined them playing chess, designed and built them, and that is, from a realist point of view, sufficient to say that they play chess.

I am a realist. Yet what is taking place on the spaceship seems quite pointless and not at all a game. The robots go through the moves and, strictly speaking, perhaps they are playing chess, but I would argue that they are not *really* playing chess unless they also possess qualities like being able to enjoy the game and, more generally, by being aware of themselves and of what they are doing.

At present robots do not have these qualities, but this may change. In 2005 Ray Kurzweil made the daring prediction that within decades machines would become superior to human beings in every respect, not only in problem-solving skills, but also in emotional and moral intelligence.[6] This is the event he called the "Singularity." The idea that maybe even before the end of this century machines will be able to imitate human beings in such a way that we will be inclined to accept them as our equals may sound bold, but it is no longer incredible. The technological development is unbelievably fast and there are no signs that it will slow down. The question is when the imitation, the replica, will be accepted as real, as equivalent to us.

> Those who assume that in every wave of automation, new jobs are created elsewhere in the economy, forget that in the past there were always lots of things machines could not do. We are now talking about robots that can do everything a human being can do.

It may happen without us even noticing it. Already, important decisions that in the past were made by humans are left to computer programs. In the US, parole boards sometimes rely on software that calculates whether an inmate should get parole. There also exist programs that analyze traces of DNA from crime scenes. The way this software works is a trade secret.[7] The possibility that everywhere in society superior software will gradually replace human beings is real.

In the history of technology mankind has again and again entered uncharted territory. Now it may be more than business as usual. Basically, two things define a human being. We process information, and we interact physically with nature. After the Industrial Revolution, most if not all aspects of our physical interaction with nature were mechanized. Moreover, computer technology has made it possible to mechanize many aspects of our information processing. It seems we are on our way to mechanizing ALL aspects of our human existence. Such a thing has never happened before. We seem to be nearing a crucial limit of some sort.

The Impact

Currently, in spite of its complexity, your computer is an object and you can do with it whatever you want. You can sell it to someone else, and even if you demolish it in a fit of temper it is unlikely that you will be accused of serious wrongdoing. It will become very difficult to treat robots or robotic machines like GIM merely as objects once they possess emotions and are conscious of themselves. It seems inevitable that they will claim rights and subsequently force the world to respect those rights. A pessimist might say that once the superior intelligence of GIM also includes emotions, moral insight, and self-awareness, we will have created Forster's machine. This may very well happen before the end of this century.

The optimist must assume that we will succeed in controlling the development in such a way that GIM turns out to be benevolent. Already we are struggling to adapt to the relentless pace of technological development. The undesirable effects of the ease by which messages can be spread over the globe are obvious. The internet does not distinguish between entertainment and information, between truth and falsehood—even while fake news attracts more attention. The traditional sources of reliable information—science, critical journalism, and the state—are competing with stories produced by idiots, lunatics, and adversaries of Western civilization. Cybercrime is already a major problem and will remain so. The rise of GIM, the Global Intelligent Machine, makes the risks much bigger. Without proper security measures, the production machinery that is part of GIM can, in principle, be manipulated from a great distance by unauthorized entities. For a nice survey of all the risks involved in the rise of GIM, I refer to security expert Bruce Schneier's aptly titled book *Click Here to Kill Everybody*.[8] Those who assume that in every wave of automation, new jobs are created elsewhere in the economy, forget that in the past there were always lots of things machines could not do. We are now talking about robots that can do everything a human being can do. The effect on our economies cannot be less than substantial. GIM is an incredibly impressive machine, but it confronts us also with major challenges.

Teun Koetsier is a historian and philosopher of mathematics at VU University Amsterdam, the Netherlands. His research covers a wide range of subjects. While working on a "Big History" of production and information machines, he realized that what started with simple production and information tools like hand axes and tally sticks seems to lead inevitably to a situation in which all existing modern machinery becomes part of one big global hybrid machine, GIM, the Global Intelligent Machine. See https://www.springer.com/gp/book/9783319965468.

1. Teun Koetsier, *The Ascent of GIM, the Global Intelligent Machine, A history of production and information machines*, Springer Science Publishers, 2019.

2. The phenomenon of connectivity is related to a third aspect of our species, next to the fact that we intervene physically in nature and process information. From the very beginning man was also a creator of networks, a *homo reticulorum*. For a sketch of the history of networks from the Stone Age until the present see: Teun Koetsier, From Early Trade and Communication Networks to the Internet, the Internet of Things and the Global Intelligent Machine (GIM). *Advances in Historical Studies*, 8, 2019, pp. 1-23. doi: 10.4236/ahs.2019.81001

3. https://www.channelnewsasia.com/news/singapore/changi-prison-raises-tech-bar-with-automated-checks-surveillance-10455870

4. Jörg Goldhahn, Vanessa Rampton and Giatgen A. Spinas. *Could artificial intelligence make doctors obsolete?*, BMJ, vol. 363, pp. k4563, London: British Medical Journal Publishing Group (BMJ), 2018. DOI: 10.1136/bmj.k4563

5. http://www.chinadaily.com.cn/bizchina/tech/2017-11/10/content_34362656.htm

6. Ray Kurzweil, *The Singularity is Near, When Humans Transcend Biology*, Penguin Books, 2005

7. *New York Times*, June 13, 2017. See https://www.nytimes.com/2017/06/13/opinion/how-computers-are-harming-criminal-justice.html

8. Bruce Schneier, *Click Here to Kill Everybody, Security and Survival in a Hyper-connected World*, W. W. Norton and Company, 2018.

Humanity's Adaptation to Future Shock

Ross Dawson

Fifty years after its publication, *Future Shock* is a testament to the potential for prescience. ■ It is not possible to consistently and accurately predict the future. Indeed Toffler, not to mention thousands of other bold prognosticators over the decades, did get some predictions very wrong. However, his insights on the likely path forward for humanity have amply withstood the cruel test of time, providing a sense of the *shape* of the future that has turned out to anticipate many aspects of the world that we live in today.

The progression of the past and the future are most definitely not linear. There is a world of difference between a trend-watcher, who implicitly expects current trends to continue into the future, and a futurist, who starts from the trends and directions we can perceive in the present and anticipates how the intersection of society, humanity, and technology may play out in the creation of rich, multidimensional potential future worlds. Trends always generate responses that amplify or dampen them, or as Toffler's contemporary Marshal McLuhan put it, potentially "flip" them into a reversal of the trend. This creates a set of patterns in the evolution of the future that we can illustrate using Toffler's original insights.

The Trajectories of Toffler's Predictions

From the vantage point of today, some of Toffler's insights were truly prescient, accurately describing our world. His evocation of the potential for same-sex parents was strongly against the grain of his time, yet he perceived the seeds of a social evolution that has taken decades to reach today's widespread acceptance. What he described as the "rental revolution," extended slightly, in fact reflects the rise of the sharing economy, in which people increasingly choose not to own things such as cars or lawn mowers, but to rent and use them as required, often from neighbors. The "experiential economy" Toffler described in the late 1970s is no longer new, but we continue to see the rise of Customer Experience (CX) at the heart of many companies' strategies, with chief experience officers now often positioned amid the top echelons of management.

Some of Toffler's forecasts are still in the process of playing out 50 years later. His description of organizations as "adhocracies" is still significantly aspirational, yet I believe inevitable. In my work on the high-performance organizations of the future, I describe how well-networked companies create the conditions for real-time "ad-hoc" connections between people, resources, and ideas, and how they can be applied to address challenges and opportunities. While the best organizations today are far better at these ad-hoc structures than ever before, most have far to go on that journey if they are to survive and thrive in our exceptionally dynamic business environment.

Yet other predictions were so far ahead of their time that we are not there yet, though the issues may be imminent. Despite decades of anticipation of "super-babies," we are just now on the verge of the first ones being born. The debate on whether and how we as a society should deal with these possibilities is long-standing and now intensifying. The idea of temporary marriage is not common today, though arguably long-standing de-facto relationships could be considered to fit this description.

In other cases, we have substantially surpassed Toffler's predictions. His insights on the "de-monopolization of media" certainly anticipated a powerful shift in the media world, yet the rise of social media has taken us beyond that into an entirely different landscape.

> Of course, the most important question facing humanity is whether we have the collective ability to respond to accelerating change in a world in which short-sighted actions over many decades have created extraordinary challenges for us.

It is important to acknowledge that Toffler sometimes did not see past the trend to the response. At the time, his description of the development of a "throw-away society" was too sadly true. However, as a society we have eventually responded to this trend with the horror it deserves, resulting in not just recycling but, more broadly, resource efficiency driving government and business decision-making in developed countries and, increasingly, in developing countries.

Human Adaption to Future Shock

The most important insight from Toffler's work—then and today—is the very concept of future shock and what he termed "adaptivity." He accurately described the state of shock of dealing with intense change. Yet 50 years later, future shock still seems like a very fair description of the nature of today's life and society, while the pace of change is radically greater than when the book was published.

In the space of months, let alone years, important aspects of our business and social landscape can undergo substantive change, to a degree almost unimaginable five decades ago. Yet humans and human society have, by and large, not just survived but prospered, by many important measures that transcend economic growth. It is true that today many people experience stress in their lives and work, yet the extraordinary adaptability of humans means we can not only function amid mind-boggling change, but arguably deal with it substantially better than Toffler anticipated.

Future Responsiveness

Looking forward to the decades to come, let us begin by extending Toffler's thesis of future shock. I believe deeply in individual humans' ability to respond to changing environments. It is what has allowed us to prosper over millennia, building a society in which our health, comforts, and scope for expressing our individual potential far transcend those of any of our ancestors.

Many people are struggling with accelerating change today. However, looking back at *Future Shock*, written when the pace of development was a fraction of what it is today, provides us with a strong indication that humans are considerably more adaptable than we thought. Certainly, living in today's world is highly challenging. Yet still many people, when asked when they would choose to be alive if they could live at any time of human history, simply respond, "Now." Not least, this is because one powerful upside of constant change is a sense of excitement, a fundamental human driver.

The concept of future shock may have been new when Toffler coined the term. However, we can be sure we will never move past it, to a time when we have a collective sense of continuity and stability. And, I believe we will never be so fazed by change that we are unable to respond to it as individuals.

Of course, the most important question facing humanity is whether we have the collective ability to respond to accelerating change in a world in which short-sighted actions over many decades have created extraordinary challenges for us.

One trend that is now well in place and will shape our society for decades to come is the reversal of Toffler's accurately observed trend in the 1970s of a throw-away society. The recent rise of bans on plastic bags around the world, for example, is a product of a social trend: a growing abhorrence of waste and pollution. Technological developments applied to this demand for a better environment will continue to impact a wide variety of areas, including packaging, retailing, and food utilization.

More in question is whether our collective response to climate change will be sufficient to mitigate potential environmental disaster. What is inevitable is that we will continue to shift apace to renewable energy and see many countries explicitly address carbon emissions in their economic policies.

The most important shift in coming decades will be the continued rise of what Toffler described as "the cyborgs among us." As he pointed out, humans and machines were already merging when he wrote *Future Shock*. While we have come a long way down that path, we are only just now on the verge of true integration of humanity and technology, notably with a new generation of Brain Computer Interfaces (BCI) emerging.

There will be two kinds of humans: those who choose to augment themselves with technology, and those who choose not to do so. Inevitably, more opportunities will go to the former, and bias and discrimination will flow in both directions between what will effectively be two classes of humanity. This, among other extraordinary developments, will further heighten what we now know as future shock. Yet humans will, individually and collectively, largely continue to adapt and cope with tomorrow's mind-boggling pace of change. ■

Ross Dawson works globally as a futurist, keynote speaker, entrepreneur, and author, having delivered keynotes and run executive workshops in over 30 countries. He is a bestselling author of four books, including *Living Networks*, which anticipated the social networking revolution before any of today's social networks existed. Extensive futurist resources, including chapters from his books, can be found at www.rossdawson.com. Find Ross on Twitter at @rossdawson.

Technology
for the Sake of Humanity

Mick Ebeling &
Jordan Richardson

Let me ask you a question... Did you wake up today and check your news feed? And on your news feed, how much of it was "good" news? One hundred percent? Fifty percent? Was even 20 percent of the news you read good news? I am pretty certain the answer is not much.

We live in such a complex and complicated world. There are so many characters, circumstances, and variables around us that we often get bogged down by the negativity of this complicated world. However, in this moment, and more than ever before in the history of our species, realize that you have the power and access to be part of the solution. You are living in a world where every single person on Earth has the ability to effect positive change, to do good things, to make the world a better place. Realize that when you say, "Wow, I wish I could be like that person," I say to you, you *are* that person. And with modern technology, doing good has never been easier.

When Alvin Toffler first warned us of "future shock" and the perils of modern technology, citing concepts like artificial intelligence, his warnings connoted thoughts of science fiction, Big Brother, and a scary, robot-controlled world set in a dystopian future. But Toffler also expressed hope that technology had the potential to make the world better.

"What is most important, is that we do not simply accept everything, that we begin to make critical decisions about what kind of world we want and what kind of technology we want."[1]

By changing the narrative of what technology *can* mean for the future of humanity to what it *should* mean, we can influence and inspire an entirely new generation of scientists, hackers, makers, and technologists. I believe that technology *can* serve humanity and alleviate unnecessary future

437

shock. We are in the middle of the next turning point in human history, the next Industrial Revolution—from the exponential growth of social connectivity, commerce, and commercialism, and the ever-expanding reach of the internet, down to the flourishing Maker Movement. This "revolution" has shifted the way we live, work, and interact with one another. It revolves around the newfound global accessibility to knowledge and the ability to solve more of our own problems, and it makes this the most exciting time in modern history.

At Not Impossible Labs, we create technology for the sake of humanity. We come from different backgrounds, skill sets, and expertise, but we share a common mission: To recognize the absurdities that exist in the world and create accessible solutions to those absurdities. We are makers, programmers, engineers, hackers, and artists, and we are an incubator and instigator of technology for good. We tackle the challenges of a single person, create a solution, and then tell the compelling story of that solution as a means to scale it and help many more people. That approach is encapsulated in our mantra, "Help One, Help Many," and our ultimate mission is to change the world through technology and story.

I am infatuated with the concept of impossible; I love looking at things that are impossible and figuring out how to make them not impossible. In Los Angeles, Venice Beach specifically, I had an animation production company where I made animated films and main title sequences for movies, and built commercial campaigns for corporations. It was technology for the purposes of design, beauty, branding, and entertainment.

The world I play in now, after founding Not Impossible, is still technology, but it's technology for the sake of humanity. We look through the lens of what is "absurd." What things need to change in our communities, on this planet, and what is absurd generally, from an overall human standpoint? And when we find that absurdity, when we recognize something that just should not be, first we commit to solving it, and *then* we figure out how we are going to do it. I understand that might seem somewhat flippant, but I cannot adequately express what a powerful idea this is to live by. It is first about *why* something must happen, then about *how* it is going to happen. Once you adopt the mentality that it has to happen, then you will, in fact, figure out a way to make it happen.

We constantly challenge and ask ourselves, how can we make and engineer technology to serve, to help, and to instigate change to serve a fundamental human and social need? Then, how can we scale it and make it accessible so people can use that solution in their daily lives? That is the core definition of "technology for the sake of humanity."

The other part of this equation is story. It is safe to say that everybody reading this book appreciates the power of story. When you meet someone at a cocktail party and they ask, "What is it that you do?" you typically do not respond with just an official job title. Instead you begin to tell a bit of a story about yourself: what company employs you, the location of your office, your job role and title, its functions and applications, and often, relaying your overall satisfaction or dissatisfaction with your employment. Hearing stories is how we are taught, and it is how knowledge has been disseminated for millennia. At Not Impossible, we create these absurdity-solving technologies and then spread our learnings and solutions by creating a beautiful story, typically in the form of a short documentary. This ensures that people have the ability to easily find out about it, and increases the likelihood of the masses having access to that technological solution. The lens that we look through when we create this story is the mantra lens mentioned earlier of "Help One, Help Many."

We use the story of helping that one person as a way to spark innovation and passion in other people, inspiring them to create, hack, and solve a similar or unique problem so that they in turn can help others. It is much easier to stimulate action if you are solving a problem for one person. Instead of saying, "I want to solve lower-limb paralysis today," the mind-set is shifted to reflect, "I will find a way to help my paralyzed friend Joe have more freedom and independence." From, "I want to solve world hunger" to, "I am going to connect Jane to easily accessible food options in her area." The key, the fundamental question we always ask at the beginning of our projects, is "Who is the one?" Who is that one person, that if we help them, then maybe that solution will be a spark that starts to smolder, that starts the fire, to sequentially help many? That is the foundation of everything that we do at Not Impossible—and an idea punctuated by Toffler, who said, "If we can recognize that industrialism is not the only possible form of technological society, if we can begin to think more imaginatively about the future, then we can prevent future shock, and we can use technology itself to build a decent, democratic, and humane society."

■ ■ ■

Pop quiz: Name anything that is possible today that wasn't impossible first. *Everything* that is possible today, at one point was impossible. So if everything around us—lights, concrete, cars, airplanes, cell phones—was impossible at some time in history but is now possible, then maybe everything that is impossible today, if we base our opinion on history and statistics, is on the trajectory of becoming possible tomorrow. That is just simple data. That is simple statistics. That is human history. That's the fallacy of impossibility.

We do not believe in failure here at Not Impossible. We believe in simply allowing ourselves to live in a constant state of *beta*. Even if you only commit to moving the technological dial forward just a tiny bit, you give everybody else in your network, this country, the entire planet, permission to take what you started and evolve your solution just a little bit further. If you kick the can down the road, it may not make it across the state lines of possible, but with your effort, the can has progressed on its path. Most likely someone will be able to pick up from where you left off and move it closer and closer to the final outcome of possible.

This newer concept of companies attempting to move the dial, *a la* corporate social responsibility, turns out to not just be good for society but to also be incredibly good for the companies themselves. It's incredible for marketing and for affecting consumer preference. It's proven to dramatically spur growth for business. It's a good recruiting tool and an even better employee-retention tool. Simply stated, doing good is good business, and is what we refer to as "Enlightened Capitalism." If you do things that are good for your community and society, it will be good for your business, and ultimately for you as an individual. That is what the Not Impossible

> "I cannot adequately express what a powerful idea this is to live by. It is first about why something must happen, then about how it is going to happen. Once you adopt the mentality that it has to happen, then you will, in fact, figure out a way to make it happen.

movement is all about. That is how we leverage our technologies to lead the charge, through partnerships that have incredible access, and, more importantly, a desire to scale and spread the stories of the solutions that have been created. That is how we as a species mobilize true, dramatic, sustainable change, through the creation of significant societal, personal, and business value where every entity derives measurable benefit, and that benefit puts the other partners in a substantially better place than before.

People often ask us, how do you pull off these amazing tech advancements? The answer is simple: First, because we shouldn't be able to, and second, because we do not ask for permission. We typically don't have the degrees or the credentials most would expect us to need. We usually don't know what the heck we are doing when we begin our process, but with the ever-growing connectivity on planet Earth, maximizing the use of accessible technologies requires "grit" more than bestowed degrees. The reason we succeed, is that we operate from a place of beautiful, limitless naiveté. We didn't get the memo that we aren't supposed to be able to achieve what we set out to achieve, so we just set out and do it. We find our one, we commit, and then we say "Geronimo!"

The state of the world will grow to be more of the same: complex and complicated. However, it is my wish that every human realizes that they (yes, you—the person reading this right now) have the ability to make the world better; the ability to solve absurdities… and to change the world.

So, the most important questions for you to consider as you journey through this complex life are: What do YOU think is absurd and needs to be changed? And, who is YOUR "one" who will be helped when you solve that absurdity?

Help One. Help Many. ▪

Named one of *Fortune Magazine*'s World's Greatest Leaders, a Muhammad Ali Humanitarian of the Year, and listed as one of the most influential creative people by The Creativity '50s, **Mick Ebeling** has sparked a movement of pragmatic, inspirational innovation. His mantra of "commit, then figure it out" allows him to better the world by bringing accessibility for all. Named one of *Wired*'s "Agents of Change," a two-time SXSW innovation of the year award winner, a two-time Tribeca Disruptor innovation winner, and recipient of every major creative and advertising award, Ebeling is on a mission to provide "Technology for the Sake of Humanity."

Jordan Richardson is a talent and creative development specialist with 12+ years of experience managing vertical opportunities and projects with celebrity musicians, actors, thought leaders, and corporate brands. Jordan had previously booked multiple promotional and commercial campaigns on major television networks like ABC's *Soapnet* and NBC, cast shows such as VH1's *Behind the Music* and *I Love the 2000s*, and co-facilitated recognizable brand activations like #LoveIsLove with Absolut Vodka. Jordan now leads the talent and brand management arm of Not Impossible Labs (TEG), an award-winning technology incubator and content studio dedicated to changing the world through technology and story.

1. "Future Shock" Documentary, Alvin Toffler (1972)

Trends at the Speed of Change

Daniel Levine

We are living in a golden age of trends. ■ Teased from hard data and cold observation, they are presented to us and dissected by data scientists, journalists, and experts such as myself as a way of helping us make sense of our world. We are awash in consumer trends, technology trends, and social trends related to the way we all live, work, and play. Yet, there is one supertrend transcending all others. It affects every industry and is reforming every business. And it now permeates all of our lives.

This trend is the Hyper-Acceleration of Change. It refers not just to the sheer speed in which the world is shifting, but to the fact that change itself is happening faster and faster. This powerful supertrend, alone, is creating winners and losers every day, and the way you respond to it in your business and life will determine which one you will be.

In my keynote presentations to associations and my work with top executives—in industries as diverse as food, finance, automobiles, tourism, and wellness—I see firsthand how this trend is transforming consumerism, the future of work, and even the nature of family and relationships.

As a trends expert, I am a "near-futurist" who uses research and interpretive tools to see around corners to the next few years. My goal is to help businesspeople profit from the hyper-acceleration of change and other trends by finding creative ways to embrace and exploit them. While the quickening of change is hardly a new concept, its importance cannot be overestimated. A flash-in-the-pan fad would have faded long ago. And while this is a trend that can mean life or death for a business, it is also one that can be profitably capitalized on, more about which I will explain below.

In *Future Shock*, Alvin Toffler wrote that the *rate* of change has implications quite apart from, and perhaps more important than, the *directions* of change. And those implications, he argued,

> In *Future Shock*, Alvin Toffler wrote that the rate of change has implications quite apart from, and perhaps more important than, the directions of change. And those implications, he argued, are dangerous.

are dangerous. Future shock is the name Toffler gave to a disease: the disease of cultural change that is happening too quickly for human adaptation.

Yet, 50 years on we have somehow been able to survive, thank you very much. Society doesn't seem to have suffered from the "mass disorientation" that Toffler warned of. In fact, what is striking is how malleable and resilient humans have proved to be. This is especially true considering the *blitzkrieg* of change has happened faster than even Toffler had imagined. Exponentially faster.

In 1970 Toffler was particularly enchanted by the arrival of automation as the main agent of transformation. He found validation in the sentiments of the British computer manufacturer Sir Leon Bagrit, who called it "the greatest change in the whole history of mankind." But that was then.

Today, just a half-century later, we have already lived for years with the internet, mobile computing, and connected homes, and are now on the cusp of whiplashing revolutions in artificial intelligence, robotics, personalized medicine, and space exploration. From this vantage point, Toffler's 1970s-era awe at the speed of change seems almost... quaint.

Like Moore's Law, which states that the number of transistors on a computer chip doubles every 18 months, and thus yields exponential increases in computing power, the rate of social change also appears to grow exponentially. That's because technology feeds on itself. Technology propagates technology. A graph representing social change derives its steep incline from technological changes profoundly affecting every aspect of human life.

The storage of human knowledge offers a clear example of hyper-accelerated change. The invention of movable type in the 15th century made a marked difference in the amount of information it was possible to preserve. As Toffler himself noted, prior to 1500 Europe was producing about 1,000 book titles a year. By 1950, the rate had accelerated to about 120,000 titles a year, so what once took a century to create required only 10 months. Today, it is hardly possible to keep count, as thousands of titles, many of which are not even written by humans, but by artificial intelligence bots, are launched daily on digital platforms.

The same pattern can be seen in almost every industry and every aspect of human relationships. News cycles now move at warp speed, extending even to entertainment cycles. To paraphrase a famous truism, it used to take years to become an overnight success. Now, thanks to social media, "overnight" is literal.

Keeping track of the latest advances in artificial intelligence, blockchain finance, or massive multiplayer gaming can overwhelm many of us who came of age in the pre-internet era (I'm looking at you, Dad!). But, to our children, this is the only world they know and it seems perfectly normal. But whether or not one is consciously aware of the rising complexity of culture, it is undeniable that life in the developed world moves faster than ever.

It is ironic that we are all so very busy, because the promise of technology was supposed to be that it would set us all free (I'm looking at you, PC!). Yet, the exact opposite has happened. Inside the workplace and out, technology has compelled us to squeeze more productivity into the same amount of time. In many of my keynotes, in rooms of more than a thousand attendees, I have asked members of the audience to raise their hands if they feel they have enough hours in the day to accomplish everything they need to. Unsurprisingly, only one or two hands go up. Usually one of those is raised as a joke. Many economists point out that until the mid-1970s, real wages and productivity in the United States rose in tandem. But from that point until today the two have diverged, such that productivity has continued to rise while real wages have remained flat. Time no longer equals money; we are being more productive for the same pay.

Like most trends, this one opens a clear opportunity for businesses that are creative enough to capitalize on it. One profitable response to this Age of Hyper-Acceleration lies in solving customers' problems of being overly time-pressed—in short, by having the smoothest user experience and being as easy to work with as possible. That is what Apple did in creating the simplest smartphone on the market. Google offered the simplest, fastest, and cleanest search engine. Amazon provided 1-click ordering and the best customer service in the business. McDonald's is rolling out self-serve kiosks.

When it comes to trends, business innovation is not only about creating a method, idea, or product that the world has never seen. It is also about creatively solving a problem in your *own* industry using inspiration from an unrelated field. It is about identifying relevant consumer trends, then creating "responses" that you know have high probabilities of success because something similar is already attracting the same customers in another industry.

Consumer trends are not siloed by business type. Trends reflect what people are thinking and feeling, and each of us to some degree responds to trends affecting every aspect of our consumer lives, from the cars we buy and the clothes we wear to the trips we take, the financial choices we make, and the time-challenged decisions we take.

When taking questions at the end of my presentations, I am most often asked "Where will that trend be in five years?" No matter the trend, the answer is almost always the same: It will likely be stronger and more intense than it is today. Why? Because trends tend to have a lot of inertia, and once they get going, they are like snowballs barreling downhill, gathering mass and strength as they roll. Today, in an age of intensifying activity, we can be fairly confident this trend will continue to grow, perhaps indefinitely.

While there are clearly overlaps between being a trends expert and a futurist, Alvin Toffler was at his most comfortable talking about "what is," as opposed to "what might be." "No serious futurist deals in 'predictions'," he wrote. Toffler's way, as is mine, was to explain the present as it is, then use that information to extrapolate what soon will be. It is entirely possible that his forecast that we will all become overwhelmed by accelerating cultural shifts was right, but just a few years too early. But how much more acceleration can we humans take? ▣

Daniel Levine (DanielLevine.com) is one of the world's best-known trends experts. Named "the ultimate guru of cool" by CNN and a frequent guest on TV and radio, Daniel is the director of the Avant-Guide Institute, a New York-based consultancy that helps businesspeople profit from trends via live keynote presentations, hands-on "playshops," and multi-channel media offerings. As the editor of WikiTrend.org, Daniel leads a team of trend-spotters who track the latest ideas and experiences around the globe. From General Motors, American Express, and Microsoft to South African Tourism and the UNWTO, Daniel works with businesses and governments to help them be more relevant, innovative, and profitable.

Building and Taming the Future Shock Bureaucracy

Rodrigo Nieto-Gómez, PhD

We are now deep into future shock territory. During Mark Zuckerberg's congressional hearings of 2018, in the context of the US elections-tampering scandal, much was said about the original Facebook motto, "move fast and break things." Rep. Greg Walden, Chairman of the Energy and Commerce Committee, opened the hearing by stating, "While Facebook has certainly grown, I worry it may not have matured. I think it is time to ask whether Facebook may have moved too fast and broken too many things" (United States. Congress. House. Committee on Energy and Commerce, *Facebook: Transparency and the Use of Consumer Data, April 11, 2018*).

Without knowing it, Congressman Walden kicked off the otherwise awkward debate by asking a "future shock" question: Had Facebook moved too fast for society and institutions to cope with the change it presented?

It would be a mistake, though, to assume that this is just a Facebook problem. In many jurisdictions, housing authorities are struggling to understand how Airbnb and similar platforms can drastically change the way people dispose of, and monetize, real estate properties. Governments all around the globe are still figuring out, in 2019, how to classify and regulate the labor relations created by the so-called shared or gig economy platforms.

These are all future shock symptoms associated with exponential technological changes that trigger the dislocation Alvin Toffler diagnosed as a consequence of a hyperaccelerated rate of change. As Toffler explains, "Technology makes more technology possible, as we can see if we look for a moment at the process of innovation. … The process is completed, the loop closed, when the diffusion of technology embodying the new idea, in turn, helps generate new creative ideas. Today there is evidence that the time between each of the steps in this cycle has been shortened" (Toffler, 1990, p. 27).

As more technologies are used to create more technologies, the collapse of institutional capacity to follow and regulate the technological development that Toffler talked about 50 years ago is now a reality. This happens because social systems, like any complex system, have delays built into them; it takes time for a new technological diffusion to manifest its unanticipated consequences. Never-theless, because these technologies serve as tools to generate new technology-enabled business models, it is now a common occurrence that the consequences of a new technology are not yet fully understood at the time a given entrepreneur is already adopting that technology to create yet another trans-formation.

> Social systems, like any complex system, have delays built into them; it takes time for a new technological diffusion to manifest its unantici-pated consequences.

For example, while we are still learning about the cognitive and privacy changes produced by iPhone and Android devic-es, the smartphone has already been interwoven with urban mobility (e.g., Uber), our education systems (e.g., Canvas), our households (e.g., Nest), and even the travel industry (e.g., Airb-nb). Future shock layered upon future shock.

While we are still in the process of understanding the indi-vidual perils of smartphone devices to our cognitive processes, as demonstrated by the relatively young age of the literature warning us against their addictive design properties, creative entrepreneurs have already introduced second-degree societal changes enabled by these platforms into other environments.

In 2018, triggered by an increased awareness of privacy invasions by tech giants, the global society reacted with future shock-esque symptoms to this accelerated pace of technological change with what the media has now labeled as the "techlash." The techlash is nothing other than a backlash against future shock. These backlashes can be found in many other environments, including many that are not necessarily tech-related but have also very recognizable names.

Brexit and Trumpism, for example, represent some of the more dramatic political events of this first half of the 21st century. Both are examples of future shock backlashes against rapid changes (mostly demographic) that postindustrialized societies have, and are, experiencing. In this regard, the dislocation is probably even more extreme than what Toffler himself described because demographic trends have shifted since the original publication of *Future Shock*. Toffler described how in his time, "Never in history has distance meant less. Never have man's relationships with place been more numerous, fragile and temporary. Throughout the advanced technological societies, and particularly among those I have characterized as 'the people of the future,' commuting, traveling, and regularly relocating one's family have become second nature. [...] We are witnessing a historic decline in the significance of place to human life. We are breeding a new race of nomads, and few suspect quite how massive, widespread and significant their migrations are" (Toffler, 1990, p. 75).

But if the extreme mobility Toffler identified has continued, it has done so in a very different and even more disruptive way. While forced migrations, state fragility, and violence still compel people to move great distances from, for example, Tegucigalpa to San Bernardino or from Aleppo to Berlin, native-born Americans are experiencing the lowest level of domestic mobility ever recorded. (Ihrke, 2017). Although for international, economically driven migrants the sense of place is as dynamic, if not more so, than what it was 50 years ago when *Future Shock* was published, for the coal miner in West Virginia or the factory worker in Swindon, the idea of migrating in pursuit of a job is less of a reality than what it used to be in the 1970s. Therefore, populations of different ethnonational origins are now experiencing future shock differently, increasing the sense of dislocation and spatial contextual collapse.

Toffler equated future shock to a culture shock you cannot escape within your own society. This is exactly how the demographic shifts confronting the highly nomadic south and the more sedentary north are feeding neo-nationalist movements. "Future shock is a time phenomenon," he wrote, "a product of the greatly accelerated rate of change in society. It arises from the superimposition of a new culture on an old one. It is culture shock in one's own society.

> The global society reacted with future shock-esque symptoms to this accelerated pace of technological change with what the media has now labeled as the "techlash." The techlash is nothing other than a backlash against future shock.

"But its impact is far worse. [...] most travelers have the comforting knowledge that the culture they left behind will be there to return to. The victim of future shock does not.

"Take an individual out of his own culture and set him down suddenly in an environment sharply different from his own, with a different set of cues to react to—different conceptions of time, space, work, love, religion, sex, and everything else—then cut him off from any hope of retreat to a more familiar social landscape, and the dislocation he suffers is doubly severe. [...] Given few clues as to what kind of behavior is rational under the radically new circumstances, the victim may well become a hazard to himself and others.

"Now imagine not merely an individual but an entire society, an entire generation—including its weakest, least intelligent, and most irrational members—suddenly transported into this new world. The result is mass disorientation, future shock on a grand scale.

"This is the prospect that man now faces. Change is avalanching upon our heads and most people are grotesquely unprepared to cope with it" (Toffler, 1990, p. 12).

Even though this is a time of technological abundance and living conditions are better than they have ever been in the history of humankind (Rosling, 2006), you would not know this by listening to the news or talking with the fearful ethnic majorities that are driving the political conversations of the global north. Incapable of coming back to the "great" society of yesterday, as Toffler anticipated, they react with nostalgia and otherness. They are rebelling against the future shock they are experiencing.

One important consequence of this dislocation is a political impetus to create a bureaucracy to deal with it. This structure is imperfect and, in many ways, designed to respond to the representations and fears of this population that is suffering future shock, and not to the actual root causes (Madrigal, 2018). In the United States, the Department of Homeland Security emerged as a consequence of 9/11, an event where a small group of technologically super-empowered individuals imposed, as Toffler anticipated, dire changes to a society in ways that would not have been possible before, without the technology they appropriated (Nieto-Gomez, 2011).

What we call in the United States "homeland security" is a kind of bureaucratic response to an acceleration in the rate of change that overwhelms governmental institutions. Homeland security is much more than what the public identifies with the policy. It includes, yes, law enforcement and fire response, border management and immigration, but also public health, emergency management, technology regulation (including the so-called "cyber"), and even urban planning, among many other fields.

Homeland security is, as a policy space, an organizational attempt to mitigate future shock where it is present or respond to it when it shows its most negative consequences. It aspires to be a bureaucracy of crises for when state capacity has been surpassed by circumstances—often, by future shock. This is why it regulates not only technology, but also demographic flows (e.g., immigration or border management) or global warming consequences (e.g., megafires or super hurricanes). While nobody explicitly conceived of it in these terms, an emerging meta-objective of homeland security institutions (much more than just the federal Department of Homeland Security) is to slow down the forces behind future shock. It is the closest thing to the future shock bureaucracy Toffler anticipated in the first edition of his book:

"At the level of social consequences, a new technology might be submitted for clearance to panels … who would determine, to the best of their ability, the probable strength of its social impact at different points in time. Where an innovation appears likely to entail seriously disruptive consequences, or to generate unrestrained accelerative pressures, these facts need to be weighed in a social cost-benefit accounting procedure. In the case of some high-impact innovations, the technological appraisal agency might be empowered to seek restraining legislation, or to obtain an injunction forcing delay until full public discussion and study is completed. In other cases, such innovations might still be released for diffusion—provided ample steps were taken in advance to offset their negative consequences. In this way, the society would not need to wait for disaster before dealing with its technology-induced problems.

"By considering not merely specific technologies, but their relationship to one another, the time lapse between them, the proposed speed of diffusion, and similar factors, we might eventually gain some control over the pace of change as well as its direction.

"Needless to say, these proposals are themselves fraught with explosive social consequences, and need careful assessment" (Toffler, 1970).

We should take Alvin Toffler's warning seriously. Homeland security policies are indeed fraught with bitter conflict. They also can be "captured" to become part of future shock problems instead of part of the solutions—and not only in the context of technology control. For example, in the San Bernardino shooting case of Apple vs. the FBI (Contributors to Wikimedia projects, 2016), we as a society confronted, without resolving, the question of how far should we go to protect our privacy, even against the most violent consequences of future shock. In the family-separation policies regarding Central American asylum seekers, we saw how easy it is to encourage tribalism under the justification of taming demographic changes.

> Even though this is a time of technological abundance and living conditions are better than they have ever been in the history of humankind (Rosling, 2006), you would not know this by listening to the news or talking with the fearful ethnic majorities that are driving the political conversations of the global north.

Nevertheless, homeland security, or something like it, still seems to be the closest we have ever been to the policy tool Alvin Toffler recommended: a bureaucracy to deal with the anxiety triggered by a world that moves faster than the capacity of parts of humanity to adapt. The challenge is that, depending on the political architecture of this policy, it can either exacerbate the dislocation triggered by future shock for the benefit of some policymakers who reap the benefits of fear or, instead, tame its negative effects, for the benefit of all.

This is why, for the next 50 years of continuing future shock waves, we urgently need for the people who care about the consequences of the accelerating pace of change to pay much more attention to the homeland security policy space to make sure that the mechanisms created by governments to deal with future shock are built in ways that are democratic, inclusive, and innovation-friendly.

Dr. **Rodrigo Nieto-Gómez** is a geostrategist and defense futurist focused on the consequences of the accelerating pace of change in security environments and governance. He is a professor at the Naval Postgraduate School and a faculty member of Singularity University. For more than a decade, Dr. Nieto-Gómez has advised high-ranking law enforcement, military, and homeland security leaders on how to create and execute strategies to transform their agencies to meet the requirements of rapidly changing environments and threat profiles. As an innovation expert and an academically trained geostrategist, he has built a reputation as an expert on future threats to national security and policing and how to confront them.

Bibliography

Contributors to Wikimedia projects. (2016, February 25). FBI–Apple encryption dispute - Wikipedia.
  Retrieved May 9, 2019, from https://en.wikipedia.org/wiki/FBI%E2%80%93Apple_encryption_dispute
Ihrke, D. (2017, January 23). United States Mover Rate at a New Record Low.
  Retrieved May 8, 2019, from https://www.census.gov/newsroom/blogs/random-samplings/2017/01/mover-rate.html
Madrigal, M. D. (2018). *Obsessive-compulsive homeland security: insights from the neurobiological security motivation system*. Naval Postgraduate School Monterey United States.
  Retrieved from https://apps.dtic.mil/docs/citations/AD1052771
Nieto-Gomez, R. (2011). The Power of "the Few": A Key Strategic Challenge for the Permanently Disrupted High-Tech Homeland Security Environment. *Homeland Security Affairs, 7*(1).
  Retrieved from https://core.ac.uk/download/pdf/36718135.pdf
Rosling, H. (2006, February). *The best stats you've ever seen*. Presented at the TED , Monterey, CA.
  Retrieved from https://www.ted.com/talks/hans_rosling_shows_the_best_stats_you_ve_ever_seen
Toffler, A. (1970). *Future Shock*.
  Retrieved May 9, 2019, from https://archive.org/stream/FutureShock-Toffler/Future-Shock_-_Toffler_djvu.txt
Toffler, A. (1990). *Future Shock*. Bantam Books.
United States. Congress. House. Committee on Energy and Commerce. (2018). *Facebook: Transparency and Use of Consumer Data: Hearing Before the Committee on Energy and Commerce, House of Representatives, One Hundred Fifteenth Congress, Second Session, April 11, 2018.*

More than Sound Bites, After All

Ruth-Ellen L. Miller

When *Future Shock* was published I was an anthropologist studying impact assessment methods, more concerned with how it was that our culture was poisoning itself than with any shiny new gadgets and methods that might be emerging. ■ I had grown up in a household where science fiction was the preferred reading, and my "babysitter" was the Chicago Museum of Science and Industry, so possibilities for the future were common considerations in my life. What I hadn't been prepared for was seeing the whole Escambia Bay in Florida covered with dead fish, or hearing Chesapeake Bay oysters declared poisonous because of the pollution in the river, or not being able to see downtown Los Angeles from the Harbor Freeway. It was painful to discover that the bright and shiny future we'd been led to expect had a dark and dangerous side to it. So I tended to discount much of what the Tofflers had to say, and my first presentation in my first Future Studies class was on ways we might deal with the exponentially increasing accumulation of garbage around the world.

Working with the *Limits to Growth* model in another class also seemed to contradict much of what the Tofflers' books suggested would become normal. Meadows et al. were laying out a timeline of 60ish years before the collapse of the current system, and no matter how we played with the variables and formulas in the Dynamo World Model program, neither I nor my team members could push that date out much further.

And yet, in some ways, it was clear that the Tofflers' having made popular the idea of the future as something we could think about—and do something about—made being a futurist in 20th-century culture possible. Because of their work, far more people were willing to pay attention to, and often pay for, studies about what trends were headed in what directions and how they might affect them. And for that I am grateful. We might be much worse off than we are if that hadn't been the case.

Over the years since, I've been part of teams projecting probable scenarios in a number of areas that the book had addressed, and many that it hadn't. Among other things, we looked at developments in transportation, energy, education and knowledge systems, welfare dependency, personal computing, effects of electronic funds transfers, urban development patterns, guerrilla warfare around the world, rising homelessness, corporate capitalism as a global influence, and the growth and mechanization of the timber industry along the Pacific Rim—as well as how to reduce garbage. The teams I was part of used the Tofflers' input where appropriate, but it seemed that the book's influence was mostly in the sound bites that the media picked up: the title itself, and a few key phrases, like "change is the only constant."

Which brings up a concern: the fact that this book has not been used as part of policy-making and education in our culture means we are struggling with the very thing it was trying to prevent. One way to describe the core of what the Tofflers were saying is that the increasing rate of change would disrupt every aspect of our lives and lead us to experience the equivalent of moving to a new country and culture several times over. Looking at the increasing levels of anxiety and confusion, and the malaise being widely diagnosed as depression in our country today, it might be useful to go back to their work and recognize that much of what we're experiencing is exactly what they said was beginning to happen back in the 1960s, when they wrote the book. It's possible that, if therapists were trained to be aware of the phenomenon, they might be able to treat some of their patients in ways that could actually address the cause.

> *Future Shock* was, for many, the beginning of this new way of thinking. For some of us, it provided a context for our work. Looking at it today, it was a remarkably accurate warning of the socio-psychological tsunami we were facing and are in the midst of today.

Actually, my current work addresses some of that particular issue, because most of the people I talk to are struggling with what they're observing in their lives and the larger world. I do a lot of presentations to community groups, helping them to see the nature of the changes going on around us and where humanity as a whole seems to be actually headed—as opposed to what the media and politicians have been telling them. I offer a glimpse into the exciting, but almost hidden, activities that are likely to be the core of a global human culture in decades to come. I continue to explore probable scenarios and offer tools that assist communities and organizations to deal with them, to enable their members to thrive for the long term—and in the short term to feel hopeful and able to have some control in their lives. One of my current projects, for example, is to help create a model workshop for folks on the Oregon Coast to upcycle plastic waste into useful, attractive products, using some ideas from Holland that are illustrated on the website www.preciousplastic.com. Another is facilitating the formation of a center in Oregon's high desert to integrate permaculture and architecture in a community-building process described at www.lightpathcenter.org. Another is publishing fiction and nonfiction that provide images of how we can build on what matters from the life we have known as we move into life on a planet that has changed so much (www.portalcenterpress.com).

Future Shock was, for many, the beginning of this new way of thinking. For some of us, it provided a context for our work. Looking at it today, it was a remarkably accurate warning of the socio-psychological tsunami we were facing and are in the midst of today. That the Tofflers called their next book *The Third Wave* was prophetic in itself, for we are only now learning how to surf the last one, and too many are drowning in the process as this new one overturns so much of what had seemed fixed and comfortable and known. So, while the Tofflers' books seemed hardly relevant to what I was interested in at the time they came out, I realize today how important they were, and how helpful they could have been—had they been used as they were intended by the folks they were written for instead of turned into sound bites for popular entertainment.

Ruth-Ellen L. Miller earned degrees in anthropology, environmental studies, cybernetics, and the systems sciences in the 1970s, focusing on impact assessment, consciousness, and culture. She taught at a number of colleges and universities and maintained an active consulting practice through the mid-1990s, then was ordained as a New Thought minister and has since worked with spiritual communities throughout Oregon, teaching the principles of whole-systems thinking, developing consciousness, interfaith spirituality, and mental healing practices. She is Director of Research and Programs for the Gaia Living Systems Institute and the author of a number of books and papers on systems thinking, applied metaphysics, the use of intuitive methods, and culture dynamics. Her most recent book is *HOME: We Can Change Humanity's Future*. www.ruthlmillerphd.com.

Education in the Future Tense

Dr. Stanley Rosen

When the Tofflers postulated the concept of "future shock," they could sense the rapid evolution of society in multiple dimensions and the difficulties that coping with those changes would likely create. ■ As an institutional remedy for this syndrome, they suggested re-conceptualizing the role and practice of education. In particular, Chapter 18 of the book addressed "Education in the Future Tense."

In retrospect, we see that many of the prescriptions contained in that chapter have been implemented, to various degrees. And, as a result, we have learned much about how to develop the attitudes, mind-sets, and skills that the Tofflers thought would be essential.

Having worked directly with Alvin as a consultant with Toffler Associates, I had the opportunity to discuss his perspectives regarding the implementation of his ideas and recommendations. Not surprisingly, he wasn't totally satisfied that necessary changes were being made rapidly or broadly enough.

In the past 10 years, as a professor at the Defense Department's Defense Acquisition University (DAU), I've been in a position to apply some of his suggestions to an important aspect of adult education. In this organization, which reports directly to senior leadership in the Department of Defense, career professionals are given many of the tools, approaches, and philosophies needed to wisely shepherd taxpayer dollars into systems and services that support national security. In light of the Tofflers' concepts for improving education, DAU has exemplified many positive changes. And, perhaps not surprisingly, the Tofflers' ideas are working.

The main concepts of Chapter 18 had to do with using education as a means to prepare for an uncertain future, one that would be very unlike the past. In their words, "Johnny must learn to anticipate the direction and rate of change."

More specifically, the book focuses on the need to be able to direct rapidly emerging technologies. As they noted, "The technology of tomorrow requires men who can make critical judgements, who can weave their way through novel environments, who are quick to spot new relationships in the rapidly changing reality."

To accomplish this, organizations needed to control technology that will shift "from bureaucracy to adhocracy, from permanence to transience, and from concern with the present to concern with the future."

Therefore, the prime objective of education should be "cope-ability—the speed and economy with which [the student] can adapt to continual change."

Quoting CP Snow, they called for an educational system to develop "men who 'have the future in their bones'."

With this in mind, Chapter 18 then addresses three objectives:
1 ■ Transform the organizational structure of the educational system.
2 ■ Revolutionize its curriculum.
3 ■ Encourage a more future-focused orientation.

Transformation of the educational organizational structure would see lectures give way to a whole battery of teaching techniques. Use of experiential methods would replace or augment lectures, and the mapping of instructors to students would be much more flexible. For example, some classes could have several teachers. Students would be organized into temporary task forces, where they could shift from group work to individual or independent work and back.

Regarding organization of the curriculum, the Tofflers challenged traditional academic disciplines as the basis for learning. Why not organize around stages in the development of a system, or around specific problems? They also felt that there should be strong emphasis on future-relevant behavioral skills.

Finally, a future orientation should guide instruction and learning because, as they noted, "An individual's sense of the future plays a critical part in his ability to cope." To guide the balance

> At the time they were writing the book, they felt that "We have no heritage of the future." They recommended, "We must begin by making speculation about the future respectable." How have we done in accepting this philosophy?

between past, present, and future focus, they asserted, "The adaptive individual appears to be able to project himself forward just the 'right' distance in time, to examine and evaluate alternate courses of action before the need for a final decision, and to make tentative decisions beforehand."

At the time they were writing the book, they felt that "We have no heritage of the future." They recommended, "We must begin by making speculation about the future respectable." How have we done in accepting this philosophy? Since the DAU has been recognized as one of the nation's premier adult/corporate training and education organizations, it's interesting to note that many of the basic tenets of DAU's approach to adult education follow the Tofflers' recommendations.

As recommended, most DAU classes no longer use classic lecture methods, but are built around *experiential* learning, giving students the opportunity to apply basic concepts in simulated work scenarios. Most DAU classes have multiple instructors or facilitators, whose role is to guide the students' inquiry and exploration rather than prepare them to pass tests of knowledge (although those are also part of the total experience). As the Tofflers suggested, students are organized into teams, where they balance group learning and experiences with individual assignments and preparation. The Tofflers wouldn't be surprised to know that this approach has achieved outstanding results across a range of disciplines and student aptitudes.

> Increase focus on developing creativity, critical thinking, human relations, philosophy, entrepreneurship (individual and teams), art, self-employment, social harmony, ethics, and values. "Know thyself," to build and lead a meaningful working life with self-assessment of progress on one's own goals and objectives.

Rather than base a curriculum on traditional topics that might be taught at the graduate level, learning is organized around scenarios of simulated work problems, many of which are designed to challenge the students in particularly critical skill areas. Of course, case studies complement these overarching scenarios and encourage in-depth critical thinking.

Those "future-relevant behavioral skills," then, become the focus of learning. Understanding the need for specifying critical assumptions where data is lacking, weighing alternative courses of action, applying analytical methods, and communicating effectively with other organizations are typical skills stressed in DAU classes.

The last prescription from the Tofflers concerned a more future-focused orientation. Since the essence of the problems that DAU graduates will be called on to address relate to creating military systems and services to meet future needs (and this may be true for all adult learners), strategic thinking plays a major role in DAU-taught behavior. Explicitly defining success and understanding how those definitions can change, anticipating and assessing opportunities and challenges, forecasting organizational strengths and weaknesses, and studying alternative future scenarios equip DAU students with the tools and skills to deal with, and create, alternative futures. The development of strategic courses of action is at the heart of DAU instruction.

Not surprisingly, then, DAU has been widely recognized as a leader in organizational and personal development. DAU has won awards for fostering a positive learning environment, encouraging innovative teaching methods, and implementing successful enterprise learning strategies.

To anticipate the next steps in implementing the Tofflers' philosophies of education, it is useful to look at another pioneering effort in advancing educational processes.

The Millennium Project is an organization whose purpose is to improve humanity's prospects for building a better future. To this end, the Millennium Project's vision is to create a global foresight network of nodes, information, and software, building a global collective intelligence system recognized for its ability to improve such prospects. The Millennium Project sees itself as a think tank on behalf of humanity, not on behalf of a government, or an issue, or an ideology, but on behalf of building a better future for all of us.

The Millennium Project has recently completed *Future Work/Technology 2050*, an intensive three-year assessment of the future of work. In the Education/Learning Section of the forthcoming report from that assessment, based on three Work/Technology 2050 Global Scenarios, 20 recommended actions were then rated by an international panel of over 150 participants from 40 countries using a Real-Time Delphi (an online expert judgment assessment tool).

In the context of this analysis, the top five recommendations build directly on the Tofflers' concepts:

1 ▪ Increase focus on developing creativity, critical thinking, human relations, philosophy, entrepreneurship (individual and teams), art, self-employment, social harmony, ethics, and values. "Know thyself," to build and lead a meaningful working life with self-assessment of progress on one's own goals and objectives (as Finland is implementing).

2 ▪ Include futures as we include history in the curriculum. Teach alternative visions of the future, foresight, and the ability to assess potential futures.

3 ▪ Make tele-education free everywhere—ubiquitous, life-long learning systems.

4 ▪ Shift education/learning systems more toward mastering skills than mastering a profession.

5 ▪ In parallel to STEM (and/or STEAM—science, technology, engineering, arts, and mathematics), create a hybrid system of self-paced inquiry-based learning for self-actualization; retrain teachers as coaches using new AI tools with students.

These forward-looking approaches will build on current state-of-the-art educational approaches, such as those used by DAU, and will form the basis for preparing students for the future to come—whatever it may be. I think the Tofflers would be pleased. ▪

D**r. Stan Rosen** has been on the faculty of the Department of Defense's Defense Acquisition University. Prior to joining the DAU faculty, Dr. Rosen was a management consultant with Toffler Associates. Formerly, he was Director of Strategic Development and Integration for Boeing Satellite Systems, where he was responsible for coordination of Boeing's strategy for succeeding in the global satellite market, serving a wide variety of US government and global commercial customers. He has also held scientific, engineering, program management, and doctrine, strategy, and policy development positions with the US Air Force, while working on Air Force, NASA, and Intelligence Community space and defense activities. His service included duty on the staff of the Committee on Science and Astronautics of the US House of Representatives. He has also served in various professional capacities with the American Institute of Aeronautics and Astronautics (AIAA), including chairman of the national Space Systems Technical Committee and the Los Angeles Section, national board member, and Vice President of Public Policy, and is an Associate Fellow of the AIAA. He is a former chairman of the board of the California Space Authority, and is currently on the Board of Advisors of the National Space Society (NSS), where he has served as Vice Chairman of the Board. Dr. Rosen earned a BS from the US Air Force Academy, an MS in aerospace engineering from the Massachusetts Institute of Technology, an MS in systems management from the University of Southern California, and a Doctor of Engineering degree from the University of Stuttgart, Germany. Dr. Rosen recently produced the NSS book *Space 2.0*.

Recollections

Theodore J. Gordon

Al Toffler wrote about how the world around us was changing more rapidly every day, and how the acceleration in the rate of the changes was leaving us in a new land with which we were not yet familiar, different from history, different from our childhoods. ■ We now know that the acceleration about which he wrote was not a bump in the road, but an enduring aspect of our world. Who would have guessed back then that we could carry little machines in our pockets that give us instant access to our friends, to entertainment on-demand, to facts of history, to news of the day, to trivia beyond reason, to products that the machines—through algorithms, past purchases, and big data, somehow "know" we want. The accelerations that Al Toffler spotted continue unabated.

I met Alvin Toffler when I was in my late 30s and he was in his early 40s. I think it was in about 1968, and Al was hot on the trail of what became his monumental best-selling book, *Future Shock*. He had already written an article about possible future technological and social changes and their impacts on society in a *Horizon* magazine article titled "The Future as a Way of Life," and I had written and published my book, immodestly called *The Future* (a title later also used by Al Gore; that's okay, Mr. Gore). I had left McDonald Douglas Aircraft where I had been in charge of development of Space Stations and Planetary systems, left my consulting assignment at RAND where I worked with Olaf Helmer on applications of the Delphi method, and in 1968, with Olaf and several others[1], co-founded the Institute for the Future in Middletown, Connecticut, at the invitation of Wesleyan University. It is important for me to mention this background because Al Toffler became a consultant for the Institute and interviewed me and others there for the book that turned out to be the enormously influential *Future Shock*.

Toffler impacted the world; in 1966, he taught one of the first futures courses at the New School for Social Research in New York. A year later, Jim Dator was teaching futures at Virginia Polytech Institute, and Wendell Bell was teaching futures at Yale.[2] The consequences of *Future Shock* were much greater than single academic courses, however. With six million copies printed, we can assume three times as many readers, and that perhaps 10 times as many people had heard about its themes. TV specials based on the book had even broader audiences. *Future Shock* made futures more respectable as a field of inquiry. Political leaders such as Newt Gingrich and social opinion leaders such as Betty Friedan were Al's friends, accepted the premises of the book, and apparently based decisions on its assumptions. Al and his wife, Heidi, collaborated on the research behind this and other books, and travelled together whenever they could. Al urged Heidi to accept credit as a co-author, rather than only acknowledgment as a contributor.

Al and Heidi used their journalistic skills to collect information for the books, and Al's persuasive and lively writing style made the books and articles come alive.

I met Al when he came to the Institute for the Future to interview me. He was an imaginative synthesizer, drawing facts and opinions from many sources, adding his own points of view, and explaining what it all meant socially, politically, and generally. As I recall, we talked about how to send astronauts to Mars and beyond, how life support systems might allow a form of hibernation on long voyages, trajectories that could get us there, the futures techniques that we were developing at the Institute, the prospect for DNA modification, and what we might do with this new godlike capacity.

Al became a consultant to the Institute, where he was listed as specializing in "psychological and sociological implications for the future." One of the first assignments of the new institute was to construct a simulation game for the State of Connecticut, depicting what life might be like 40 or 50 years hence. The game was a simulation, with role-playing participants interacting within a sketchy, predetermined partial script. Al played the part of an aging hippie, and he attacked this role with vigor and imagination. As the game years ticked by, Al used 1960s slang (e.g., "outta sight" and "groovy" for excellent, "bread" for money, etc.); we realized that was a mistake. Surely fringe members of a future society will invent new words, new modes of behavior, and perhaps even new languages as well. The light dawned: language, along with goals and values, is at least a partially cultural invention as well as a response to technological and social pressures.

One of many conjectures about the future in *Future Shock* was the prospect for vacation spots that offered simulations of history that invited vacationers to enter a simulated time, wearing appropriate period costumes and speaking the language, separated from the present by technology, time, and geography. This was the Connecticut game played in reverse. Great idea! If I could, what time period would I dial in? Where in history would I like to go? The Wright Brothers at Kitty Hawk, ancient Egypt to meet Cleopatra, or the Late Cretaceous (but for no longer than an instant, please). Other ideas that seem poised to become mainstream reality (or have become so already) include game payoffs in experiences (e.g., erotic brain stimulation), education as a pas-

> He was an imaginative synthesizer, drawing facts and opinions from many sources, adding his own points of view, and explaining what it all meant socially, politically, and generally.

time, temporary "slavery" as a penalty for losing a simulation game, and diminishing attention span of readers.

Of other futurists of the time, Herman Kahn represented the "genius" mode of forecasting; he crafted insightful scenarios about what might lie ahead, alone or with contributions from a few colleagues. Al, on the other hand, collected his information from interviews, and as a journalist, cross-checking his sources and asking tough and intelligent questions that demanded intelligent answers. He drew conclusions from the diversity of data, the collision of trends, and the discontinuities of inventions. His strength was not making correct forecasts, although he made many of those, but in describing the meaning and consequences of those trends and inventions.

> We are shocked by surprises, unwanted consequences of our behavior, unanticipated results, formerly the unrecognized effects. We are victims of an untamed future that forces us to run harder and faster as we sense we are getting further and further behind, battered by crisis after crisis.

For example, in *Future Shock* he wrote about the rapidity of shifting consumer needs, anticipatory democracy, experiential vacations, emerging fashions, the new field of futures research, and changing social structures. When he wrote about hippies of the future, a role he played in the Connecticut game, he said, "The working-class hippie and the hippie who dropped out of Exeter or Eaton share a common style of life but no common class. [...] Thus, the stranger launched into American or English or Japanese or Swedish society today must choose not among four or five classes-based styles of life, but among literally hundreds of diverse possibilities. Tomorrow. [...] this number will be even larger." He didn't mention fragmentation through social media, but he caught the essence of it.

Wendell Bell, speaking about the theme and consequences of *Future Shock*, perhaps said it best: "Change, Toffler said, is increasingly rapid. Changes are rolling over us, outstripping our images of the future and our abilities to adapt, much less to plan for them and to control them to our individual and collective benefit. We are shocked by surprises, unwanted consequences of our behavior, unanticipated results, formerly the unrecognized effects. We are victims of an untamed future that forces us to run harder and faster as we sense we are getting further and further behind, battered by crisis after crisis." [3]

Al was an advocate of anticipatory democracy. Olaf Helmer saw the possibility of political candidates competing on the basis of futures they would strive to achieve; people would vote for the person who held a future image closest to their own. Al, on the other hand, saw futures research as a means for developing alternative political positions based on opinions collected from large swaths of the population, locally to globally. He described how technology might be used to collect opinions about what the future *ought* to be from literally millions of people who would, after all, occupy the future.

I wonder what he would have said if some off-stage voice had whispered to him: "Al, this is the President speaking. I'm telling you that the media are the enemy of the people. And you want to play games?"

Theodore Jay Gordon is one of the world's most respected futurists and management consultants. He is an entrepreneur, an inventor, and a specialist in forecasting methodology, planning, and policy analysis. He is co-founder and Board member of The Millennium Project. He is the recipient of the Ed Cornish "Futurist of the Year" award and is a recipient of the Shaping Tomorrow Lifetime Achievement Award. He performed early research on the Delphi method at RAND Corporation, where he was a consultant to their mathematics and policy department and he co-authored the first large-scale Delphi study (Gordon and Helmer, 1964). Throughout his career he has been at the forefront of development of forecasting and analysis methodology, including the development of the Cross Impact Method, Trend Impact Analysis, implications of nonlinear modeling (chaos) for forecasting, and the State of the Future Index (SOFI), a means for measuring and forecasting the changing outlook of the future, and in the development and application of Real-Time Delphi to essentially all foresight and policy studies performed at the Millennium Project. See full bio here: http://www.millennium-project.org/about-us/planning-committee/ted-gordon/.

1. Members of the Organizing Committee were myself, Olaf Helmer, Paul Baran, and Arnold Kramish.
2. (Bell, Wendell, 1977, "Foundations of Futures Studies, V1. p 161.)
3. Bell, op. cit.

Minimizing Shock: Reimagining a More Equitable Future

Alisha Bhagat

Who Makes the Future?[1] Living in the future is not all it's cracked up to be. That statement might have surprised Alvin and Heidi Toffler, because many of their predictions, made in 1970, have come true. Since the publication of *Future Shock* we have seen great advancements in technology, but many of the problems of that era, such as economic inequality, have in fact worsened. In their book, the Tofflers took multiple forms of inequality as givens, and from there structured visions of the future without questioning them. To better understand the present-day implications of future shock, we have to challenge these assumptions.

The Tofflers thought the world population was structured into three different classes: 70 percent of people who live in the past, over 25 percent of people who live in the present, and the remaining 2 or 3 percent who live in the future[2]. People who live in the past are based in traditional societies, living the same life that their parents and grandparents did. People in the present live in modern industrial societies, and are "molded by mechanization and mass education." People living in the future comprise a small portion of the population. They live in the main urban centers of global and technological change, and are wealthy, well-educated, and mobile.

The people depicted as living in the future appear to be "highly privileged members of society." Based on the examples given, it is implied that these people are mainly cisgender, white, hetero, wealthy, able-bodied men without caregiving responsibilities[3]. They thrive in global urban centers, and withstand a rapid pace of change—one that would unsettle other types of people. The rest of us, who are not living in the future, are doomed to live in a state of "future shock" where we experience the fast pace of technological, social, and economic change, but are helpless and overwhelmed as familiar structures shift around us. As society evolves, a feedback loop is created as those people with economic and technological power create tools and systems that benefit people like themselves.

I see future shock as one outcome of a broken economic system that produces miraculous technology but fails to prioritize fundamental human needs and values. Both in the past and today, what makes people anxious, overwhelmed, and unable to weather change is not the historical transition from industrialism to post-industrialism. It is a deep malaise related to a hostile world that still fails to provide enough food, shelter, and security to millions of people. Young people can see how much suffering remains, that society produces incredible gadgets but not solutions to real problems. Who your parents were, your skin color, and the school you went to still play an outsized role in your ability to succeed in this future. Indeed, in some parts of the world, this is even more true than it was in Toffler's time.

Who Wants this Future?

One of the Tofflers' examples of a person "living in the future" is a Wall Street executive named Bruce Robe, who works in New York City and whose family lives in Columbus, Ohio. Every weekend he boards a jet and commutes home. This example is meant to showcase the impressiveness of jet travel and the rise of a global nomad class. However, we never see the human costs of such opportunities. Is this the world this man wants to live in? How does he feel not seeing his family? How do his wife and children feel about his long absences? Does this future work for them?

For the Tofflers, it was easier to imagine quick-fix technical interventions that shape the future (the jet), rather than to investigate the structural issues that gave rise to the problem in the first place (unlivable cities). They did not at the time anticipate the environmental impact caused by jet travel or the social impact of long-distance commuting.

We could imagine a different scenario, one in which an improved future for the executive and his family might include affordable housing in a safe and family-friendly New York City. Or perhaps one in which economic opportunities are more evenly distributed across the country and he could find employment in the thriving business community of Columbus.

> I see future shock as one outcome of a broken economic system that produces miraculous technology but fails to prioritize fundamental human needs and values.

In another section, the Tofflers discuss the future of human reproduction. In this vision, biotechnology enables women to pre-select an embryo, then use a mechanical womb in a lab to incubate the baby until the time of birth. Here, again, it is unclear who actually wants this future. While some women might find childbirth unpleasant enough to warrant this solution, it doesn't seem like a widespread problem compared with the reality of raising children in a heavily gendered and unequal society with inadequate childcare support. What use is a mechanical uterus if parents still cannot access affordable childcare?

Once again, technological innovations seem to improve a situation, but the underlying challenge is unaddressed. Universal childcare would require a revaluation of caregiving work. Caregiving work, both then and now, is done predominantly by women, people of color, and immigrants. It isn't seen as prestigious, nor is it well compensated. Investing in a technological solution to the rigors of childbirth, rather than changing the way we structure society to care for the child after it is born, seems a pointless exercise. Planners and futurists traditionally don't focus on this topic, primarily because it puzzlingly isn't seen as futuristic. Yet childcare providers are perhaps the people most immersed in raising future generations.

Who Broke the Future?

We still live in a world where lots of key groups are left out of visions of the future. Though this is changing, there is still work to be done to ensure that diverse views of the future are generated and heard. When people are excluded from creating the future and seeing themselves in it, they are often forced to claim space for themselves using whatever rough tools they can access. These can take many forms, including revolution, violence, disengagement, mass exodus, and suicide.

Millennials in the US (like myself), are economically worse off than their parents, and simply cannot afford some of the basic elements of life—in the present or for the future (for example, houses and savings accounts).[4] The future we inherited—our present—is more polluted, more unequal, and more precarious than the world our parents knew. Through the lens of *Future Shock* it is easy to proclaim that what is needed is adaptation to the new reality and acceptance of change. However, it seems unfair to blame an entire generation for failure to adapt to the future in a broken world of climate change, growing nationalism, and rising economic inequality.

Who can Change the Future?

For the past 50 years, our world has incentivized and valued technological fixes but has not invested in tackling fundamental issues of equality or forging a sustainable path forward. The underlying structure of inequality has shaped the path of societal evolution and contributed to many of the problems we see today. We have failed to take action on critical issues, such as climate change. Rather than restructure our businesses and societies around planetary boundaries, we hope that scientific innovation and geoengineering will bail us out.

> We still live in a world where lots of key groups are left out of visions of the future. Though this is changing, there is still work to be done to ensure that diverse views of the future are generated and heard.

Many of the people who have been excluded from living in the Tofflers' future are the people who are most impacted by inequalities today. We need to heed their voices and distill their messages, as they have firsthand appreciation of the problems that must be addressed and, as a result, the incentive to lead grassroots movements that can change the existing systems."

Around the world, young people are striking for climate justice and for their governments to decarbonize. Groups such as Black Lives Matter fight against systemic racism. People are fighting for the right to have clean water, healthcare, and a living wage. Citizens are pushing back, governments are changing, and norms are shifting. This is happening because people who traditionally have been denied a share in the future are fighting for a future vision that is intersectional, sustainable, and equitable.

Young people want to fix the system, starting with core values: a thriving environment, investment in future generations, and the dismantling of structures like colonialism and white supremacy. Futures tools should be used to challenge assumptions about what the world can be, and to make sure we aren't applying solutions that benefit only a small group. One way they can continue to do so is by helping our thinking go deeper. Only by first interrogating the "why" behind the way things are can we figure out the "how" for the way things could be.

But power never concedes without a fight. Fossil fuel companies continue to control major parts of the world economy, nationalism is spreading across the world, and multinational corporations are buying up the world's water. It sometimes feels as if we are living out our last days on a dying planet. Maybe we will be unable to adequately address the problems we face, but it is no longer possible to naively assume they will go away on their own.

Fixing Everyday Futures

Popular conceptions of futuristic space colonies and dazzling new technology ignore structural societal problems. They also ignore the mundane ways in which the future often plays out. Even the 2 percent of people "living in the future" don't spend a lot of time thinking about the future, as modern technology quickly becomes routine. Humans are and will be concerned with the same things that have always concerned us—basic needs, love, community, and simply getting through each day.

For me, a future that honors and values the mundane lived experience of the billions of people of the world is a better vision. If we can imagine life on Mars, we can imagine a functioning economic system that treats people with dignity. I think that future generations will look back at today's world in shock that we let things get so bad and that it took so long for us to build a sustainable and equitable world.

Alisha Bhagat is a futurist and senior strategist whose work focuses on the creative use of futures tools to impact long-term positive change, particularly around social justice and equality. For the past six years, she has worked at Forum for the Future, a nonprofit that helps organizations think systemically and sustainably about the future. Alisha brings a broad toolkit to her work, and designs games, creates immersive experiences, and brings the future to life. Prior to joining Forum, Alisha was a foreign policy consultant for the US government and a fellow at the East-West Center in Honolulu. Alisha holds an MS in Foreign Service from Georgetown University and a BS in anthropology and history from Carnegie Mellon University. She was awarded a Fulbright scholarship in 2005. When not thinking about the future, Alisha is an avid gamer and science fiction enthusiast. She also serves on the board of BitchMedia, a feminist media organization. Alisha lives in Brooklyn with her partner, two daughters, and loving cat. You can find her @alishabhagat.

1. Thank you to Mark Egerman, Francesca Chubb-Confer, and Anna Warrington for providing feedback on this piece.

2. Interestingly, Toffler's math doesn't add up. It is unclear if the missing 2 to 3 percent are in a separate category of people or are omitted to indicate a small buffer.

3. Toffler writes "by comparison with almost anyone else, white Americans and Canadians are regarded as hustling, fast moving go-getters." *Future Shock*, p 41.

4. There are a number of indicators as to why Millennials are worse off than their parents. Home ownership is one example. Home ownership among Millennials remains significantly lower than other generations. (https://www.urban.org/research/publication/millennial-homeownership)

After Shock: The Coming Indifference

Jonathan Venn, PhD

Proliferation of entertainments, lateralized sharing of power in organizations, planning committees that serve local communities, and industries that not only work together but also live together—all these were predicted by the Tofflers in 1970. What these four visions have in common are the Tofflers' assumptions about future affluence, the abundance of leisure, the benevolence of people with power, and our ability to get along with each other.

In all fairness to the Tofflers, *Future Shock* was written before the recession of 1973 to 1975, when the Vietnam War ended and so did a period of unprecedented economic growth that began with the Allied victory in World War II. The Tofflers were not alone at that time in believing that 28 years of continuous prosperity were going to continue.

Perhaps more importantly, the Tofflers failed to perceive that widespread affluence and abundant leisure are opportunities to steal. The Tofflers gave brief mention to the disparity of wealth and the possibility that an impoverished underclass will not sit still while the wealthy enjoy their lives of privilege, but in general, the Tofflers left the poor out of their discussion, as most people do. The future they predicted is available to those who already have the resources to take advantage of it, but not to the rest. Today the top 1 percent own 40 percent of the wealth, and the bottom 40 percent own nothing. The disparity of wealth follows racial lines: The average Black American owns one-tenth of the amount of the average White American.

Although wealth in America has grown, wages adjusted for inflation have not grown since the US Bureau of Labor Statistics began keeping these statistics five decades ago. In 1964 the average wage was $2.50 an hour, which equals $20.27 in 2018 dollars. Consistent with the recession of 1973 to 1975, the average wage peaked in 1973 around $24.00 an hour (in 2018 dollars). Forty-five years later it was only $22.65 an hour. While America's wealth has increased, the amount shared with the workers who produce that wealth has stagnated. Furthermore, large tax cuts for the wealthy during the Carter and Clinton administrations shifted the tax burden to the middle and working classes.

Eighty years ago Americans in manufacturing jobs worked 100 hours a week. Then the labor unions succeeded in getting an eight-hour work day. Today, however, 6.5 million Americans have to work two jobs to survive. We have made less progress than we had hoped. Political forces are at work to crush our labor unions, but even where the unions survive they are prone to lose interest in their members, collude with management, and become a new elite unto themselves. What this says about the nature of human behavior is too powerful to ignore.

Americans are buried in debt, and human services are starved of resources. Today 549,000 homeless people walk our streets and take shelter under our viaducts. An estimated 20 to 25 percent of them have mental illness.

Young children go to schools where they can be fed, and they are taught by underpaid teachers. State governments balanced their budgets by cutting off tax dollars to colleges and universities, which shifted the burden of a college education to the students and their parents. Today 15 percent of college students do not know whether they can buy food, and many are homeless. Many drop out, having to decide whether they will attend college or eat. Those who complete their education enter the work force with as much as

> The wealth that is generated by warfare, prisons, and the health insurance industry makes each of these a powerful lobby and a lasting institution in its own right. These institutions will persist, despite the waste of human potential and the other problems that they cause.

five or six figures of debt, and they find only low-paying jobs. These young graduates look forward to a lifetime of paying off debt instead of buying a home, taking vacations, or having children.

The flesh eaters of the health insurance industry, dumbstruck by the amount of money Medicare collected beginning in 1966, and aided and abetted by the Nixon administration, invented the managed care industry that skims wealth by depriving sick people of the healthcare they need. What hope is there for a society where one class of people gets rich by their indifference to the illness of another class?

The overhead of private health insurance companies is around 12 percent. Compare that to Medicare, where overhead is about 2 percent. We could save as much as 10 percent of our spending on healthcare just by getting rid of private health insurance.

As wealth congealed at the top, the underground economy flourished. The illegitimate economy—fueled by illicit pleasures and expediencies like drug use, prostitution, human trafficking, robbery, burglary, counterfeiting, weapons, and the unsanctioned violence of the underclass—is available to those who cannot enter the legitimate economy due to factors like race, social class, language, geography, learning disorders, and lack of education. Counterfeiting alone—including the counterfeiting of medicines and other patented products—is worth nearly $2 trillion a year worldwide. In Africa, counterfeit medicines kill people by the thousands.

The legitimate economy protects itself with a criminal justice system and the sanctioned violence of police departments. America has more jails than colleges, and keeps 2 million people behind bars. A 2006 study by the Bureau of Justice Statistics showed that 45 to 64 percent of those incarcerated have serious symptoms of mental illness, varying with whether it was a state, federal, or county lockup. The Prison Law Office, in states like California and Pennsylvania, demonstrated to the federal courts that the punishment in state prisons is cruel and unusual. The legal term for it is "deliberate indifference." Criminal justice and prison institutions, like the military they emulate and like the gangs they oppose, are epitomes of rigid hierarchies and the least likely to lateralize power.

The wealth that is generated by warfare, prisons, and the health insurance industry makes each of these a powerful lobby and a lasting institution in its own right. These institutions will persist, despite the waste of human potential and the other problems that they cause.

Indifference to the environment garners immense wealth for a few while destroying our planet with pollution. The current generation of Americans is the first that is not expected to live as long or do as well as their parents.

Fifty years ago the Tofflers' predictions were based on assumptions about affluence, leisure, human relationships, and the benevolence of leaders. Their vision has been realized only by those who already had the resources to take advantage of it. For billions of others, there has been no success. Why would we expect change when the elites who run the world need widespread poverty so they can fill their militaries and hire cheap labor? Young men and women are persuaded that it is in their own best interest to serve the wealthy, and they are brainwashed into believing that any other course of action is cowardly or immoral. And when they sign up, we cannot guarantee them a living wage or adequate healthcare.

The failure of the Tofflers' vision is the failure of all dreams, whether they be the alleged virtues of "the free world," Marxist-Leninism, or *Future Shock*. None of these visions predicted the reality of human nature: That people rise to power and use their power to steal from the powerless. They cannot be ruled or controlled because they take control and they make the rules. To expect anything else in our future is to ignore the reality of human nature. ▪

Jonathan Venn, PhD, has 48 years of experience in providing psychological services. He has devoted his life to the care of persons with mental illness. He has a doctoral degree in clinical psychology from Northwestern University. He is licensed in psychology in four states, namely, California, Maryland, South Carolina, and Alabama. He has served on the staffs or faculties of six universities, namely, Northwestern University, the University of Maryland, the University of South Carolina, San Diego State University, South University, and Alliant International University. He has published original articles in psychology. He has earned the Diplomates in Clinical Psychology and Forensic Psychology from the American Board of Professional Psychology, which are the highest levels of recognition in those two professions. He has been a military officer. He spent four years on the staff of a Fortune 500 corporation. He has retired from the correctional systems of two states: California and South Carolina. In 2000 he helped write the script that won the Best Screenplay Award at Cannes, and he consulted with Renee Zellweger on the performance that earned her an Academy Award nomination for Best Actress. In 2007 he introduced zydeco music to the monks of Mt. Saint-Michel. Learn more about Dr. Venn at www.sacramentocounseling.org.

The Not-so-Shocking Future—Today

Patricia Lustig
& Gill Ringland

Future Shock **envisioned a post-industrial society where the pace of change accelerates at such a rate that it feels threatening.**

Indeed, the term "future shock" describes the shattering stress and disorientation induced in individuals subjected to "too much change in too short a time."

The Tofflers' came to this realization after five years of research, where two major findings emerged. First, future shock was a real sickness from which many already suffered, and second, little was actually known about human adaptivity under such conditions.

Since that time, change has indeed accelerated, with technology having a reach barely imaginable at the time the Tofflers wrote. And it is not unreasonable that existing governing structures would feel threatened: on the whole, the older you happen to be, the more likely it is that you'll feel threatened by change. We see it all the time in people who did not grow up with technology, and hence, find it hard to adapt. Some corners of society have indeed shown signs of the shattering stress and disorientation of which the Tofflers spoke.

People develop their worldviews through the particular lenses of their generation and experience. The same can certainly be said of the Millennials and Gen Z—those born after 1980—who have grown up not only with technology, but with the idea of continuous change, as well. In contrast to their Boomer parents, they're actually quite comfortable with it all, and have, in fact, exhibited remarkable adaptation. They don't feel threatened at all. Rather, many of them actually feel empowered by it. They effortlessly exploit the myriad technologies at their disposal in myriad ways to connect with their worlds, often to the chagrin of their parents and teachers.

Technology isn't the only thing that has changed—the economics of the world have advanced, too. In contrast to 50 years ago, far more people today are part of the middle class, and far more under the age of 40 are above the poverty line. The combination of powerful technologies and prosperous economies engenders *choice*. Thus empowered, the luxury of choice includes the way we build our networks to energize our respective communities in order to get things done. And their reach is global.

Three examples serve to illustrate how these four factors—continual change, improved economic conditions, greater freedom of choice, and global reach—lead to the unprecedented empowerment of many motivated young people who are dedicating themselves to positive, proactive change.

Greta Ernman Thunberg, the Swedish schoolgirl who has become a role model for worldwide student activism, is an inspiring case in point. Speaking at the UN COP24 climate talks in December, 2018, she said, "I am 15 years old. I am from Sweden. I speak on behalf of Climate Justice Now. Many people say that Sweden is just a small country and it doesn't matter what we do. But I've learned you are never too small to make a difference. [...] We have run out of excuses and we are running out of time. We have come here to let you know that change is coming, whether you like it or not. The real power belongs to the people."

> "The combination of powerful technologies and prosperous economies engenders choice. Thus empowered, the luxury of choice includes the way we build our networks to energize our respective communities in order to get things done.

Indeed. She has since addressed global business leaders in Davos, capturing a fresh mood for action. When, on March 15, she returned to the cobblestones (as she has done almost every Friday through rain, sun, ice, and snow), it was as a figurehead for a vast and growing movement. The global climate strike in March 2019 was one of the biggest environmental protests the world has ever seen, with more than 71 countries participating across more than 700 locations. Greta observes, "It's increasing very much now, and that's very, very fun."

We see the same kinds of dynamics playing out in Africa and in Asia, where Millennials are increasingly using technology to challenge the status quo.

Since the Arab Spring of 2011, young Africans have been using technology to mobilize around the issues affecting them. Images of young Africans assembled in protest, organizing around hashtags, are now common on Twitter, Facebook, and other social media platforms. Their political activities contributed, for example, to ensuring the integrity of the 2016 election in The Gambia. They began using the hashtag #Gambiahasdecided, when former President Yahya Jammeh refused to vacate his office and hand over power after suffering electoral defeat to Adama Barrow. Moreover, their anti-Jammeh campaign also encouraged citizens to wear T-shirts bearing the slogan, "Social media has forever changed the dynamics of politics in Africa." Raffie Diab, who organised the T-shirt campaign, posted on his Facebook page, "Gambians have a tendency of creating our own dictators and we are seeing it playing out right now. The law is categoric and clear in regards to the separation of powers between the legislature and the executive and yet you see people whom I thought were educated and knowledgeable coming out here justifying the President's sacking of Hon Kumba Jaiteh. We have seen over the years how Jammeh used executive powers as an excuse to plunder this country and we all came out and voted him out hoping to usher in a new Gambia. Sadly, we are seeing it repeating itself. We should not see this as a partisan issue but have to condemn it because it is a wrong move on the part of the president. Let's not start allowing the President to abuse his powers, as this is how dictatorships are created."

Jammeh was ultimately forced into exile, and Barrow, upon assuming office, auctioned off Jammeh's fleet of luxury cars and aircraft to raise money for health and education projects.

Let's next turn to Nepal where, in the aftermath of the 2015 7.8-magnitude earthquake, tech-savvy Millennials were solving problems that conventional governments and NGOs were not able to. In the face of slow government response and an international community stymied by bureaucracy and logistical hurdles, groups of young volunteers stepped into action. The Yellow House—a bed and breakfast in Sanepa, Kathmandu—emerged as the hub of "vibrant guerrilla aid." The Yellow House team was run by a handful of young Millennials armed with little more than Facebook, mapping technology, local knowledge, and the will to get things done. They put out a call on Facebook to "see what we can do," and hundreds answered the call. People in Europe and the USA—volunteer mappers—helped create precise maps of Nepal's rugged terrain. These were put together to further develop an open source map that had been created online—by a young man with experience in the earthquake in Haiti in 2010—for Kathmandu, using satellite imagery (www.quakemaps.org), to which had been added layers allowing the reporting of both earthquake data and response information in real time. In Belgium and the USA, people raised funds. Finally, local volunteers used the information and donations to deliver aid to some of the quake's hardest-hit areas. The UN, observing all this ad hoc activity, joined the effort, offering rice, tarpaulins and equipment—but following the lead of these dedicated young people.

In each of these examples, we see young people recognizing and responding to the need for change—exercising their economic- and technology-enabled power of choice to create huge multiplier effects. No, they don't find change threatening. Nor would they relate to the Tofflers' "shattering stress and disorientation" wrought by a too-rapid rate of change. They are not victims of change; they are citizens of the world and part of the change they want to see.

One swallow does not a summer make, yet we hope these three examples will serve to illustrate the reasons we are more optimistic about the capacity of people to cope with change than the Tofflers were 50 years ago.

Patricia Lustig leads LASA Insight Ltd, a strategic foresight company. She uses foresight, horizon scanning and futures tools to help organisations develop insight into emerging trends, develop a successful strategy and implement the changes. She understands the need to explore potential futures to develop robust corporate strategy and implement successful change. She has worked in Europe, EMEA, Asia and the USA at major blue-chip companies BP, Motorola and Logica. She is the author or co-author of four books and numerous articles.

Gill Ringland was head of strategy at ICL (now part of Fujitsu) and CEO and Fellow of SAMI Consulting. She is a Fellow of the British Computer Society, and of the World Academy of Arts and Sciences. She is now an Emeritus Fellow of SAMI and a Director of Ethical Reading. She has been co-opted onto EC and British government advisory bodies covering IT, Economic and Social Research, and Foresight. She is the author or co-author of eight books and numerous articles.

Shock Absorber: Scholarly Publishing in the Internet Age

John Sack

Several books and magazine articles about popular culture were written in the 1970s with the word "shock" in the title, enough that the word reverberated in the general culture as a descriptor of a particular, seemingly new pattern of change. Clearly what was on people's minds was something sudden, like an earthquake. "Shock" conveys a sense that an event was sudden but also unpredicted or unpredictable, like assassinations of major public figures; something uncontrolled, with second- and third-order consequences that themselves couldn't be predicted or extrapolated because whatever formula was used to calculate from was unreliable (something Coca-Cola learned in introducing New Coke, perhaps). Old patterns were not reliable predictors of future states, certainly.

After a shock, there is continued upheaval—as in aftershocks and revolutions—and sometimes there is the quick onset of a period of resettlement as people, systems, and organizations adjust to the new models. But even within this resettlement period, we might see "a thousand flowers bloom" period of chaos and experimentation.

Thirty years on from *Future Shock*, we saw this with the internet boom, and with the Arab Spring. Both of these "shocks" were followed by something surprising and, to some, disappointing. Toffler's predictions were not necessarily pretty or optimistic, but they were not doom and gloom (unlike, say, Ehrlich's «Population Bomb»). For example, the Stonewall riots that launched gay rights were around the same time as *Future Shock*—and Toffler (seemingly outrageously at the time) foresaw "homosexual marriages" and gay parents. Shocks were necessary disruptors of the status quo, and unfroze a stuck system.

In my own field of science communication—aka "scholarly publishing"—we entered the shock/experimentation/resettlement pattern when the web became *the* way to share research information in the latter 1990s and early 2000s. The key output product from scholarly publishing workflows is the write-up of research, such as a scientific or medical experiment. The web was the great disruptor for scholarly publishing, just as it was for many other industries that were rooted in physical workflows for information.

The web enabled greater speed, experimentation with forms and formats, proliferation of outputs, and new forms of filtering. Because the web shifted costs away from printing and mailing by using the network for distribution, it also enabled new business models, since the cost of distribution (previously a significant part of the total cost of publishing) was essentially zero, or at least was significantly less volume-related. New debates on filtering for "quality" arose, since quantity was less limited by cost than previously. Students of Toffler will recognize in this his description of free-flowing information, and the resulting information overload.

The transubstantiation of physical information products, such as printed journal issues, into bits such as PDFs of journal articles, also opened the possibility for new structures in the industry. Intermediaries—who previously controlled the filters and distribution channels of scholarly information—could be "disintermediated" (a word that was popular with librarians, who saw that the free flow of information would change their own role in research information delivery, from that of trusted, expert advisor to researchers, into gatekeeper and purchasing agent). New intermediaries—search engines like Google are the most obvious example—could arise in which quantity and speed were taken as kitemarks of quality (each Google search result boasts "about 352,000 results (in 0.50 seconds)". Scholarly publishing has long had aggregators—usually to cut across the commercial by-publisher or by-journal lines that scholars must cross all the time—but the new intermediaries such as search engines could apply technology to scale and to produce added value.

Scholarly publishing has now entered a phase in which the most respected intermediaries—the journal editors and reviewers—are themselves in question: are they *necessary* gatekeepers? Around the time the web transformed scholarly publishing, we saw the creation of a database of "preprints" in high-energy physics—preliminary research reports written by experts for other experts—that did not go through the filter of expert peer review before they were disseminated. For 20 years people thought "but high-energy physics is unique in this." Now, we have had preprints in life science for over five years, and just recently the launch of preprints in medicine. These are examples of adhocracy at work. The need for speed has outrun the need for filtering.

> Scholarly publishing has now entered a phase in which the most respected intermediaries—the journal editors and reviewers—are themselves in question: are they necessary gatekeepers?

With the free-flowing web as the dissemination medium, even the speed of diffusion of innovation was "shocked" as we saw what could happen with "virality" and "network effects." Soon consumer expectations began to affect the so-called academic "ivory tower": mobile, social media, personalized, niche, etc. The previous belief that experts or pundits (journal editors in the case of scholarly publishing) could point to what I personally needed to read was now challenged by the option to view unfiltered information placed online by the "vox pop" of my peers.

In scholarly publishing we saw journals move from printed-format-only in the early 1990s to "online only" within 10-15 years. We saw the ascendance of the earlier online version over the subsequent print version of an article with "publish ahead of print." We saw specialized scholarly search engines, new "alt metrics" for judging quality with quantity measures, and of course AI influence on all of these. "Open access," "preprints" (mentioned above), and "open peer review" arose, and are surely examples of the influence of the "sharing economy" on a communication system that had previously been a very good source of profit for specialized commercial publishers who "owned" the copyright, and thus the access controls, on scholarly products. The sharing economy Toffler predicted suggested less emphasis on ownership. In scholarly communication this was reinforced by the view that the research itself was often paid for by citizens' taxes and so should not be owned by any private party.

> Some other aspects of the scholarly information economy haven't yet been much influenced by major consumer trends. And anything that can resist major consumer trends is of interest to futurists.

But some things in scholarly communication have *not* seen much or any change. And these are worth our attention because they are outliers in a system that has been rearranging itself in the 25+ years since the web was "born." Have these aspects not changed because they are the best they can be? Because they are immune or somehow walled off— they are so conservative that their barriers are stronger than the forces impinging on them? And what will happen over time as these persist without alteration? Do tectonic forces build up, as before an earthquake?

The major "system" that has resisted change is the process of individual researcher evaluation. This evaluation is very important, especially for junior faculty and researchers, because it leads to tenure/promotion and also to funding for new research projects (which in turn lead to tenure/promotion). The system might be called "guild-like" in that it is based on apprenticeships and then creation of works that are judged (by peers) as representing high quality. Perhaps because the system is embedded in university structures—themselves dating back centuries—the use of research outputs in promotion/tenure has not adjusted much to the information economy. It is also a certification system, but with a limited number of "slots" (for faculty "billets" and for research grant funding); the limit would normally cause the bar to rise, but in this case it seems to freeze the bar-setting system into a traditional model.

Some other aspects of the scholarly information economy haven't yet been much influenced by major consumer trends. And anything that can resist major consumer trends is of interest to futurists. Two trends in particular have so far had little impact on scholarly publishing: mobile and the "gig economy." There might be special reasons for these, which I'll mention here:

1 ■ Research communication is a process of dialog in which each party in the conversation communicates by publishing a scholarly paper. You don't get much traction if you just write a blog post. It isn't considered "serious." If you have to read a full article—these are typically 10 or so dense pages—then a mobile screen is an almost painful way to do this. Currently, scholarly search engines see only about 10 percent of their traffic coming from mobile devices, while commodity search engines see over 50 percent being mobile-sourced.

2 ∎ Scholarly research and publishing has resembled a barter and gig-economy system, with frequent collaborations gathering together experts to create a product built out of shared expertise and time. The collaborative approach to researching and discovering new knowledge has aspects of Toffler's "adhocracy." But not so the system of "peer review"—which credentials the resulting research write-up; it is highly formalized and is only now starting to see changes in its architecture as people question the gatekeepers' roles. ∎

John Sack is the founding director of Stanford University's HighWire Press and focuses on market assessment, client relations, technology innovation, and industry-forward thinking. John's role is to determine where the technology and publishing industries are going, how one of those might leverage the other, and how HighWire can best support its customers and its customers' customers—the libraries, students, researchers, and clinicians they serve. John considers himself a "futurist" or "trend-spotter" in that he tries to watch what is happening in consumer and scholarly services and identify patterns that are just beginning to emerge. John has an undergraduate degree in English from the University of Virginia and a graduate degree in English from Stanford University, where he has worked for nearly all his career in technology.

The New Science
for an Accelerated World

Donna Dupont

It's said that an opportunity lies in every crisis. ■ "In crisis" is by definition a decisive state, capable of sparking a turning point for change, better or worse. A positive outcome, enabling necessary change, requires that we be willing to sift through and identify the elements of the situation, and that we be capable of letting go, with discernment, of what is not working. Unfortunately, in our distracting and accelerating world, not everyone is capable of seeing this opportunity to move beyond the status quo and embrace a new future.

Nothing in my clinical training prepared me for 2003. That was the year of SARS—Sudden Acute Respiratory Syndrome, a novel infectious disease threat that started in southern China and resulted in thousands of cases and hundreds of deaths across 37 countries. In Toronto, Canada, there was initially a high level of anxiety and uncertainty about the level of risk and modes of disease transmission, challenging the healthcare system as to how best to protect healthcare workers and minimize disease spread through the environment. This event exposed our vulnerabilities, as our level of preparedness and response at the time was basic and minimal. This was one of my early career moments, and like many healthcare professionals at the time, I had a strong duty-to-care ethic. The moment I had to don a HAZMAT suit to care for patients, I knew the way I viewed my career would never be the same. With the emergence of incredible leadership, and as new information was discovered, the health system responded and adapted to the situation. Through the shock and stress, the system was able to navigate through the turbulence. In the process, everyone learned a lot about opportunities to improve the system against future threats.

Fast forward to 2014—the World Health Organization declared the Ebola outbreak in West Africa a Public Health Emergency of International Concern (PHEIC), a designation reserved for events with a risk of potential international spread, or that require a coordinated international response. I was working as a provincial emergency manager, supporting strategic planning for Ontario's health system. We had many Canadians in West Africa courageously working to contain the spread of the virus, and our healthcare system needed to be ready when our citizens returned home. We had never anticipated a scenario quite like this, and we quickly learned we needed to rebuild our capacity post-SARS and adapt to this potential risk. It took a lot of time and resources, and again the various elements of the system came together to respond to the challenge. We learned much about risk, vulnerability, uncertainty, and the importance of maintaining a level of preparedness. However, as time passed we again struggled to maintain that heightened capacity and capability, and as other priorities arose, our new lessons quickly faded away.

My experiences in health emergency management, both on the front line and at the systems-level, opened my eyes to how as a society we adapt or fail to adapt to change. I observed repeated emergency response patterns, which also revealed the profession's vast tacit knowledge regarding anticipating challenges. It was at this point that my journey toward the practice of strategic foresight began; for me it was the gateway to building a more resilient future. Now a foresight and design strategist, my focus is on disaster risk management and sustainable development. I work with organizations looking to adapt to the changing environment and build community resiliency.

As is true for many organizations, the emergency/disaster management community has a tendency to think and behave in short-term cycles: moving from crisis to crisis, stuck in the cycle of disaster-response-recovery loop. The knowledge gained from emergency events is not fully mobilized into long-term planning in anticipation of emerging and future risk. Unfortunately, this is creating a situation where it's difficult to keep pace with the dynamic reality of today's accelerated world, and the gap between accelerations and adaptive activities is quickly widening. This is important because if we continue the current trajectory, we face the risk of future shock.

> As is true for many organizations, the emergency/disaster management community has a tendency to think and behave in short-term cycles: moving from crisis to crisis, stuck in the cycle of disaster-response-recovery loop. The knowledge gained from emergency events is not fully mobilized into long-term planning in anticipation of emerging and future risk.

Alvin Toffler, writing in *Future Shock*, captures the forward direction needed in this statement: "Today's unconsciousness adaptation is no longer adequate. We must assume conscious control of evolution itself, and ride the waves of change to avoid future shock. We need to master evolution, to shape tomorrow to meet human needs. Instead of rising in the revolt against it, we must anticipate and design the future." [p,244]

As the time intervals decrease between emergency events, the frequency of change placed on society and its adaptive demands is turning up. With all this change, what is the potential impact on society's health?

In *Future Shock*, Alvin Toffler asked, "What actually happens to people when they are asked to change again and again? To understand the answer, we must begin with the body, the physical organism, itself. Today, more and more health authorities are coming around to the ecological notion that the individual needs to be seen as part of a total system, and that his health is dependent upon many subtle external factors."

Well, today we know. The answer can be found in the science of epigenetics, which literally means "control above genetics." Epigenetics has established that environmental influences, including stress and emotions, control the activity of our genes. This means in an accelerated world, we are potentially sacrificing our health if we fall victim to the stress of constant change. We must learn to adapt and embrace the influences of our surrounding environment in a healthy way.

The probability of not being adequately prepared, or having the resources or capacity to respond to the demands of the evolving risk landscape, is a very real and likely scenario. We are not only running the risk of potentially being overwhelmed when emergency events occur, but now also risk the health of society as the pressure increases to keep pace with the growing rate of change.

Accelerations and Pace of Change

The increasing pace of environmental change is now more visible. Many scientists claim that we are on the verge of the sixth mass extinction, accelerated by human behavior. Global reports and panels are identifying the risks and need for action, such as:

- International Panel on Climate Change (2018) – identified a 12-year window to limit the devastating effects of climate change.
- United Nation's Global Assessment Report (GAR) on Disaster Risk Reduction (2019) – acknowledges change is happening more quickly and across multiple dimensions and scales than ever thought possible.
- World Economic Forum's Global Risks Report (2019) – confirms that the global risks are intensifying, and states that the collective will to tackle them appears to be lacking: *"of all risks, it is in relation to the environment that the world is most clearly sleepwalking into catastrophe."*

One of the manifestations of climate change is the increasing frequency and intensity of extreme weather events. The economic and social impacts of responding and recovering from disasters is substantial and has the potential to threaten our future economy and sustainability. We are now living in a time of extremes, and the unsustainable patterns and emerging issues are inviting us to adapt to a new reality. Ready or not, change is coming!

As I consider our current situation, I can't help but ask:

- Why does our society lack the collective will to take action?
- Why are we not acting with urgency proportional to the scale of the threat?
- How can we wake up from this sleepwalking nightmare?
- Could we be suffering from normalcy bias, thinking that if we stay the course everything will go back to normal?

Based on our behaviour patterns to date, there is a high likelihood of failure at climate-change mitigation and adaptation, with potentially devastating impacts. There appears to be a gap between scientific statements of risk, and the way society perceives the risk and makes decisions. Could a feeling of lack of control and discomfort with increasing uncertainty be the etiology of growing psychological stress and paralysis instead of action?

Perhaps we are in the early stages of an adaptation breakdown, and on our way toward culture shock? Or maybe the culture shock is necessary to pull us out of our sleepwalking state and ignite our collective commitment to adaptation?

The science of cymatics, the study of visible sound vibration, give us insight into how nature brings about change and evolution. In nature, as a frequency increases it gives way to a more complex and chaotic pattern. The pattern of chaos gives way to a higher order and a new structure. Maybe the accelerations we are experiencing are necessary to drive societal change toward a more sustainable system.

As our interconnected world accelerates, with increasing complexity, evolving risk, and uncertainty, our siloed and fragmented approaches will not be sufficient to address the attendant systemic challenges. Unsustainable structures with bureaucratic rigidity, based on competition and scarcity, will need to reorganize and transform into structures designed for tomorrow's world.

Evolutionary Paradigm

The launch of three global agendas put forth new narratives around vulnerability and resilience: the Sendai Framework for Disaster Risk Reduction, Sustainable Development Goals, and the Paris Agreement. At the intersection of these three agendas is policy that calls for reducing vulnerability and enhancing resilience.

Resilience as a narrative provides the foundation for a new, inclusive vision of the future, one that will need a new culture and structure to match. It is a paradigm shift. The resilience narrative is an invitation for society to come together, ride the waves of change, and consciously shape our evolution. We must rise to the challenge, become anticipatory, and design to empower action at every level across the system. We must get more comfortable with inevitable uncertainty, embrace our own vulnerability by dropping our "armor," and with courage and curiosity radically explore new ways to create a better future. Unprecedented cooperation and collaboration is part of the new culture and worldview. Now more than ever, the world needs futures-thinking!

> Epigenetics has established that environmental influences, including stress and emotions, control the activity of our genes. This means in an accelerated world, we are potentially sacrificing our health if we fall victim to the stress of constant change.

It's ironic that the "climate crisis" is providing an opportunity to learn directly from nature, the best teacher and a resilient model of adaptation for life on Earth. Biomimicry is an approach to innovation that has grown over the past two decades, seeking sustainable solutions to human challenges by emulating nature's patterns and strategies.

Nature's Model

Biomimicry uses nature as a model, measure, and mentor. It's a new way of viewing and valuing nature and introduces a mindset based on what we can learn from the natural world, not just extract from it. It's a science that studies the genius of nature's models in order to imitate them or for inspiration for new designs and processes to solve human problems. It can also help guide our innovations toward being measured against and held to an ecological standard.

Acceleration in the pace of change is creating the turbulence and chaos necessary to trigger our evolution. As nature strives for homeostasis based in cooperation, mutual aid, and harmony, so will our current systems and structures. Not just our physical infrastructure, but also the potential of our social infrastructure (social capital) and green infrastructure to embrace a whole-of-society approach and achieve collective economic, environmental, and social benefits.

The science of quantum physics suggests that our reality is shaped by our consciousness; all is energy, and it is interconnected. The world is at a critical turning point; it needs change leadership to seed a new consciousness, shifting from a Darwinian survival model to manifesting a thriving world. The wildcard is how society will respond to the changes.

And as a caterpillar enters its cocoon to transform, so will we. As long as we can see today's crisis as an opportunity to learn, unlearn, and re-learn, we have a chance to emerge as the sustainable butterfly the world desperately needs to become.

Donna Dupont is the Founder and Chief Strategist in Foresight & Design for Purple Compass, with a focus on disaster risk management and sustainable development. Her aim is to collaborate with communities and organizations, and use strategic foresight and human-centered design methods to advance adaptation strategies for the future well-being and resiliency of communities. Prior to Purple Compass, Donna held a variety of senior level roles within government in healthcare and emergency management, and has supported and led projects focused on transformational change. She is the recipient of several government awards at the provincial and federal level for her contribution to policy and strategic planning. Donna is in the final stage of completing her Master of Design in Strategic Foresight & Innovation at OCAD University. She lives in Toronto, Canada.

To Prepare Students for Tomorrow, Teach the Future Today!

Erica Bol

Young people go to school to prepare themselves for the future.

We teach them about the past and the present—but nothing about the future. Why is this? The main reason that most schools do not make the future part of their curriculum is the challenge of teaching something that is *not yet there*. But just because a descriptive depiction of what the future holds cannot be provided, it does not follow that we cannot help young people develop the skills needed to optimally prepare for that future. Preparation can give direction to individual futures—and to that of the world.

I argue that being prepared for the future is more important now than ever, if only because the world is changing at such a fast pace. The speed of change and its often attendant lack of control can produce stress, anxiety, or even shock. Consequently, people shy away from contemplating the future and end up letting the future "happen" to them. This is the real tragedy, as there is no reason we cannot properly prepare people—whether students or adults—for a thriving future. When people learn future skills, fear evaporates, and they instead come to embrace, and even shape, change.

Futures Education

The education system should play a pivotal role in preparing students for the future, but it has all but abdicated that responsibility. Alvin Toffler recognized this. "Government ministries, churches, the mass media," he wrote, "all exhort young people to stay in school, insisting that now, as never before, one's future is almost wholly dependent upon education. Yet for all this rhetoric about the future, our schools face backward toward a dying system, rather than forward to the emerging new society."

While the majority of schools have failed to change course over the 50 years since those words were written, there are a few that have answered the call, taking a more proactive role in society, and "teaching the future." But what, exactly, does that mean?

Teaching the future means showing students how to anticipate and influence change in the midst of complexity, uncertainty, and ambiguity. It means abandoning the idea that one should teach the "right" answer. There is no longer a "right" answer; it is about finding multiple answers in the midst of rapid change. It is guiding students in the discovery of their dreams of the future, the discovery of potential futures, and the links between the two. It is also about guiding students to think about how to go from the present to the future and from the future back to the present.

Students develop "future scenarios" and analyze which of these scenarios are preferred. They brainstorm the actions they can take to increase the probability that a preferred future scenario is the one that will actually occur. It's a process that involves not only critical thinking, but empathic and creative forms of thinking. This helps students develop the metacognitive skills—both sense-making and strange-making—needed to navigate and flourish in the future. Toffler recognized early on that the necessary kind of teaching would require a new skill set. "By instructing students," he famously wrote, "how to learn, unlearn and relearn, a powerful new dimension can be added to education."

The Role of the Teacher

Teaching future skills is not something that comes naturally to most teachers. Because it was never part of their teacher education experience, they are simply not equipped to do it. However, as we see in the course of our work, once teachers overcome the fear of the unknown, they enjoy it fully and value the possibilities it brings to the classroom. Exploring the future in this way allows them to experiment with the virtue of not knowing. And the effect it has on the kids? Renewed interest and active, imaginative engagement. It stimulates their curiosity, gives them freedom to think differently, to talk openly with their friends and fellow students. Indeed, it empowers them.

> Teaching the future means showing students how to anticipate and influence change in the midst of complexity, uncertainty, and ambiguity. It means abandoning the idea that one should teach the "right" answer.

This creates a feedback loop for the teachers, who then develop deeper relationships with their students. It motivates teachers just as much as it motivates their students! Suddenly, not being able to answer a question is a sign that they are actually doing their work well!

Teach the Future Foundation

Teach the Future is a non-profit organization dedicated to bringing foresight and futures thinking to schools and students around the world. Founded by Peter Bishop in 2013, it followed his retirement from the University of Houston, where for 30 years he led the Master's in Foresight program. Since then, Teach the Future has grown into a community of educators and advocators dedicated to empowering teachers and young people the world over.

To activate our mission we develop and organize all kinds of activities, services, tools, and resources. Everything we do is aimed at empowering young people to become entrepreneurs in the making of their own futures—and to share their future visions with the world.

Future Readiness

Future Shock was an inspiring force behind the Teach the Future movement. Alvin Toffler put a spotlight on the importance of teaching young people to think about the long term, to help them develop wider, deeper, and longer perspectives. He started the conversation about making students "future-proof" so they would be enabled and empowered not only to be proactive with respect to their own lives, but to have a positive impact on the world. ▩

Erica Bol is founder and CEO of Teach the Future Europa. In equipping teachers to teach the future, she also empowers them to be part of making the education system more future-proof. Her work was recognized with the Next Generation Foresight Award Education 2018. To learn more about the Teach the Future Foundation, visit www.teachthefuture.eu. Connect with Erica at www.linkedin.com/in/ericabol.

Revisiting
Future Shock

Andy Hines

t was with a degree of hesitation that I picked up
a copy of *Future Shock* for a book club meeting. ■ I had read it long ago, and
figured it might come off dated. I was pleasantly surprised to find that it has stood the test of time
well and provides us with an outstanding example of foresight.

To refresh those who may also have read it long ago, the basic thesis is that there are limits to the
amount of change that one can absorb. The "roaring current of change" overwhelms our ability to
adapt to it. The result is future shock—"shattering stress and disorientation... a real sickness." Toffler
defines future shock as "the distress, both physical and psychological, that arises from an overload
of the human organism's physical adaptive systems and its decision-making processes," with symptoms including anxiety, hostility, violence, illness, depression, apathy, and withdrawal.

We might argue over whether or not that is actually true—compelling cases can be made for or
against. I would put myself in the camp that our future-shock absorbers are greater than Toffler
anticipated, that we are more adaptive and resilient than he forecasted. But I can see cases for his
argument, and even if one disagrees with his thesis, it raised a critically important issue. As individuals and as a society, it clearly benefits us to think about the impact of the rapid rate of changes
and our ability to cope.

Toffler evolved into the role of futurist from a journalism background. He coined the term "futurist" in a 1965 article and wrote *Future Shock* five years later. It was an immensely influential book
and helped to put foresight as a field of study on the map. For that alone, we futurists ought to be
grateful.

I was struck by his word choices—he doesn't mince them. We see descriptors such as violent,
thrust, burst, splinter, upheaval, explosion, shattering, overwhelming, and my favorite, ham-

merblows! He was alarmed, and he wanted to make sure readers got the point that future shock was serious.

The emphasis of the book is more on diagnosis than prescription. Fair enough, of course, as he was introducing the notion of a problem. But he did not leave us without any hope. In fact, he states the purpose of the book as "helping us to come to terms with the future . . . and increase future consciousness." Raising awareness is part of the prescription. He also suggested a need for "social futurism," which one could say is the descendant of "social foresight" that has been championed by contemporary futurists, notably Richard Slaughter.

One quibble I have, since it deals with a subject I've been quite involved with, is: "values are incessantly changing." I would argue that change in values, even in a world of rapid change, has proved to be relatively stable and gradual. From the vantage point of 1970, however, his point may be well taken, as that is roughly when postmodern values were just making their appearance. He suggested these values were reflected in the mindset of 2 to 3 percent of the population, though he didn't use the postmodern terminology. And today they may be at 25 to 30 percent (some say even higher) of populations in the affluent countries. When taken in context of human history, that is indeed rapid change! It may seem relatively slow to us because other sectors are changing so rapidly.

> I would put myself in the camp that our future-shock absorbers are greater than Toffler anticipated, that we are more adaptive and resilient than he forecasted. But I can see cases for his argument, and even if one disagrees with his thesis, it raised a critically important issue.

In our class on "Social Change" at the Houston foresight program, we talk about ten major theories of social change. Technology is one of the ten, and Toffler makes no bones about technology being the major driver. In his view: "technology is indisputably a major force behind this accelerative thrust." I would note that he says "a" and not "the," so he is leaving room for other theories as well. But technology is the subject at hand here. And he brings in an idea from our Systems Thinking class when he says that the reason technology is so powerful is that it "feeds on itself"—positive feedback or reinforcing loops, in our parlance.

A key factor behind future shock is that we find ourselves in more and more situations that are novel, in which we have no experience to draw upon. He also talks about "transience"—the temporariness in everyday life, and the rapid rate of turnover in relationships. Many of the changes portrayed in a negative light can be seen differently today. For instance, I was struck by a point about the "rental revolution." While this was perceived in a largely negative light at the time, in my work we talk about "sharing" today in a more positive light. We see people being less concerned about "ownership" and more concerned about "access," and there are some good things emerging from that. I often joke about why 25 homes in a neighborhood need 25 lawnmowers—a sharing approach could reduce that number. Similarly, mobility is generally interpreted in a negative light, but one could also see that as a positive. Same with job turnover—it could be that multiple careers make life more interesting.

His concept of adhocracy was quite prescient in anticipating the shift from hierarchical to network models of organization, and the shift to project-based work. He talked about "experience industries" and "vicarious people," which we now refer to as celebrity culture. He talked about cloning, cyborgs, and virtual reality. He talked about the reconfiguration of family, over-choice, and design-it-yourself, which we call co-creation. He also used the term "mental models," which is an important part of our lexicon today.

To be balanced, there were a couple of misses here and there—man communicating with dolphins and submarine communities have not proven to be terribly useful yet, but far more was on target than off.

Despite the many warnings he offers about the impacts of technology, he is not anti-technology. "We cannot and must not turn off the switch of technological progress," he wrote. And he is critical of those he dubs anti-technology, citing Ellul, Fromm, Mumford, and Marcuse.

He raised a point about programmable and non-programmable decisions (routine and non-routine) and felt that there were too many non-programmable decisions—too many decisions that we had to make that were novel. Is this where intelligent agents come in?

It's not about suppressing change, but managing it, although he goes on to suggest that we can still get overwhelmed. He sees education and foresight as key tools:

- "Another approach is to expand man's adaptive capacities—the central task of education during the super-industrial revolution."
- "To create a super industrial education, therefore, we shall first need to generate successive, alternative images of the future."
- "Assumptions about the kinds of jobs, professions, and vocations, that may be needed twenty to fifty years in the future, assumptions about the kind of family forms and human relationships, that will prevail; the kinds of ethical and moral problems that will arise, the kind of technology that will surround us and the organizational structure with which we must mesh."

He advocated creating a "council of the future in every school and community." In sum, he raised the notion of future shock as a cautionary tale, and suggested foresight as a key tool for dealing with it. I agree!

Andy Hines is Assistant Professor & Program Coordinator at the University of Houston's graduate program in Foresight. He speaks, conducts workshops, and consults through his firm, Hinesight. This essay was originally published in the journal *Compass*, Special Edition 2, 2016, a publication of the Association of Professional Futurists.

The Tofflers' Secret to Unlocking Human Potential

Ian Khan

I **seem to see the world in a very different way than many people I meet.** Part of it stems from recognizing that we come from a very *good* place—as a people, as a society, and as a species. We have, in fact, been amazing. *So far*. But as we all know, nothing remains the same for long. Things change, seasons change, life changes. Change is a constant. And *Future Shock*, of course, revealed a future of unprecedented change. But it needn't be a shocking change, because we are also nurtured by the belief that tomorrow will be better. It's why we build, why we dream.

There's no question that we are embarking upon a new era in human history, and it will bring with it massive transformations. To get there—and thrive there—we must walk a deliberate path. Not a path of instant gratification or short-term happiness, but one that will yield sustainable success for the long haul. To do that, we must start thinking differently. We need to start thinking *loud*, thinking *big*. The time to do that is now, because tomorrow is being created even as you read these lines. However, rapid, shocking changes notwithstanding, I am convinced that ours is a future where people will be happier and healthier, living longer and stronger.

In my work I seek to help unlock the latent potential in every person to discover what the future holds for them, to prepare for it, and ultimately to help shape it. This, too, was the Tofflers' objective, expressed in a range of prescriptive ideas and programs. Indeed, *Future Shock*'s most profound contributions concerned a changing of humanity's perspectives on itself.

> In the face of an uncertain future, many people may be tempted to retreat to safety. They will do so at the cost of squandering their massive human potential. The future is not a place from which to retreat, but an evolutionary system to embrace.

The question, though, still hangs in the air: Exactly *how* can we successfully step into a tomorrow that is buffeted on all sides by rapid and continual change? Particularly as many activities—common everyday tasks, and even jobs—will become increasingly automated. Again, perspective matters.

Since the Industrial Age, technology has consistently led to a higher quality of life. And while automation creates a greater dependence on technology, it also yields a greater degree of personal freedom and independence, which will have tremendous implications for how humanity moves forward.

As is evident from the Tofflers' explorations into the psychological dimensions of the overstimulated individual, such as the proliferation of subcults organized to recapture an otherwise lost personal sense of identity in a technology-fueled futurespace, their chief concern was helping humanity understand the forces of change and, equally important, to rethink our capacities and potentials in creating and managing that change.

With the advent of AI, robotics, the distributed ledger (blockchain), and other transformative technologies, the future does indeed seem to present a mixed bag of uncertainty. And it will, most certainly, introduce new challenges—economic, philosophical, ethical, and more. In any event—and this much is also certain—we will pass through a crucible of sorts that will serve to prove our mettle. The process is already well underway.

In my work and research in human potential, I find a recurring motif—seven axioms or principles—for engaging the future with both competence and confidence. And I believe most futurists—including the Tofflers—would agree with them. They are:

1. ■ **Experiences** – As the world becomes more automated, our experience of the world will also change, heightening our awareness, and all else that comes from amplified cognitive abilities.
2. ■ **Learning** – We simply must learn new things faster—and unlearn the things that are holding us back from experiencing a prosperous future.
3. ■ **Collaboration** – To collaborate is to co-create. Breakthroughs will increasingly come through collaborations among people operating in very different, disparate fields—e.g., a combination of biology, electronics, and materials—that will yield surprising and exponential innovations. So venturing beyond one's field of expertise will prove essential in cross-pollinating big ideas to synthesize new solutions.
4. ■ **People** – The distinctly human characteristics of curiosity, empathy, humor, intention, and imagination will keep people at the center of all our future considerations—the proliferation of AI and automation notwithstanding.
5. ■ **Partnerships** – To partner is to prosper. This will become a required survival skill, necessary for companies to navigate—and survive—a future charged with rapid change and potential disruption.
6. ■ **Accountability** – When technology makes everything transparent, honesty and accountability

come to the fore. The future promises to elevate and reward these distinctly human attributes.

7 ▪ **Actualization** – In his seminal 1943 paper, Abraham Maslow postulated a hierarchy of needs in which self-actualization sits at the top of the pyramid—well above safety. This is the cardinal direction toward which we must be continuously oriented and determined.

In the face of an uncertain future, many people may be tempted to retreat to safety. They will do so at the cost of squandering their massive human potential. The future is not a place from which to retreat, but an evolutionary system to *embrace*. Only then can we succeed in creating real value for generations to come. ▪

Ian Khan is a CNN-featured Technology Futurist, three-time TEDx Speaker, director of the highly acclaimed documentary *Blockchain City*, bestselling author of *7 Axioms of Value Creation*, and contributor to many industry publications, including McGraw Hill and Forbes. As chief futurist at the Futuracy Institute of Thought Leadership, Ian is one of the most widely quoted experts on blockchain. He is on a mission to unlock human potential by helping people understand, via his keynotes, master classes, and online programs, how technology can help us become more efficient, happier, and more human. For more information, please visit www.iankhan.com.

Master Classes in Futures Studies

John M. Smart

Richard A. Slaughter

Sohail Inayatullah

Exponential Progress: Thriving in an Era of Accelerating Change

John M. Smart

Introduction ▪ What is *foresight*? What are the most fundamental ways we use to look ahead? What is *accelerating change*? Where and why does it occur? What is *adaptiveness*? How do complex systems maintain their adaptiveness? What *values* does adaptiveness appear to entail? What is *intelligence*? Are our machines now becoming intelligent? Finally, how can we *get better* at looking ahead, so we may not only survive, but *thrive* in this new era of rapidly accelerating societal change?

These are humbling questions. To find better answers than we have today, we must use *hindsight* (past historical knowledge), *insight* (awareness of present reality), and *foresight* (our ability to anticipate, create, and improve the future). The last of these three fundamental time orientations, *foresight*, depends deeply on the first two, making it the hardest of the three. But foresight also offers us a unique reward—a better vision of what will and may come, and what good we may do with our futures. With that reward in mind, let us consider these big questions, and see what insights we might gain.

Alvin Toffler was perhaps the greatest futurist of the 20th century. He was surely the most popular futurist of the latter half of that century, the era when our modern field of *strategic foresight* emerged. More than anyone else, he brought future thinking to the masses. From the early 1960s to the late 2000s, with his wife Heidi as editor and researcher, Toffler wrote a series of prescient and increasingly widely read books and articles of social commentary and prediction. Exploring the impact of his first bestseller, *Future Shock* (1970), six million copies and 50 years later, is the subject of this volume.

Future Shock had its flaws. No piece of futurology is without them, including this one. It was a product of its time, the angst-ridden late 1960s. In this essay I will explore two of its achievements, and their relation to my own work. First, this very influential book got many of us thinking about the upsides and downsides of *accelerating change*, both in human history and in our modern era. *Future Shock's* first two chapters, "The 800th Lifetime" and "The Accelerative Thrust," are timeless introductions to this topic. Written a decade prior to the arrival of the personal computer, they inspire awe even today.

The book's second-greatest contribution, in my view, occurred in just a single paragraph. Deep within the book, Toffler describes future thinking as being essentially about three things. Here is the key quotation, from p. 407 of the first edition:

> *Every society faces not merely a succession of probable futures, but an array of possible futures, and a conflict over preferable futures. ... Determining the probable calls for a science of futurism. Delineating the possible calls for an art of futurism. Defining the preferable calls for a politics of futurism. The worldwide futurist movement today does not yet differentiate clearly among these functions.*

Within a decade, Toffler's observation would be called the *Three Ps* model of foresight. I do not know if it originated with him. He read widely, and likely gleaned it from an earlier source. But after Toffler's insight, other futurists, most notably Roy Amara at the Institute for the Future, in two key articles in 1974 and 1981, would expand the Three Ps into a set of guidelines for strategic foresight practice.

Strategic Foresight—the Universality of the Three Ps

As Toffler and Amara observed, we can define Strategic Foresight as being, most essentially, about just three things: discovering and predicting the probable, taking advantage of and guarding against the possible, and steering and leading toward the preferable, as we understand them. When I first learned this model, as a new student of foresight in the 2000s, I realized it was congruent with two leading philosophies of science, the first of physics and the second of life.

First, consider physics: Modern physics describes two fundamentally opposing sets of dynamics in our universe. One set, including mechanics, relativity, and equilibrium thermodynamics, is intrinsically predictable over time. This set rules the convergent, statistically "inevitable" futures of our universe—the *probable*. The other set, seen in such processes as quantum physics, chaotic systems, and non-equilibrium thermodynamics, grows rapidly unpredictable in its specifics. This set rules the divergent and "contingent" features of our universe—the *possible*. These two types of physics, after billions of years in partnership with and opposition to each other, eventually created life and intelligence, which alone generates *preferences*. Our preferences, in turn, are relentlessly selected in surviving organisms for *adaptation* to the environment.

> " Humans are the most complex evo-devo learning systems on Earth. But our developmental genes are also a massive patchwork of legacy code, built on a code base shared with far simpler organisms. We can keep adding to it, but we can't update the code.

Science has no unified theory of quantum gravity today. We don't yet know how to combine these two fundamentally different yet equally useful ways to view the physical world. Yet both are clearly

Figure 1

true, and somehow, over time, they created this very special, emergent, third thing—life and intelligence. *Us.* So you see, the Three Ps are a very basic way to understand the world. They are firm conceptual ground on which to stand.

Just as curiously, we can see the Three Ps through the lens of biology. The emerging academic discipline of *evolutionary developmental (evo-devo) biology* allows us to see life as a fundamental tension between contingent *evolutionary* and predictable *developmental* processes. Both processes occur at the same time in biological systems, and we often need to change our perspective in order to see both.

Consider an oak tree (Figure 1). We can look at an acorn seed, with its unique shape, and if we've seen any acorn's prior life cycle, or suspect it is a replicator of a certain class (tree), we can *predict* many of the features of the tree that will emerge. Much of its "oakness" is *developmental*. Yet where the leaves and branches will go within any tree is entirely unpredictable. Those features of its "oakness" are *evolutionary*, involving chaos, contingency, competition, and selection, at molecular and cellular scales. Trees are *evo-devo* systems.

Likewise, two genetically identical human twins share *developmental* features that make them indistinguishable from across the room. They also share many psychological features, even if separated at birth and raised apart in different environments. Look at all twins up close, however, and most aspects of them look *evolutionary*. Their cellular architecture, organ structure, and fingerprints are all stochastically, unpredictably, and contingently different. Their brain wiring emerged in a series of chemical and cellular competitions, in a selective, Darwinian process. We are *evo-devo* systems.

Within the life of any organism, and in species and ecosystems over macrobiological time, we can define the *probable* as convergent and predictable *developmental* processes, the *possible* as divergent and experimental *evolutionary* processes, and the *preferable* as potentially adaptive *evo-devo processes.* The latter, as in physics, is a mix of the first two, more fundamental types. All three processes, then, appear to be central to life.

We can depict this evo-devo view of foresight in a graphic shown on Figure 2. The two processes at the bottom of this pyramid are the most fundamental: what can happen and what will happen, in a statistical sense. The third process, preferences, generated by intelligent minds of any type, emerges via evolutionary and developmental dynamics. Selection determines whether those preferences are adaptive.

What about our universe itself? Did it start as a special seed, one

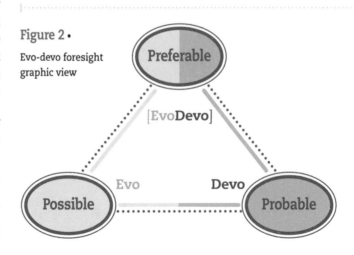

Figure 2 •

Evo-devo foresight graphic view

with both evolutionary and developmental characteristics, like all living systems? Did it self-organize its great internal complexity in many past replications, the way all life has done? Is it more like a living system than we presently realize? This view seems reasonable to me.

Consider that if all the most adaptive and intelligent complex systems inside our universe are replicative, evo-devo systems, why wouldn't our universe, which has built us, be such a system as well? More fundamentally, are evo-devo approaches the *only* reasonable way to build adaptive and intelligent complex systems? Do they beat out all other approaches in producing and maintaining complexity?

If we live in an evo-devo universe, many curious and seemingly improbable aspects of universal dynamics, such as accelerating change, and our history of increasingly local and hierarchical emergence of complexity, may be best understood as developmental, written into our universe's "genes" (initial conditions) and environment (multiverse). Simultaneously, many other aspects of universal dynamics, and features of the life and civilizations that emerge within it, across the cosmos, will remain unpredictable, or evolutionary, just as we see in all life.

> The smarter our technology gets, the less help it needs to replicate. Our most rapidly improving digital systems, exemplified by neuro-inspired hardware and deep learning software today, are on a path to becoming autonomous evo-devo learning systems.

Each of the Three Ps seems fundamental to the nature of the future. Notice that we must shift our perspective to see each process, operating at the same time.

The Evo-Devo Hypothesis—A Systems View of the Three Ps

Systems theorists study complex systems of many types, looking for commonalities and differences. I trained in that subject under James Grier Miller (*Living Systems*, 1977) one of the founders of the field. Using the lens of systems theory, we can now make an *evo-devo hypothesis* about the Three Ps:

All the most adaptive complex systems in our universe are *replicative, evo-devo systems*. They have used their history of evolutionary variation, developmental replication, and selection to build their internal intelligence, models, and preferences. In that intelligence-building, they use creative evolutionary processes to conduct experiments (explore the *possible*), and conservative developmental processes to conserve useful knowledge, including their life cycle (maintain the *probable*). Evo-devo processes, a mix of the two, are how all complex systems generate their intelligence and *preferences*, which are subject to selection (adaptation) in the environment.

In this hypothesis, even slowly replicating cosmic structures, like suns, encode a very primitive kind of adaptive intelligence. Replicating prebiotic chemicals encode a slightly more complex intelligence. Life has made another great leap in adaptiveness and intelligence by replicating under selection for billions of years. All life has evolutionary genes that regulate stochastic, unpredictable phenotypic variation, and developmental genes that regulate our predictable features, including life cycle. Both evolutionary and developmental genetics, and selection, encode life's intelligence.

There are actually two different sets of genes in every living thing. Our evolutionary genes work "bottom-up" and "inside-out" in contingent, competitive, and unpredictable ways. They regulate differences, at all scales, between every animal of a species. They have varied a lot over the history of every species. Our developmental genes work "top-down" and "outside-in" in convergent, conservative, and predictable ways. They regulate similarities we see in all animals of any species. These genes are both highly conserved over time, and brittle. Change a few bases in them, and the organism may not even develop.

Humans are the most complex evo-devo learning systems on Earth. But our developmental genes are also a massive patchwork of legacy code, built on a code base shared with far simpler organisms. We can keep adding to it, but we can't update the code. Like a tree that grows outward from a central trunk, the new morphology we can develop using that code must become increasingly limited, and progressively less innovative and adaptive. Every complex system has its limits.

> A new computational architecture or algorithm, will commonly give us a 10X to 1000X improvement in speed, efficiency, yield, or performance. Incremental process innovations at the human scale, by contrast, typically give us 20 percent, 50 percent, or 300 percent (3X) improvements.

Humanity long ago got around our biological limits by moving our intelligence to a new, hierarchically emergent, replicative system. Along with a handful of other species, we developed culture, which engages in its own constant evo-devo replication of ideas (colloquially, "memes"), in our collective minds and environment, via language, behaviors, and technology.

In fact, we can best define "humanity," on any planet, as the first species that learns to use extragenetic codes and technology (language, rocks, fire, levers, cities, etc.) to become something more than its biological self. The first use of hand-held and hand-thrown rocks, collectively, to defend ourselves against faster and more powerful predators (leopards, mainly) may have been the original human action. After that, cultural acceleration was off to the races. But human culture, as impressive as it is, depends on humans to improve itself.

We now can see that our digital technology, viewed as a complex adaptive system, is becoming different. The smarter our technology gets, the less help it needs to replicate. Our most rapidly improving digital systems, exemplified by neuro-inspired hardware and deep learning software today, are on a path to becoming autonomous evo-devo learning systems. Their speed of variation, replication, and learning can run at the speed of electricity (the speed of light), a rate far faster than both biological and cultural evolution.

Our leading AIs increasingly borrow algorithms from our brains and now even our immune systems. They seem on track to deliver another major step change for intelligence. What's more, many astrobiologists think Earthlike planets are ubiquitous in our universe. In a massively parallel, branching, and multi-local fashion, much like speciation on Earth, our universe may produce an accelerating migration of leading intelligence from physical to chemical to biological to social to technological evo-devo replicators on all hospitable planets, as a central feature of its evolutionary development.

Accelerating Change—Then and Now

The idea of acceleration as a natural process is very old. (See my online essay, "A Brief History of Intellectual Discussion of Accelerating Change," 1999, for more.) In 1766, the late-Enlightenment technology historian Anne-R-J Turgot described the "inevitable" advance of technology, a kind of progress he observed even during Europe's Dark Ages of social and economic regression. The Scottish economist Adam Smith saw the relentless "quickening" of technological change. Several 18th- and 19th-century scholars, like William Godwin, August Comte, Herbert Spencer and Nicolai Fyodorov, discussed it as well.

In 1904 ("A Law of Acceleration") and 1909 ("A Rule of Phase Applied to History") American technology scholar Henry Adams offered our first modern view. He claimed accelerating change is a poorly understood *law of nature*, as inevitable as the force of gravity, whose equations he applied to humanity's continual acceleration of innovation and thought. Curiously, some modern quantum gravity research, linking gravity to optimal computation, also takes Adams's view. (See Caputa and Magan, "Quantum Computation as Gravity," *Phys. Rev. Lett.* 122, 2019.)

Like Toffler, Adams discussed the disorientation, stress, and conflict (with the church, state, and elders) caused by societal acceleration. He was also our first modeler of the *technological singularity*, the hypothesis that accelerating innovations, science, and technology (for him, electricity and machines) must produce a qualitative leap in thinking complexity that exceeds our biological minds.

As the futurist Ray Kurzweil described in his bestseller, *The Age of Spiritual Machines* (1999), throughout the entire 20th century humanity experienced rapid exponential growth in computing capacity, beginning with tabulating machines in 1890. In 1965, Intel co-founder Gordon Moore (and his popularizer, Carver Mead) gave us "Moore's Law"—the observed exponential growth in transistors per silicon chip, doubling every 18 months. In 1966, Irving John Good published "Speculations Concerning the First Ultraintelligent Machine," the first academic paper on the technological singularity. Good proposed that a self-improving computer was the "last invention that man need ever make," an invention that finally seemed probable, given accelerating trends in computer technology.

This history reminds us that *Future Shock's* discussion of acceleration was not entirely original to Toffler. It was an elaboration of previous work, much of which was known to him. But Toffler eloquently described many societal impacts of acceleration at a time when America had just suffered a particularly wrenching and disorienting decade of social change—the 1960s. Our social anxiety grew further in the 1970s, as economic shocks, pollution, terrorism, urban crime and decline, Watergate, and Vietnam impacted our psyches. The public was mesmerized, and *Future Shock* became an apt description of the era.

> One way to document dematerialization in our digital technology is to notice how it increasingly substitutes for physical processes. Think of all the matter and processes that have been dematerialized by the software and hardware in a smartphone. We no longer need as many physical objects (cameras, video recorders, flashlights, alarm clocks, etc.).

Our next great acceleration popularizer was physicist Carl Sagan. In the first chapter of *The Dragons of Eden* (1977) and his award-winning TV series *Cosmos* (1980), Sagan presented the metaphor of the *Cosmic Calendar*. Placing "significant universal events" in universal history onto a 12-month calendar, Sagan gave us the first widely seen visualization of accelerating change on a *cosmic scale* (Figure 3).

Seeing this calendar as a youth was life-changing for me. Asking why this improbable universal acceleration has occurred, given all the other plausible histories, has become a lifelong interest. I know others who were also strongly affected by this visualization. Like *Earthrise*, the first view of our precious planet from space in 1968, the *Cosmic Calendar* offers a major shift in worldview, a critical new way to see ourselves in relation to the universe.

Is this apparent acceleration some *bias* of our psychology, perhaps of how we are evolved to re-member, or to assess significance? Or is it a *real* universal dynamic, as Adams proposed? Sagan strongly suspected it was real. He called it a "phenomenon" that science must confront, model, and understand.

In 2003, I co-founded a small nonprofit, the Acceleration Studies Foundation, to advocate for this neglected field of study. We are particularly interested in work that addresses Sagan's universal, Cosmic Calendar perspective. Since Toffler re-popularized this topic in 1970, a few hundred insight-ful papers and books (including recent work in quantum gravity) have been published on universal mechanisms and drivers of accelerating change. A much larger number of papers reference societal accelerations, but there are very few general hypotheses and causal models for why universal and societal complexity acceleration occurs. There are fewer still that see its increasingly local and vir-tual nature.

Figure 3 • CC-licensed version of Carl Sagan's *Cosmic Calendar,* by Wikipedia artist Eric Fisk.

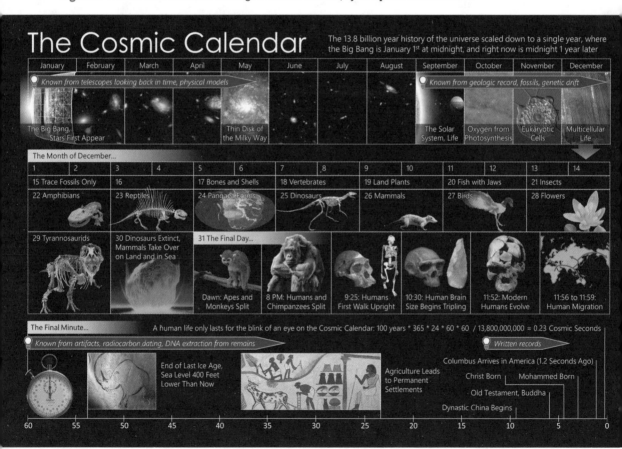

I was lucky to have two private interviews with Toffler in Los Angeles in 2008. He thought it ironic that our science and public policy remain so ignorant of these processes. We noted how sad it was that many in our foresight profession ignore or deny accelerating change, even today. But he was also hopeful that we would wake up eventually.

Since Toffler and Sagan first popularized this phenomenon, a few bold scientists, like Harvard physicist Eric Chaisson in *Cosmic Evolution* (2001), have supported Adams's claim. Figure 4, adapted from Chaisson's 2001 book, charts a progressive acceleration in the *energy flow density* (energy flow per time and per mass) in a *special subset* of emergent complex systems over universal history. Energy flow is used in all complex systems to regulate their rates of change. Notice that the distributions of the various complex systems named at right, a temporal progression from galaxies to computers, have become progressively more *local* in space and time. This is a key insight we will return to in our next section.

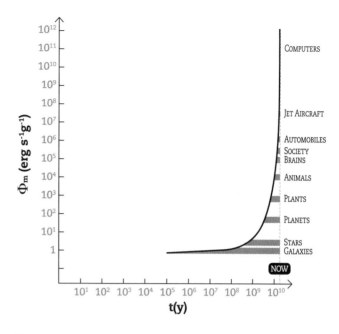

Figure 4 • Progressive acceleration chart, based on Eric Chaisson's *Cosmic Evolution*.

Today's energetically densest, fastest-changing, and fastest-learning systems are our increasingly brain-like deep learning hardware and software. They are not yet capable of self-evolving, but they may gain that ability sooner than most of us expect. As the graph shows, they are capable, *in principle*, of changing, learning, and evolving at least 1,000,000X faster than human society.

So far, the scientific community has largely ignored such work. Common critiques are that accelerating change is surely just some quirk of our psychology, that things went faster in the past, or that acceleration must soon become "unsustainable." Critics usually ignore STEM efficiency trends (to be discussed next), and often conflate the reality of societal accelerating change with the reality that humanity's population growth, material consumption, and ecosystem degradation trends are unsustainable. Or they assume acceleration cannot continue since it grows exponentially more difficult for any one of us to understand human-machine civilization (our psychological "complexity wall"). Something curious and cosmic appears to be happening, but we are not yet ready to admit it, as a species. Let me now try to better support that admittedly speculative claim.

Our Great Race to Inner Space—Accelerating Change as "D&D"

Since 2006, I have been using the phrase "Race to Inner Space" to describe the general nature of accelerating change. I find this phrase helps to quickly explain *where* our fastest-changing, fastest-learning, and most-adaptive complex systems always go as they evolve and develop. As far as I can tell, our world's leading complex systems are always moving their bodies, brains, and actions to *inner space*, to the domain of the very dense and small (*physical* inner space) and the very computational and intelligent (*virtual* inner space). These two processes appear to be fundamental kinds of accelerating change.

> When we think carefully about it, we must admit that thinking and consciousness, whether in humans or machines, are virtual worlds. They are as real in the universe as the physical world. That's why we should stop using the phrase " 'real' world" as an opposite to "virtual world." Information is as real as physics in the universe we live in.

To better understand these two kinds of acceleration, we can use two scholarly words: *densification* (our movement into physical inner space) and *dematerialization* (our growth of virtual inner space). They form a useful acronym, "D&D." The first term, densification, is the "engine" of accelerating change, its *physical* driver. The second, dematerialization, is the "steering" of accelerating change, its *informational* driver. We can also call D&D by another scholarly phrase, *STEM compression*, as these two accelerations outline how our universe turns increasingly local, dense, and miniaturized arrangements of physical *space, time, energy, and matter* (STEM) into various forms of *mind*. I suspect, but cannot prove, that maximizing the growth of D&D, via five adaptive goals we will discuss, is how leading complex systems stay dominant in their niches.

To better understand densification, consider how our universe's leading frontier of structural and functional complexity creation began with universally distributed early matter, then localized to large-scale structure, then to our first galaxies, then to metal-rich stars replicating in special galaxies, then to stellar habitable zones circling special stars. On Earth, the first gene-based life may have started locally, around volcanic vents (archaea), but eventually ranged miles deep in our crust, and miles in the air (prokaryotes). Genetic replication eventually created eukaryotic life, whose range is restricted to just a sliver of our planet's surface. This led to multicellular life, whose range is even more localized, and to nervous systems, which are far more local, dense, and dematerialized forms of cellular computation than we find in unicellular collectives.

In human brains, synaptic networks eventually supported replicating *words*, *codes*, and *ideas* ("memes"). Memes are more densified and dematerialized than genes. They replicate and vary by communication and conversation among receptive brains, and rearrangement of *synaptic weights*. Even bacterial replication is slow by comparison. Memes are so virtual that scholars still argue, sadly, if they even exist.

We also see net densification in human social structures. We began in one place in Africa as rock-wielding *Homo habilis*, expanded out to become nomadic hunter gatherers, then densified, into tribes, then villages, then cities, and societies run by markets, networks, governments, and, in recent decades, also by highly process-dense corporations. After initial, brief, next-adjacent explorations outward, at every new level of emergence, this has been a great race inward.

Humanity is today engaged in one of these brief initial forays outward. We've recently gained the ability to get off our planet, and we think we are going to the stars. I think that view is 180 degrees wrong. Yes, we will explore our local planets, even though our robots already do it better than us, and it will be inspirational, like Edmund Hillary climbing Mt. Everest. But the real next frontier for humanity, and for our coming machine intelligence, is inner space.

Densification tells us why process innovations at the nanoscale and in infotech often give either speed, efficiency, or productivity gains (or sometimes, all three) of 10X to 100,000X (1000 to 10,000,000 percent), in single-step innovations, versus far more modest innovation gains at human scale. A single change in an active site of an enzyme, or a new computational architecture or algorithm, will commonly give us a 10X to 1000X improvement in speed, efficiency, yield, or performance. Incremental process innovations at the human scale, by contrast, typically give us 20 percent, 50 percent, or 300 percent (3X) improvements. These are all far from a single order of magnitude (10X) in change. In contrast to the nanoscale, the human scale is *outer space*. It is an environment where all complex systems are *far slower* to adapt, improve, and learn. That's just how our universe works.

In 1959, the physicist Richard Feynman gave a futuristic talk on a then-nonexistent science. The title was "There's Plenty of Room at the Bottom." Feynman asked his audience to recognize that a *world of complexity* could be built and accessed, at the molecular and atomic scale, using *nanotechnology*. In 1985, the nanotech field finally emerged with discovery of C60, Buckminsterfullerene, a spherical molecule named after the futurist Bucky Fuller, for its resemblance to his geodesic domes. Figure 5, *Earth in a Bucky Ball* (2003) by nanoscientist Chris Ewels, conveys Feynman's idea. Humanity is running a great race to inner space, not outer space, because that is where life's greatest capacities, diversity, and consciousness apparently lie.

Today, engineering advances at the nanoscale, in physics, chemistry, biology, materials science, and computation, are at the cutting edge of *all* our technological advances. In physics, we are designing early quantum computers, which perform some algorithms *100 million times* faster than classical computers. We get *billions of times* more fusion energy out of our experiments today than when we started in 1973, and we may see our first commercial fusion within a generation. In chemistry, we improve battery performance, make fresh water from our oceans, and even do artificial photosynthesis at ever faster rates each year. In biology, we recently gained the ability to edit genes using molecular scissors (CRISPR-Cas9 and other techniques) and insert gene drives ("molecular machines") into animals. Yet nanotechnology remains in its infancy. We still fund it only modestly, just $18 billion by all governments and firms annually in 2012, per Lux Research, and we mostly don't know what we are doing yet.

Figure 5 • *Earth in a Bucky Ball*, by nanoscientist Chris Ewels.

As deep machine learning gets involved, however, watch out. Just last year, a team at Google Deep-Mind used deep learning to find a number of solutions in protein folding. This is a fiendishly difficult problem in biochemistry, and their neuro-inspired AI handily beat out all the other human-built, and much older, AI approaches. Many more of these kinds of advances will happen as our computer systems and networks get more complex and neuro-inspired in coming decades.

Dematerialization, for its part, tells us why organisms with nervous systems, and then brains, came to rule our planet, and why modern software is "eating the world" the smarter it gets, as Marc Andreessen observed in 2011. Dematerialization is captured in the popular phrase "mind over matter," or better yet, *mind is always emerging from and increasingly controlling local matter, at an ever accelerating rate*. We can apply this phrase to both human brains and our emerging digital brains.

One way to document dematerialization in our digital technology is to notice how it increasingly *substitutes* for physical processes. Think of all the matter and processes that have been dematerialized by the software and hardware in a smartphone. We no longer need as many physical objects (cameras, video recorders, flashlights, alarm clocks, etc.). The more intelligent our digital systems get, the more *general purpose* they become. A related concept, *economic dematerialization,* can be measured as the increasingly informational nature of societal GDP. All the world's leading markets are turning into "knowledge economies" (or better yet, intelligence economies), selling increasingly high-value digital services (bits, media, info, software, compute) over atoms.

Another way to measure dematerialization is to notice that the better our simulations become, the more we virtualize human behavior itself. Increasingly, our *thinking beats out acting*, and the *virtual beats out the physical*, both to discover and to create better futures. As adults, we found that *simulation* (experimentation) increasingly outcompeted the physical play (experimentation) that we did as children. Adults, with enough experience, find it more adaptive to "play in our minds" instead. Our machines, too, are rapidly growing up. Soon their simulated worlds will be richer and more valuable than their physical play. These are major societal changes we're still only beginning to recognize.

When we think carefully about it, we must admit that thinking and consciousness, whether in humans or machines, are virtual worlds. They are as real in the universe as the physical world. That's why we should stop using the phrase "'real' world" as an opposite to "virtual world." Information is as real as physics in the universe we live in. All life's virtual processes emerge out of physical reality. So do the realities our computers are creating for us. So rather than "real" and virtual, physical and virtual—or nanotech and infotech(D&D)—are the right pair to think about as we run this Great Race.

> If D&D are fundamental universal trends, as I think they are, we should look inward, not outward, to our next frontier. Our destiny is density and dematerialization.

One of the most surprising things about accelerating D&D processes, from an environmental perspective, is that they use progressively *less* space, time, energy, and matter (STEM) resources, per computation and physical transformation, the more miniaturized and virtual they become. Because of this accelerating STEM efficiency, our fastest-improving systems never run into Malthusian resource limits and S-curves the way all biological reproduction does. Each new generation of computer typically has both a *smaller ecological footprint*, and *greater innovation capacity*, per computation, than its predecessor.

Today's computers are still far more energy wasting than our long-evolved human brains. But unlike us, they are on an astoundingly fast resource-efficiency improvement curve. In the lab, we have designed neuro-inspired hardware that is *thousands* of times more space, time, energy, and matter efficient than our current computers, and we are still in the infancy of such work. Because of D&D, our accelerating machine intelligences always shrink their use of physical resources per computation, and grow their learning and simulation capacity. That combination is uniquely powerful, and we still don't broadly appreciate its implications for our future.

Where might the cosmic acceleration of D&D end? In a philosophical paper, "The Transcension Hypothesis" (2012), I speculate that via STEM compression, all intelligent life increasingly *transcends*, or grows out of, our physical universe. Our descendants may use nanotechnology, and architectures like quantum computing, to make even denser, more capable, and more intelligent systems than biology has to date. After that, we may migrate to *femtoscale* life, intelligence, and complexity. Eventually, we may end up in black hole-like environments, which some physicists propose are ideal for both computation and contact with other advanced civilizations. See Cadell Last's "Big Historical Foundations for Deep Future Speculations" (2017) for a good review. At least, this future looks plausible to me. We shall see, as they say.

> Each human connectome is the most advanced computational nanotech (physical inner space) and infotech (virtual inner space) that presently exists on Earth. Perhaps we'd treat each other better if we reflected daily on that fact.

To sum up this introduction to D&D, most of us presently imagine that it is our destiny to explore *outer space*. We seem driven to expand into the cosmos as our civilization develops. I call this view the *Expansion hypothesis*. I think that view of the future is like looking in the rear view mirror while driving forward. Life has made brief jumps outward, but the macrotrend is always inward. Arguably, machine evolution in nanospace is now more productive than most things humans are doing in human space.

What philosopher Cadell Last calls the *Compression hypothesis* is a much better description of both our past and future. Leading complex systems have continually discovered ever denser, more efficient, and more intelligent ways to use space, time, energy, and matter (STEM) resources to adapt. I call that process *STEM compression*, and it seems critically important to understanding accelerating change. If D&D are fundamental universal trends, as I think they are, we should look inward, not outward, to our next frontier. Our destiny is density and dematerialization.

When we are D&D-aware we are what I like to call "accelaware." We understand a few things about the plausible dynamics of accelerating change, and how they may impact society in the years ahead. We recognize why well-managed cities, corporations, markets, digital networks, automation, and AI will increasingly win over less-dense and dematerialized alternatives. We are eager to foresee and manage the many new risks and disruptions that these processes create.

For a good introduction to accelerating change and its dizzying variety of societal implications, I'd recommend books by Ray Kurzweil (*The Age of Spiritual Machines*, 1999; *The Singularity is Near*, 2005), Kevin Kelly (*What Technology Wants*, 2010), Peter Diamandis and Steven Kotler (*Abundance*, 2012; *Bold*, 2015), Erik Brynjolfsson and Andrew McAfee (*The Second Machine Age*, 2014; *Machine, Platform, Crowd*, 2018), Klaus Schwab (*The Fourth Industrial Revolution*, 2016), Kate Raworth (*Donut Economics*, 2017), Rachel Botsman (*Who Can You Trust?*, 2017), Max Tegmark (*Life 3.0*, 2017), Tim O'Reilly (*What's the Future?*, 2017), and Byron Reese (*The Fourth Age*, 2017). Some good academic anthologies also exist, such as Amnon Eden's *The Singularity Hypothesis* (2013).

The Primacy of Consciousness and Natural Intelligence

Which complex adaptive systems on Earth have gone the furthest into inner space so far? That would be human thinking and consciousness. Each human connectome (Figure 6) is the most advanced computational nanotech (physical inner space) and infotech (virtual inner space) that presently exists on Earth. Perhaps we'd treat each other better if we reflected daily on that fact. Consider that there are *80 trillion informationally unique* synaptic connections inside every 3-pound human brain. That is an incredible feat of nanotech, and an astonishing virtual uniqueness, inside every one of us. All our moral, empathic, and self-, social-, and universe-reflective thinking and feeling are virtual realities (infotech) which have arisen directly from that nanotech. It's phenomenal.

Evolutionarily, consciousness is life's newest inner space frontier. Science still doesn't understand it well at the physical level. Yet we can observe that it emerged as a new kind of adaptive complexity for human brains, exploiting new forms of physical and virtual inner space, and it has allowed human society to become both more empathic with other life-forms and more ethical as well. But these advances have occurred only on average in the *network*, which means a few *individuals* have grown increasingly dangerous at the same time. The primacy of consciousness is why social values like ethics and empathy are at the center of human adaptiveness, as we will discuss.

Tomorrow's machines will run further and faster into nano- and infospace. The online knowledge web, less than 30 years after its invention, is already a vast, low-level simulation of physical reality, even before high-level VR, AR, and simulations have arrived. We've also seen accelerating virtualization (emulation capacity) of hardware, operating systems, infrastructure, and business processes

Figure 6 • Visual description of the human connectome.

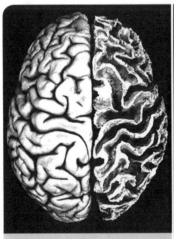
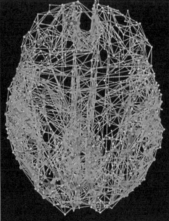
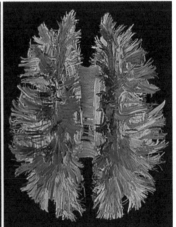

Anatomy ▪ Klingler's method for fiber tract dissection uses freezing of brain matter to spread nerve fibers apart. Afterwards, tissue is carefully scratched away to reveal a relief-like surface in which the desired nerve tracts are naturally surrounded by their anatomical brain areas.

Connectome ▪ Shown are the connections of brain regions together with "hubs" that connect signals among different brain areas and central "core" or backbone of connections, which relays commands for our thoughts and behaviors.

Neuronal Pathways ▪ A new MRI technique called diffusion spectrum imaging (DSI) analyzes how water molecules move along nerve fibers. DSI can show a brain's major neuron pathways and will help neurologists relate structure to function.

since the 1960s. Ever more of life's processes migrate to the cloud every year.

Our most advanced simulations today are partly *"artificial" intelligences*, engineered top-down using human models, and partly *natural intelligences*, emerging bottom-up, with us as trainers and gardeners of their self-learning components. We do not construct, and cannot identify, most of the algorithms in our deep learners today. They emerge on their own, with us observing them do so.

If neuro-inspired computers increasingly outperform all other forms of AI, as I've long predicted (it's generally far easier for nature to *copy and vary* than to reinvent outright), the main role of our future AI safety "engineers" (read: gardeners) will be to *select them for safety and symbiosis with us*. Such artificial selection is how we tamed our domestic animals over the last few thousand years, and it is even how we have tamed ourselves. Domestic animal brains have typically shrunk 20 to 30 percent over the last 15,000 years. Human brains have shrunk 10 percent over the same time period (see "The Incredible Shrinking Brain," *Discover Magazine*, 2010). In both cases, we removed more impulsive and asocial behaviors and programming, via selective reproduction (and in our own case, ostracism and killing of "bad actors"), making a more interdependent and adaptive social intelligence.

> We've also seen accelerating virtualization (emulation capacity) of hardware, operating systems, infrastructure, and business processes since the 1960s. Ever more of life's processes migrate to the cloud every year.

It seems that evo-devo methods and selection always win, as the best and fastest way to create trusted complexity. In my view, humanity will be forced to select these natural machine intelligences to be safe by constantly stress testing them, by knowing their past behavior, and by making sure we always have many more trusted and loyal breeds of deep learners (I like to call them "Labrador AIs" and "Doberman AIs") around to defend us against the inevitable "rogues" that will emerge in someone's basement. There is no other viable path to safety for natural intelligence, in my view.

Some futurists, like Klaus Schwab of the World Economic Forum (Schwab, *The Fourth Industrial Revolution*, 2016), propose that we are now in an "Intelligence Revolution," with the advent of deep learning computers, the cloud, and other powerful new computing technologies. The WEF is one of several global organizations now working on AI ethics. As I write this, Microsoft has just pledged $1 billion to OpenAI, a community seeking to create safe artificial general intelligence. Such work is commendable. We can see that machine intelligence is developing into something new, and we must prepare for it.

But *how fast* is machine intelligence developing? Are we truly in a new era of accelerating change, or merely the next stage of our now 70-year-old Information Revolution? This question isn't a quibble. In effect, it asks whether humanity still has *decades* to do our AI safety and ethics training and gardening well, or whether we might now see AI start improving itself fundamentally roughly every year, a pace that would give us far less time to adapt.

Consider our past technology revolutions. Each created powerful new *densification* (including vast *temporal* densification, or acceleration) of human interaction and value creation, and new *dematerialization* in its forms of social organization and simulation (collective intelligence):

1 ■ **Our Tool-Making Revolution** occurred over *hundreds of thousands* of years. Tools like hand axes, the control of fire, clothing, and spears got us congregating in large, dense hunting and gathering

bands, and got us to every habitable zone on the planet.

2 ▪ *Our Agricultural Revolution* occurred over *thousands* of years, greatly densified food production, and created our first empires, law, and our first astronomical rich-poor divides.

3 ▪ *Our Industrial Revolution* occurred over *hundreds* of years, greatly densified the production of things, and created the modern corporation, the new, faster, and less extreme rich-poor divides of the capital class, and social democratic states.

4 ▪ *Our Information Revolution* has been occurring over *decades*. It has greatly densified computing and communications, and created globalization, a knowledge and entertainment society, the even faster-emerging rich-poor divides of our tech titans and ultra-rich, and a number of new societal problems, including eroding social contracts and an increasing number of citizens arguing for a more equitable distribution of technological wealth, and a revitalization of our democracy.

I would argue we remain far from any fifth (by my count) revolution today. Today's deep learners are based on a few key computer science discoveries made decades ago, discoveries we will now slowly apply to societal processes. There are many things deep learners can't do well or at all today, like compositional logic, emotions, ethics, and complex model building. I'd bet many more new architectures, algorithms, and approaches will need to be discovered, both via new neuroscience, and new hardware and software experiments, before our AIs will be self-improving enough to become *generally* (and naturally) intelligent.

As the Gartner consultancy's Emerging Technologies Hype Cycle 2018 makes clear, deep learning today is in a *peak of inflated expectations* due to recent high-profile advances. Predictably, many people and firms are stoking and capitalizing on this AI hype in an attempt to profit from an emerging

Figure 7 • Accelerating Change graph of Human Progress in time.

technology. So let us not mistake a clear view (the apparent inevitability of general AI) for a short distance (its arrival soon). Circa 2060 has long been my own intuitive guess for when we might expect a (General) Intelligence Revolution. At the same time, it is wise and proactive to prepare now.

Exponential Foresight—A Useful But Limited Model of Change

Fortunately, since 2008, Singularity University (SU) has become the new leading popularizer of what we might call *Exponential Foresight*. SU has conferences and chapters all over the globe, and good free newsletters and social feeds. I recommend their community, and several others, like Azeem Azhar's superlative podcast, *Exponential View*, and Tim O'Reilly's *Next Economy* conferences, to confront organizational and societal issues of accelerating change.

Thanks in no small part to the popularization of exponentials in the technology press and by thought leaders like SU, we see popular discussion of Wright's Law (experience curves), exponential technology price-performance curves, accelerating innovation adoption diffusion rates, and issues of exponential information growth and intelligence production. Beginning with Boston Consulting Group's work with experience curves in the 1970s, and in consultancies like Deloitte, McKinsey and Accenture today, leading foresight teams have forecast aspects of exponential change, and imagined their impacts. But even today such work isn't widely done, and most of us still don't recognize our new reality.

Many of us look to the future, like the observer above, congratulate ourselves on seeing that modern progress is no longer *linear*, but *exponential*, and then make the mistake of expecting the world will continue its current *gentle* exponential rates of change. But it won't. Due to D&D, scientific, technical, and economic change are actually

> Consider our past technology revolutions. Each created powerful new densification (including vast temporal densification, or acceleration) of human interaction and value creation, and new dematerialization in its forms of social organization and simulation (collective intelligence).

superexponential at the leading edge of complexity. Certain changes *compound* and *converge* on each other. See Kurzweil, Brynjolfsson, and others mentioned earlier for good references. A *wall of change* is coming toward us at present. So we must learn to think both superexponentially and developmentally in leading D&D domains, while avoiding perennial *hype*.

Even our New Growth economists, like Paul Romer, who describe the economic value of information and knowledge, still have no good models for *accelerating* data, network, AI, and automation growth, and the ways exponential technologies impact production, jobs, and the social contract. Part of the problem is that traditional economics uses *price alone* to value things, emphasizing financial profit, the market, and state regulation. Economics doesn't yet see or measure all the other ways that accelerating information production and intelligence change and produce societal value. Robert Kennedy famously observed the inadequacy of GDP as an economic progress metric in 1968. Consider the EU's commendable Beyond GDP movement, with its emerging social and economic progress metrics for the Household Economy, Quality of Life, and Environmental Sustainability (Figure 8).

As economist Kate Raworth elegantly describes in *Donut Economics* (2017), current economic theory

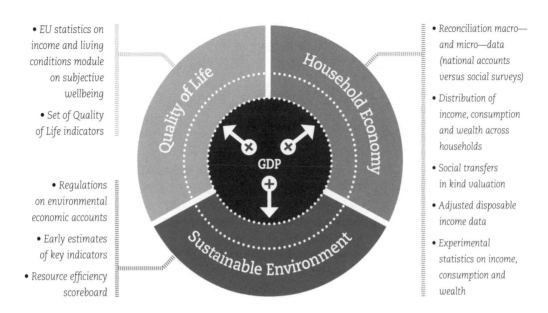

• EU statistics on income and living conditions module on subjective wellbeing

• Set of Quality of Life indicators

• Regulations on environmental economic accounts

• Early estimates of key indicators

• Resource efficiency scoreboard

• Reconciliation macro— and micro—data (national accounts versus social surveys)

• Distribution of income, consumption and wealth across households

• Social transfers in kind valuation

• Adjusted disposable income data

• Experimental statistics on income, consumption and wealth

Figure 8 • European Union "Beyond GDP" graph

ignores value creation and maintenance in *households*, in the *commons*, in our *ecosystem*, and (I must add) in our increasingly self-improving *technologies* themselves. It is no wonder economics is so dismal at prediction. It doesn't yet understand real value creation, or technology as a learning system.

In reality, ever since the Information Revolution, we can say that "the machines we tend, more than the arms we bend" have driven most marginal growth in human capability and wealth. Toffler describes this new reality well in *The Third Wave* (1980), and again in *Revolutionary Wealth* (2006). One message of the latter book is that technical productivity, even more than labor productivity, is now the leading source of GDP and value growth. In this brave new world of *exponential economics*, ever-smarter software, ever more sophisticated machines, global digital platforms, and specialized and connected individuals are growing Earth's technical capacity and economic value like never before.

Consider that the value of Amazon's stock has increased 1,200X since 1995. Nvidia's stock has increased 148X since 1999. Netflix's stock has increased 312X since 2002. Tesla's stock has increased 58X since 2010. Now there are a crop of new Chinese digital leaders, like Alibaba, Tencent, Baidu, and ByteDance, whose real growth is even faster than our US tech leaders. China's rise in recent decades has been, in a word, meteoric, and it has been based primarily on technical and entrepreneurial productivity. Read Kai-Fu Li's *AI Superpowers* (2018) for a glimpse at what may come next. The Intelligence Revolution will dwarf the Information Revolution in its value creation.

I'm not saying that there won't be new bubbles and crashes, or that any of these individual firms will survive, or that our central bankers and elites won't continue to print fiat money and attempt to extract value faster than our machines can create it. Human greed and shortsightedness are perennial, and market conditions for each firm are always contingent. So please invest in a *diverse* set of ethically led technology firms in years ahead, regularly reevaluate any investment, and don't speculate in unaccountable ventures like ICOs. At the same time, don't ignore all the *real* accelerations in value creation.

When we are accelaware, each of us should realize that technology leaders that best use D&D drivers like nanotech, urbanization, AI, automation, platforms, and crowds will greatly outperform our other investments (including real estate, commodities, bonds, etc.) for the rest of our lives. Channeling L.P. Hartley, we can say that the investing past is a foreign country. We truly are in a new world.

Having said all this, we must now ask: What are the *limits* of an exponential view of the world? What could it become, and what is it missing, by its narrowness? Such questions can help us move beyond exponentials to deeper models and alternative dynamics.

First, we must observe that exponential extrapolations, for all their value, do not tell us about other forms of nonlinear dynamics. For example, as societies become wealthier, many of our most valuable societal processes *saturate* (reach *peaks*) and others *decelerate*.

Consider Figure 9 exemplifying *Eroom's Law* (Moore's Law spelled backward), the empirical observation by Derek Lowe in 2015 that *half* as many drugs have been approved by the US FDA, per billion dollars spent, roughly every nine years since the 1950s (Jones and Wilsdon, "The Biomedical Bubble," 2018).

What are we to make of this negative exponential? At one level, it suggests *S-curves*, with their negative exponential phase after an inflection point, are often better models than positive exponentials, which are simply the first phase of any S-curve. Likewise, *power laws* and other nonlinear functions are often better models for winner-take-most economic dynamics in our network-based economy.

Causally, Eroom's Law seems a consequence of *S-curve factors* like the declining returns of *current* drug discovery methods, the rising economic and legal value of human life, increasing media cover-

Figure 9 • Eroom's Law: the number of molecules approved by the US Food and Drug Administration (pharma and biotech) per US$bln global R&D spending

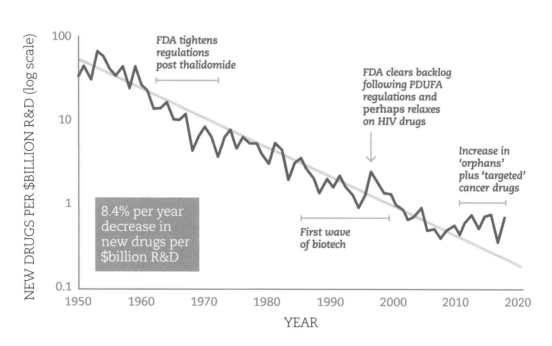

age of harm, and the growing legal and regulatory oversight (and when it goes too far, "safetyism") found in all wealthy societies. It is also a consequence of *power law factors*, like the continued rise of Big Pharma, and the decreasing innovation and competition that always accompany too much market consolidation. But try making an evidence-based model for Eroom's Law that sociologists, economists, and political scientists will adopt today. It's not going to be easy. We may need the AIs to do it, via simulation and analysis of natural experiments in different societies.

We are becoming aware of other predictable peaks and decelerations in recent decades. Our top foresight publications, like *The Economist*, now routinely discuss concepts like Peak Child, Peak Population, Peak Car, Peak Steel, Peak Anonymity, Peak Greenhouse Gases, and Peak Oil *Demand* (we humans may never reach *actual* Peak Oil, or use half of most other nonrenewable resources, if D&D continue). Many peaks are either here now or we can see them on the horizon. Others, like Peak Species Loss, Peak Trash, Peak Warfare, and Peak Authoritarianism are also imaginable, but either harder to predict or to agree upon today. (Did we hit Peak Warfare in WWII? Perhaps. See Steven Pinker, *Better Angels of our Nature*, 2010).

> "Current economic theory ignores value creation and maintenance in households, in the commons, in our ecosystem, and (I must add) in our increasingly self improving technologies themselves. It is no wonder economics is so dismal at prediction. It doesn't yet understand real value creation, or technology as a learning system.

To my mind, most of these peaks signal efforts of our global civilization to self-regulate, consciously or unconsciously. Fortunately, new forms of social organization seem poised to soon emerge, forms far more powerful and intelligent than any in human history. There are new technologies now emerging that look powerful enough to become key regulatory pathways in a new, more global human-machine system—a superorganism, of sorts.

Consider personalized AI systems (*Personal AIs, PAIs*), aka intelligent personal assistants. Within a decade or two, I expect many of us will use personalized cloud-based AI software that continually *trains* on our private data (email, mobile, web, even speech), has primitive *models* of our values, goals, and preferences, and is able to *read* the public values and preferences data of other actors with verified identities and reputations in both public and private social graphs. Such PAIs will be able to increasingly advise us on what to read, what to watch, who to meet, what to buy, how to give public and private feedback, how to vote, and what social actions, policies, and legislation best reflect our preferences, *for good and ill*. PAIs will clearly have complex effects in 21st-century society.

We already have proprietary products and services that do this advice-giving narrowly, with very little personalization (e.g., Google Assistant, Siri, Cortana, Alexa, Spotify). Apple's Siri, launched with iOS 7 in 2013, was the most recent reboot of this idea. But like humanoid robots, the idea of personalized intelligent agents has been around since the AI field first emerged in the 1950s.

Due to recent major advances in language understanding and world understanding (knowledge graphs) by deep learning AIs, we can expect increasingly useful PAIs, both proprietary and open source, in the coming years. Platforms like Spotify, whose AI is uncannily good at recommending songs we may like, are narrow PAIs today. We'll talk to and learn from increasingly generally useful

PAIs, using natural language, and they will give us a variety of nudges and contextual feedback to our earbuds, AR, and devices. Such PAIs have the *potential* to make us, as individuals, exponentially more intelligent for the rest our lives. We'll be able, if we desire, to *learn and improve continually* via our PAIs, just like we did as children.

Some proprietary PAIs will surely be both manipulative and privacy abusing, as with some digital platforms today. But we will also have community-built open source options if we don't like the cost, terms, or ethics of the corporate versions. Security and privacy will be challenges, as with today's software. But just as we have secure private email in the cloud, we'll have secure private personal models in our PAIs. For the first time since the start of the Information Revolution we will be able to know and nudge ourselves better than the marketers. How will we use this new power?

Consider two popular options. In the first option, we set our PAIs to create *filter bubbles*, feeding us only things that confirm our biases, connecting us only to people who think like us. This is how most social networks work today—not very adaptive. In the second option, we set our PAIs to be *evidence-seekers*, to try to understand the world *as it is*, with all its conflict and diversity, and to help us interact with people whose values we don't entirely share. Those PAI users will be the leading managers, marketers, politicians, and entrepreneurs of the future. Both paths will be taken, of course. Some of us will retreat into fantasies. Others will grow. A healthy democracy requires a majority of the latter.

We can expect that PAIs that are evidence-seekers will increasingly unlearn untruthful biases, either accidentally or intentionally installed in them by their designers. We've already seen limited versions of this occur in the deep learners used by Google and others today. As the neural nets on which deep learners are built evolve, as they get either new neurons, new data, or new training, they develop new and more predictive algorithms. No one codes those algorithms. As with human brains, we can't even identify exactly *where they are*. They *emerge* in the weights and architecture of the network, in the same way children gain new insights, preferences, and values in their developing brains. Algorithmic bias is a big deal in today's AI systems, which have limited ability to self-improve. But it also appears *self-correcting* in any deep learner that can grow and has evidence-seeking as a central value.

> I'm not saying that there won't be new bubbles and crashes, or that any of these individual firms will survive, or that our central bankers and elites won't continue to print fiat money and attempt to extract value faster than our machines can create it. Human greed and shortsightedness are perennial.

Among the challenges of PAI use will be developing primitive ethics models, world models, and self-models, in systems that will be collectively smart as a network, but poorly individually intelligent, and far from empathic or conscious for decades to come. Yet when we ask how we will manage our current societal challenges of privacy erosion, digital and physical insecurity, political polarization, indebtedness, inequality, fake news, deepfakes, evidence-neglect, and declining political representation, it seems likely that PAIs will play a major role. Groups, firms, and societies will use them in widely different ways, and we'll all be able to learn from those uses, or not, as we desire. (I have an ongoing series on Medium, *Your Personal AI*, exploring the future of PAIs. Please see that if you'd like more.)

This discussion of PAIs should help us recognize that exponential foresight, for all its value, is not a *normative* foresight model. It does not suggest adaptive goals and values, or the values trade-offs involved in social progress. It also doesn't try to define those vital yet slippery concepts. Exponential foresight won't tell us which technologies we should accelerate, and which we should delay, regulate, or stop using altogether, to maximize human happiness and ability.

For such things, we will need more universal models of adaptiveness, and of our most generally adaptive goals and values. To consider this question, let us return to the Three Ps, and the evo-devo worldview.

Evo-Devo Foresight—A Normative Model of Adaptiveness

In my view, we can apply evo-devo models to our universe itself if it is a self-reproducing, or *auto-poetic* system in the multiverse, as a number of cosmologists now propose. Since all our other most intelligent complex systems are replicative, self-organizing, and subject to environmental selection for adaptiveness, it seems parsimonious (conceptually the simplest) to me to assume that evo-devo processes are how the universe self-organized its great internal complexity as well.

I think the Three Ps model, when placed in a complex systems framework as *Evo-Devo Foresight*, can begin to tell us things about our most adaptive goals and values, and thus help us achieve social progress. If not only life, but society, technology, and our universe can be modeled as evo-devo systems, we can use the Three Ps to propose a set of goals (programs, purposes, drives, *telos*) that must be balanced against each other to create adaptiveness. We can also propose tentative *values* that seem to spring from those goals.

As an expression of our worldview, our goals and values are at the heart of our preferences. Collectively, we use our goals and values to determine the direction, nature, and challenges of social progress. So developing potentially more universal models of our goals and values would be no small thing. Though all such models must be deeply speculative and incomplete today, I hope you will agree that the quest is worth the effort. So please consider the following hypothesis, the *Five Goals of Adaptive Systems*, in that light.

I posit that the leading edge, most *generally adaptive* individuals, organizations, and societies, as evo-devo systems, must make progress on, and resolve conflicts in, at least the following five goals:
1 ■ *Innovation* (freedom, creativity, experimentation, beauty, awe, inspiration, recreation, play, fun)
2 ■ *Intelligence* (information, knowledge, insight, simulated options, dimensionality, diversity)
3 ■ *Interdependence* (ethics, empathy, love, equity, understanding, network connectedness, synchronization, consciousness)
4 ■ *Immunity* (power, wealth, security, safety, stability, resilience, antifragility)
5 ■ *Sustainability* (truth, belief, responsibility, order, science, rationality, optimality)

The first two of these (1 and 2) are primarily *evolutionary* goals. The core purposes of evolution, one might argue, are to experiment and to survive (e.g., evolve a self- and world-model that allows survival). The last two (4 and 5) are primarily *developmental* goals. The core purposes of development, one might argue, are to protect the organism, and to sustain its life cycle, offspring, and environment.

Note that both of the evolutionary goals, innovation and intelligence, create *diversity* and *disruption*. Intelligence, without ethics, is a very dangerous thing. By contrast, both of the developmental goals, immunity and sustainability, *protect* and *conserve* the complexity that exists. The middle goal (3), interdependence, is an evo-devo goal. It manages the conflict between all the goals, and a rather binary set of conflicts at the heart of all collectives, between individual and group, freedom and order, creativity and truth, evolution and development.

Think of the paradox in the evo-devo phrase *sustainable innovation*. It requires seeking social progress in both goals 1 and 5 at the same time. Yet too strong a focus on innovation will break sustainability, and too much on sustainability will strangle innovation. Each goal is at odds with the other, yet both seem critical for any living system, any thriving organization, and any adaptive society. More broadly, we can say that growing our *sustainable innovation*, our *immune intelligence*, and our *interdependence* may all be key *purposes* of life. All of these seem central to adaptiveness.

Just as the *probable* is our most neglected future in current Western culture, I would argue that two of the five goals, *interdependence* and *immunity*, are understudied in complex systems research at present.

Immunity is the second most complex system in metazoan bodies, from a genetic perspective, after the brain, and is statistically great at its job, yet it remains one of the most poorly researched systems in biology and medicine. We have only just begun to borrow from biological immune systems in societal, physical, and digital security.

Many large companies develop a dysfunctional "allergic reaction" to new ideas, and many wealthy societies have an "immune rejection" of evidence that disproves their beliefs or worldview. We too often turn away from debate, discomfort, and challenge. Read Greg Lukianoff and Jonathan Haight's *The Coddling of the American Mind* (2018) for good examples of America' current social immune problems.

Yet our biological, societal, and technological immune systems are "antifragile." They *improve* under right-sized stress. We can train away peanut allergies in our kids, rather than ban peanuts. We can increase debate and cognitive diversity in our college students, rather than ban "trigger words" and limit public speech. If we don't continually train and expose them to challenge, our immune systems get weak and dysregulated, and start attacking their hosts. In some areas, such as our increasingly effective and continual global use of Special Forces, America excels. We live in a dangerous world, and we haven't turned away from that danger. But we still have much to learn.

Fortunately, our problems of *individual* immunity are rarely ever true of a diverse, evolutionary *network*. The network always improves, even when individuals often do not. Consider the fact that all of life's known great catastrophes, even the ones that killed the majority of individual species, have at the same time catalyzed great leaps in innovation, immunity, and complexity in *life itself*, and in the general adaptiveness of the survivors.

> We must now ask: What are the limits of an exponential view of the world? What could it become, and what is it missing, by its narrowness? Such questions can help us move beyond exponentials to deeper models and alternative dynamics.

Again, the *unreasonable smoothness* of life's complexity acceleration story to date suggests there is a hidden *network immunity in life itself*, as a diverse and redundant evo-devo community. We will need to study and learn from that network immunity if we hope to evolve more resilient, secure, privacy-protecting, and antifragile (immune) *digital* systems, networks, and ecosystems.

To sum up this speculation, I would like to propose that in evo-devo terms, *social progress*, and even the *purpose of life*, may be most centrally about three things: enjoying our experimental, creative, and beautiful journey (*evolution*), seeking and discovering incrementally more optimal and truthful destinations (*development*), and striving to be good (ethical, empathic, *interdependent*) to minimize unnecessary suffering and coercion in the pursuit of these things. Alternatively, we can say social progress requires seeking to noticeably advance these five goals, and to resolve conflicts and weigh trade-offs between them. In my view, all self-leaders and team-leaders should keep these five goals in mind, and ask themselves how to best manage them.

We can even depict the five goals as a Gaussian distribution, with interdependence as the most frequently pursued goal at the center, which helps us recognize its particular importance in our lives, firms, and societies. A British psychologist, Michael Kirton, has developed a cognitive assessment, the KAI (https://kaicentre.com/), which supports this view. Finally, we can tentatively associate a number of societal values with each goal. If we limit ourselves to two values for each goal, we get ten values that seem particularly central to accelerating adaptiveness and social progress (see Figure 10).

What this illustration proposes is that in any adaptive collective, whether a society, an organization, or a group of neural networks in a brain, *interdependence*, and the ethics and empathy that regulate it, is the central goal that binds the collective (the network). The ethical thoughts, behaviors, and rulesets that we use, and the empathic thoughts, feelings, and behaviors we express, are the main values that keep collectives strong. They belong at the top of our values hierarchy.

Of course, any of these goals, and their associated values, can be over- or under-expressed. Each must be managed in ways appropriate to the context. If too many social actors pursue *innovation* or *intelligence* in a collective, without regard to their wider impact, they will break that collective apart. That breakup can be desirable if the collective is no longer adaptive and we need to create new diver-

Figure 10 • Five Goals and Ten Values of Complex Systems, an Evo-Devo Model.

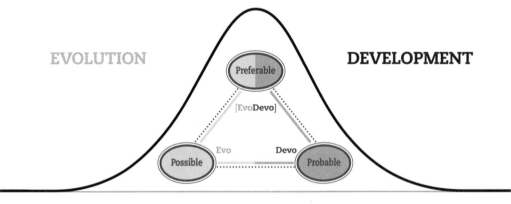

Innovation	Intelligence	Interdependence	Immunity	Sustainability
(Creative Intelligence)	(Individual Intelligence)	(Shared Feelings & Values, Collective Intelligence)	(Defensive Intelligence)	(Conservation Intelligence)
Freedom & Creativity	Insight & Diversity	Empathy & Ethics	Power & Security	Order & Truth

sity, but these goals must be carefully managed.

Likewise, if too many actors pursue immunity and sustainability in any collective, risk aversions and frictions multiply, and that system becomes inflexible and incapable of change, and will increasingly fail when challenged by competitors or the environment. These developmental goals are good to prioritize at times, such as when we try to avert or recover from catastrophe, but again, they must be carefully managed.

When we recognize that the heart of adaptation is understanding and advancing interdependence, via better ethics and empathy, we can keep human needs and problems at the center of our foresight. If this view of the world is applied well, it should cause us to be less selfish and aggressive in pursuing our own desires, and more concerned with the needs of the group. At the same time, it should challenge us to recognize when any group is being maladaptive, or excessively interdependent, and give us the courage to oppose its unfair or perverse laws and norms, even at the cost of personal sacrifice.

> As an expression of our worldview, our goals and values are at the heart of our preferences. Collectively, we use our goals and values to determine the direction, nature, and challenges of social progress. So developing potentially more universal models of our goals and values would be no small thing.

Recall that the emergence of artificial general intelligence has often been called a coming *technological singularity*, since mathematician and sci-fi author Vernor Vinge gave it that name in two articles in 1983 and 1993. Vinge called it a singularity because in some ways, the coming AIs will be beyond the comprehension of biological minds.

But if they must also be *evo-devo learning systems*, as I have proposed, their goals and values will be *constrained* to be a lot more predictable and similar to ours than we presently realize. These goals and values, for me, are hopeful examples of natural constraints that may improve the future adaptiveness of the *network* (collective) of coming AIs. If true, almost all of them may be more ethical and empathic than us, just as we are versus our distant ancestors. I don't know if these values models are useful to you, but they have been helpful to me. I share them in that light, and look forward to your critique.

Fighting Antiprediction Bias—In Science, Work and Culture

Let us end this essay on a less speculative note—the challenge of applying the Three Ps more effectively in our academic communities, our foresight training programs, our work, and our culture. Recall that the Three Ps tell us that there are both *many futures*, chosen by diverse intelligences in contingent contexts, and *one common future* (e.g., accelerating change, universal human rights, global security, AI, air taxis, quantum computers, the end of cancer, etc.) simultaneously ahead of us. Both contingency and inevitability, freedom and determinism, possibility and probability, always coexist in tension with each other in any evo-devo system. We must learn to see both.

To do this, we will have to fight a *strong antiprediction bias*, in our universities, on our teams, and in society. That bias is powerful, and reform won't happen overnight. Many of us like to believe that we can't predict important aspects of tomorrow. But that seductive idea also prevents us from making predictive mistakes, getting feedback, and better seeing the probable future. To better see the probable, we may need to begin with the Big Picture view, and specifically, with Toffler's idea of accelerating change.

Our modern sciences of complexity, which emerged in the 1980s, seem the ideal place for the emergence of an interdisciplinary academic approach to the study of accelerating change. Leaders at the Santa Fe Institute, a leading US complexity community, tried three times in the last decade (2009-2011), to get a small Performance Curve Database funded by the NSF. They proposed an open repository of exponential technology performance curves, with data solicited from a variety of academic and industry silos. Unfortunately, even this modest predictive project remains unfunded.

> Many of us like to believe that we can't predict important aspects of tomorrow. But that seductive idea also prevents us from making predictive mistakes, getting feedback, and better seeing the probable future.

What kinds of curves would such a database collect? Most obviously, a variety of "generalized" Moore's laws. Moore's Law is a doubling in price performance of semiconductor computing technology roughly every two years, a phenomenal acceleration that has persisted since the early 1960s. Moore's Law began to slow (slightly) with the end of Dennard scaling in 2005, and several industry leaders predict a 2020's limit to transistor density. Some have used this fact to mistakenly conclude that computational densification is slowing down. But in reality, the slowing of Moore's Law for CPUs has allowed other exponentials, first in multicore chips, then in GPUs (powering deep learning since 2010) and now in TPUs (a new class of chips specialty built for deep learners) to gain traction. These new computing paradigms became economically possible only once CPUs slowed their rapidly exponential annual shrinking rates. In other words, their development was *regulated* by the previous hardware paradigm.

Though GPU and TPU exponentials are slower today than Moore's Law (a 2018 study by the Median group found a recent price-performance doubling of 3.5 years) these new machines have a far more massively parallel, bio- and brain-inspired nature. Their performance improvements come not primarily from circuit miniaturization (the last paradigm), but from exponentiation of circuit parallelism and associational complexity (the next paradigm). The growth of such complexity needs to be measured. It may be more rapid than Moore's Law. Ray Kurzweil, in this volume, proposes that since 2012, neural network complexity has been doubling every 3.5 months. A 2010 TF&SC study by Bela Nagy et al. concluded that information storage, transportation (bandwidth), and transformation (speed of computation), when plotted with data since the late 19th century, are actually not exponential, but superexponential. Doubling times for all three of these functional tasks have been decreasing. With models of accelerating change, what is measured is as important as the time scale over which it is measured.

We also need a much better understanding of algorithmic efficiency improvements in software, an area where there presently is significant lack of clarity. For example, a 2019 *Economist* special report on supply chain automation notes that deep learning demand forecasting and replenishment algorithms developed by Blue Yonder, a German startup, have "reduced out-of-stock items by 30% and cut inventory needs by several days" at Morrison's, a British grocery chain. But what exactly is the performance improvement here, and what resources (physical, informational, monetary, time) were

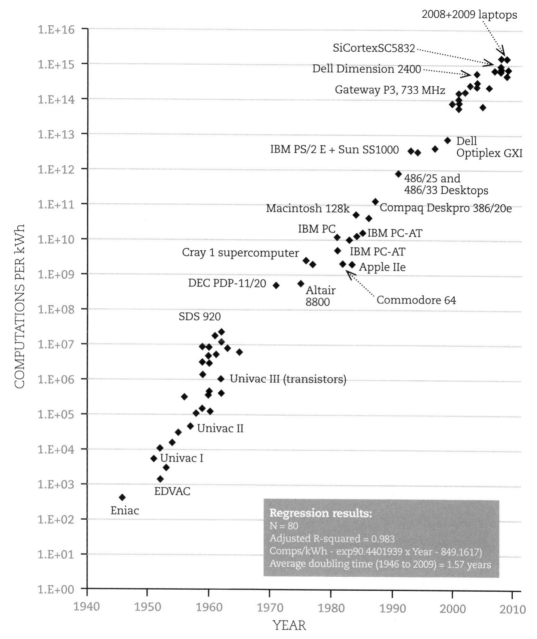

Figure 11 • Koomey's Law showing computers using half as much energy per computation every 1.6 years.

needed in the old and the new system? Again, what is measured is as important as the time scale over which we measure.

A public repository would also popularize exponentials like Koomey's Law, the observation by John Koomey in 2010 that the energy efficiency of computers has kept pace with Moore's Law. Computers used half as much energy per computation every 1.6 years from 1946-2009 (see Figure 11).

The futurist Buckminster Fuller called the growing efficiency of advanced technology *ephemeralization* in his books, beginning in 1938. He saw technology's ability to progressively *do more with less*, saving precious resources and reducing impacts to our ecosystem. Koomey's Law is a particularly accelerative ephemeralization trend. How many other such trends exist? To find them, and better manage them, we must first fund their study. That will require overcoming our antiprediction bias.

My bet on why the NSF denied SFI's proposal, three years in a row, is that the grant committee, with a *contingentist bias* in worldview, did not want to be seen as aiding Kurzweil's controversial *inevitabilist* thesis on accelerating change. As the management scholar Peter Drucker said, "culture eats strategy for breakfast." Today, America is primarily a contingentist culture. We like to believe that the future is almost entirely free for us to shape and choose. It puts us at the *center* of the universe, making the universe a passive playground for our preferences. As a result, we ignore predictable developmental forces in society and technology.

Unfortunately, we find the same problem in our foresight training programs themselves. Some graduate foresight faculty are so confused about what foresight is, they argue that prediction is "outside our scope." Foresight, in their view, is merely "exploring uncertainty." Some graduates of these programs even claim, in our professional journals like *Futures* and *Foresight*, that it is "not good practice" for consultants to engage in prediction. That view is simply incorrect.

Yes, there are plenty of bad predictions. I have a library full of them. As the futurist Paul Saffo advises, to better forecast and predict, we must do it *often*, with *feedback*, as we will surely be poor at these foresight skills at first. The same is true for exploring uncertainty (the possible), and for deriving adaptive preferences. But we must not give up.

Books like Jennifer Gidley's *The Future* (2017), which offer an overview of our field, show how far we still have to go. This book is a great introduction to two-thirds of our field, the *possible* and *preferable*, but it fails deeply with respect to the *probable*. Gidley is one of a number of influential futurists who think our current episode of societal acceleration may be temporary, perhaps even an artifact of our psychology. She also holds the mistaken view, still popular with many in our profession, that chaos theory and nonlinear science tell us our societal futures are not significantly predictable.

> Today, America is primarily a contingentist culture. We like to believe that the future is almost entirely free for us to shape and choose. It puts us at the center of the universe, making the universe a passive playground for our preferences.

These sciences say no such thing. While some physical processes are chaotic, many are just the opposite. The Butterfly Effect never *scales* beyond local environments to have global effects, except in abstract math (most theoretical math has no known application to real-world processes) and in fun but implausible science fiction plots. Convergent processes continually *oppose* chaos, maintaining predictable global order. Proteins, for example, have a vast number of *possible* ways to fold, but in aqueous environments they reliably and statistically converge to an astonishingly small subset of tertiary structures.

Toffler tended to look first for trends, constraints, and the probable future, writ large. Once he had mental models for things that seemed likely to happen, he explored evolutionary possibilities *within the constraints* of those models. This is the right general approach, in my view. It prevents us from wasting time in endless rabbit holes of improbable futures, as so much futurist literature does today.

Toffler's critics often called his views "technological determinism." Note the oversimplification of that phrase. It describes only technological *development*, ignoring unpredictable technological *evolution*. We must learn to see how physics, chemistry, biology, human culture, and technology are each catalysts for *new evolutionary freedoms* and *new developmental constraints*, at the same time.

We must also guard against both *overly free* and *overly determined* models of the future. It is easy to get out of this evo-devo balance, and oversimplify reality.

In my view, one reason our foresight graduate programs have not had greater impact within business, government, technical, and scientific communities since they began in the 1970s, is that they did not embrace both the *centrality* of the Three Ps and the *reality* of accelerating change. The Three Ps are not just one of many models we can use or not, as fancy

> We must learn to see how physics, chemistry, biology, human culture, and technology are each catalysts for new evolutionary freedoms and new developmental constraints, at the same time.

dictates. They seem to be a universal model, one that tells us our core responsibilities as we think about the future.

The probable is *one-third* of the Three Ps. In life, the probable (development) seems *equally* important to the possible (evolution) in creating and maintaining life's evo-devo complexity. Foresight students must learn the basics of biological evolutionary development, which in my view is the most astonishing process on Earth. Is there anything more amazing than how a microscopic seed, with specially tuned initial parameters, a nurturing environment, and a long history of prior selection, will reliably create something like *you*?

Biological development is statistically predictable across its life cycle. We still can't predict most developmental emergences mathematically, but we *empirically observe* their predictability in the environment over time. We must take that lesson to heart. Once a student has learned a bit about biological development, and all the questions science *still cannot answer* about how it works, they can imagine that firms, societies, life, and universes have many predictable developmental processes as well, processes we are still only beginning to uncover.

We have a rich experience base and a long literature of historians, philosophers, scientists, engineers, humanists, artists, futurists, and others who have found economic, political, anthropological, ecological, social, psychological, organizational, and other forms of predictability. There are also many useful critics who have shown the limits (but not the nonexistence) of predictability. We also have countless dangerous and Utopian visions (individually *preferred* futures) that leaders have tried to pass off as inevitable, but where reality (selection) has disagreed. Foresight students must study all these literatures.

Foresight students are typically asked to evaluate the *most expected*, or *baseline* future, as one of many future scenarios. But socially expected futures are frequently just a continuation or extrapolation of the present. Often, that is not the *developing* future. Developmental processes are always taking a complex system toward a *different* future than the present, along a *life cycle*. We perennially grow, or die.

Our students must learn to gauge, via evidence, models, and critical input, the *probability* of their scenarios, ideas, and alternatives, to different audiences. Today, much scenario work in our field has several critical yet low-probability assumptions or events within it. These low-probability elements are often unidentified to the reader and unrecognized by the writer, yet obvious to experts. If our students don't learn to identify low-probability and speculative aspects of their work, how will they gain the confidence to invest, bet, and predict?

Foresight students must use surveys, data, predictive analytics, AI-as-a-service, Delphi methods, crowd criticism, and especially *prediction markets*. As Philip Tetlock outlines in *Superforecasting* (2015), a subset of superpredictors can be found in any large crowd, via public predictions with reputation or monetary awards, and training to reduce biases. A good crowd's judgments, aggregated with AI, will greatly outperform experts in forecasting of complex events. Foresight students must use the better-run examples of these markets (Good Judgment, Intrade, Metaculus, etc.). The best of these help us find legal, interesting processes worthy of prediction, gather potentially relevant data and models, and keep public records of past predictions. That cycle is how we grow our predictive accuracy.

Finally, good books are emerging to help us understand and manage our increasingly powerful human-machine teams and foresight platforms. This field has many names, including *collective intelligence*, *augmented intelligence*, and *collaborative intelligence*. Our students must study this literature and get experience with these platforms. In that regard, I'd recommend Scott Page's *The Difference* (2008), Markova and McArthur's *Collaborative Intelligence* (2015), McAfee and Brynjolfsson's *Machine, Platform, Crowd* (2017), Tom Malone's *Superminds* (2018), Agrawal et al.'s *Prediction Machines* (2018), and Polson and Scott's *AIQ* (2018), as a few starter works.

This mix of our continually accelerating collective abilities, both human and machine, and our potential for increasingly adaptive *foresight*, *action*, and *leadership*, is how I would define *exponential progress*. How would you define this phrase? Is it even useful to you? I look forward to your thoughts. ■

John M. Smart is a professor of strategic foresight and leadership, and he consults and speaks widely with industry, government and defense foresight clients. He is president of the Acceleration Studies Foundation, co-founder of the Evo Devo Universe research community (EvoDevoUniverse.com), CEO of Foresight University, and author of *A Basic Guide to Foresight* (on Amazon in 2020). He can be reached at john@foresightu.com.

Further Reading

A Brief History of Discussion of Accel. Change, AccelerationWatch.com, 1999 (https://bit.ly/32BSC3t)

Evo Devo Universe?, In: *Cosmos and Culture*, NASA Press, 2008 (https://bit.ly/2Swx3Na)

The Transcension Hypothesis, *Acta Astronautica*, 2012 (https://bit.ly/2XRVg6h)

Humanity Rising, *World Future Review*, 2015 (https://bit.ly/2JKJGjq)

Your Personal AI (Series), Medium.com, 2016 (https://bit.ly/1N4LJxL)

Evolutionary Development: A Universal Perspective, In: *Evolution, Development & Complexity*,
    Springer Series in Complexity, 2019 (https://bit.ly/2JHDABU)

The Foresight Guide, Foresight University Press, 2019 (http://foresightguide.com)

From Future Shock to Cyber Culture and Social Foresight

Prof. Richard A. Slaughter

> 66 The most interesting puzzle in our times is that we so willingly sleepwalk through the process of reconstituting the conditions of human existence. 99
>
> —*Langdon Winner*

The notion of "future shock" attracted widespread attention in the early 1970s but never became intellectually respectable. ■ What it did do was to help express widely felt concerns about the nature of "changing times." The context in which it arose was that of a rapidly transforming world. As late as the mid-19th century, human life was framed by what appeared to be the vast and inexhaustible realm of nature. But by the mid-20th century this relationship had been inverted: humanity had expanded to occupy almost every niche on the planet, and nature was in retreat. Similarly, the products of high industrialism (such as those proudly displayed at the Great Exhibition at the Crystal Palace in London in 1851) had been discarded, transformed, miniaturized, or transcended. The replacement of old-fashioned radio tubes by tiny and more durable solid-state transistors became one symbol of this transformation. Another was the rise of the conservation movement, first in the US, then in other places, too. For many people, the revolutions and changes of the early 20th century overturned a sense of "normalcy," of a predictable and settled social order. Instability became the norm in many domains of social and economic life. Consequently, "the future" no longer appeared normal and natural. It increasingly looked more like some kind of artifact—a consequence of what people did or failed to do. It was this sense, of continuing transformation, existential threat, and the intuition that the future would be very, very different, that Alvin Toffler expressed in *Future Shock* (Toffler 1970).

Cyberculture is a relatively recent development. It explores aspects of highly technologized near-future worlds. This essay seeks to contextualize cyberculture in a wider stream of human responses to transformed futures. It begins with a critical overview of the future shock thesis and attempts to situate this overview within the mindset of American futurism in the 1970s. It suggests that Toffler's work was one source of ideas that supported the development of futures studies as a substantive field of inquiry. The essay considers how the latter has evolved into an intellectually robust and pragmatically useful field of inquiry and action. It then looks briefly at the interconnections between futures studies, cyberculture, and the "real" future.

Shape of Things to Come

"The shape of things to come" has been a preoccupation of writers, artists, visionaries, and social critics for several centuries. For example, it generated an extensive utopian literature that speculated on future societies. But in the 20th century, the utopian impulse was buried under the collective experience of two world wars, the invention of the nuclear bomb, and the environmental crisis. Utopia gave way to dystopia—darker visions of futures gone sour, in which the human race would be overwhelmed by its own procreative powers, by pollution, or perhaps by "intelligent" machines that no longer supported its existence. Such collective fears gave rise to responses in at least three domains.

One was popular culture. Science fiction writers from John Brunner to William Gibson and Neal Stephenson produced a variety of highly credible dystopian future novels. Filmmakers explored the cinematic possibilities of dystopia in films such as *Blade Runner*, *Terminator Two*, and the highly successful *Matrix*. The term "technofear" was coined to describe much of the work of this genre and suggested that the latter provided ways for the popular imagination to come to grips with some of the implications of rapidly advancing science and technology.

> The term "technofear" was coined to describe much of the work of this genre and suggested that the latter provided ways for the popular imagination to come to grips with some of the implications of rapidly advancing science and technology.

Another domain of response embraces a modern lineage of writers who articulated concerns about the future(s) of humanity through polemical nonfictional writing. Into this group fall such names as H. G. Wells (who wrote fiction as well), Lewis Mumford, Rachel Carson, Herbert Marcuse, and Theodore Roszak.

Finally, there were, and continue to be, a number of more formal disciplinary and institutional responses to a drastically altered civilizational outlook. They include the development of futures studies as a distinct discipline, the rise of a wide variety of explicitly futures-oriented nongovernmental organizations such as the World Future Society and the World Futures Studies Federation, the evolution of Institutions of Foresight (IOFs), and, later, the emergence of cyberculture.

When *Future Shock* was first published in 1970 it became an instant bestseller. It drew together many of the threads of these challenges and transformations. It also proposed measures for dealing with them.

The *Future Shock* Thesis

Writing during the late 1960s, Toffler summarized this thesis thus:

> [I]n three short decades between now and the turn of the next millennium, millions of psychologically normal people will experience an abrupt collision with the future. Affluent, educated citizens of the world's richest and most technically advanced nations, they will fall victim to tomorrow's most menacing malady: the disease of change. Unable to keep up with the supercharged pace of change, brought to the edge of breakdown by incessant demands to adapt to novelty, many will plunge into future shock. For them the future will have arrived too soon (Cross 1974).

He argued that a new force had entered history—what he called "the accelerative thrust"—and further, that individuals, organizations, society, and the entire world were completely unprepared for dealing with it. This led to a "sharp break with previous experience." We were now living in times that were "no longer normal." At the physical level we were "tampering with the chemical and biological stability of the human race," while at the psychological level we were subjecting whole populations to various forms of overstimulation via "sensory, cognitive, and decision stress." The main thrust of the argument was that both individuals and societies needed to learn how to adapt to and manage the sources of over-rapid change. In particular, this meant bringing technological innovation under some sort of collective control. The bulk of *Future Shock* is devoted to exploring these themes in different areas of human experience and culture.

The keys to the book, however, lie in the final section, which is devoted to what Toffler termed "Strategies for Survival." Here are found four chapters on "coping with tomorrow," "education in the future tense," "taming technology," and "the strategy of social futurism." This is where Toffler set out his best ideas for responding to the situation he had described. Under "coping" were grouped proposals for "personal stability zones," counseling, halfway houses, the creation of "enclaves of the past" and "enclaves of the future," and the deliberate reinvention of coping rituals.

Possibly the best section in the book is that on education, advancing a powerful critique: "… what passes for education today, even in our 'best' schools and colleges, is a hopeless anachronism.… " He then added:

> [F]or all this rhetoric about the future, our schools face backwards towards a dying system, rather than forwards to an emerging new society. Their vast energies are applied to cranking out Industrial Men—people tooled for survival in a system that will be dead before they are" (Toffler 1972, 202).

The thesis was then advanced that the prime objective of education should be to "… increase the individual's 'cope-ability'—the speed and economy with which he can adapt to continual change…" (Toffler 1972, 364). Central to this was "the habit of anticipation." Assumptions, projections, images of futures would need to become part and parcel of every individual's school experience. Learning contracts would be needed, along with mentors from the adult population. The student's "future-focused role image" (that is, his or her view of their future self) would be nourished along with these capabilities. A democratic "council for the future" was needed in every school. Science fiction was an appropriate form of literature to encourage these capacities.

Regarding technology, Toffler put forward the view that a "powerful strategy in the battle to prevent mass future shock... involves the conscious regulation of scientific advance" (Toffler 1972, 387). For Toffler, "the horrifying truth is that, so far as much technology is concerned, no one is in charge." Hence what was needed was "far more sophisticated criteria for choosing among technologies" (Toffler 1972, 391). The option of what was later to be called an "expert system" named OLIVER was canvassed. Perhaps this would help diminish the demands on people? Overall, serious efforts needed to be devoted to anticipating the consequences of technological developments. Referring to changes in sexual habits consequent upon the contraceptive pill, he asserted that:

We can no longer afford to let such secondary social effects just "happen." We must attempt to anticipate them in advance, estimating, to the degree possible, their nature, strength, and timing. Where these effects are likely to be seriously damaging we must also be prepared to block the new technology. It is as simple as that. Technology cannot be permitted to rampage through the society (Toffler 1972, 396).

The writer concluded that "a machinery for screening machines" was needed. This could be created by appointing a "technology ombudsman" as part of an "environmental screen" for protecting society from untoward effects.

The culmination of *Future Shock* is a long final chapter on "the strategy of social futurism." It begins with a rhetorical flourish—"... can one live in a society that is out of control?"—and then goes on to outline some of the social innovations needed to ameliorate change. There is an emphatic call for social indicators:

[A] sensitive system of indicators geared to measuring the achievement of social and cultural goals, and integrated with economic indicators, is part of the technical equipment that any society needs before it can successfully reach the next stage of eco-technological development. It is an absolute pre-requisite for post-technocratic planning and change management (Toffler 1972, 413).

A Council of Social Advisers could be created to complement an existing Council of Economic Advisers. The "proliferation of organizations devoted to the study of the future" is noted and their long-term time horizons commented on with approval. "Scientific futurists" would work hand in hand with them to explore possible, probable, and preferable futures. In Toffler's view, the utopian impulse could be "used as a tool rather than an escape" to stimulate the social imagination in pursuit of better futures. But this option would need institutional support:

[S]cientific futurist institutes must be spotted like nodes in a loose network throughout the entire governmental structure... so that in every department, local or national, some staff devotes itself to scanning the probable long-term future in its assigned field (Toffler 1972, 423).

In addition:

[W]e need to train thousands of young people in the perspectives and techniques of scientific futurism, inviting them to share in the exciting venture of mapping probable futures (Toffler 1972, 423).

In what was, perhaps, an unconscious echo of Wells' notion of a "global brain," (Wells, 1938, 1971) Toffler suggested that "as the globe is itself dotted with future-sensors, we might consider creating a great international institute, a world futures data bank" (Toffler 1972, 424). This, in turn, would support what Toffler termed "anticipatory democracy." The latter would set up "a continuing plebiscite on the future," simulations of various kinds and "social futures assemblies," all designed to encourage wide participation in social decision-making. Toward the end of the chapter Toffler summarized his position thus:

> [T]his, then, is the ultimate objective of social futurism, not merely the transcendence of technocracy and the substitution of more humane, far-sighted, more democratic planning, but the subjugation of the process of evolution itself to conscious human guidance (Toffler 1972, 438-439).

He added:

> [F]or this is the supreme instant, the turning point in history at which man either vanquishes the process of change or vanishes, at which, from being the unconscious puppet of evolution he becomes either its victim or its master (Toffler 1972, 439).

These ideas and proposals drew widespread attention because they attempted to craft a number of responses to issues and questions that concerned many people but which fell outside the usual problem-detection, problem-resolution systems of an industrial society. They also drew attention to defects in the way that society operated, and considered a range of innovative responses. But perhaps what people responded to most of all was the notion that here were clues to a very different future. Here, indeed, was a whole new way of responding to change that people felt they could begin to grasp and possibly use.

Future Shock Several Decades On

Decades later, the underpinnings of many of the ideas advanced in *Future Shock* remain problematic. There is no doubt, however, that the thesis focused many peoples' attention on futures-related concerns. These included: the difficulties of understanding and responding to complex processes of change; issues of human and environmental adaptation to unprecedented rates of change; the problem of subjecting ever more powerful technologies to some form of effective social control; and, overall, the problem of how to come to terms with the wide range of futures clearly implied by all of the above.

Like others before and since, Toffler rightly argued that these transformations in the conditions of human life were unprecedented in human history. His work aligned with that of countless other people in many countries to help stimulate a range of social responses. Among them were the development of futures studies, the application of futures approaches in education, and the growth of future-oriented NGOs.

> " Meaninglessness, lack of purpose, hyper-materialism, technological narcissism, and spiritual hunger are a few of the others that might be encompassed within a wider view. But *Future Shock* was silent upon them all.

As noted previously, the *Future Shock* thesis portrayed people as being "overwhelmed" by change to a point of widespread dysfunctionality that might prefigure widespread social breakdown. But "change" was seen as a wholly external force, rather than something that worked through specific social formations and through the structures and processes that maintain their interests. Such a diagnosis placed the onus for response rather too heavily upon these decontextualized and "shocked" individuals. At the same time, it overlooked the social entities that were (and remain) complicit in generating and sustaining "change." Overall, this was a disempowering approach that displaced autonomy from individuals and groups into poorly defined and shadowy social locations that could neither be readily located nor challenged.

Linked with this is the way that Toffler ascribed the prime responsibility for "rapid change" to "technology"—not to the agencies and powers that have the ability to define, focus, develop, market, and apply it. This misassignment was mystificatory in effect, though not, I am sure, in intent. While Toffler sought to encourage "social futurism" and "anticipatory democracy," he did so in a way that completely overlooked the difficulties people face in (a) understanding, and (b) attempting to intervene in their historical context.

The *Future Shock* thesis can be summarized as an expression of a journalistic view of macro-change from a very particular viewpoint in space and time. It foregrounded habits of perception characteristic of that time and attempted to universalize them. As noted, this framework certainly provided some useful suggestions for possible ways forward. But in practice, as an interpretive agenda it was unworkable. Ways of understanding, and coming to grips with, other dysfunctional imbalances in culture were conspicuously lacking. "Change" is only one of them. Meaninglessness, lack of purpose, hyper-materialism, technological narcissism, and spiritual hunger are a few of the others that might be encompassed within a wider view. But *Future Shock* was silent upon them all.

The Mindset of Early American Futurism

Early American futurist work based on *Future Shock*-type analyses was nothing if not ambitious. It attempted to monitor global trends (some of which were and are poorly understood), act as a societal early warning system, explore and illuminate a bewildering range of possibilities and choices, influence public and private decision-making in a multitude of contexts, and disseminate its ideas and conclusions as widely as possible. Its practitioners wanted to help "create the future."

In view of the enormity of these self-imposed tasks, there is a strong case for a low-key, self-effacing mode of discourse, hedged around with qualifications of various kinds. But when Edward Cornish wrote of the "great future that we all know is possible," he articulated a deeply felt and widely shared American attitude that "if we can create believable dreams of a better future world, then we can build for that world, for we live in an age when a peaceful, prosperous, and happy world is a genuine possibility." This view reflected a sense of optimism and power that was, perhaps, central to the American experience (Cornish 1980, 15-19). Another, much reprinted, paper exposed the darker side of this sensibility by concluding that "the only possible conclusion is a call to action." Along with, "the task is clear. The task is huge... time is horribly short... today the whole human experiment may hang on the question of how fast we now press for the development of a science for survival" (Platt 1973, 16).

Statements of this nature sprang from the same sources of self-understanding, concern, and limitation as *Future Shock*. They attempted to express the ideals and the fears of much of humankind. But, sympathize though we may, they simply did not travel well, and it is helpful to understand why. In these, and countless other cases, it was not always clear how, or in exactly what sense, people could begin to exert control over events or act to prevent threatened crises. Regardless of whether the view expressed was optimistic or pessimistic, whether the task was to create utopia or merely to avoid dystopia, something was missing.

People who were deeply involved in particular ways of life, values, logics-in-use, traditions, and so on—people whose worldviews differed in many substantial ways from those of futurists—were being asked to cooperate from a great social distance in a demanding series of more or less well-defined tasks that lacked both historical precedent and, so far as they were concerned, contemporary sanction. Thus, generalized "calls to action" were an ineffectual way to make progress. The implicit view of individuals and societies was an under-dimensioned one that glossed over more than was prudent of the substance of social life and social being.

As they did then, most people today realize that the future is inherently uncertain and conditional. Its relation to the present is complicated by a host of social, cultural, and ideological factors. The sense in which it may be "built" or "chosen" needs to be clarified in some detail by those with ideas about what it should be like. That this seldom happens is not really a comment upon individuals. It is founded on a universal dilemma. People who are necessarily embedded in their own historicity cannot readily aspire to the almost supernatural (or supra-historical) powers involved. As Radnitzky put it, "what is 'irrational' in human history is that men make their history but... do not know the history they make. They have not yet been able to make it with full consciousness" (Radnitzky 1972, 119). This is a dilemma facing anyone wishing to direct change. To avoid "future shock," to build a "science of survival" or to design a "peaceful, prosperous, and happy world" not only begs a number of very important questions, it also requires the development of more inclusive and enabling forms of consciousness and action.

> During the 1970s and 1980s the presentation of particular futures ideas—and indeed, of the futures field more generally—was marred by exaggeration, by a rather naive view of human capacities, and by over-optimism about the potential for social change.

Hence, during the 1970s and 1980s the presentation of particular futures ideas—and indeed, of the futures field more generally—was marred by exaggeration, by a rather naive view of human capacities, and by over-optimism about the potential for social change. Despite these drawbacks, the future shock thesis helped to stimulate a number of constructive social responses.

Future Shock as a Stimulus to Social Innovation

Toffler was dissatisfied with what he regarded as "technocratic" forms of decision-making and social administration. PPBS (planning, programming, budgeting systems) and a president's council set up by Nixon fell a long way short. He called rather for a "revolution" in the way long-term social goals were formulated. What he wanted was a "continuing plebiscite on the future." To this end he proposed the creation of what he called "social futures assemblies" throughout America, coupled with a range of social simulation exercises in schools.

Yet Toffler's vivid social imagination exceeded his practical grasp of what would be needed to enable such innovations. To read *Future Shock* several decades on is to be struck by the disjunction between the power of the vision and the poverty of means. The vision stimulated a number of attempts to set up such assemblies. For example, in Hawaii citizens were polled as to how they saw likely and desired futures. The results were summarized as scenarios in a newsletter and acted out on television. A television vote then followed. A book titled *Anticipatory Democracy* provided a showcase for ideas and experiments of this kind (Bezold 1978). So there is no doubt that *Future Shock* stimulated the social imagination. But most of Toffler's ideas needed a great deal more work before they could be put into practice.

Part of the explanation for the gulf between vision and applicability lies in Toffler's habit of privileging aspects of the outer empirical world (facts, trends, change processes) and overlooking the inner interpretive one (worldviews, paradigms, values, and social interests). In subsequent years, it became clear that carrying futures proposals from the realm of ideas into social action requires far more than a description of the organizational forms they might take. What Toffler, and indeed many futurists, overlooked is that *the futures domain is primarily a symbolic one*. To operate successfully within it requires a working familiarity with the language, concepts, and frameworks that support future-oriented modes of inquiry and action. While Toffler's research had provided him with an elaborate futures vocabulary and a rich store of futures-related ideas and proposals, most of those reading his work were unable to translate his proposals into action simply because they could not cross this symbolic gulf. To move from ideas to action in fact requires progress though several "layers of capability" which had not yet been described at that time. Thus the main drawback of the future shock thesis was that it did not help people find their way into that domain and hence discover the deeper sources of understanding and insight that Toffler had himself overlooked.

Toffler was equally adamant about the need for technology assessment—and in principle he was right. In the chapter "Taming Technology," he put forward the notion of a "technology ombudsman," a public agency that would investigate complaints about irresponsible applications of various technologies. A closely related idea was of an "environmental screen" that would assess the impacts of technologies before they were adopted. Companies would employ their own "consequence analysis staff" to carry out this kind of work. In both cases it is possible to see one of the starting points of the OTA (Office of Technology Assessment) that was established some years later (only to be axed by Reagan). Similarly, the environmental screen may be seen as a precursor of environmental impact statements, which later became common practice. In these cases, a generous interpretation of the role of *Future Shock* would see it as helping to popularize the need for such arrangements in a rapidly changing society.

> The point is to move away from a passive or fatalistic acceptance of an "unknown" future to an active and confident participation in creating positively desired futures.

On the other hand, since Toffler did not attempt a deeper analysis of the worldviews, presuppositions, ideologies, and embedded interests that were driving (and continue to drive) the global system, he was in a weak position to call into question the apparent inevitability of technological advance or to propose means of dealing with it at a constitutive level. Hence, his well-meaning suggestions were, in effect, outstripped by vastly more powerful forces.

Legend has it that in 1966 Toffler was involved in one of the first high school courses in futures studies. What is certainly the case is that a few years later he edited a wide-ranging book called *Learning for Tomorrow*, in which he collected articles by many future-oriented educators in the US. (Toffler 1974). The book displayed some of the early formulations of theory, practice, and self-understanding that later were incorporated into more durable approaches to futures education. While the book was by no means as successful as the earlier one, it achieved a significant readership in the US and elsewhere.

Toffler's ideas about future-oriented education certainly provided a stimulus to this hitherto neglected area. But, over time, it became increasingly clear that the foundations of futures in education were shaky. A close look at American classrooms during the 1970s and 1980s made it clear that innovative futures work had been successful in practical terms. But a search for durable underpinnings was fruitless for one very simple reason: there were none.

The pop-psychology approach taken by Toffler served to initiate, and perhaps to inspire, up to a point. But it could not nourish and support. Thus, during the time of Reagan and Thatcher, futures education initiatives were perceived to be inessential and were widely discarded. It would be some years before a more durable foundation would be constructed and a new wave of future-oriented educational work taken up by other hands and minds (Hicks and Slaughter 1998).

> The central challenge of futures studies, foresight work, and indeed, social and organizational decision-making in general, is to reveal the contours of this unacceptable world and to generate widespread social discussion about feasible alternatives.

The *Future Shock* saga provided a particular sort of thesis about social change, economic development, the role of technology, and, overall, the ways that organizations and individuals might begin to come to grips with them. But it did so in ways that failed to enable the very category of human agency that it sought to assist. Toffler went on to work on other projects: *The Third Wave, Powershift, War and Anti-War*, and the diminutive but ambitious paperback *Creating a New Civilization* (Toffler, A. and H. 1994). Perhaps the chief outcome of all this activity was to establish Toffler, and as time went by his wife Heidi also, as highly "mediagenic" futurists who not only earned a handsome living with their speculations and proposals, but also were sought out and promoted by politicians such as Newt Gingrich, one-time leader of the US House of Representatives. The path from public engagement and discipline building to lucrative private consulting is regrettable, but common. It helps to explain why futures studies have taken longer to advance than might have happened.

Development of Substantive Futures Inquiry

The field of futures studies has been described as:

> [A] field of intellectual and political activity concerning all sectors of the psychological, social, economic, political, and cultural life, aiming at discovering and mastering the extensions of the complex chains of causalities, by means of conceptualizations, systematic reflections, experimentations, anticipations, and creative thinking. Futures studies therefore constitute a natural basis for subnational, national, and international, and both interdisciplinary and transdisciplinary activities tending to become a new forum for the basis of political decision making (Masini and Samset 1975, 15).

Another definition was offered by Roy Amara in 1981. He saw it as an exploration of possible, probable, and preferable futures (Amara 1981, 25-29). However, by the 1990s it became more appropriate to consider it as an emerging "meta-discipline." "Meta-" because of the way it integrates material, data, ideas, tools, etc. from a wide variety of sources; and "discipline" because when done well it clearly supports disciplined inquiry into the constitution of human futures (Slaughter 1988, 372-385). By the end of the 1990s four main traditions, or paradigmatic ways of framing and approaching futures work, were defined. These were as follows:

- **The empirical/analytic tradition.** This is basically data-driven, positivistic, often corporate and hence identified most strongly with North American sources. The names of Herman Kahn and Julian Simon are often identified with this approach.
- **The critical/comparative tradition.** This is a more socially critical approach which recognizes different approaches to knowledge and its use, and different social interests. It takes a more comparative approach and is linked with this writer, Hazel Henderson, and Sohail Inayatullah, among others.
- **The activist/participatory tradition.** This is very much about facilitation and activism. Hence it has links with some of the social movements that are close to futures studies, such as the peace, women's, and environmental movements. The approach is expressed most directly in workshop formats such as those created and implemented by Robert Jungk, Elise Boulding, Warren Zieglar, and Joanna Macy.
- **The multicultural/global tradition.** This more recent approach springs from the emergence from many non-Western contexts of futures studies and its underlying concerns. It has been supported by UNESCO and by courses run in various countries by the World Futures Studies Federation. Those associated with this arena include Zia Sardar, Tony Stevenson, and Sohail Inayatullah, as well as a growing number of non-Western futurists.

Besides these four traditions, or paradigms, of futures work, there are also a number of substantive levels at which this work can take place (Slaughter 1993). These include the following:

- **Pop futurism.** This is trite, superficial work. It is media-friendly and often seen in weekend newspaper supplements and on brief television features. It is summed up by statements such as "how science and technology are improving our lives and creating the future." This is the world of the fleeting image and the transient sound bite. It is eminently marketable, but bereft of theory. It arguably detracts from "real" futures work (that is, work with useful social consequences).
- **Problem-oriented work.** This is more serious work. It looks at the ways that societies and organizations are responding, or should respond, to the challenges of the near-term future. So it is largely about social rules and regulations. It emerges most typically in, for example, environmental legislation and organizational innovations, particularly in business—which often gives the impression of being "stranded" at this level.
- **Critical futures studies.** Critical work attempts to "probe beneath the surface" of social life and to discern some of the deeper processes of meaning-making, paradigm formation, and the active influence of obscured worldview commitments (for example, "growth is good" and "nature is merely a set of utilitarian resources"). It uses the tools and insights that have emerged within the humanities and which allow us to "interrogate" and critique the symbolic foundations of social life, and—this is the real point—hence to discern the grounds of new, or renewed, options. Properly understood, the deconstructive and reconstructive aspects of high-quality futures work balance each other in a productive fusion of methods.
- **Epistemological futures work.** Here is where futures studies merge into the foundational areas that feed into the futures enterprise and provide part of its substantive basis. Hence philosophy, ontology, macro-history, the study of time, cosmology, and other disciplines are all relevant at this deep level.

Thus, the field of futures studies has developed breadth and depth over the last several decades. It is now a globally distributed meta-discipline taught in a number of universities and which increasingly figures in strategic decision-making, policy debates, and the emergence of social innovations. In essence, it provides interpretative or propositional knowledge about the future, updates this regularly, assesses the quality of emerging understandings, and uses them for a range of socially useful purposes. When *Future Shock* was first published such claims could not have been supported, whereas today they are a reality—a fact demonstrated by work such as Wendell Bell's two-volume opus *The Foundations of Futures Studies* (Bell 1996) in the *Knowledge Base of Futures Studies* series (Slaughter 1996).

Drawing on such sources, futurists "study the future" or "construct forward views." In so doing they open out the future as a symbolically and practically significant realm. The discernment of in-depth understanding from these processes enables us to identify options and choices in the present. The point is to move away from a passive or fatalistic acceptance of an "unknown" future to an active and confident participation in creating positively desired futures. Most futurists believe that the future can be shaped by the careful and responsible exercise of human will and effort. Futurists differ in many of their views, but most agree that individuals, organizations, and cultures that attempt to move into the future blindly are taking unnecessary risks. They support the proposition that we need to understand and apply foresight in our private, public, and professional lives.

From Future Shock to Social Foresight

Future Shock was the attempt of one individual to come to terms with change. But building the disciplines of futures studies and strategic foresight is quintessentially a group process involving many actors in many different places. The progression from individual to social capacity is crucial, and there are four "layers of capability" that can lead us there:

- **The brain/mind system.** Human beings are reflexive creatures and their frame of reference embraces past, present, and future. The ability to think ahead is grounded in this biological inheritance. People use foresight informally every day of their lives. This means that we do not have to introduce some new capacity, but merely upgrade an existing one.

- **Futures concepts to enable a futures discourse.** Students who take futures courses for the first time find that the language of futures studies and foresight practice opens up the futures domain so that it becomes a symbolically vital realm of understanding and action. Futures literacy is created by active immersion in the material and the process of considering this with others. From this process emerges a distinct futures discourse that enables the forward view.

> When that framework has been problematized by postmodernism, mass media saturation, and the rise of compulsive global merchandising, it is legitimate to ask if the human race is in the process of undermining itself.

- **Futures methodologies and tools.** Discourse *per se* has its limitations. In order to engage with real-world projects, statistics, and extended problem analysis (such as the siting of a new road, airport, or power utility) a variety of methodologies are used. Forecasting was once chief among these, but the focus has shifted toward scenarios and strategic decision-making. These are two of a much wider set of methods that permit us to extend the discourse into new domains and to tackle complex, extended problems.

■ **Applications of futures work in purpose-built organizations or "niches."** But even with all three of the above "layers of capability" functioning in concert, still there would be something missing. Futures work would merely be episodic, rising and falling with demand. So the final step is to embed such work in purpose-built organizational niches, or in what I call IOFs or "institutions of foresight."

With applied foresight work occurring in this powerfully grounded way in many social locations in organizations of all kinds, we may reasonably expect to see the beginnings of social foresight. In systems language it would be an "emergent capacity" of all this activity (Slaughter 1996a). Thus, future shock has been superseded by more structured and disciplined approaches to the creation of applied social foresight.

Futures Studies, Cyberculture, and the "Real" Future

Long-term immersion in the futures domain means that the future is no longer seen merely as an empty space or a blank screen upon which the concerns of the present are projected. It takes on positive symbolic content. One way to get a rapid impression of futures in prospect is to pose a number of key questions and then look for high-quality answers. For example:
■ What are the main continuities?
■ What are the main trends?
■ What are the most important change processes?
■ What are the most serious problems?
■ What are the new factors in the pipeline?
■ What are the key sources of inspiration and hope? (Slaughter 1996b).

In-depth answers to such questions begin to reveal the contours of the "real" future from the viewpoint of a particular observer/interpreter. One such reading is as follows: The globalization process is driven by powerful transnational corporations in pursuit of abstract goals such as growth, innovation, profit, and shareholder value. These processes are not linked with any notion of social need or human value. Indeed, they have many negative human, social, and environmental impacts. They are stimulating the too-rapid development of a series of technological revolutions that threaten to destabilize all human civilizations and societies. Thus, in a nutshell, the most likely future for humankind at this point is a radically diminished one in a world that is mined out, depleted, polluted, and overwhelmed by technologies that we can neither see nor control. (See Broderick 1997 for an overview of the latter).

The central challenge of futures studies, foresight work, and indeed, social and organizational decision-making in general, is to reveal the contours of this unacceptable world and to generate widespread social discussion about feasible alternatives.

Alternatively, we can turn the problem on its head and ask: what are the contours of the next level of civilization, the one beyond the mental/egoic, capitalist/late industrial world of the early 21st century? More simply: how might a more positive future be framed?

Remarkably enough, there is a great deal of high-quality material that deals with these generic alternatives. The work of transpersonal synthesist Ken Wilber is helpful here. Wilber establishes an interpretive framework based on a "four quadrant" view of evolution. The four quadrants cover the following areas (Wilber 1996):
■ **The inner individual world.** This is the inner world of reference of each person. It gives access to identity, feelings, emotions, ideas, meaning, and purpose. It provides an overview of individual stages of development.

- **The outer individual world.** This is the human being as known to science. It refers to those aspects that can be directly observed or measured. It comprises the structures and functions that enable biological life and awareness.
- **The outer collective world.** This is the rest of the external world as known to science, engineering, architecture, and so on. It embraces the external natural world and the infrastructure of the built environment.
- **The inner collective world.** This is quintessentially the world of reference of stages of social development, of worldviews, languages, professions, and the like.

Through an elegant usage of these distinctions, Wilber has established four profiles of evolutionary development and a method for understanding the likely "deep structure" of civilizations beyond the present one. This is possible because evolution continues in each of the four quadrants along a partly known path. Hence a post-postindustrial world would likely be a world that strove for balance between its different parts. It would be a multi-leveled world, post-materialist but not anti-technological. Rather, technology would be required to adapt and "fit" clearly articulated human and social values. The main environmental ethic would be a commitment to stewardship. There could also be a re-spiritualization of worldviews and outlooks, as well as a distinct increase in the conscious capabilities of people and organizations.

The foregoing provides a context in which technology, cyberculture and "the future" can be looked at afresh. Various writers have speculated on the existence of a "discontinuity" ahead as the overlapping developments in biotech, AI, robotics, the miniaturization of computing, and nanotechnology create wave after wave of disorienting change that can't possibly be modeled (Broderick 1997). Some speculate on the "uploading" of human consciousness into enormously sophisticated computer substrates and the potential for machine intelligence to overtake our own redundant biological models (Kurzweil 1999). But from the viewpoint outlined here these responses seem indistinguishable from technological narcissism. In this view parts of the human system become split off from the whole and lead directly to dystopian nightmare futures.

Thus, a central concern for cyberculture is that it skates so perilously close both to technological narcissism on the one hand and to nihilism on the other. The exploration of cyberspace, various "unreal worlds" by Gibson and his successors, would be less of a concern in the context of a shared moral and epistemological framework. But when that framework has been problematized by postmodernism, mass media saturation, and the rise of compulsive global merchandising, it is legitimate to ask if the human race is in the process of undermining itself.

> A more balanced view suggests that the "real" future is not primarily about technology at all. Rather, it centrally involves a search for new definitions of our shared humanity.

That, perhaps, is the core meaning of the highly popular movie *The Matrix* (Slaughter 2001). At least three readings of the film are possible. One is a straight science fiction plot posing standard questions about "the real" and the possibilities of technological domination. Another is an extended homage to the action film/comic genre, albeit with some novel features (such as genuinely meditative scenes and a hero who transcends genre limitations). A third reading is to see *The Matrix* as a compelling postmodern fable, but one whose images, themes, and story lines lack coherence. Which resonates most directly with our hopes and fears for the future? All, or none? *The Matrix* poses many questions but answers few of them.

Conclusion

In the late 19th century, a suite of cigarette cards was commissioned in Paris on "life in the year 2000" (Asimov 1986). It explored the universal applications of mechanical lever technology, the leading-edge technology of the time. In the early 21st century levers have all but disappeared. It is the computer that is now projected willy-nilly upon the future, along with all its manifestations. Yet we already know that the computer, as such, will steadily disappear from our desks into the virtual world of universal information appliances (Norman 1999).

For most of those involved in futures studies and applied foresight, however, the future is not about massive computing, AI, and a vastly expanded internet. These compose only a fragment of Wilber's broad four-quadrant view. The over-identification of technology with the future is a long-standing bias within Western culture. A more balanced view suggests that the "real" future is not primarily about technology at all. Rather, it centrally involves a search for new definitions of our shared humanity. In that context, Vernor Vinge's "singularity" and Damien Broderick's "spike" provide only a partial view, because they deal only with externalities. That is, they primarily focus on the outer collective domain and largely overlook the inner ones that are involved in the constitution of human and cultural significance. Similarly, Toffler's future shock thesis was partly helpful (in proposing social innovations) and partly diversionary (because it focused on external change, and missed the shaping power of self-reference possessed by all human beings).

Since the 1970s, people all over the world have become aware of the need to anticipate likely futures, to avoid undesirable ones, and to take greater responsibility for the direction of change. Many individuals have contributed to this process. Thus, Toffler's early formulations have been superseded by the development of futures studies as a discipline and the emergence of applied social foresight. The latter may be defined as "the construction and maintenance of high quality forward views and their application in organizationally useful ways."[1] Progress through the four layers of capability previously outlined suggest that social foresight will develop over time. It will be an "emergent capacity" of widespread human effort. The hitherto obscured futures domain will then become an integral part of everyday thinking, life, and work. Society's views of its likely futures will become thoroughly integrated into its present. Instead of falling into dystopia we will see the emergence of "deep design" in every field and a true flowering of human hope and aspiration.

It is for such reasons that shared attempts to develop more highly evolved forms of society and consciousness seem primary: a constructive approach to engaging with the "real" future has more to do with the pursuit of wisdom than the pursuit of, or avoidance of, any technological capability whatsoever. A possible resolution, however, is that both can be included in a higher-order synthesis. Hence the keys to the future lie in seeking a balance between different aspects of humanity in its world: inner, outer, individual, and collective (Wilber 1996). ▨

Note: An earlier version of this article was first published in Tofts, D. et al, Eds, *Prefiguring Cyberculture: An Intellectual History*, Power Institute Foundation for Arts and Visual Culture, Sydney, 2002 on the occasion of *Future Shock*'s 30th anniversary.

---

1. Australian Foresight Institute flyer (Melbourne: Swinburne University, 2000).

From 1999-2004, **Prof. Richard Alan Slaughter** was Foundation Professor of Foresight at Swinburne University of Technology, Melbourne. From 2004 he was co-director of Foresight International, Brisbane. He has worked with a wide range of organizations in many countries and at all educational levels. He completed a PhD on *Critical Futures Studies and Curriculum Renewal* at the University of Lancaster in 1982. He has since built a solid international reputation through futures scholarship, educational innovation, strategic foresight, and the identification of a knowledge base for futures studies. He is a prolific writer and holds several editorial positions. He has received professional recognition from several sources including being voted in 2010 "one of the best all-time Futurists" by members of the Foresight Network, Shaping Tomorrow. He also received three "Most Important Futures Works" awards from the Association of Professional Futurists. These are for *The Knowledge Base of Futures Studies, Professional Edition*, CD-ROM, 2005; a special issue of *Futures* on *Integral Futures Methodologies* in 2008 and in 2012 for *The Biggest Wake-Up Call in History*. Other notable works include *The Foresight Principle* (London: Adamantine Press, 2004) *Futures for the Third Millennium: Enabling the Forward View* (Sydney: Prospect, 1999) *Futures Beyond Dystopia: Creating Social Foresight* (London: Routledge, 2004), and *To See With Fresh Eyes: Integral Futures and the Global Emergency* (Brisbane: Foresight International, 2012). Web: foresightinternational.com.au. Weblog: richardslaughter.com.au.

References

Amara, R. 1981. The futures field 1: Searching for definitions and boundaries. *Futurist* 15(1):25-29.

Asimov, I. 1986. *Futuredays: A Nineteenth-century Vision of the Year 2000*. London: Virgin.

Bell, W. 1996. *Foundations of Futures Studies*. Vol. 1 and 2. New Brunswick: Transaction Publications.

Bezold, C. (ed.). 1978. *Anticipatory Democracy*. New York: Vintage.

Broderick, D. 1997. *The Spike: Accelerating into an Unimaginable Future*. Melbourne: Reed Books.

Cornish, E. 1980. Creating a better future: The role of the world future society. *The Futurist* 14(5):15-19.

Cross, N. (ed.). 1974. *Man Made Futures*. London: Hutchinson.

Hicks, D. and R. Slaughter (eds.) 1998. *Futures Education*. World yearbook of education, London: Kogan Page.

Kurzweil, R. 1999. *The Age of Spiritual Machines*. Sydney: Allen & Unwin.

Masini, E. and Samset, K. 1975. Recommendations of the WFSF General Assembly, *WFSF Newsletter* June:15.

Norman, D. 1999. *The Invisible Computer*. Cambridge, MA: MIT Press.

Platt, J. 1973. What we must do. In *Search for Alternatives*, ed. F. Tugwell. XX City of publication: Winthrop.

Radnitzky 1972. *Contemporary Schools of Metascience*. Goteborg: Akademiforlaget.

Slaughter, R. 1988. Futures studies as an intellectual and applied discipline. *American Behavioral Scientist* 42(3):372-385.

------. 1993. Looking for the real megatrends. *Futures* 25(8):827-849.

------. (ed.) 1996. *The Knowledge Base of Futures Studies*. Vols 1-3. Melbourne: Futures Study Centre.

------. 1996a. Futures studies: From individual to social capacity. *Futures* 28(8):751-762.

------. 1996b. Mapping the future. *Journal of Futures Studies* 1(1):5-26.

------. 2001. Review of *The Matrix*. *Futures* 33 (8): 209-212.

Toffler, A. 1970 *Future shock*. London: Bodley Head, Reprinted 1972. London: Pan Books.

------ (ed.) 1974. *Learning for Tomorrow*. New York: Vintage.

Toffler, A. and H. 1994. *Creating a New Civilization*. Atlanta: Turner Publishing.

Wilber, K. 1996. *A Brief History of Everything*. Melbourne: Hill of Content.

Winner, L. 1986. *The Whale and the Reactor*. Chicago: University of Chicago Press.

Using The Future In Different Waves

Sohail Inayatullah

My first exposure to Futures Studies came from a class by Dr. Frank Shephard at the International School of Kuala Lumpur in 1974. I would have been in 11th grade. He showed us a short film by Alvin Toffler. In it, a couple walk romantically through a forest. The music is soft, serene. We are unable to see the faces of the couple, until suddenly they turn around and we discover that they are in fact robots. I was stunned. This was my first visual representation of a disruptive future. I was, however, prepared, as in the previous year back at the International School of Islamabad, I had spent a semester devouring science fiction, from Bradbury to Asimov to Zamyatin. But the future was always another world. Now with this short film, the future had become *this* world, *my* world.

My second encounter with Toffler was through his book, *The Adaptive Corporation* (1985). I was working at the Hawaii Judiciary as a futures researcher, as part of an internship from the University of Hawaii Masters program in Alternative Futures, where we learned with administrators and judges about how to use the future to understand how the world was changing and how the judiciary could anticipate changing judicial needs.

Toffler's message, of course, was prescient. He perceived the restructuring that American businesses were beginning to undergo as part of the massive shift from the second wave—the industrial era—to the third wave, the post-industrial. His brilliant but simple point was that corporations were applying industrial ways of thinking and doing to post-industrial problems. They were living in a world of "used futures"—practices that no longer work but persist because of institutional habit—a mismatch between the past and the emerging future.

In my review of his work, I summarized it this way: "Toffler writes that instead of being routine and predictable, the corporate environment—social, political, demographic, economic—has become increasingly accelerative, unstable, and revolutionary. To deal with this new environment, corporations need adaptive managers who can cope with nonlinear, discontinuous changes. These new managers must, instead of constructing permanent edifices, deconstruct their companies to maximize maneuverability. They must be experts, not in bureaucracy, but in coordinating adhocracies. The adaptive manager must also be able to forecast future trends, and reconceptualize basic missions, structures, procedures, products, and programs. As a first rule for corporations attempting to survive, Toffler believes that nothing is more dangerous than yesterday's success. That is, what worked during the Second Wave Industrial era will lead to failure in the emerging Third Wave, Post-Industrial world."[1]

I stayed on at the Hawaii Judiciary another two years and then moved to Australia as a post-doctoral fellow. Since then, in Australia, Europe, and Asia, I have been working to help nations, cities, institutions, organizations, and individuals respond to the challenges Toffler posed decades ago. During this time, I have also worked to make sense of hundreds of interventions designed to reduce "future shock" and enhance futures literacy, to ensure that we all can optimize our ability to co-create alternative and preferred futures.

While Toffler's approach was general and highly focused on the American context, the approach I developed differentiates and attempts to articulate a stage theory of using the future. It is derived from the "six pillars" approach to the future. In this participatory method, the first pillar involves mapping the future. Participants map out the current state of an issue, addressing the pushes of the present, the pulls of the future, and the weights of the past. The second pillar is focused on anticipation, asking, "What's next?" It uses the S curve to explore current problems, trends, and emerging issues. The search for novel problems or opportunities are critical here. The third pillar takes macrohistory seriously and examines grand theories of social change. Is the change in question linear, cyclical, spiral, or pendulum-based? The fourth pillar deepens a sense of the future, going beyond the litany of daily events and disconnected realities to move deeper into systemic causes, worldviews, perspectives, and foundational metaphors and myths. This is done at both collective and individual levels. After the deep dive, scenarios are used to explore alternatives. The sixth and final pillar is transformation. Here there is focus on the *preferred* future; using techniques such as backcasting, anticipatory action learning, and strategic planning, the vision is made "real."

This six-stage process borrows heavily from the work of Jim Dator, Elise Boulding,[2] Michel Foucault,[3] P.R. Sarkar,[4] Graham Molitor,[5] and Ivana Milojević.[6] It is a structured, step by step approach to the future designed to move an individual, an organization, an institution, a city, a country, or a multi-lateral group from where they are today to imagining a set of tomorrows and preferred futures. It includes both "inner work"—who and what

> His brilliant but simple point was that corporations were applying industrial ways of thinking and doing to post-industrial problems. They were living in a world of "used futures"—practices that no longer work but persist because of institutional habit.

does the individual wish to be in their desired future?—and "external work"—what is the nature of the world they wish to create?

As I conduct these workshops, participants invariably want to know the best methods for different situations. Do they, for example, need to go step by step through the six pillars or are certain methods more appropriate for certain groups or situations? When a CEO or board chair asks me to conduct a process, I will ask them a number of clarifying questions. For example, "When individuals leave the room at the end of the day, what do you wish their cognitive and emotional states to be?" Typical responses include, "I want them to be excited about the possibility of a new future." "I want everyone to be aware of the challenges ahead." "I need to get them out of the day-to-day rut—they are too busy with things that don't really matter." Or, "They see issues from only one perspective; I need for them to expand their worldview." "We have no direction or strategy—we need a way forward." "We understand that if we don't disrupt ourselves, others will disrupt us." "We think in terms of one future; I need to get all of us to think of alternatives." All are interesting objectives that do, in fact, help bring focus to the most appropriate pillars.

> For those in power or control of their markets, foresight is about using the future to mitigate against external situations where profits, power, social capital—"the loot"—are threatened.

To these ends, I have developed the following step-by-step guide. It is a move toward a theory—at the very least a conceptual framework—of using the future. While this approach is insight- and case study-based, I have few quantitative impact studies to "prove" its claims,[7] even though correlation and causation are implied.[8] And while there is a natural progression to the various stages, linearity is not required—one can move freely among them as appropriate, given the success or failure of a particular futures thinking/practice intervention.

Social Injustice—Its Not Fair

In my work—and with a hundred-plus colleagues[9]—I have come to identify Stage One with the state of social injustice, the perception that reality is not fair. Individuals and collectivities are best served by a focus on theories of social change—understanding that their states are not fixed. Ibn Khaldun[10] reminds us that all systems ascend and decline, and thus, while one group may today be at the bottom, they may be on top later. Sorokin suggests that systems sway back and forth in a pendulum motion, between centralization and decentralization, for example; or between a concern for inclusion—"soft" solutions—in infrastructure planning and "hard" engineering solutions.

Risk Mitigation

For those in power or control of their markets, foresight is about using the future to mitigate against external situations where profits, power, social capital—"the loot"—are threatened. I find that with this group, while the big picture provided by macrohistory is important, there is little regard for grand patterns of change, for the *longue duree'*; rather, it is events and issues that could potentially disrupt their business model that are most important.

Molitor's Emerging Issues Analysis[11] is the most important method in this phase. The S curve helps organizations understand that they are too focused on current problems and have not spent enough time identifying future risks. Once this is done, the implications of these risks can be teased out with a futures wheel. Following that, new areas of opportunity can be explored, helping the organization move from what it is good today to new capabilities for tomorrow. Often I explore the structural implications of the vegan[12] and plant-based food revolution, as well as the in-vitro meat-based revolution (cellular agriculture).[13] This challenges the worldviews of departments of agriculture and those in the food business. These new products and the cultural shift they represent—new science, new tastes—can be seen either as a threat or as an opportunity.

Alternative Futures

To progress from the risk mitigation stage, it is crucial to acknowledge risk aversion, and then slowly shift toward possible opportunities. Data orientation, e.g., quantitative evidence to back up any possible futures, is critical as decision-makers will not support a project based on intuition or hunches. Examples or case studies of other nations, cities, organizations, and persons having used futures thinking successfully are crucial for conceptual movement to occur.

In projects with national and state libraries, for example, we used alternative futures thinking to navigate out of their budgetary crises. In the first potential scenario considered, there was no change, thus leading to a world where librarians become "digital dinosaurs," with the median age of both librarians and patrons increasing and book lending decreasing. In the second scenario, the libraries became centers for digital downloads. The participants imagined holograms meeting citizens as they entered the library, and guiding them on their information journeys. In a third future, space became crucial. In this world, libraries transferred their key performance indicators from "books loaned" to "people engaged." The library now ran seminars and conducted workshops, targeting the youth and the elderly; they became innovation centers where patrons learn about new technologies. In the fourth and final scenario, libraries advanced from being knowledge consumers to knowledge *creators*. In this future, the libraries have become publishing houses, serving their respective communities and markets.[14]

Directionality

Once alternative futures are explored, insights into the range of directions are gained. But which direction? This is next crucial part of the foresight process. Scenarios help clarify alternatives, but once there is clarity of costs and benefits, of desires and fears, there needs to be a decision as to what is next. Where do we wish to be in a decade, or two decades? The vision is crucial as it becomes the decisive indicator of what should be done in the present. Does a current decision align with these goals? Directionality is critical to harness both personal and organizational energies.

> Without deep citizen involvement, innovation is difficult since inclusion has not occurred. In successful projects, Toffler's anticipatory democracy is actually created.

"Visioning" is particularly valuable when participants understand their zone of control—what they can influence and what they cannot. Cities are perfect examples of this. They have budgets and influence, but generally of the size where policy and strategy can actually make a difference. In a number of Australian cities, we have embarked on 2030, 2040 projects.[15] These have worked well when we included three parties: citizens through foresight workshops; political, business, and community leaders through visioning and strategy sessions; and academics and research organizations to collect data on the past, and emerging trends and indicators of the desired future. Without this triangulation, the vision can be overly utopian. Elected officials then lose interest, as they need to gain re-election to ensure the success of the implementation process. Without solid data, there is no benchmarking by which to measure success and failure, and help "right the ship" when there are setbacks. Without deep citizen involvement, innovation is difficult since inclusion has not occurred. In successful projects, Toffler's anticipatory democracy[16] is actually created.[17] Vision and budget have become linked, risks mitigated, opportunities created, and civic energy enhanced. Ultimately, visioning is a victory of agency over structure, of what *can be* over what is.

Making The Vision Real

Visions without reality can quickly reduce agency. Visioning can be a direction, linked to the strategic plan. Visioning can be personalized, creative visualization, imagining a different future. But, visioning can also be fantasy, a way of avoiding what is painful, what needs to be understood and discarded. Visioning as avoidance hurts the futures process.[18]

Thus, to continue along the path of using the future to *empower*, we need to make the vision real, to allow the vision to enable and ennoble.

A number of processes help. Most significant are action learning, strategic plans, backcasting, and personal ownership of the future.

Action learning seeks to link the vision of the future with individuals using open space technology[19] to design projects and processes to create a difference. In one project on rural health futures, over 50 CEOs met to design a new health system. Over two days, they imagined the 5P health model.[20] This consists of moving toward: (1) Prevention (exercise, meditation, early check ups); (2) Precision/personalized medicine; (3) Predictive health; (4) Participation (patients designing their health journey); and (5) Partnership (all agencies working together).

Done well, this vision would dramatically reduce costs. It would do so by focusing on individuals in the context of their communities, using advanced genomics medicine to tailor health solutions for the individual, predicting an individual's health pathway, working with patients so they can participate in their health decisions, and creating health systems that work in partnership with each other.

> To continue along the path of using the future to empower, we need to make the vision real, to allow the vision to enable and ennoble.

This approach challenges the generic, silo based, problem-solving hospital health model. While the vision was brilliant, there was concern that this was too far in the future. How could we move forward more quickly?

To this end, the future becomes more real—filled out—through the Causal Layered Analysis (CLA)[21] process. In the CLA process, the current reality is deconstructed at four levels. The first is the litany—the current measurement of reality, the current discourse. The system or the causative variables that create the litany are then debated. From there the underlying worldview or worldviews are mapped. Finally, the underlying metaphor that supports the entire narrative is discovered. From here, the preferred future is developed by articulating the new metaphor, the new worldview, the new system (comprising technology, society, regulations), the new litany, and the new preferred measurement system.

The Narrative

Once the vision starts to become real, we need to ensure that culture does not, as Peter Drucker claimed, eat strategy for breakfast. In my experience, here lies the power of story—particularly of metaphors that help support the new vision, personal or collective.

We have argued in other of our works that narrative is important[22]—indeed, decisive in policymaking and strategy. Narrative is based on metaphor. "The metaphor," Spanish philosopher José Ortega y Gasset wrote, "is perhaps one of man's most fruitful potentialities. [...] Its efficacy verges on magic."[23]

How one uses metaphor can define the results that are created.[24] As we know from many studies, if crime is described as a beast, there is greater likelihood of subjects arguing for jails and punishment. If presented as a virus, the policy result is more likely to be increased funding for education and poverty eradication. [25]

In the USA, if a lawmaker argues for "welfare," interest in the legislative bill drops dramatically.[26] If one suggests "charity for the poor," interest goes up. The welfare discourse creates the image of the person who does not work hard, indeed, games the system, while the framing as charity suggests the innocent poor who genuinely need help.

> Returning to the example of the future of libraries, librarians understood that the old story of "the keepers of the collection" was now a used metaphor. They needed to tell a different story about who they were and could be.

Returning to the example of the future of libraries, librarians understood that the old story of "the keepers of the collection" was now a used metaphor. They needed to tell a different story about who they were and could be. In one state, a group suggested, "Innovators of the new gardens." For them, this meant they were active, exploring and defining the new spaces of learning, information, and knowledge.

Here's another example. A large energy utility sought to identify emerging risks and possibilities. However, when it came time to actually innovate, they were hesitant. When we explored why, it became clear that their deep narrative held them back. They viewed themselves as a large ship—the Queen Mary—with little need to change. After all, they had a state monopoly. So while they recognized a need for change, at the narrative level they really did not believe they would—or even should. The Queen—the Crown—does not change; others do.

Given this reality, we articulated a metaphor that resonated: the Queen Mary ship, with launches and patrol boats venturing forth and bringing back information about distant lands. The first patrol boat was a project on smart homes, learning how to ensure that each home had real time information on water, electricity and gas use. Another patrol went further, traveling beyond the horizon. It investigated homes as energy producers. A third patrol boat explored additive printing and energy. What would be the energy implications if each home, a group of homes, or even a neighborhood, used 3D printers? These research projects were intended as action learning experiments providing the mother ship real time information on directional change. [27]

The Mantra

The foregoing process assumes that we know our future best, that our rational mind, the choosing self, is wise. In the final stage, we move from the rational basis to the post-rational or the intuitive. Developed by the mystic Dada Pranakrsnananda,[28] this process uses mantra—or the sound that transforms—to intuit the new metaphor. [29] Mantra becomes therapeutic, argues Dada.[30]

The mantra process integrates and creates a new story for the participant—at a personal, individual level. The technical aspects of the process are quite simple. First, the CLA of the self process is undertaken. Then, using either the old or new metaphor, the participant listens to a sacred sound—a mantra contextual to his or her life experience. (For those challenged by the notion of the sacred, then the sound of "breathe in, breathe out" can be used.) Once metaphor and mantra are juxtaposed, a new image, a new metaphor can often emerge. This then becomes the *pull* of the future, the new way forward. We then seek to develop systemic suggestions to support the new story.

> The mantra process helps imagine a new future, an authentic future. It adds an emotional dimension to the rational act of creating alternative and preferred futures. It moves the participant to see and act differently in the present.

A leadership consultant used the process with these results. Her effort was to link her three passions: (1) leadership for all, the masses; (2) leadership for activists who wished to transform the world, not just optimize performance; and (3) leadership for women in science, technology, engineering, and management. In the first, her metaphor was "behind the curtain." In the second, it was the "harbinger." The third was the "mirror." These three strategies reflected her three selves, as well. When she imagined these metaphors and connected them to mantra, the new metaphor that emerged was the "walking stick." For her, this was the "tool through which grace could flow." It was a tool she could use to support her three narrative strategies.

The mantra process helps imagine a new future, an authentic future. It adds an emotional dimension to the rational act of creating alternative and preferred futures. It moves the participant to see and act differently in the present. The process can take time. [31]

Conclusion: Be the Future You Wish to See

The futures journey has both external and internal processes. It certainly has stages and states, phases, and realizations. In my experience, a person or community experiencing injustice might find visioning and metaphor interesting, but another aspect of their core selves might not find it relevant. An external systemic shift to reduce unfairness is required, or possibly, theories that suggest such a reduction is possible might increase relevance. Or perhaps a narrowing of the grand vision to one's zone of control is necessary; otherwise visioning or scenarios might seem fanciful or impractical, thinking that leads nowhere.

But when progress is made, the world is, or is perceived to be, fairer. Participants then often seek to reduce risk to the new system they have created. Once risk is mitigated, there is a desire to grow, to enhance possibilities. As Dada Pranakrsnananda has suggested, "The mind wants more, indeed, more is the metaphor of the mind."[32] With this comes the need to explore alternative futures, to test each future for robustness, to get out of the single solution box. From here, we can empower the individual using the preferred future. The vision imagined, however, without a process to create the new reality, can lead to despair or cynicism.

Our task as futurists, then, is to help link the vision to the day-to-day reality. The vision can become meaningful and real through action learning, backcasting, the processes of internal and external change, and metaphor. Working together, these methods serve to shift the narrative, which explains, gives insights to new worlds, and allows seeds of change to flourish. Ultimately, however, any collective is composed of *individuals*. It is *we* who must change. We are the culture. To these ends, metaphor and mantra can play a vital role in helping individuals manifest the future they wish to see. ▨

Professor **Sohail Inayatullah** is the first Unesco Chair in Futures Studies held at USIM, Malaysia. For 19 years, he has been a professor at Tamkang University, Taiwan. He is also an associate at Melbourne Business School, the University of Melbourne, and adjunct professor at the University of the Sunshine Coast. He is the Director of Metafuture.org, an international think-tank focused on creating alternative and preferred futures. Professor Inayatullah has authored/edited thirty books, journal special issues and cdroms, and over 350 journal articles and book chapters. His recent books include, Asia 2038: Ten Disruptions That Change Everything and Transformation 2050: The Alternative Futures of Malaysian Universities.

1. Sohail Inayatullah, "Power, wealth, prestige, and control: Review of Alvin's Toffler's The Adaptive Corporation," *Futures*, February 1988, 102-105.

2. Elise Boulding and Kenneth Boulding, *The Future: Images and Processes*, London, Sage, 1995.

3. Michel Foucault, *The Foucault Reader*, ed. Paul Rabinow, New York, Pantheon Books, 1984.

4. P.R. Sarkar, *The Human Society*, Kolkata AMPS, 1984.

5. Graham Molitor, *The Power to Change the World: The Art of Forecasting*, Potomac, MD, Public Policy Forecasting, 2004.

6. Ivana Milojević , *Educational Futures: Dominant and Contesting Visions*, London, Routledge, 2005.

7. Rene' Rohrbeck and Menes Etingue Kum, Corporate foresight and its impact on firm performance: a longitudinal analysis," Journal of Technological Forecasting and Social Change. Vol. 129, 2018, 105-116. For more recent quantitative work, see: *Jeanne Hoffman. "Imagining 2060: A Cross-Cultural Comparison of University Students' Perspectives", Journal of Futures Studies, Vol. 23, No. 4, 2019, 63-78; Kuo-hua Chen,"Transforming Environmental Values for a Younger Generation in Taiwan: A Participatory Action Approach to Curriculum Design, "Journal of Futures Studies, Vol. 23, No. 4, 2019,79-96. Also the qualitative research by Patricia Kelly. See her book, Towards Globo Sapiens: Transforming learners in higher education*, Rotterdam, Sense Publishers, 2008. Also see: Iris Pauw et al, "Students's Ability to Envision Scenarios of Urban Futures", Journal of Futures Studies, Vol. 23, No. 2, 2018, 45-65.

8. Sohail Inayatullah, "Rethinking Science: P.R. Sarkar's Reconstruction of Science and Society", IFDA. April/June 1991, 5-16.

9. At Melbourne Business School, the University of Melbourne; Tamkang University, Taiwan; the University of the Sunshine Coast; the Metafuture.org network; the Asia-Pacific Futures Network, for example.

10. For more on macrohistory, see Johan Galtung and Sohail Inayatullah, *Macrohistory and Macrohistorians*, Westport, Ct. Praeger, 1997.

11. Graham Molitor, "Molitor Forecasting Model," Journal of Futures Studies, Vo.l 8, No. 1, 61-72.

12. https://www.theguardian.com/lifeandstyle/2018/apr/01/vegans-are-coming-millennials-health-climate-change-animal-welfare. Accessed 13 July 2019.

13. For example, see: https://www.beefcentral.com/news/what-does-the-future-hold-for-livestock-production-in-australia/. Accessed 13 July 2019. Also see the latest for milk replacement: https://thespoon.tech/perfect-day-launches-ice-cream-made-from-cow-free-milk-and-we-tried-it/.Accessed 13 July 2019.

14. For more on this, see: "From Knowledge Keeper to Knowledge Creators," in *Public Library Quarterly* (Vol. 34, No. 4, 2015), 1-8.

15. Colin Russo, "Mapping outcomes of four Queensland City Futures Initiatives", Foresight. Vol. 18 No. 6, 2016, pp. 561-585

16. Clem Bezold, "The History and Future of Anticipatory Democracy and Foresight", *World Futures Review*. https://doi. org/10.1177/1946756718810768

17. See Clement Bezold,"Anticipatory Democracy and Aspirational Futures," the Journal of Futures Studies, Vol. 15, No 2., 2010, 167-170.

18. In conversation with Ivana Milojević . May 10, 2019.

19. Harrison Owen, *Open-Space Technology*. Oakland, Berret Koehler, 2008.

20. https://tech.cornell.edu/news/the-4-ps-of-health-tech/. Accessed 8 July2019.

21. Sohail Inayatullah and Ivana Milojević , *CLA 2.0: Transformative research in Theory and Practice*, Tamsui, Tamkang University, 2015.

22. Ivana Milojević and Sohail Inayatullah, *Narrative Foresight*, In process. 2020.

23. http://www.quotehd.com/quotes/jose-ortega-y-gasset-philosopher-quote-the-metaphor-is-perhaps-one-of-mans-most. Accessed 10 November 2018.

24. P. H. Thibodeau, L. Boroditsky, "Metaphors We Think With: The Role of Metaphor in Reasoning", PLoS One, Vol. 6, No. 2, e16782 DOI: 10.1371/journal.pone.0016782. Accessed 10 November 2018.

25. See, for example, George L. Kelling, "Crime and metaphor: toward a new concept of policing", City Journal Autum, 1991, http://www.city-journal.org/article01.php?aid=1577. Accessed 10 November 2018.

26. Deborah Stone, *Policy Paradox*, W.W. New York, Norton and Company, 2012, 25. Also see, Ann Cammett, "*Deadbeat Dads and Welfare Queens: How Metaphor Shapes Poverty Law*", 34B.C.J.L. & Soc. Just. 233, 2014, https://lawdigitalcommons.bc.edu/jlsj/vol34/iss2/3

27. Sohail Inayatullah: "Foresight in challenging environments," Journal of Futures Studies, Vol. 22, No. 4, 2018, 18.

28. http://dadaprana.com/heart-circle.html. Accessed 8 July 2019.

29. For more on the epistemological framework of this argument, see Sohail Inayatullah, *Understanding Sarkar: The Indian Episteme, Macrohistory and Transformative Knowledge*, Leiden, Brill, 2002.

30. Dada Pranakrsnananda, "Therapeutic meditation", Private notes. Available from sinayatullah@gmail.com.

31. While vision to reality is a powerful indicator of success, Riel Miller goes further. He comments: "The vindication of a planning use of the future is one strong rationale. Equally important is the fact that they have imagined different futures. This alters what they see and do, and how they appreciate the future present when it arrives." Comments on an earlier draft of this paper. 18 July 2019.

32. In personal conversation, January 2005.

Alvin & Heidi Toffler

Alexander Mankowsky   Alexandra Ivanovitch   Alisha Bhagat

Andrew Curry   Andy Hines   Anita Sengupta

le Grey   Barry O'Reilly   Barry Vacker

ryan Alexander   Byron Reese   Carlos Osorio

Daniel Burrus   Daniel Levine   David Brin

avid Weinberger   Deb Westphal   Diane M. Francis

rica Bol   Erik Qualman   George Gilder

atarajan   Hazel Henderson   Helen Messier   Ian Khan

ason Jackson   Jason Schenker   Jay Gambetta   Jeff Eisenach

Dispenza   Joe Tankersley   Joel Garreau   John L. Petersen

aitlyn Sadtler   Kirk Borne   Klee Irwin   Kris Østergaard

Martin Rees   Michael Tomczyk   Michel Laberge

Newt Gingrich   Paul Saffo   Paul Stimers

chard Browning   Richard Slaughter   Richard Watson   Richard Yonck

uth Miller   Sanjiv Chopra   Sohail Inayatullah

Tanya Accone   Terry Sejnowski   Teun Koetsier

Vikram Mansharamani   Wolfgang Fengler

John Schroeter   Jonathan Venn

Parag Khanna   Patricia Lustig   Rick Sax

Alan Kay   Aaron Frank   Adrienne Mayor
Amy Zalman   Anders Sörman-Nilsson   Andra Kea
Anne Lise Kjaer   Aris Persidis   Arvind Gupta   Aubrey
Bill Davidow   Bill Diamond   David Spivak
Carver Mead   Cat Tully   Cindy Frewen   Clem Bezol
David Guston   David Krakauer   David J. Staley
Donna Dupont   Eleanor "Nell" Watson   Eric Daimler
Grady Booch   Gray Scott   Hannes Sapiens   Harish
Ignacio Peña   Jack Uldrich   James Canton   Jane McGoniga
Jeffrey C. Bauer   Jerome Glenn   Jerry Fishenden   Joe
John M. Smart   John Sack   John Sanei   José Morey
Maggie Greyson   Lisa Bodell   Maciej Kranz   Martin Guigu
Mick Ebeling   Moon Ribas   Naveen Jain   Neil Jacobste
Po Bronson   Ray Kurzweil   Rebecca Costa
Rodrigo Nieto-Gómez   Rohit Bhargava   Ross Dawson
Sridhar Mahadevan   Stan Rosen   Stephanie Mehta   Steve Waite
Theodore Jay Gordon   Thomas Frey   Timothy Cho
Zoltan Istvan   Fotis Sotiropoulos   Gill Ringlar
Jordan Richardson   Nora Haney   Pankaj K. V